International Yeats Studies

vol. 9.2

W. B. YEATS'S RAPALLO NOTEBOOKS

Descriptive & Analytical Examinations of the Five Notebooks (NLI 13,578-82)

by Neil Mann and Wayne K. Chapman

ISBN 978-1-63804-200-6 paperback
ISBN 978-1-63804-201-3 hardcover

Published by Clemson University Press in Clemson, South Carolina

To order copies, contact Clemson University Press at 116 Sigma Dr., Clemson, South Carolina 29634, or order via our website: www.clemson.edu/press.

Table of Contents

Volume 9, Issue 2

W. B. Yeats's Rapallo Notebooks

The Rapallo Notebooks: A Special Issue
Wayne K. Chapman and Neil Mann 1

Yeats's Rapallo Notebooks: General Overview
Neil Mann 5

Rapallo Notebooks A and B: *A Packet for Ezra Pound*, *A Vision*, and Articles
Neil Mann 31

Rapallo Notebook C: *A Vision*, Poetry, and Sundry Writings
Wayne K. Chapman 119

Rapallo Notebook D: Diary Notes, Poetry, and Other Writings
Wayne K. Chapman and Neil Mann 181

Rapallo Notebook E: Supernatural Drama, New and Revisited
Neil Mann and Wayne K. Chapman 275

Appendices by Neil Mann and Wayne K. Chapman
A. Tabular Summary: Rapallo Notebook A (NLI 13,578) 377
B. Tabular Summary: Rapallo Notebook B (NLI 13,579) 388
C. Tabular Summary: Rapallo Notebook C (NLI 13,580) 401
D. Tabular Summary: Rapallo Notebook D (NLI 13,581) 413
E. Tabular Summary: Rapallo Notebook E (NLI 13,582) 424

Notes on Contributors 438

FRONTISPIECE: W. B. Yeats, bearded and recuperating (c. March–May 1930), is seated outside at the restaurant Albergo Rapallo (Lungomare Vittorio Veneto, 32), next door to the Caffè Aurum in the same building. Photograph courtesy of the Stuart A. Rose Manuscripts, Archives, and Rare Books Archive, Emory University. (See Massimo Bacigalupo, *Tigullio Itineraries: Ezra Pound and Friends* [Rapallo: Azienda Grafica, 2008], 382).

W. B. Yeats's Rapallo Notebooks: A Special Issue

Wayne K. Chapman and Neil Mann

This special number of *International Yeats Studies* appears by courtesy of the editor, Rob Doggett, and by provision of the publisher, Clemson University Press. The authors acknowledge with gratitude the initial suggestion from its director, Alison Mero, to make the essays on the Rapallo Notebooks available in a single place. This themed issue is thus the culmination of the *IYS* series of analytical digests on W. B. Yeats's five Rapallo Notebooks and includes (1) a new overview of the full set, (2) a reprise presentation of the essays on the first four notebooks, published previously in *International Yeats Studies*, and (3) a new account of the fifth notebook (Rapallo Notebook E).

The project emerged conceptually from several informal discussions in late 2017 between *IYS* founding editor Lauren Arrington and fellow Yeats specialists Margaret Mills Harper, Wayne Chapman, Neil Mann, and Warwick Gould. Arrington finished her tenure as editor with *IYS* 3.1 (2018) but thereafter published her biographical study *The Poets of Rapallo: How Mussolini's Italy shaped British, Irish, and U.S. Writers* (Oxford University Press, 2021), which provides valuable biographical and cultural background to these essays. Our Rapallo project took shape under the editorship of Rob Doggett, as the team worked to prepare a reliable, detailed map of the notebooks from direct observation in the National Library of Ireland, supported by microfilms held at Harvard University, an almost complete set of digital facsimiles provided by Catherine Paul, and photographs from the NLI itself (largely work conducted by Neil Mann). The first article in our series, on Rapallo A and B by Neil Mann, appeared in *IYS* 6.1 (2022); one on Rapallo C, by Wayne Chapman, followed that in *IYS* 7.1 (2023); another one, on Rapallo D, by Chapman and Mann, appeared in *IYS* 8.1 (2024). As noted earlier, the final essay, on Rapallo Notebook E by Mann and Chapman, appears for the first time in this special issue of *IYS* 9.2 (2025). We are grateful to Margaret Mills Harper and Warwick Gould for their continued support and occasional input into the project although, in the end, it has been the two of us who have had the time to dedicate to the research, writing, and production of the series with the staff of Clemson University Press.

The objective of this series has been to guide readers through the varying landscapes of the notebooks while remaining faithful to the principle that, together, they must be valued as artifacts, evidence for textual specialists involved in the analysis of contents, on the one hand, but also as reflections of Yeats's broadly creative process, on the other. To that end, we hope our work will be of service well into the future as a guide to the wonderful collection of manuscript workbooks that Yeats's idiosyncratic composing process has left.

The assembled essays adhere to a high standard of collaborating scholarship anticipated by numerous precursors. Given the hybrid nature of the essays as a cross between documentary editing and a newer variety of literary criticism beholden to textual biography as a form of life study, we have been granted by the publisher an unusually direct role in oversight and production of the printed presentation of the *IYS* "Rapallo" series. For example, the layout and documentary apparatus are largely in accordance with what we as authors have felt to be dictated, respectively, by the organization of the notebooks themselves (each one varying according to differing needs and content) and by the necessity to introduce customized principles of transcription and abbreviation at variance with the house style used more generally by *IYS* and by the publisher (often, again, because of Yeats's erratic spelling and the accidental events affecting the notebooks). These principles were severally introduced with the essays published in 2022, 2023, and 2024, when former *IYS* production editor Charis Chapman was enlisted to typeset the essays on Rapallo Notebooks A through D as a freelance designer and a *de facto* member of our team, entrusted to manage the complicated coordination of texts (ours and Yeats's), numerous facsimile images and blocks of transcription, as well as the multicolumn tabular summaries, here presented together as a single set of appendices, which constitute the subsidiary component of this issue.

For the few of us who have published documentary scholarship in this way, the reality is that so much depends upon collaborating with people conversant with the technology of the day and who are on hand to pitch in as needed. Hence, special thanks are owed to Charis Chapman for establishing software templates for all manner of text design and visuals used in the series. Thanks are owed to Catherine Paul for her generosity in sharing her photographs and permitting selected digital images to be used as illustration. Thanks, too, are due to Jack Quin for re-checking the physical descriptions of the Rapallo Notebooks at a time when Covid restrictions made travel to Dublin impossible for either of us. And, of course, we are much indebted to the Trustees of the National Library of Ireland, which owns and curates the physical notebooks and has consented to their use in this series, with authorization granted by United Agents LLP on behalf of Caitríona Yeats and the W. B. Yeats Estate.

We had hoped to publish this compendium in book form, to make it available for reference in academic libraries, especially in the Manuscripts Reading Room at the NLI, beside the volumes of the Cornell Yeats Manuscript Series and those that Chapman has published on the W. B. and George Yeats

Library. But a book *as such* was not in the stars. Instead, we were offered the next best thing in the present themed issue of the journal; this means that there has been no recasting or shifting of notes to the end, nor an index, though that is scarcely necessary in PDF format, which is so readily searchable electronically (Ctrl + F). In fact, as copies of the journal will shortly be available for order to be printed on demand (as was formerly the case for *IYS* volumes 1–3), it will be possible for any interested party, whether institutional or individual, to go to Clemson University Press's collaborating vendor for a paper version. A paperback or hardcover edition of *The Rapallo Notebooks: A Special Issue* may now be ordered by selecting one of the purchase links provided on the *IYS* journal's webpage for this issue.

Gathering together the essays published in *IYS* volumes 6 through 8 without re-editing inevitably entails a small amount of repetition in certain places (always in the first few pages, where defining transcription methods and half a dozen of the most cited abbreviations are necessary to understand the commentary). Rapallo Notebook E is, therefore, introduced in the same way, under the assumption that readers will not necessarily read the entire issue straight through. Similarly, supplied folio numbers are placed in square brackets in the first and last essays, but for greater readability they are not included in the second and third essays, where the need for line numbers in the many poetry drafts and the interjection of cued lines would create confusing clutter. Also for the sake of enhanced readability, we report whenever we have simplified the transcription of a passage with revisions by omitting cancellation or other accidentals, to ensure that Yeats's meaning is not obscured by a jumble of stricken words or false starts. Since the process of Yeats's writing and revision is at the heart of the project, we have, on the whole, not interceded very often but, rather, as far as possible, used photographs and other visual aids, such as tables and diagrams—not least in the final essay on "Rapallo Notebook E: Supernatural Drama, New and Revised," which features twelve figures (including two redrawn diagrams) and a table, as well as the tabular summary of the notebook in the appendix. For the entire special issue, the number of facsimile images comes to a total of thirty—a prodigious number for any scholarly book of around 400 pages (counting notes and appendices). So, in many respects, we *have* delivered a book.

Mann's introductory piece, "Yeats's Rapallo Notebooks: General Overview," opens the way for all readers. For those who are encountering the series for the first time, it puts the whole in perspective. For those who have been following from *IYS* 6 onward, it can be taken as the sort of peroration that is presented before last arguments—in this case Rapallo E—with comments on the remaking of *A Vision* (from 1925) and *The Resurrection* (from 1927), and the rapid making of an immediately successful play, *The Words upon the Window-Pane*

(1930). In either case, the "General Overview" provides a fresh footing for our readers, who are introduced to Rapallo from 1928, given physical accounts of the notebooks purchased there, including a general summary of their contents and a comprehensive summary of dating logic, which is discussed in the other essays more individually but in greater detail. Finally, after considering manuscripts in relation to criticism, we hope that our readers will appreciate why we believe that the Rapallo Notebooks show a kind of *extraordinary ordinariness*, as their pages bear the traces of the operation of an extraordinary mind involved in the everyday struggle with words and meaning, and witness the alchemy of the creative process that shapes new and precious works of art.

Yeats's Rapallo Notebooks: General Overview

Neil Mann

1. Rapallo

The Yeatses first arrived in Rapallo on February 17, 1928. Early in October 1927, W. B. Yeats had caught a cold that developed into pneumonia, so that he "was ordered to a warm climate for a time" (WBY to Kazumi Yano, November 18, [1927], *CL InteLex* 5049). He and George sailed to Gibraltar at the beginning of November 1927, but they found the weather in Spain unexpectedly cool and Yeats's health was still precarious, with bleeding lungs and high blood pressure. Having travelled north to France, they reached Cannes in late November and, shortly after arriving, Yeats wrote how he felt "staggered by my first serious illness—I hardly expected to recover but now I do expect to" (WBY to Olivia Shakespear, November 27, [1927], *CL InteLex* 5055).[1] Because of his poor health, they spent over two months in Cannes, with Lennox Robinson visiting and the children joining them for Christmas, but in January they were already planning to be in Rapallo for February, as Ezra and Dorothy Pound were now established there.[2] Once in Rapallo, they were sufficiently taken with the town to find an apartment "with balconies & the most lovely view imaginable" (WBY to Olivia Shakespear, February 23, [1928], *CL InteLex* 5079) and sign a five-year lease, evidently confident enough to plan their Mediterranean winters for some years to come. They lunched and dined with the Pounds regularly, and W. B. Yeats's health gradually revived (*BG* 396). Reinvigorated, he started a notebook and a prose essay provisionally headed "Siris," later retitled "Rapallo in Spring." The original title shows that he intended to follow the tangential and exploratory method used by George Berkeley in *Siris: A Chain of Philosophical Reflexions and Inquiries Concerning the Virtues of Tar-water, And divers other Subjects connected together and arising one from another,*[3] substituting Berkeley's tar-water with a poem by Guido Cavalcanti and the view from his window.[4] This was the first of five notebooks, referred to collectively as the Rapallo Notebooks.

The details of the notebooks and their specific concerns will be left for the individual essays that follow; this general overview sets out to describe the notebooks and to outline their contents in broad terms, considering them as a group and focusing on the relationships between the individual books and what they show about Yeats's habits of composition. The essays that follow and the appendices with tabular page listings aim to provide a reference resource for readers who want to consult either the originals at the National Library of Ireland or microfilm copies. Together, the essays and appendices also give context to the published transcriptions and facsimiles for those who want to construct a clearer sense of the notebooks in their original form than is possible from the published material currently available (mainly in the excellent Cornell manuscripts series). But we also hope that the accounts here can convey something of the fascination, excitement, and texture of these notebooks and of the manuscripts they contain for more general readers.[5]

2. Physical Description

In his biography of Yeats, Roy Foster emphasizes the importance of these notebooks:

> The "Rapallo Notebooks" which contain the drafts of so many of his new ideas are sacred objects in the great Yeatsian mine of manuscripts. The entries and outlines, jammed together in close proximity, show how freely and excitedly he was writing in his sunny eyrie above the road to Portofino. (*Life2* 385)

Yet the uniqueness of these five notebooks should not be exaggerated, and talk of "sacred objects" hints at veneration of relics rather than an interest in content.[6] To some extent, all of Yeats's notebooks show a jostling of interests and creativity,[7] first ideas and fuller drafts, letters and poems; those preceding the Rapallo Notebooks are almost as rich though briefer, while one of those that follows soon after, the White Vellum Notebook (WVN), is if anything even more crammed, such that it too has been described as "a talisman among Yeats manuscripts."[8] However, the Rapallo Notebooks come at a particular point in Yeats's career, when he was redrafting *A Vision*, writing the poems of *The Winding Stair* and plays such as *The Resurrection* and *The Words upon the Window-Pane*, and their shared format integrates their concerns, even if a little accidentally. This group gives any reader a direct and vivid sense of Yeats's mind and thinking in a way that almost nothing else can.

Curtis Bradford notes that "Very often when Yeats was away from home he used a bound manuscript book as a workbook" rather than loose paper,[9] and David R. Clark gives a good summary of Yeats's practice when using such notebooks:

> Yeats usually wrote on the right-hand page first and then added or corrected or substituted on the facing left-hand page, so that the order becomes 1r, 2r, 1v,

> 3r, 2v, 4r, 3v and so on. Occasionally the verso was left blank, and occasionally a portion of a play or a note on some other subject would interrupt the sequence.[10]

The Rapallo Notebooks are typical in this way—they are portable compendia of work and, though named for their Italian center of gravity, they bear internal records of their journeys between Rapallo and Dublin and London and Galway, like old luggage labels or passport stamps. The basic pattern of usage also conforms to Yeats's usual practice, proceeding from recto to recto, the pages sometimes numbered in sequence, with the versos usually left blank in the first instance and reserved for later revision.

They are five large-format notebooks, 30 × 22 cm (c. 12 × 8.5 in), originally with a hundred leaves made up of five signatures of ten folios sewn and folded into twenty leaves, but all have pages removed, whether torn out or cut out with a blade.[11] They are now labeled with the letters A, B, C, D, and E: Notebook A has a large "D" on the cover, but an "A" on the flyleaf; Notebook B has "B" on the flyleaf; Notebook E has an "E" on the cover; neither of the notebooks now designated C or D has any identifying letter on or in the notebook itself. Notebooks A, B, and E have the same cover design, while C and D have a different one,[12] and all contain unruled paper of relatively low quality,[13] about 20 lb. weight,[14] and they are probably of Italian origin.[15] Yeats numbered the pages in some sections of Notebooks A, B, and E, but C and D have no numbering.

Table 0.1. Leaves in the Rapallo Notebooks and blank leaves.

Rapallo Notebook	No. of extant leaves	Blank leaves*	Leaves with a blank recto*	Leaves with a blank verso*
A	86	23	2	24
B	96	1	0	38
C	70	0	0	5
D	53	0	0	0
E	72 + 4†	11	0	23 + 2†

* Blanks, both whole leaves, rectos, or versos, are specified here, as microfilms often omit blank pages unless they are part of a spread. The location of the blank pages is made clear in the tabular summary for each notebook (see appendices).

† Four leaves were inserted loose into Rapallo E and are probably not an intrinsic part of the notebook.

Notebook B was actually the first to be used, with A following a little later, and the notebooks are not in any real sense sequential, as Yeats, at least initially, intended some books for one particular area of activity, while others were more general. The notebooks also overlap considerably: Notebook A redrafts material from Notebook B, and both are devoted largely to *A Vision*, while Notebook C runs in parallel with them for a while, having been started as a "Diary of Thought | begun. Sept 23. 1928 | in Dublin." Notebook D appears to have been started at the same time as Notebook B, in March 1928, but then left for a year and a half until autumn 1929. Notebook E appears to have had a good part of its initial contents removed and opens with undated notes on Leo Frobenius, but on the second verso it has an entry on London clairvoyants that appears to be from May 1929, while Notebook C was still in use and before D was picked up again. The diary that Yeats kept during 1930 (NLI 30,354)[16] overlaps with both Notebooks D and E and, when it was full, Yeats retrieved Notebook A and used one of its blank pages to extend one of the diary's October entries. Notebook E also overlaps with the White Vellum Notebook, "Begun Nov 23 1930 at 42 Fitzwilliam Square, Dublin," and it contains a later version of *The Resurrection* than the draft in the WVN. Notebook D also contains a brief late addition "On a recent incident," which ties in with a letter to Augusta Gregory in April 1931, and also a stray line of dialogue that seems destined for *The Words upon the Window-Pane.*[17]

Though there are dates scattered through most of the notebooks, dating is not always entirely clear; the questions involved are outlined briefly in Section 3 (below) and are examined fully in the individual essays that follow.

3. The Notebooks' Contents

The first notebook with entries dated to Rapallo is actually a leather notebook (NLI 30,359) containing drafts, some quite advanced, of "A Dialogue of Self and Soul" part I (as "Silk, Sword & Tower"), "In Memory of Eva Gore-Booth and Con Markiewicz," "From the 'Antigone'" ("Oedipus Child"), "Death," "Before the World Was Made," and what Yeats entitles "part II of 'Silk, Sword & Tower,'" which is dated "Dec 1927." There is no clear indication of when the poems on the volume's earlier pages were written, but, as some of them appear to be relatively fair copies, they may well be (as David Clark proposes) advanced drafts that were transferred into the notebook to be taken abroad.[18] Later on, this notebook records "Sleeps"—trance-like states in which George Yeats appeared to talk to her husband while asleep—three in Cannes and two in March in Rapallo; it also contains "suggested first paragraph of system," which is an early version of the draft that was taken up as "First Things" in Rapallo Notebook B, then further redrafted as "First Things" in Notebook A.

Although significantly longer than this slim but elegant notebook, Rapallo B and Rapallo A will probably disappoint those whose primary interest in Yeats is poetic. Despite the felicities of "Rapallo in Spring," which would become the first part of *A Packet for Ezra Pound*, Notebook B is devoted exclusively to *A*

Vision and its associated material. Notebook A is also largely concerned with *A Vision*, but contains other drafts of articles and a letter, as well as some late changes for *The Player Queen*. Only in the later three notebooks do poetry and drama come to the fore. Rapallo C opens with diary and *Vision* material but then moves on to poems such as "Meditations upon Death,"[19] published and unpublished poems from the two series later called "Words for Music Perhaps" and "A Woman Young and Old," before returning to *A Vision* in the last pages. Rapallo D is the shortest but probably the richest of the notebooks, with a little of everything. Started in March 1928 in Rapallo,[20] only the first three pages were filled at that time, before it was picked up again in Dublin in August 1929 with a draft of "I am of Ireland." This is followed with notes on Yeats's esoteric reading, draft letters, the list of a week's engagements, drafts of poems such as "Coole Park 1929" and "Byzantium," a testimonial for Wyndham Lewis, a memorial for John Quinn, aphoristic propositions drafted as "Astrology & the Nature of Reality," as well as, inevitably, material for *A Vision*. Notebook E opens with notes taken from Leo Frobenius's *The Voice of Africa*,[21] before moving on to a note on clairvoyance, drafts for *A Vision*, sketches and drafts for *The Words upon the Window-Pane*, the final handwritten draft of *The Resurrection* (including its songs), and drafts of a poem, "For Anne Gregory."

One of the striking elements in the notebooks is their variety, showing Yeats's mind shifting from one topic to another, both within a notebook and between notebooks. He tried to dedicate particular books to a single purpose: for example, on its first page, Rapallo C declares itself to be a "Diary of Thought," but Yeats drifted from that original aim within a few pages; at the back of the same notebook there are signs of an (earlier?) attempt to start the book in the opposite direction as a "Diary" (Yeats writes "diary" and then a larger, clearer "Diary" over it but nothing else, and may have decided to restart more cleanly at the other end, now the front end). Rapallo D also opens as a "Diary" but, after three pages, the book appears to have been abandoned for some sixteen months before being used for other non-diary material. With the smaller leather-bound diary that was "Begun in April, 1930, at Rapallo, or rather near it" (NLI 30,354), Yeats managed to keep to his intended purpose more singly, and the diary runs alongside the later stages of Notebooks D and E, while a late page in Notebook A contains the continuation of an entry he was unable to fit into the final pages of the diary itself.[22] Though Yeats clearly started a new notebook with a plan for a particular focus, such purpose was difficult to follow when reaching for paper on which to sketch ideas or work out his thoughts, so that each book potentially gathers together many of the disparate elements going through Yeats's mind at the time.[23]

4. Dating the Notebooks

As mentioned above, the notebooks contain enough dates to give a clear idea of their composition in many instances, but not always. Extraneous evidence often helps—whether contemporary letters or publication of items—as do more subjective criteria, such as the precedence of drafts or a reconstructed order. More detailed analysis of dating will be found in the treatments of the individual notebooks, so the following survey simply aims to give an overview of the five notebooks.

Notebook A contains two explicit dates, one at the end of the first long draft of material related to the Great Year in *A Vision*, "Nov 1928," and an isolated late entry of "Oct 20" that continues from the 1930 diary. Yeats must have started it before August 14, 1928, as a letter to George on August 17 says that he had "found those notes you have been searching for in one of those Italian MSS books," which he had brought to Coole, rather than the leather book he had asked her to examine (*CL InteLex* 5145; *YGYL* 194). He was referring to notes on Plotinus found on the second recto of Rapallo Notebook A, evidently made before he arrived at Coole on August 14. The November date for the *Vision* material, squeezed vertically into a lower corner, must relate to revision and possible additional material, as it is followed by drafts for two articles on censorship published in September 1928 (*CW10* 211–18; *UP2* 477–85); an essay on the Irish coinage (finished, according to a letter, by August 28, [1928], *CL InteLex* 5150); and a letter responding to Annie Horniman's querulous intervention in the *Irish Statesman* on October 6, 1928 (WBY's letter was published 13 October 1928, *CL InteLex* 5176; *UP2* 485–86). The notebook was then put aside and taken up two years later to continue an entry from the diary of 1930 (NLI 30,354), dated October 20, but the extension was almost certainly added after November 18 when the diary was finished and leaving no space for the revision to be added there.

Notebook B is devoted to material for *A Vision*. The earliest date comes at the end of "First Things": "March 1928." "Introduction" is dated "May 1928"; and the cover states that it was "Finished, Oct. 9, 1928." Started in Rapallo, Notebook B was apparently taken to Dublin and was in relatively continuous use until finished. Some material on *A Vision* was redrafted in Notebook A, and, given this and earlier dates that the notebook contains, it is evident that Rapallo B was actually begun before A, although they overlap.

Notebook C declares its starting date to be "Sept. 23. 1928 in Dublin" and that it was intended as a "Diary of Thought." Separate items are given dates from January, February, March 1929—when the Yeatses were in Rapallo—and May 1929—when they were in Dublin—again indicating relatively continuous use. On the outside back cover, is the note "Finished June or July

1929," evidently written later on and with details uncertain. This notebook was originally started at the other end (and "upside down"), and a preliminary table of contents that Yeats roughed out lists some eight leaves dedicated instead to drafting for *A Vision*, all of it removed. The first recto (now the last verso), however, is inscribed "Diary," possibly indicating that once he had torn out the *Vision* material, Yeats was repurposing the book but then decided to start at the other (cleaner) end. Alternatively, he may have deviated from his declared aim almost immediately. Either way, Yeats may have begun the notebook earlier than the date of September 23 that was inscribed once Notebook C was turned around (see also Rapallo E).

Notebook D was started in Rapallo in March 1928 (cf. Notebook B), with the first page also declaring it a "Diary." Yeats wrote to Ottoline Morrell, on March 20, 1928: "I put things in a diary — sometimes a lot of things & then nothing for months. The other day I was writing there that certain moments in Abbey plays had been a principal part of my education," and he goes on to summarize the opening entry of Rapallo D (*CL InteLex* 5093).[24] Even "nothing for months" was sanguine in this case, as Yeats appears to have stopped using the notebook after three pages and to have put it aside for a year and a half—although it was no longer a diary when he resumed. Presumably work in Notebooks B and A was continuing, and Notebook C became the main creative outlet in early 1929. After it was finished, Yeats picked up Notebook D again in Dublin in August, using it during September, October, and November 1929, while he was in Dublin, at Coole, and in London. The Yeatses left for Rapallo at the end of November 1929; however, Yeats was suffering from Malta fever and wrote little over that winter, jotting a comment in the notebook in late March 1930 to the effect that he had "written nothing but one poem." Between drafts of "Veronica's Napkin" and "Byzantium," the next date is "July Renvyle" for an "Open letter to [Wyndham] Lewis"[25] and then a copy of "A lyric written in 1923 & lost | have just found August 1930." A memorial piece on John Quinn is dated "Oct 1930." Two separate groups of drafts of "Crazy Jane on the Day of Judgment" appear to be spaced almost a year apart, the first group dated "Oct 29" [1929] and almost sixty leaves later,[26] following the Quinn essay, the second dated "Oct." A brief "Subject for a poem" is dated "Nov 18 1930" and this appears to mark the end of sustained usage, but in April 1931, when Yeats had probably finished with Notebook E (see below), a blank space at the top of an early verso ([4v]) in Notebook D must have offered the most convenient space for a stray item, a squib on a child custody case involving a Protestant mother and the Roman Catholic Church.[27] This late addition, as with the diary entry inserted after a gap of almost two years into Notebook A, shows that Yeats kept the notebooks at hand at least some of the time, possibly consulting them even after he was no longer adding to them.

Notebook E contains few dates and no years, which leads to the widest variance in terms of critical dating, depending on whether the focus is on the few dated elements or greater weight is given to the discerned sequence of drafts of *The Resurrection*. There are also four leaves inserted into the notebook, with a separate scenario entitled "Ressurection" (sic), which may have belonged to the original notebook but probably did not. These once-loose pages are almost certainly earlier than anything that remains in the notebook proper, but opinions on dating vary from 1925 to January 1929.

Our dating of the notebook, explained fully in the essay on Rapallo E, is at variance with that given in the Cornell manuscripts censuses,[28] and we attribute the first extant entries in Notebook E to spring 1929, with the notebook in use until early 1931. As with Rapallo C, what was probably the earliest work in Rapallo E (or at least part of it) has been removed, but the first pages of the book are taken up with notes on Frobenius, whom Yeats mentions in a letter to Sturge Moore from Rapallo in April 1929 (*CL InteLex* 5328), and this seems indicative, if far from conclusive. On the verso of the second leaf, following an account of "Clairvoyance on May 9," there is a reference to getting a spirit photograph, and both indicate that Yeats was in London (see Rapallo E, p. 287, below), pointing to May 1929, when Yeats was in London until May 16, as he was in Dublin in early May of every year from 1923 to 1928.[29] We know from Yeats's correspondence that *The Words upon the Window-Pane* was written between August and October of 1930. "For Anne Gregory" is referred to in a letter of September 1930. The draft of *The Resurrection* reworks the version in the White Vellum Notebook (a notebook only started in November 1930), and it was ready for dictation to a typist in March 1931. Moreover, drafts for *A Vision* follow this play, so the notebook was almost certainly still in use during early 1931.

Although a large part of the first gathering has been torn out, the cover bears a cancelled three-line inscription: "Principle [sic] symbols | hourglass and diamond | T[?he] [?Diagram of the] Great Wheel"), as well as a large letter "E." This "E" is similar in appearance to the "D" that appears on the cover of Notebook A, drawn with many strokes of a fine nib (see Rapallo E, Figure 4.1, below at 280), and the cover matches the designs of Notebooks B and A. None of the topics listed appears in the book, where the treatment of *A Vision* starts at a more complex level on a page numbered "17." The material is clearly another version of the introductory presentation for *A Vision* that Yeats was working on in Notebooks B and A, so quite possibly dating, like them, to 1928, though the sequence of letters on the covers would indicate that Rapallo E was probably started after Rapallo A (formerly "D").

The other dates in the book come from the four leaves, a loose pair of bifolia (with six pages of writing), that have been inserted. These have no material bearing on the dating of the notebook itself, as they almost certainly come from a different—though similar—notebook.[30] They contain a scenario titled "~~Ressurection~~ | Dance Play"—actually one scenario in two slightly different versions—which Curtis Bradford takes as preparatory material for *The Resurrection*, as do Jared Curtis and Selina Guinness. Above the title comes a date: "~~Sunday~~ Jan ~~20~~ 21 & 22"—or just possibly "Jun." If this is a scenario for *The Resurrection*, it is very different from the form the play would later take, so would almost certainly have to pre-date it, placing it in early 1925. Yet there is no date in 1925 that would make the combination in the heading possible, and in fact there is a single typed sheet based on the scenarios in Rapallo E and with the same dates of "(Jan 21 & 22)," with "1929" added in ink in Yeats's hand.[31] On the last recto of the four leaves, there is a separate note on Masefield, Synge, and Pound dated "Jan 22," with "(?1929)," also added later.[32] And the day and date combination would work for January 1929. The arguments involved in unraveling the knot are convoluted and will be left for the appropriate section of the treatment that follows below (see p. 342ff below). But, put simply, when we began this project, we followed previous writers in taking the scenario to be a rejected approach to the themes of *The Resurrection* with problematic dates; we now take this inserted material as dating from 1929 and unconnected with the play except for the problematic duplication of its title. Hence, these leaves are largely irrelevant to Rapallo E, though there is a real possibility that they actually came from Rapallo C (see pp. 345–46, below), tying these notebooks together even more closely.

The accompanying table offers a rough conspectus to give an idea of the timing relating to the five notebooks, as well as the preceding notebook (NLI 30,359) which ends in Rapallo, the 1930 diary (NLI 30,354), and the White Vellum Notebook (formerly MBY 545).

Despite the overlaps, the only notebooks that run simultaneously for most of their span are D and E, along with the diary. The first prose draft of "Byzantium," for instance, appears in the 1930 diary, dated "April, 30," while subsequent drafts are in Rapallo D.[33] Thus, even the diary, which Yeats kept almost exclusively for philosophical thought and political ideas, could be brought into use for poetry if it was the closest to hand, though he then tried to keep the diary consistent and moved the poetic drafts into the notebook. "Byzantium" was completed during the summer, the more final versions appearing after a draft of an open letter to Wyndham Lewis dated "July."[34] In August 1930, Yeats copied into the notebook a poem from 1923 that he had recovered, "The Crazed Moon," and drafted a tribute to John Quinn in October 1930; in between these two items appear undated drafts of "Veronica's Napkin" and a page of *The Cat and the Moon*. Between August and October 1930, Yeats was also using Rapallo E for drafts of *The Words upon the Window-Pane*,

Table 0.2. Dates of Use of the Notebooks. The location given on the left is approximate for the month and based on John S. Kelly's *A W. B. Yeats Chronology*. Darker shading indicates active use, lighter shading temporary disuse. In the cases of Rapallo C and E, the lighter shading indicates possible earlier use indicated by the excision of contents.

year	*month*	*main places*	Leather NB 30,359	Rapallo Notebooks A	B	C	D	E	1930 Diary 30,354	WVN (MBY 545)
1927	Nov	Spain								
	Dec	Cannes								
1928	Jan	Cannes								
	Feb	Cannes								
	Mar	Rapallo								
	Apr	Rapallo to Dublin via Switz. & Paris								
	May	Dublin								
	Jun	London								
	Jul	Dublin								
	Aug	Coole								
	Sep	Dublin								
	Oct	Dublin								
	Nov	Rapallo								
	Dec	Rome/Rapallo								
1929	Jan	Rapallo								
	Feb	Rapallo								
	Mar	Rapallo								
	Apr	London								
	May	Dublin								
	Jun	Glendalough								
	Jul	Coole								
	Aug	Dublin								
	Sep	Sligo, Dublin								
	Oct	Dublin, London								
	Nov	London, Rapallo								
	Dec	Rapallo								
1930	Jan	Rapallo								
	Feb	Rapallo								
	Mar	Rapallo								
	Apr	Portofino, Rapallo								
	May	Rapallo								
	Jun	Rapallo								
	Jul	London, Dublin								
	Aug	Dublin, Galway, Coole								
	Sep	Dublin								
	Oct	Dublin								
	Nov	London, Dublin								
	Dec	Dublin								
1931	Jan	Coole								
	Feb	Coole								
	Mar	Dublin								
	Apr	Dublin								
	May	Dublin								
	Jun	Oxford								
	Jul	London								
	Aug	Coole								
	Sep	Coole								
	Oct	Dublin, Coole								
	Nov	Dublin, Coole								
	Dec	Coole								↓Mar 1933

interrupted by "For Anne Gregory" in September. One stray line intended for *The Words upon the Window-Pane* appears in Rapallo D, whether by accident or just to commit the idea to paper.[35] Rapallo D was used on November 18, 1930, to outline the idea for a poem, asserting philosophy as drama,[36] and the White Vellum Notebook (WVN) was then "begun Nov 23 1930," with a draft for the introduction to *The Words upon the Window-Pane*.[37] Further on in the WVN, Yeats started to rework a published play, *The Resurrection*,[38] which was then further redrafted in Rapallo E, so this final handwritten draft dates probably (and the following *Vision* material more certainly) from 1931. Then, in April 1931, Rapallo D was used for a satirical quatrain. It seems likely, therefore, that there was some distinction between the notebooks in Yeats's mind, with one viewed as dramatic and the other perhaps more poetic, but not necessarily any clear division.

The five Rapallo Notebooks may be differentiated from the other notebooks that Yeats used more by the accident of their physical form than by their content, but they are closely connected in time and use, despite their individual characters. As a group they cover roughly three years of Yeats's creative life, running from spring 1928 to the spring 1931. Convenient and robust, these workbooks traveled with the Yeatses between Italy and Ireland, serving for everything from engagement lists and notes of reading to the drafts of major poems and plays.

5. Publication of the Notebooks' Contents

Almost all of the poetic and dramatic material contained in the Rapallo Notebooks has been reproduced and transcribed, whether in the comprehensive Cornell manuscripts series or in other studies of the genesis of Yeats's works, starting with Curtis Bradford's and Jon Stallworthy's pioneering surveys.[39] Some of the more philosophical and pensive material—such as the consideration of Pound and skepticism,[40] "Seven Propositions"/"Astrology and the Nature of Reality,"[41] or the nature of Yeats's belief in the system of *A Vision*[42]—has also been mined by critics and biographers to reveal Yeats's thought and its development. Yet a large proportion of the notebooks' material has remained untranscribed (except perhaps in private papers) and unpublished. Some of this includes drafts of prose, such as articles or letters, or notes of Yeats's reading, whether short jottings or more thorough summaries. Much, though, relates to *A Vision*, a work that is hard enough to approach in the pruned and tidied form of the published books, but bewildering in the tangle of tentative and cancelled material scrawled in handwriting only ever intended for the author's own eyes. It is understandable that it has not been reproduced or transcribed, if only because of the limited appeal of the topic and the economics of publishing. However, the even more knotty automatic script has been transcribed and published, as have the earliest drafts, and the later formulations of these notebooks are arguably more fully part of Yeats's own thought and his attempt to understand the world through his system than the early papers and even *A Vision A* (1925) itself. Certainly the notebooks confirm the continuous presence of *A Vision* in Yeats's thought during this period, as he notes in Rapallo B: "This book has filled my imagination for so many years, that I can never imagine myself studying anything without in some [*way*] relating it, or incorporating it with what is here[. . .]."[43] In the published version of *A Packet for Ezra Pound* (1929), this sentence becomes: "I will never think any thoughts but these, or some modification or extension of these; when I write prose or verse they must be somewhere present though not it may be in the words."[44] And both formulations reflect the depth of Yeats's intellectual immersion in the system.

So far, only isolated parts of Notebook B have been quoted or transcribed, and only the uncancelled material related to *The Player Queen* in Notebook A has been transcribed.[45] For Notebooks C, D, and E, however, substantial portions are transcribed and much of this material is also reproduced photographically, mainly in the Cornell manuscripts series. Vital though these volumes have been in bringing a sense of Yeats's creative process in the poetry and plays to readers, they are necessarily abstracted from the process that the notebooks embody. Extracted and organized to illustrate the development of each poem, the treatment inevitably ignores the sequence and structure of the notebooks themselves, which have a very different, often random and organic form. Particularly in the cases of Notebooks C and D, the lyrics that would be published in *Words for Music Perhaps* appear in the Cornell edition in the order of the Cuala volume rather than the sequence in the notebooks: the recto drafts are usually placed before their facing verso to reflect the order of composition, and separate bouts of composition that were interspersed with other material are corralled into a single sequence. The original juxtapositions of heterogeneous writing can be significant, not least when we are looking to date works by examining surrounding material.[46] Yet even here, we can only partially reconstruct the sequence of revision or the processes involved, and it is often impossible to tell definitively how much time passed between drafts or separate entries. Absence is also significant, as a blank leaf or stretches of two, three, or more leaves without any writing are integral to the book as object and may indicate space left for extension that did not happen or that the poet felt the need for a gap between one set of concerns and another. These voids are invisible in the extracted formats, and even microfilms, concentrating on written text, often omit them.[47]

6. "... but out of what began?": Manuscripts and Criticism

The fascination of drafts and their relationship to the process of composition is indisputable, but critics over the years have taken different approaches to the relationship of discarded versions to the published work and their intrinsic value. As in other aspects of literary criticism, attitudes towards manuscripts often betray conceptions of creativity and artifice, authorial voice or death, and will vary depending upon the writer or the writing in question.

There has been an almost unavoidable tendency to take a teleological approach, as if the poem were a shape within a mental form of marble awaiting the Quattrocento sculptor to liberate it, or an organic process growing through the lines and shifts in wording towards a destined final form.[48] Even with less artistically wrought material such as essays or expository prose, the drafts may be seen to show the writer's struggle to find the right words to express an idea and communicate with the audience, progressing towards a more perfect state. Zachary Leader refers to this as the "old dispensation in which rejected drafts and variants were seen as false starts happily rectified on the road to a work's final form, which was an incarnation of the author's final intention," and, in this kind of reading, the drafts or "pre-texts"[49] are studied to trace how the author improves prosody or music, usually assuming the superiority of the final form.[50]

Stephen Parrish dubbed this approach "The Whig Interpretation of Literature," following Herbert Butterfield's characterization in *The Whig Interpretation of History* (1931), where history is written privileging the tendencies and events that have led to the current order.[51] Parrish was presiding editor of the multi-volume Cornell edition of the works of William Wordsworth and many of his arguments in that essay were evidently responses to Wordsworth's very particular practices—keeping works unpublished, revising them over gaps of many years, and leaving many still unpublished at his death. Parrish judged "that the early Wordsworth was a better poet than the late Wordsworth," because "closer to the sources of his inspiration and less inhibited by the various orthodoxies [. . .] that he succumbed to in his later years."[52] In such a reading, therefore, later work may not rectify false starts but mar the original fire, with discarded forms closer to a creative impulse that is at least partially unconscious, and with a poet's more conscious, later involvement possibly changing that conception. As such, "earlier 'intentions' will command independent interest, especially as they reveal the poet's persistent struggle to redefine, and perhaps even to understand, his purposes."[53] Here drafts stand as almost autonomous works, unsanctioned by print, but otherwise showing aspects of the writer's vision and craft. This reading makes the author a conduit for (a suitably Romantic) inspiration,[54] acting in the first stages almost automatically with successive layers of mental intervention reaching a point of aesthetic equilibrium, as adjudged by the critic.[55]

Such considerations apply less obviously to Yeats's work in general, although readers may vary in their opinions about the aesthetic value of Yeats's revisions to *published* works. Despite some critics' apparent hankering for a general unified heuristic, applicable to all (or at least most) situations, it is almost impossible to find a single approach that works for all the manuscripts of any one poet or writer, let alone one that applies to all writers (whose drafts survive). The validity and usefulness of approaches will also depend upon the purposes of study: are we examining the manuscripts to achieve a better "final text," to explore the text's development, to address the manuscript on its own, or to understand the ideas it embodies?[56] With the Rapallo Notebooks, all approaches are possible and rewarding in different places as appropriate. The notebooks show poems emerging from relatively confused and partial beginnings with the only steady states or stages of completion being the final or near final forms. They also show prose and drama in first drafts that are very close to the versions that were published, while rejected expressions of the ideas in *A Vision* can sometimes illuminate a concept better than close reading of the final text.

Within the notebooks here, each individual draft offers insight into both the field of ideas and forms of expression that were in play during the process of creation, enabling us to explore the "stitching and unstitching" that precede and produce the illusion of lines that "seem a moment's thought" ("Adam's Curse," *VP* 204). In the understanding of Jean Bellemin-Noël, a draft shows "the written word *in transformation*, and in an open system, the writer not knowing in advance exactly where he is going," and in order to avoid introducing a false sense of direction towards a determined end-state into either our writing or reading, "we need to treat the draft not as the gradual approach towards a state of perfection, but as a field of work, a workshop where everything can be made manifest."[57] He goes on to summarize that "The difference between *the Text* ('*finished*,' i.e., published) and what we call the *pre-text* [*avant-texte*] lies in the fact that the former is offered to us as a whole, fixed in its destiny [*son destin*], while the latter carries within it and reveals its own history. One is stopped, the other on the move."[58]

For Yeats, at least, that concept of textual destiny is both an illusion and real: art exists as the illusion created by the much-worked lines that must seem a moment's thought, but also as an attempt to express a *daimonic* ideal reality that has a completeness and unity, where nothing can be added or taken away without marring the whole.[59] "Destiny," in Yeats's understanding, retains a sense of a perpetually receding challenge, the shifting *Mask* and *Image* that lead the artist on through the challenge of what is most difficult but not impossible.[60] The *Mask*, which comes from the *Daimon*, is the goal that the *Creative Mind*—"the intellect," both as "the mind that is consciously constructive" (*AVA* 15, *CW13* 15) and also "in the most *antithetical* phases [. . .] imagination" (*AVA* 76, *CW13* 64; *AVB* 142, *CW14* 106)—helps the artist to achieve. Yeats's artist is inspired, but then works to realize the "vision of reality" (*VP* 369) until, ideally, arriving at a moment where the "poem comes right with a click like the closing of a box" (to Dorothy Wellesley, September 8, [1935], *CL InteLex* 6335).

The arrested motion of the "finished" text did not mean that Yeats was satisfied—not all boxes clicked quite as resoundingly as others—and he continued to revise and recast works often long after their first publication. This was, perhaps, even more common for his non-poetic writing, whether in prose (the same letter noted that "The correction of prose, because it has no fixed laws, is endless" [*CL InteLex* 6335]) or in drama, where, amongst other factors, performance and theatrical experience influenced the vision. These notebooks contain various examples of further correction of details in *The Player Queen*, a major revision of *The Resurrection*, and, of course, repeated reworking of *A Vision*. In this context, Wim Van Mierlo draws attention to a letter to A. H. Bullen, in which Yeats explained why he wanted "to substitute" revised texts in his *Collected Works*,[61] asserting that, otherwise, "It changes the volumes from being a collection [of] precisely those things I wish to be my permanent self, into a collection of odds and ends including some that should not have been published" (February 22, 1913, *CL InteLex* 2094).[62] These terms proleptically echo those he would use in the unpublished Introduction for the Scribner edition of his work, conceiving of the poet himself as "something intended, complete," separate from the "bundle of accident and incoherence that sits down to breakfast," and therefore the conception of the work of art as something intended and unified.[63]

Examining earlier variants and even more, of course, drafts, means looking at precisely those things "that should not have been published," yet these earlier versions certainly exist,[64] and the manuscripts were preserved, enabling us to view the process of making and remaking, as well as gaining insight into the remade work or self. Though the artist may prioritize the goal, the process is also part of the art. Within the context of genetic criticism, therefore, the draft is given greater independence, such that the pioneering French critic Louis Hay declared that "the perspective of genesis shows us" that a first draft was "one of the *possibilities* of the text," even in the cases where "it was neither integrated nor subsumed" into the later versions: "In other words, the writing is not simply consummated in the written work. Perhaps we should consider the text as *a necessary possibility*, as one manifestation of a process which is always virtually present in the background, a kind of third dimension to this written work."[65] In this approach, the manuscript points to other directions and indicates branchings of potential forms that did not materialize further. It is not an inevitable step to the realization of the final text, but a moment with its own ramifications. This is particularly useful when drafts give us images or information that is subsequently lost from the published version, but may remain as a subterranean connection. In Yeats's case, this often applies to his reworking of *A Vision*, where the many formulations of an idea point to possible expressions of a theme, even though the ones that reached publication must be seen as closer to definitive. We can see Yeats's own understanding of his material developing and changing, so that ideas that were superseded may inform the poetry or drama that was written at that date. And, given that the system extends beyond what Yeats was able to include in the published versions, there are also elaborations and ideas that fall outside the core contained in the confines of *A Vision*. Other information can be contextual, such as evidence of dating or the sequence of creation.

Hay also draws attention to "The ways in which the text is laid out on the page, with marginal notations, additions, cross-references, deletions, alterations, in different handwriting styles, and with drawings and symbols, texture the discourse, increase the significations and multiply the possible readings."[66] Yet, while manuscripts may open up possibilities, they can also close down or delimit possible ambiguities found in a final text, perhaps through an alternative formulation or further detail and context that is subsequently lost. While the final textual surface may not indicate where certain elements came from, thus allowing critics some speculative space, the draft may show the exact route by which a particular formulation reached its final form, curtailing speculation.

Specifically examining Yeats's manuscripts, in four volumes of the Cornell Manuscript Materials series, Robin Gail Schulze acknowledges Hay's "*possibilities*" but also emphasizes how non-verbal aspects of manuscripts can delimit meanings:

> rather than merely endless[ly] multiply available readings, such manuscripts reveal instead the absolute material limits of any such freeplay. The physical features of the document—the doodles, the pictures, the rushed scrawls, the marginal insertions, the strenuous lines of cancellation, the balloons and arrows—rather than announce the endless deferral of meaning, stand witness to the difficult and very human attempt to contain meaning and to utter it [. . . .] The physical marks circumscribe the flow of text on the page and, as with published texts, help to determine what meanings are "operable" in any given version.[67]

This is particularly true for the construction of a complex argument or exposition such as those that Yeats undertakes with *A Vision*, where the drafts sometimes resolve ambiguities more decisively than parsing the syntax of the final wording or exploring the claims of logic. A spread of Yeats's drafts sometimes resembles the thorny tangle of a briar patch (see, for example, "Rapallo Notebooks A and B," Figure 1.5 at p. 70, below), yet, paradoxically, this forbidding mass of scrawls, insertions, cancellations, balloons, and arrows may well exclude interpretations arising from ambiguous phrasing and clarify uncertainties of meaning that exist in a published text, where defining details have been pruned for concision.[68]

Manuscripts, in Hay's words, force us to "come to grips with their heterogeneity, since they are diverse by nature,"[69] and such diversity applies all the more to the inherent nature of a notebook that gathers a range of drafts and times together. Heterogeneity and multiplicity are essential to what Yeats celebrated in his own terms as the "terrestrial" and "*antithetical*." *Per Amica Silentia Lunae* (1917) proposes that the human, terrestrial condition is the source of power in part by virtue of the heterogeneity it allows and in contrast to the simplicity of the condition of fire (*Myth* 356–57, *CW5* 25). In the condition of fire, like only meets like, whereas the terrestrial enables the meeting of the things that are unlike. Yet once the new combination is enabled, the terrestrial is then refined towards the condition of fire—the incoherence of "one's own life as symbolised by earth, the place of heterogeneous things, the images as mirrored in water, and the images themselves one could divine but as air; and beyond it all [. . .] the fire that makes all things simple"—with poetic imagery partaking of all four levels in differing degrees, or even of a fifth, "the veil hiding another four, a bird born out of the fire" (*Myth* 346, *CW5* 18–19).[70] This fifth level of spirit reveals a whole world beyond that mirrors but transcends the realms accessible to human thought.

And the intermingling of terrestrial and empyrean is a recurrent theme of the later poetry, whether in voices such as Ribh's, Old Tom's, or Yeats's own: "Natural and supernatural with the self-same ring are wed" (*VP* 556); "Things out of perfection sail..." (*VP* 530); "Those masterful images because complete / Grew in pure mind but out of what began? / A mound of refuse or the sweepings of a street" (*VP* 630). The "foul papers" of manuscripts may be the remains of the first meeting of pure mind with the loam of human language and the mechanics of writing, and notebooks often retain something of the miscellany of "Old kettles, old bottles, and a broken can, / Old iron, old bones, old rags" (*VP* 630). In "The Statues," Yeats maintains that the numbers of Pythagorean harmonies are characterless until given form in stone by the sculptor and then given life by the viewer, becoming realized ideals in the work of the sculptors and in the dreams imbued into these statues by the living (*VP* 610). The notebooks show the chisel marks and the rejected stone, preserving both the richness of possibilities and their limits, along with the contiguity of disparate concerns.

7. Conclusion

The Rapallo Notebooks bring together a unique record of Yeats's creative processes at a key period of his artistic and personal life. Roughly half of their pages are given over to work related to *A Vision*, representing an essential intermediate stage between *A Vision A* and *A Vision B*, as Yeats wrestled with both his understanding and his exposition of the material; and, though we can only wonder about what was on the pages that were removed, it seems that in most cases they related to *A Vision*. Other prose writing, including prefaces and essays, caused less of a problem in conception, usually taking a form that reflects the final organization more or less from the first, while the actual formulation of sentences and expression shows relentless effort to express the ideas with elegance and effect, and usually—but not always—greater clarity. These notebooks also contain important later works of poetry and drama that we are fortunate to see in genesis and development: this labor sometimes seems an evocation that starts with little more than a wisp of language, with a gradual aggregation of substance; often it starts from a block of prosy pondering, an attempt to capture a conception or perception, which is recast, modified, elaborated, and refined; and occasionally a fully formed Pallas Athene emerges with little or no preliminary sketching.

Jon Stallworthy emphasizes how the manuscripts from the late 1920s and 1930s bear witness to a process of exteriorizing thought:

> As he grew older he wrote, I believe, often with no intention of reading what was before him on the page: his fingers were simply turning the dials. He did not watch them, but rather listened to the stirring of the cog-wheels in his brain. He was in fact *thinking* on paper, and this gives his manuscripts their especial fascination. Reading them, one seems to be at his elbow, with the great voice chanting in one's ears.[71]

This is doubly true of the notebooks, where their physical form captures aspects of writing that may otherwise be lost. In contrast with loose papers, the notebooks sometimes preserve the very earliest germs of later works and show a variety of interests and impulses. Referring to them as sacred or talismanic indicates the frisson that the reader feels through such direct and unmediated contact with the creative mind. But what makes the Rapallo Notebooks special is their very ordinariness, showing the ferment of Yeats's creativity in its daily exercise. What is not ordinary is the poetry and thought that emerges in their pages.

Notes

1 George Yeats had written to Lennox Robinson that "WB of course is making his last will & testament at all hours of day & night—Hurrying to finish a poem—but has not been able to begin yet. 'Of course I shall never be able to go on with the autobio: now—' etc. etc. All poppycock—However in the same breath he talks of writing a poem on the Herons at Algeciras in 'a few years time'" (c. November 19, 1927; cit. Ann Saddlemyer, *Becoming George: The Life of Mrs W. B. Yeats* [Oxford: Oxford University Press, 2002], 387; hereafter cited as *BG*).

2 The Yeatses had visited Sicily in the winter of 1925/26, partly because the Pounds were there too, and Ezra Pound had not been the best of company then, either (*BG* 340–42; *Life2* 279). Roy Foster notes that, in the event, "The Pounds' complicated ménage made Rapallo less idyllic than expected" (*Life2* 357).

3 George Berkeley, *Siris* (London: C. Hitch; C. Davis, 1744; Dublin: R. Gunne, 1744).

4 See WBY's letter to Lennox Robinson, March 10, 1928 (*CL InteLex* 5088), cited in "Rapallo Notebooks A and B," *International Yeats Studies* 6.1: 106 (and p. 64 below); hereafter *IYS*.

5 A version of this general overview appears as "Yeats's Rapallo Notebooks," in *YA22* (forthcoming). Originally foreseen as a prelude and advertisement for the individual essays in *IYS*, delays in publication of *YA* mean that most of the essays appeared earlier. We have removed, especially from these notes, material that is repeated in the later essays.

6 Apart from the oddity of locating sacred objects in a mine, the metaphor also risks confusion with Yeats's own concept of the "sacred book of the arts": see Warwick Gould, "Yeats and His Books" (*YA20* [2016], 3–70) and "Conflicted Legacies: Yeats's Intentions and Editorial Theory" (*YA21* [2018], 479–541). See also Ian Fletcher, "Poet and Designer: W. B. Yeats and Althea Gyles," *Yeats Studies* 1 (1971), 42–79, and "Crafting the Book" in the National Library of Ireland's exhibit on W. B. Yeats (www.nli.ie/yeats/), especially "Althea Gyles and the Talismanic Book."

7 Conrad A. Balliet's census lists some thirty-two under "Miscellany—Diaries and Journals," *W. B. Yeats: A Census of the Manuscripts* (assisted by Christine Mawhinney; New York and London: Garland Publishing, Inc., 1990), 181–87, including the Rapallo Notebooks, with six additional, distinct cross-references to "Books" (187), and a signed but blank notebook given to Lady Gregory (187). See Neil Mann, "Yeats's Notebooks" (Appendix), *YA22* (forthcoming).

8 Jared Curtis and Selina Guinness, "*The Resurrection*": *Manuscript Materials* (Ithaca, NY: Cornell University Press, 2011), p. xxx. See Wayne K. Chapman, "Yeats's White Vellum Notebook, 1930–1933," *IYS* 2: 2 (2018), 40–59. Much that Wayne Chapman writes about the WVN, esp. 42–43, can be applied here, both in terms of each notebook's uniqueness and in drawing attention to David Clark's "appendix" (consisting of four lists) entitled "The Contents of the Notebooks," which he provided "to sort through the numerous threads that connect "The Large Notebook Bound in Vellum (MBY 545)" with Rapallo Notebooks C (NLI 13,580), D (NLI 13,581), and E (NLI 13,582)" in his "*Words for Music Perhaps and Other Poems*": *Manuscript Materials* (Ithaca, NY: Cornell University Press, 1999) (*IYS* 2:2, 43).

9 Curtis Bradford, *Yeats at Work* (Carbondale, IL: Southern Illinois University Press, 1965), 101 (hereafter *YAW*). He notes more generally that "Yeats nearly always wrote in a book either bound or looseleaf; apparently he liked the two page spread each opening provided" (xiii).

10 David R. Clark, *Parnell's Funeral and Other Poems: Manuscript Materials* (Ithaca, NY: Cornell University Press, 2003), xxiii. See also Bradford, *YAW* xiii.

11 See David R. Clark's descriptions in *Yeats at Songs and Choruses* (Amherst: University of Massachusetts Press, 1983), 243ff. Anomalously, Rapallo B appears to have had 102 leaves originally.

12 Notebooks A, B, and E have a vertical design of chains of small black diamonds and dots on a pale yellow ground (see "Rapallo Notebook E," Fig 4.1, p. 280), while Notebooks C and D have an olive-green ground covered with small white circles containing blue flowers, with smaller white dots between. NLI MS 13,577, containing the "Stories of Michael Robartes and His Friends," has the same cover as C and D, but is cased in a leather sleeve.

13 WBY was frequently given or used books with fine bindings, often in leather or vellum, and appropriately heavy paper, but these are very much ordinary notebooks, with no watermarks on the paper—hence the conservation problems attendant upon the relatively poor materials of the Rapallo Notebooks.

14 See *"Words for Music Perhaps and Other Poems": Manuscript Materials*, xvi–xvii.

15 In a letter to GY from Coole, WBY refers to some notes on Plotinus "in one of those Italian MSS books," clearly referring to the notes at the opening of Rapallo A ([August 17, 1928], *CL InteLex* 5145; *YGYL* 194).

16 Later, this was partially published as *Pages from a Diary Written in Nineteen Hundred and Thirty* (Dublin: Cuala, 1944).

17 WBY to Lady Gregory, April 24, [1931] (*CL InteLex* 5462); see R. F. Foster, *Life2* 417–18.

18 David R. Clark, ed., *The Winding Stair (1929): Manuscript Materials* (Ithaca NY: Cornell University Press, 1995) dates the drafts to "between September 1927 [. . .] and 13 March 1928" (xviii), basing the first date on comments in WBY's letter to Olivia Shakespear of October 2, [1927] (*L* 728–29; *CL InteLex* 5034). Clark considers it in more detail in the Introduction (xxiii–xxvi), suggesting that "the NLI 30,359 notebook was begun by the time of the October 2 letter, probably even 'two or three weeks ago' in September" (xxvi).

19 This poem (later split into "At Algeciras—A Meditation upon Death" and "Mohini Chatterjee") was published as "Meditations upon Death" in *A Packet for Ezra Pound* (Cuala, 1929), *The London Mercury* (November 1930), and *The New Republic* (January 1931), and "A Meditation written during Sickness at Algeciras" in *Words for Music Perhaps* (Dublin: Cuala, 1932) (see *VP* 493 and 495).

20 The first entry ties in with a letter sent to Ottoline Morrell on March 20, 1928, *CL InteLex* 5093. I am grateful to Wayne Chapman for alerting me to this match and correcting the dating originally proposed.

21 See Matthew Gibson, "Yeats's Notes on Leo Frobenius's *The Voice of Africa* (1913)" in *Yeats, Philosophy, and the Occult*, edited by Matthew Gibson and Neil Mann (Clemson, SC: Clemson University Press, 2016), Appendix II, 305–325.

22 These continuations in Notebook A were included in the published *Pages from a Diary Written in Nineteen Hundred and Thirty*.

23 Curtis Bradford similarly observes, "Yeats eventually used all his Journals as manuscript books, though often he began them intending to restrict their use, say, to a record of esoteric experiences," *YAW* 340.

24 The first part of the opening "Diary" was also reused in "A Note on Illness" found on loose-leaf pages associated with drafts for *A Packet for Ezra Pound* (NLI 30,319(5)). This passage looks back to convalescence in "Sevill, Cannes Rapallo," and focuses on four moments that remained as clear images that had "entered into my soul." The following section refers to a conversation "The other night [. . .] in some western farmhouse" about the Censorship Bill, so it may have been written in Ireland at the end of 1928 or in 1929.

25 WBY was staying at the Gogartys' "Renvyle House Hotel" in Connemara and sent the "open letter" to GY for typing on July 27, 1930 (*CL InteLex* 5363; *YGYL* 220), though this letter

was delayed and, on August 3, WBY announced that, instead, he would ask Lady Gregory to type it for him when he arrived at Coole (*CL InteLex* 5367; *YGYL* 221).

26 Some forty pages have been cut out of Notebook D between leaf [41] and leaf [84], but they are counted in the numbering of the folios in Clark's *"Words for Music Perhaps and Other Poems": Manuscript Materials* and (slightly differently) in the NLI's electronic version at the *Yeats* exhibition (2006–). It is probable that the first draft of "Veronica's Napkin" was written on [41v] after the pages were excised, with subsequent drafts on [84v], [85r], and [93v] (see *"Words for Music Perhaps and Other Poems": Manuscript Materials* 228–35), but the gap between the drafts of "Crazy Jane on the Day of Judgment" appears to be real.

27 A copy of the quatrain was sent to Lady Gregory on 24 April [1931] (*CL InteLex* 5462), but a successful appeal made the satire obsolete; see *Life2* 417–18 and 736n76.

28 In the Cornell manuscripts series, David R. Clark states that Notebook E contains "entries from about 9 May [1928] to about January 1929," *"Words for Music Perhaps and Other Poems": Manuscript Materials*, xvii. Mary FitzGerald's wording is almost identical in *"The Words Upon the Window Pane": Manuscript Materials* (Ithaca, NY: Cornell University Press, 2002): "*NLI 13,582 Rapallo Notebook E* containing entries from about May 9, 1928, to about January 1929" (xii), as is that of Richard Finneran, Jared Curtis, and Ann Saddlemyer in *"The Tower": Manuscript Materials* (Ithaca, NY: Cornell University Press, 2007). It is probable that the untimely deaths of FitzGerald and Finneran led to Clark's text simply being repeated. In the volume dedicated to *The Resurrection*, editors Jared Curtis and Selina Guinness state that "The notebook appears to have been in use from about May or June 1926, perhaps as early as May 1925" (*"The Resurrection": Manuscript Materials*, xvi) and, though they give no explicit end date, indicate the book's use in early 1931 (see page xxx).

29 See John S. Kelly, *A W. B. Yeats Chronology* (London: Palgrave, 2003). WBY wrote to GY on [May 9, 1929] that he had "been to a couple of mediums" (*CL InteLex* 5251), and though the account of the letter and the notebook do not quite match, they are very close, whereas on May 9, 1928, WBY was at the Abbey writing to Seán O'Casey about the success of *The Plough and the Stars*.

30 Curtis and Guinness note that the "four leaves" of the earliest scenario "were at some time removed from the notebook and [are] now tipped into it at the stubs that follow the holograph revision of the play" (xvi). As shown in the essay "Rapallo Notebook E" below (p. 337), there is no realistic way that the pages could have come from Rapallo E itself, so they almost certainly came from one of the other Rapallo notebooks or from a notebook that is no longer extant. As for the position of these pages in the book, the conjugate leaves were loose and were inserted just *before* the later drafts of *The Resurrection* when the notebook was photographed for the microfilm at Harvard's Houghton Library, which appears to be from the late 1940s. Wayne Chapman argues convincingly that these microfilms were prepared at that time for Richard Ellmann; see "Yeats's White Vellum Notebook, 1930–1933," *IYS* 2:2, 58 n18.

31 NLI 30,769, described in *"The Resurrection": Manuscript Materials*, xviii, and photograph on page 14.

32 NLI 13,582, [63r].

33 WBY later told Thomas Sturge Moore that the poem originated in "a criticism of yours" (October 4, [1930], *CL InteLex* 5390; cf. *TSMC* 164), expressed in a letter dated April 16, 1930 (*TSMC* 162).

34 The final MS draft on loose paper, NLI 13,590 (17), was paper-clipped and kept at the back of Rapallo D, photographed there on the Harvard microfilm.

35 The line is evidently intended for the character of John Corbet: "I prove in an essay for my Cambridge lecture that there is only one plausable explanation for the celibacy of

Swift— dred that his children might inherit madness," NLI 13,581 [17v], cf. *VPl* 955. See p. 204 below.

36 "All the great philosophies, Plato, Spinoza, Hegel, are but drama [. . .]" NLI 13,581, [97v]. See pp. 254–55, below.

37 See Chapman, "Yeats's White Vellum Notebook, 1930–1933," 48.

38 This is item 51 in Chapman, "Yeats's White Vellum Notebook, 1930–1933," covering the pages that Curtis Bradford numbered 185–230 ([93r] to [115v]), though WBY could easily have plunged into the middle of the notebook relatively early on, and almost certainly did.

39 Curtis Bradford's *Yeats at Work* (Carbondale, IL: Southern Illinois University Press, 1965) is cited in note 9 above; *The Writing of "The Player Queen"* (DeKalb, IL: Northern Illinois University Press, 1977) is referenced in note 45. Jon Stallworthy's first examination of Yeats's drafts was *Between the Lines: Yeats's Poetry in the Making* (Oxford: Oxford University Press, 1963), see note 71; his second was *Vision and Revision in Yeats's "Last Poems"* (Oxford: Clarendon Press, 1969).

40 Rapallo C (NLI 13,580), [6r–8r], used in Richard Ellmann, *The Identity of Yeats* (rev. ed. London: Faber and Faber, 1964), 239–40.

41 Rapallo D (NLI 13,581) in Neil Mann, "'Everywhere that antinomy of the One and the Many': The Foundations of *A Vision*," in ed. Mann, Gibson, Nally, *W. B. Yeats's "A Vision": Explications and Contexts* (Clemson, SC: Clemson University Press, 2012), 8–9; for its relation to the "Seven Propositions," see https://www.yeatsvision.com/7Propositions.html.

42 Rapallo B (NLI 13,579), last page [94v] and [83r], cited in Catherine Paul, "W. B. Yeats and the Problem of Belief," *YA21* 295–316, at 297–98, 307; see also Mann, *A Reader's Guide to Yeats's "A Vision"* (Clemson, SC: Clemson University Press and Liverpool University Press, 2019), 300.

43 Rapallo B (NLI 13,579), [102v].

44 *A Packet for Ezra Pound* (Dublin: Cuala, 1929), 32–33.

45 See Curtis Bradford, ed., *The Writing of "The Player Queen"* (DeKalb, IL: Northern Illinois University Press, 1977).

46 Adjacent material is not always a reliable guide for dating. Although WBY generally uses the rectos of the leaves as his main sequence, with the opposing versos available for revisions and insertions, he sometimes filled them with entirely separate material as he took advantage of a blank page for notes, possibly weeks, months, or even years later.

47 We are extremely grateful to Jack Quin for checking the original notebooks to confirm gaps and blanks at a time when travel to Dublin was not possible.

48 See David Holdeman, "Manuscripts and revisions," in ed. Holdeman and Ben Levitas, *Yeats in Context* (Cambridge: Cambridge University Press, 2010), 365–75.

49 Jean Bellemin-Noël's term "*avant-texte*" is usually translated as pre-text (see below).

50 Zachary Leader, "Daisy packs her bags," review of *Trimalchio: An Early Version of 'The Great Gatsby' by F. Scott Fitzgerald*, ed. James L. W. West III, *London Review of Books* 22: 18 (September 21, 2000).

51 Stephen M. Parrish, "The Whig Interpretation of Literature," *Text: An Interdisciplinary Annual of Textual Studies 4* (1988), 343–51. Leader describes this title as a "belittling tag," see note 50 above.

52 Ibid., 346.

53 Ibid., 345. Taking Wordsworth as a pattern, Parrish "would plead the autonomy and the validity of each steady state of the text as it changes in confused, unpredictable ways, through patterns which the author may never have foreseen, let alone 'intended'" (ibid., 350). The key word here, though, is "steady," which applies more readily to Wordsworth—who kept unpublished drafts with him for years, leaving them and reworking them at intervals—than most other writers.

54 See, for instance, Shelley on the role of inspiration in "A Defence of Poetry": "Poetry is not like reasoning, a power to be exerted according to the determination of the will[. . . .] for the mind in creation is as a fading coal, which some invisible influence, like an inconstant wind, awakens to transitory brightness; this power arises from within [. . .] and the conscious portions of our natures are unprophetic either of its approach or its departure"; thus, "when composition begins, inspiration is already on the decline, and the most glorious poetry that has ever been communicated to the world is probably a feeble shadow of the original conceptions of the poet," *Essays, Letters from Abroad, Translations and Fragments*, 2 vols. (London: Moxon, 1840), 1: 47–48. See also WBY's early essays on "The Philosophy of Shelley's Poetry" (*E&I* 65–95, *CW4* 51–72) and "William Blake and His Illustrations to the *Divine Comedy*" (*E&I* 116–45, *CW4* 88–107).

55 The Cornell Wordsworth therefore aimed to present the "texts of a poem as it stood at successive stages of its completion." Stephen M. Parrish, "Versioning Wordsworth: A Study in Textual Ethics," *The Wordsworth Circle* 28: 2 (Spring 1997), 98–100, at 98. The editors went further, in also pledging themselves "to show all readings in all other texts, including the final one, in all manuscripts and all lifetime editions" (98).

56 The first two of these are the focus of the Cornell series, where Stephen Parrish and the Editorial Board initially declared, in the statement of intent prefacing each volume of the Cornell series of *Manuscript Materials by W. B. Yeats*, that the manuscripts "help to illuminate Yeats's creative process," enable "scholars who wish to establish definitive texts of the published works," and provide "many passages of biographical interest" (*Manuscript Materials by W. B. Yeats*, "The Cornell Yeats," v). This objective was repeated in seven volumes of the series until 1994, when in the volume on *Michael Robartes and the Dancer* the statement substituted "authoritative" for "definitive" and dropped reference to biography. A more significant overhaul took place in 2000, in *New Poems*, where it was said that the editions would "present, comprehensively and accurately, the various versions behind Yeats's published poems and plays, including versions he left unpublished" and "be of use to readers who seek to understand how great writing can be made, and to scholars and editors who seek to establish and verify authoritative final texts"; this wording continued in use until 2005 in *Diarmuid and Grania*, where "can be made" became "take shape." These changes, no doubt, reflect shifts in general editorial policy, especially the decision not to include Prose or Family Papers as originally envisaged, signaled in removal of these areas from the series outline on page ii from the year 2000 onward.

57 Jean Bellemin-Noël, "*Lecture psychanalytique d'un brouillon de poème : 'Été' de Valéry*," *Essais en critique génétique* (Paris: Flammarion, 1979). My translation of: "*l'écrit* en transformation, *et dans un système ouvert, l'écrivain ne sachant pas à l'avance où il va exactement, nous le voyons en train de se frayer un chemin, c'est la suite de ses options qui détermine l'itinéraire du texte* [. . .] *il faut traiter le brouillon non comme la progressive approximation d'un état de perfection, mais comme un champ de travail, un atelier où tout peut venir à réalisation*" (116).

58 Ibid. "*La différence entre* le Texte ['achevé,' *entendons: publié*] *et ce que nous appelons l'avant-texte réside en ceci que le premier nous est offert comme un tout fixé dans son destin tandis que le second porte en lui et révèle sa propre histoire. L'un est arrêté, l'autre en marche.*" Addressing the idea of the *pre-text* with respect to WBY's work, Daniel Albright writes (in thought-provoking but less than perspicuous terms) of "the tendency of modern semiotics [. . .] to regard the text as a coordination of written words temporarily paralyzed, stunned into Roman or elite quiescence, but liable to reassume a state of extreme fluidity, infinite semantic possibility, at the instant when the reading Medusa averts her gaze. The tendency is to regard the pre-text as either (1) a bundle of rough drafts, slowly dissolving into a heat-sink of related documents—as Coleridge's 'Kubla Khan' disperses into travel literature in Lowes's *The Road to Xanadu* (1927); or, more breathtakingly, (2) the aggregate of all possible

propositions in all possible languages—the Gibraltar of diction out of which any finite set of sentences is quarried," *Quantum Poetics: Yeats, Pound, Eliot and the Science of Modernism* (Cambridge: Cambridge University Press, 1997), 3.

59 The relation of artistic unity to the *Daimon* is seen in two passages from Rapallo Notebook B, in a description of the spiritual condition where "flame is eternal" and potentially attained through art: "the mystery remains, that the daimon is alone is real, that nothing can be added to it, nothing taken away; that all progressions are illusion; that all things have been born from it like a ship in full sail" (NLI 13,579, [34r & 33v], dated "March 1928" [see "Rapallo Notebooks A and B," *IYS* 6.1: 176 (and p. 80 below); cf. NLI 36,272/18/4, p. 26, dated "May 5 1928," and cf. Ellmann, *The Identity of Yeats*, 221]); and in a passage on *A Vision*: "A single thought has expressed itself as if it were a work of art," with each detail tested "by its relation to the whole, each completed movement by its reflection of the whole, & the value of that single [*thought*] and therefore of the whole, lies in the daimon, which I can express but cannot judge" (NLI 13,579, [102v], see *IYS* 6.1: 183 (and 99 below). See also Mann, "Yeats's *Daimonic* Art and Unity of Being," (forthcoming).

60 See Mann, "The Mask of *A Vision*," *YA19* (2015) 167–189, esp. 173–74.

61 WBY was referring to *The Collected Works in Verse and Prose of William Butler Yeats* (Stratford-upon-Avon: Shakespeare's Head, 1908) and was particularly concerned here with *Deirdre*.

62 Wim Van Mierlo, "Vision and Revision in the Manuscripts of William Wordsworth and W. B. Yeats," in ed. J. Bloom and C. Rovera, *Genesis and Revision in Modern British and Irish Writers* (n.p.: Palgrave Macmillan, 2020), 18.

63 WBY had already indicated, in his epigraph for the second volume of these same *Collected Works*, "what issue is at stake: / It is myself that I remake" (*VP* 778). Although "authorial intention" may be a problematic term in criticism, intention and will also have different but important connotations in the context of ritual magic as used by the Golden Dawn.

64 Warwick Gould cites WBY's exasperation with those who favored superseded versions, to the point of inscribing an American collector's copy of *Poems* (T. Fisher Unwin, 1895) with a reproach: "Mr Young why do you like first editions. This edition is much less agreeable than the later ones. It has a cover which has nothing of the beauty or meaning of Althea Gyles's covers, some misprints & none of the dramatic verse is in its final shape. Some day will not writers have a mortal quarrel with their readers over this business of first editions." "Bibliophilia and Descriptive Bibliography: The Case of Yeats's Books," *Studi Irlandesi: A Journal of Irish Studies* 14 (2024), 109–10.

65 Louis Hay, "Does 'Text' Exist?" translated by Matthew Jocelyn, revised by Hans Walter Gabler, *Studies in Bibliography* 41 (1988), 64–76, at 76. Though this is an official translation, Hay's "*se consumer*" would be better translated as "is consumed" or "consumes itself" (in the sense of "burns itself up") than "is [. . .] consummated"; furthermore, "*l'un des* possibles" is less "one of the *possibilities*" than one of the possible expressions, manifestations, or realizations, almost a possible embodiment of an ideal form. See "'*Le texte n'existe pas.*' *Réflexions sur la critique génétique*," *Poétique* 62 (1985), 147–58: "*Mais la genèse nous révèle en même temps que cette œuvre première et différente était l'un des* possibles *du texte, sans se trouver pour autant inclus ou subsumé dans l'œuvre seconde. Autrement dit : l'écriture ne vient pas se consumer dans l'écrit. Peut-être faut-il tenter de penser le texte comme un possible nécessaire, comme une des réalisations d'un processus qui demeure toujours virtuellement présent à l'arrière-plan et constitue comme une troisième dimension de l'écrit*" (158).

66 Hay, ibid., 69: "*L'organisation sur la feuille, les marginales, ajouts, renvois, les textes croisés, les graphismes divers, les dessins et symboles entrelacent les discours, dédoublent les systèmes de significations et multiplient par là les réseaux de lecture*" (151).

67 Robin G. Schulze, "The One and the Many: Reading the Cornell Yeats," ed. W. Speed Hill, *Text: An Interdisciplinary Annual of Textual Studies* 10 (Ann Arbor: University of Michigan Press, 1997), 323–37, at 336. She notes: "The volumes, by virtue of their photofacsimiles, stress the materiality of the texts they record, even if they cannot truly reproduce such materiality," although, in the case of bound notebooks, they actually dematerialize the physical object containing the manuscript.

68 Examples in *A Vision B* include an ambiguity about where the *Meditation* fits into the afterlife (see Rapallo E, [58v], p. 347 below, clarified further in NLI 36,272/22), whether "imminent" (*AVB* 263, *CW14* 192) should read "immanent" (see Rapallo A, [20r], *IYS* 6.1: 146; and p. 44 below), and major aspects of the *Daimon* and the *Principles*, which WBY treats cursorily in *A Vision*, despite stating their centrality (much of the *Vision* treatment in Rapallo A, B, and E).

69 Hay, "Does 'Text' Exist?" 69: "*Ils nous imposent une réflexion sur l'hétérogène, puisqu'ils sont par nature divers*" (151).

70 WBY's thinking here is clearly based on the Cabala of the Golden Dawn, with the four levels of the Tree of Life—material Assiah, formative Yetzirah, creative Briah, and archetypal Atziluth—corresponding to the four classical elements (see Israel Regardie, *The Golden Dawn*, 4 vols. [Chicago: Aries Press, 1937–1940], 1: 125–26). The G.∴D.∴ taught about a fifth element of Akasa (spirit or ether, drawn from Indian thought; see *The Golden Dawn*, vol. 4: 12–14), the quintessence. This was reflected in the transitional "Grade of the Portal" between the outer order of the Golden Dawn—where each grade was attributed to an element and a sephirah on the Tree of Life—and the inner order of the Red Rose and the Golden Cross; this "Grade" was associated with Akasa and the Veil *Paroketh*, the Veil of Temple (see *The Golden Dawn*, vol. 1: 65–66).

71 Jon Stallworthy, *Between the Lines: Yeats's Poetry in the Making* (Oxford: Oxford University Press, 1963), 9–10.

Figure 0.1. The waterfront at Rapallo in the region of Liguria on the Italian Riviera, c. 1926, from a prospect familiar to the Yeatses, looking eastward.

Figure 0.2. The waterfront at Rapallo, c. 1920s, from the eastern side of the harbor, looking westward.

Rapallo Notebooks A and B

Neil Mann

The Rapallo Notebooks

This is the first of a series of essays in *IYS* covering the five notebooks that W. B. Yeats kept between 1928 and 1931, referred to as "Rapallo Notebooks," which are now held by the National Library of Ireland as MSS 13,578–13,582. As well as the Italian town of Rapallo, the notebooks bear traces from other places, including Dublin, Coole, and London, as Yeats tended to use bound notebooks as a portable means of keeping his work together when traveling, preferring loose-leaf notebooks when at home. However, the name is apt, as W. B. and George Yeats returned to Rapallo for three successive winters for Yeats's health,[1] and it is also likely that the notebooks were purchased in Italy.[2] They were not the only notebooks used when the Yeatses were in Rapallo, and others overlap with them, including, for instance, the diary that Yeats kept in 1930, but these five have a uniformity of dimensions and paper,[3] and were early on treated as a group, now labeled A, B, C, D, and E.[4] Notebooks A, B, and E are identical, with a yellow cover decorated with vertical lines made of lozenge shapes, while C and D have a cover design in olive green, blue, and white, with small flowers.

The overview of the five notebooks that prefaces this collection was written to appear in *Yeats Annual* 22 in advance of the individual essays in *IYS*.[5] As that essay indicates, it is in fact likely that Rapallo Notebooks A, much of B, and E were all started in 1928, with B being the first, while E had the early material removed.[6] Because of particular overlap of time and material between Rapallo Notebooks A and B, they are presented together here, though treated separately for the sake of clarity. And, although Rapallo Notebook B precedes Rapallo Notebook A in terms of starting date and, to a large extent, of use, they are examined in the order of their labeling. Subsequent essays address the notebooks singly and are by Wayne Chapman, or are collaborations between Chapman and myself.

If there is a common thread to the notebooks, it is in the drafts and notes where Yeats was struggling with a new exposition of the system of *A Vision*. After publication of the first version of *A Vision* in 1925,[7] he had immediately started to revise his thinking about important elements, to read more widely in philosophical literature, and to rewrite sections of the book. By 1928 he was seriously drafting for a new edition, and all five Rapallo notebooks contain

Vision material—though Rapallo Notebook D has relatively little, while Rapallo Notebook B is almost exclusively dedicated to such drafts. Some of the material is completely new, but much could be termed "intermediate" between the formulations of *A Vision A* and those of *A Vision B*. For students of *A Vision*, therefore, they often reveal how the thought itself was developing, so that what is expressed concisely and sometimes too laconically in *A Vision B* (1937) may be explained a little more fully or tentatively here, or even in completely different ways. In fact, relatively little of the material contained in the notebooks' drafts appears in the 1937 edition without significant transformation, with the exception of material for *A Packet for Ezra Pound* and some of what became "The Great Year of the Ancients."

The notebooks also bear witness to the poetic creativity of the late 1920s, including poems that would appear in the Cuala Press's *Words for Music Perhaps* (1932) and Macmillan's edition of *The Winding Stair and Other Poems* (1933), drafts for *The Words upon the Window-Pane* (first staged in 1930) and *The Resurrection* (the revised version of 1931). There are also minor emendations for *The Player Queen*, material associated with *The Cat and the Moon*, drafts for essays, prefaces, letters to the press, and unpublished material, both poetry and prose, including ideas for poems that were probably never written. Mixed in with these are diary entries and analyses of friends, reading lists, notes from Yeats's reading and researches, a week's appointments, calculations, and a record of payments.

Because of their binding, the notebooks preserve a fuller record of the genesis of poetry and drama than Yeats's preferred format of loose leaf, though all of the notebooks show signs of pages having been torn out or removed with a blade. Above all, it is the heterogeneity and the miscellaneous quality of the material in the notebooks that makes them a singular and very immediate record of Yeats's mind and concerns at a crucial stage of his career. The poet may not be "the bundle of accident and incoherence that sits down to breakfast," but rather someone who "has been reborn as an idea, something intended, complete" (*E&I* 509, *CW5* 204), yet both poet and bundle of accident are present in the notebooks' ferment of the esoteric, the poetic, and the day-to-day. Indeed, just as some alchemists claimed that the raw material for the Philosophers' Stone was to be found on the common dungheap,[8] Yeats acknowledged that the poet's "masterful images" began in "A mound of refuse or the sweepings of a street" (*VP* 630, *CW1* 355), and, though it would be unnecessarily disparaging to describe the notebooks as such sweepings, they do show the jostle of disparate elements.

This disparateness is lost when drafts are removed from their context. Most of the poetry and drama is now readily available in facsimile in the Cornell manuscripts series, but in extracted form, presented page by page and often reordered, as Yeats tended to use the right-hand side of a spread first, with the left-hand side for later revisions.[9] The Cornell series's presentation, of course, serves well the purpose of showing how the works evolve and brings together drafts from a variety of places, but it risks creating a false sense of teleology or smoothing over the cross-fertilization of other interests.[10] These notebooks may contain multiple drafts of a single poem, just one, or even just a few lines adumbrating something filled out elsewhere, but this version is placed not with any preceding states nor with later typescripts and more final versions, but rather with the mix of other writings and concerns.[11] The tables presented in the Appendix make it possible to map how this material appears in the notebooks, at least partially, and they also indicate some other places that offer relevant transcriptions.[12]

Because almost none of the material in Rapallo Notebooks A and B has been transcribed or reproduced before, I have erred on the side of fullness when presenting transcriptions in the following essay. This has made the article significantly longer than originally projected, but I trust that there is enough of interest to students of Yeats to justify the length and the detailed—though far from exhaustive—treatment of the material.

Note on Transcription Principles, Conventions, and Symbols

The transcriptions in this examination seek to illustrate the wealth of material contained in the notebooks, most of it not published before.

In general, readability is paramount. Cancelled text is not included in the transcription, unless a cancelled word makes the syntax more comprehensible. Where the line striking content through does not reach a word that is evidently no longer intended, that word is omitted as if it had been struck through. However, in examples where the process of composition is a point of consideration, the cancellations are, of course, included, to show how Yeats rethought and refined his expression. In cases of multiple levels of cancellation, I have tried to indicate these as far as possible with standard typography, with single strikethrough, double strikethrough, and lines drawn in.

Similarly, in text for reading, insertions are usually included silently, but when the process of writing is important, they are indicated by placing the text in <pointed brackets>, omitting any caret mark or lines. Material inserted from the opposite verso is placed in {curly brackets}.

Punctuation is only added in [brackets] when the reader might otherwise stumble over the construction, so the text is usually left with Yeats's very light and slightly wayward punctuation. Uncertain readings show the word(s) [?queried in brackets]. Supplied words and clarifications are in [*italics in brackets*], as is the occasional [*sic*] where the reader might suspect a misprint, although most misspellings and repetitions are given as they appear without comment. As Yeats occasionally uses his own ellipses, my ellipses signifying omitted text are also placed in brackets, with three [. . .] or four points [. . . .] according to standard convention of whether or not at least one period is omitted. In transcriptions where cancelled text is being shown, repetitious material that is cancelled is sometimes omitted and shown as [~~....~~].

Yeats's spelling was never conventionally strong and, while his handwriting is seldom easy, in these personal notebooks it is sometimes little more than gestural shorthand: paradoxically, therefore, words with clearer lettering appear with Yeats's (mis)spelling, while those with outlines that are understandable only in context appear more conventionally.

The illustrations of the pages from the notebooks are intended to give some instances of how the transcriptions relate to the real material, in particular the appearance of the pages, and to show readers some words that have remained impossible for me to transcribe with confidence.

The Sequence of Rapallo A and B

Both Rapallo A and B are dominated by material associated with *A Vision*, Rapallo A significantly, and Rapallo B almost exclusively. From internal dating, it appears that Rapallo B was started in March 1928, while it is likely that Rapallo Notebook A was started in July 1928. The two notebooks ran in parallel during the summer and early fall of 1928; Rapallo Notebook B was finished in October and Notebook A a month later in November 1928, only for a blank page to be used two years later to extend an entry from the 1930 diary.

The sequence and relationship of the notebooks can be illustrated by one section from the Rapallo Notebooks' immediate predecessor, and the versions that developed in the two notebooks themselves. Prior to the Yeatses' arrival in Rapallo, W. B. Yeats had been using a leather notebook, which he had probably brought along with him when his health problems led the couple to sail for the south in November 1927.[13] It contains drafts of poems that would go into *The Winding Stair* (1929), some of which appear to be in relatively fair form while others are still very much in progress.[14] At the end of these poems Yeats gives a date of "Dec 1927"; they are followed by notes relating to the system of *A Vision* and records of "Sleeps" in Cannes, where the Yeatses stayed from the end of November 1927 until the middle of February 1928. The last date in this book (though not the last entry) is "Sleap March Rapallo."[15]

One of the more extended notes in this volume is titled "suggested first paragraph of system," two pages after the date of "Dec 11," 1927. In this projected opening for the new edition of *A Vision*, Yeats starts with the *Daimon*. Realizing that he had not stated the subject of the paragraph clearly, Yeats indicated the insertion of an introductory sentence stating, "all that can <need> be said of the daimon in this place can [*be*] put into a few sentences."[16] This prefaces the following presentation:

> It is a self creating power none is like another, for what in a man personally is unique is from the daimon and this daimon seeks to unite itself now with one now with another daimon but can only do so through the human mind it has neither reflection nor memory. We represent it thus
>
> 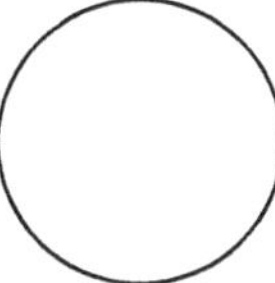
>
> because it does not perceive, as does the linear mind of man, object following object in a narrow stream, but all at once & because it perceives objects arranged about as it were in order of their kinship with itself, those most akin the nearest & not as they are in time & space.[17]

The treatment goes on to consider the relation between human and daimon in some depth, with many cancellations and second thoughts.

The next draft in Rapallo B, titled "First things" and dated March 1928 at the end, shows more confidence, though Yeats decided to insert yet another introductory paragraph in front of the text, indicating its insertion from the opposite verso.[18] The few sentences about the *Daimon* are introduced by the disclaimer, "I begin with the daimon & of the daimon I know little," a lack of knowledge that is brushed aside in characteristically Yeatsian style by piling up quotations from a proto-Christian heretic, the Upanishads, and a Zen koan (see the section on Rapallo B below). He then recounts an argument with the instructor, in fact very recent as it was one of the last entries in the previous, leather-bound notebook, "Sleap March Rapallo." Yeats comments that the instructor was "cross because I did not realize that the daimon was perfect" and had explained to him how *Daimons* could be both unique and perfect.[19] Yeats records in Rapallo B:

> I did not dare to ask why, if the daimon is perfect, ~~it was necessary to create man~~ <man comes into existence>; I did not want another scene & besides one cannot know everything. I accept his thought & say that nothing can be taken from or added to the daimon & being a symbolist & no philosopher I declare that this is its shape[20]

This comes at the bottom of a page and the following page was torn out, but Yeats appears to remove the explanation of why the *Daimon* is symbolized by the circle; further explanation is separated into the following section and consideration of how the *daimonic* mind connects to and differs from the human mind is briefer. This whole page was later completely cancelled.

In Rapallo A, the list of contents on the book's first verso notes that the section titled "First Things" has the "first page lacking."[21] Because of this, the notebook does not show how the opening section developed, but the text of its section II echoes Rapallo B:[22]

> I did not dare to ask why if each be perfect man should come into existence; I did not want another scene & besides one cannot know everything. I accept his thought & say <to introduce the chief person of my ~~play~~ drama> that nothing can be taken from or added to the Daimon & being a symbolist <dramatist> & ~~know~~ ~~no philosopher~~ <~~logician~~> <not a dialectician> declare that this is its shape[23]

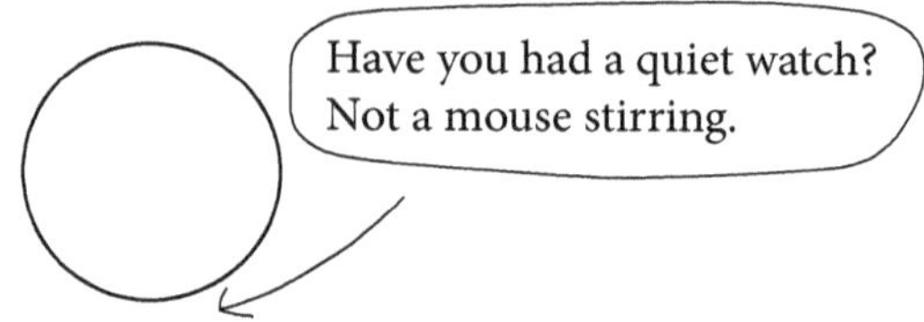

Have you had a quiet watch?
Not a mouse stirring.

What were additions and corrections to the text of Rapallo B are incorporated into the text of Rapallo A, with slight changes, generally in the direction of more formal language, so that "why if the daimon is perfect man comes" is amended to "why if each be perfect man should come." Further elaborations are added, so that Yeats declares the *Daimon* "the chief person of my drama," and refines his thinking, deciding, for instance, not to disqualify himself as a philosopher but to admit that he is no dialectician. The miswriting of "know" for "no" may indicate that the text was being dictated directly from its source, whether Rapallo B or the associated typescript. He also adds a gnomic quotation from *Hamlet*, alluding to the presence of a spirit, which persists through a series of drafts.[24]

These three extracts show the relatively straightforward development of a single concept,[25] and also indicate the order of the Rapallo Notebooks, which is also indicated by the first bloc of material in Rapallo A being listed as "Great Year (final version),"[26] while the fourth bloc of material in Rapallo B is listed as "Great Year (early version)," with the text in Rapallo A adopting the later versions of Rapallo B's drafts, though there are relatively few points of direct contact between the two.[27] The "Great Year" section in Rapallo B follows a bloc dated "May 1928" (after a few intervening notes),[28] and takes up more than twenty-four leaves, so it is unlikely that "The Great Year" that opens Rapallo A was started before June of that year, and July seems more probable.

The following tabulation sets out the approximate periods during which the three notebooks examined above were in use.

Table 1.1. Approximate dates and places of use of Yeats's notebooks NLI 30,359, Rapallo A, and Rapallo B.

year	*month*	*main places*	Leather NB NLI 30,359	Rapallo A NLI 13,578	Rapallo B NLI 13,579
1927	Dec				
	Jan	Cannes			
	Feb				
	Mar	Rapallo			
	Apr	Rapallo / Dublin			
	May	Dublin			
	Jun	London			
1928	Jul	Dublin			
	Aug	Coole			
	Sep	Dublin			
	Oct				
	Nov	Rapallo			
	Dec	Rome / Rapallo			
1929					
1930					
	Nov	London / Dublin			

RAPALLO NOTEBOOK A

Rapallo Notebook A is, therefore, probably the second of the Rapallo Notebooks Yeats started, and its main period of use was from before August 1928 until later that year, when Yeats put one of the notebook's two explicit dates at the end of a long draft of material related to the Great Year for *A Vision*, "Nov 1928."[29] The other date contained in the notebook actually comes from 1930 and relates to an isolated late item dated "Oct 20," continuing an entry from the 1930 diary. However, much of the other material in Rapallo A is clearly datable by external factors including letters and periodical publication.

The November date for the *Vision* material is squeezed vertically into a lower corner and evidently relates to revision and possible addition, as it is followed by material from before that date: drafts for articles on censorship published in September 1928;[30] early drafts for his essay on the Irish coinage (the final draft finished, according to a letter, by August 28, [1928], *CL InteLex* 5150); and a draft letter responding to Annie Horniman's carping criticism in the *Irish Statesman* on 6 October 1928 (Yeats's letter was published 13 October 1928, *CL InteLex* 5176).[31] The notebook also contains revisions to *The Player Queen* for upcoming performances at the Abbey in September 1928, as well as notes from reading Stephen MacKenna's translation of Plotinus and on the long ages of Indian tradition. It appears to have been treated as finished and put aside at the end of 1928, but it was taken up two years later to take advantage of the plentiful blank space at the end of the notebook to add to the diary of 1930,[32] which had been filled up; Yeats extended the diary entry dated "October 20" and also added a coda to a later undated entry. As the diary was finished in November 1930—its final entry is dated "Nov 18"—it is likely that the extension was actually added after that date.

Contents: Overview

Over half of the notebook is taken up with revisions for *A Vision*, focused on two areas that changed significantly: the vastly expanded treatment of the "Great Year" and Yeats's continuing struggle with how best to start his presentation of the system.[33] The main treatment of the Great Year in *A Vision A* (1925) had been a lengthy exploration in Book II, section "X | The Great Year in Classical Antiquity," which is supplementary to the system as such, illustrating how Yeats's idea relates to its many precedents (*AVA* 149–58, *CW13* 121–28). The drafts in Rapallo A and B build on this material but contain further research on ancient cosmology, furnished by wider reading, although Yeats had yet to be introduced to some of the illustrations he would use, such as the work of Leo Frobenius that was Ezra Pound's enthusiastic recommendation.[34] Many pages of the drafts also relate the Great Year to more technical aspects of the system, but little of this material reached the published version. Like its slighter predecessor in *A Vision A*, therefore, much of "Book IV: The Great Year of the Ancients" as published in *A Vision B* (1937) is not particularly connected to the esoteric system. Rather, it is mainly concerned with drawing parallels between the long periods of *A Vision*'s historical cycles and various schemes of antiquity—whether the return of all the planets to the same positions or the precession of the equinoxes—as well as more modern anthropological research and discussion of writers such as Oswald Spengler and Henry Adams.

As alluded to in the earlier examination of the notebooks' order, Rapallo A's section on "First Things" redrafts the material of Rapallo B, intended for the new edition of *A Vision*. It opens with the *Daimon* before moving to the intersecting cones and the presentation of the gyres—drawing on Plotinus, Heraclitus, Proclus, and Cavalcanti—to explain the underlying foundations that Yeats felt he had avoided in *A Vision A*. Convinced of the *Principles'* more fundamental importance, Yeats also decides to explain the gyres in terms of the *Principles* rather than the *Faculties*, describing the movements of *Husk* and *Passionate Body* instead of *Will* and *Mask*, along with *Spirit* and *Celestial Body* instead of *Creative Mind* and *Body of Fate*. This treatment breaks off in a tortuous swirl of cancellation and correction as Yeats struggles to work in the opposition of Christ and St. John in the Christian year, already included in *A Vision A* (cf. *AVA* 164, *CW13* 133; *AVB* 212, *CW14* 156), and pages have evidently been removed.

Interjected between these two drafts comes the first of two essays relating to the Censorship Bill that was going through the Dáil, which had had its first reading the day after Yeats last spoke in the Senate in July 1928.[35] The two articles appeared in September 1928, and the drafts here probably date from late July or August (there are later, fuller typescripts).[36] They show Yeats's continued interest and activism in national politics, despite his physical infirmity and frustrations with the state of affairs. The notebook also contains a draft of a letter connected to the first article: Yeats mentions Wagner's inspiration by the Palatine Chapel in Palermo, which prompted a letter to the editor from Annie Horniman—and this subsequent rejoinder.[37] There are also pages drafting parts of the "Editorial" or introduction to *The Coinage of Saorstát Éireann*, giving an account of the process involved in deciding on the designs for the new Irish coins, another aspect of his engagement in the public life of the Free State.[38]

The only direct reference to any poetic or dramatic work comes in some revisions to *The Player Queen* so that "no dancer has to speak" (to George Yeats, August 17, 1928, *CL InteLex* 5145; *YGYL* 194). These changes appear to have been undertaken in preparation for the Abbey's production of the play in September 1928 alongside dance programs given by Ninette de Valois' company.[39]

Other pages of the notebook are taken up with stray notes on his reading, and there are many blank pages. The only real date in the notebook comes after Yeats apparently returned to revise and probably add to his drafts on the Great Year, and this is followed by three completely blank leaves, so Yeats had clearly left empty pages available for finishing off this section, possibly recognizing the need to start drafting something on censorship. There is a similar gap after the article on censorship and Aquinas,[40] probably showing Yeats again starting a new project while still expecting to add to the preceding material. As there are no obvious changes in handwriting or ink, it is impossible to say how many pages he originally left and subsequently used, but they do show the need to move from one area of interest to another, while knowing that there was still work to do. Indeed, the date of "Nov 1928" at the end of the notebook's first large bloc, "The Great Year," may well indicate that revising and adding to this section was the last sustained work in the notebook. However, as mentioned earlier, in the plentiful space towards the end of the book,[41] a single blank page was convenient when Yeats wanted to expand on one of the entries toward the end of the diary he kept during 1930, thus briefly bringing the notebook back into service.

Rapallo Notebooks A and B contain no poetry. Yeats had told Olivia Shakespear in October 1927 that he had undertaken to provide "sixteen or so pages of verse" for a New York publisher for £300, adding later that "These new poems interrupted my re-writing of 'A Vision'" (*CL InteLex* 5034; cf. *L* 730). Having contended with ill health over the winter and having fulfilled his poetic commitment when the typescript of the poems went off to the press on March 13, 1928,[42] Yeats appears to have restarted work on *A Vision* in Rapallo B with redoubled focus, and in July he was telling Lady Gregory that he had "snatched every moment to finish 'A Vision' & put off till tomorrow everything else" (July 30, [1928], *CLInteLex* 5137; cf. *L* 745).

Despite this focus, timeliness was obviously crucial for his contributions to the censorship debate, and other commitments such as the report on the currency had some urgency too, as did rehearsals for the Abbey's new season, so that these intruded into the notebook he began slightly later, Rapallo A, but only insofar as they were pressing. Rapallo A is thus largely confined to the prosaic, albeit essential aspects of Yeats's life in the 1920s, both the private esoterica of *A Vision* and public politics, represented here by censorship and coinage. The only aspects of the poet or dramatist glimpsed are those of the practical man of the theater adapting a play for particular upcoming circumstances and perhaps the lyrical prose of "Rapallo in Spring" that opens Rapallo B. However, the following year, when, "in the spring of 1929 life returned to me as an impression of the uncontrollable energy and daring of the great creators," as Yeats recalled in the introduction to the *Winding Stair and Other Poems* (1933, *VP* 831), renewed inspiration would fill subsequent notebooks with poetry.

In Greater Detail

[Cover][43]

This notebook has a large letter "D" on the cover, the relic of a previous labeling system that was certainly in operation in late 1930: at the end of the entry for October 20 in the 1930 diary, Yeats indicated where to locate the continuation: "see book D."[44] The only other notebook to have a letter written on the front cover is Rapallo E,[45] and indeed these two could well have been "neighboring" volumes in a different sequence of notebooks. It is very probable that Rapallo E was started before the current Notebooks C and D, and contained the *Vision* material that is indicated in the cancelled list written on the cover above the letter "E." Though the three lines have been scratched through to the point of illegibility, they appear to read "Principle [*sic*] symbols | hourglass & diamond |

T[?he Diagram of the] Great Wheel." This content does not appear in Rapallo E as it now is, but a significant number of pages have been removed from the beginning of the notebook.[46] The relabeling of notebook "D" as "A" appears to have been done by the Yeatses, with "A" and "B" appearing on the first rectos of these notebooks, even though this ordering is out of chronological sequence.[47]

[1r–3r]

The rebinding of the notebook has added two leaves at the front of the notebook, but the first page proper bears a large letter "A" on the recto, while the verso gives a list in W. B. Yeats's hand of the book's "Contents":

> Great Year (final version) 20 pages
> Censorship & Thomas Acquinas
> First Things 12 pages (first page lacking)
> Player Queen (corrections) 6 pages
> Essay on Coinage 3 pages
> Censorship 10 pages
> letter in Reply to Miss H 1 page

This table of contents reflects fairly accurately the notebook's main material, and the list was evidently drawn up after the book was finished, probably in 1928 and before the addition of the 1930 diary entry. The pages were counted and it was possibly at this stage that Yeats numbered or renumbered the pages of each section, usually restarting at "1" for each new stretch and occasionally skipping numbering for pages with rejected material or moving out of sequence to reflect changes in order (in Rapallo B).[48]

The brief chain of notes below these contents shows, however, part of the provocative juxtaposition that comes in Yeats's bound volumes: he links with vertical lines "One absolute," "manifold one. Int Prin," "Each one among many. soul (individuals)," jottings that evidently relate to his notes on Plotinus on the facing page [2r]. Brief though they are, Yeats was looking for them in August 1928, writing to George from Coole:

> I am so sorry but I have found those notes you have been searching for in one of those Italian MSS books. They were not in the leather bound book I put you looking for. I am ashamed of myself. Next time you are in Dublin send me the fourth Plotinus volume for it is to that they refer. ([August 17, 1928], *CL InteLex* 5145; cf. *YGYL* 194).

This letter indicates that Yeats must certainly have started the notebook before he arrived at Coole on August 14, 1928, and if the volume of Plotinus was located in Dublin, Yeats had probably made the notes while there—he and George had arrived in April 1928 and he spent much of his time there.[49] The notes refer to MacKenna's *Plotinus: The Divine Mind, Being the Treatises of the Fifth Ennead*, noting the symbolism of "intellection symbolized by [*circle*] | sensation by line" and locating such connections as "p12 par[*agraph*] 3 | sphere," which gives an account of Parmenides, comparing his unity "to a huge sphere in that it holds and envelops all existence."[50] Such notes show Yeats writing only for himself and a full blank leaf left before the following item, [3r/3v], may indicate that he contemplated more notes on Plotinus or other reading.

[4r–26r] "Great Year (final version) 20 pages"

The leaf that follows [4r] starts a formal draft of "The Great Year" for *A Vision* and, after rejecting at least two openings, begins with what would be the second paragraph of "Book IV: The Great Year of the Ancients" in *A Vision B*—"To the Time when Marius sat at home planning a sedition that began the Roman civil wars, popular imagination attributed many prodigies" (cf. *AVB* 243, *CW14* 177)—but there is much correction, cancellation, and insertion. The general shape and text are relatively close to the published version for the first five pages (two sections), while also including ideas that were incorporated into the introduction for *The Resurrection* in *Wheels and Butterflies* (1934), such as the comment on the Great Year, that "To measure it according to Proclus we should know the life period of all living things gods, whales & gudgeons for when it ends all must end[,] when it begins all begin."[51]

Section III, however, starts on a provocative tack that was not included in *A Vision B*, and the implications, though characteristic of Yeats's thinking, are slightly confused and confusing, albeit clearer than the version outlined in Rapallo B:

> I delight in a symbolism that can thrust Christianity back into the crises where it arose & then display it not as an abstract ideal but united to its opposite, & thrust it forward in crissis after ~~criss~~ crisis, where the actors must change roles, & the defeated Tincture triumph in its turn. An ideal separated from its opposite is lyrical & its fantastic immobility ~~appals us~~ palls upon us but an ideal united to its opposite is tragic & stays always like the poetry of Dante. I am tired of Shellean Christianity—I prefer to any song in the air a Phoenix, that rises twelve times from a body twelve times consumed to ashes.[52]

The opposition of lyrical and tragic—the two forms most characteristic of Yeats's own poetry and drama—is slightly strange, as it seems to disparage his lyric mode, though there is evidently some of the bravura provocation that would later inform *On the Boiler*. Though this formulation went through drafts in Rapallo B and then A, this approach and tone were not used in *A Vision*. In general, the drafting here shows signs of hurry in the handwriting, which is often illegible or intelligible only from context, sentences that are ungrammatical as they change course with deletion and substitution, and thinking that is exploratory, even muddled. Yeats is possibly, as Jon Stallworthy suggests, "*thinking* on paper," projecting ideas provisionally in an act of discovery rather than statement.[53]

Yeats also shows uncertainty about how to relate various elements of *A Vision*'s scheme of historical gyres and the phases of the moon to the solar year, with tables presenting significantly different alignments of various cycles within the system, as his examination passes into more technical aspects of the symbolic year. Several schemes that place the phases and zodiac signs in correspondence with the 2,200-year months of the Great Year are all rejected, as Yeats abandons all but the simplest arrangement. The draft proceeds to an exposition of the *Principles* showing "the different phases of the wheel of month or year" in the geometrical arrangement of the cones,[54] before differentiating the historical Great Year from "the great wheel of incarnations."[55] The treatment then provides an explanation for the special arrangement of the diagram prefacing "Dove or Swan" which survives into the version published in 1937, discussing how "My instructors have adopted this arrangement of the cones & gyres . . . because it enables them in figure [*gap for number*] to stretch out in a line four periods which are in Spengler's sense 'contemporaneous,'" noting that the instructors "scrawled it once or twice on the margins of a manuscript, while writing something else & left me to discover its meaning. They seem to play with their abstractions as we do with words" (cf. *AVB* 256, *CW14* 187).[56]

The following section expands on the concept of the Phoenix mentioned earlier, comparable to the divine avatars of Hinduism:

> VIII.
>
> The Twelve beings who start the twelve months of my year are called incarnations of Buddha in the east but as we have [*no*] name for them I shall call them the twelve Phoenixs because a Phoenix rises from its predecessors ashes. Each must create itself, so fully that all the past is taken up into its nature, & upon completeness of this act not upon any reality beyond the mind depends the stability of civilization, & only through this act which leaves nothing beyond itself can the will of man be free. We approach a multiform Phoenix because antithetical revelation though its Master may show certain dominant types can never be the same for any two personalities. Its God is immanent, Shelleys Demigorgan rising from the earth as from the daimonic sphere to overturn quantative nature, transcendant law, his serpent struggling with an eagle.[57]

The next pages return to diagrammatic representations of the Great Year mapped to the zodiac, the possibility of spiritual release from the wheel of incarnation, and Plotinus's "Three Authentic Existants" (Yeats's very partial reading of MacKenna's translation of *The Enneads*):[58]

IX

The diagrams frequently make each of these months a half month, a bright or dark fortnight, that they may turn the 26 000 years we have thought of as the great year into the first half of a year of 52 000. When they do this they still enumerate the zodiac twice over. The *Spirit* of the year of 52 000 years moves twice through the zodiac

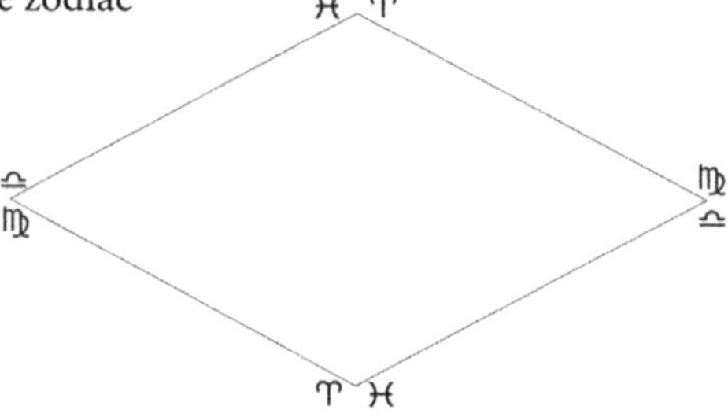

before it completes its circle.[59] The object is to get the second half of the greater, a new zodiac a new series of twelve cycles, which may contrast with the first as primary with antithetical but — being preceded by a kind of death p[*hase*] 22 — may[,] should the soul have earned its freedom, be a spiritual existence. If a spiritual existence they are no longer twelve [?then/?there], no longer gyres but spheres one within an other. The Three Authentic existants of Plotinus & from the first of these — called the thirteen cycle [—] the Antithetical Tincture is reflected, from the second the Primary[,] while in the third is the union of the first two. It is from this 3 fold world that the greater spirits descend. It will be present[*ly*] seen that ~~they are~~ being related to those in the first twelve cycles as the principles are to the faculties and come without intermediary not being means to an end.[60]

This treatment, which continues onto the next page, shows Yeats still thinking in terms of the stages beyond incarnation as three "cycles" or spheres (cf. *AVA* 176, 236; *CW13* 143, 194), a formulation that was in the process of being assimilated into a single *Thirteenth Cone* or *Sphere*. He writes of the Great Year as containing all the lesser cycles within it (see Figure 1.1), stating that:

Sometimes my instructors have compared the great year to a whole number, & the months or days of the other wheels, where all wheels finish at the same moment to integers that multiply into the whole number, as 1, 2 & 3 multiply into 6, to a work of art where every thing is a part of everything, flows back as it were into the whole, & the days & months of those wheels where the wheels do not coincide to numbers, where the integers do not multiply into the whole number but pass as it were beyond [?indefinitely], & to all kinds of practical & scientific work that is a means to something else, information as distinguished from knowledge. Indeed their whole morality, when they speak of the soul liberating itself, they mean that ~~it can at last enter~~ the sphere, escapes from the gyre into the sphere because it has so lived that the clocks chime midnight at the same instant.[61]

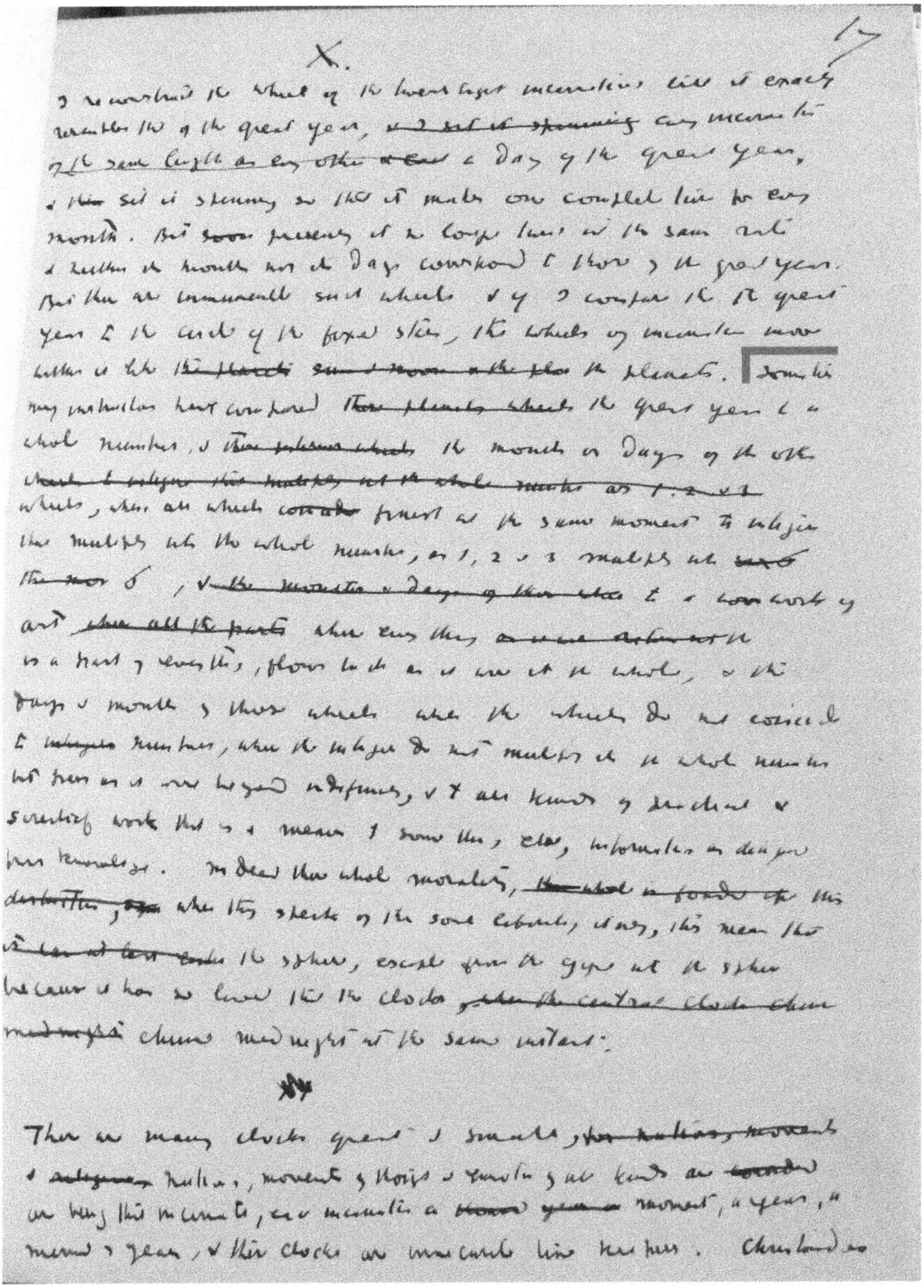

Figure 1.1. Rapallo Notebook A, NLI 13,578, [22r], page numbered 17. This photograph shows the actual appearance of the page transcribed and discussed; the mark ⌜ indicates where the quotation "Sometimes my instructors . . ." starts. The original includes cancellations that are not transcribed, as well as illustrating some of the problems with deciphering Yeats's hand. Courtesy of NLI; photograph courtesy of Catherine E. Paul.

This image is magnified even further in *A Vision B*, to embrace "innumerable dials" all completing "their circles when Big Ben struck twelve upon the last night of the century," while he also offers "a symbol of the less unities that combine into a work of art and leave no remainder" (*AVB* 248, *CW14* 181), but, with the removal of the spiritual meaning for the individual soul, the import of these Platonic numbers is harder to appreciate in *A Vision.* Even if Yeats decided to reject the concept of the soul's liberation as an aesthetic act determined by Pythagorean integers, this vision of mathematical congruence provides a missing context—or the memory of one—that helps to explain a rather cryptic section of the published book.

Yeats consistently prefers mystical mathematics, where integers multiply into perfect numbers, to the messy fractional values of scientific reality. In terms of the harmony of cycles, he also makes the useful clarifying comment (see the last four lines of Figure 1.1):

> There are many clocks great & small, & nations, movements of thought & emotion of all kinds are all beings that incarnate, each incarnates a moment, a year, a miriad of years, & their clocks are [?innacurate /inncarnate] time keepers.[62] Christendom is now passing from phase 22 to phase 23, but a nation or individual or movement may be at any phase, though that phase must always work within the general phase &[,] even if opposing[,] express that phase.[63]

A consideration of the Great Year's relation to the precession of the equinoxes leads to observations about when the Great Year, and therefore the current *primary* dispensation, began. Hipparchus discovered equinoctial precession in the second century BCE (cf. *AVB* 252, *CW14* 184) and Yeats appears to see this as falling in some fated way at the opening of the eras:[64]

> XI
>
> My instructors have told me repeatedly without explaining it the Great Year began not at the birth of Christ when these diagrams seem to begin it. I think it probable, they hold that Hipparcus chose the Equinox place of the sun during his own life time as our 0 of ♈ [=*0° of Aries*], not because it was during his life time but for a more profound reason. The Alexandrian Greeks who founded Astrology as it has come down to us must have considered that the great year began during his life time, for their successors judged the positions of the stars not in relation to the constellations but to 0 of ♈ long after 0 of ♈ had ceased to coincide with the begging [=*beginning*] of the constelation Ares [=*Aries*]. They considered 0 of ♈ as the ascent [=*ascendant*] in the horoscope of the epoch
>
> { a point that remains fixed like the ascend of the individual horoscope }

& related all their calculations to it. Astrology does not rely as is generally supposed upon the ~~influence~~* [?devine] influence of stars but upon that of certain mathematic relation between stars & a point mathematically ascertained. My instructors spoke of ten generations from the start of the Great Year to Christ, & if I count 15 years for a generation that being the length according to Heraclitus one gets a date during the life time of Hipparcus.

Footnote

* Each astrologic aspect is the distance between two ancles [=*angles*] of one of the regular polygons, & their polygon must have some relation to those described in the Timeus, though the ancles of those in the Timeus [?lie] within a sphere not within a circle.

Plutarc thought so for he confused the twelve sided figure in the Timeus with the zodiac. Astrology had its theoretic foundation in some part of great mathematic philosophy that has been lost, but now
{ that Mr Wyndham Lewis can acuse Mr Bertram Russell of substituting Mr 4.30 in the afternoon for Mr Smith we may recover it. }[65]

This is a first draft toward *A Vision B*'s Book IV, section VIII, which endorses "the conviction of Plotinus that the stars did not themselves affect human destiny but were pointers which enabled us to calculate the condition of the universe at any particular moment and therefore its effect on the individual life" (see *AVB* 253; *CW14* 184).[66] Yet almost the only element of the draft that survived intact into *A Vision B* itself is Yeats's strange interpretation of *Time and Western Man* as presaging a return to an astrological sense of timing: "has not Mr. Wyndham Lewis accused Mr. Bertrand Russell of turning Mr. Smith into Mr. Four-thirty-in-the-afternoon by his exposition of space-time," giving the idea a cast that neither Lewis nor Russell—nor Bergson, who was actually the more immediate target in this excerpt—would have recognized (*AVB* 253n; *CW14* 184n).[67]

The final two pages of this section deal with the difference between *primary* and *antithetical* revelation, though in different terms from those used in *A Vision*, using Gautama Buddha as an *antithetical* contrast to Christ.[68] Through many reformulations, Yeats struggles with the expression of a distinction between *primary* and *antithetical* by considering representations of Buddha, the landscape art of China, and the sainted scholar-artist-official-engineer, Kōbō-Daishi, founder of Shingon Buddhism in Japan.[69]

As explained in the note on "Transcription Principles," I have omitted cancelled text in most previous quotations for the sake of readability; here, however, I include the cancellations (even though some readings are uncertain) in order to give an idea of the drafting process as seen in the notebook, with rephrasing, false starts, repetitions, and Yeats's clarifications of his own handwriting (Figure 1.2 shows the second page transcribed here). It may be difficult to follow (for a reading text, see note 71), but shows the mind turning over an idea and seeking its best expression, only for most of it to be rejected later on.[70]

(19

XII

They tell me that the primary revelation comes soon after the opening of the year, & the antithetical considerably before its close & that East & West are ~~a~~ Primary & Antithetical respectively, ~~two & that they~~ <each> one dying the others life living the others death. I do not know [*why*] the Primary revelation should not begin its year but image that the antithetical comes before its close, though it is the inspiration of ~~the~~ its successor because out of human intellect & not from beyond it & so needs a mature tradition. As antithetical Europe at the end of an antithetical year [?approached] primary revelation, primary Asia, at the end of a primary year brought forth antithetical revelation in Buddha. Christ speaks to & is born of the primary masses, but Buddha is a kings son & speaks to kings, & Buddhism grows by its effect upon kings courts. ~~Its appeal It offers nothing but long & audacious intellect no consoling god~~ <~~the world is the separation~~> ~~that all immortal souls each but a~~ if the world [?~~use~~] comes from the sepparation of the knower & the known, ~~if this can be united~~
~~birth itself~~ being born is the supreme crime, but after many incarnations ~~or after one life of incredible self denial~~ – we may escape into nothing, or into a ~~some~~thing that the most [?po]
~~to the common man~~ No god no consoling heaven, ~~nothing for the common man, no [?on] & to even the most audacious intellect something that seems~~ so little common man can understand that generations ~~dispute whether its supreme reward is being or not being~~ as to whether ~~has promised anything~~

Nothing for the common man, no god no consoling heaven. ~~Generations must dispute before men are certain that its rewards for may [?reward]~~ men dispute as to whether it [?gnows] of any punishment but life any reward but extinsion. ~~It took~~ <take> <Having taken> from the sculptor of Alexander the high bred ~~faces &~~ face of a god ~~&~~ it moulded ~~it not that of~~ <~~express~~> ~~the contemplative Buddha~~ from it ~~a face~~ the symbol of a solitude more terrible than that of Oedipus.

(20

~~Then it sings [=*sinks*] into the primary soul of Asia~~

When Christianity ~~was taken up into the Antithetical European soul~~ <lost its first character>, ~~when a~~ when eclesiastic became princes, but Buddhism ~~sa~~ as Buddha sank down <~~in Primary Asia,~~ ~~thus~~ ~~India, the~~ ~~sec~~ ~~sculpture faced became~~ ~~grew vague, & the bodies many armed~~ into Primary Asia, ~~the scu~~ ~~the Indian scultors gave their gods~~ the abstraction of the Vedas, that something that seems to disolve all form away coarsed into India ~~sculpt~~ sculpture, gave it vague pleasant faces & a multitude of arms. ~~Only in~~ <~~in China~~> In Japan <& China alone> could ~~it~~ <Buddhism> prolong its Antithetical nobility, ~~for~~

for there <it was> ~~its constant St Agustine its Sankara no abstract philosophy~~ <~~commissioner & saint~~>, ~~no primary~~ Sankara no abstract philosopher, but ? . . — Daishi, ~~painter & saint philosopher,~~ who was a great artist & commissioner <& saint>, united it to the common faith by making it thought centred, the inspiration & defe ~~with thought~~ <joined ~~it~~> to the common belief ~~by great artist & commissar, who made the inspiration~~ by great works of art ~~yet even there & created an art~~ where one can study ~~the antithetical~~ the primary <primary> soul in its antithetical moment. ~~The~~ Their style defines <defining> a ~~subject matter~~ theme rather than a personality ~~& it~~ passes ~~from generation to generation in~~ on, in the same family from generation to generation, or ~~will be~~ is taken up or laid down when the narrative selects a new ~~subj subject~~ theme, & it is ~~primary~~ <above all> an art ~~in~~ of landscape, ~~mountains & cloud great mountains without names, the mountains, th & cattaract~~ <~~mountains that have no names, cattaracts that plunge into holy descend from clouds~~> ~~that stream of mist~~ <~~great sheets of mist~~> ~~that old saint by the road side~~, ~~wrought its~~

{ great ~~namely~~ <nameless> mountains, ~~cattacts~~ <cattaracts> falling through cloud into cloud an old saint climbing to some mountain shrine, & all}

& all caught up <into> a ~~rythm~~ powerful <rythm>, that unlike the rythms of European art, carries <us> beyond ~~the work~~ <its scene> that we may share ~~Buddha~~ <the> contemplation of Buddha.

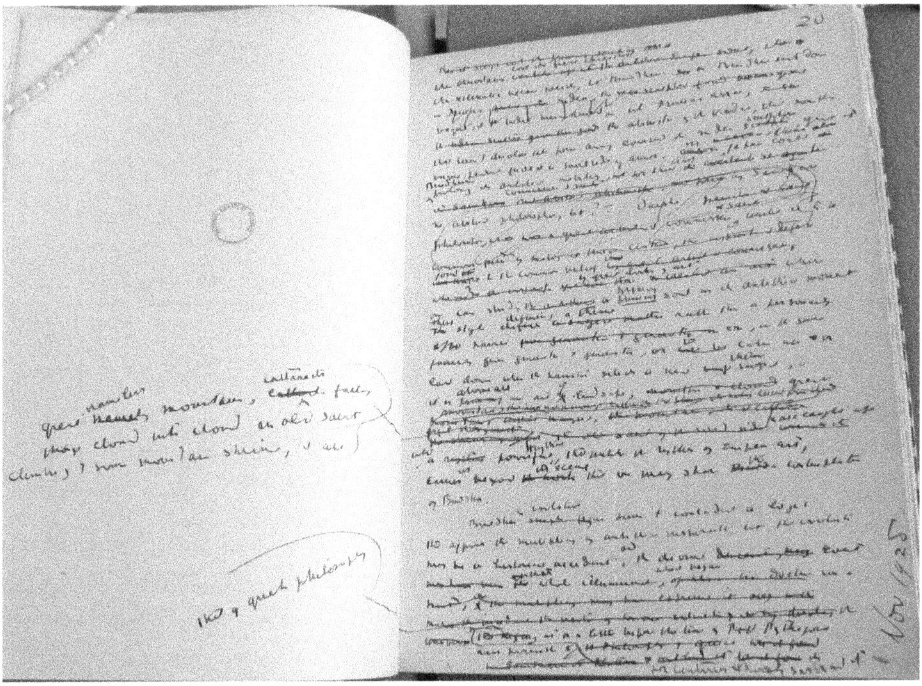

Figure 1.2. Rapallo Notebook A, NLI 13,578, [24v–25r], page numbered 20. Courtesy of NLI; photograph courtesy of Catherine E. Paul.

> Buddhas ~~single figure~~ <in isolation> seems to contradict a logic that affirms the multiplicity of antitethical inspiration, but that isolation may be a historical accident, <and> the devine ~~descent, may~~ event ~~may have been that all~~ that whole illumination <which began> ~~of which his doctrine was a part, &~~ <~~or~~> ~~the multiplicity may have expressed it self in the making the invidual that vents of his own salvation of it by desolving the universe, that beging~~ at or a little before the time of ~~Pith~~ Pythagoras ran parallell to
> { that of Greek philosophy }
> ~~the philosophy of Greece till it found in Sankara its Plotinus & outlived it [?but] it found its~~ for centuries & hardly survived it.
>
> [*vertically*] Nov 1928[71]

The exact thread of argument is difficult to follow. Indeed, even if there were less revision, the thinking would probably be rather incoherent, yet the gist is clear, as is the relation to the system. An inchoate mix of ideas, it was never intended for another reader, and, though very little is present in *A Vision*, elements adumbrate themes that appear later in the poetry—the old Chinese saint climbing to the mountain shrine in "Lapis Lazuli" (1936), the solitary meditator dissolving the universe in "Meru" (1934), and the *antithetical* proportions and sculpture of Greece related to the *primary* Asian sculpture of Buddha in "The Statues" (1938)—showing that these ideas remained with Yeats and ripened with time.

Much of the treatment seems to draw on Laurence Binyon's writings on Asian art, particularly "Some Phases of Religious Art in Eastern Asia," published in G. R. S. Mead's *Quest*. Elements, and even phrases, that Yeats seems to have borrowed include Binyon's focus on Alexander and Hellenistic influence on "the type of the Buddha which Gandhara sculpture evolved," "the Chinese genius for rhythm," "the effort to concentrate in figures, usually isolated, all that the self-liberated soul of man can conceive of loftiness and intellectual peace," and "paintings of mists and mountains."[72] One of Yeats's reasons for rejecting this material may have been doubts about whether Buddha, a figure of the fourth or fifth century BCE, or the Buddhism of China and Japan effectively bore out *A Vision*'s pattern of history.[73]

While the date "Nov 1928" is fitted into the bottom right-hand corner, there are three cancelled lines on the next recto, isolated in an otherwise blank spread. The fragments on [26r] appear to follow on from "that whole illumination which began at or a little before the time of Pythagoras ran parallel to the philosophy of Greece till it found," continuing: "~~Plotinus in Sankara, but a Plotinus~~ | ~~in Sankara its Plotinus~~ | ~~for so many~~ <~~a few~~ many> ~~centuries & survived hardly survived it.~~"[74] It seems likely that, realizing this line of thought did not go any further, Yeats decided to squeeze the concluding phrases into the space at the bottom of the previous page—"~~in Sankara its Plotinus &~~

~~outlived it~~ ~~but it found its~~ for centuries and hardly survived it," before rejecting the connection between Plotinus and Sankara.

It also seems more probable that this material was added during the later revision, when Yeats knew that this was the end of the section, and so put his customary finishing date there in November 1928. After leaf [26] with the fragments on it, there are a further three blank leaves [27–29]. As the material that comes after this is from August, September, and October, Yeats evidently left a number of blank pages in the knowledge that he would be returning to revise and add to the *Vision* material, though in the end he did not need all of them.[75]

[30v–33r] "Censorship & Thomas Acquinas"

The next draft is the first of two articles in response to "The Censorship of Publications Bill," continuing Yeats's involvement in Senate business even though he had made his "last Senate appearance" on July 18, 1928, "A little speech of three sentences, [which] was followed by a minute of great pain," as he wrote to Lady Gregory on July 30 (*CL InteLex* 5137).[76] The following day James Fitzgerald-Kenney, the Minister for Justice, introduced the Censorship Bill to the Dáil, and it was read for the first time.[77] Yeats told Lady Gregory that he had "arranged two interviews & other things to fight the censorship so I am still in public life & shall be till I get to Rapallo" (*CL InteLex* 5137).[78] His opposition to the proposed bill was based on a mixture of reasons, and he was particularly suspicious of any attempts at legal definitions or criteria, which he addressed in the article, "The Censorship and St. Thomas Aquinas," which appeared on September 22, 1928, in the *Irish Statesman*, under the editorship of George Russell (AE).[79] Characteristically, Yeats contrasts "Byzantium & Platonic Theology,"[80] which separate and isolate the soul from the body, with the Thomist view that "the soul is wholly present in the whole body and in all its parts,"[81] and he sees Thomism as lying behind the emergence of Renaissance art and "that art of the body, that is an especial glory of the Catholic Church."[82] Though very much a first draft, with cancellations and insertions throughout, and gaps left to be filled later, it is almost complete and close to the final text used, showing Yeats honing his expression and adding focus to this short essay.

The article's final section gives a good example of the process involved in the drafting, which I try to reflect in the transcription here, though the accumulation of cancellations and insertions cannot be properly conveyed in print (see Figure 1.3).

III [=IV]

There is such a thing as immoral ~~art~~ <painting> & immoral literature, & ~~a criticism~~ <~~an historical~~> <~~critical~~> <~~method~~> <~~a criticism~~> <& a criticism always growing more profound> <establishes> ~~[?shaped] by~~ [?~~shaped] by the cen~~ ~~as ex~~ ~~evolved through centuries established that is as exact as a science has established~~ that ~~it~~ <they> is bad ~~art~~ painting & bad literature ~~but it cannot be defined in a senten~~.

{ ~~but unless one say that does not some [?sense ?gave] the~~
~~but though one can say of it, that~~
but ~~apart from~~ though it may be said of ~~it~~ <them that they> ~~does~~<~~do~~ sin ~~in some way>~~ always ~~some how seem~~ <in some way> gainst “in toto corpore”, ~~it~~ <they> cannot be defined in a sentence }

If you ~~find~~ <think> it neccary to exclude certain books or pictures, leave <it> ~~the church exclusi~~ to men learned in the ~~arts~~ <art & letters> & ~~if you can find them & if you cannot~~ <~~if you cannot find them in such will leave it to~~ if they will serve you & if they will not> <to> average educated men. ~~They will make~~ ~~may blunder & may be [?often ?in] the wrong [?after~~ each] ~~<whatever choice you make, your censors will often blunder>~~ ~~but a legal definition often~~ <choose what men you may they will make blunders> blunder but you need not compel them to by a definition.[83]

There were further modifications, but stripped to the undeleted material, this passage is very close to the final copy that appeared in the *Irish Statesman*, and indeed the essay kept the four sections and their concerns unchanged from this first rough draft.

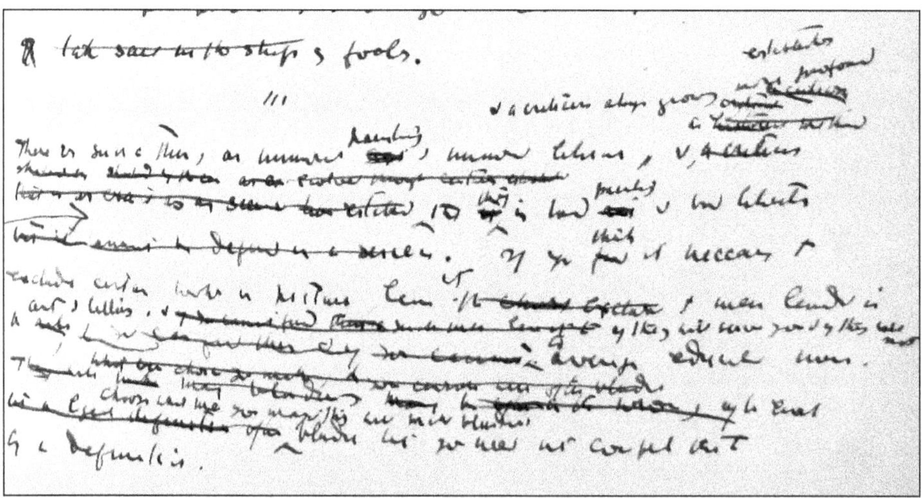

Figure 1.3. Rapallo Notebook A (NLI 13,578), [33r], page numbered 2; cf. *CW10* 213, *UP2* 479–80. The transcription is the passage starting “There is such a thing . . .”. Courtesy of NLI; photograph courtesy of Catherine E. Paul.

Another stretch of three blank leaves [34–36] follows the end of this draft, before the next section (dedicated to *A Vision*), so it is possible that Yeats envisaged extending this essay or starting on the one intended for the *Spectator*. Whereas this *Irish Statesman* article (September 22, 1928) argued from Catholic doctrine as understood by Yeats, the *Spectator* was a London journal; in the article published there the following week (September 29, 1928), the argument took a different tack (see [66v–76r], below).[84]

[37v–48v] "First Things 12 pages (first page lacking)"

The first eight leaves of "First Things" evidently became loose because the leaves on the other side of the gathering—coming at the end of this bloc of draft—were torn out. This must have happened relatively early on, since the loss of the first leaf was already recorded by Yeats when he listed the contents [1v], though, as with other removed pages that can be ascertained, the folio numbering used here counts it, as leaf [38] (see Appendix). The remaining pages, though now secured in the rebinding, are visibly discolored and more damaged at the edges than the rest of the notebook. The verso of the undamaged preceding page [37v] also contains an insertion, and this appears to connect to a line with an arrow on the extant page opposite numbered "2" [39r], so is presumably a revision made after page "1" was lost.[85]

Apart from the missing opening, the text follows the draft in Rapallo Notebook B, incorporating the revisions and changes made there and with further additions, as outlined above in "The Sequence of Rapallo A and B." For instance in Rapallo B, Yeats wonders "why if the daimon is perfect ~~it was necessary to create man~~ man came into existence" and Rapallo A "why if each be perfect man should come into existence"; Rapallo B's "being a symbolist & no philosopher" becomes Rapallo A's "being a symbolist ^dramatist ~~& know no philosopher~~ ^~~logician~~ not a dialectician."[86] The diagram of the circle symbolizing the *Daimon* has no caption in Rapallo B, whereas it is given a line from *Hamlet* in Rapallo A and subsequent drafts: "Have you had a quiet watch? | Not a Mouse stirring."[87] A paragraph that was a late addition on a verso in Rapallo B ("Between this symbol and the next. . . .") is brought up to the beginning of Section III,[88] and there are major changes in phrasing and order. There are also corrections, such as Rapallo B's "Guido Valentanti" (the exact lettering is not clear) to "Guido Cavalcanti."[89] The exposition of the gyres and cones is revised at each step.

The presentation relies heavily on the pre-Socratic philosophers Empedocles and Heraclitus, with further references to "Greco-Roman Stoics," Plotinus, Proclus, Cavalcanti, and Grosseteste, in an approach that is broadly similar to that taken in the final version of *A Vision B*, though different in most particulars. Most importantly, this initial presentation of the gyres and cones is in terms of the *Principles*: *Spirit*, *Husk*, *Passionate Body*, and *Celestial Body*. Seeking to explain the relationship of the *Principles*, Yeats gives a fascinating insight into his reading of Berkeley and Coleridge, together with the symbolism of *The Cat and the Moon*. (In this case I transcribe cancelled material, but omit some as [~~.....~~], in cases where it is simply reformulated and repeated in the following text.)

> It is customary to deney or affirm a "substratum" behind the irrational film or smudge but we who begin all with the full & perfect daimon discover this substratum behind the ~~completed thing,~~ the picture as mastered by the intellect, ~~not only behind~~ and [*not*] behind the picture only, behind fruit or tiger[,] but behind all their functions & capacities. This substratum, ~~the daimon itself~~ <Passionate or Celestial Body>, imeasurably exceeds our knowledge, for only what Husk desires ~~reflects itself as~~ <is transformed into> light or nature and only that so ~~reflected~~ <transformed> can arrouse our Spirit into contemplation. It must however be considered later whether in Spirit [~~.....~~] [,] which no longer lives, or living has been aroused by desire that [~~.....~~] exceeds our own[,] can, to use a metaphor employed by Betheus [=*Boethius*] to describe the intercourse of angels, cast its light into our Spirit as into a mirror.
>
> [~~....~~] Some ~~old~~ Buddhist preacher of the first or second century described the ~~body~~ mind ~~depending upon the body as~~ in relation to the body as a lame man upon a blind mans back. That metaphor must have been Christian as well as Buddhist for the people of my ~~neighbours~~ Galway neighbours, say that our Holy Well, the Well of St Colman was discovered by lame man, ~~who had dreamed that night & found where~~ who had seen himself ~~[?cast] in a dream, & found the right spot, mounted~~ & ~~his friend~~ a blind man cured at a certain spot, & found it mounted on the blind mans back. I turned the story into a little comedy called "The changes of the moon" ~~for which I h~~ picturing as in some obscure & grotesque tapestry the ~~depends~~ dependence of ~~the Known Spirit & Celestial Body, the Knower & the Known, upo upon the Husk & Passionate Body, the Is & the Ought; & needing requiring for performance actors who can sing & dance and/to play a drum.~~
> ~~Spirit & Celestial Body, up Thought or Spirit & Celestial Body~~ upon one another of ~~Thought Spirit & Celestial Body & Will or Husk & Passionate Body~~ Will (~~Spi~~ Husk & Passionate Body[)] & Thought (Spirit & Celestial Body) [90]

Most readers will recognize the outline of *The Cat and the Moon*, though Yeats's memory of his own title was shaky and recalls the phrasing used by Owen Aherne, "Sing me the changes of the moon once more" in "The Phases of the Moon" (*VP* 373, *CW1* 164).[91] As the first version of the play was written in the summer of 1917, before the Yeatses' marriage and the beginning of the automatic script, the play was not created out of the system, but originally reflected the basic duality of mind and body, with some of the concerns about the mind seeking its opposite expressed in *Per Amica Silentia Lunae*.[92] The play had been published in magazine form and by the Cuala Press in 1924, and in the notes to the Cuala volume, Yeats connects the play with the *antithetical* and *primary tinctures* of *A Vision*, stating that "when the Saint mounts upon the back of the Lame Beggar he personifies a certain great spiritual event which may take place when Primary Tincture, as I have called it, supersedes Antithetical" (*VPl* 805, *CW2* 896). This refers to the transition from the third into the fourth quarter of the Wheel, described in *A Vision*, where "Before the self passes from Phase 22 it is said to attain what is called the 'Emotion of Sanctity,' and this emotion is described as a contact with life beyond death. It comes at the instant when synthesis is abandoned and fate is accepted," a description that Yeats actually places in his description of the culmination of this process in Phase 27, the Saint (*AVA* 114, *CW13* 92; *AVB* 181, *CW14* 134). Evidently in this image, the Saint mounting on the back of the Lame Beggar, or mind, expresses the attainment of "Emotion of Sanctity."

In Rapallo A's examination in 1928, this scene is now analyzed further and in terms of the spiritual *Principles* that Yeats was trying to integrate into the system: the solar pair—*Spirit* and *Celestial Body*—are associated with mind or spirit and the figure of the Lame Beggar, while the lunar pair—*Husk* and *Passionate Body*—are associated with incarnate life as the Blind Beggar. The lunar *Principles* are effectively the vehicle that makes incarnation possible—*Passionate Body* is the emotional matrix, *Husk* the link with the physical, and their light is nature—so that the Blind Beggar carries the Lame Beggar; meanwhile the solar *Principles* are mind, *Spirit*, and spiritual reality, *Celestial Body*, and their light is thought, so that the Lame Beggar directs the Blind Beggar carrying him (cf. *AVB* 190, *CW14* 140). The notebook also refers to them as Knower and Known, Is and Ought—*Spirit*, *Celestial Body*, *Husk*, and *Passionate Body* respectively[93]—exactly as in "A Dialogue of Self and Soul," which explored the same distinctions at the end of 1927. Like the Lame Beggar choosing the Saint's blessing, the mind or Soul can become one with the supernatural environment and "ascends to Heaven" (*VP* 478, *CW1* 239), while body, *Will*, or Self, like the Blind Beggar, chooses physical healing—and to have revenge on his companion—effectively pitching "Into the frog-spawn of a blind man's ditch, / A blind man battering blind men" (*VP* 479, *CW1* 240). However, as the Lame Beggar, by choosing blessing, is also healed,[94] the Self may "cast out remorse" and become in its turn "blest" (*VP* 479).[95]

The following page describes the *Principles* as finding a unity in the *Daimon*, an idea that reappears in Rapallo E but is present only as a shadow in the published version of *A Vision B*, where Yeats describes "the *Four Principles* in the sphere" (*AVB* 193, *CW14* 142).

> X
>
> When the Four Principles are one in the daimon there is no greater or lesser, no decrease or increase because no time & space, & therefore but one of a form and no conflict between form & forms, & life in action lacking hope & memory because all but itself has been consumed. Some such thought passed through my mind when I wrote the last stanza of ["]the Withering of the Boughs" & described that King & Queen "so happy and hopeless, so deaf & so blind with wisdom, they wander till all the years have gone by"[.] But before the union the Celestial Body, still discordant, or undefined, it preserves all the acts of struggle in what my instructors have called the Record. The Record is accessible to Spirit but it is no memory for what comes into memory does so voluntarily or by association, in a context not its own, & is always abstract. When we are not content to say "so & so was dark or fair, round or long faced,["] & call up a concrete image that image, however like the old, is a new creation. The Record upon the other hand contains the actual event in its own context. When we are in Spirit & Celestial Body alone we must pass through these events in reverse order to that of Time, & it is this inverted life of the dead that in contemplation compells us to trace all things to their source.[96]

The association of the *Principles* in the *Daimon* with a timeless state of Platonic Ideas, with only the divine Idea, is significant, as is the way in which Yeats rereads earlier poetry in the light of his new ideas.[97] The explanation of the *Record* here may be no fuller than that of *A Vision*, but it is distinctly clearer in its description. By the time he writes of it in *A Vision B*, Yeats has brought in a quotation from Blake and a remembered sentence from an Indian writer that may express similar ideas but do so more obliquely.

Generally, the draft of "First Things" shows the tension between an attempt to be more methodical in the presentation of the system's central ideas and Yeats's naturally more discursive approach and allusive style. As ideas are added and links elided, the exposition becomes less disciplined and structured, and it ranges from enigmatic comments on the nature of the *Daimon* to pre-Socratic thought and the mechanics of the cones, then to the interactions of the *Principles* and *Faculties* and the avatars or incarnations associated with the start of a religious dispensation, as well as the symbolism of the Christian year, reminiscent of the erratic chain of loosely connected ideas that characterized the approach of much of "What the Caliph Refused to Learn" in *A Vision A*.

The last material in this section consists of two versions, both cancelled, of Yeats's attempt to use the idea that St. John the Baptist and Christ represent a form of opposition, with appeals to Coventry Patmore and Leonardo da Vinci.[98] These form part of a series of drafts, which will be considered more

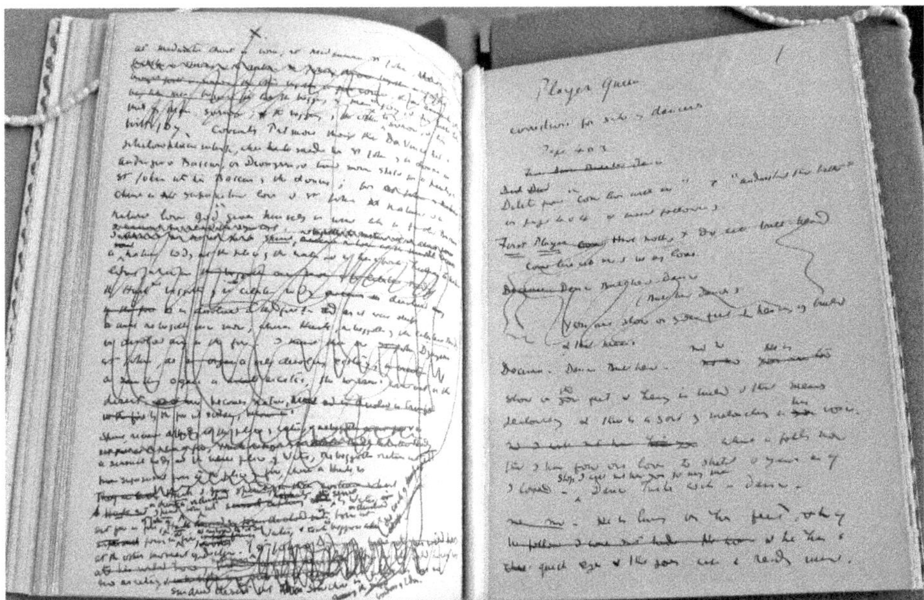

Figure 1.4. Rapallo Notebook A (NLI 13,578), [49v] and [58r], page numbered 1. Courtesy of NLI; photograph courtesy of Catherine E. Paul.

fully in the context of Rapallo Notebook B, but the final page here is so vigorously cancelled that its gestural energy brings it close to expressionist art (see Figure 1.4). This verso [49v] was probably not the last page of this section of draft, as some eight pages were removed from the book, before the next section on *The Player Queen*, and at least one of the lines appears to indicate that text was originally to be inserted onto a facing recto that is no longer there.

[50–57] [8? stubs of pages]

The rebinding by the National Library of Ireland and the Delmas Conservation Bindery, carried out in 2006, includes eight stubs of Japanese paper used to bind in the loose pages on the other side in. These represent some of the leaves removed from the notebook that led to earlier pages of this gathering [38–45] being loose, as well as probably two in the following one [74–75].[99]

[58r–63r] "Player Queen (corrections) 6 pages"

The following pages, titled "Player Queen | corrections for sake of dancers," offer a stark contrast to the tangle of the preceding drafts, with well-spaced writing, albeit still with many changes and second thoughts (see Figure 1.4). These pages constitute "Draft 32" in Curtis Bradford's *The Writing of "The Player Queen"*—the last of the play's drafts and, because they were made after the play's publication, rather adrift from the rest of the material in Bradford's book. As such, this is one of the only parts of this notebook that has been transcribed and published (see Appendix).[100]

A few questions that perplexed Bradford are clearer now with more evidence available, especially from letters. Bradford was puzzled as to why Yeats was revising and suggested that Yeats "may have made these changes, which he labeled 'corrections for sake of dancers,' for the revival of the play by the Cambridge Festival Theatre in the week beginning May 16, 1927."[101] The dating of the notebook makes this impossible, but the experience of the Cambridge production may well have inspired Yeats to make a necessary revision, though the immediate incentive was undoubtedly rehearsals for the Abbey's staging of the play in September 1928, when it was put on with ballets choreographed by and starring Ninette de Valois.[102] In his letter to George from Coole on August 17, 1928, Yeats wrote: "I have finished all my 'Player Queen' revision & now no dancer has to speak" (*CL InteLex* 5145; *YGYL* 194).[103] He also told Maud Gonne on September 6, 1928, that he was being held up in Dublin by, among other things, "a revival of my 'Player Queen' which I have so modefied that the new Abbey Ballet can dance abundantly in the middle & at the end" (*CL InteLex* 5158).

Another riddle for Bradford was that "The page numbers to which Yeats refers in Draft 32 do not correspond to any printing of *The Player Queen*," leading him to speculate that they might have been the 1934 page proofs, noting that Yeats "included the substance of these but not too many of the actual words in the text of the play printed in *Collected Plays*, 1934."[104] However, these page numbers correspond exactly to the American printing of Macmillan's *Plays in Prose and Verse: Written for an Irish Theatre, and Generally with the Help of a Friend* (1924). Though not the most obvious printing of the play to have used, it was an appropriate volume to be using at the house of that very friend, Lady Gregory.[105]

[62v–65r] "Essay on Coinage 3 pages"

The draft of "Introduction to *The Coinage of Saorstát Éireann*" is an early one, starting with a version of what would be section IV—"What advice should we give the government. on the choice as artist? No good could come of a competition open to everybody"—and petering out after the first sentence of section VI—"We did not allow ourselves to see the designs till we saw them all together, the name of each artist, if the medal had been signed covered with a piece of stamp paper."[106] Writing to his wife from Coole, Yeats announced on August 28, 1928, "I have finished my coinage essay" (*CL InteLex* 5150), evidently referring to a version later than this one, which is incomplete, so this initial draft must date from earlier in the month. Yet, if the uncancelled text is extracted from the web of insertion and revision, the text that emerges is relatively close to the final version that was published, as is the case with the censorship essay.

II

> ~~To design sometimes~~ When ~~art~~ an artist takes <up> some task for the first time ~~his work he has~~ he must sometimes experiment before [??] he has mastered the new tecnique, we therefore advised that the artist himself should make every alteration necessary, & that if he had to go to London — ~~if by chance th must chose might to~~ his expenses should be paid & the Government accepted our advice. An Irish artist ~~had made~~ [?was asked &] had made an excellent design for the great seal of the <Dublin> National Gallery & that design founded [*upon*] the seal of a ~~medieval~~ Irish Abbey had been altered by the Mint, <& round> academic ~~design~~ <contours> substituted for the flat planes ~~& [?still] forms of~~ <of a> medieval design, & we felt ~~confident that the authorities of the London~~ confident that the [?adjunct] head of the London <Mint> recently appointed ~~as the rest of~~ to satisfy the [?critic] of art would think the better of us for protecting the ~~artist~~ artist, who ~~not seen may not seem not perhaps [?as ?mast ?of] not completely a craftsman from the craftsman who can be never be an artist~~.
>
> { quote Blake— }
>
> who many not ~~be~~ seem, or ~~may~~ as yet may not be a master of the craft, from the crafts man who never be an arttist,
>
> As the deputy master of the mint has commended, a precaution which protects the artist, who ~~may not seem, or as yet may not be a m who turning~~ set to a new task, & not as yet ~~its master~~ ~~from the~~ a craftsman from the crafts man who will never be an artist. One remembers the rage of Blake, when his designs for Blairs Grave came smooth & lifeless from the hand[107]

Yeats invests considerable care in finding the exact ordering of his phrases to express the need to protect the expression of the artist from the technique of the craftsman, turning over in his mind the progressive refinements, happily preserved on paper.

[66v–73r, 75r–76r] "Censorship 10 pages"

The following pages draft the article "The Irish Censorship" for the *Spectator*.[108] It is difficult to ascertain if Yeats returned to the subject of censorship after starting his draft on the coinage, but this seems more likely than his leaving blank pages and jumping to a point somewhere in the latter half of the book to start the article once he had finished the other essay on censorship and Aquinas. This version is more complete, though still very much a first draft.[109] Written for a London magazine, it has a rather different approach from the Thomist arguments of the article for the *Irish Statesman*. It starts with the scandal over "The Cherry-Tree Carol," a medieval song that the Christian Brothers deemed blasphemous because, when asked for cherries by the pregnant Mary, Joseph says "Let them gather thee cherries / That brought thee with child."[110] While saying that government ministers sponsoring the bill were "full of contempt for their own words,"[111] Yeats also notes that the law "will give one man, the Minister of Justice, absolute control of what we may or may not read," rephrased in the printed version as "control over the substance of our thought," removing the word "absolute" but going further than simple reading matter.[112] Thinking of what could be banned, he notes that the Government intends no general prohibition, but that "in legislation intention is nothing, & the letter of the law is everything."[113]

Two leaves, [74] and [75], became loose with the removal of other leaves, and when the notebook was photographed for the microfilm held at Harvard in the late 1940s, leaf [74], containing notes on Indian ages, was placed as the final page of the notebook, though the cancelled first line of section VI of the *Spectator* article at the top of the leaf indicates its original position, which has now been restored. However, it was obviously already out of position when Yeats was numbering the pages, as [73r] is numbered "8," [75r] "9," and [76r] "10." Leaves [74] and [75] show characteristic damage to the edge of the page, whereas [76], the first leaf of the next gathering, secured by its sewing and corresponding folio, is undamaged.

[74r & v] [notes on Indian ages]

Interjected before the last two leaves of the censorship article is a leaf with notes on the great ages of Hindu tradition, "Indian ages of world," including various kalpas, mahayugas, and manvantaras. These notes were probably taken from H. Jacobi's article in Hastings's *Encyclopaedia of Religion and Ethics*—which Yeats had consulted for *A Vision A* and cites in Rapallo D—as the material follows the same order.[114]

[75r–76r] ["Censorship" continued]

At the head of [75r], before the start of section VI, there is a brief observation, which may continue the preceding section or be a note: "There is no remedy but better education, & taste for reading, & enough mature [?purpose] [?to] . . . ." a comment that Yeats leaves unfinished. At the end of section VI on [76r], Yeats has placed his signature to indicate that the work was completed, even if still in very rough form.

[77r] "letter in Reply to Miss H 1 page"

The *Spectator* article is followed by a single page with a draft a letter to the editor of the *Irish Statesman* in response to A. E. F. Horniman's claim that Yeats's article on censorship and Aquinas displayed ignorance in suggesting the Palatine Chapel in Palermo as the inspiration for Richard Wagner's Chapel of the Grail in *Parsifal*. She had written to the editor on October 6, 1928 that, "It would be unreasonable to expect you to correct the mistakes of your contributors, but you may like to know that the Byzantium Chapel at Palermo, spoken of in the article on The Censorship and St. Aquinas, has nothing whatever to do with the Grail Temple scene in 'Parsifal' at Bayreuth,"[115] and accused Yeats of confusing Palermo with Pavia. Yeats's response was published on October 13 and dismisses Pavia as merely the inspiration for the painted scenery, while the people of Palermo would "~~tell her that Wagner~~ was there day after day seeking—unless local patriotism deceive it self—an idea powerful enough to call into his hearers mind the chapel of the Grail."[116]

[78r] [note on Coinage]

Page [78r] contains an isolated note for the essay on the coinage concerning the Croatian sculptor Ivan Meštrović, noting that he was away from the address to which they had sent their invitation to compete. This may well have been drafted at the stage of correcting galleys or proofs to be added to the pamphlet, and a version of it appears in the published text.[117]

[79r] [entry to be inserted in the 1930 diary]

Yeats appears to have returned to this notebook late in 1930 to use a blank page to continue his diary entry for October 20. The main entry was started on the penultimate leaf of his 1930 diary, where it is given the Roman numeral X in the diary (published in *Pages from a Diary Written in 1930*, it is grouped together with other entries as XL).[118] It considers the relations of Protestant Anglo-Ireland and Catholic Ireland, and starts by asserting that: "We have not an Irish Nation until all classes grant its right to take life according to the law & until it is certain that the threat of invasion, made by no matter who, would rouse all classes to arms" (cf. *Ex* 338). In the diary, the entry finished:

> Will the devout Catholicism and enthusiastic Gaeldom commit the error commited at the close of the close of [*sic*] the 18th century by dogmatic protestantism. All I can see clearly, bound as I am within my own limited art[,] is that every good play or poem or novel <that is characteristically> binds the opposing Irelands together.[119]

The rest of this page and the diary's remaining two blank pages contain an undated entry that opens with a comment on Seán O'Casey's *The Silver Tassie* (XI in the diary and XLI in *Pages from a Diary Written in 1930*), along with a further two sections dated "Nov 16" (not published) and, on "Nov 18," the final epigram: "Science, separated from philosophy[,] is the opium of the suburbs" (cf. *Ex* 340).[120] At some stage—presumably once the diary was already full—Yeats went back to the diary and wanted to extend the ideas leading to the conclusion of entry numbered X, so he cancelled the last sentence with a single line, adding the instruction to "see book D," the label on the cover of Rapallo A and evidently its designation in 1930.

Diary (Oct 20 continued)

> . . . . Dogmatic protestantism. Much of the emotional energy in our civil war came from the ~~refus~~ indignant denial of the right of the state, as at present established to take life in its own defense, whether ~~by~~ <by> arms or by process of law, and that right~~, & the~~ is still denounced by a powerful minority. Only when ~~both conditions all grant the right & when~~ all ~~that grant to the state the rxxx right to~~ permit the state to demand the voluntary or involuntary sacrifice of ~~xxx~~ ~~the lifes~~ its citizens lifes ~~wh~~ will Ireland prossess [*sic*] that moral unity to which England according to Coleridge, [?~~are awar~~] owes ~~so~~ a large part of its greatness. All I can see clearly, bound as I am within my own limited art is that <our moral unity is brought nearer by every> ~~evry~~ play or poem or novel that is characteristically Irish ~~binds classes into one~~ [?~~mass~~][121]

This addition was duly published in *Pages from a Diary Written in 1930*, but the paragraph that follows it was not. This latter continues from the entry on the *Silver Tassie* in the main diary, numbered XI, taking up the themes of "moral unity," of "the Irish Salamis" and Mallarmé's denunciation of the attempt "to build as if with brick and mortar within the pages of a book" (*Ex* 339).

(This follows XI)

XII

> ~~We seek~~ ~~We mus~~t <It is not enough to> have moral unity; we must have unity of a particular kind. We must recognize that our Salamis has been fought & ~~one~~ won. An [*sic*] commercial empire can afford to build in brick & mortar with[*in*] the pages of a book, but a small <or week [*sic*]> nation must fall back upon its self, must encrease its ~~energy~~ <unity> that it may encrease its [?~~oness,~~] energy.[122]

In writing these final entries from 1930 in Rapallo A, Yeats was clearly using a blank page that was to hand, and they are fully integrated into the diary's thought, for instance repeating the final sentence "bound as I am within my limited art" with slight modifications. Both diary and notebook were probably with Yeats in Dublin, as Yeats returned to Dublin from London in mid-November.

[80–97] [blank pages]

Yeats was probably aware that there was plenty of space available at the end of this notebook as the final eighteen leaves of the notebook are blank. Yet in late 1928 there was considerable overlap in the use of different notebooks. Rapallo Notebook C was "begun. Sept. 23. 1928 in Dublin," just a day after the publication of the first censorship essay, and it was initially designated a "Diary of Thought."[123] Rapallo B's cover declares that it was "Finished, Oct 9, 1928," while Yeats was evidently also using Rapallo A, as the draft of the letter in response to Annie Horniman's letter of October 6 shows; he also returned to revising the material on the Great Year in Rapallo A as indicated by the date of "Nov 1928" at the close of that draft. Rapallo D was started at the end of 1928, in other words, roughly as he was finishing that revision, and the two new notebooks (Rapallo C and D) probably account for the unused space at the end of Rapallo A. In fact, Rapallo D was put aside after a few pages, and Rapallo C was the main workbook for the first half of 1929 until July, after which Yeats took D up again in August.[124]

Although we usually value Yeats most for his poetic invention and genius, the prose style that he had developed over the years is vigorous and distinctive. Yeats was aware of Coleridge's "homely definitions of prose and poetry; that is, prose = words in their best order;—poetry = the *best* words in the best order."[125] Yeats's poem "Adam's Curse" explains the labor of poetry, but good prose is almost as demanding in the "stitching and unstitching" (*VP* 204, *CW1* 78) required to organize words into their best order. It has only been possible to show a few instances of the drafting process that is visible in Rapallo A, but no one who has examined these pages could doubt the attention that Yeats paid to the precise placing of words and phrases, to the movement of the argument, or his commitment to expressing ideas as effectively as possible.

The Appendix (following the treatment of Rapallo B) gives a tabular overview of the notebook, offering a slightly clearer idea of how the various pieces of work stand in relation to each other. And, as noted in the introduction and summary, part of the interest of Rapallo A in particular is seeing Yeats's obsession with *A Vision* running up against the demands of the public man—whether senator, involved in the controversies and the symbolism of the state, or man of the theater, addressing the practicalities of a new production.

Rapallo Notebook B

As far as we can tell, Rapallo B was the first notebook that Yeats started in Rapallo.[126] As outlined above in "The Sequence of Rapallo A and B," Yeats appears to have arrived in Rapallo with a leather notebook (NLI MS 30,359) that he was using for Crosby Gaige's commission of "16 pages to be privately printed in America" (to Frederick MacMillan, September 16, 1927, *CL InteLex* 5029). However, Yeats was already complaining to Olivia Shakespear in October 1927 that the "new poems interrupted my rewriting of 'A Vision'" (*CL InteLex* 5034; cf. *L* 730) and David R. Clark notes that the leather "notebook was probably to be devoted to *The Winding Stair*, but already on leaf 9 Yeats seems to have had enough of poems, and his occult investigations start to crowd the poetry out."[127]

Once he had fulfilled his obligation to provide the poetry—and quite probably before George Yeats dispatched the corrected typescripts to New York on March 13, 1928[128]—Yeats evidently felt at liberty to return to his "occult investigations." At some point after arriving in Italy in February, it seems that the Yeatses bought "those Italian MSS books,"[129] very possibly with the purpose of using them for the postponed work on *A Vision*.

The writing in this notebook is frequently a form of shorthand, with the endings of words in particular left as suggestions rather than actually written. Terminations such as -ly, -er, -tion, or -ment are sometimes even non-existent and their presence indicated only by syntax. Yeats was never overly concerned with spelling, and these are private notebooks intended for no one's eyes but his own or possibly George's, so that it is frequently almost impossible to be certain of a word except by context or, in some cases, from later, clearer versions of the same passages, or, even more helpfully but only occasionally, typescripts, often dictated from the manuscripts.

Contents: Overview

Initially, however, this first notebook was not focused on *A Vision*, at least not directly, stating on the title page that it was "Prose" and suggesting "? Siris," the title which also heads the prose on the following recto. This was originally intended, as he explained in a letter to Lennox Robinson on March 10, 1928, to be:

> a comment on a philosophical poem of Guido Cavalcantis, translated by Ezra Pound, which I hope to make a book of to follow your Anthology. I think of calling the book "Siris"; it is about Rapallo, Ezra & the literary movements of our time all deduced from Guido's poem, as Berkeley in his "Siris" deduced all from tar-water. (*CL InteLex* 5088)[130]

Destined for his sisters' press, to follow Robinson's *A Little Anthology of Modern Irish Verse* (1928), Yeats evidently hoped to create a work of philosophical and associative prose along the lines of George Berkeley's *Siris: A Chain of Philosophical Reflexions and Inquiries Concerning the Virtues of Tar-water, And Divers Other Subjects Connected Together and Arising One from Another.*[131] Yeats echoes the last phrase of that title when he describes the project to Lady Gregory as "a little book I am writing for Lolly, an account of this place, & Ezra & his work & things that arise out of that" (March 12, [1928], *CL InteLex* 5089).[132]

The poem Yeats refers to is Cavalcanti's "Donna Mi Prega," a work that has fascinated and baffled readers and critics for centuries. Yeats seems to have remembered the "obscure canzone upon the origin of things" as expressing a form of the antinomy of his own system's "opposing gyres" through the roles of "it may be Mars & Venus," both astrologically and mythologically, in Cavalcanti's poem.[133] He continued with the intention of using the poem until the summer of 1928, when he re-read Pound's translation, at which point he seems to have realized that his projected structure relied either upon a misunderstanding of the poem or that it would require too much explication to be elegant.[134] However, even in the spring of 1928, when the poem was still conceived of as the central element, Yeats deliberately started his chain of reflections with the setting of Rapallo and Ezra Pound himself.

The impressionistic vision of the Italian town and its bay in these opening pages very fittingly inaugurates the Rapallo notebooks, evoking this "indescribably lovely place—some little Greek town one imagines—there is a passage in Keats describing such a town," as he had rhapsodized to Lady Gregory shortly after their arrival ([February 24, 1928], *CL InteLex* 5081, *L* 738). The closeness of the notebook's prose to the descriptions filling his letters at the time show how immediate the inspiration was. After central sections covering most areas that he was rewriting for *A Vision* itself, the notebook concludes with a first draft of "Introduction to the Great Wheel" that would explain the truth about the "incredible experience" of the automatic writing.[135] In contrast to the sensuous presence of Rapallo, these other drafts for *A Packet for Ezra Pound*, coming at the end of the notebook, look backwards over the preceding ten years with a mix of autobiography, essay, and speculation, in a style that Yeats had been making his own since the unpublished journals, the *Reveries over Childhood and Youth*, *Per Amica Silentia Lunae*, and *The Trembling of the Veil.*[136]

As just noted, the remainder of the notebook is taken up with the material for the revised edition of *A Vision*. Yeats had already decided to retain the delineations of the twenty-eight typical temperaments ("The Twenty-Eight Embodiments" became "The Twenty-Eight Incarnations") and the survey of history ("Dove or Swan") largely intact (see [40r–41r] and [96v] below), and there is evidence that, at this stage, he also hoped to retain other sections with revisions (see [43v–44r] below).[137] However, the rest was to be recast, and this notebook contains examples of all the new material: two sections of introductory material, titled "First Things" and "Introduction," as well as sections on "The Soul in Judgement" and the Great Year in antiquity. Much of this is tentative, showing long passages revised, recast, replaced, and rejected, and indeed little of the material presenting the gyres and their movements or the afterlife was used in the form Yeats attempted here, so that its main interest is as a stage in the evolution of his thinking and his struggle with how to present the ideas most clearly and effectively. The drafts are frequently illuminating on problematic elements, such as the *Daimon*; other aspects are clearly intermediate and superseded by later reformulations, though even in these cases seeing the process by which Yeats reached the later presentation can clarify his general approach or specific details.

Rapallo Notebook B is thus of particular interest to those studying *A Vision*, including in this context *A Packet for Ezra Pound*, and the development of these writings. Perhaps because of its relative focus, it is the most complete of the Rapallo notebooks, with ninety-eight extant leaves, though there are still some pages torn out. Conversely, it shows little of the cross-fertilization that gives added interest to other notebooks, and rather bears witness to the frequently Sisyphean labor involved in the attempts to revise *A Vision*. Many of the drafts here are repeated in other versions both in manuscript (including Rapallo A) and typescript, some eventually reaching published form, but most abandoned. The more the drafts are explored, the clearer it is that the published version of *A Vision* itself, in either version, is only the visible tip of an iceberg, and that Yeats was not stretching the truth when he wrote that "this book has filled my imagination for so many years, that I can never imagine myself studying anything without in some [*way*] relating it or incorporating it with what is here."[138]

In Greater Detail

[Cover]

The notebook's cover declares that it was "Finished, Oct 9, | 1928," a date that seems to be borne out by the contents, though there is no specific date internally. Yeats noted in the contents that the notebook's final bloc of material—what would become "Introduction to the Great Wheel" in *A Packet for Ezra Pound*—was continued in a loose-leaf notebook. Certainly on November 23, 1928, he informed Ezra's mother-in-law:

> I am finishing a little book for Cuala to be called either "A Packet" or "A Packet for Ezra Pound". It contains first a covering letter to Ezra's saying that I offer

> him the contents, urging him not to be elected to the Senate of this country & telling him why. Then comes a long essay already finished, the introduction to the new edition of "A Vision" & telling all about its origin, & then I shall wind up with a description of Ezra feeding the cats ("Some of them are so ungrateful" T. S. Elliott says) of Rapallo & Ezras poetry — some of which I greatly admire. (to Olivia Shakespear, *CL InteLex* 5191; cf. *L* 748)[139]

Though this reverses the final order, the drafts in this notebook are often very close to the version that was published and show Yeats as an assured writer of prose for evocation, description, and autobiography, yet continually redrafting to achieve the desired finish.[140]

[1r–1v] [title page and "Contents"]

Titling the first page as "Prose" indicates that this was perhaps not, in the first instance, a book for *Vision* material, and the title "? Siris" indicates his model in Bishop Berkeley's chain of associations that starts with the medicinal qualities of water mixed with pine resin and ends with the ancient philosophers' conceptions of the divine. Having moved through the links of 368 sections, the final sentence admonishes: "He that would make a real progress in knowledge, must dedicate his age as well as youth, the latter growth as well as first fruits, at the altar of Truth";[141] for Yeats such a dedication was perhaps more important in "Decrepit age" than youth, as he wondered whether he must "Choose Plato and Plotinus for a friend" (*VP* 409, *CW1* 198).

Apart from the unsuitability of Cavalcanti's poem as a central text, Yeats may also have realized that part of the strength of *Siris* is the gradualness of the ascent from the mundane to celestial, entailing some length and some philosophical depth. At any rate, "Siris" was rejected as a title, and Rapallo itself was brought to the fore; the contents give two versions, as the rather flat "Note on Rapallo" is cancelled, and replaced with "Rapallo in Spring," the phrase which also replaces "Siris" on the following page, and this may indicate that the revision happened as Yeats was creating the list of contents.

Contents.
~~Note on Rapallo~~
Rapallo in Spring. 9 pages. First 4 to be used
First Things. 15 pages.
~~Book I "Great Wheel"~~
Additions ~~to Book I~~ & corrections of Vision Book II
7 pages (dated May 1928)
Great Year 21 pages. (early version)
Soul in Judgement ~~(first draft)~~ 10 pages
Introduction. 12 pages (continued in loose leaf book.

Rapallo A and B are the only Rapallo notebooks to have a list of contents, and Yeats's listing is relatively accurate, even to the point of indicating some false starts.

[2r–10r] "Rapallo in Spring 9 pages First 4 to be used"

This first draft of *A Packet for Ezra Pound*'s "Rapallo" opens with an evocation of the Riviera town before focusing on the resident of most interest to Yeats. As the contents page indicates, the first four pages were used with relatively little revision for the Cuala volume, making up the first three sections of "Rapallo." Both published versions—the Cuala Press edition and the prefatory material to *A Vision B*—continue this section with a consideration of Rapallo's English-speaking church and the finishing of *A Vision*, while the Cuala version also has a further section on Ezra Pound's poetry.

These are not included in the notebook, which instead has further sections that explore the "the literary movements of our time" (*CL InteLex* 5088) partly through Balzac's *Chef d'oeuvre inconnu* [5r–7r], and considerations of the nature of imagination and poetry. Since these drafts show a range of aspects of Yeats's drafting and how he worked on his material, I shall give particular attention to these few pages.

There are in fact three sections all numbered "V": the first one on [5r–6r] is brief and replaced by the second on [6r and 5v], which is itself completely rewritten on [7r], while the third on [8r–10r] is different material and appears to be a mistake for "VI," but none was used for publication. Elements touching on Balzac from the earlier versions were, however, salvaged and added to the earlier Section II, in a jigsaw of elements keyed for insertion from the facing versos. In the published versions of *A Packet for Ezra Pound*, the references to Balzac's short story are applied to Pound's *Cantos*.

As well as *Siris*'s chain of reason, Yeats's train of thought often seems to follow "the crooked road of intuition" that he symbolized as a butterfly (*VP* 827), zigzagging through a range of topics and references, often within the space of a sentence or two. The drafts, however, reveal that these allusive paths often started with a slightly more hawk-like "straight road of logic" and sequence as part of a more expansive treatment of the topic, which successive revisions gradually telescope into briefer forms that are often harder to follow. This process was seen with the symbolism of the sphere in relation to the *Daimon* in Rapallo A above, but, whereas those drafts never reached publication in recognizable form, with the treatment of Balzac's *Le chef d'oeuvre inconnu*, we can trace the evolution backward from the published version, through the drafts of insertions to Section II, to the original formulation in the abandoned Section V. Writing of what Yeats perceives as Pound's aim in the Cantos, the published version suggests that:

> There will be no plot, no chronicle of events, no logic of discourse, but two themes, the Descent into Hades from Homer, a Metamorphosis from Ovid, and, mixed with these, mediaeval or modern historical characters. He has tried to produce that picture Porteous commended to Nicholas Poussin in *Le chef d'œuvre inconnu* where everything rounds or thrusts itself without edges, without contours—conventions of the intellect—from a splash of tints and shades; to achieve a work as characteristic of the art* of our time as the paintings of Cézanne, avowedly suggested by Porteous, as *Ulysses* and its dream association of words and images, a poem in which there is nothing that can be taken out and reasoned over, nothing that is not a part of the poem itself.
>
> * Mr. Wyndham Lewis, whose criticism sounds true to a man of my generation, attacks this art in Time and Western Man. If we reject, he argues, the forms and categories of the intellect there is nothing left but sensation, "eternal flux" [. . . .][142]

It would seem that Yeats was citing from memory, substituting Balzac's Porbus with Porteous,[143] without checking his sources—but this is not quite true, as we shall see. He also appears to reshape several ideas related to painting in Balzac's story—of which more below—in much the same way as he had made a very personal interpretation of Pound's translation of "Donna Mi Prega," which had not stood up to rereading. At the same time, putting these considerations to one side for the moment, this short passage traces a rapid zigzag of thought and allusion where aspects of contemporary art jostle one another: the poetry of the *Cantos* is compared to a painting described by Balzac, the post-Impressionist painting of Cezanne,[144] and James Joyce's *Ulysses*—although the supposed "dream association of words and images" seems more applicable to Joyce's *Work in Progress*, which had started appearing in 1924. There is also a reference to Wyndham Lewis in a note. And yet Yeats conceives this "art of our time" as having "nothing that can be taken out and reasoned over, nothing that is not a part of the poem itself," showing an inner coherence, similar perhaps to that described by Balzac's Frenhofer, "the unity which simulates the conditions of life itself."[145] There are, however, a series of ideas and connections, elided or suppressed in this final version, that are clarified considerably by the drafts.

This passage first takes its published form in a pencil draft on the notebook's third recto, corrected in ink and with insertions from the verso of the second leaf, in four separate impulses of thought, a first treatment of hypnagogic visions, a second, on artistic unity, to be inserted in the first, and a third section on "Porteus," for insertion in the second, along with a footnote on Wyndham Lewis that refers to *Ulysses*, all to be inserted in the text on the recto.

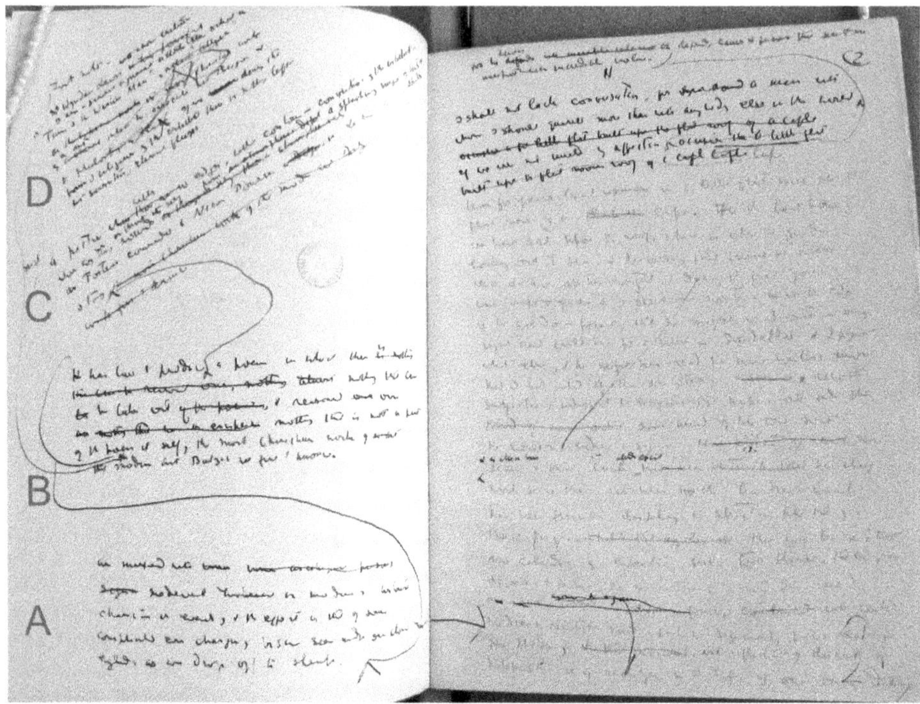

Figure 1.5. Rapallo Notebook B, NLI 13,579, [2v–3r]. The insertions on the verso are labeled here in probable order of composition. Courtesy of NLI; photograph courtesy of Catherine E. Paul.

The relevant text can be assembled as follows:

> [3r] There will be no plot, no calendar of events but two themes, the Odysse[*a*]n descent into Hades, the metamorphosis of a god from Ovid, ~~as repeated~~ <~~come~~> ~~& again~~ <[~~xxx xxxxx~~]> ~~in different forms, combined with certain medieval archetype mind—perhaps Sigismond, perhaps Lorenzo De Medici & this archetypal with reflection of descent of [?perhaps plan] as of archetype in the life of our own day~~.
>
> [2v]
>
> [**A**] and mixed with ~~various archetypal persons segments~~ modern ~~historical~~ or modern & historic characters or events, & the effect is that of some complicated even changing vision seen under our closed eyelids as we are dropping off to sleep.
>
> [**B**] He has tried to produce
>
> [**C**] <such> a picture ~~where there are no~~ without edges, without contours—conventions of the intellect—where everything rounds or thrusts itself from a splashing surge of tints or shades as Porteus commended to Nicolas Poussin in his story~~, the most characteristic work of the modern art Balzac was to first anounce~~

> [**B**] a poem in which there ~~is nothing that can be reasoned over, nothing almost~~ is nothing that can be taken out ~~of the poem~~ & reasoned over ~~and nothing that has an existence~~ nothing that is not a part of the poem itself, the most characteristic work of ~~an art~~ that *modern art Balzac was first to anounce.
>
> > [**D**] [*]Foot note
> > Mr Wyndam Lewis ~~in his powerful~~ <with whose criticism> <I am in general agreement attacks the school in> "Time and Western Man" ~~attacks "Ullyses" as the typical work~~ its most characteristic work of ~~a school~~ an art which he associates with Bergson & the philosophy of Time. If we ~~rxxxxx~~ deny that form & categories of the intellect there is nothing left but sensation, eternal flux. [146]

In layering these thoughts together, Yeats adds to the complexity of his treatment, suggesting many aspects of what he considered the art of his own time "at this 23rd Phase," though earlier in *A Vision A* he had appeared to see dissociation of "the *physical primary*" and "the *spiritual primary*" (*AVA* 211–12, *CW13* 174–75) as the modern characteristic, rather than works where there "is nothing that can be taken out" (draft and published text). With the cancelled reference to *Ulysses*, all the elements of the final version are included, except that of the painter Paul Cezanne, while the draft's hypnagogic vision is removed.

The contrast of a pencil draft [3r] corrected in ink [2v] suggests a later revision, and it seems likely that Yeats returned to section II after deciding to abandon section V ([5r–7r]), in order to reuse the elements he wanted to preserve. As outlined above, there are effectively three versions of the passage under discussion, and to continue tracing backward, I shall start with the last:

> (6
>
> A friend tells me that Cezanne deduced his art from certain passages in Balzac Chef D'oeuvre Inconnu & I discover in those passages what divivides [*sic*] the school most dominant today from that [?art] which is now born. Nicholas Poussin an unknown art student called upon his friend the painter Porbus in the year 1612 & met in his studio a strange old man whose criticism [~~. . . .~~] was by its effect upon the mind of Cezane to destroy impressionism & to be first word of all this discussion, which has establisht among the most audacious of a new generation a school of literature opposed to that I was born in.[147]

It is evident here that Yeats had gone to check the story, as the date, given in the story's first sentence, is correct, and the name Porbus appears to be spelled correctly—twice, including a cancelled instance—but Yeats's "b" is easily mistaken for an "l" or an uncrossed "t," so it seems that the mistake came from Yeats misreading his own handwriting later on. However, Porbus is not Poussin's friend at the start of the story, so it is unclear whether Yeats actually refamiliarized himself with the story or just checked details, and the immediate focus is an adaptation—possibly on the part of the "friend"—of an anecdote about Cezanne.

In Balzac's story, the fictional Frenhofer, the only pupil of Jan Gossaert (Mabuse), impresses the younger Frans Porbus and even younger Nicholas Poussin—all of whom are historical—with his fascinating theories about art and his brilliant retouching of Porbus's canvas. They learn that Frenhofer has been working on a canvas of surpassing mastery for over a decade, which he keeps secret while he perfects it. By offering Poussin's beautiful young girlfriend as a model, Porbus and Poussin are finally able to enter Frenhofer's studio and see the painting of *Catherine Lescault, La Belle Noiseuse*. Poussin "can see nothing there but confused masses of colour and a multitude of fantastical lines that go to make a dead wall of paint," though in a corner there is a beautifully realized "bare foot emerging from the chaos of colour, half-tints and vague shadows that made up a dim formless fog" that "had escaped the incomprehensible, slow, and gradual destruction."[148] Though they are horrified, Frenhofer seems unaware and asserts that he has "succeeded in softening the contours of my figure and enveloping them in half-tints until the very idea of drawing, of the means by which the effect is produced, fades away, and the picture has the roundness and relief of nature."[149] Porbus declares that "There [. . .] lies the utmost limit of our art on earth," but Poussin tactlessly lets drop that "sooner or later he [Frenhofer] will find out that there is nothing there."[150] Accusing them of jealousy, but thrown into dejection, Frenhofer drives them out, and that night he dies as his studio is destroyed by fire.

The story is, of course, full of ambiguities. Has Frenhofer's mad perfectionism led him to ruin a near-perfect masterpiece—as indicated by the remaining foot and the preparatory works on the walls—or has he simply gone beyond the conventions of his day to something so radical that his more orthodox colleagues fail to recognize its genius? Is the master, who is able to breathe life into Porbus's canvas with a few touches of the brush, unable to see where to stop, marring his own creation? Or is this truly the "utmost limit" of art? Frenhofer's work has been taken as the forerunner of the Impressionists, the post-Impressionists, or abstract art.

The story had particular resonances for Cezanne, and the ambiguities only multiply. A friend of his recorded how Cezanne once pointed to himself in a self-accusatory manner as Frenhofer, and in a questionnaire, Cezanne named "Frenhoffer" as the literary character he was most drawn to.[151] Yet when Cezanne identified himself with Frenhofer, was he identifying with genius ahead of his time, with failure, or both?[152] Critics vary. Yeats, however, understands the anecdote differently, seeing Cezanne as taking Balzac's descriptions as a guide or manifesto for his own artistic practice, turning self-accusation into a *modus operandi.* Cezanne is seen as the "first word" of a new school encapsulated in the words that Balzac puts in Frenhofer's mouth and those that describe his painting.

In Yeats's preceding draft, this idea followed an examination of "the art of my generation, 'pure art' as men have come to call it, with sentences the young Hallam wrote of the Tennyson of the Lotos Eaters and the early poems"—referring to Arthur Hallam's review essay "On Some of the Characteristics of Modern Poetry, and on the Lyrical Poems of Alfred Tennyson"—all of which was later cancelled.[153] Here, in the context of "pure art," Yeats comments:

> I am to day dissatisfied with <that> descri[*p*]tion & remember that Cezanne — or so I am told — turned his own art to Chef-d'oeuvre inconnu of Balzac....

This was cancelled and taken up again a few lines later:

> A friend tells that Cezzane deduced his art from some passage in Balzac's Chef-d'oeuvre inconnu & ~~Frenhofer's~~ ~~describing of what he has attempted~~ <that passage, if indeed I have found it>, ~~describes the words~~ describes the art to day more accurately ~~than those of Hallam~~ <that [=*than*] Hallam[*'s*] words>, which turn the soul into a mirror.[154]

Yeats was evidently looking to find a way to express the theme of schools and movements in art and time, which he was adapting from the final pages of *A Vision A*'s "Dove or Swan" to his projected "Spring in Rapallo."[155] Alighting on Cezanne as the expression of a modern spirit, inspired by a novella written more than half a century earlier,[156] Yeats wrestled with how to express the connection of ideas with elegance and economy. And he was consulting Balzac's story in search of the passage alluded to by his friend.

The very first draft of the material actually starts with Cezanne—cancelled—moving, on second thought, to Wyndham Lewis and the Modernists, cancelled in its turn:

> V
>
> ~~A friend tells that Cezanne traced~~ ~~art~~ ~~the~~ ~~his most characteristic~~ ~~his art~~ ~~painting to his reading~~ ~~to Balzacs Chef-d'oeuvre inconnu~~
> Sometimes I have discussed with Pound those ~~powerful~~ ~~mighty~~ books in which Mr Wyndham Lewis ~~has attacked him~~ ~~confounds to geth~~ ~~describes him, as of the same school as Jame Joyce, Gertrude, Stein, Charly Chaplin & Henri Bergson & Ezra Pound~~
>
> (5
>
> ~~confounding all together in his powerful invective~~ ~~symbols according to powerful~~ ~~rhetoric~~ ~~invect~~ ~~invective, of an anarchic sexual emotional art~~

> chooses him ~~out for analys~~ & James Joyce, & ~~as the two most representative of a an~~ to represent a whole school ~~—Gertrude Stein, Henri B Lawrence, &~~ which seem to him emotional & anarchic.[157]

This, then, is the first expression of the idea that was finally published as the footnote. Yet that footnote is no afterthought, being rather the tip of an iceberg of thought and labor, which so often underlies even minor elements within the published work.

The references to Frenhofer's words and his work were also salvaged, though mixed together and assigned to Pourbus/Porteous instead. If modern readers have created some of the ambiguities in Balzac's story, Yeats's misremembering blurs things further. While Yeats has Porteous commend a picture "where everything rounds or thrusts itself without edges, without contours—conventions of the intellect—from a splash of tints and shades,"[158] in Balzac's story it is Frenhofer who says:

> there are no lines in Nature, everything is solid[. . . .] So I have not defined the outlines; I have suffused them with a haze of half-tints warm or golden, in such a sort that you can not lay your finger on the exact spot where background and contours meet. Seen from near, the picture looks a blur; it seems to lack definition; but step back two paces, and the whole thing becomes clear, distinct, and solid; the body stands out; the rounded form comes into relief; you feel that the air plays round it.[159]

And it is not "Porteous' disastrous picture,"[160] as Yeats writes, but Frenhofer's that shows "a bare foot emerging from the chaos of colour, half-tints and vague shadows that made up a dim, formless fog. Its living delicate beauty held them spellbound."[161] It is all the more surprising that Yeats occludes the role of Frenhofer—who is mentioned in these drafts—since in some respects he is a *daimonic* artist: while Frenhofer is adding his masterful touches to Porbus's painting, "it seemed to the young Poussin as if some familiar spirit inhabiting the body of this strange being took a grotesque pleasure in making use of the man's hands against his own will" and later, when Frenhofer falls into abstraction, Porbus comments "he is in converse with his *dæmon*."[162]

There is a subterranean element to Yeats's use of Balzac, with his forgetfulness enabling greater freedom and serving his own purposes better. In using the art of Frenhofer and Cezanne to write of Pound and his younger contemporaries, Yeats is perhaps able to enjoy the ambiguity of the story: the *Cantos* may be at the "utmost limit" of art, unrecognized as yet in their genius, or maybe Pound is like Frenhofer and "sooner or later he will find out that there is nothing there."[163] Certainly *A Packet for Ezra Pound* contains comments that could be subtle barbs; as Catherine Paul remarks, when Yeats advised Pound not to "be elected to the Senate of your country,"[164] "there are few things Pound would have preferred to having his own government require his expertise."[165]

Although there is no sign in the drafts in Notebook B that "Rapallo in Spring" was yet conceived of as material directly associated with the new edition of *A Vision*, connections were inevitable, and indeed at the back of this notebook Yeats would create a first draft of the introduction itself, declaring, as already cited: "I can never imagine myself studying anything, without in some [*way*] relating it, or incorporating it with what is here" in *A Vision*.[166] Thus, his examination of recent movements in art and literature inevitably relates to the treatment of the current period that he had outlined in *A Vision A*, extending and building on those earlier perceptions.

The rest of the notebook is dedicated to the new material for *A Vision*, rethinking the initial presentation, the descriptions of the afterlife, the expanded material on the concept of the Great Year, and an account of the automatic script and its origins.

[10v–33r] "First Things 15 pages"

"First things" is a projected introductory text for the revised system of *A Vision*, and it would later be redrafted in Rapallo Notebook A. As mentioned earlier, elements of the first page or so had already been outlined in the leather notebook that Yeats had brought with him to the south of Europe,[167] where he titled a brief treatment "the daimon" "suggested first paragraph of system."[168] There he had inserted a sentence at the beginning—"all that can <need> be said of the daimon in this place can [be] put into a few sentences," and the new opening in the Rapallo B draft is an elaboration of this theme:

> I begin with the daemon & of the daimon I know little, but comfort [myself] with this saying of Marc[*i*]on's "neither can we think, know, or say anything of the gospels'['], & with this cry from the Indian sage Behold the exposition of God – the lightening fills the sky – ah – ah – my dazzled eyes are shut – ah – ah – the exposition of god is finished & that cry of the Japanese attaining Nirvana "You ask me what is my religion & I hit you on the mouth". At the same time I remember that an Arian theologian once wrote "I know God as he is known to himself" & write out with confidence what my teachers have said, or what I have inferred from their messages [*and*] diagrams.[169]

As commented already, Yeats's rapid delivery of gnomic fragments here both dazzles and befogs. The quotations may illustrate the problem of speaking about the ineffable but would do little to help the reader at the start of a complex exposition, except that they are characteristic of Yeats's range of reference. This group of quotations was retained through a long series of drafts, and the two Eastern examples—one Japanese and one Indian, both taken from

Daisetz Suzuki's *Essays on Zen Buddhism*—were retained into the published version, though moved to the end of the exposition of "The Completed Symbol" (*AVB* 215, *CW14* 158).[170] Critics have commented more on Yeats's references to Eastern thought than his knowledge of Christian thinkers, but this is nonetheless impressive, if usually focused less on the writers themselves than their heretical targets. The two examples from early Christianity were used again the following winter in Rapallo C in a short examination of what "Ezra Pound bases his scepticism upon. . . ."[171] Again they form a contrasting doublet of "a Church father [who] said 'we can never think or know anything of the gospel'"—a vaguer but rather more credible attribution than Marcion, whose views about the gospels were very decided—and "some Arian [who said] 'I know god as he is known to himself.'"—referring to Eunomius, Bishop of Cyzicus, who scandalized the Church Father John Chrysostom: "A mere human has the boldness to say: 'I know God as God himself knows himself.'"[172]

Even though Yeats may have little in common doctrinally with the Church Fathers, he shares something of their approach to philosophical questions and abstract reasoning, and, as the Pre-Raphaelite Brotherhood identified Raphael as the beginning of a deterioration in art, Yeats treats René Descartes as the pivotal figure in a detrimental shift in thinking. This is adumbrated in a new opening section that he sketches on the opposite page to be inserted as the very first section of the new presentation:

> I
>
> ~~This book~~ ~~de~~ ~~cannot~~ help
> ~~What I have to say,~~ This book ~~cannot~~ would be different if it ~~did not~~ ~~come from~~ ~~if~~ ~~if were not founded upon the words~~ had not come from those, who claim to <have> died many times, ~~& so begin &~~ & ~~did not~~ ~~assume~~ ~~must assume their~~ in all they say assume their own existence. In this it resembles ~~not~~ ~~some ancient books of philosophy, xx but none~~ ~~no book~~ ~~no modern book, but some~~ ~~that are ancient no book xxxx~~ nothing since Decartes but much that is ancient.[173]

This is both a clear statement of the central role of the automatic script and yet a scrupulous distancing from any declaration about what or who the voices are—they "claim to have died many times" and "assume their own existence," but Yeats withholds giving greater credence to their claims than is strictly warranted. They may assume their own existence yet still be the figures of dream, appearing as projections or dramatizations from the medium's mind.[174]

After these preliminaries, which include the initial presentation of the *Daimon* as outlined earlier in "The Sequence of Rapallo A and B" [11r and 12v], Yeats moves on to explain the gyres. The redrafting was far from clear and the process of composition of the following twenty pages is particularly complex. Right at the outset, three pages have been torn out prior to section III [12–14], so that this page [15r], numbered "2," is clearly already a reworking of rejected material, and the following pages are a thicket of cancellations at various levels, with the page numbering, evidently added at a relatively late stage, moving forwards and backwards (through verso revisions; see Appendix) and on to recapitulations or substitutions: for example, the exposition of how Plotinus supplies a connection between the *Daimon*'s sphere and the double vortex, first drafted on [15v], is repeated or moved into a new arrangement on [26v].

The treatment shows some of the features of the distinctive presentation in *A Vision B*, including a drawing of a cone with "Time" and "Subject" at its apex and "Space" and "Object" at its base ([15r], cf. *AVB* 71, *CW14* 52). However, it also seeks to frame the dualism in terms of a "universal self, or daimon of daimons, consciousness itself [?presenting] through time & mirroring space & a separate self set in the midst of space & struggling for room to live & mirroring the Daimon passions. Thought is from the first movement, emotion & sensation from the second."[175] These categories and formulations were not included in *A Vision* itself, yet the ideas are present in further formulations, including the Seven Propositions ("Astrology and the Nature of Reality" in Rapallo D),[176] and they clearly underlie Yeats's deeper understanding of the system.

After presenting the opposing gyres in terms borrowed from Proclus, Cavalcanti, and Heraclitus, Yeats proceeds to introduce their movements in terms of the *Four Principles*: "To the Two in the unshaded cone we give the names Husk & Passionate Body.... The Two gyres In the shaded cone, which are called Spirit & Celestial Body have an exactly corresponding movement."[177] This contrasts with both versions of *A Vision*, which present the movement of the gyres in terms of the temporary *Faculties*. As Yeats stated further on in this notebook, his understanding of the *Principles* as the permanent spiritual forms of the *Faculties* had come after he wrote "The Twenty-Eight Embodiments" of *A Vision A*,[178] and evidently he was seeking to remedy this misunderstanding by presenting the material related to the gyres in terms of the *Principles*.

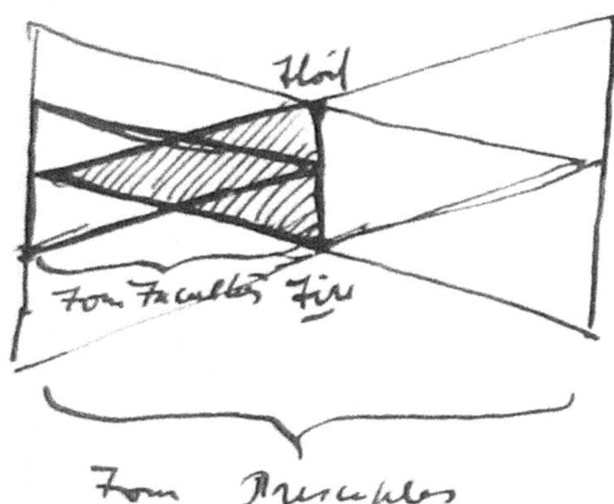

Figure 1.6. Detail from Rapallo Notebook B, NLI 13,579, [29v]. The cones of the *Four Principles* contain the cones of the *Four Faculties* (here on the left). The two crisis points are "Flood" (top) and "Fire" (bottom), mirroring the two manners of destruction of the universe. Courtesy of NLI.

In the end, this approach was not adopted, however, with the result that many readers have found the *Principles* unnecessary duplicates and insufficiently clarified or differentiated.[179] Some of the material that Yeats outlines here—such as the *Principles* in relation to light and to "their unity in the daimon"[180]—was included in *A Vision B*, not in the initial presentation as envisaged here, but delayed until the second "book," "The Completed Symbol," where it is treated so summarily that readers have not found it very illuminating. Yet the ideas here, worked through as part of the system's technicalities, still underlie imagery and poetry. The following draft, for instance, suggests the foundation of the poem "Chosen," while Yeats also recalls the transcendent close to "Among School Children" understood as Unity of Being:

> It was a Greco Roman fancy, that the soul could at ~~the po~~[*int*] where the zodiac is crossed by the Milky Way turn aside from its path & become a sphere; & the whole aim of the soul is to become a sphere, to allow such a harmonious confluence of all the principles & faculties, that the whirling ends for ever, & all return into the daimon. Some shaddow of its final achievement is found at every point of the vortex, but only complete union at one or other extreme limit, either when Husk may be absorbed in <u>Passionate Body</u> & all be beauty, or when <u>Spirit</u> may be absorbed in Celestial Body & all be Truth, and then only to the supreme Soul. Because <u>Spirit</u> & Celestial Body are human life alone when united to Husk & Passionate Body, & so nourished by particular reality; because all search is through the Four Faculties the union of the Faculties must accompany that of <u>Spirit</u> & <u>Celestial Body</u>. Once that supreme union is attained, Celestial Body & Passionate Body, the known & the ought are our body, the <u>Spirit</u> & the Husk, the knower & the Is our soul, & body & soul are one "How shall we know the dancer from the dance?"[181]

At the same time, the symbolisms involved in the relationship between the sexes, the church calendar, and the Great Year jostle in the treatment, as Yeats's attraction to favorite ideas draws him into characteristic streams of association. One that first appeared in *A Vision A* and is repeated in more than one context in Rapallo A and B is the idea of John the Baptist and Christ as complementary opposites. In *A Vision A*, John's midsummer birth is contrasted with Christ's midwinter nativity, and their conceptions placed at the respective equinoxes nine months earlier, an idea attributed to St. John Chrysostom (*AVA* 164, *CW13* 133). Yeats compares Leonardo da Vinci's painting of John the Baptist to a Dionysus, as he is conceived when the grapes are picked and born when the wheat is harvested. Each of these points is elaborated in the new treatment:

> At midwinter—"the generation of all things with water" Porphyry wrote—Christ is born, at summer St John, Christ begotten in Spring, & in the Autumn

St John, one begotten in joy & brought forth in sorrow, one begotten in sorrow & brought forth in joy.

[. . .]

Coventry Patmore called St John "Natural love" & so a preparation for "supernatural love" following doubtless some father of the Chuch, & did some member of the Platonic Academy of Florence first suggest to Da Vinci a St John with the likeness of Dionysus a form emerging perhaps, not from ~~a sandy desert but~~ some wilderness like that of Eden. The Spirit—supernatural love—begotten a [?new] at the midpoint, receives a natural body when the year brings round the Water – the natural flux; the Husk anew self, instinct, natural love, begotten at the opposing point receives a supernatural body when the year brings round the fire – the purifying ecstacy. Did [?early] Christian [?revery] turn Dyonysus into a saint & mistake his wild honey for the food of an ascetic.

{ ~~Christ is always antithetical to man~~

The God, "boundless love" the universal self is always the antithetical portion of the vortex, but when the year or month of the Faculties is primary it is antithetical, & when antithetical primary; & escaped from the whirl of month or year, the soul born in purifying in flame, rebegotten in the [?su[*pe*]rcelstial] body is Nature itself. }[182]

This draft brings in the cataclysms of flood and fire, which Yeats had read about in Duhem's *Le système du monde* and Plato's *Timaeus*,[183] along with the regeneration of the *Principles*, as well as the transformed body purified in flame, that recalls the spirits "on the Emperor's pavement" of fire in "Byzantium" (*VP* 498, *CW1* 253). The introduction of Coventry Patmore looks forward to the treatment that survived into *A Vision B*, where Patmore is said to have "claimed the Church's authority for calling Christ supernatural love and St. John natural love, and took pleasure in noticing that Leonardo painted a Dionysius like a St. John, a St. John like a Dionysius" (*AVB* 212; cf. *CW14* 156, which corrects the misspelling of "Dionysus"). Yeats attributes to Patmore much that he had already found elsewhere or thought himself: "The Precursor" does speak of St. John and Christ as natural and supernatural love, but none of the essays in *Religio Poetæ* mentions Leonardo's painting, though Walter Pater's *Renaissance* does.[184]

Yeats returns to this group of ideas later in this same notebook in the context of the Great Year, presenting God and man as two wheels that oppose each other, with the spring of one being the autumn of the other (see below).[185] And, in another version later in this notebook (see below, p. 91) and redrafted in Rapallo A, Yeats goes so far as to include a quotation from Patmore—"Christ is supernatural love & St John natural & in natural love God 'gives himself in wine like the fabled Baccus [*sic*]'"—using a phrase wrenched from a completely different essay and context.[186] This last addition was dropped, but, whether the conflation was consciously contrived or not, Yeats evidently found it convenient to ascribe his own mythopoeic mix to the Catholic convert Patmore.

Yeats's repurposing of this idea in different contexts within the construction of the book and its arguments is a larger-scale version of the way he moves clauses around in a sentence and rephrases the elements. Just as he evidently wanted to include the material on Balzac's *Le chef d'oeuvre inconnu* somewhere in "Rapallo in Spring," he seems to have been set on putting some version of the knot of ideas about Christ and John somewhere in *A Vision*. Eventually he included it among a variety of "the symbols of the relations of men and women and of the birth of children" (*AVB* 211, *CW14* 155), but immediately after presenting the contrast between Jesus and his cousin, Yeats cuts off further exploration: "But I need not go further, for all the symbolism of this book applies to begetting and birth, for all things are a single form which has divided and multiplied in time and space" (*AVB* 212, *CW14* 156).

Rapallo B's draft of "First Things" ends with the question "How are we different at the years end from what we were at its beginning?" answering in terms of Blake's illustrations to the Book of Job. I include cancelled material for clarity:

> What in his designs to the book of Job ~~represents~~ showing that begin & end shows of a necessity a year. At the begging [=*beginning*] is Job surounded by his children ~~xx all have~~ que [*?=quiet*] at prayer, their stringed instruments hanging on the tree[,] their faces, ~~gentle,~~ passive, <timid> emotional, like the faces of good children who attend to their duties, do what they are told never open a book but in the two last pictures, his new family is about him their faces more beautiful, because full of intellect & daring & in the last of them they stand in triumph playing upon many instruments.
>
> { At first we are subject to Destiny, ~~or Husk and~~ or Passionate Body, to ~~Husk Fa Fat~~ Fate or Cellestial Body, but in ~~the end we attain~~ that ~~that state~~ we may escape from the constraint of our nature, & from that of external things, by entering upon ~~that condition~~ <a state> ~~where there is nothing but the condition itself~~ where all fuel has become [*flame*], & where ~~seeg~~ seeing that there is nothing outside the state, nothing to constrain it[,] flame is eternal. We attain <it ~~for a moment~~> in the creation, or enjoyment of a work of art but the moment ~~passes, because its circle~~ though eternal in the daimon passes from us, because it does not contain our whole being. Philosophy has always explained as in some such way & yet the mystery remains, }
>
> ~~Do we not at first rebel without~~ [?~~meaning~~] <~~a purpose~~> ~~&~~ [?~~obey~~] ~~the universal self without understanding . But however one explain it, & the philosopher & the misty~~ <[?~~the mustery~~]> [?~~remains~~] that the daimon is alone real, & that nothing can be added to it, nothing taken away; that ~~change & progress are~~ <all ~~progression is~~ progressions> are allusion [=*illusion*]; that all things have been born from it like a ship in full sail.
>
> March 1928[187]

At the end of the year or after a series of incarnations, Yeats contemplates a transformation from a dutiful innocence to vigorous experience, like the children of Job, which implies a form of progress. Yet paradoxically, it seems, nothing is added, as the later self rather approaches closer to its own archetype or *Daimon*. There is a momentary intimation of this *daimonic* eternity in creating art, where the numbers fold in on themselves, and the integrity can be seen in the modern art he had contemplated in "Rapallo in Spring," where "there is nothing that can be taken out & reasoned over nothing that is not a part of the poem itself, the most characteristic work of that modern art Balzac was first to anounce."[188] It is also—as Yeats writes at the end of Rapallo B—like *A Vision* itself, in which the value of the "single thought has expressed it self as if it were a work of art," with the clarity of "a smokeless flame" and a unity that "lies in the daimon."[189]

Little of this construct finds direct expression in *A Vision* itself, however, but, as mentioned earlier, there are clear echoes in the poetry. Purifying fire and "escape from the constraint of our nature" had been a theme in "Sailing to Byzantium,"[190] and the hard-worked struggle with words here would also feed later into in the fuelless flame of "Byzantium" (see Rapallo Notebook D) and the opening of "Old Tom Again": "Things out of perfection sail / And all their swelling canvas wear. . . ." (*VP* 530, *CW1* 274).

This treatment is dated March 1928 and, as Yeats usually seems to have dated his work after revising it, these drafts were probably created during the Yeatses' earliest days in Rapallo.

[34v–43r] "Additions & corrections of Vision Book II | 7 pages (dated May 1928)"

The folios from [34v–38r] contain various fragmentary paragraphs, including two or three false starts to the revised version of "Book II | 1. The Great Wheel." To some extent these seem to rework "First Things," containing some of the same material, but mainly seek to build on the exposition of the double vortex, or interpenetrating cones, moving on to the more flexible symbol of the Great Wheel.

Though brief and fragmentary, even these *disjecta membra* contain insights into Yeats's thinking and how he viewed his material, and Yeats numbered the pages, which generally indicates that he saw the material as useful. In the first introduction, he heads the paragraph, "~~Religio Poetae~~ | Book II | I. The Great Wheel"; since he had just quoted Coventry Patmore's *Religio Poetæ* on John the Baptist, this may be no more than a note that was rejected, but its size and position make it look like a title, so he might have been considering borrowing the title for some less than orthodox musings. Certainly, the opening paragraph he drafts below it focuses on the double vortex and the wheel (confusing Empedocles with Heraclitus, as he often did):

> The double vortex of Heraclitus was too simple, we know of it from a metrical fragment & when Heraclitus spoke to his pupils, he may have used some form that showed more of actual history. Things do not move gradually in one direction & then as gradually in another, as the narrowing & then expanding gyres suggest.[191]

Yeats evidently recognizes that the gyres might seem inadequate to "An Explanation of Life," as offered by the subtitle of *A Vision A*. Even if he considers that his instructors' version of the "double vortex" is more complex than that of Empedocles, many readers presented with *A Vision*'s single supreme diagram may well have felt that, however much it is modified by epicycles of complexity, the scheme is "too simple."

On the opposite verso, so probably later, Yeats also drafts one of his recurrent disclaimers, explaining, perhaps more clearly than elsewhere, what he means by the metaphor of the *dramatis personae*, a phrase which became the working title for these opening sections through a series of drafts:

> I am a dramatist & symbolist & often content with such definition or describtion [*sic*] as one can in list of Dramatis Personae, ~~preffering that "Principles" or "Faculties" "Daimon" "[?emotion]" "thought" "man" "God" or Da that my matters to reveal them selves in action~~ leaving my matter to display itself in action.[192]

The analogy does not seem particularly sound, as there is relatively little action within which to observe how these various actors behave, but it does show that Yeats's sparse definition and "character sketch" of his players is a deliberate choice. Again, many readers find the lack of delineation of *Faculties*, *Principles*, *Daimon*, man, or God something of a barrier to understanding.

In the following opening, the recto shows again "Book II | I. The Great Wheel," but preceded by two rejected titles, "~~Siris~~| ~~A Foundation~~." Like "Religio Poetæ," the cancelled title "Siris" at the head may hint that Yeats considered embarking on more literary and discursive writing, which was then pushed aside by the expository material of "A Foundation," a title repeated on the following recto too. The text describes how the instructors gave the Great Wheel before the double vortex, explaining how it "is a pictorial ~~simpl~~ representation of a form of the Double Vortex" and gives a presentation that presents the *Principles* with their corresponding *Faculties*, "Husk and P[assionate] B[ody] or Will and Mask" in an initial section that runs out of steam on the second page.[193] The text continues from the diagrams and explication of the preceding page, yet, at the top of the page, Yeats has cancelled "~~A Foundation~~ | ~~I~~ | ~~This book would be different~~," evidently using the new opening that he had drafted for "First Things."

Though these two rectos, [36r] and [37r], are numbered, Yeats's numbering skips the following recto, which has only a few abandoned efforts:

> ~~When for many weeks, after~~
> ~~When my instructors first taught me, they~~
> ~~For~~
> ~~For the first <couple of> years my instructors based the greater part of their instruction upon what "The Great Whel Wheel", & some weeks of that time had passed before I connected with it, certain gyres & cones used~~[194]

The rest of the page is blank. Though completely fragmentary, these false starts—and the more substantial one before—appear to show something like a practice run-up to a jump or pitch, and the following pages launch into a sustained exposition, drawing on these feints at starting.

> I. Introduction
> ~~When my instructors began I was taught to measure character & emotion by the movements of what I have called "The Great Wheel" movements that seemed as arbitrary as those in some game of chance [. . . .]~~ The Great Wheel is a circle of 28 lunar phases, or of 27 phases and a moonless night, each symbolized by a circle & a crescent, the circle for the convenience of an arbitrary symbol representing the sun, but for convenience of representation and symbol alike made dark.[195]

The exposition is presented now almost exclusively in terms of the *Faculties*, as the focus is on the character of the various incarnations, and the material is a variation on the presentations that would appear in the published version of *A Vision B*. Yeats had clearly decided to repeat the descriptions of *A Vision A*'s "The Twenty-Eight Embodiments," explaining:

> When I first wrote my second Book for the first edition of this book I had not mastered all the geometrical symbolism & was so persuaded of its difficulty that I tried [*to*] interest my reader as I had been interested in the Great Wheel, as something unexplained but yet explaining the world. Somewhere in the Arabian Nights an Arab boy becomes a Zizier [=*Vizier*] & explains his wisdom by saying "O brother I have taken stock in the desert sand and of the sayings of antiquity"; & compelled to my great regret as I have explained to invent for my symbols an imaginary origin I thought I could draw attention to [*the*] most important of them by pretending this was the marks made upon the sand by certain enigmatical men & women, dancing to amuse & instruct

> a tyrant of Bagdad. What I had been told about the Four Principles meant nothing to me, because the geometry that explained it was still unintelligible, so I gave to each Faculty the quality of the corresponding Principle together with its own. Had I understood that the Principles are value & attainment, & the Faculties process & search I could not perhaps have done other without innumerable cumbersome explanatory sentences. During embodied life the Principles are brought into existence by the Faculties, & only when we speak of the state after death is it necessary to constantly distinguish one from the other. I wrote this book in my first excitement, when it seemed that I understood human nature for the first time, & leave it unchanged except for a few passages crossed out because their matter is somewhere in book I & three or four sentences added to sharpen a definition or correct an error.[196]

The repetition of the quotation about the Vizier and desert sand that he had used in *Per Amica Silentia Lunae* (*Myth* 343, *CW5* 17)—different from any of the translations but with exactly the same wording as the 1917 essay—shows how essential a part of Yeats's mental stock it was,[197] and how clearly he connected the ideas of that earlier essay with the Arabian fantasy of *A Vision A*, the diagrams made in the sand by the Judwalis, and Kusta ben Luka's young bride in "The Desert Geometry or the Gift of Harun-al-Rashid."[198]

Yeats also admits that the descriptions of the twenty-eight incarnations should in fact be more complex and labored in explanation, as he is only including half of the relevant elements, yet many readers probably find even that half difficult enough to accommodate when they read about the different types. It is, indeed, unlikely that the description of the incarnations corresponding to the phases of the moon would gain any clarity or insight by adding the more spiritual layer of the *Principles*, though it would probably have helped readers to grasp how the two groups of his *dramatis personae—Faculties* and *Principles*—interacted on the stage in action, instead of the relatively abstract accounts of the *Principles* that are given in "The Completed Symbol" of *A Vision B*. Yeats clearly recognized that the description of "the 28 types of incarnation" was among the more approachable and attractive sections of the book, so worth keeping without alteration, even as he was attempting to integrate the *Principles* more fully into the system elsewhere.

He also admits to the many shortcomings of his presentation, only some of which are mentioned in the published version:

> As each gyre of 28 incarnations is succeeded by another of an opposite, & creates itself, by a struggle with predecessor or successor, it is impossible [*to*] explain any particular incarnation without knowing which among the twelve gyres it belongs to and this I cannot do. Again & again my instructors spoke of some man or woman, as belonging to the 4 or 5th or 6th, let us say, but my imagination has not been able to follow. I cannot even master in its detail the single type of

> gyre of this book. The list of attributes in "The Table of the Four Faculties" or "character in certain phases" [*is*] not my work, nor could I replace it if it was lost. It was dictated nine or ten attributes at a time, & all I have done is to change two or three words for reasons of style, after I had asked permission, or to fill a blank space with that somewhat vague description "Player on Pans pipes".
>
> A phase or type recurs until the soul has attained a proximate unity of being — unity of Spirit and Celestial Body "nourished" by that of the Faculties & the moment of this possible attainment "could be fixed mathematically" had I the power of abstract thought.
>
> May 1928[199]

The dating of May 1928 shows that a few months had passed since he had started on "First Things" and two since revising it. This date also appears on a typescript that appears to have been dictated from this, while the corrections are dated July 1928,[200] and both appear to pre-date the equivalent material in Rapallo A.

Folios [44–50]

These folios are not accounted for in Yeats's table of contents. The spread of [43v–44r] gives notes for amending pages 12, 13, 14, and 15 of *A Vision A*, "The Great Wheel" (the last in fact relating to page 14). Clearly, in 1928, when presenting the concept of the Great Wheel, Yeats still intended to modify parts the presentation of *A Vision A* rather than rewrite the material completely, as eventually happened.

While [44r] repeats the page number of the preceding recto [43r]—"7"—the following three leaves, [45–47], have been removed, and the numbering on [48r] follows with the number "8." However, the following two rectos, [49–50], are unnumbered and, on these three pages, all the material is cancelled. The figure "II" at the beginning of the draft appears to relate to section II of the Great Wheel, and these pages outline rejected considerations of the Wheel, the latter parts relating to civilizations and the birth of Christ.

Following a diagram where Christ is placed at the center of a gyre (see Figure 1.7), the final line, which Yeats struck through along with the rest, ominously states that "My instructors have preferred a more complicated symbol,"

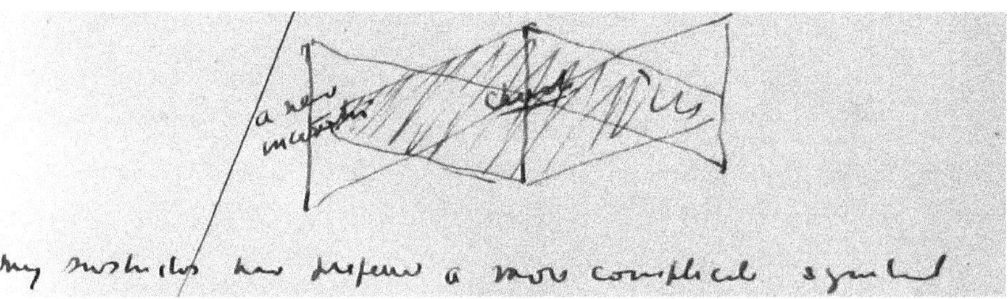

Figure 1.7. Rapallo Notebook B, NLI 13,579, [50r]. The annotations read "a new incarnation" and "Christ." Courtesy of NLI; photograph courtesy of Catherine E. Paul.

no doubt referring to the double cone that precedes "Dove or Swan" in both versions of *A Vision*.

[51r–74r] "Great Year 21 pages (early version)"

Although the next page appears to follow its predecessors as rejected text, it marks the beginning of the book that Yeats was preparing for the new version of *A Vision* on the Great Year of the Ancients, and the text is recognizably that of the published version: "'By common custom,' Cicero wrote in the Dream of Scipio 'men measure the year merely by the return of the Sun, or in other words by the revolution of one star. . . .'"[201] The following page is numbered as the first of the new section, which continues over the next twenty-two folios (numbered 1–8, one blank page, 8[bis]–21). Yeats attributes the 26,000-year period of the Great Year to his instructors, noting that with respect to the astronomical details involved, "I got this all wrong in the first edition of this book thinking that it must have begun between Taurus and Ares," rather than Aries and Pisces.[202] Personally, his purpose appears to include providing a framework that makes Christianity a phenomenon of a particular time and combination of cycles rather than a revelation for all time. (Part of the treatment here was reworked in the first section of Rapallo Notebook A: see the transcription from [8r] above, p. 42.)

> I myself seek a symbol that can thrust Christianity back into the crises where it arose, and there display it not as an abstract ideal but united to its opposite, or thrust it forward into the crisis where the actors must change robes & the defeated Tincture triumph in its turn. ~~An abstract ideal is lyrical.~~
>
> ~~VI~~
>
> ~~An ideal separated from its opposite is lyrical~~ ~~acquires a~~ ~~is lyrical;~~ ~~has a phantastic imobility like that of the Greek figures in Keats Ode & palls upon us po;~~ ~~has a phantastic imobility like that of the gr figures Keats saw upon the Urn & therefore xxx palls upon us, the exceptional moment past;~~ ~~whereas~~ ~~but an idea united to its opposite is tragic & stays always like the poetry of Dante~~
>
> ~~VII~~
>
> ~~and like the poetry of Dante needs no exceptional moment & always stays like the poetry of Dante.~~
>
> I am tired of Shellean Christianity. An ideal separated from its opposite is lyrical, & its phantastic imobility palls upon us, but an ideal united to its opposite is tragic & stays always like the poetry of Dante.[203]

It seems strange for a lyric poet to decry lyrical poetry, and to characterize it by an "imobility like that of the figures Keats saw upon the Urn," especially when he had referred to the very same poem and image in his evocation of Rapallo, which had brought "to mind the little Greek town described in 'An Ode to a Grecian Urn.'"[204] Yet evidently he sought to attain the grandeur and movement of drama, and to place religion within this context, by uniting *primary* Christianity to its *antithetical* counterparts.

The treatment includes a schematization that links the months of the Great Year to the signs of the zodiac, the months of the year, and the phases of the moon, as well as the seasons and points of the compass. He would continue to struggle with these schemes when he reworked this material in Rapallo A, and though he eventually abandoned all but a vague identification of the months of the year with the twelve "gyres" of the lunar phases, these correspondences evidently informed how he approached and thought about the process of development in time and history.

The treatment of history presents God and man as two wheels that oppose each other, spring to autumn and *Mask* to *Will*, in cancelled material that was reworked and incorporated into "The Completed Symbol" (cf. *AVB* 210n; *CW14* 154) rather than "The Great Year of the Ancients." The seasonal contrast brings Yeats back to the opposition of St. John's Day on June 24 and Christmas on December 25, while Blake's "Mental Traveller" is invoked in both contexts. A cancelled page elaborates the idea further, though with some jumps of thought that only make sense if one knows the earlier treatments. Some of the associations appear in the material already examined, but, yet again, Yeats elaborates ideas that do not appear in *Religio Poetæ*, connecting "natural love" to the desire for a transcendent object, the *Mask*, or more unexpectedly God as woman. He again alludes to the lush background of the St. John/Bacchus at the Louvre and to his use of St. John Chrysostom in *A Vision A*.

> I am puzzled by a symbolism which Patmore must have thought that of the medieval church unless I can understand "natural love" as all man does for a transcendant object, God is woman, an accepted discipline, a self lacerating ecstacy. I cannot transform a sun dried desert into the wilderness of eden. I do not know Chrisostom accept [=*except*] from what other[*s*] quote of him he has perhaps some passage, that explains what the early church ment by the Four Seasons. My instructors have warned me, not to consider theirs as the only possible symbolism.[205]

This last sentence forms something of a complement to the statement Yeats would include in *A Packet for Ezra Pound*—"but then there are many symbolisms and none exactly resembles mine"[206]—replaced in the version in *A Vision B*.

[66v]

In the following pages, amid exposition of the movements of the gyres of the solar diamond and the lunar hour-glass, and of how to read the positions of the *Faculties* in the cones preceding "Dove or Swan," there is a fragment of a plan for a lecture or an essay on a blank verso (Figure 1.8), possibly the only page in the notebook not directly connected to *A Vision*, though even here the line "My philosophy" may indicate the connection.

[?General].

Influence from Sligo.
folk & faery } Origins
Lady G s book

? Materlinck do not touch me.
? what about Lang Etc

Chance Choice – | difference from other | ? [?~~desire~~] [?~~of~~] [?~~dicipline/deception~~]
Pater. V de l Adam ([?contrects][207]

Michel R & Mathers

Cambridge Neo Platonists

My philosophy

plays & self dicipline & public work
Castiglione

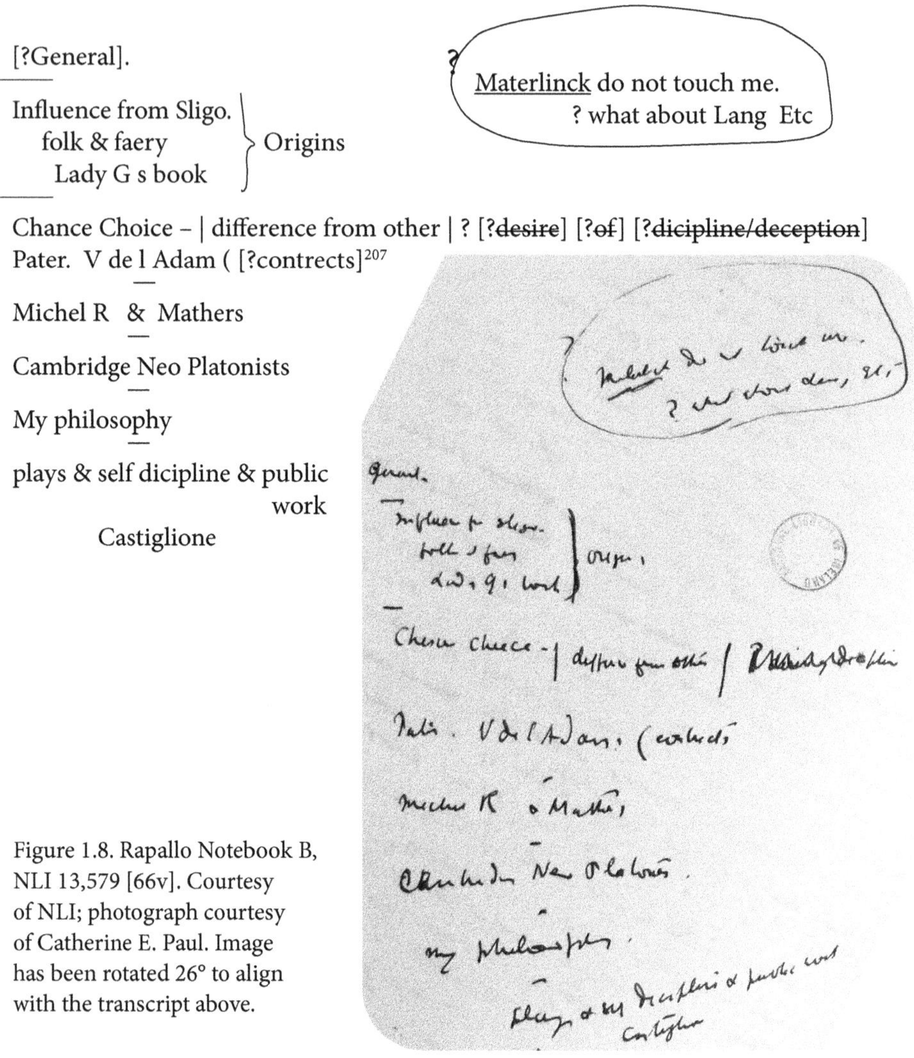

Figure 1.8. Rapallo Notebook B, NLI 13,579 [66v]. Courtesy of NLI; photograph courtesy of Catherine E. Paul. Image has been rotated 26° to align with the transcript above.

Despite some doubtful readings, the plan appears to outline a presentation or lecture. Much of it seems to relate to the growth of the poet's mind, recognizing important influences in Sligo's folklore and Lady Gregory's work on Irish myth, as well as his reading of Walter Pater and Auguste Villiers de l'Isle Adam's play *Axël*.[208] Chance and Choice, fate and destiny, had become an important element of the duality inherent in the system of *A Vision*, while the pairing of Michael Robartes with MacGregor Mathers points to what the fictional Robartes owes to the former leader of the Golden Dawn. *Per Amica Silentia Lunae* gives some indication of the significance that the Cambridge Platonists such as Henry More and Ralph Cudworth held for him, and the category of "My philosophy" could be as extensive or brief as Yeats chose. The inclusion afterwards of the theater work seems to imply that the "philosophy" was not the sole or even main focus, as it looks outward to Yeats's public work, citing the influence of Castiglione's *The Book of the Courtier*.[209]

The circled queries above these notes are even more enigmatic. In Maeterlinck's *Pelléas and Mélisande*, Mélisande's first words on stage are "Do not touch me," a phrase she repeats through the play, but it could be applied here in any number of ways, depending entirely on what aspect caught Yeats's interest.[210] His Deirdre also uses the phrase twice to King Conchubar after Naoise has been killed (*VPl* 383, 384), and it was a theme repeated in nineteenth-century literature, particularly drama, with both biblical and sexual connotations.[211] Andrew Lang had written on many folkloric themes, including taboos, which may indicate a possible approach. However, there is no clear relation with the more personal focus of the other notes.

[67r–74r] ["Great Year" continued]

The following pages continue the treatment of the Great Year uninterrupted, turning to more technical considerations of all the cycles coming together and how art partakes of the whole, as was redrafted in Rapallo A.[212]

> My instructors sometimes talk as if all were calculable, & then again insist upon mans freedom[,] though only at the moment [?some] reaches its climax[.] I have sometimes thought there were two parties among them[,] more often that there is one that can free themselves from the Kantian antinomy. Some times they compared the sphere to a number made of integer numbers whose multiplication make that number with no fraction over, & contrasted it to those others which are like the separate phases, made up of numbers that never constitute a whole, of clocks that do not chime when the central clock strikes midnight or strike some other hour. They compared the first kind of number to a work of art, because in the work of art each separate line, color or thought is related to whole, is as it were multiplied into it, & called both a "sequence", as the second kind they called a "recurrence" meaning I think that the units multiplied themselves but did not constitute a whole. Every phase, every act of the Four Faculties was such a "recurrence", & every such "recurrence" began with an "allusion" an unrelated fact or image which is like the 0 which precedes 1 & is the thing multiplied.
>
> { In pure "sequence["] there is no "allusion," no 0[,] all is from the whole & flows back into the whole. The spirits at phase 1, who are wholly passive, percieve [*sic*] "allusion" only. Others think & create through them but they themselves have neither "recurrence" nor sequence. }

> The subject however was never developed, owing to my mathematical incapacity, I touch upon it here because it echoes Platos perfect numbers, & because the anxiety of my instructors, as to the date of my childrens birth—I speak of that elsewhere—reminds me of the passage in the Republic, where when the rulers forget the perfect numbers, the wrong children come to birth.[213]

Again, the significance of symbolic or Pythagorean number seems to connect to slightly more practical numbers, with the birth of children and Yeats's sense that there is a mystery he has not penetrated. These thoughts are included at the end of "The Completed Symbol" in *A Vision*:

> There are certain numbers, certain obscure calculations in Plato's *Republic* meant to suggest and hide the methods adopted by the ruling philosophers to secure that the right parents shall beget the right children [. . . .] Will some mathematician some day question and understand, as I cannot, and confirm all, or have I also dealt in myth? (*AVB* 212–13, *CW14* 156–57).

Such eugenic concerns—both esoteric and more political—are also evident in "Under Ben Bulben" and *On the Boiler*.

After further consideration of the complementary wheels of Europe and Asia, Yeats addresses the question of his similarity to Spengler's historical scheme, material that was, in the main, eventually published in *A Packet for Ezra Pound* rather than *A Vision* itself.

> I have left what follows, except for the changes of Fountain into Phoenix on page [*blank*] exactly [*as*] it was when first published in 1925, some two or three months before the publication of an English translation of Spenglers ["]decline of the West". When the diagram on which it is founded came in 1917 while Spenglers book, was still at the german printers, & that was unfinished. I read no German, I knew nothing of Spengler except something about his general scheme of thought [?as was first/an Irish priest] told me during a [?comity] <in 1922 or 1924>, & his outline of European civilization resembles so closely that I have read him in astonishment. Not only are our dates & their significant [?contours] the same but we have both used the drilling of the eyes of <statues> at the time Hadrian to prove the same contrast between Greek and Roman character, & described the staring eyes of Byzantine icons in almost the same sentence – I have "staring at miracle" he or his ~~English~~ translator has "staring at the infinite" & we both draw the same conclusion form how the portrait heads [*of*] Roman sculpture screw on to stock bodies. ~~I certainly though I wrote~~ The dates were from my diagram but I certainly thought I wrote those sentences myself. Yet why should I say "astonished"[:] that mind can know of mind without the intervention of speech or print does not astonish me; it has been my familiar thought, sometimes my experience, these many years.[214]

As is often the case, this final declaration is deflected away from personal disclosure in the published version, though possibly made more magical:

> I knew of no common source, no link between him and me, unless through
> 'The elemental things that go
> About my table to and fro'.[215]

The remaining three pages of this section consist of rewriting of the material already included in *A Vision A* about the Etruscan year and Hipparchus's observation of precession. They are headed by the instruction "insert at A," evidently earlier in the section, though that insertion point and symbol seem to have been lost with the removal of a page or pages.[216] They are followed by a completely blank leaf, [75].

[76r–90r] "Soul in Judgement ~~(first draft)~~ 10 pages"

The drafts next move on to a new version of the section dealing with "Life after Death," the cancelled title that is replaced with the ambiguous but more satisfying "Soul in Judgement." Though the section is new, Yeats again repurposes the treatment of St. John as Bacchus and natural love juxtaposed with Christ as supernatural love, though the idea has become so familiar perhaps that the writing is rather careless:

> Coventry Patmore thought Da Vinci had a philosophical intention when he painted a St John like a Baccus [*sic*], a Baccus like a St John, for Christ was supernatural, & Baccus natural love – "God give[*s*] him[*self*] in wine like the fable[*d*] Baccus["]. He had doub[*t*]less some tradition of the Church in his head, for he was an orthodox Catholic and no doubt remembered that early church symbolism attributed to Christ an annunciation at the Vernal Equinox, & a birth at midwinter, & to St John an autumn conception & a birth at midsummer, the one begotten in joy brought forth in sorrow, the other begotten in sorrow brought forth in joy.[217]

The pairing is now interpreted as a rather strained allegory of the *Principles*' cones of life and death, with St. John mirroring the *Husk* and Christ *Spirit*. In many ways, though, this obsessive repurposing of ideas (almost none of which ever crossed Patmore's mind) illustrates how Yeats views the myth of *A Vision*'s geometry: it is the underlying structure rather than the final form, the skeleton rather than the living bird, which "signifies truth" when it goes through the processes of life (*AVB* 214, *CW14* 158). It is perhaps to be regretted that Yeats did not include more of the mythic vision which seems to match the associative movement of his thought between supernatural Christ and the natural Bacchic Baptist:

> I do not quarrel with Patmores thought but must restate it. I read in the cones of the Four Principles & identify St John to Husk: for Husk is begotten when at Lunar North Solar West, when in the middle moment between Life & Death it is called back into life to reject a Celestial Body and find some new Celestial Body the antithesis of the old, as the new Celestial Body is born at the summer solstice or with the death of man; & identify Christ to Spirit for Spirit [*is*] begotten, or announced, when in the middle moment between birth & death, it rejects Passionate Body, & seeks some new Passionate Body the antithesis of the old, & the Passionate Body comes with phisical birth at the winter solstice. Christ, Spirit, identifies himself with the new body as an act of will, being of the Sphere, not of the gyre, the [*point?*] where Creative Mind, at its corresponding moment is en forced, Husk upon the other hand, perhaps given the cup of oblivion Porphyry talks of, intoxicates the soul[.][218]

This passage appears on leaf [77r], which is numbered "2." Although the treatment in the following four pages moves on to the processes involved in death, all are cancelled with a vertical line and are unnumbered, so that the page numbered "3" is actually [82r]—and even then most of the text is scored through. Yeats sets out to explain the movements of *Faculties*, representing the period between birth and death, and *Principles*, representing the whole circle from birth to birth—or death to death.

> Only the cones between Will & Mask represent our present life in them move the Four Faculties as well as the Four Principles, & within the other cone something more unexplained & mysterious. When the twelve cicles that began as Will reached 8 upon the circle reach their end with Will at 22, life will pas into the cone, to which we given the main[=*name?*] of the 13th cone. This is the same change that takes place with the Faculties, when the consciousness is transferred from the Will to the Spirit & the change from the bright fortnight to the dark; & The 13th spere [*sic*] is the present dwelling place of those [*who*] are set free from life.[219]

The *Thirteenth Cone* was an idea that evolved significantly between the two published versions of *A Vision*, and here Yeats seems to be moving away from the earlier idea of three further cycles beyond incarnation to that of a single state or being, the *Thirteenth Cone* or *Sphere.*[220] Calling it a "dwelling place" implies that it is, in this context at least, closer to state than being.

Since Yeats's thought works by analogy, and since he was still trying to clarify his thought about the nature of the *Principles*, at least in draft he seems to see an analogy between the *Principles* and the *Thirteenth Cone.* He also enters into significant speculation on the nature of mind, seeing waking consciousness as a relatively limited portion of a greater whole, both individually and as part of a unified whole. Some of the sentences run on and appear to shift from one construction to another, without making clear sense—as private notes they are part of the process of discovery, not an end in themselves—so I have not attempted to punctuate beyond the very basic level. (Handwriting is also a factor, so it is not always clear whether verbs or nouns are singular or plural.)

> That the Principles contain in their complete movement life and the state between lives means, if I understand my symbol[,] that they limit consciousness, which contains within it but is not contained by that of the Faculties. I have learned from Plotinus to consider the universe as a consciousness, & that the individual man is a movement—or change of quality—within it but not in himself conscious. My instructors tell me that to every phase, at a moment mathematically calculable[,] a man has the opportunity of unity of being—unity of Spirit & Celestial body "nourished" by unity of the Faculties, but that even if attained Antithetical man knows nothing of it or has at best a momentary knowledge; I admit that I am in my Principles a living conscious being of whose acts I know little for my Faculties are limited by memory. Beyond the limit of the Principles are yet greater limits up to that being that has none & contains all. The Principles themselves are related to the thirteenth cone, as the Faculties are to the Principles, the Faculties are a process not a value, a method of discovery not a beauty or truth, & Spirit though separated [?power/from] the Faculties bring to us always, if they bring anything, what comes from beyond themselves, what descends perhaps through Spirit after Spirit [—] only those in the 13 cone need no intermediaries. This was shown to me by a symbol. I was told that a Spirit of the 13 Cone was present I was asked to notice that whereas when other Spirits [*were there*] the house often smelt of some light scent, or of garden flowers, or some scent produced by burning church incense or the sweet or fragrant odour of some burnt wood or brack[,] it smelt now sea water. They would use always I was told such symbols, selected from our memories, as did not suggest artificial preparations.[221]

Part of these speculations inform "The Completed Symbol" of *A Vision*, while some of the account of the smells associated with spirits was used in *A Packet for Ezra Pound*. The more extended meditation upon how consciousness relates to the various aspects of being is never really given in the published versions, replaced by oblique references to Valéry's "*Le cimitière marin*," Iseult dancing on a beach in Normandy, and the Upanishads (*AVB* 219–23, *CW14* 159–62). However confused these musings of this draft may be, they genuinely illuminate an important aspect of how Yeats viewed the nature of mind.

After three sections of introduction, Yeats finally broaches the subject of the afterlife, only to admit that he will not really broach it.

IV

The first edition of this book contains a long section called the Gates of Pluto that now fills [*me*] with shame. It contains a series of unrelated statements, inaccurate deduction from the symbols, & was little but notes [*I*] [?have] recorded for my own future use. I postpone the theme till my instructors come to me again or my own thought take fire, & for the moment content my self with a few rambling comments.

My instructors declare that soon after death the Spirit seeks to separate it self from the Husk & Passionate Body that should disapear, & to unite itself to the Celestial Body but that it is continually drawn back into the Passionate Body which compells it live over & over again the events of life that have most moved it or the delusion of its terror. It is the Homeric contrast between Heracles moving through the night bow in hand, & his happy spirit,

"And Heracles the mighty I saw when these went by;
His image indeed, for himself mid the gods that never die
Sits glad at the feast, & Hebe fair-ancled there doth hold,
The daughter of Zeus the mighty & Here shod with gold."[222]

Here, the ideas are already approaching the form that Yeats would publish in 1937 (*AVB* 226; *CW14* 164–65), contrasting the *Spirit*'s attraction to the memories of mortal life and to a more transcendent life (which would become the subject of a poem in Rapallo C, "Imagination's Bride").[223] This exposition does not use the anatomy of six stages that Yeats evidently developed later, nor the related terminology,[224] focusing on the processes of dreaming back—without using that term—and gradual separation from the previous life, but relatively cursorily in the course of a few pages. At the conclusion of this draft, the final stages of the afterlife (what would later be called *Beatitude*, *Purification*, and *Foreknowledge*) are then summarized in a few sentences:

Then comes ~~a state of freedom~~ ~~states of~~ a condition I have been told little of, & I have learned little of unity, & brief beatitude, corresponding to phase one, followed by a long period when the soul [?~~can move] its own life~~ can take what form it please — one thinks of the shape-changers of folk lore — live a life planned by itself — being a Priest in its own house as Blake said — & await birth.

{ While so waiting it can foresee its future & through the living prepare for it, I was told by an an [*sic*] instructor who compared [*it*] to one of my Canaries at that moment [*it*] gathers down, grass & moss for its nest, ~~& be at such moments full of love & hate beyond anything known to the living. Porphyry spoke of such souls as drunk with the honey of generation~~. }

In all these states, except that of union with the [?shade] the <u>Spirit</u> may become a messenger of the 13th cone to the living. Some few souls saints or sages may break away at the Beatitude[,] like a gyring bird that has seen its prey[,] & return to life no more.[225]

Though some readers of *A Vision* may feel that the treatment of the afterlife, particularly the latter stages, is rather scant, it is at least fuller than this outline would have given, though the final image provides the most striking feature, implying that the widening gyre may lead to escape from the constraints of nature when the falcon swoops through the center.

[91r–102v] "Introduction. 12 pages (continued in | loose leaf book[)]."

The final block of writing in the notebook is entitled "Introduction" and is the first—or a very early—draft of the "Introduction to the Great Wheel" of *A Packet for Ezra Pound*.[226] In fact, the first paragraph about Lady Gregory commenting that he was "a much better educated man," appears in an earlier version on the final recto of the notebook [102r], titled "Beginning for account of origin of system," implying that Yeats started this at the back of the notebook and then realized he would have rather more material than he had originally thought and might need more space, so moved back further into the book.[227] The text throughout is remarkably close to the final published version, though the paragraphs that explain the first automatic writing show some telling changes and second thoughts in the writing process, especially over the initial motivation or plan for attempting automatic writing.

> ~~Four days after my marriage~~ On the afternoon of October the 24, four days after my marriage[,] my wife ~~& I were~~ my wife ~~suggested~~ ~~said~~ ~~proposed that~~ said she would like to ~~try & do~~ attempt automatic writing. She told me afterwards that she ~~intended to amuse me by some invented message~~ had meant to make up messages & having amuse me for an afternoon say that what she had done. She wrote ~~one or two vague~~ did invent a few line, some name & some imaginary addres when her hand was, as it were, grasp by another & there came ~~in an almost unintelligible~~ ~~in disjointed sentences & in~~ in disjointed sentences & in almost illegible handwriting ~~certain [?]startling sentences~~ ~~disjointed sentences that excited my imagination~~ ~~that were~~ what was at first a ~~development &~~ comment upon my ~~essay~~ little book ["]Per Amica Silentia Lunae", but so passed far beyond my thought ~~We sat gave up~~ From that on we gave some part of every day, when ~~my wifes strength permitted~~ ~~my wife felt that she that she could bear~~ what ~~was soon a heavy drain upon her vitality~~ my wife had strength enough for such a drain upon her vitality. ~~This~~ ~~We returned to Ireland & lived generally in solitary places absorbed in this task~~. We spent ~~much~~ part of 1918 ~~& part of 1919~~ then at Sligo Glendalough, & our house Thur Ballalee, Coole solitary places ~~absorbed in this task. At the begging of 1919~~ my wife bored & fatigued by her almost daily task I think & talking of little else. ~~Whe we had returned to England~~ Early in 1919 the communicating spirit said they would shortly change the method ~~to words~~ from the written to the spoken word as that would be less exausting for my wife, but The change did not come however ~~until late~~ until *[gap for*

> *date*] while I was on an american lecture tour. We had one of those little compartments on the train with two beds, & one night my wife began to talk in her sleap. ~~From~~ ~~At once it began became the principal & soon the only means of [?delivery] a little later the automatic writing ceased altogether, & the communicating spirits spoke [?talking for] my wife [?talking through] my wife while a sleap.~~[228] When ever they wished to ~~do so~~ <talk ~~in her sleap~~> in this way they would ~~give me an~~ signal ~~to me sometime during the day that~~ during the day — I will explain later what these signals were — & I would have pen & paper & my questions ready.[229]

In the course of revision, Yeats honed certain phrases and added more detail and anecdote—most notably the "metaphors for poetry"—but also glossed over George's idea of playing a game with invented script. Though this aspect was evidently true, and matches what George Yeats told Richard Ellmann,[230] Yeats was clearly aware of the impression that it would create. He himself was comfortable enough with the fictions surrounding mediumship, which he viewed as aspects of dramatization by the medium, but, perhaps suspecting that this would be seized on by skeptics to dismiss everything that followed, he eventually omitted it.[231] In contrast the simple phrase "what was at first a comment upon my little book [']Per Amica Silentia Lunae'. . . so[*on?*] passed far beyond my thought" is expanded to give a characterization of *A Vision*'s system of phases and cycles of history in relation to *Per Amica Silentia Lunae*, with allusions to Browning's Paracelsus and Goethe's Wilhelm Meister (elided in the parallel passages above).

The continuing exposition follows a similar pattern, so the communicators' direct speech becomes indirect and a phrase such as "they said I must not read philosophy until they had finished their exposition" becomes "they asked me not to read philosophy until their exposition was complete," and "They were always in a hurry, because as they explained before long they must leave, & there were others who knew this, who tried to confuse us or in some way to waste time & were called Frustrators"—"Because they must, as they explained, soon finish, others whom they named Frustrators attempted to confuse us or waste time."[232]

His account of the genesis of *A Vision A* has a few variations of interest, particularly his refusal to publish it as his own work and the suggestion that the Instructors forbade the use of dialogues between Robartes and Aherne as a method of exposition.

> When I prepared for publication the first confused inconsistent edition of this book I had to invent a phantastic setting about one Robartes, the hero of an [?early] story of mine[,] bringing the philosophy from Arabia because I could not tell the real origin. My wife hated the idea of its origin becoming known, & I could not, though the spirits urged me, permit it to seem my own

> work, I had begun to write it as a series of diaglolgs [*sic*] between Robartes & other [?vaguer] characters, but that they forbid lest some one or other of them should mistake an imaginary person for himself. They had compelled me to write, though my thought was still confused, & a hasty arangement with a publisher compelled me to publish [?early] in 1925. Had I delayed no one would have believed that much of the section "Dove or Swan"—repeated in this book without alteration[—]was not a plagiarism from Spenglers "Decline of the West" of which an English translation appeared later in the year.[233]

He implies that the Instructors contrived a rather premature publication because they foresaw that the translation of Spengler would fatally undermine *A Vision* otherwise.

Writing about the communicator that came when they were in Cannes, just before they moved to Rapallo, Yeats notes that the visits were "almost nightly" and explained the circumstances in which these renewed sessions came.

> In Ireland I had rewritten a good deal of the "Vision", but there was a whole section of [*it*] that deals with the "<u>Four</u> <u>Principles</u>["] which I could not understand[.] I had put it aside to finish a book of verse "The Winding Stair["] & had worked at this at intervals through my illness, & by [?luck] I had I had [*sic*] taken it up again. He made me read what I had written to my wife that he might hear it, & now while my wife slept he went over it bit by bit. I had forgotten how powerful in thought was the communicator, how completely master of a system in its minute details, which I could but hope to master in outline[.] [a]s my embarrassment was increased by his irrasibility—some term from Plato, & a phrase from a modern realist enraged him—why was I not satisfied to get my tecnical term from him. He & his he explained were not always at their best—anger I had long noticed was a signal that [*they*] were at their best but that made it no pleasanter at the moment—presently some communicator not at his best would accept some false reasoning from me & all would be confused.
>
> { It was [?obvious], that though he tolerated my philosophical studies out of respect for freedom, he hated it, & later on}
>
> he was to tell me my present illness & another that preceeded it, were the result of my preoccupation with abstract thought. [?Altho] these quarrels within[=*with him?*] [?alarmed] me, & made my question[*s*] vague & confused I gained for the first time ~~an understanding of the Principles, which enabled me to get the geometry correct~~ to distinguish between the "<u>Principles</u>" between all [*that*] comes in Thomist philosophy from "revelation", & "Faculties" which construct it supporting Will & abstracting reason. I felt that I had known nothing & began that study which tests even Buddhist philosophers, the contemplation of the void, & struggle to substantiate the last conception which made the Japanese saint say of himself after the supreme experience of his [?riglen (=*religion?*)] "He comes no more from behind the embroidered

> screen, amid the sweet incense clouds, & goes among his friends & among the lute players: something very nice has happened to the young man but he will only tell it to his sweet heart.["][234]

This passage is relatively close to the version in *A Packet for Ezra Pound*'s section XI,[235] though in *A Vision B* the reference to the Zen poem was moved to the end of "The Completed Symbol," placed together with the other material drawn from Suzuki's *Essays in Zen Buddhism*.[236]

As mentioned, the suggestion that the reason for abandoning the Robartes–Aherne dialogues was not creative difficulties or problems with the framing fictions but because the instructors feared that they might identify with these characters underlines the closeness between the voices that spoke through George Yeats and the figures of W. B. Yeats's personal "phantasmagoria" of fictions (*VP* 821): both are dramatizations, names attached to certain words spoken that create the illusion of character. On the following page, Yeats continues exploring this theme in a different sense, stating how, "When I try to understand the means of communication I am struck by all it has in common with dreaming."[237] As in the published version of section XII, he recounts an incident of George's meaningless sleep-talking, which yet evinced "tricks in speach used by one or other of the philosophic voices," and, comparing the experience of the communications to a shared dream, he comments that "I feel that the 'spirits' would prefer such an explanation to one attributing all to themselves," which allows for the fact that the "spirits" can be allowed a preference and yet that dreaming is also a valid explanation.[238]

In further sentences dropped from the final version, he questions what benefit the communicators might derive from the intercourse, citing one answer that the spirit would have "'a short life', but what[?=*why*] that reward, if reward it can be called[,] for serving me."[239] Looking at the exchange from another angle, he notes that:

> One indeed ~~said~~ explained that I brought my questions & that though the answers came through them they were as startling ~~to them as much as~~ as greatly as they did me, but then seeing they have daimons of their own, are indeed being dead in a sense those daimons, why do they need my questions. The answer lies somewhere within the statement made in different forms, that all creation comes from the living.[240]

The idea that creation comes from the living is in fact a theme that Yeats had formulated in *Per Amica Silentia Lunae*, distinguishing the simplicity of the condition of fire, where selfhood is possessed in a single moment, from the heterogeneous complexity of earth, yet emphasizing that "All power is from the terrestrial condition" (*Myth* 356, *CW5* 25). And the dead, as he later explained in the introduction to *The Words upon the Window-Pane*, "can create nothing, or, in the Indian phrase, can originate no new Karma. Their aim, like that of the ascetic in meditation, is to enter at last into their own archetype, or into all being: into that which is there always" (*VPl* 968–69, *CW2* 720, *Ex* 366). Increasingly, and certainly by the time he wrote these lines in 1931, Yeats came to identify that archetype, "that which is there always," with the *Daimon*.

Rapallo B closes with the first of many drafts in which Yeats sought to express his attitude towards the system of *A Vision* and how far he believed in it, the precursor of the Introduction's different final sections in *A Packet for Ezra Pound* and *A Vision B*. As the contents at the beginning of the notebook indicate, this draft is "continued in loose leaf book," yet the contours of the whole "Introduction" are already here. The nine sections would become fifteen, as the points were elaborated and illustrated further, but the introduction itself is already substantially formed and, whether Yeats yet saw this introduction being put together with "Rapallo in Spring" or not, the outlines of *A Packet for Ezra Pound* are clearly discernible.

There are at least five or six different versions of Yeats's statement of belief about *A Vision*, which vary and elaborate different aspects, and the version that appeared in *A Vision B* casts the coolest eye on the nature and possibility of belief.[241] This first outline is not necessarily the most committed, but it is the most inward-looking. Most of the later versions start with the phrase "Some will ask. . ." or a variation on it, focusing on what others will think, but this draft is a question of his own attitudes, as Yeats struggles to understand his own reluctance to speak of belief and the act or state of believing.

> IX
>
> Sometimes I have asked my self do I believe all this book, or only some part of it; ~~or do I believe different parts with different degrees~~ or do some parts of it seemed ~~ser~~ certain & some parts probably, & I always find my self loth to answer. ~~What I write in future, will~~ This book has filled my imagination for so many years, that I can never imagine myself ~~reading or xx~~ studying anything, without in some [*way*] relating it all incorporating it with what is here, & yet I do not want to answer because what ever else ~~it is~~ may be it is a dream. A single thought has expressed it it self as if it were a work of art, whether man or centaur, & I have tested each detail by its relation to the whole, each completed movement, by its reflection of the whole, ~~& though I am always conscious that there is a unity beyond that which I have found, a smokeless flame that I cannot reach~~, & the value of that single [thought], & therefore of the whole, lies in the daimon, which I can express but cannot judge.[242]

He acknowledges the time and commitment that the project has involved, and the impact it has had on his thinking, yet, as if discovering his feelings, he *finds* himself "loth to answer." Whatever else it "may be[,] it is a dream," shared with his wife and others and peopled by the *dramatis personae* of the spirits and fictions of their shared phantasmagoria. *A Vision* and its system has for Yeats the integrity of the numbers that multiply into the whole, the work of art not of science. The hybrid figure of the centaur may represent an impossible fusion, stand for mythic imagination, or symbolize wisdom,[243] but it has a unity born of integrity. Ultimately the work's value "lies in the daimon" and is therefore not a matter of believing but of being. The phrasing and expression of this declaration is perhaps too personal to be understood readily, and later versions remove both centaur and daimon, yet this is a fascinating glimpse of the personal ambiguity that Yeats grappled with. It is also an aspiration, for not only the poem but also the poet—"reborn as an idea, something intended, complete" (*E&I* 509, *CW5* 204)—aspires to the *daimonic* state, where the "flame is eternal. We attain it in the creation, or enjoyment of a work of art but the moment though eternal in the daimon passes from us, because it does not contain our whole being."[244]

The final work of art or system may be like a perfect number "where every thing is a part of everything, flows back as it were into the whole,"[245] aiming for the simplicity of fire, the smokeless flame, but the notebooks have much of the heterogeneity of the terrestrial, the "mound of refuse or the sweepings of a street" (*VP* 630), where opposites meet and there is choice, a fluidity of form. While Rapallo B may have a certain consistency of theme and purpose, the other notebooks do not even have that, but they all provide that essential creative meeting of things that are not already alike. The details are not related to the whole, because what form and order they may have are provided only by the physical form of the notebooks. That is, of course, what makes them unique.

Notes

1 Having arrived in Rapallo in February 1928, the Yeatses took a five-year lease on an apartment in via Americhe in March. They then spent the winters of 1928–29 and 1929–30 there, as well as time in April and June 1930. In their absence, the apartment was burgled in 1931, and they only returned to Rapallo in June 1934 to clear it out. See John S. Kelly, *A W. B. Yeats Chronology* [hereafter *ChronY*] (Basingstoke: Palgrave, 2003), 258–88, and *Life 2* 356–501.

2 See letter to George Yeats [hereafter GY], [August 17, 1928] (*CL InteLex* 5145; cf. *YGYL* 194), cited p. 41.

3 They measure 30 × 22 cm. (ca. 12 × 8.5 in.); the paper is unruled, unwatermarked, and about 20 lb. weight; see David R. Clark, ed., "*Words for Music Perhaps and Other Poems*": *Manuscript Materials* (Ithaca, NY: Cornell University Press, 1999), xvi–xvii. Uniform with Rapallo C and D are the notebooks which W. B. Yeats [hereafter WBY] used to draft *Stories of Michael Robartes and His Friends* (National Library of Ireland [hereafter NLI], Dublin, MS 13,577); see Wayne K. Chapman, *W. B. Yeats's Robartes-Aherne Writings* (London:

Bloomsbury, 2018), 167ff. This notebook was further "mounted inside a heavy, ornately embossed, leather attaché cover with enlaced edges" (167).

4 Rapallo A (NLI 13,578) has a large "D" on the cover but an "A" on the first recto; Rapallo B (NLI 13,579) has "Finished Oct. 9. 1928" on the cover and "B" on the first recto; the cover of Rapallo C (NLI 13,580) is labeled "DIARY" and "Diary of Thought" is on the first recto; Rapallo D (NLI 13,581) has nothing on the cover and "Diary" on the first recto; Rapallo E (NLI 13,582) has a large letter "E" on the cover along with a cancelled three-line caption and no title on the first extant recto.

5 Neil Mann, "Yeats's Rapallo Notebooks," *YA22* (forthcoming). I use a capitalized "Notebook" when it acts as the title of a particular book or books, as in "Rapallo Notebook A" and "the Rapallo Notebooks"; the lower-case "notebooks" is used where it is simply a descriptive term. However, the shortened forms of "Rapallo A," "Rapallo B," etc. are the main forms used to refer to the five notebooks in the essay for reasons of clarity and brevity.

6 As the presentation that follows shows, Rapallo B contains drafts that pre-date versions in Rapallo A. Rapallo A was originally labeled "D" on the outer cover in the same way that E is labeled (they are the only two with external letters). A large number of pages have been removed from the beginning of E, and the cancelled, barely legible caption on the cover bears no relation to its current contents.

7 *A Vision A* is dated 1925 but was actually released on January 15, 1926 (see Wade item 149, p. 152).

8 "Our most precious stone is thrown in the dung heap, most dear, cheap, and most vile," "Tractatus aureus," *Ars Chemica . . . Septem Tractatus seu Capitula Hermetis Trismegisti, aurei* ([Strasbourg]: [Emmel], 1566), 21.

9 The relevant volumes are: Clark, *"Words for Music Perhaps and Other Poems": Manuscript Materials*; Mary FitzGerald, ed., *"The Words Upon the Window-Pane": Manuscript Materials* (Ithaca, NY: Cornell University Press, 2002); and Jared Curtis and Selina Guiness, eds., *"The Resurrection": Manuscript Materials* (Ithaca, NY: Cornell University Press, 2011).

10 The Cornell volumes are inevitably selections of the manuscript material and the editorial approach varies across the series, so that some editors prioritize the process and the untaken roads, while others are more focused on the final versions. See Robin Gail Schulze, "The One and the Many: Reading the Cornell Yeats," ed. W. Speed Hill, *Text: An Interdisciplinary Annual of Textual Studies 10* (Ann Arbor: University of Michigan Press, 1997), 323–37.

11 There is one partial exception, in that a fair copy of "Byzantium" (now NLI 13,590 [17]) on two sheets of loose paper was kept at the back of Rapallo D and was photographed there for the Harvard microfilms, probably in the late 1940s; see Wayne Chapman, "Yeats's White Vellum Notebook, 1930–1933," *International Yeats Studies* [hereafter *IYS*] 2, no. 2 (2018): 58 n18.

12 These other sources include transcriptions by Richard Ellmann in *The Identity of Yeats* (1954; London: Faber and Faber, 1964), 239–40; David R. Clark, "Yeats: Cast-offs, Non-starters and Gnomic Illegibilities," in *Yeats: An Annual of Critical and Textual Studies* 17, 1–18; and Matthew Gibson, "Yeats's Notes on Leo Frobenius's *The Voice of Africa* (1913)," in *Yeats, Philosophy, and the Occult*, eds. Matthew Gibson and Neil Mann (Clemson, SC: Clemson University Press, 2016), 310–12. The Cornell manuscript series contains no material from Rapallo A and B, as they contain very little poetry or drama.

13 This leather-bound notebook is NLI 30,359.

14 WBY, *The Winding Stair* (New York: Fountain Press, 1929). See David R. Clark, ed., *"The Winding Stair" (1929): Manuscript Materials* [hereafter *WS29*] (Ithaca, NY: Cornell University Press, 1995). He proposes: "All drafts probably written between September 1927 . . . and March 13, 1928" (xviii); the starting date is suggested by WBY's letter to Olivia Shakespear of 2 October [1927] (L 728–29, *CL InteLex* 5034) explaining the arrangement

with Crosby Gaige (see *Life2* 350), and the end date is that of GY's letter (*WS29* xxv–xxvii) accompanying the typescript sent to New York (*WS29* xiii–xiv).

15 Leather notebook, NLI 30,359, [19r]. The sleeps are the version of "communication" from the instructors of *A Vision* that superseded automatic script in 1920. GY spoke in sleep or trance, while her husband listened, questioned, and noted the exchanges.

16 Leather notebook, NLI 30,359, [9v]. This sentence is inserted from the opposite verso; above "can" WBY has written "need" without cancelling the first. And the word transcribed as "put" may be "fit," but the form of the letter is closer to the surrounding p's than the f's.

17 Leather notebook, NLI 30,359, [10r].

18 The date comes on [30r]; as "First Things" takes up forty-one pages of large format paper (Rapallo B, NLI 13,579, [9v]–[30r]), it would likely have taken many days, and probably weeks, to draft.

19 Leather notebook, NLI 30,359, [19r]–[20r].

20 Rapallo B, NLI 13,579, [11r], page numbered 1. This appears in typescript form in NLI 36,272/11.

21 Rapallo A, NLI 13,578, [1v].

22 Typescript NLI 36,272/18 is based directly on Rapallo A, however, and it repeats Rapallo B's convoluted disclaimer largely intact. The typescript numbers the section quoted here "II"; this section precedes section "III" in the notebook.

23 Rapallo A, NLI 13,578, [39r], page numbered 2. The typescript NLI 36,272/18 corrects the Shakespearean quotation.

24 Another (probably later) manuscript draft explains the enigmatic quotation at least partially. See n87, below.

25 An even later typescript draft titled "Principal Symbols" telescopes this introduction, suppressing a useful connecting sentence: "All begins with what my instructors have called, probably taking the term from PER AMICA SILENTIA LUNAE the daimon. ~~Each Daimon is unique and perfect and has for its symbol the sphere.~~ One thinks of those words of Parmenides Plotinus has incorporated in his own system 'it is complete on every side equally poised from the entire in every direction like the mass of a rounded sphere' and of those of Empedocles 'so fast was the God in the close covering of harmony, spherical and round, rejoicing in his circular rest.'" It then gives a succinct description of the *Daimon*. (NLI 36,272/13, [1]).

26 Given WBY's handwriting, it is possible that "final version" could be read as "first version." It does not make sense in context, unless WBY made a mistake about priority (which might also explain the labeling of A and B on the fly-leaves), but the evidence points to Rapallo A's version coming after Rapallo B's "early version." It would, however, be dangerous to stake much on either reading.

27 Section V of Rapallo A ([12r] ff) is a direct redrafting of Section IV of Rapallo B ([61r] ff), clarifying and simplifying the earlier formulation. For example in Rapallo B, WBY writes: "Hitherto we we [sic] have had ~~two~~ three symbols of change ~~a double cone what I have called the double cone of Heraclitus~~ that of ~~the~~ a double cone,~~ when or where we can right [?subje] Antithetical at the one side Primary of the at the other,~~ that of the wheel formed from a double cone, & we can write Antithetical at one side Primary at the other of ~~both x~~ each. There ~~is a third symbol~~ are however two other symbols found from the ~~whel~~ wheel. . . across whose center we can write Primary or Antithetical. One is a figure like an hourglass. . . passes through centre of the wheel & joins Will & Mask representing Nature [. . . .] The other is a diamond shaped figure which passes through the centre of the wheel ~~& unites the~~ joins Creative Mind & the Body of Fate, ~~& represents xx the~~ all that is ~~the supernatural or spiritual.~~" (NLI 13,579, [61r–62r], pages numbered 8 and 9). In Rapallo A, this becomes: "~~Hitherto~~ we have ~~had three two three~~ four symbols of change, ~~that of~~ the

double cone, ~~that of~~ the wheel formed from the double cone {the two cones like an hour glass or like a diamond that cross the centre of the wheel uniting the Faculties to its centre [. . . .]}" (NLI 13,578, [12r], page numbered 8, and [11v]).

28 The date appears at the end of the draft of "Introduction," Rapallo B, NLI 13,579, [43r]. Some notes amending the printed text of *AVA* follow, and then the draft on the Great Year. There is no later date except the one that appears on the cover, "Finished Oct. 9, | 1928."

29 The reason for hesitancy in declaring it unambiguously the second notebook to be started is the label "D" on its cover, which may indicate lost notebooks.

30 WBY, *Uncollected Prose by W. B. Yeats*, vol. 2 [hereafter *UP2*] (New York: Columbia University Press, 1976), 477–85; cf. *CW10* 211–18.

31 *UP2* 485–86.

32 The diary kept in 1930, NLI 30,354, served as the basis for WBY, *Pages from a Diary Written in Nineteen Hundred and Thirty* (Dublin: Cuala, 1944).

33 The notebook has ninety-five leaves, counting nine removed leaves and twenty-three that are blank on both sides, so that sixty-three of them are used. Twenty-three leaves [4–26] are devoted to the Great Year and eleven leaves [39–49] to the new beginning of *A Vision*.

34 WBY was spurred on particularly by reading the early volumes of Pierre Duhem's *Le système du monde*, 10 vols. (Paris: Hermann, 1913–59); vols. 1–5 appeared between 1913 and 1917 and the remaining five volumes appeared posthumously between 1954 and 1959. Also important was WBY's discovery of Spengler and his further reading of Hegel. See "Editors' Introduction," in *CW14* xxvi–xxvii, and notes, 433 n59; Matthew Gibson, "'Timeless and Spaceless'?—Yeats's Search for Models of Interpretation in Post-Enlightenment Philosophy, Contemporary Anthropology and Art History, and the Effects of These Theories on 'The Completed Symbol,' 'The Soul in Judgment' and 'The Great Year of the Ancients,'" in Neil Mann, Matthew Gibson, and Clare Nally, eds., *W. B. Yeats's "A Vision": Explications and Contexts* [hereafter *YVEC*] (Clemson, SC: Clemson University Press, 2012); Matthew Gibson, "Yeats, the Great Year, and Pierre Duhem," in *Yeats, Philosophy, and the Occult*, eds. Matthew Gibson and Neil Mann (Clemson, SC: Clemson University Press, 2016), 171–224.

35 See *Life2* 373. His final appearance, without speaking, came a week later on July 25, 1928 (*ChronY* 261).

36 See n79 below. These drafts take up twelve of the notebook's sixty-three written leaves: three leaves [31–33] and nine leaves [67–73, 75–76].

37 The draft occupies a single page, [77r].

38 These take up more than three leaves [63v–66r] and a fragment on [78r]. On August 12, 1928, WBY told Olivia Shakespear that he was going to Coole and had his "notes upon the new coinage to write" (*CL InteLex* 5142; *L* 746); on August 25, 1928, he was dictating part of the essay to Augusta Gregory at Coole (*ChronY* 262) and on August 26, had a "first draft of my coinage essay" (to GY, *CL InteLex* 5148; *YGYL* 196); and on August 28, he told his wife that he had finished the essay (*CL InteLex* 5150; *YGYL* 198).

39 These take up most of six leaves [58r–63r].

40 These come specifically between the material on "The Great Year" and the article on censorship and Thomas Aquinas (leaves [31–33]) and between that article and "First Things" for *A Vision* ([38v–49v]), with a single blank page also left at the beginning of the notebook, [3], between the Contents and notes on Plotinus and "The Great Year."

41 Sixteen blank leaves remain at the end of the notebook (80–95), with two more added during conservation.

42 The date comes from GY's covering letter, cited in *WS29* xxvi–xxvii; see n14 above.

43 The descriptions are divided into the book's natural sections, many of them indicated by Yeats's own list of contents. Descriptions taken from the contents are given in quotation marks; other supplied details are given in brackets.

44 The 1930 diary, NLI 30,354, [64r].
45 The "D" on the cover of Rapallo Notebook A (NLI 13,378) and the "E" on Rapallo E (NLI 13,582) are both drawn with multiple lines to create a thicker, wider capital letter.
46 See "General Overview," p. 12 above. Two loose bifoliums associated with Rapallo E have an early draft for *The Resurrection* and also a brief line of personal material from the first month in Rapallo in 1928, though these pages could have come from another notebook.
47 The "new" ordering of the other three notebooks is roughly chronological, though Rapallo C and D have no explicit labels.
48 The missing page "1" of "First Things" (Rapallo A, NLI 13,578, leaf [38]) could indicate that the page numbering was done as Yeats wrote; however, if he was numbering later, he may well have omitted this number deliberately to remind himself of the missing material. Rapallo C and D have no page numbering by Yeats, while in Rapallo E only the *Vision* material and the draft of *The Resurrection* have numbered pages.
49 They had returned from Rapallo in mid-April (see *ChronY* 259). It is, however, also possible that he had made the notes earlier in Italy, traveling with the Plotinus; two years earlier, referring to an earlier volume of MacKenna's translation, he had written from Thoor Ballylee: "I have brought but two books Beadelaire, & Mackenna's Plotinus" (to Olivia Shakespear, May 25, [1926], *CL InteLex* 4871).
50 *Plotinus: The Divine Mind, Being the Treatises of the Fifth Ennead*, trans. Stephen MacKenna (London: Medici Society, 1926), 12.
51 Rapallo A, NLI 13,578, [5r], page numbered 2. Cf. "a Greatest Year for whale and gudgeon alike must exhaust the multiplication table" (Notes on *The Resurrection* [*VPl* 934, *CW2* 724]). The corresponding sentence in Rapallo B declares that "Aristotels Annus Maximus . . . is incalculable, because as Proclus thought we cannot reckon the life cycles of all living things, man, whale and gudgeon" (NLI 13,579, [73r], page numbered 20).
52 Rapallo A, NLI 13,578, [8r], page numbered 5. See below for the earlier treatment in Rapallo B, NLI 13,579, [53r–54r], including the image of Keats's Grecian Urn (see p. 86, n203).
53 Jon Stallworthy, *Between the Lines: Yeats's Poetry in the Making* (Oxford: Oxford University Press, 1963), 9–10, emphasis in Stallworthy's original. See "General Overview," p. 23 above.
54 Rapallo A, NLI 13,578, [14r], page numbered 10. The cones are presented in the form of the hourglass and diamond in most instances.
55 Rapallo A, NLI 13,578, [17r], page numbered 12.
56 Rapallo A, NLI 13,578, [19r], page numbered 14.
57 Rapallo A, NLI 13,578, [20r], page numbered 15. The serpent struggling with the eagle is an important symbol from Shelley's *The Revolt of Islam* (*Laon and Cythna*), Canto I. The figure of Demogorgon rising from earth in Shelley's *Prometheus Unbound* is used in connection with the *Thirteenth Cone* in *AVB*, Book II, Section XIV (*AVB* 211, *CW14* 155). WBY's use here of "immanent" (clearly written) in opposition to "transcendent" helps to confirm the correction that most commentators have felt warranted in *AVB* of substituting "immanent" for "imminent" when WBY contrasts "a *primary* dispensation looking beyond itself towards a transcendent power," with "an *antithetical* dispensation [which] obeys imminent power" (*AVB* 263, *CW14* 192); see Neil Mann, *A Reader's Guide to Yeats's "A Vision"* [hereafter *ARGYV*] (Clemson, SC: Clemson University Press, 2019), 321 n16; 353 n12.
58 See *ARGYV* 169 and Neil Mann, "Plotinus and *A Vision*, Part II," in The Widening Gyre (March 1, 2020), https://yeatsvision.blogspot.com/2020/03/plotinus-and-vision-part-ii.html, addressing WBY's conflation of the hypostases and "Authentic Existants," an error from which several critics have tried to rescue him.
59 This diagram shows the solar diamond (associated with *Spirit* and *Celestial Body*), with two complete zodiacs running clockwise around the edge. Starting at the right-hand side at the

top is the symbol for the first sign, Aries ♈, with the sixth and seventh signs, Virgo ♍ and Libra ♎, at the right-hand point, and the twelfth, Pisces ♓, at the base; the same sequence then ascends on the left-hand side from Aries to Pisces again.

60 Rapallo A, NLI 13,578, [21r], page numbered 16. Though omitting cancellations in general in this transcription, I leave one of the deleted phrases to show how the syntax originally worked.

61 Rapallo A, NLI 13,578, [22r], page numbered 17. Although cancelled text is omitted, one stricken phrase is included to make the remaining text comprehensible. I have not tried to reproduce the letters on the page exactly, as a number of words are even more gestural than is usual for WBY—"information as distinguished from knowledge" is actually closer to reading "ınfomalxn as dılıgxxd fxxx knowlxge," with "t's" uncrossed and "i's" undotted, and the "x" standing for an indeterminate character (see Figure 1.1).

62 The phrasing here may recall the closing song from *The Resurrection*—"Everything that man esteems / Endures a moment or a day. . . ." (*VPl* 931)—or the play's notes, in which WBY writes of "these souls, these eternal archetypes, coming into greater units as days into nights into months, months into years" (*VPl* 935). Also relevant are *AVB*'s observations that the "wheel is every completed movement of thought or life, twenty-eight incarnations, a single incarnation, a single judgment of act of thought" (*AVB* 81, *CW14* 60), and, "It is as though innumerable dials, some that recorded minutes alone, some seconds alone, some hours alone, some months alone, some years alone. . . ." (*AVB* 248, *CW14* 181).

63 Rapallo A, NLI 13,578, [22r–23r], pages numbered 17–18.

64 For the discovery, Pierre Duhem gives a date of 129 BCE in *Le système du monde* 2:182, though Emmeline Plunket, in *Ancient Calendars and Constellations* (London: John Murray, 1903), refers to the "Initial Point of the Grecian Zodiac fixed by Hipparchus at equinox 150 B.C." (Plate III, facing p. 40). Plunket's volume was in the Yeatses' library, see Wayne K. Chapman, *The W. B. and George Yeats Library: A Short Title Catalog* [hereafter *WBGYL*] (Clemson, SC: Clemson University Press, 2019), item 1608, and Edward O'Shea, *A Descriptive Catalog of W. B. Yeats's Library* [hereafter *YL*] (New York: Garland, 1985), item 1596. O'Shea records that WBY annotated a correction on this page, but WBY seems to have taken Plunket's date; he also appears to view Hipparchus's whole lifetime (c.190–c.120 BCE) in a more symbolic sense in the draft cited here. The precession of the equinoxes is a consequence of Earth's extremely slow wobble, whereby the sun's position at the year's two equinoxes drifts backwards in relation to the constellations, going through a complete circle of the zodiac in some 26,000 years. At the vernal equinox the sun was located in the constellation of Aries in Hipparchus's day, but is in Pisces in our day—yet the equinoctial point retains the name "The First Point of Aries" (WBY's "0° of Aries") despite the drift.

65 Rapallo A, NLI 13,578, [23r], page numbered 18, and [22v]. One cancelled word is included as the anchor for WBY's footnote, and the first sentence of the footnote is moved from its position in the text to the note, as indicated by WBY's balloon and arrow. WBY appears to confuse polygons and polyhedra. Plutarch, in "The Platonic Questions," speculates that Plato related the solid "dodecahedron to the globe," as, like "globes made of twelve skins, it becomes circular and comprehensive" and, by the subdivision of its faces, "it seems to resemble both the Zodiac and the year, it being divided into the same number of parts as these"; *Plutarch's Morals*, 5 vols., ed. W. W. Goodwin (Boston: Little, Brown, 1878), 5:433. Like WBY, A. E. Taylor commented on Plutarch's mistake, which was to see "a circular band" rather than the "twelve angular points" of the solid, in Taylor, *A Commentary on Plato's 'Timaeus'* (Oxford: Clarendon Press, 1928; *WBGYL* 2121, *YL* 2107), 377. According to the half-title page, WBY's copy of Taylor's commentary was "Read Sept 1929 etc," so WBY either knew the objection already, or he came back to make the note later.

66 Claudius Ptolemy (c. 90–168 CE) had sought to establish a rational Aristotelian basis for astrology, with a chain of cause and effect working through the inflow of stellar "influence"; Plotinus (c. 204–270 CE) argued against this, stating that the stars were signs not causes in *Ennead* 2:3 "Are the stars causes"; see Stephen MacKenna's translation, *Plotinus*, vol. 2 (London: P. L. Warner, 1921; *WBGYL* 1602; *YL* 1590), 159–77. WBY's treatment here also prefigures some of the aphorisms in "Astrology and the Nature of Reality" in Rapallo D (later called Six or Seven Propositions); see Neil Mann, "Seven Propositions," (revised September 2008, corrections April 2009), https://www.yeatsvision.com/7Propositions.html.

67 Wyndham Lewis, *Time and Western Man* (London: Chatto and Windus, 1927; *WBGYL* 1136, *YL* 1126). See *CW14* 430–31, n43; see also Katherine Ebury, "'A new science': Yeats's *A Vision* and Relativistic Cosmology," *Irish Studies Review* 22, no. 2 (2014): 167–183; 170.

68 Rapallo A, NLI 13,578, [24r], page numbered 19. WBY had contrasted the Buddha and the Sphinx in "The Double Vision of Michael Robartes" but was told that he "should have put Christ instead of Buddha, for according to my instructors Buddha was a Jupiter-Saturn influence" (*AVB* 208, *CW14* 153); i.e., Buddha was *antithetical*, like the Sphinx.

69 The passage leaves a question mark and blank in front of "Daishi," indicating that WBY partially remembered and partially forgot Kobo Daishi, the title given posthumously to Kukai (774–835); see *E&I* 236 (*CW4* 173 adopts a mispunctuation from *Essays* [1924] that originates in the Cuala volume, putting a comma between Kobo and Daishi). The passage contrasts Kobo-Daishi with the eighth-century Indian teacher Sankara (Adi Shankara-charya), whose works are the foundation of Advaita Vedanta in Hinduism, and the third-century Neoplatonist Plotinus, whose works influenced both Christian theology and pagan philosophy.

70 The material about the differing lengths of *primary* and *antithetical* dispensations is used in modified form in *AVB*, Book II, Section XII (*AVB* 208, *CW14* 153–54).

71 Rapallo A, NLI 13,578, [24r–25r], pages numbered 20–21. *Reading text*: "They tell me that the primary revelation comes soon after the opening of the year, & the antithetical considerably before its close & that East & West are Primary & Antithetical respectively, each one dying the others life living the others death. I do not know [why] the Primary revelation should not begin its year but imag[in]e that the antithetical comes before its close, though it is the inspiration of its successor because out of human intellect & not from beyond it & so needs a mature tradition. As antithetical Europe at the end of an antithetical year [?approached] *primary* revelation, primary Asia, at the end of a primary year brought forth antithetical revelation in Buddha. Christ speaks to & is born of the *primary* masses, but Buddha is a kings son & speaks to kings, & Buddhism grows by its effect upon kings courts.

"Nothing for the common man, no god no consoling heaven. Men dispute as to whether it [?grants] of any punishment but life any reward but extinxion. Having taken from the sculptor of Alexander the high bred face of a god it moulded from it the symbol of a solitude more terrible than that of Oedipus.

"When Christianity lost its first character when eclesiastic[s] became princes, but Buddhism as Buddha sank down into Primary Asia, the abstraction of the Vedas, that something that seems to disolve all form away coarsed [=*coursed?*] into Indian sculpture, gave it vague pleasant faces & a multitude of arms. In Japan & China alone could Buddhism prolong its Antithetical nobility, for there it was joined to the common belief by great works of art where once can study the primary soul in its antithetical moment. Their style defining a theme rather than a personality passes on, in the same family from generation to generation, or is taken up or laid down when the narrative selects a new theme, & it is above all an art of landscape, great nameless mountains, cattaracts falling through cloud into cloud an old saint climbing to some mountain shrine, & all caught up into a powerful rythm, that unlike the rythms of European art, carries us beyond its scene that we may share the contemplation of Buddha.

"Buddha in isolation seems to contradict a logic that affirms the multiplicity of antitethical inspiration, but that isolation may be a historical accident, and the devine event that whole illumination, which began at or a little before the time of Pythagoras ran parallel to that of Greek philosophy for centuries & hardly survived it."

72 Laurence Binyon, "Some Phases of Religious Art in Eastern Asia," *The Quest* 2, no. 4 (1911); the four quotations are found on pages 657, 662, 662 (again), and 666, respectively. The essay mentions Kobo Daishi and a painting of him as a child, which is generally regarded as anonymous but, in *Painting in the Far East*, 2nd ed., (London: Edward Arnold, 1913; *WBGYL* 201; *YL* 194). Binyon attributes it to Nobuzane, and WBY repeated this in "Certain Noble Plays of Japan" (*E&I* 236, *CW4* 173). See Louise Blakeney Williams, *Modernism and the Ideology of History: Literature, Politics, and the Past* (Cambridge: Cambridge University Press, 2002), especially chapter six, "'Our own image': the example of Asian and non-Western cultures."

73 WBY potentially saw them as comparable to fifth-century Athens (Buddha and Confucius were also active in this century) and the period from Justinian's Byzantium (in which Chan Buddhism developed in sixth-century China and moved to Japan as Zen) to Charlemagne, whose dates (748–814) make him a little older than Kobo Daishi (774–835).

74 Rapallo A, NLI 13,578, [25r]. On Sankara and Plotinus, see n69.

75 There is no point in the drafts where WBY is obviously restarting after a considerable break.

76 See *Life2* 373. His final appearance, without speaking, came a week later on July 25, 1928 (*ChronY* 261).

77 See https://www.oireachtas.ie/en/debates/debate/dail/1928-07-19/16/ (accessed July 2019). The bill reached its Second Stage and was debated in October 1928. It was enacted on July 16, 1929 (see https://www.oireachtas.ie/en/bills/bill/1928/41/). This is explored extensively in Warwick Gould, "'Satan Smut & Co': Yeats and the Suppression of Evil Literature in the Early Years of the Free State," *YA21* (2018), 123–212, which focuses particularly on "The Cherry-Tree Carol," dealt with in WBY's second essay.

78 WBY was interviewed for the *Manchester Guardian* by the paper's Irish Correspondent, and "Censorship in Ireland. The Free State Bill. Senator W. B. Yeats's Views" appeared on August 22, 1928 (p. 5); see Appendix to Gould, "'Satan Smut & Co.,'" 203–05. The next day, in rejoinder, the *Irish Independent* published "Censorship: Mr Yeats's Peculiar Views" (August 23, 1928), 5.

79 WBY, "The Censorship and St. Thomas Aquinas," *Irish Statesman* (September 22, 1928), 47–48 (*CW10* 211–13, *UP2* 477–80). There are two typescript versions in NLI: NLI 30,170 and another typescript, NLI 30,867, dated September 1928.

80 Rapallo A, NLI 13,578, [32r], unnumbered page; cf. "the Platonizing theology of Byzantium," *CW10* 212.

81 *CW10* 212, *UP2* 478. The draft does not include this text as it gives: "Cardinal Mercier writing in his 'Manual of Modern Scholastic philosophy,['] vol I; page 314, English Edition | ' (quote marked passage) [']"; Rapallo A, NLI 13,578 [31r], page numbered 1. The volume is in the Yeatses' library (*WBGYL* 1318, *YL* 1305), with the passage marked as indicated.

82 Rapallo A, NLI 13,578, [32r], unnumbered page. Cf. *CW10* 212, *UP2* 479.

83 Rapallo A, NLI 13,578, [33r], page numbered 2, and [32v].

84 WBY, "The Irish Censorship," *The Spectator* (September 29, 1928), 391–92 (*CW10* 214–18, *UP2* 480–85).

85 On the loose pages, see n99. The cancelled and unfinished paragraph on [37v] appears to relate to the formulation of "being a symbolist <dramatist> ~~& know no philosopher~~ <~~logician~~> <not a dialectician>" on [39r]. The sentences on [37v] read: "In obedience to

their will I remain a dramatist and if I define a thing my definition is summary and casual as in a list of a dramatis personae. I wish it to unfold itself as the actor unfolding, & no more expect, & seeing that . . ." where it breaks off (this transcription ignores earlier cancellations, which repeat the same material).

86 Rapallo A, NLI 13,578, [39r], page numbered 2, and Rapallo B, NLI 13,579, [11r], page numbered 1. The spelling of "know" for "no" may indicate that someone—perhaps GY?—was dictating from the earlier draft.

87 Rapallo A, NLI 13,578, [39r], page numbered 2, and Rapallo B, NLI 13,579, [11r], page numbered 1. Later drafts correct the quotation to "Have you had a quiet guard?" (*Hamlet* I:1). Its application is rather enigmatic, but partly explained in a stray sheet of loose-leaf manuscript developing this draft: "I accept his [*the instructor's*] thought, & being a symbolist & dramatist not a dialectician, apply to the daimon ~~the words~~ Parmenides description of the universe. 'It is complete on every side, equally poised from the centre in every direction like the mass of a rounded sphere'[.] But as ~~he~~ Parmenides ~~applies the~~ means some kind of philosophical object & I some kind of a ghost add the opening words 'Have you had quiet guard? Not a mouse stirring'" (NLI 36,272/3). Its significance seems personal, probably alluding to the time he spent on watch or waiting for GY's "Sleeps" to start.

88 Rapallo B, NLI 13,579, [15v], and Rapallo A, NLI 13,578, [39r].

89 Rapallo A, NLI 13,578, [39r] and [42r], pages numbered 2 and 5; and Rapallo B, NLI 13,579, [15v] and [16r] unnumbered verso and page numbered 3. A line or two earlier on in Rapallo B, NLI 13,579, [16r], WBY had cancelled a more correctly spelled "~~Guido Cal Cavilanti~~."

90 Rapallo A, NLI 13,578, [47r–48r], pages numbered 10–11. The manuscript has been interpreted with the help of a typescript, probably dictated from this draft (NLI MS 36/272/18/1, page numbered 13, section IX).

91 The dictated typescript (see previous note) has the correct title. Andrew Parkin observes that the connection of the play to its title is not immediately obvious and had baffled "that doggedly faithful Dublin playgoer, Joseph Holloway: 'What the name given to the piece had to do with it, I could not fathom,'" in *"At the Hawk's Well" and "The Cat and the Moon": Manuscript Materials* (Ithaca, NY: Cornell University Press, 2010), xlvii. The poem "The Cat and the Moon" follows "The Phases of the Moon" in WBY, *The Wild Swans at Coole* (London: Macmillan, 1919), but was first published in *Nine Poems* (privately printed by Clement Shorter, 1918).

92 See A. Norman Jeffares and A. S. Knowland, *A Commentary on the Collected Plays of W. B. Yeats* (London: Macmillan, 1975), 172. Parkin gives the full reasoning behind this dating in *"At the Hawk's Well" and "The Cat and the Moon": Manuscript Materials*, xlix.

93 In these Rapallo notebooks, all of WBY's presentation was expressed in terms of the *Principles*, but in *AVB* these descriptions are applied to the counterpart *Faculties* (*Husk–Will*; *Passionate Body–Mask*; *Spirit–Creative Mind*; *Celestial Body–Body of Fate*): "It will be enough until I have explained the geometrical diagrams in detail to describe *Will* and *Mask* as the will and its object, or the Is and the Ought (or that which should be), *Creative Mind* and *Body of Fate* as thought and its object, or the Knower and the Known, and to say that the first two are lunar or *antithetical* or natural, the second two solar or *primary* or reasonable" (*AVB* 73, *CW14* 54).

94 The Lame Beggar's cure is far more clearly indicated in the revised version of 1934, apparently written in 1930 or 1931; see *"At the Hawk's Well" and "The Cat and the Moon": Manuscript Materials*, 241ff. See Mann and Chapman, "Rapallo Notebook D," *IYS* 8.1: 186–89 (rpt. at 94–97, below).

95 For an examination of how "A Dialogue of Self and Soul" draws on the categories and thinking of *A Vision*, see Neil Mann, "Yeats's Visionary Poetics" in Matthew Campbell and

Lauren Arrington, eds. *Oxford Handbook of W. B. Yeats* (Oxford: Oxford University Press, forthcoming).

96 Rapallo A, NLI 13,578, [49r], page numbered 12.

97 "The Withering of the Boughs" dates from 1900 (*VP* 203–204).

98 Rapallo A, NLI 13,578, [48v] and [49v], section X. *AVA* had made the connection (*AVA* 164, *CW13* 133), but it was developed in *AVB* (*AVB* 212, cf. *CW14* 156).

99 The Harvard microfilm appears to indicate that seven leaves of "First Things," numbered 2–8 [39–45], were loose, as were [74], the leaf with Indian kalpas on it, and [75], the penultimate page of the *Spectator* article draft, numbered 9. Together with the missing leaf [38], these total ten leaves, but the paper anchors used in restoration appear to number eight (my thanks to Jack Quin for checking this in a time of COVID-19 restrictions). I have chosen the lower number as more clearly verifiable, but recognize that the counting of phantom leaves is somewhat arbitrary, especially as we are uncertain how many leaves each notebook originally contained.

100 Curtis Bradford, *The Writing of "The Player Queen"* (DeKalb: Northern Illinois University Press, 1977), 447–51.

101 Bradford, *The Writing of "The Player Queen,"* 447; see WBY's letter to GY of [May 23, 1927], *CL InteLex* 4999.

102 The play opened on September 24, 1928, for seven nights, and was directed by Lennox Robinson, with Sara Allgood as Nona and Arthur Shields as Septimus (see the Abbey Theatre website, https://www.abbeytheatre.ie/archives/production_detail/3227/, accessed March 2020). Various ballets were performed alongside *The Player Queen* (see https://www.abbeytheatre.ie/archives/production_detail/8363/, accessed March 2020).

103 This is the letter, written shortly after arriving at Coole, in which WBY apologized to GY for making her search for notes on Plotinus in the wrong notebook; it is possible that he stumbled on the notes when he reached for Rapallo A to sketch out the revisions.

104 Bradford, *The Writing of "The Player Queen,"* 447.

105 Wade item 137; the second impression (1928) had some variations of pagination, but these do not affect *The Player Queen*. There were two copies in the Yeatses' library, the first with the notes and music torn out (*WBGYL* 2425; *YL* 2399) and the second from a limited edition of 250 (*WBGYL* 2425a; *YL* 2399A).

106 Rapallo A, NLI 13,578, [64r], page numbered 1, and [66r], numbered 3.

107 Rapallo A, NLI 13,578, [65r–66r], cf. section V of the final version, *CW6* 168–69.

108 WBY, "The Irish Censorship," *CW10* 214–18, *UP2* 480–85.

109 There are three typescripts in NLI 30,105, and a fourth in NLI 30,116.

110 See *English Folk-Carols*, collected by Cecil J. Sharp (London: Novello, 1911), 8 (first version). Gould, "'Satan Smut & Co.'" reproduces the center spread of the carol in *Pears' Annual* 1925, illustrated by Richard Kennedy North (127). The carol draws on chapter twenty of the apocryphal *Infancy Gospel of Matthew*, popular in the Middle Ages, where Joseph chides Mary for pining for dates, but the infant Jesus makes the tree bow.

111 Rapallo A, NLI 13,578, [67r], cancelled, numbered 1, and *CW10* 214.

112 Rapallo A, NLI 13,578, [71r], numbered 6, and *CW10* 215.

113 Rapallo A, NLI 13,578, [72r] and *CW10* 216.

114 Hermann Jacobi, "Ages of the World (Indian)," in *Encyclopaedia of Religion and Ethics*, ed. James Hastings (Edinburgh: T. & T. Clark, Jacobi's article is referred to in notes on the same topic in NLI 13,581 [10r–12v], along with Sepharial's book, *Hebrew Astrology* ([6v] ff.).

115 Cit. *UP2* 485.

116 Rapallo A, NLI 13,578, [77r], cf. *UP2* 486, *CL InteLex* 5176.

117 See *CW6* 297 n10.

118 The 1930 diary, NLI 30,354, [63v]. WBY, *Pages from a Diary Written in 1930* (Dublin: Cuala, 1944), reprinted in *Explorations* (London: Macmillan, 1962).
119 The 1930 diary, NLI 30,354, [64r].
120 The 1930 diary, NLI 30,354, inside back cover [65r].
121 Rapallo A, NLI 13,578, [79r], with cancellations omitted; cf. *Ex* 338–39.
122 Rapallo A, NLI 13,578, [79r]. The entry for November 16 was also omitted, passing directly to November 18; see Mann, *ARGYV* 298–99.
123 Rapallo C, NLI 13,580, [1r].
124 See Mann, "The Rapallo Notebooks."
125 Samuel Taylor Coleridge, in his *Table Talk* of July 12, [1827]; the edition in WBY's library is Coleridge, *Table Talk, and the Rime of the Ancient Mariner* (London: Routledge, 1884; *WBGYL* 417, *YL* 406), 63.
126 A formerly loose double bifolium, bound in what is now Rapallo E, contains some material that could be as early, or even earlier, but its original source is unclear.
127 *WS29* xxvi.
128 *WS29* xxvi–xxvii.
129 Letter of [August 17, 1928], *CL InteLex* 5145; cf. *YGYL* 194. The same letter refers to a "leather bound book I put you looking for," which could have been NLI MS 30,359.
130 The reference to Lennox Robinson's *A Little Anthology of Modern Irish Verse* (Dublin: Cuala Press, 1928) shows that the book was conceived with the Cuala Press in mind.
131 George Berkeley, *Siris: A Chain of Philosophical Reflexions and Enquiries Concerning the Virtues of Tar Water, and Divers Other Subjects Connected Together and Arising One from Another* (London: C. Hitch; C. Davis, 1744; Dublin: R. Gunne, 1744).
132 This was repeated some weeks later: the "essay . . . . takes a poem of Guido Cavalcanti's for text & discusses the latest movements in contemporary literature" (WBY to Augusta Gregory, April 1, [1928], *CL InteLex* 5097; *L* 739).
133 Rapallo B, NLI 13,379, [15r].
134 See Catherine E. Paul, "Compiling *A Packet For Ezra Pound*," *Paideuma* 38 (2011), 29–53, for everything touching *A Packet for Ezra Pound*. In a note on WBY's letter of April 1, 1928, to Lady Gregory, Allan Wade claims that "Yeats wrote [the essay] and then destroyed it, finding it, he said difficult to make clear or even readable" (*L* 739n). Whether Wade was relying on personal information from WBY or upon letters he did not publish, the situation that emerges in the letters appears a little more complex. Writing from Coole on August 26, 1928, WBY told Ezra Pound, "I came down here some ten days ago to complete that essay begun in Rapallo on you and your work. I toiled away at it and then . . . I got suddenly the thought I wanted. I went at it again and all was going beautifully until George sent me your Cavalcanti translation which I hadnt looked at since I left Rapallo. I read it and it was almost clear to me, but the meaning I found had no relation at that time. I dare not risk it without a whole apparatus of learning, for they would either accuse you of bad translation, or me of bad scholarship. If I am to use my essay about you I must use it without the Cavalcanti which uninterpreted would be without meaning to the Cuala readers and interpreted would get me out of my depth at the best" (*CL InteLex* 5147). A month later, he seems to imply that Pound's translation, with its deliberate archaisms, was not direct enough for him to use: "I worked hard until I found myself plunging into solutions that seemed impossible for the period, & realised that as I could not read the Italian & even if I could lacked historical knowledge, nobody would accept me as interpreter. On the other hand your verse translation is far from explaining itself, & people would want to know why what they regarded as a work of art — verse translations are always so regarded — was not sufficient to itself. I wish you could make yourself do another & purely conjectural version which was clear. I would delight to comment upon it in this strain 'Whether this is

Cavalcanti or not I neither know nor care — it is Ezra & that is enough for me.' I would then go on, all out of my own head & without compromising you in any way, & say that it was your religion, your philosophy, your creed, your collect, your nightly & morning & prayers, & that with it F and Buckler you faced a Neo-thomist, Wyndam-Lewis, Golden Treasury World in Arms" (September 23, [1928], *CL InteLex* 5161). Pound did not rise to the bait.

135 Rapallo B, NLI 13,579, [87r]; see also *AVB* 8, *CW14* 7.

136 *Reveries over Childhood and Youth* (London: Macmillan, 1916), *Per Amica Silentia Lunae* (London: Macmillan, 1918), and *The Trembling of the Veil* (London: T. Werner Laurie, 1922).

137 "I wrote this book in my first excitement [. . .] & leave it unchanged except for a few passages crossed out because their matter is somewhere in book I & three or four sentences added to sharpen a definition or correct an error" ([41r], p. 84, n196); "the section 'Dove or Swan'—repeated in this book without alteration" ([96v], p. 97, n233); cf. [71r], page numbered 18, n214); and the changes proposed for pages 12–14 of *AVA* ([43v–44r], p. 85).

138 Rapallo B, NLI 13,579, [102v], see p. 99, n242.

139 Viewing the photograph of the letter at the NLI (https://catalogue.nli.ie/Record/vtls000816026) leads me to favor the reading of Wade's *Letters*, "his country" (indicating the United States), over *CL InteLex*'s "this country" (implying Italy). This also agrees with the published version, "Do not be elected to the Senate of your country," in WBY, *A Packet for Ezra Pound* [hereafter *PEP*] (Dublin: Cuala, 1929), 33.

140 See Paul, "Compiling *A Packet For Ezra Pound*."

141 Berkeley, *Siris*; the work passed through some six editions in just six months in 1744. The word σειρίς "*siris*" is a diminutive or variant of "*sira*," meaning cord or chain, and Berkeley notes it is applied to the Nile; see A. A. Luce, "The Original Title and the First Edition of 'Siris,'" *Hermathena* 84 (1954): 45–58; 52.

142 *AVB* 4, *CW14* 4; cf. *PEP* 2.

143 Frans Pourbus the Younger was the last of three generations of painters surnamed Pourbus or Porbus, the spelling favored by Balzac and used in the translation owned by WBY; Honoré de Balzac, *The Unknown Masterpiece (Le Chef d'oeuvre inconnu) and Other Stories*, trans. Ellen Marriage, vol. 37 in the Temple edition of the *Comédie humaine* (40 vols.), ed. George Saintsbury (New York: Macmillan, 1901; *WBGYL* 109, *YL* 109).

144 Paul Cezanne's surname did not have an acute accent in his native Provence, though Parisian orthodoxy added one, which was customarily used through most of the twentieth century. The Société Paul Cezanne and surviving family, however, advocate the Provençal spelling; see Anna Brady, "Drop the accent? Cézanne's acute dilemma," *The Art Newspaper* [London and New York] (January 9, 2020), https://www.theartnewspaper.com/news/drop-the-accent-cezanne-s-acute-dilemma. While WBY's publishers tend to give the accent, his own manuscripts omit it (albeit probably through inattention), so the unaccented spelling is used here.

145 Balzac, *The Unknown Masterpiece*, 7.

146 Rapallo B, NLI 13,579, [2v] and [3r], page numbered 2. In the text on page 3r is written in pencil, there are a few cancellations in ink in the last lines (double strikethrough here), and two vertical ink strokes cancelling all four last lines (single strikethrough here), to be substituted by the text from the opposing page.

147 Rapallo B, NLI 13,579, [7r]. This is just the uncancelled text, omitting several sentences relating Balzac to Keats, Tennyson, and Hallam (see below).

148 Balzac, *The Unknown Masterpiece*, 29–30.

149 Balzac, *The Unknown Masterpiece*, 30.

150 Balzac, *The Unknown Masterpiece*, 31.

151 Émile Bernard visited Cezanne in 1904: "One evening, when I was talking to him about the *Chef-d'œuvre inconnu* and Frenhofer, the hero of Balzac's drama, he rose from the table, stood up in front of me, and, striking his chest with his index finger, pointing to himself without a word, but repeating this gesture, indicated in a self-accusatory manner that he was that very character from the story" (my translation); Bernard, "Souvenirs sur Paul Cézanne et lettres inédites," *Mercure de France*, 69 no. 247 (October 1, 1907), 403, https://gallica.bnf.fr/ark:/12148/bpt6k105566f/f19.item. As reshaped by Joachim Gasquet, this anecdote took the form that became more current: "Frenhofer, he declared one day with a silent gesture, pointing a finger at his own chest, while the *Chef-d'œuvre inconnu* was being discussed, Frenhofer is me" (my translation); Gasquet, *Cézanne* (Paris: éditions Bernheim-Jeune, 1921), 42–43, https://gallica.bnf.fr/ark:/12148/bpt6k1521407h/f83.item. The French, "*Frenhofer, c'est moi*," recalls Gustave Flaubert's statement "*Madame Bovary, c'est moi*," but with very different implications. Both articles, with the questionnaire, "Mes Confidences," are collected in P. M. Doran, *Conversations avec Cézanne* (Paris: Macula, 1978). For full consideration of the theme, see Bernard Vouilloux, "«Frenhofer, c'est moi»: Postérité cézannienne du récit balzacien," in *Tableaux d'auteurs: Après l'*Ut pictura poesis (Saint Denis: Presses universitaires de Vincennes: 2004), https://books.openedition.org/puv/6183. See also Dore Ashton, *A Fable of Modern Art* (Berkeley: University of California Press, 1991), especially chapter two, "Cézanne in the shadow of Frenhofer," http://ark.cdlib.org/ark:/13030/ft8779p1x3/.

152 Bernard contrasts Balzac's Frenhofer with Claude Lantier, a painter based on Cezanne in Émile Zola's *L'Œuvre* (Paris: G. Charpentier, 1886): "Oh—there is a huge distance between this Frenhofer, impotent through genius, and this Claude, impotent by nature, that Zola unintentionally saw in [Cezanne]!" (my translation) (Bernard, "Souvenirs sur Paul Cézanne," 403).

153 Aspects of this material echo what Yeats had written on Hallam, Tennyson, and the Romantics in his 1913 essay "Art and Ideas," especially section II (*E&I* 346–55, *CW4* 250–56).

154 Rapallo B, NLI 13,579, [6r].

155 The material in *AVA* dealing with contemporary art and the near future (*AVA* 210–15; *CW13* 174–78) was not used in *AVB*, and WBY had projected another ending, rather more focused on politics and society, which was never used; a relatively final version dated "September 1932" is given in *CW14*'s Appendix II, 293–98. The artists mentioned in *AVA* had included Lewis, Pound, and Joyce, taken up in these drafts.

156 It first appeared in 1831 in a periodical, *L'Artiste*, in two parts, before being published in book form later that year. Influenced by Théophile Gautier, it was heavily revised for inclusion in Balzac's *Études philosophiques* (1837), gaining more detail and artistic theorizing, and it was incorporated into the grand scheme of *La Comédie humaine* in 1845. A further version with a minor variations appeared in 1847 in *Le Provincial à Paris* (vol. 2), while Balzac's personal copy of the story in *La Comédie humaine* has corrections. See René Guise, introduction to Balzac, *Le Chef-d'œuvre inconnu*, in *La Comédie humaine*, vol. 10, Pléiade edition ([Paris]: Gallimard, 1979), 399 ff.; see also Ashton, *A Fable of Modern Art*, chapter one. WBY would have known the version published in *La Comédie humaine* in Ellen Marriage's translation, which bears the date 1845 (*The Unknown Masterpiece*, 1).

157 Rapallo A, NLI 13,578, [5r–6r].

158 *AVB* 4, *CW14* 4; cf. *PEP* 2.

159 Balzac, *The Unknown Masterpiece*, 16.

160 *AVB* 5, *CW14* 5; cf. *PEP* 4.

161 Balzac, *The Unknown Masterpiece*, 30.

162 Balzac, *The Unknown Masterpiece*, 12, 16.

163 Balzac, *The Unknown Masterpiece*, 31.
164 *PEP* 33, *AVB* 26, *CW14* 19.
165 Catherine E. Paul, "A Vision of Ezra Pound," in *YVEC*, 263. Pound could have retorted that WBY was never elected.
166 Rapallo B, NLI 13,579, [102v]. See n138 and n242.
167 Leather notebook, NLI 30,359.
168 Rapallo B, NLI 30,359, [9v]. This sentence is inserted into [10r] from the opposite verso. See above, p. 34.
169 Rapallo B, NLI 13,579, [11r], page numbered 1.
170 See Daisetz Suzuki, *Essays in Zen Buddhism*, first series (London: Luzac, 1927; *WBGYL* 2045; *YL* 2033), 230, 242n. The metaphor of lightning actually comes from the *Kena Upanishad* (IV:29), while "Chōkei (Chang-ching, died 932)" was the author of the short poem: "'How deluded I was! How deluded indeed! / Lift up the screen and come see the world! / 'What religion believest thou?' you ask. / I raise my hossu and hit your mouth" (233–34). The author is given as his master, Seppo (822–908), in the original article *The Eastern Buddhist* 1, no. 3 (Sep.–Oct. 1921), 213, https://archive.org/details/in.ernet.dli.2015.283162/page/n223/mode/2up.
171 Rapallo C, NLI 13,580, [6r], dated "Jan 1929," cited by Ellmann, *The Identity of Yeats*, 239.
172 St John Chrysostom, *On the Incomprehensible Nature of God*, Homily II, §17, in *The Fathers of the Church*, vol. 72, trans. Paul W. Harkins (Washington, DC: Catholic University of America Press, 1984), 77. There are several nineteenth-century sources from which WBY might have gleaned the saying, though none is more obvious than another.
173 Rapallo B, NLI 13,579, [10v].
174 See *ARGYV* 32–34.
175 Rapallo B, NLI 13,579, [15v].
176 For a summary of the four versions of the propositions, see Mann, "Seven Propositions." Concerning the Seven Propositions, see *ARGYV* 81–84 and 323 n5. See also Neil Mann, "'Everywhere that antinomy of the One and the Many': The Foundations of *A Vision*," *YVEC* 8–9 and Margaret Mills Harper, "Words for Music? Perhaps," *IYS* 1 no. 1 (2017), 3–5.
177 Rapallo B, NLI 13,579, [16v]–[17v].
178 See Rapallo B, NLI 13,579, [40r–41r], numbered 4 and 5 (p. 84, n196) and [100r–101r], numbered 10 and 11 (p. 97–98, n234).
179 See *ARGYV* 94.
180 Rapallo B, NLI 13,579, [17r], page numbered 6.
181 Rapallo B, NLI 13,579, [30r–31r], pages numbered 11 and 12. Cf. "It was a Greco-Roman phantasy that at a point in the Zodiac where it was crossed by the Milky Way the vortex changed into a sphere, and when man and woman turn from domination and surrender to love their vortex becomes a sphere, the union of spirit and celestial body fed by that of the faculties, and all things are at an end. Because the two passive faculties are the reflection of the two active principles Guido Cavalcanti is justified in finding in the beloved his body of science, and every lover of a beautiful woman in that form drawn as with a diamond, the symbol or image of his undiscovered wisdom." NLI MS 36,272/18/4(f), pages 24–25.
182 Rapallo B, NLI 13,579, [32r–33r], pages numbered 13 and 14, and [32v]. Most cancelled text is omitted, except for two instances that are included for clarity. The last paragraph's opposition to the cone of the month or year alludes to the opposition of the *Thirteenth Cone* explained in *AVB* 209–10, *CW14* 154–55.
183 The destruction of the world by conflagration when the planets are all in Cancer and by deluge when they are in Capricorn goes back to some of the earliest astrological writings, the *Babyloniaca* of Berossus (fl. 280 BCE); see Duhem, *Le système du monde*, vol. 1, 70, 276.

Stanley Mayer Burstein, *The Babyloniaca of Berossus*, Sources from the Ancient Near East, vol. 1, fasc. 5 (Malibu, CA: Undena, 1978), 15.

184 Coventry Patmore, "The Precursor," in *Religio Poetæ* (London: George Bell, 1898; *WBGYL* 1553, *YL* 1542), 17, refers to Renaissance painters only to point out that John the Baptist is paired with John "the Divine." Walter Pater comments on "the so-called Saint John the Baptist of the Louvre" and its "strange likeness to the Bacchus, which hangs near it" in Pater, *The Renaissance* (London: Macmillan, 1873), 111–12, though the observation about the lush wilderness may well indicate that WBY was drawing on his own viewing of the paintings too.

185 Rapallo B, NLI 13,579, [60r], entirely cancelled, unnumbered page.

186 Rapallo A, NLI 13,578, [49v]. The version later in Rapallo B is very sketchy: "Christ was supernatural, & Baccus natural love – 'God give him in wine like the fable Baccus[']" (NLI 13,579, [76r], page numbered 1). Patmore's actual formulation is: "When God makes Himself as wine to the Beloved, like the fabled Bacchus, the one thing He resents is inattention, and when she [the Soul] has fallen into this offence, she has to recover her favour with Him by tears and prayers" (Patmore, "Dieu et Ma Dame," in *Religio Poetæ*, 171).

187 Rapallo B, NLI 13,579, [34r], page numbered 15, and [33v]. The word "flame" is missing following "where all fuel has become" but is supplied from a typescript closely based on this MS and dated "May 5, 1928," NLI 36,272/18/4, pages numbered 25 and 26. Similarly, although "allusion" has a special meaning in the system of *A Vision*, the typescript gives "illusion."

188 Rapallo B, NLI 13,579, [2v], cf. *AVB* 4, *CW14* 4; cf. *PEP* 2.

189 Rapallo B, NLI 13,579, [102v]. See p. 99, n242.

190 Warwick Gould convincingly suggests inspiration in the Stella Matutina's ritual for 7=4 Initiation, which required the aspirant to repeat a meditation, "Earthborn and bound our bodies close us in"; Gould, "Byzantine Materiality and Byzantine Vision: 'Hammered Gold and Gold Enamelling,'" in *Yeats 150*, ed. Declan Foley (Dublin: Lilliput, 2016), esp. 111–13. WBY made at least two attempts at rewriting the poem, one in the PIAL Notebook, dated to November 1915 (NLI 36,276, [36v]) and another on writing paper headed "18 Woburn Buildings," which was inserted in a copy of *Responsibilities and Other Poems*; see *YL* 356 for a very inaccurate transcription, and Wayne Chapman's "*Something that I read in a book*": *W. B. Yeats's Annotations at the National Library of Ireland* (Clemson, SC: Clemson University Press, 2022) 2: 106 provides a better version. See also Nick Farrell, *King Over the Water: Samuel Mathers and the Golden Dawn* (Dublin: Kerubim, 2012), 139–40. R. W. Felkin's original version reads: "Planets encircle with their spiral light, / Stars call us upward to our faltering flight – / Thus we arise. / Sun-rays will lead us higher yet and higher / Moon-beams our souls scorch with their purging fire, / Thus we arise," while WBY cuts this back to "The stars & the planets sumon [sic] us / The sun calls the moon is a purging fire" (writing paper) or even more concisely "The stars call & all the planets / and the purging fire of the moon" (PIAL Notebook, [36v]).

191 Rapallo B, NLI 13,579, [35r].

192 Rapallo B, NLI 13,579, [34v].

193 Rapallo B, NLI 13,579, [36r–37r], pages numbered 1 and 2. The cancelled "simpl" seems to indicate WBY balking at the word "simplification."

194 Rapallo B, NLI 13,579, [38r].

195 Rapallo B, NLI 13,579, [39r], page numbered 3.

196 Rapallo B, NLI 13,579, [40r–41r], pages numbered 4 and 5. Cancellation omitted. Cf. a corrected typescript dated May 5, 1928: "What I had been told about the Four Principles meant nothing to me because the geometry that explained it was still unintelligible, so I gave to each Faculty the quality of the corresponding Principle together with its own. Had

I understood that the Principles are value and attainment, the Faculties process and search, I could not perhaps have done otherwise without innumerable cumbrous explanatory phrases." "Book II: Introduction," NLI MS 36,272/18/4(f), pages numbered 4 and 5. A few minor variations may indicate it was dictated from Rapallo B; WBY sometimes introduced minor changes during dictation.

197 The tale "King Wird Khan, his Women and his Wazirs" (in Richard Burton's translation), is not included in all collections, but rather than WBY's vague wording about "sayings," the translations specify a particular "saying of the ancients." Burton gives, "The boy replied, 'O brother, I know this from the sand wherewith I take compt of night and day and from the saying of the ancients, "No mystery from Allah is hidden; for the sons of Adam have in them a spiritual virtue which discovereth to them the darkest secrets."'" *The Book of the Thousand Nights and a Night*, 16 vols., trans. Richard Burton (London: Kamashastra Society, 1885–87), 9:117. In John Payne's version: "'O brother,' answered the boy, 'I know this from the sand wherewith I tell the tale of night and day and from the saying of the ancients, "No mystery is hidden from God;" for the sons of Adam have in them a spiritual virtue which discovers to them hidden secrets.'" *The Book of the Thousand Nights and One Night*, Cashan edition, 13 vols., trans. John Payne (London: privately, 1901), vol. 8, 276.

198 See Warwick Gould, "'A Lesson to the Circumspect': W. B. Yeats's two versions of *A Vision* and the *Arabian Nights*," in *The "Arabian Nights" in English Literature: Studies in the Reception of "The Thousand and One Nights" into British Culture*, ed. Peter L. Caracciolo, (London: Macmillan, 1988), 245–46.

199 Rapallo B, NLI 13,579, [42r–43r], pages numbered 6 and 7. The typescript NLI 36,272/8/4 gives "'could be fixed automatically,'" but that is probably because WBY or the person dictating misread the handwriting.

200 NLI 36,272/8/4, the date appears on page numbered 6.

201 Rapallo B, NLI 13,579, [51r], cf. *AVB* 245, *CW14* 179.

202 Rapallo B, NLI 13,579, [53r]. WBY repeatedly writes "Ares" (the Greek name for the planet that rules Aries) for "Aries." He also consistently writes about the sun "rising" at the Equinox, which shows remaining confusion about the meaning of the Equinoctial Point, which is unconnected with any time of day.

203 Rapallo B, NLI 13,579, [53r–54r]. Cf. Rapallo A, NLI 13,578, [8r], page numbered 5, cited above p. 42 (n52).

204 Rapallo B, NLI 13,579, [54r] and [2r].

205 Rapallo B, NLI 13,579, [60r], all cancelled, unnumbered page. Though not struck through, the word "by" in "understand by 'natural love'" goes with a cancelled formulation, substituted by "understand 'natural love' as," so it has been omitted in the transcription.

206 *PEP* 33.

207 The word after "V. de l Adam" is probably "context" or "contacts"—or possibly "extracts"—though none quite fits the outline of the letters; however, neither do readings like "Cambridge" or "Platonist"—this is WBY's handwriting at its most personal.

208 In *The Trembling of the Veil* (see n136), WBY noted that "Villiers de l'Isle Adam had shaped whatever in my *Rosa Alchemica* Pater had not shaped" (*Au* 320–21, *CW3* 247), and in the poem "The Phases of the Moon," he has Michael Robartes speak of how Mr. Yeats wrote "in that extravagant style / He had learned from Pater" (*CW13* 4 and 230–31 n7, *CW14* 42 and 341 n6); see also n182. Though it had appeared in fragmentary and serial form in periodicals from 1872 onwards, Auguste Villiers de l'Isle Adam's symbolist play *Axël* was not published in book form until the year after the author's death (Paris: Quantin, 1890); it had a great impact on WBY, who wrote a preface to H. P. R. Finberg's 1925 translation (*CW6* 156–58).

209 Corrina Salvadori's *Yeats and Castiglione, Poet and Courtier: A Study of Some Fundamental Concepts of the Philosophy and Poetic Creed of W. B. Yeats in the Light of Castiglione's "Il Libro Del Cortegiano"* (Dublin: A. Figgis, 1965) is still the principal study of the connection.

210 Maurice Maeterlinck's *Pelléas and Mélisande* (Brussels: Paul Lacomblez, 1892) premiered in 1893. Writing about it in 1905, Joseph Holloway recorded "Mr. Yeats said he never understood its meaning clearly until he saw Mrs. Patrick Campbell and Madame Bernhardt enact the roles of the lovers as if they were a pair of little children" (*CL3* 614 n1). In *Per Amica Silentia Lunae*, Mrs. Patrick Campbell was a point of reference for the opposition of her boisterous daily self to the roles she played of "those young queens imagined by Maeterlinck who have so little will, so little self, that they are like shadows sighing at the edge of the world" (*Myth* 327, *CW5* 5), though he was later contradicted in this supposition by GY's instructors; see George Mills Harper (general editor), *Yeats's "Vision" Papers*, 4 vols. (Iowa City: University of Iowa Press, 1992), vol. 1, 181; vol. 2, 17; vol. 3, 419. Michael McAteer draws parallels with Villiers de l'Isle Adam, Ibsen, and Maeterlinck in McAteer, *Yeats and European Drama* (Cambridge: Cambridge University Press, 2010), especially chapter one, where he outlines the influence of *Pelléas et Mélisande* on *The Countess Cathleen*, and also makes a connection with Andrew Lang's work on totemism (30–31); see also McAteer, "Music, Setting, Voice: Maeterlinck's *Pelléas et Mélisande* and Yeats's *The Countess Cathleen*," *IYS* 2, no. 1 (2017), article 2.

211 Guy Ducrey traces the phrase's use by writers including Balzac, Ibsen, Maeterlinck, and D'Annunzio in Ducrey, "'*Ne me touchez pas!*' Transgressions decadentes d'une parole biblique," *Nordlit* 28 (2011), 141–157. WBY may indeed be thinking of Christ's words to Mary Magdalene, "Touch me not: for I am not yet ascended to my Father" (John 20:17), usually given in Latin as "*Noli me tangere*"; this could in turn relate to *The Resurrection*, which was originally conceived ca. 1925 (*CL InteLex* 4725) and written in two versions of 1927 and 1932. This was drafted especially in Rapallo E, NLI 13,582, and the White Vellum Notebook (in private hands; see Chapman, "Yeats's White Vellum Notebook," *IYS* 2, no. 2 (2018), article 4); see Jared Curtis and Selina Guinness, *"The Resurrection": Manuscript Materials* (Ithaca, NY: Cornell University Press, 2011). The question of the substance of the resurrected Christ fascinated WBY and was linked to psychic phenomena: the Greek's horror that "The heart of a phantom is beating" (*VPl* 931) draws on Sir William Crookes's experience when "he touched a materialised form and found the heart beating" (*VPl* 935).

212 See p. 87 above, on Rapallo A, NLI 13,578, [22r], page numbered 17.

213 Rapallo B, NLI 13,579, [68r–69r with insertion from 63v], pages numbered 15 and 16. Cf. Rapallo A, 13,578, [22r], page numbered 17, p. 44 (n60). In the phrase "called both a 'sequence,'" both appears to relate to the "kind of number" and the "work of art"; my thanks to Wayne Chapman for helping with this reading.

214 Rapallo B, NLI 13,579, [71r], page numbered 18. Following ". . . read him in astonishment," a cancelled sentence starts: "A phrase of Sir Thomas Brown comes into my mind," almost certainly alluding to Browne's opinion, "I do think that many mysteries ascribed to our own inventions have been the courteous revelations of Spirits. . . ."; see *Religio Medici* (London: J. M. Dent, 1896; *WBGYL* 297, *YL* 289), 46 (section 31). WBY used this quotation in "Swedenborg, Mediums, and the Desolate Places" (*Ex* 60, *CW5* 66), as well as in the drafts of the Robartes-Aherne dialogues, where it is rendered as "the courteous communication of spirits"; see *Yeats's "Vision" Papers*, vol. 4: *"The Discoveries of Michael Robartes," Version B ("The Great Wheel" and "The Twenty-Eight Embodiments")*, ed. George Mills Harper and Margaret Mills Harper, with Richard W. Stoops, Jr. (London: Palgrave, 2001), 45.

215 *PEP* 25; cf. *AVB* 18–19, *CW14* 14.

216 There is an unrelated paragraph tagged "A" on leaf [24], numbered 8, a cancelled section, itself intended for insertion "at page 6 (or rather at back of p. 5" (i.e., 2 or 3 pages earlier in the notebook).
217 Rapallo B, NLI 13,579, [76r], page numbered 1.
218 Rapallo B, NLI 13,579, [76r–77r], pages numbered 1 and 2.
219 Rapallo B, NLI 13,579, [83r–84r], pages numbered 4 and 5.
220 A passage from Rapallo A quoted above still speaks of "this 3 fold world" (Rapallo A, NLI 13,578, [21r], page numbered 16; see p. 44 n60). For more detail on this topic, see Neil Mann, "The *Thirteenth Cone*," in *YVEC*, 159–93, and *ARGYV*, chapter ten.
221 Rapallo B, NLI 13,579, [87r], page numbered 7[bis].
222 Rapallo B, NLI 13,579, [88r], page numbered 8. The accurate quotation of Morris's version of the *Odyssey* (down to Morris's idiosyncratic spelling of "ancled" and, probably, also of "Here" rather than Hera—the letter is unclear) suggests that he had the book to hand; Morris, *The Collected Works of William Morris*, 24 vols. (London: Longman, Green, 1910–15; *WBGYL* 1401, *YL* 1389), 13:169.
223 Clark, "Cast-offs, Non-starters and Gnomic Illegibilities," 7–12. See Chapman, "Rapallo Notebook C," *IYS* 7.1: 261–63 (rpt. at 169–71 below).
224 Later termed *Meditation*, *Return*, *Shiftings*, *Beatitude*, *Purification*, and *Foreknowledge* (*AVB* 223–235, *CW14* 162–171), WBY's presentation of the nomenclature has proven confusing, with sub-stages placed in parallel with the main stages (*ARGYV* 253–54).
225 Rapallo B, NLI 13,579, [90r], page numbered 10, with insertion from [89v]. The reference to Blake is to the marginalia in *An Apology for the Bible* by R. Watson, Bishop of Llandaff (London: F. & C. Rivington, 1797); see D. V. Erdman, *The Complete Poetry and Prose of William Blake*, rev. edn. (New York: Anchor, 1988), 615. WBY had used the word "Shade" as a synonym for the *Passionate Body* in the notes to *The Dreaming of the Bones* (*VPl* 777–78, *CW2* 692–94), but the reading is uncertain.
226 *PEP* 11–33; later "Introduction to 'A Vision,'" *AVB* 8, *CW14* 7.
227 Rapallo B, NLI 13,579, [102r].
228 This cancelled sentence is replaced by a long insertion from the facing verso, which is largely the same as the closing section of the published section III.
229 Rapallo B, NLI 13,579, [91r–92r], pages numbered 1 and 2. Cf. *PEP* 12–14, and also *AVB* 8–10, *CW14* 7–8.
230 Richard Ellmann, *Yeats: The Man and the Masks*, 2nd edn. (1979; Harmondsworth: Penguin, 1987), xiv–xv; see Ann Saddlemyer, *Becoming George: The Life of Mrs W. B. Yeats* (Oxford: Oxford University Press, 2002), 102, and *ARGYV* 29–30.
231 See *VPl* 967–68, *CW2* 719–20, and *ARGYV* 32–34.
232 Rapallo B, NLI 13,579, [93r–94r], pages numbered 3 and 4; *AVB* 12–13, *CW14* 9–10.
233 Rapallo B, NLI 13,579, [96v], insertion to replace text on [97r] numbered 7. Cf. section IX (*AVB* 19, *CW14* 15). An earlier cancelled version on the same page has: "because my wife has a great distaste for spiritism in its common form, & hated being thought of as a medium, I introduced it by a piece of make believe, which could not & was not intended to deceive any body. The philosophy had been found in the Arabian desert by Michael Roberts the hero of an early story of mine. The spirits had wanted me to represent the system as my own creation but that I would not do."
234 Rapallo B, NLI 13,579, [100r–101r], pages numbered 10 and 11, insertion from [100v]. The passage contains much cancellation, but only one is transcribed to make sense of the structure.
235 *PEP* 28–29; cf. *AVB* 21–22, *CW14* 16–17.
236 See above, p. 76. The Cuala edition has almost exactly the same wording with "screen" and "lute-players" (*PEP* 29), while the transposed version in *A Vision* has "curtain" and

"flute-players" (*AVB* 215, *CW14* 158). Suzuki's version has a "brocade screen" and "flute-playing" (*Essays in Zen Buddhism*, 230).

237 Rapallo B, NLI 13,579, [102r], page numbered 12; this is the first draft of section XII in *PEP* 29–31 (*AVB* 22–23, *CW14* 17).

238 Rapallo B, NLI 13,579, [102r–101v], page numbered 12 and facing verso; cf. *PEP* 29–30; *AVB* 22–23, *CW14* 17. In a slightly later draft WBY glosses "'the guides' those greater beings whose messengers are communicating spirits" (NLI 30,319(4), page numbered 20).

239 "He said also that when a spirit is given a special mission in 'state before birth' it is compensated by having a short life after," September 5, 1921, *Yeats's "Vision" Papers*, vol. 3, 97; see also Card File R1, vol. 3, 383.

240 Rapallo B, NLI 13,579, [102v]. Cancelled text included to clarify syntax.

241 See Catherine E. Paul, "W. B. Yeats and the Problem of Belief," *YA21* (2018), 297–311.

242 Rapallo B, NLI 13,579, [102v]. See Paul, "Problem of Belief," 298, whose readings differ in a few places; see also *ARGYV* 300.

243 In the early drafts for *A Vision*, the centaur seems to be associated with the unity or wisdom of Phase 4. Phase 18 is referred to as having "a wisdom as emotional as that of the Centaur Chiron was instinctive" (*Yeats's "Vision" Papers*, vol. 4, 200). Phase 18 is in the emotional quarter, standing opposite Phase 4 in the instinctive quarter, and there is a possible reading under Phase 4 (*Yeats's "Vision" Papers*, vol. 4, 172). In the draft of his introduction to *Selections from the Poems of Dorothy Wellesley* (London: Macmillan, 1936), WBY writes of her poem "Matrix" as "the most moving philosophic poem of our time, and the most moving precisely because its wisdom bulked animal below the waist. In its abrupt lines, passion burst into thought without renouncing its dark quality" (September 8, [1935], *CL InteLex* 6335), and it seems that this combination of passion and wisdom suggests the centaur in his mind. In the typescript "Images" III, the fighting centaurs provide a contrast to Christ preaching his Sermon on the Mount (NLI 30,434); see Neil Mann, "Images: Unpublished Tableaux of Opposition," *YA8* (1992): 313–20. Elsewhere there are the "holy centaurs of the hills" (*VP* 344, *CW1* 146) in "Lines Written in Dejection" or the "Black Centaur by Edmund Dulac" stamping "my works . . . into the sultry mud" (*VP* 442, *CW1* 219), conveying a sense of wildness and freedom, as well as violence. See also Warwick Gould, "Afterword: The Centaur and the Daimon," *YA21* (2018): 312–13.

244 Rapallo B, NLI 13,579, [33v]; see above, p. 80 (n187).

245 Rapallo A, NLI 13,578, [22r], page numbered 17.

Rapallo Notebook C: *A Vision*, Poetry, and Sundry Writings

Wayne K. Chapman

1. Introduction

This essay continues on the path established by Neil Mann, recently, in *International Yeats Studies*, where his analytical digest "Rapallo Notebooks A and B" appears as the first in a series of articles to outline the contents of Yeats's several Rapallo notebooks.[1] The present article, like the first one and the two that are projected for later issues, is the product of collaborating scholarship transacted over a number of years.[2] As there are five nominal "Rapallo Notebooks," designated by letters A to E, this article is about the third notebook, "Rapallo Notebook C." Although full treatment of notebooks "D" and "E" will come later, they are also incident to discussion when relevant to Rapallo C. Generally speaking, diary entries, notes, and philosophical prose related to *A Vision* 1925 and 1937 are common to all five notebooks. Even so, poems that became part of the lyric sequences of *The Winding Stair* are distinctive in defining Yeats's principal use of notebooks C and D. Thus, the objective of the essays in this series is to guide the reader along lines of contiguity that exist in the notebooks while remaining true to the principle that manuscripts are artifacts involved in an investigative procedure. They are properties, in this case, curated by the National Library of Ireland, quoted and reproduced with the consent of its Trustees, and authorized by United Agents LLP on behalf of Caitriona Yeats and the W. B. Yeats Estate.[3]

In 1985, when I first encountered the Rapallo notebooks, my favorite book on the poet's creative process was David R. Clark's *Yeats at Songs and Choruses* (Amherst: The University of Massachusetts Press, 1983). That beautifully illustrated book sharpened the focus for me with respect to several lyrics Yeats wrote in the late 1920s for *The Winding Stair*. Moreover, Professor Clark's presence during much of my initiation that summer as an "interpretative"[4] reader of manuscripts was a startling coincidence. As an exemplar, he was a consummate craftsman, a teacher by example with great skill navigating the nebula of archival materials in Dublin at that time, and probably the most gifted paleographic authority on Yeats anywhere.[5] Thomas Parkinson and Jon Stallworthy were my next-favorite idols in this vein, being among the earliest students of Yeats's poetry to acquire experience working under Mrs. W. B. Yeats's watchful eye. Poets in their own right, they had perhaps less adroitly than Clark trawled the manuscripts in quest of Yeatsian luminous matter, secrets of the trade, or "vestiges of creation," as Parkinson aptly called it.[6] But Clark and Parkinson had won the confidence of the National Library and of Mrs. Yeats, respectively, so that, in the years 1957–1958, Clark worked with staff at the NLI to begin sorting the manuscripts of Yeats's plays, while Parkinson worked directly with George Yeats at her home to prepare the manuscripts of Yeats's "later poetry" for the gift she eventually made to the library in 1964. Appropriately, Clark went on to edit *The Plays* (*CW2*), with his daughter, Rosalind E. Clark (2001). With publication of Parkinson's *W. B. Yeats: The Later Poetry* in 1964, the NLI adapted its cataloguing system to the organization of the poetry manuscripts—from *Responsibilities* through *Last Poems* (including fragments, miscellaneous, and unpublished material)—which Parkinson had worked out with Mrs. Yeats and left with her in a typescript known as "Parkinson's list" (NLI 30,214).

This list is in two parts, the first entitled "Loose material (manuscript, typescripts)." Part II gives thumbnail listings (from "a." to "m.") of fourteen "Bound manuscript books," of which items II.g.–k. are correspondent with the five Rapallo notebooks. That segment of "Parkinson's list" is presented here, with subsequent NLI numbers and accession date italicized in brackets:

g. "Rapallo" notebook with notation "Diary" on cover. Diary of Thought begun Sept. 23, 1928 in Dublin. Contains many working versions of poems in The Winding Stair. *[Also known as "Rapallo C"; NLI 13,580 in 1964]*
h. "Rapallo" notebook. Diary begun in Rapallo, 1928. Contains many versions of poems in The Winding Stair, including "Byzantium." *[Also known as "Rapallo D"; NLI 13,581 in 1964]*
i. "Rapallo" notebook designated "A" and containing rewritten sections of A Vision. *[Also called "Rapallo A"; NLI 13,578 in 1964]*
j. "Rapallo" notebook designated "B," finished Oct. 9, 1928. Almost entirely prose. *[Also called "Rapallo B"; NLI 13,579 in 1964]*
k. "Rapallo" notebook containing ms of Resurrection, work on A Vision. *[Also known as "Rapallo E"; NLI 13,582 in 1964]*

By 1985, when I reviewed the contents of Rapallo C, NLI 13,580 (or "Parkinson's list" II.g"), I had the benefit of Clark's description in *Yeats at Songs and Choruses* (243–44) for its chapter on "Three Things":

> The manuscripts of "Three Things" may be found in [NLI] 13,580, "Rapallo notebook ('Diary') finished June or July 1929, containing Diary of Thought, Vision material, Poems (drafts, etc.) from Winding Stair and Words for Music Perhaps, including Cracked Mary (later Crazy Jane) poems".... This is a notebook bound with a greenish tan paper with a design of large and small

> spots with blue flowers with nine white petals in the large spots. The word "Diary" is in black ink in the upper right-hand corner. The book measures 30cm. x 22cm. and contains four signatures of 30cm. x 44cm. paper folded in half and sewn together at the fold. These signatures are in turn sewn together and then the paper cover glued. The binding is now quite loose and torn. The inside of each cardboard cover is covered with the same paper as the outside.

With only Clark's reference to the Stony Brook archive omitted in the ellipsis (due to later amendments), the description continues for three additional paragraphs of precise observation on missing folios, stubs, the condition of paper ("heavy but cheap pulp paper now turning yellow and brittle"), location of poetry, and the absence of lines, chains, or watermarks. On such matters, the reader is directed to the "Tabular Summary" appended to this article, because, like Rapallo notebooks B and E, Rapallo C was rebound during conservation in December 2005, somewhat altering its original construction.[7] Rapallo notebooks A and E, however, bear evidence of their relation to "Parkinson's list" in that typed slips have survived in their collation, either tipped in where they happened to lie when rebinding occurred (in February 2006 for Rapallo A), or remaining loose (as in Rapallo E). For example, a cover notice for Rapallo A was typed out by Parkinson to serve the whole notebook as a short summary of its contents. Formerly paper clipped at a prominent location, the notice is now incongruously tipped in (at folio 39r, page "2"), appearing as follows amid materials otherwise related to *A Vision*:[8]

> From
> Rapallo Notebook designated "A" (on inside and "D" on cover) and containing rewritten sections of "A Vision". (Parkinson's List II, I)
>
> Contains notes on system including comments on THE CAT AND THE MOON, Passages of THE PLAYER QUEEN, Prose entitled THE IRISH CENSORSHIP, a letter about Wagner.
>
> None of this material may be used without the express permission in writing of Mrs. W. B. Yeats, 46 Palmerston Road, Dublin, or of her executors.

Similar instances in Rapallo E (overtly relating it to "Parkinson's List II, K") will be noted in the final essay of this series. Suffice it to say here that the survival of Parkinson's typed slips, like those in Rapallo notebooks A and E, are not unknown elsewhere in the Yeats Collection—for example, in NLI 30,336, "Red loose-leaf note book containing a version of A Full Moon in March and some prose," item II.m on "Parkinson's list")—and that labeling with clipped slips almost certainly occurred in notebooks B–D, as well, in 1958, but have since been lost in handling.[9]

2. Contents Overview (September 1928–July 1929)

Although given to diverse purposes and not the only notebooks Yeats acquired in Rapallo, Italy, during the period of their use, between 1928 and 1931, the five manuscript notebooks referred to as the "Rapallo Notebooks" (NLI 13,578–13,582) share differing degrees of distinction as tools used in rewriting *A Vision* (1925). As Neil Mann has said, "it is in fact likely that Rapallo Notebooks A, B, and E were all started in 1928" to that end, "with B being the first, while E had all the early material removed."[10] Certainly, E was started before notebooks C and D if E had carried the *Vision* material indicated on its cover. Similarly, B contains drafts that predate A and declares on its cover that it was "Finished, Oct. 9, 1928." Clark notes that entries in Rapallo E show that it was in use between c. May 9, 1928, and January 22, 1929, but it has been argued, too, that its use in remaking *The Resurrection* and writing the introduction for the play in *Wheels and Butterflies* (1934) makes it the earliest and latest of the five notebooks on date of use.[11] Still, Rapallo Notebooks C and D, both significant in the making of poetry, are the most serially related to one another in that respect. Rapallo C was "begun. Sept. 23. 1928 in Dublin" (as noted in its initiating diary entry) and "Finished June or July 1929" (as noted on its cover), whereas Yeats began to use notebook D in Rapallo in March of 1928, paused for a time, and then took it up again in Dublin in August 1929 (its last dated entry being "Nov 18 1930").

Between September 23, 1928, and July 1929, Yeats's whereabouts can be traced from Dublin to Rapallo and back to Dublin in Rapallo Notebook C. In September 1928, he finished his term in the Senate and, in November, moved to Rapallo for the winter, remaining there until early May 1929 (save for a visit to Rome in January), thereafter returning to Dublin by way of London. During those six months, he sent accounts periodically to Olivia Shakespear and Lady Gregory on his progress writing. In settling into the flat at Via Americhe 12/8, Rapallo, Italy, he wrote, on November 23, 1928: "I write each morning and am well….I am finishing a little book for Cuala to be called either *A Packet* or *A Packet for Ezra Pound*."[12] By March 1929, he had just begun to think of a series of poems to be called *Twelve poems for music*, but their number soon increased to the point whereby, on April 10, 1929, he was able to boast that "[s]ince I came here I have written 14 [lyrics] besides some little scraps of satirical verse," and "[t]his has all been in three months I think—for at first I wrote prose."[13] Nearing his departure from Rapallo, he reported, on April 26, 1929: "I am well and more cheerful than I have been for years—[and] have written 19 lyrics for the numbers keep on mounting."[14] Once back in Dublin, on May 19, 1929, he was relieved to find there "life sufficiently tranquil" and pledged "that it may continue so I shall keep away from politicians."[15]

There is a story in Rapallo C better told, I think, by addressing first its prose and then its poetry. Initially, this procedure mirrors the way Yeats began by writing prose into it as in a "Diary" (noted on the front cover) and then, for the better part of three months, wrote nothing but poetry in an apparent frenzy. That shift to poetry-writing involved a slight transition in the notebook before it became sustained, yet it failed to last to the very end of the notebook, where his latest entries in prose return to speculations (as in a "Diary of Thought") on the fundamentals of *A Vision*. The prose, in other words, *frames* the story and is first to speak of Yeats's intentional use of the notebook. The burst of poetry, surprisingly sustained once it began, had not been anticipated; and there was literally no room for a second burst, when that eventually came, except in another notebook, Rapallo Notebook D.

Before describing in detail the contents of Rapallo C below (in parts 4 and 5), the following list is provided as a scratch outline of the notebook's prose frame, with locations cited by folio (recto and verso) to assist the conceptualization of content in spatial terms. "Diary of Thought" begins with three numbered entries, dated "Sept 23. 1928" (1r–2r), on Kevin O'Higgins's last words, the idea of "national mind," and a French quotation copied from Pound, followed by dates of past significance regarding the development of the automatic script and an anecdote on Italian pictures and British propaganda. (2v is left blank.) Then revisions are drafted in paragraph blocks for insertion into *AVA* copy for *AVB*, dated "Jan 1929" (3r–5r). Also dated "Jan 1929," the draft of an essay on Ezra Pound and skepticism occupies the next six pages (5v–8r, with 8v left blank). The prose subject for a "Lyric sequence" is introduced (on 9r), prior to two pages of verse (9v–10r) and a blank page (10v; see next paragraph). This is followed by the continuation of prose inserts (on 11r–11v, like those on 3r–5r) for "End of Cuala book" (i.e., *A Packet for Ezra Pound* [1929]) and a footnote on Spengler to be added to a typescript on the "Great Wheel." Thereafter, until folio 59v, the central core of Rapallo Notebook C (12r–59r) is entirely devoted to poetry. Folios 59v–69v are filled with notes and speculations about the rudiments of *A Vision* as informed by such Instructors as Dionertes and by readings in the aesthetics of Benedetto Croce and others. After that, up to eight leaves (70r–77v) have been removed and possibly discarded from the notebook. The concluding portion of the prose frame (59v–69v) was written after Yeats returned from Rapallo, as indicated by the dates "May 26 [1929]" (on 61r) and "June [1929]" (on 67v).

To outline the body of poetry-writing in Rapallo C, even a thumbnail sketch of it, is complicated because of the crisscrossing of draft material from leaf 12 through 59, but also including the transitional subject of three poems ("At Algeciras—A Meditation on Death," "Mohini Chatterjee," and "Nineteenth Century and After") found at 9r. The poetic core of Rapallo C may be defined by the following inventory, where titles are listed only once and parenthetically accompanied by their folio location as ranging from recto to verso: "Meditations upon Death" (9r, 10r, 12r, 13r, 14r–15r); "Nineteenth Century and After" (9v, 25r); "Mad as the Mist and Snow" (13v, 14r, 16r); "Crazy Jane on the King" (unpub.; 16v–20r, 23v–24v); "Three Things" (20v–23r); "Crazy Jane Grown Old Looks at the Dancers" (25v–28r); "Those Dancing Days Are Gone" (28v–30r, 31r–31v); "Lullaby" (32r–35r, 36r–36v); "Wisdom & Knowledge" (unpub.; 35v); "Crazy Jane & the Bishop" (36v–37r, 39r); "Crazy Jane Reproved" (37v–38r); "Mrs. Phillamore" (unpub.; 38r, 43v); "The Scholars" (rev.; 38v); "Girl's Song" (39v–40r, 41r); "Young Man's Song" (41v–44r, 45r); "Love's Loneliness" (44v, 50v, 55v–56v); "His Confidence" (45v–47r, 48r); "Her Anxiety" (47v); "Her Dream" (48v–49r, 50r, 51r); "Symbols" (49v, 51r); "[Heavy the Bog]" (unpub.; 51v–52r); "His Bargain" (51v–55r); "The Two Trees" (rev.; 55r); and "[Imagination's Bride]" (unpub.; 56v–59r, first titled "The Daimon & the Celestial Body" [at 57v] and then "The Passionate & Celestial Body" [at 58r]).

3. Transcription Protocol and Key to Abbreviations

Transcriptions are meant to preserve the idiosyncrasies of Yeats's spelling, punctuation, and revising as much as possible. The whole word is given when that seems intended, even though letters are missing or elided with a stroke, as often with the "-ing" ending. When a precise spelling is unclear, a standard one may be substituted. A word will be left incomplete if Yeats seems to have abandoned it that way. Illegible words are represented thus: [?]. A conjectural reading thus: [?word]. And partly conjectural readings thus: every[?thing]. Yeats's scribal additions are indicated within angle brackets < > whereas mine are given in editorial square brackets [ ]. Yeats's underlinings are retained as are his strikeouts, which are everywhere indicated with a line through the deleted word, parts of words, parts of lines, whole lines, or sentences, as the case may be. Except in literatim transcriptions presented as block quotations, commentary follows the convention of punctuated matter entered in quotation marks (""). Hence, embedded quotation is indicated by a set of single inverted commas (''), according to American convention; and end-stop punctuation such as periods will occur within close quotation marks except in instances where end punctuation is lacking in Yeats's writing. As a rule, use of the slash mark (/), or virgule, follows *The Chicago Manual of Style* (17th ed., section 6.111). However, vertical line marks (|) are used to represent instances of accidental line breaks within texts.

Aside from secondary sources introduced above and in notes thus far, several studies are cited frequently enough in the remaining sections of this essay—either on the dating of poems or for the drafts they present from Rapallo C—that for economy they are identified in the following list of abbreviations:

"CCP" Wayne K. Chapman, "Appendix A: A Chronology of the Composition of the Poems," *YPM* 229–45 (also *YA* 15 [2002]: 138–58).

"CNGI" David R. Clark, "Yeats: Cast-offs, Non-starters and Gnomic Illegibilities," *YAACTS* 17 (1999; pub. 2003): 1–18.

Genet Jacqueline Genet, *William Butler Yeats: Les fondements et l'evolution de la creation poetique* (Villeneuve-d'Ascq, FR: Universite de Lille III, 1976).

WFMP W. B. Yeats, *Words for Music Perhaps and Other Poems: Manuscript Materials*, ed. David R. Clark (Ithaca and London: Cornell University Press, 1999).

Other acronyms are used as directed in the "List of Abbreviations" posted on this journal's website[16] or as introduced in the endnotes of this essay. Abbreviations cited here are mainly used in part 5, on the poetry.

4. Diary Entries, Notes, and Prose Fragments (in Detail)

[Covers][17]

In caps, black ink, and superimposed upon the patterned front cover, the inscription: "DIARY" (in right-hand corner as defined by all entries up to leaf 78 and the exceptional back cover). Likewise, on the patterned back cover (and at the top as defined by the upside-down positioning of the entries on 78r and 78v) is superimposed the inscription in ink: "Finished June or July 1929." The exceptional entries seem to have been made at a later date and partly in error as an effort was made but soon abandoned in listing the notebook's contents as had been introduced at the beginning of Rapallo Notebooks A and B.[18] Therefore, to approach Rapallo C from the back, one first encounters the rough completion date, next the inscription "Diary" (written twice, on 78v, the one over the other to make the title more prominent), and then, as in a book (on 78r), the words: "Contents | ~~Introduction to Great Wheel. page 13 (detach from rest)~~ | Soul in Judgement (continued from loose leaf book | 12 pages." (See 3v and 59v–69v accounts, below.)

[1r–2v] "~~Contents~~ || Diary of Thought | began. Sept 23. 1928 | in Dublin"

Yeats's first three entries, or "thoughts," are numbered, the first one reflecting his political life in Dublin on this date, or literally the day before the entry, when he had been told by the widow of Ireland's assassinated minister of justice Kevin O'Higgins (1892–1927) what his last words were on being carried into his house to die: "'my beautiful home' & | later 'my dear, I did try to save myself I could not | help it.'" Yeats later praised his friend in "The Municipal Gallery Revisited" and "Parnell's Funeral" but here wonders about O'Higgins's motive behind the words: "[He] must <have> felt that he was deserting her & that | he had tried to excuse himself."

In entry "(2)," to fill most of first page, Yeats recalls a conversation with "Someone," perhaps an American, about the "small intellectual production of some great nation" likened to the tone and volume of John King,[19] a manifestation in séances of the buccaneer Henry Morgan "with deep muscular voice." If voice is great, "[p]erhaps the national mind at each epoch is limited also to a few types" "dramatized most easily by voice alone" since "those capable of vigorous expression must be but few." To bring an abstruse thought to its conclusion, Yeats reasons that, "Probably[,] when an epoch gives us a sense of it[s] greatest possible intellectual power each dramatization has expressed itself through a single mind, & so retained its fullness & unity."

On leaf 2r, copied as entry "3," is a French passage quoted "on Ezra's authority" for the "new Vision — ~~pa[rt]~~ book 1." The quotation is from one of two volumes of Etienne Gilson's *Philosophie au Moyen Age* (Paris, 1922), yet almost certainly Yeats's source was Ezra Pound's essay "Medievalism and Modernism (Guido Cavalcanti)" in *The Dial* LXXXIV.3 (March 1928), only later retitled "Medievalism" for reprinting in *Guido Cavalcanti Rime* (1932), *Make It New* (1934), and *Literary Essays* (1954).[20] The quotation is an abridgement, defective in spelling, on "~~Grosseteste's~~ Grossetestes idea on light": "Cette substance extrêmement ténue est aussi l'étoffe dont toutes choses sont faites; elle est la premiere forme corporelle et ce que certains nomment la corporéalé." (That last word should be "corporéité.") Gilson's French came to be paraphrased in Yeats's English of *A Vision B*, Book II (191n): "Grosseteste, Bishop of Lincoln, described Light as corporeality itself, and thought that in conjunction with the first matter, it engendered all bodies" (*AVB* 191n; *CW14* 140n).

The remaining two entries on 2r are unnumbered although a short line has been drawn between them. The first is a cluster of notes on significant dates in the development of the System, ranging from "Script began Oct 24, 1917" to "March <23> 1920 first sleep." Between those events, in heavily revised notation, Yeats observes that, from mid-November 1917 to December 6 ("when first cone is drawn") "& through much of 1918," the spirit guides ("they," including the Yeatses) focused on "exposition [of] great wheel" and "life after death &

the Four Principles." Much is cancelled, except for the following after the date of Mrs. Yeats's "first sleep" in 1920: "& from June 3 to June 7 the Christian Era with | Spenglerian dates, & then back to life after death." On the otherwise blank facing page (1v), these notes are appended with the sentence: "Anne came Feb 3 1918." This is not Anne Butler Yeats, but Anne Hyde, late Countess of Ossory, a spirit much discussed in the "Sleep and Dream Notebooks" after communicating her desire to reincarnate a dead son from the seventeenth century.[21] Generally, the dates on 2r correlate with those in the earliest account of the System's origin, which Yeats drafted in Rapallo Notebook B (91r–92r) for *A Packet for Ezra Pound* (1929). That first draft is transcribed in Mann's essay "Rapallo Notebooks A and B" (95–96 below; also *IYS* 6.1 137–38).

The final "Thought" on this page returns to national politics before Yeats's departure for Italy in late November 1928:

> I have just heard the following of the Lord Chief Justice [Hugh Edward Kennedy]. He said to Bodkin | —Bodkin tells me. "I don't think we should put any more of those Italian | pictures into the gallery. I think that is all British Propaganda. & | Gaelic Ireland has no afinities [*sic*] with those Mediteranean [*sic*] nations."

Yeats's source for this anecdote is his friend Thomas Bodkin, son of jurist Matthias McDonnell Bodkin and director (later governor) of the National Gallery of Ireland. Soon, Thomas Bodkin became the author of *Hugh Lane and His Pictures* (1932, 1934), and he was one of few correspondents to receive word from Yeats to confirm both his arrival in Rapallo and his renunciation of political office: "I have ceased to be a Senator" (*L* 749, WBY to TB dated "Dec 20 [1928]" from Via Americhe 12-8, Rapallo). Thought "(2)" on leaf 1r (see above) and this concluding anecdote of 2r, conveyed by Bodkin, are vaguely related to one another on the idea of "national mind." Yeats came to own both editions of Bodkin's book.[22]

At this point, leaf 2v has been left blank, partly to mark a departure from diary entries to a series of prose drafts that follow from that opening, and partly because this page was not used to revise text for leaf 3r in the notebook.

[3r–3v] "Book II. Correction[s]" [to be introduced into *A Vision A* text]

Yeats's heading is misleading here as no correction actually applies to Book II in *AVA* (121–76). His first instruction is to "Delete all up to end of first paragraph on page 17" (i.e., to the word "quality") in Book I and then to make the following changes "at opening of paragraph 3": in "Between Phase 12 and Phase 13," numbers "11" and "12" were to be substituted; thereafter, "at" was to substitute for "between" for the rest of the paragraph. Also on page 17 of *AVA*, he directed that paragraph 4 (on "The geometrical reasons" in *AVA*) was to be deleted and replaced by the following, in parentheses:

> (~~The opening & closing of the Tincture has have been~~ I have never been | given a di[a]gram of the opening & closing of the tinctures. It must ~~I think~~ | have represented the Antithe[tical] half [...] of the Great Wheel one separate | double cone, with ~~the~~ <its> phase 8 [...] at the opening & its phase 22 at the closing of the | Tinctures. That one tincture opens [...] & closes before the other | would be represente[d] on the diagram by the ~~fall of the~~ place of the | gyre, which would pass through phase 12—say—& then through phase 12 | but I have not the details. The Primary half ~~of~~ would be anoth[er] double | vortex, at phase 22 <of this vortex>, ~~at between phases at the~~ The closing, ~~it~~ <at> its phase | 8 ~~its~~ <the> opening ~~The [?dividing] of the [?two] tinctures into four preceeds | the Marriage of Husk & Passionate Body, & the [?]~~ | Jan. 192[9])[23]

Another Book I correction is made to "Delete the whole of Section XI" ("The Daimon, the Sexes, Unity of Being, Natural and Supernatural Unity," *AVA* 26–30), followed, on another line, by instructions to introduce "Foot note to 'Then the * last gyre'" at "Page 218" in Book III, though Yeats means page 213 at line 10 ("Then with the last gyre"), as Laurie's heavy type makes a "3" look like "8." The note Yeats wanted to insert there is another roughly constructed approximation, but one reflecting recent encounters with contemporary work by Wyndham Lewis:

> ~~If I have~~ It is easier now than when I wrote to forget what forms the gyre will | take. Mr Wyndam Lewis in the ~~enemy[=essay]~~ <"Art of Being Ruled"> ~~he~~ in "Time & the Western Man["] | has studied ~~various forms of~~ [?antecedent] ~~personality~~ <sexuality>, ~~& found emotion~~ <constructed simplicity, & simulated childhood> in art | & life, which are phase 26, & in those admirable first hundred pages | of his "Children Mass" groups all <these> ~~those [?articent] personalities or [?forced] emotions~~ | round his crook backed bailiff, the phase complete meaning & symbol alike. ~~The gyre is not yet due but its fore-runners are~~. | Jan 1929. | P.T.O. [that is, "Please Turn Over" to the next insertion for *AVA*, written on 3v]

This footnote was intended for section IV ("A.D. 1050 to the Present Day") of *AVA* Book III ("Dove or Swan"), but, eventually, by the time Book III became Book V in *AVB*, Yeats had cropped the last five pages, abruptly ending "Dove or Swan" just short of material that had been there on Wyndham Lewis, Brancusi, and other contemporaries. A reference to *Time and Western Man* survives in a footnote in *AVB* 4 only because of its position in *A Packet for Ezra Pound*. Yeats's reading acquaintance with Lewis by January 1929 obviously included

Time and Western Man (1927; *WBGYL* 1136) and *The Childermass* (1928; *WBGYL* 1129), copies significantly annotated by Yeats or bearing an enclosure from Lewis.[24]

Continuing in this vein to leaf 3v, another short amendment for *A Vision* is penned beneath the heading: "Page 180 | Foote note [to] 'The Great Wheel & * history.'" The designated location in *AVA*, at the beginning of Book III, "Dove or Swan," shows that Yeats thought a simple headnote might be linked to the last word of the subtitle "2. THE GREAT WHEEL AND HISTORY." This would acknowledge similarities to his own work that he found when he read Spengler's two-volume opus *The Decline of the West* (1926–1929; *WBGYL* 1989 and 1989A), much-studied in Yeats's personal library.[25] The tone of the note suggests that Yeats was reticent about making the acknowledgment:

> * I ~~send these pages out &~~ cannot turn these pages without | these pages without [*sic*] ~~the sense of shame~~ <alarm> [....] The learned Spengler has | committed many errors, | I have been told ~~in the expo~~ in his historical exposition of | his analogous theory; & I have no learning at all[....] | If I know little of a man or | period I must use that little. I do not offer proof but the only <possible> illustration & explanation of what others must prove or | dispro[ve]. <I could amend much> Even ~~by ex~~ as explanation & illustration—now that | [I] know the system better—~~more than I have written~~ but if I do not leave | all as it was in Feb 1925 I shall seem Spengler['s] plagiarist[.]

Compare this with treatment of Spengler in *A Packet for Ezra Pound* (as borne into *AVB* 11 and 18; also *CW14* 9 and 4). Pound might well have been one source of reticence in his disparagement of Spengler's insufficient knowledge and "rubber-bag categories," as Pound called it in his essay "How to Read," first published in the *New York Herald Tribune* in 1929.[26]

[4r–5r] [A passage on "Husk & Passionate Body" for *A Vision B*]

On these pages, Yeats takes up matter beyond the 1925 edition, largely destined for "The Soul in Judgment," Book III, in 1937. The way in which *Husk* and *Passionate Body* "affect one another," or are combined in a "Marriage" of perception in which "desire & the object of desire are indistinguishable," is subject to *Will* and described with some difficulty here. Fraught with false starts and cancellations, it does seem to enlarge upon the brief suggestion in *AVA* Book II that, in man's experience after death, "if *Husk* and *Passionate Body* be sublimated and transformed—he may enter through *Spirit* and *Celestial Body* into the nature of both" (160; *CW13* 130). These three pages are the last that Yeats devotes to the subject (4v being a thorough rewriting of 5r) until he picks up the thread again with the series of notes that begin on 59v and continue with speculations to the end of Rapallo C. Perhaps anticipating the breakthrough we witness on poetry-making, beginning on 9r, Yeats draws analogy here between the "Marriage of Husk & Passionate Body," as indistinguishable merger of desire and its object, and, roughly, the last verse of his poem "Among School Children": "how shall we know the dancer from the dance" (4r).

On 5r, he struggles with the first sentence, reducing it (in four lines) to a fragment: "The Husk [...] makes perception, medieval 'matter,' makes all concrete particular [?multitudinous] & living (quote Swift),[27] whereas the Spirit is ~~an abstract and empty form~~." Remaining text on this page is then cancelled, sixteen lines on the Marriage of *Spirit* and *Celestial Body*, or (as his "instructors have called" the latter) "'a cloak lent to the Spirit,'" but thereafter succeeded by a second draft from the top of the facing page (4v). This revision begins by completing the sentence fragment from 5r, line 4, as follows: "is abstract empty unity. It cannot act [and] would change the Celestial Body ~~to the Passionate~~ to the object of desire" etc. The writing becomes more confident describing movements "in opposite directions" within familiar geometry. Anticipating diagrams ahead, yet to be drawn, the entry ends paradoxically: "It will be seen | however when I study these diagram[s] that[,] though Husk & Passionate Body | Spirit & Celestial Body prevail in turn, [...] the conquered pair remains, though to do the conquerers' will, [...] & that we can separate neither from the Faculties. Unity of Being which | alone stops the whirl is the harmony of all."

[5v–8r] [A short theme on Ezra Pound's skepticism, January 1929]

Sufficient ambiguity exists in accounts that Yeats made to Olivia Shakespear and Lady Gregory (on November 23 and 27, 1928) to allow that the "entry" (as Ellmann calls it),[28] begun on 6r, might have been intended to be more than a note, perhaps even one of the articulated units that constitute *A Packet*. In the letter to Shakespear, Yeats described a book that "shall wind up with a description of Ezra feeding the cats ('some of them are so ungrateful' T. S. Eliot says)," and then discussed Pound's poetry (*L* 748; *CL InteLex* 5191). In the essay "Rapallo" (dated "March and October 1928" in *A Packet* and *A Vision*), Ezra and the cats are featured in part III, with discussion of poetry thereafter in section VI, which resembles in certain respects features of Yeats's argument in Rapallo Notebook C, 5v–8r. Eliot makes an appearance there, too (on 6r and 8r), although part VI in *A Packet*—together with Yeats's "Meditations upon Death" I and II (dated February 4 and 9, 1929)—came to be deleted, much later, in setting copy he prepared for *A Vision* 1937.[29] Hence, similarities between this draft and "Rapallo" part VI strongly suggest an affinity in content as well as chronology. If the former was not a rehearsal, it is a proximate, discarded theme with a very similar textual topography to that of the eventually deleted section of *A Packet*.

The entry begins with the date "Jan 1929" and is succeeded, on 9r, by the poem's prose subject (labeled "Lyric Sequence" and dated "Jan 23"). Thereafter, on 10r, appears the first draft of "Meditations upon Death" (dated "Feb 4. 1929"). Catherine Paul sees a connection between the opening sentence of the "Introduction to the Great Wheel" XV—"Some will ask if I believe all that this book contains" (*A Packet* 32; cf. *AVB* 24; *CW14* 19)—and the first sentence of Rapallo C, 6r, which she takes to be "an exploration of the question of belief, generated, it seems, by a conversation with Pound, as Pound's own thinking is frequently laid out as something with which Yeats agrees or disagrees."[30] She seems to be right about that and finishes her summary concisely: "Yeats," she says, "goes on to disagree with Pound's understanding. Here he also considers what Pound means by 'belief,' and uses Pound's definition to examine how he himself understands that word—taking up the word again in the final section of 'The Introduction.'"[31] In Neil Mann's treatment, the essay "Rapallo" (originally entitled "Rapallo in Spring") consists of leaves 2r–6r in Rapallo Notebook B, and in relation to parts I–V only, confirming my belief that part VI came to be written after that, at this point in Rapallo C. *A Packet for Ezra Pound* was published in August 1929, after Yeats had returned to Dublin from Italy. He had written in January to Oliver Gogarty to report finishing the book ("re-written and corrected") and acknowledged to Lady Gregory great fatigue after laboring over proof sheets in late March 1929.[32] In the interval defined by those dates, then, the last section of the essay "Rapallo" must have been rewritten, typed, and amended in proof without leaving a trace in the archive.

The partial transcription here accepts much of the wording in Ellmann's presentation (*IY* 239–40). The composition is in three paragraphs, with verso pages left for revisions or additions to be inserted into the pages on their right—Yeats's ordinary procedure when writing prose. "Ezra Pound," it begins, "bases his […] scept[ic]ism upon the statement, that we know nothing but sequences."[33] "'If I touch the button the ~~light will shine~~ lamp will light up—all our knowledge is like that.' But this statement […] is not true of […] [insert from 5v:] any philosophy, which holds the universe [is] but a sequence in the mind." After cancelling several lines, 6r continues with a quotation from "some Asian ~~[?]~~," "some Church father," who has said: "I know god as he is known to himself." In this respect, the Church Father "had […] like Ezras transcendent object of thought […] [insert from 5v:] though his arose ~~from self~~ <out of> self-surrender, Ezras ~~from~~ out of search [back to 6r:] for complete [?undisturbed] self possession." Eliot and Wordsworth are brought in, as they are in "Rapallo" VI, as well as Lewis and Blake: "In Elliot, & perhaps in Lewis[,] bred in the same […] scepticism this is a tendency <to exchange search for sub-mission> ~~one mystery, one transcendence for the other~~. Blake […] denounced both the nature & the god <considered> ~~conceived of as~~ external like nature […] as mystery; ~~& yet~~ he was enraged with Wordsworth for passing Jehovah 'unafraid.'" (Yeats amends this sentence, on 5v, by inserting the clause "not because ~~he he appeared in~~ <Jehovah is> Mystery but because the passage from potential to actual man can only come in terror"—in place of cancelled lines on Joban terror "before the incomprehensible" on 6r.) The paragraph concludes with a Blakean trope ("I have been always a ~~worm~~ <insect> in the roots of the grass"), a metaphor turned to self-effacing effect: "~~perhaps~~ my form of it perhaps."

The second paragraph of the theme begins with a concession that extends in friendship the humor of the first, although words begin to fail:

> I agree with Ezra in his dislike of the word beleif [*sic*]. | Beleif implies an unknown object, a covenant ~~perhaps signed with my blood~~ | attested with a name or signed with my <with> blood. ~~If I am all~~ | ~~[?that] I affirm that such & such is so my proof is~~ | [continuing to the top of 7r:] ~~my exposition, & the more the exposition [...] | expounds my own nature the more certain it is. Mathematics | & such has and [?] so much more~~ <and being more> moral than intellectual | that it may pride it self on ~~lack~~ <lack> of proof.

The writing on 7r seems not to have come with ease. On the notion of making "the more complete proof" while acknowledging limits and the necessity to "kill scepticism in myself," Yeats evidently jotted "~~When Copernicus [?re]~~" (on facing page 6v) but abandoned it. Turning to "my style," the second paragraph's reflection on the revision of poetry advances haltingly: "~~Sometimes of recent years~~ I have felt ~~wh~~ <when> ~~rewriting~~ <re-writing> some early poem—'The Sorrow of Love' for instance—that by assuming a self of past years, ~~a self~~ as remote from <that of today> ~~that which I now am~~ as some dramatic creation, <I ~~found~~ touched> a stronger passion a greater confidence." No less labored are the last ten lines of the paragraph, where Pound is compared, as in "Rapallo" VI, because he "re-creates Propertius or some Chinese poet" and "escapes his scepticism." But words again falter. To simplify after Ellmann's example, we hear Yeats confess that he "must, though [the] world shriek at me, admit no act beyond my power, nor thing beyond my knowledge, yet because my divinity is far off I blanch and tremble" (*IY* 240).

The third paragraph on skepticism begins at the top of leaf 8r, where Eliot and Pound exemplify the contemporary projection of modern man in lyric poetry. The strategy of concession seems more like agreement at first: "<~~Even~~> ~~We like,~~ <We even more than> Elliot require tradition & though ~~[?ours]~~ it may include much that is his, it is not a <beleif in> submission or ~~a beleif~~, but exposition & [?intellectual] meads [= ?needs]."[34] But for himself, Yeats continues: "I recall a passage in some Hermetic writer on the increased power that a god finds on getting into a ~~stattue~~ <statue>. I feel as neither Elliot nor Ezra do[,] the need of old ~~forme~~ <forms>, […] old situations that, as when I re-write some early poems of my own, ~~an~~ <I may> escape from scepticism." Considering "years past," when seized by "the first vague impulse" to write verse with "the quality of a ballad," he cites "The Tower," a poem of 1925–1926, imagining himself "in some small sea side inn," awaiting "the hour to embark upon some eighteenth or seventeenth century merchant ship." The words begin to cloud. Is it a "Song" that he read or "A scene" that he "read of" as "a boy"—one or the other (or both) "that returns the ~~simpler~~ <simpler rhythms and> ~~forms of~~ emotions <~~& of rhythms~~>"?[35] Sensing that he might be overstating a premise (that "~~The Modern Man of contemporary poetry is an illusion~~"), four vigorously cancelled lines are amended on the facing page (7v), producing a conciliatory clause to attach to the preceding sentence—that is, "nor do I think that I differ from others ~~for this~~ except in so far as my preoccupation with poetry ~~inspired~~ makes me different." The remainder of the paragraph on 8r (and the entry as a whole) summons a picture at best only suggested at the outset (on 6r): that of friends arguing the question of belief at an outdoor table in Rapallo,[36] sometime in January 1929. Figure 2.1 shows that Yeats gives some effort to confer charm with sympathy for both the café scene and, implicitly, one particular opponent.

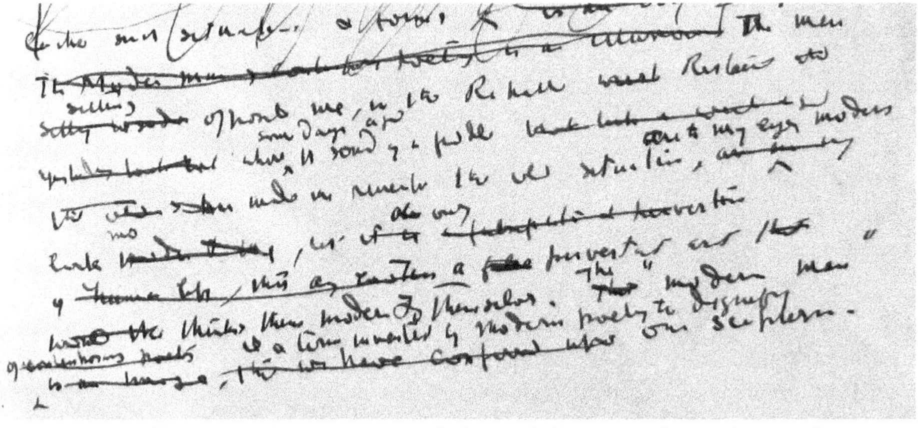

Figure 2.1. Rapallo Notebook C, NLI 13,580, [8r], detail. Courtesy of NLI; photograph courtesy of Catherine E. Paul.

As we see, the scene is depicted in dramatic present tense although belabored with revisions:

> The men | ~~sitting beside~~ <sitting> opposite me, in the Rapallo ~~wrest~~ Restaurant ~~which~~ | ~~yesterday look[ed] [?evil]~~ where <some days ago> the sound of a fiddle ~~brou[g]ht back a worl[d] &~~ such | ~~that older I hear~~ made me remember the old situation, <are to my eyes modern> ~~are in my~~ | book <mo[dern]> ~~modern to me~~, but ~~it is~~ <also only> ~~a falsification & pervertion~~ | ~~of human life, that any emotion~~ a ~~false~~ perverted art ~~that~~ | ~~would th~~ thinks them modern

> to themselves. ~~That~~ <The> "Modern Man" | <~~of contemporary poetry~~> ~~is an image, that we have conferred upon~~ <is a term invented by modern poetry to dignify> our scepticism.[37]

[8v–10v] "Jan 23" [A prose outline for a "Lyric Sequence" and first-draft versions of two poems]

The poems are "The Nineteenth Century and After" (untitled and undated) and "Meditations upon Death" (dated "Feb 4. 1929"). Leaves 8v and 10v are blank because the writing occurs between the discrete units of prose, above and below it, intended for *A Packet for Ezra Pound*. For details on this first departure into poetry writing from Rapallo C's purpose as a "Diary of Thought," see section 5 (below).

[11r] "End of Cuala book" [for *A Packet for Ezra Pound*]

This entry follows the precedent of short addenda prepared for *A Vision* (as on 3r–3v and 11v). Yet the heading indicates a "Cuala book," which might indicate either *October Blast: Poems* (1927) or the work in progress, *A Packet for Ezra Pound*. The postscript inscription ("PS."), beneath the heading, directs that the note was to be inserted (plausibly as a note on "From Oedipus at Colonus") in the former or be added as a footnote or afterword at the end of *A Packet*. Either location makes sense. However, this short piece of scholarship on Oedipus found its place in the latter (*A Packet* 36n) and subsequently enhanced in *A Vision B* (*AVB* 28n; *CW14* 21a). Yeats seems to have made use of the material in a radio broadcast for BBC Belfast (September 8, 1931), "Oedipus the King," but does not recall there Raftery and Oedipus as an outcast, wandering "from road to road, a blind old man"; instead, he concludes the broadcast with a recitation of the eponymous poem in its entirety (*CW10* 221–22).[38]

[11v] "Foot note to Book I of Great Wheel page 21"

Here, Yeats picks up a strategy executed earlier, on 3v, regarding similarities between *A Vision* and Oswald Spengler's *The Decline of the West*, except reference to Book I of "The Great Wheel" is misleading because "page 21" is not a cue to *A Vision A* but, as a parenthetical note stipulates, to "Type script in orange envelope." If extant, the typescript's location is a mystery. However, the content of the entry on 11v suggests affinity with Grosseteste's "idea on light" copied on 2r from Pound's 1928 essay in *The Dial*. The proposed footnote, streamlined by the omission of its accidentals and few cancellations, is as follows:

> * Spengler considers perception or light as spatial and the dark—our Spirit and Celestial Body—as Time because he finds there all that is sensual or rhythmical; and this makes his attribution something that [?resembles] mine;

> even our meaning is the same. His system is related to Bergson[']s, very much as that of Karl Marx (which it reverses) is [related] to Hegel['s], and he [Spengler] thinks of all beyond "the light world" as imperceptible, or as he puts it: the world has no meaning outside the great cultures.

To compare this note with Yeats's eventual discussion of Spengler and Marx (sans Bergson and Hegel) in *A Vision B* (261; *CW14* 191) is to mark how far, by 1937, overt treatment of Spengler shifted from Book I, "The Great Wheel," to Book IV, "The Great Year of the Ancients." In the vicinity of that later passage, coincidentally, there is a footnote (hung from an asterisk) that weighs in Yeats's favor the authority of his "instructors" against "Spengler's vast speculation" (*AVB* 259, *CW14* 189).

[12r–59r] [Lyrics mostly for *Words for Music Perhaps,* February–April 1929, Rapallo]

See section 5, below, "Poetry Writings (in Detail)."

[59v–69v] [Thoughts and notes for *A Vision B*, May–June 1929, Dublin]

Apart from the first three notes, on matters at issue in the poem "[Imagination's Bride]" (56v–59r)—or "The Daimon & the Celestial Body" and "The Passionate & Celestial Body" in the working title—the remaining prose entries in Rapallo Notebook C were certainly written after Yeats's departure from Rapallo (on April 27, 1929), his arrival in London (on April 29), and the week he lodged at the Savile Club to look up friends (Olivia Shakespear, Wyndham Lewis, and others) and to catch a meeting of "my 'Ghosts Club'" at Pagani's Restaurant.[39] Entry number "4" (of eight) in this section is dated "May 26" (on 61r) and the last date inscribed in the notebook (on 67v) is simply given as "June." Notably, by mid-May, the occult papers and philosophical books of Yeats's library would have been available to him once more; and he seems to have consulted both types of authority while writing many of these entries. At first, up to May 26, they are written with confidence and with surprisingly few cancellations or rephrasings. After that, they seem increasingly tentative, hypothetical, and dependent upon references to external authorities such as the spirit Dionertes and poets and philosophers such as Paul Valéry and Benedetto Croce from any number of texts. Streamed from verso to recto pages without reserving versos for improvements, the remaining effort in the notebook may be viewed as a kind of prewriting or informal rehearsal for a body of new writing destined for *A Vision B*. Given the limited number of pages left in Rapallo C, entries here are listed by headings "Note. (1)," "(2)," "(3)," "(4)," "(5)," "(6)," "7," and "8," until the progression of topics breaks down into a loosely related potpourri of ideas that one finds after 65r, reflecting Yeats's heterodox reading and ongoing activities as a creative mystic.

On leaves 59v–60r, "Note. (1)" begins with a retrospective: "When automatic script began, a spirit ~~spoke of~~ <said> the 'Funnell' contained 'no images.' But at that stage in the exposition there was only one after death cone [....] We have now the ~~narrowing~~ cones of P B [i.e., *Passionate Body*] & Husk." Like much in the remaining pages on the topic of afterdeath phenomena, this note seems to anticipate matters taken up in Book III, "The Soul in Judgment." "Death is the separation of the Spirit from the particular stream of images—a personality— [...] as in a dance except that this action is not Aesthetic [...] —it is as it were somnambulistic." The *Spirit* experiences a "coherent somnambulism" distinctive from living sleep, since "we seek in dreams experiences of pleasure & pain" whereas *Spirit* only experiences those things while it "remains united to the Husk." This thought leads to the question at the end of the note: "Is it perhaps that the Husk depended upon the body?"

Paradoxically, in note "(2)," "Husk is light," which "seeks it self," and "Spirit is consciousness—attention," which also "seeks itself." However, "[i]n the end there is only light, only consciousness" (60r).

Note "(3)" is longer and continues in this vein for more than two pages (60r–61r): "After death the Spirits act in common but not all in common. They are drawn—I will not say with Swedenborg [—] by their ruling love—but by their ruling fate, or ruling truth, into communities." They are the satisfaction that "we seek through thought & sense & do not find. 'I stand by you' Etc."" (60r). This leads to thinking about the relationship between *Spirits* and the living in a new paragraph on 60v: "Identical with the ends of human endevour[,] they are ceaselessly present to the human mind, but they know nothing of that mind except in so far as that mind [?realizes] ~~that~~ <those> end[s]." They "are always in the future here," yet in our sleep "they can use our faculties [to] create temporary personalities" and "may retain ~~knowledge~~ their identity with our ends & yet recover knowledge of time & space." In such cases, the "conscious effect" of *Spirits* is "abnormal & rare," for "it must be considered as a development from the Normall sub-conscious influence." As if to sum up, a paragraph of one sentence follows, shifting simultaneously from plural to a singular count-noun and defining *Spirit* by process: "Spirit is only ~~Future~~ future during the activation of Husk & P B, ~~for it is~~ for only then is it contrasted with past & present." Thereafter, in a new paragraph on 61r, testimony is cited from the automatic scripts: "A spirit spoke of the forms of art as 'correspondential' to the states of the dead." Therefore, "the scenery of the other world changes as spiritual states change." Accordingly, note "(3)" concludes: "A universal [...] must be understood[,] not as something thought or argued, but as a state lived. We live in that which is common [...], yet in reality this common life is but altered for a moment & approximately [...] until B V [= Beatific Vision] & after that a growing struggle in which the object of desire gradually wins."

The next entry, beginning at the middle of 61r and titled "May 26 (4)," recalls an exchange of the night before: "The spirit last night[,] after giving sign[,] confirmed [the] statement spirits come in to our sleep as the dramatis Personae of our dreams." This will become "all spirits inhabit our unconsciousness or, as Swedenborg said, are the Dramatis Personae of our dreams" (*AVB* 227; cf. *CW14* 165, 407n37). It happens in "the sleep state of the Shiftings at night[,] insisting that they came 'involuntary' whereas our dreams were 'voluntary' ('emotional'). [...] He reminded me that there is however 'for[e]knowledge.' Their equating voluntary & emotional is the first clear statement that relegates emotion to the Faculties" (i.e., "Husk tinged with Will" just as "[e]vidently 'abstract' is Spirit tinged with C. M. [*Creative Mind*]" (end 61r). This logic leads to an important question about procedure in Book III, "The Soul in Judgment":

> Can I consider "dream as our emotion acting connected | with what remains "~~sensuous~~ sensuous" as the dead remember the | word "sensuous" here may mean an "image" or that personality | is still impressed—an image which in the waking state of the | dead is "correspondential" but here steps back into personal | consciousness[?] "Sensuous" here does not mean pleasurable | unless the Spirit is still united to the husk—an image like a | remembered image. (61v)

Note "(5)" takes up the question: "Who are the Teaching Spirits of the Return?" Whereupon the response (also on 61v) is tentative, exploratory, and leads to additional questions about how the author might proceed to write compellingly on the subject. Clearly, Yeats is engaging elements of the subject that will dominate Book III, such matters as "*Shiftings*," "*Teaching Spirits*," and "the *Return*" as initially defined in the automatic writings and sleeps before codification in the card file prior to reworkings here, in fragments of parts V and VI in typescript (see *CW14* 281–91, Appendix II, "Earlier Versions"),[40] and in the final version of *AVB*. As to the *Teaching Spirits*, Yeats writes: "I think they are the being of the group to which the soul tends. [...] Behind all is the conception [...] of the union of Spirit & C B constituting Christ, divine humanity, but that divine humanity only effect [=affects] the spirit when in the Shifting it is taken up into the universals—is taught by C B alone." In a new paragraph (on 62r), he asks: "Am I to assume that the teaching spirits are beings who have passed beyond our sphere & who form the great groups [...] & draw forth from them the images of their past actions Etc so as to make them conscious of the causes of their acts Etc"? To which there is a rejoinder: "The necessity for teaching spirits is that the dead before B V are fated—are chosen—they do not choose." So, Yeats reasons: "I may have to simply state that the group [of] beings who <govern> ~~constitute~~ the group lie outside my field of study, in the world of Angels Etc upon which the script has touched but left unexplored"—the matter of the *Thirteenth Cone*, which is indeed the tack that will be taken.

Note "(6)" defines itself as a retrospective on note "(2)" although with hesitation on terms more recently employed in note "(4)": "In comment on (2), the images (P B) grow contingent ~~after~~ more & more after death—being separated from ~~Husk which~~ Will, which gave them ~~personality~~ sensuousness [continuing on 62v:] & from Husk which gave them separate existence." As "(2)" is about "Light [that] seeks itself" and "(4)" involves images "'sensuous' & 'abstract,'" note "(6)" introduces one of the most important images in Book III for "that state of absolute light" of Beatific Vision. For the next few pages, Yeats continues to toil with a figure that he eventually chooses to introduce "The Soul in Judgment." He writes here (in parenthesis): "I think of Paul Valerys description of the mid day reflected in the ~~still~~ sea—each wave with the image of the sun" (62v). In *A Vision B*, the image occurs in the opening sentences:

> Paul Valéry in the *Cimetière Marin* describes a seaside cemetery, a recollection, some commentator explains, of a spot known in childhood. The midday light is the changeless absolute and its reflection in the sea "les œuvres purs d'une cause éternelle". The sea breaks into the ephemeral foam of life; the monuments of the dead take sides as it were with the light and would with their inscriptions and their sculptured angels persuade the poet that he is the light, but he is not persuaded. (219; *CW14* 159)

In the note, Yeats wonders first if Valéry's symbols can be accommodated with his own since emphasis in the poem "is on change—mine on the perfection of the moment"; yet the prospect of building on Valéry's example held promise, as Yeats extended and then closed that parenthetical thought: "Perhaps I may even use the metaphor of things being born each out of its perfection—a ship born at full sail under a full moon—future & past, its building & its wreck [?illusions] that fall from it like a double shadow" (62v).

By contrast, on 63r, note "7" begins unpromisingly by acknowledging a possible mistake: "My association of Husk & light is perhaps [an] error. The true association may be P. B. & light." The problem was significant enough that eighteen lines were circumscribed and cancelled—matter being "the cause of all difference (Valery['s] sea)." Below the cancelled entry, a horizontal line was then drawn across the page, after which Yeats began to write the note afresh, reintroducing the centered number "7" (perhaps at another sitting): "I am tempted ~~by~~ <to> transfer light from Husk to P. B. by the fact [that]

Spirits speak of dreaming back forms Etc as in light." As he turned the page, he conceded to himself the difficulty: "I am back at the old problem. ~~I am not sensi~~ I have ~~untimely se~~ sensation (light) which [continuing to 63v:] seems [both] unlimi[ted] & limited perception." Then note "7" breaks again with verbal equations that are used occasionally on later pages of the notebook. The first two are an aphoristic pair: "The light knows it self in Husk & P B | consciousness knows it self in Spirit & C B." A third instance is figurative and looks mathematical and perhaps Blakean: "Light & Perception (Husk) = the spark from the anvil | the moment perpetual creation. The shower of sparks." Followed by space and strokes resembling an equals sign (=) in the left margin, the interrupted paragraph continues with the sentence "Supernatural light (p[hase] 15) is light completely expressed because set free from Spirit & C B." Light has two supernatural moments—"moments which have only ideal reality—that of its complete expression at [phase] 15" (voluntary), and "that at phase 1" (involuntary). A concluding paragraph on 63v takes issue with a philosophical reading to which Yeats was strongly opposed: "This ideal existence" (of phase 15) accounts for "natural beauty," for "[w]ithout it one has Croce's unsatisfying aesthetics."[41]

The last designated note in the notebook (an entry numbered "8." on leaf 64r) investigates light as understood to be "Astral Light." At this point and "for the first time," Yeats claims, "I see the derivation of astral light from that light which Grosseteste called corporeality it self or that of which corporeality is made, and from that light which Bonaventura identified with all senses." Previously, we encountered this idea on 2r (entry "3"), where Grosseteste on light is noted in connection with a quotation from Gilson's *Philosophie au Moyen Age* (cf. *AVB* 191n; *CW14* 140n), as well as on 11v in the footnote prepared for Book I, "The Great Wheel" (cf. *AVB* 259, *CW14* 189). Such "corporeality" is "matter as in Swift's verse & Husk is [...] form, form being understood as shaping, not as a shape." But here, just as in the passage on *Husk* and *Passionate Body* on leaf 5r—where confusion clouds Yeats's writing about the Marriage of *Spirit* and *Celestial Body*—a dozen lines of labored prose on "the daimonic moment" are abandoned, to be followed by an incomplete paragraph ("Astral Light in popular usage is applied to dream ~~like~~ images, & vision images rather than to natural images—though Levi used it in the last sense also"[42]), after finding himself confused. Cancelled sentences and paragraph starts follow onto the next page (64v): "This is a matter for ~~the spirit~~ <Dionertes> for it confuses me."[43] An if/then construction fails to generate either a sentence or paragraph. So Yeats turns to his spirit guide Dionertes to make a third stab at the meaning of "astral light," when "[t]he point about the dream images may not be that they are sensuous but that they are images—concrete image. I must ask Dionertes." Not to put too fine a point on this, but it is obvious from the appearance of leaf 64v that Yeats had written himself into a corner. So he broke off, temporarily (see Figure 2.2), to pose the questions he needed to have answered in this Platonic dialogue with himself:

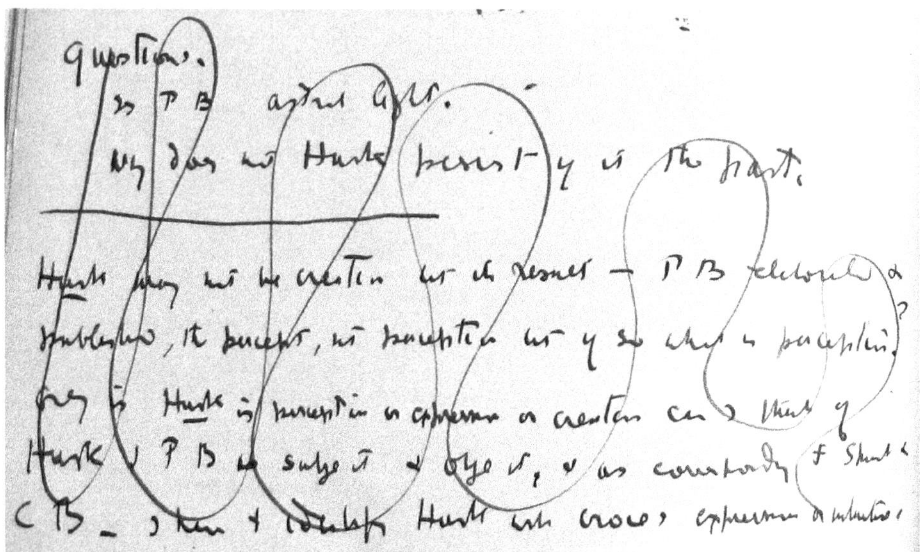

Figure 2.2. Rapallo Notebook C, NLI 13,580, [64v], detail. Courtesy of NLI; photograph courtesy of Catherine E. Paul.

> Questions.
> Is P B astral light.
> Why does not Husk persist if it [is] the past.
>
> ---
>
> Husk may not be creation but its result—P B elaborated & | published, the percept, not perception but if so what is perception? | Only if Husk is perception or expression or creation can I think of | Husk & P B as subject & object, & as corresponding to Spirit & C B. I have to identify Husk with Croces expression | or intuition.

This cancelled part of a continuing argument stipulates possible reconciliation between Yeats's thinking and that of "elaborated & published" accounts by Benedetto Croce and contemporary philosophers whose work Yeats had been reading on the distinction between "percept" and "perception"—for example, works by Bernard Bosanquet, John H. Muirhead, and Bertrand Russell.[44]

On leaf 65r, Yeats joins his discussion of the mechanics of *Husk*, *Passionate Body*, and *Spirit* to that of the afterdeath state called the "Dreaming Back," a term introduced in *A Vision A*, Book II, Part XIV, "Life After Death," and discussed in greater detail in Book IV, "The Gates of Pluto." *Dreaming Back* as a concept he believed to be confirmed by Henri Bergson in *Matter and Memory* (1919),

Theodor Fechner in *On Life after Death* (1914), and Hermes Trismegistus in *Hermetica* (1924) as suggested by the marginalia in Yeats's copies.[45] On leaf 65r, Yeats again finds himself in trouble after resuming note "8," now on the persistence of *Passionate Body* in the *Dreaming Back*. "I am back at my old difficulty. I want to make P B the creator. ~~Can I do so~~. But that is impossible. Can I make it [?protean]—endless change—fixed by Spirit according to its eternal forms. [...] No for the astral image recurs. Can I identify Husk with endless ~~change~~ creation—no for it is the past." Consequently, these lines in the notebook are crossed out and succeeded by as many in a series of interrogative sentences beginning with "Is" and "If" on the behavior of *Passionate Body*, *Husk*, and *Spirit*. Similarly, as on the facing page, a series of equations are inscribed as if to help clarify:

Once more Material
Husk = expression. P B = the ~~expressed~~ (Matter)

~~Spirit = the mould or form expressed~~.
~~or~~
~~Husk = expressed = P B expression~~] ~~no for then the~~ [bracketed lines are
~~Spirit = the mould~~] ~~Husk would persist~~[46] vigorously stricken]

Yeats's writing in the next opening of the notebook (65v–66r) stumbles forward in much the same manner, three-quarters of it cancelled and punctuated with formulae, intermittently: "Husk = senses" and "P B [=] matter, ~~of light~~ <or undivided> light" on 65v; and "Husk = expression" and "P B = Matter" on 66r, concluding the page with the entirely cancelled equation "Daimon = ~~form~~ <forms> expressed." Aside from dispiriting references to mystical authority, such as "But I dare not go to Dionertes with abstractions like 'transformation'" (on 65v) and "Only those our spirit knows [...] are so expressed" (on 66r), the most promising element on both of these pages is the Valéry thread from notes "(6)" and "7" (leaves 62v and 63r). Here, "life is a meaningless flux, a sea—as in Valery poem—where the Sun—Spirit—is mirrored" (65v). "Valery man sitting in [a] dark theatre, [h]is eyes on the lighted square of the stage[,] except that we are the lighted stage" (66r). After cancelling most of the page, Yeats asserts that expressed forms are from the *Daimon*, neither *Husk* nor *Creative Body* "but their perfect union. Absolute expression[, as a] flame without ark [i.e., arc]," like "the spark from the anvil" on 63v.

But a formula at the top of leaf 66v offers an alternative explanation: "or perhaps | Husk ~~Express~~ = Expression. B. B. [i.e., P. B.] [=] Potential form." This alternate turn in thought does not develop very far in the ensuing paragraph ("In which case the daimon is [...] in its full expression only"), almost all of which is cancelled. After a new start ("Husk & ~~daimon~~ P B expresses the daimon & impose their form upon the Spirit, & so realize its end. End & form imply one another"), even that small remnant was also stricken. Beneath that, a horizontal line has been drawn across 66v to divide the page, providing space for Yeats to recall "an unpleasant but important interview with Dionertes" (see Figure 2.3).

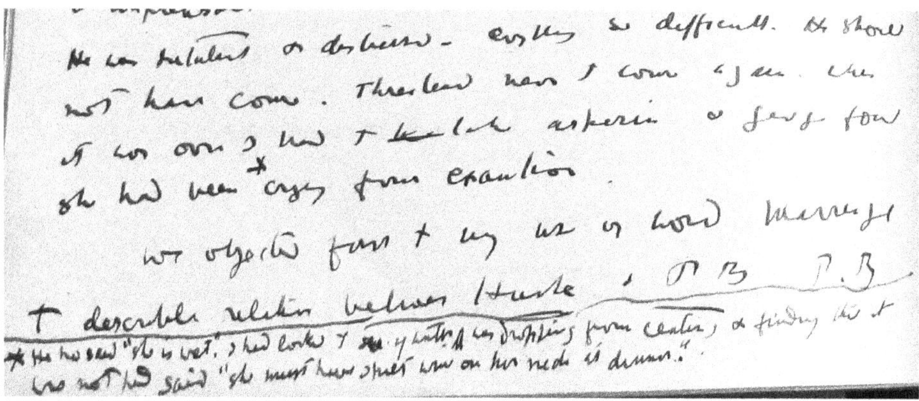

Figure 2.3. Rapallo Notebook C, NLI 13,580, [66v], detail. Courtesy of NLI; photograph courtesy of Catherine E. Paul.

> He was petulant & distressed—everything so difficult. He should not have come. Threatened never to come again. When | it was over I had to ~~tke~~ take asperin & George found | she had been *crying from exhaustion.
>
> We [= He] objected first to my use of [the] word marriage | to describle [*sic*] relation between Husk & P B[.] PB | [continuing to 67r:] was to[o] ephemeral for such a word. [. . .]
>
> ---
>
> * He had said "she is wet." I had looked to see if water [?] was dropping from cealing & finding that it | was not had said "she must have spilt wine on her [?neck] at dinner."

As one of the Yeatses' chief Communicators, Dionertes presided on several occasions, during the winter of 1919/1920, when George Yeats's function as medium was impaired by acute fatigue (see *YVP2* 519, 525, and 528), directing them, in effect, to end the automatic scripts: "I do not really want script here [in Pasadena, California]—I prefer to use other methods—sleeps" (539). And that is just what they did until the end of George's "philosophical sleeps" on November 27, 1923.[47] In Dublin, in late May 1929, Yeats recalled an evidently more recent episode in which Dionertes had intervened on her behalf and gone on to object to the wording of questions put to him. In Rapallo Notebook C, the objection relates to the entry introduced on "the Marriage of Husk & Passionate Body" (4r–5r) but qualified here (on leaf 66v) from memory and for the next two pages. On 67r, objections are enumerated: "He objected to a certain phrase of mine about Husk 'bringing forth' the forms from P B. Implied much too [= to] intention. (He meant I conclude that 'the marriage' is a kind of correspondence or image & [...] something ephemeral & unconscious. He meant also that [....] Husk is life—~~sea foam~~ the wind that makes waves.)" Dionertes's "most important statement" on that subject may be interpreted as an endorsement of the efficacy of sleep. After *Beatific Vision*, "they do not ossilate [*sic*] between sleep & waking but can still sleep" (cf. *AVB* 238, *CW14* 174: when "[t]he expiation is completed and the oscillation brought to an end for each at the same moment"). Yeats notes that, although this statement corrects a "previous" one by the Communicator, they agree that "images seen in dreams are a continuance of the dreaming back" and that images made by one spirit may be "used by a different spirit to communicate through." However, Dionertes "refused to speak of 'the Teaching Spirits' & with great emphasis to say anything of that state between BV & birth that I [continuing to 67v:] must think out for myself."

Left to think the matter out for himself, Yeats brings to an end a movement he may have intended for part of note "8." He had also reached the end of a sitting, partly indicated by the long line that he drew beneath this paragraph:

> ~~When speaking of "M~~ When I was asserting that I was right | in using the phrase "Marriage of Husk & P B" he | had said "What comes of it?" He meant that it was | barren. The point is I think is that ~~uni~~ antithetical | unity of being, or even phase 15, implies the faculties | ~~—it is even~~—it is as it were human. ~~That which is | given there~~ <there> ~~is barren nature—man through nature~~ | ~~—Husk & P B—is an abstraction from it~~. Perfection of form | —p 15—comes through the effort of the individual soul | & its Faculties. We create our bodies & our scenery. (67v)

After that, the remaining prose entries in Rapallo C form a somewhat broken landscape of writing on the subject of "expiation." Below the drawn line on 67v, the date "June" is inscribed (at left) halfway toward the vertical center of the page. To the right of the date, a small figure has been drawn, juxtaposed semicircles, perhaps to symbolize persons A and B (soon discussed on 68r–69r), who are bound in "the continuous circling" of expiation. The figure is notched, possibly to suggest motion by degrees:

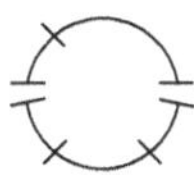

Below the date, aligned at the left margin, are the heading and opening lines:

> Expiation.
> A soul which expiates ignorance in the "shiftings" | had its "abstract memory" in the Return but has not | that memory now. I think not[,] for I think | that now its knowledge must be positive knowledge | of the contrary of the self so remembered—of the | self of its dreaming back. Its oppressor if he has | now returned to life will upon the other hand live | through that which had inflicted. Is he affected | by his ~~oppressors viscetims~~ <victims> dreaming back state? (67v)

This much, though cancelled, very much resembles the definitions and notes in the Card File on Expiation (E2, E3, and E10–12; *YVP3* 297–98 and 300). But then Yeats begins anew in a way resembling the draft of an essay: "A Spirit joined to its C. B. lives through its life in the order of the events, that is to say growing younger until childhood comes; but these words 'younger' 'childhood' [continuing to 68r:] are symbols, or metaphors because it is ~~separated~~ from the Record & has memory alone." In "The Soul in Judgment," part XI (*AVB* 237–39, *CW14* 172–74) we find the treatment of "expiation for the dead." In typescript (NLI 36,272/6/2a), it occurs in part XIII with a brief notice at the end of part XV (*CW14* 288–89). In Rapallo C (68r), spirits travel according to rule: "If Principles are placed on Wheel [?instead] of cone C B [*Celestial Body*] of course travels back ~~from~~ 22-~~12~~-21-19 Etc & reaches 8 at rebirth." Maturity (the middle), not the source, is correspondent with the *Beatific Vision*, where a spirit realizes itself as "one with the Spiritual whole," at first separating from *Passionate Body*, then sinking back into it again—"a New P B—images which are purified of personal associations[....] It is only after the new birth that they are the objects of its thought. Before birth thought summons the image, after birth [thought] is summoned by it."

In a new paragraph, victim and oppressor are discussed in relation to the *Shiftings*: "In expiation the two persons[,] being symbols to one another, are not—taken as symbols—bound to the continuous circling. [...] A wrongs B & B cannot pass the Shiftings until the active wrong is expiated in life of <A> ~~B~~, & that of ignorance by <B> ~~A~~ himself in Shiftings" (68r; cf. *AVB* 237–38; *CW14* 173). "~~B re~~ A returns to life again & either to repeat the act[,] being still caught in the Dreaming Back[,] or to expiate it by the reversal[.] <He> ~~it~~ longs to suffer what he has inflicted." The account continues for interpretation on the next page (68v): "The system denies[,] I think[,] the existence of anything which we know unconsciously. When A reverses the act, ~~that~~ he does so that he may complete something, something which is therefore known in its details." Recalling the myth of Eros and Anteros, to which Michael Robartes alludes in "The Phases of the Moon" as he delivers his recitation of the phases, beginning at line 30,[48] Yeats asserts, here, that A and B "have changed natures, & yet each is made whole in the other. ~~This [is] called Expiation for the Daimon~~"; but correction is necessary because this change is painful: "The two might have been one through sympathy, but instead theirs has been [a] struggle in which one has been victim & afterwards that exchange of nature which Russell foretold for England & Germany."[49] Even so, "All this dissatisfies me," Yeats observes at the end of the paragraph, "but for the moment I can do no better" (68v).

From here on, procedure reverts to that of question and short-answer follow-ups. To wit:

> [68v:] B remains in "Shiftings" because something checks | the living back. What does? In some form | it must be drawn down into the Dreaming Back. | If so[,] does its dreaming back effect [*sic*] the living man? | Does a dreaming Back ever effect [*sic*] the living except by the | re-birth of the dreamer—or by some obvious haunting.
>
> [69r:] Is not sympathy itself a reversal of being | but voluntary whereas that in expiation is involuntary[?] | One must not forget that human life is but | the ground where the friendship or anim[osity] of the | daimons is displayed.
>
> What is expiation for ghostly self? How does it | differ from that for daimon? B & A expiation is | not for one another but for daimon. I conclude [this] because | it is the daimon not the individual that is denied completeness. | The individual may get nothing but strain & pain. What is | the daimon during embodied life—as an actual existence[?]
>
> Is not the Daimon <in some sense> that being which can stretch | its memory—both Record & abstract memory— | through 28 incarnations & man that being | whose memory includes one only? If so[,] the significant | moment for the man is that [of] when the Daimon | changes phase—the Mans B. V.[?] | If so[,] the great passions arise from the Daimons | phasal relations—& are to the man "subconscious" | whereas those that arise from (say) the phasal | relations of a life in its passage are conscious & ephemeral. ~~The Daimon of the~~ || If so[,] the distinction between the Daimon of | the man when embodied by that of the man disembodied | looses [*sic*] meaning. All mans <28> incarnations are <a> single | [continuing to 69v:] phase of the daimon [~~...~~] -its life constituting a year—28 phases divided into 12. | We are in the midst of a powerful incomprehensible | death corresponding to the daimons death to birth state.

All that is left, after this, are several scratch notes that direct our attention to the end of part XI and the beginning of part XII in "The Soul in Judgment" as it was eventually written. "The Daimon or its essence is always the timeless moment, the symbolic sphere [...] —the fullness which includes ever[y] moment" (69v). "Every ex[p]iation is conscious. When A reverses his nature he does not starve his Karma because his suffering is not from ignorance, but the desire to suffer. Expiation for the ghostly self" (the next point, made on 69v between centered, parallel strokes laid horizontally). The reference to "Karma" could be an indication that Yeats had in mind the "ascetic schools of India" cited in part XII (*AVB* 239, *CW14* 174). Then, after another pair of strokes to set off the following point, he weighs in the logic of the foregoing statements on 69v: "Can I take 'ghostly self' as daimon here[?] ~~Daimonic~~ Then the refusal to experience, starves the daimon, but is followed by Daimonic living—conscious experience for the Daimons sake, & so by [?initiation]—a guide." Although fuzzy here, the relevant elements of part XII are (1) "refusal of experience itself" that "starves" a *Spirit of the Thirteenth Cone* and (2) the acquisition of a "supernatural guide" (*AVB* 239, *CW14* 174).

[70r–78v] [Missing pages and end matter]

The facing stubs of omitted leaves 70–77, presumably on the "Introduction to the Great Wheel" for *A Packet for Ezra Pound* and therefore cancelled in the "Contents" list on 78r, are correspondent with entries on 2r, 6r–8r, and 11r, just as the entries on 59v–69v relate to draft materials cited in the "Contents" as belonging to "Soul in Judgement ([as]continued from loose leaf book[)] | 12 pages"—that is, roughly, from the beginning of part VI to the end but not in final order. Leaf 78v confirms that the entire notebook was considered to be a "Diary."

5. Poetry Writings (in Detail)

[8v–10v] "Jan 23 [1929]" [A prose outline for a "Lyric Sequence" and first-draft versions]

Notably, leaves 8v and 10v are blank because the writing between these two points is flanked by discrete units of prose, before and afterward intended for *A Packet for Ezra Pound*. The poems conceived here in planning become, in a few days and pages later, "Meditations upon Death" (dated "Feb 4. 1929" on 10r, continuing on 12r, 13r, 14r–15r) and "The Nineteenth Century and After" (untitled and undated on 9v, continuing on 25r). As a prose subject, "Lyric Sequence," as it was called, appears in three parts on 9r and has been transcribed accordingly (cf. *WFMP* 208–209):

I

Slowly ~~the circle narrowed—at Al[g]e~~ciras | At Al[g]eciras where ~~I~~ <are> the long [?beaked] herons, they [?settle] [?with] | [?out] clamour in the dark pines, & ~~& I cry out~~ <I see the rock have no desire to climb it—I love them near at hand> an old man is | ~~like a child—he turns to god as a child to his nurse~~. | ~~[?Death] with me is [?terrible] spirit make sweet the trouble~~ | ¶ An old man is like a child & turns to god as to his | The [?circle] — I look [?back] upon my life—I have a little [?wisdom]. | Platos king—something of Sankarya, & something has been spoken | to me alone—. Hence forth I shall seek from

~~searching~~ <searching>, & | turn it over & over, as if I were a child turning over & over | a handful of shells. | ¶ ~~At Cannes. Ka | Algeciras I I could walk a couple of miles & now a~~ mile

II

~~I have been & am being~~ || What preyers should I play [= pray], Do not prey said the Brahmin but say | I have been <I been man & women> king & slave , <I have been man> Mirriad of beloveds have sat | on my knees, I have sat on a mirriad knees [?"] & shudder | thinking that soon I must change again [?"] Always an insect in the roots of | the grass.

III

What I have built grows from me— | Don't deceive yourself exorbitant soul—<the> [~~?if~~] greater men are gone | You have been a rattle of pebbles in a receeding wave.

From part III of these scratch notes, Yeats wrote the first draft of "The Nineteenth Century and After" (on 9v in four stages, the first three cancelled in left column) and began fashioning a longer poem (on facing leaf, 10r, based on part I of the outline; see Figure 2.4). This longer poem was entitled "Meditations upon Death," which resonates with the dedicated general purpose of Rapallo Notebook C as a "Diary of Thought" (the heading given the first entry on 1r) and echoing such celebrated sequences of meditative lyrics as "Thoughts upon the Present State of the World" (afterward "Nineteen Hundred and Nineteen") and "Meditations in Time of Civil War," masterworks of the kind in Yeats's recent collection *The Tower* (1928). One notices by viewing the fourth stage of the quatrain, appearing in the upper right-hand corner of 9v, and then by skimming the first-draft version of "Meditations upon Death," with which it aligns on 10r, that there is commonality in imagery, at first elemental, compressed, and suggesting "pebbles which the waves draw back" and famously "fling" in Arnold's "Dover Beach"—

Though the
~~The~~ great men return no more
~~I make~~
I take delight in what I have
The rattle of pebbles on the shore
Under the out going wave—

a scene set in apposition to the particularity of images in the second poem, emerging on the facing page (10r): a "heron-billed pale Cattle Bird, / That feeds on some foul parasite / of an African flock or herd," that "Crosses the narrow straits to light / In Algeciras gardens and there rest / Until the mourning break as on a Dark breast." Thereafter, we have Yeats as "a boy," the "actual shells of Rosses level shore" (rhymed with "Newton's metaphor"), and young Yeats bidding "imagination run" on "What matters he [Newton] may question" but with the confidence that "befits a man." The thought-chain and stream of images, from the yet unfinished quatrain on 9v to the welling up of memory and imagination on 10r, seems consistent with the technique of *scrying*, "a form of meditation," Yeats said, "that has perhaps been the intellectual chief influence on my life up to perhaps my fortieth year" (*Mem* 26–27). This technique is captured in the following reproduction of those two, extraordinary, facing pages in the notebook:

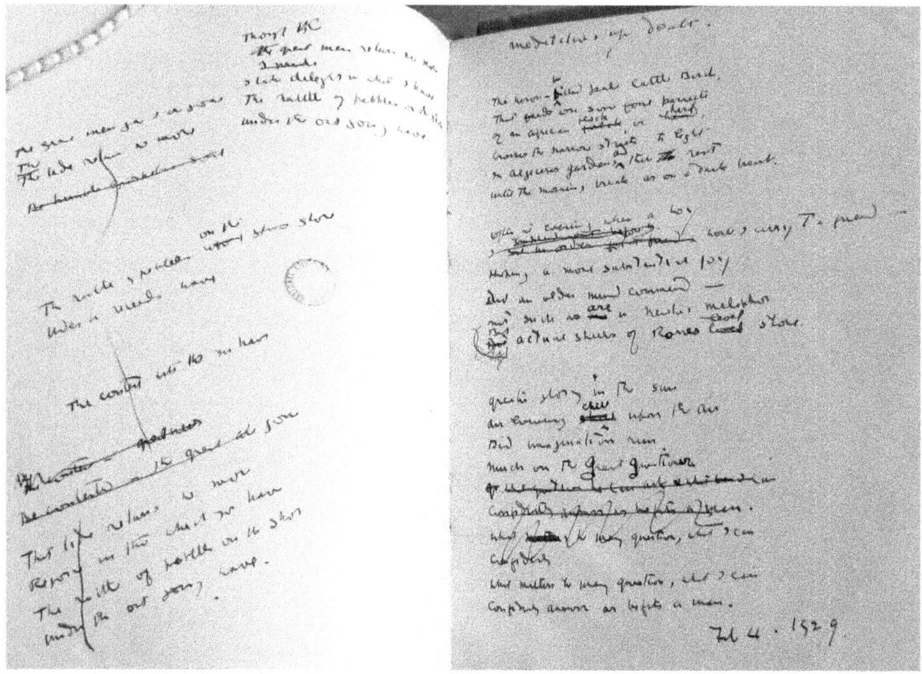

Figure 2.4. Rapallo Notebook C, NLI 13,580, [9v and 10r], in full. Courtesy of NLI; photograph courtesy of Catherine E. Paul. (See *WFMP* 262–63 and 210–11.)

From references to Browning and Morris in a letter Yeats wrote to Olivia Shakespear on March 2, 1929 (*L* 758–59, *CL InteLex* 5221), Stallworthy infers that in "Nineteenth Century and After" "Yeats has 'loaded every rift with ore'" without attempting to pinpoint sources, and that example is best to follow here.[50] Though Yeats had intended the poem to be third in a three-part sequence, the reason the plan was not carried out is indicated by the poem's displacement for many pages, until 25r, where he finished and dated it "~~Feb 2~~ March 2 [1929]" (see below). There is a good chance that he simply forgot the lyric as he concentrated on the other two movements, which would become "Meditations upon Death" I and II in *A Packet for Ezra Pound* (9–11) and later two poems in *Words for Music Perhaps and Other Poems* (Cuala Press, 1932): "A Meditation written during Sickness at Algeciras" (12–13; afterward "At Algeciras—A Meditation upon Death") and "Mohini Chatterji" (13–14). February 2, 1929, is almost certainly the date on which the draft on 9v was made, facing the "Feb 4. 1929" draft of "Meditations upon Death" I on 10r. After the notes for *A Packet* and *A Vision*, on 11r–11v, the focus on "Meditations upon Death" II would be broken only by "Mad as the Mist and Snow" and by the intervention of Crazy Jane around mid-February. Both "Meditations" I and II are misleadingly dated in *The Collected Poems* (e.g., "November 1928" and "1928"), perhaps from later recollection of Yeats's travels and illnesses rather than from recorded dates of composition. The dates Yeats recorded in Rapallo Notebook C are fairly dependable (see "CCP" 240).

For practical reasons, it is unnecessary, hereafter, to give literatim, or detailed, transcriptions of the poems in Rapallo C because David R. Clark has provided both facsimiles and reliable transcriptions in *WFMP*. These will be cited in every case, even as they are noted in the Appendix. Exceptionally, there are instances in which reproduction or quotation may be necessary to make clear the sense of Yeats's process, as when the Cornell series' arrangement of titles and pairings of facsimiles and transcriptions disrupt the actual physical (and often cognitive) relationship between compositions on facing pages in the notebook (verso-to-recto). Figure 2.4 is an example of one such exceptional case (cf. *WFMP* 262–63 and 210–11).

[11r–11v] [See entry in part 4 above]

The note "End of Cuala book" bears project relevance to "Lyric Sequence" and "Meditations."

[12r–16r] ["Meditations upon Death" II and "Mad as the Mist and Snow"]

As "Meditations upon Death" I and II were destined to complete the essay "Rapallo" in *A Packet for Ezra Pound* (9–11), facing pages at 14v–15r of Rapallo C were used to preserve essentially finished versions of those lyrics for that project (see *WFMP* 225n and 224–25). Yeats seems to have felt satisfied with "Meditations" I just as it stood on 10r, dated "Feb 4. 1929," for he inscribed the title "Meditations upon Death | I" at the top of 14v, leaving the remainder of the page blank opposite an amended fair-hand copy of the second lyric, entitled "Meditations upon Death | II" and, at the end, dated "~~Feb 8. 1929~~ Feb 9 1929" (February 9 being coincident with a substitution of nine lines). The refinement of those nine lines seems to have been as easy for the poet as were the first half of stanza 1, which began, "I asked if I should pray / But the Brahman ~~say~~ said" (etc.) and seems to have been a fairly simple matter of versifying from part II of the prose subject on 9r. The notion of "myriad" lives and loves had taken longer to develop and was a bit harder to render in several drafts. Together, the two lyrics, when finished, can be seen as part of Yeats's philosophical objection to the idea of "modern man" as an invention, in contemporary poetry, "to dignify our scepticism" (8r).

On 12r, 12v, and 13r (*WFMP* 216–17, 218–19, and 220–21), we witness an uninterrupted effort to write the poem eventually entitled "Mohini Chatterjee," although the Brahmin by name and spelling are approximate at this stage—matters for the second stanza. The three-stress lines of stanza 1 are fortunate but are not enough for cadence to marshal thought coherently to anything like a stable second stanza for two more pages (through 13r), in spite of the emergence of old soldiers in "strategic thought" (fourteen lines cancelled on 14r, compressed on 15r, and then reduced to the line "The old troops parade"). From the four stresses of "Meditations" I to the three stresses of "Meditations" II, the latter poem in progress was temporarily arrested before it could be completed, engulfed by stanzas of a new poem, a ballad. This event occurs on facing pages 13v–14r in Rapallo C (*WFMP* 498–99, 222–23, and 500–01), where the three stanzas of "Mad as the Mist and Snow" took shape comparatively quickly, starting with an unnumbered stanza 1 on 13v, followed by numbered stanza "~~II~~ | III" (also on 13v) and stanza "II" written in the space beneath those fourteen cancelled lines from "Meditations" II on 14r.

With the planned "Lyric Sequence" nearly finished for the "Rapallo" essay in *A Packet for Ezra Pound*, and with an unanticipated ballad nearing completion, Yeats had only to set out in fair-hand state the poems that he had written thus far. This was done for "Meditations" I and II on 14v (from 10r) and on 15r as cited above. Part II (afterward "Mohini Chatterjee") was then dated "~~Feb 8. 1929~~ Feb 9 1929" (see "CCP" 240). The three stanzas of "Mad as the Mist and Snow" were written out in correct order on 16r (with the initial lines of stanza 2 revised on 15v) and officially dated at the end: "~~Fb~~ Feb 12. 1929" (see "CCP" 241 and *WFMP* 503n and 503–04). This was the first lyric written for Yeats's "Words for Music Perhaps" sequence, anticipating such personae as Crazy Jane and Tom the Lunatic.

[16v–20r, 23v–24v] ["Crazy Jane on the King"]

The unpublished lyric "King Nuala," retitled "Cracked Mary's Vision" and, finally, in typescript "Crazy Jane on the King" (see Clark's exceptional genetic commentary, reproductions, and transcriptions in Appendix I of *WFMP* 577–603) confirms Yeats's renewed interest in the ballad while in Rapallo at this particular time. The majority of the poems collected under the rubric "Words for Music Perhaps" in 1932 were written in this interval. Although "Crazy Jane on the King" seems to have been typed directly from the advanced draft on 24v, or from Yeats's dictation (probably at Coole on August 5, 1929, according to Mrs. Yeats),[51] Yeats decided to withdraw the poem from publication, at the suggestion of friends, despite the apparent role he thought it might play as an introduction to the sequence. From 24r in the notebook to the typescript, the title given is "Cracked Mary's Vision" until changed, in Yeats's hand, to "Crazy Jane and the King || (Words for Music)" (*WFMP* 600–01). The base text (on 24r) is dated "Feb 24," which is consistent with the dating of poems up to this point, except for intervening, undated verses on leaves 20v–23r. Not at cross-purposes, the writing of "Three Things" was not even the chronological interruption one infers from standard scholarly sources (see below). As "Words for Music," they confirm the premise that Yeats, like the expatriate poets of his circle in Rapallo, had begun to emulate the unvarnished balladry of Robert Burns.[52]

So "Crazy Jane on the King" begins without title but conscious of form at the first two openings devoted to the poem in the notebook, where rhyme patterns are noted beside the lines on 17r ("A | B | B | A | ~~C | D | D | C~~" and "A | B | B | A | C [circled] | D | D | A | C [circled]") and on 17v ("A | A | B | C | D | D | C | B"). The refrain line changed very little, from "The devil take King George" to "May the devil take King George," as one would expect. Yeats's right-handedness is evident in the way entries tend to slope, roughly from 30 to 45 degrees, except at stages where written text needed to be copied out and revised, presumably on the flat surface of a table. The content itself was quite malleable. As Clark points out, by leaf 19r, Yeats had managed to write one "impressive stanza" (discarded after 20r) from "a daring mix of Blakean symbolic topography with misremembered Irish legend" (*WFMP* 579):

Did Nuala's ship of glass
Over Udan Adan pass?
Did the gloomy river Storge
Bear that great mouth &
~~Carry his great~~ lucky eye
That
^ Magnanimity of rage
Towards his
~~To that~~ ^ famous anchorage
(When I think of him I cry
May the devil take King George) (NLI 13,580, 20r)

The mixed Blake topography involves the lake Udan Adan from "Vala or the Four Zoas" and the river Storge from "Milton"; and the "misremembered Irish legend" involves Yeats's confusing King Nuada with Queen Nuala. On 23v and 24v, the names are gone (the Blakean as well as the Irish) except for the English King George V, of course, and the "Long bodied Tuatha de Danaan." Still, the transgender error in the poem and its title, on 20v, may have partly inspired the invention of a persona expressly not that of the poet himself:

The bad girl's
A ~~The Childs~~ refusal to Cheer for the King
^
~~King Nuala~~

On this page, the whole poem is stricken with a long diagonal line. Afterward, at the first opportunity following the writing of an intervening lyric, "Three Things," the "bad girl" poem was rewritten from 23v to 24v, christened "Cracked Mary's Vision" on 24v (taking the name of an eccentric woman who lived in Galway near the Gregory estate),[53] and dated, at the bottom of the same page, as completed on "Feb 24."

[20v–23r] ["Three Things"]

Between the "King Nuala" and "Cracked Mary" versions of "Crazy Jane on the King," Rapallo C shows that in an unspecified number of days Yeats had conceived and largely completed work on a minor gem for "Words for Music Perhaps," then envisioned as a sequence of twelve lyrics, as he said in a letter to Olivia Shakespear: "no[t] so much that they may be sung as that I may define their kind of emotion to myself....One of the three I have written is my best lyric for some years I think. They are the opposite of my recent work and all praise of joyous life, though in the best of them it is a dry bone on the shore that sings the praise" (*L* 758; *CL InteLex* 5221). The date of this letter is "March 2 [1929]," and the best of three lyrics so intended is the song "Three Things" (the other two being "Mad as the Mist and Snow" and "Cracked Mary's Vision"). Until now, the standard date assigned to "Three Things" has been "March 1929" ("CCP" 241). In a memoir, Bridgit Patmore recalls a particular scene of Yeats and his wife, strolling along the seashore at Rapallo, when Yeats becomes transfixed by an object at his feet. Two days after that, she and her companion, Richard Aldington, are present for tea and a recitation of the poem at Via Americhe 12/8: "after every two lines, he raised his head a little and, over his spectacles looked at me and then, after the next two lines, at Richard."[54] Unfortunately, dates are not provided for either scene, although, more precisely, George Yeats later typed out a select list of dates headed "Sequence of poems written at Rapallo Feb & March 1929," which places the composition of the poem as occurring between February 14 (two days after "Mad as the Mist and Snow") and "Cracked Mary's Vision (King George) Feb 24" (NLI 30,891, 1 page).[55] Patmore's telescoping Yeats's sudden inspiration and subsequent reading of "Three Things" makes a good story thirty-nine years after the fact, although possibly without too much exaggeration.

If Yeats's discovery was indeed a *bone* on the beach, the writing of the poem gained from recent exercise in the notebook. "The Nineteenth Century and After," with its "rattle of pebbles on the shore," remained in suspension until

"March 2" (on 25r). "Mad as the Mist and Snow" anticipated the three-part structure of the new ballad, each stanza of which gained in effect by the addition of an extra refrain. As in "Crazy Jane on the King," each stanza's closing refrain was quickly found in early draft; likewise quickly obtained were refrain lines 2, 8, and 14. In fact, the whole poem came with relative ease at first, from the first opening devoted to the poem, on 20v–21r (*WFMP* 458–61), until Yeats took a bit longer to resolve a problem that stanza 3 posed for him.

On 21v–23r (*WFMP* 463n, 462–67), we see him reverting to a planning strategy last employed in launching the "King Nuala" phase of "Crazy Jane on the King": namely the jotting down of rhyme notes to remind himself of words he thought might be effective as he made the bone sing of the third thing that a woman holds dear. In *Yeats at Songs and Choruses*, Clark argues that *that* thing is sexual arousal rather than heterosexual consummation: "Yeats achieves his aim of ending climactically with excitement of the mind and spirit by going back to the time of desire rather than fulfillment" (64). Clark's case depends to a large degree on multiple instances in which the words "stretch and yawn" occur in his poems from 1914 onward.[56] Such intricate reading from multiple contexts is impressive. Moreover, Clark's interpretation is most convincingly made after providing a transcription of the relevant folios in Rapallo C. Although the basis for his work in *WFMP*, this transcription is streamed without reference to location and broken into five separate drafts. By draft 4 (on 23r), the problem of dwelling on a woman's pleasure to a man comes to no satisfactory end, and Yeats strokes through the entire poem after making two stabs at the last stanza. Then, on 22v (to the left of draft 4), he works out the final version (draft 5) in the notebook. The stanzas are assigned numerals, stanza I on point as a mostly fair-hand copy, followed by a reworking of stanza II. But when he copied out and revised stanza III from 23r, where the speaker recollects past intellectual and spiritual congress with "wise" Solomon, the stanza is decisively rejected and followed by substitution of an "~~Alternative last verse~~":

third III
The ~~third~~ thing that I think of yet
<u>Sang a bone upon the shore</u>
Is — that morning when I met
Face to face my right ful man
And did after stretch and yawn
<u>A bone wave whitened & dried in the wind</u>

As an afterthought, the new stanza III provides strength to the voice of the woman who speaks, because, as Clark saw, "to be nostalgic about her former role as ignorant muse does not make a convincing climax to the poem" (56). Fortunately, Yeats chose the option that most affirms the woman's role.

[25r] ["The Nineteenth Century and After" concluded]

More a revisiting than an afterthought, since 9v, the unfinished fulcrum of four lines on which the first part of "Meditations upon Death" had been leveraged on February 4 was now copied out at the top of leaf 25r, amended slightly there, dated "~~Feb 2~~ March 2," and then cancelled. Beneath that, Yeats drew a long line across the page horizontally. Below the line and the heading "On re-reading," he toyed with the idea of adding a line at the beginning: "~~Thinking of all they have~~" > "~~Abashed at all that greatness gone~~" > "Abashed at all they had & gave" (25r). (Six vagrant lines from stanza 3 of "Cracked Mary's Vision"—facing on 24v from February 24—were penned just to the right on 25r.) However, this five-line option for the quatrain was cancelled with a vertical stroke through the whole thing. Below that, the final version in Rapallo C, including the poem's title, was inscribed in the lower margin of the page (see *WFMP* 264–65):

~~The end of~~ The Nineteenth Century & After
~~The old poetry & the new~~

Though that great song returns no more
There's
~~Theirs~~ keen delight in what we have
~~The~~
A ~~A~~ rattle of pebbles on the shore
Under the receeding wave

[25v–28r] ["Crazy Jane Grown Old Looks at the Dancers"]

In his letter of March 2 to Olivia Shakespear, extolling the creation of "Three Things" as "my best lyric for some years," Yeats went on to relate to her a strange dream that, brooding upon it, seemed likely to produce a new poem:

> Last night I saw in a dream strange ragged excited people singing in a crowd. The most visible were a man and woman who were I think dancing. The man was swinging round his head a weight at the end of a rope or leather thong, and I knew that he did not know whether he would strike her dead or not, and both had their eyes fixed on each other, and both sang their love for one another. I suppose it was Blake's old thought "sexual love is founded upon spiritual hate"—I will probably find I have written it in a poem in a few days—though my remembering my dream may prevent that—by making my criticism work upon it. (*L* 758; *CL InteLex* 5221)

The poem "Cracked Mary and the Dancers" emerged over the next four days (later retitled "Crazy Jane Grown Old Looks at the Dancers"). Its genesis resembles the pattern of "Cracked Mary's Vision" and "Three Things" in that it began with snatches of song (or chanting) striving to be formally and metrically completed in three stanzaic movements (this time in tetrameter verse)—all regimented according to jotted rhyme notes and to a refrain-line (once discovered). The process began on leaf 26r of the notebook, where successive efforts to launch the poem as the writer's dream vision of a man and woman "dancing there" in "Some sort of Indian dance" on a theme established by the refrain "Love is like the flower of the lilly." In four cycles of drafting, the first stanza progressed to a full revision on the facing page (at left), 25v. Three additional efforts were attached to that refrain—perhaps due to Yeats's affection for the biblical *Song of Solomon* 2.1 ("I am the rose of Sharon, a lily of the valley," a lily among thorns). But, without striking out those efforts, a new direction was forged in the space between first and second trials (and at a slant); and this departure substituted a new refrain ("<u>Love is like the lions tooth</u>"), which would require a completely different set of end-rhymes ("Youth | truth | both | uncouth") to perpetuate it over three stanzas. From lily of the valley in the floral world to dandelion, a common weed (in French, *dent-de-lion*, or lion's tooth),[57] Yeats made a formally exacting first stanza on leaf 26v—noting (at right) rhyming words "there," "hair," "scream," "dare," "gleam" in relation to lines 2 ("youth") and 7 ("tooth")—rendering the poem's notable a-b-a-c-a-c-b pattern. With the stanza established, a first trial of lines for stanza 2 was made next, with a new set of rhymes for the a- and c-lines. After that, he copied, amended, and expanded stanza 2 onto leaf 27r (adapting Blake's idea to the line "There must be sweetness in such hate"), and, with ease, set down a fair-hand version of stanza 3, entered at a slant after composing off the page, it appears, and superseding two false starts. The three stanzas coalesce as a poem of three complete stanzas, designated by numerals I–III and given the title "Cracked Mary & the Dancers" on 28r. Consequently, on 27v (facing left), a fair-hand copy of the poem was neatly inscribed, bearing the same title, few corrections, and the date "March 6" (see "CCP" 241). For corresponding facsimiles and transcriptions, see *WFMP* 376–87.

[28v–31r] ["Those Dancing Days Are Gone"]

This poem was written on two consecutive days—March 7 and 8, 1929—and included in Yeats's account to Lady Gregory, on March 9, in which he boasted, "I have written seven poems—16 or 18 lines each—since Feb 6 and never wrote with greater ease. The poems are two 'meditations' for *A Packet for Ezra Pound* which Lolly is printing and the first five of *Twelve Poems for Music*. The getting away from all distractions has enriched my imagination" (*L* 759–60; *CL InteLex* 5225). Unlike the "meditations" and "Cracked Mary's Vision," which took longer, and the epigrammatic "Nineteenth Century and After" (not included in this count), "Those Dancing Days Are Gone" was composed apparently without competition from of other poems as its drafts are located at three contiguous openings (see *WFMP* 506–515).

Remarkably, finding the closing refrain of this ballad seems not to have been especially an aim when Yeats began writing the poem, on 29r, for it appears ready-made at the end of the first full draft of stanza 1 (at the foot of the page: "I carry the sun, <in> the gold[en] cup / The moon in a silver bag"; cf. "*I carry the sun in a golden cup, / The moon in a silver bag*"; *VP* 525). In his later note in *The Winding Stair and Other Poems* (1933), he acknowledged that the first refrain-line, but not the second, "is a quotation from the last of Mr. Ezra Pound's *Cantos*" (*VP* 831). The reference is to "With the sun in a golden cup" (line 19 in *Canto* XXIII) as Yeats encountered it in *A Draft of the Cantos 17–27* (1928). The next line in *Canto* XXIII ("and going toward the low fords of ocean") might have suited a sunny beach scene in the manner of "Three Things," but expropriating most of a single line from Pound must have seemed enough to complement with an echo from any number of Yeats's early lyrics (e.g., "The Man who dreamed of Faeryland"). After two preliminary runs at the first five lines in active voice ("I sing…"; "I cry…"), both cancelled, the speaker shifts to passive in addressing "that old woman there," a "sorry crone" although at one time dressed in "silken gear," "silk & satin gear," "Before her dancing days were gone" ("…done"). The a-b-a-b-c-d-c-d stanza has been defined in ballad form without resorting to rhyme notes of any kind. Already on the left-hand facing page (28v) he has begun jotting phrases ("husband," "song," "sons…so tall & strong," "sleeping like a top / Under a marble fla[g]") relevant to stanza 2. From there, Yeats turned to the next opening in the journal and copied stanza 1 from 29r as far as line 6, stopped there, cancelled the fragment, and then reintroduced the stanza, amending lines and changing "That is a wretched crone" to "Sits there upon a stone" before going on to make a draft of stanza 2. On facing page 29v, he worked out corrections for stanza 2 and then, I believe, stopped for the day. Entered at a 45-degree slant, a fair version of stanza 3 is inscribed in full beneath a drawn line, possibly from a discarded sheet. Finally, on leaf 31r, the entire poem was copied out (untitled but in segments I–III) with interlinear revisions mainly in stanza 3. (Leaf 30v is blank, save for an almost vertical column of numbers—"5 | 6 | 7 | 5"—nearly in alignment with lines revised on 31r, suggesting syllable counting in that region.) This final version bears the date "March 8 [1929]" ("CCP" 241). The title "Those Dancing Days Are Gone" was decided much later, when in typescript it was substituted for "A Song for Music."

[31v–35r, 36r] ["Lullaby"]

The writing of this poem seems both delayed and impeded by other work, which came with the arrival of proof copy for *A Packet for Ezra Pound*. In letters written in dictation due to fatigue brought on by proofreading, he also blamed failing eyesight as well as poetry writing, noting that in "writing a great deal of poetry … even a few lines [will] expend my vitality" (WBY to Shotar Oshima, March 24, 1929, *CL InteLex* 5228); on the same day, he also alleged that a trip to Monte Carlo, "just before" proofreading his "little Cuala book," had contributed to his run-down condition (WBY to Lady Gregory, *CL InteLex* 5227). Hence, "Lullaby" took nine notebook pages to emerge, triumphantly, in three stanzas of six lines each. Yet, even then, progress seems to have been offset (as Figure 2.5 indicates; see below) by the intervention of an unpublished poem on leaf 35v. As usual, reproductions of the folios, paired with Clark's transcriptions, are available in *WFMP* 470–87; however, in this instance the first page of drafting is also reproduced and briefly discussed by Genet in a note (n1095, 696–97).

The writing begins on 32r with jotted lines about Paris and Helen, at daybreak, after their first sleep together—two stresses, three stresses, and finally four stresses per line. From there, Yeats moved to the facing page at left (31v) to work on stanza 1, eliminating Helen, working from rhyme notes "sleep || alarm | deep | bed | arms," and allowing three stresses to dominate. Turning the leaf to 32v, the matter of sleep shifts to "Hunter Trist Tram" (*sic*) and a new set of rhyme notes jotted diagonally on the right side of several mainly three-stress lines. In writing for stanza 2, all lines are cancelled by a vertical stroke. On facing page 33r, Yeats returned first to recast stanza 1 into tetrameter verse, drew a horizontal line below that, and then began recasting stanza 2 in the same way. All of the latter work was rejected, as indicated by a long vertical line. Turning the leaf to continue work on stanza 2, Yeats made two unsuccessful stabs at it on 34r, striking out half of the lines individually and then everything, together, by means of a vertical stroke from top to bottom. Shifting left, then, to facing page 33v, he copied out and corrected stanza 2, cancelling all of it but two lines: "Found the potions work being done / When birds could sing, when dear could weap." A diagonal line also passes through numerous rhyme notes anticipating stanza 3. Similarly cancelled on 34v are a pair of couplets (the most advanced being "Such a sleap as Leda saw / When upon Eurotas bank") that straddle a cluster of rhyme notes related to stanza 3. On facing leaf 35r, the couplet is reduced to "Such sleap, as on Eurotas ~~bank~~ banck" before Yeats uses this space to copy and revise stanzas 2 and 3 at a new sitting, writing at a 20-degree slant in relation the slight amendment of stanza 3 at the top of the page. It may be that he considered transposing the order of stanzas by introducing the numeral "I" over this draft of stanza 3. However, as the right-hand leaf in Figure 2.5 shows, by 36r, when he copied out the complete poem for the first and last time in the notebook, he either decided against rearranging the stanzas or had caught the error. A degree of indecisiveness is suggested in the correction and "Stetting" of lines 3–4 in stanza 1. Also noteworthy in Figure 2.5 is confusion in Yeats's dating the poem, though there can be little doubt that it was "March 1929," and (on Mrs. Yeats's authority) it was probably March 27, 1929 (see "CCP" 241).

On March 29, with his wife and children away in Switzerland, he felt fit enough to write to Olivia Shakespear to say that he was "filling up … time by sitting in the sun when not reading or writing" and to share the poem with her as an example of the "wilder and perhaps slighter" work that he had been writing for "Words for Music." By that time, the tally was up to nine poems.[58] As a lullaby "that I like," the lyric was highlighted among recent accomplishments, which included "two or three others that seem to me lucky and that does not often happen." In confidence, he added a confessional note to the letter without signing:

> Yet I am full of doubt. I am writing more easily than I ever wrote and I am happy, whereas I have always been unhappy when I wrote and worked with great difficulty. I feel like one of those Japanese who in the middle ages retired from the world at 50 or so…to devote himself to "art and letters" which are considered sacred. If this new work do[es] not seem as good to my friends then I can take to some lesser task and live very contentedly. The happiness of finding idleness a duty. No more opinions, no more politics, no more practical tasks[.] (*L* 761; *CL InteLex* 5236)

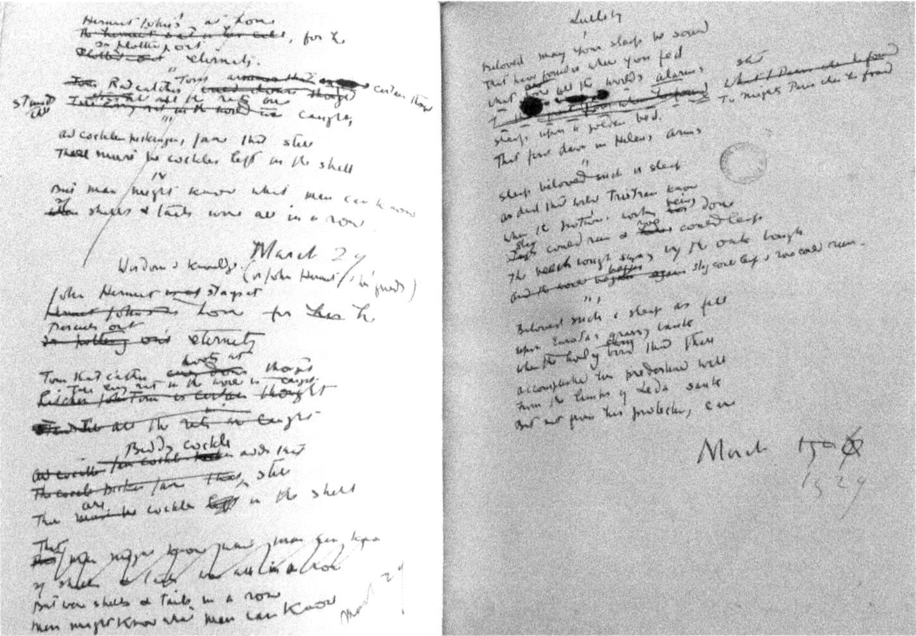

Figure 2.5. Rapallo Notebook C, NLI 13,580, [35v and 36r], in full. Courtesy of NLI; photograph courtesy of Catherine E. Paul. (See *WFMP* 486–87 for "Lullaby," right. At left, "Wisdom & Knowledge" is reproduced for the first time; see below.)

[35v] "Wisdom & Knowledge (or John Hermit & his friends)" [an unpublished poem]

A transcription without facsimile of the two drafts shown at left in Figure 2.5 (just above) appears in "CNGI" (2–3), from which Clark produced a "reading text" of the second (lower) draft "by omitting the cancelled words" (4). This procedure projects a final version of four rhymed couplets in tetrameter, the first featuring the persona John Hermit introduced in the parenthetical subtitle. Couplets 1–3 are given to three characters (Hermit and friends Tom Ratcatcher and Biddly Cockle), reminiscent of Cracked Mary (later Crazy Jane), Tom the Lunatic, and a trio of eccentrics from the epigraph Yeats attached to "Stories of Michael Robartes and His Friend" in *AVB* 32: Huddon, Duddon, and Daniel O'Leary.[59] Clark is silent on the matter of dating this and three other unfinished poems from Rapallo C. Possibly, this is because of their relation to similar work in Rapallo Notebook D and the White Vellum Notebook. He only ventures to say: "I have not attempted to date these poems. They are all converging on 1930, either somewhat before or after" (1). In relation to "Lullaby" (on 36r), however, it follows that "Wisdom & Knowledge" was written on March 27 or 29, 1929, either before or after "Lullaby" was posted to Olivia Shakespear in Yeats's letter. Also, there is a problem with Clark's "reading text" in that a fair-hand copy of "Wisdom & Knowledge" exists (entitled "Knowledge & Wisdom | ~~John Hermit & his friends~~"), filed in a large green, loose-leaf notebook (NLI 13,583) into which Yeats saved various non-starters. Recast as a single stanza on "Swift Brook Bond" typing paper (perhaps meant for the typist), Yeats circumscribed the first two lines ("John Hermit stays at home for he / Parcels out eternity") and instructs their "transfer" to the end of the poem—an intention also indicated by an arrow. Below that, another cast-off poem was copied there for safe keeping, a quatrain in ballad measure entitled "Heart on sleeve."[60]

[36v–37r, 38v–39r] ["Crazy Jane and the Bishop" and "The Scholars" (revised)]

The poem that began at the next opening of the notebook (36v–37r), entitled "Cracked Mary & the Bishop," is not dated although it must have been written around March 27, given its location between "Lullaby" and the untitled stanzas of "[Crazy Jane Reproved]" dated March 27 (on 37v). Until now, the date attributed to "Crazy Jane and the Bishop" has been March 2, 1929, on Mrs. Yeats's authority (see "CCP" 241), perhaps owing to the point-position the lyric has maintained in "Words for Music Perhaps" as a sequence since 1932. But George Yeats was uncertain, confident that it was sometime in "1929" and that one should "See letter to O.S. | March 2. 1929"—that it was "undated but March."[61] The fair-hand copy taken down on 39r (in stanzas arranged I–IV), following the disorder of 36v, also appears undated as the ceremony of dating poems began to give way to a clustering of lyrics that Yeats wrote in rapid succession (several to remain unpublished).

On viewing the draft material on facing pages 36v–37r, one's first impression is how much more advanced the first three stanzas are already when compared with poems of earlier date, such as "Cracked Mary's Vision" or "Cracked Mary and the Dancers," which relied on rhyme notes to define stanzas, each following from the first. Such devices are absent here, suggesting either that the two drafts of stanzas 1 and 3 (appearing side by side on 37r) and the slightly amended middle stanza had been drafted elsewhere (in source material now lost), or that the poem was written with great ease in the voice of Cracked Mary (i.e., Crazy Jane). The multiple efforts on stanzas 1 and 3 were revised and circled on 36v, and, over that, a much more labored draft of stanza 4 (labeled "IV") was worked out for the first time. The finished text of "Cracked Mary & the Bishop," save for a stricken mistranscription of the opening line, was copied out and punctuated on leaf 39r—prepared in a suitable state for typing (see *WFMP* 328–33).

For some reason Yeats copied to the page facing that finished text a new version of his epigram "The Scholars." Written in 1915 and published in magazines, as well as in *The Wild Swans at Coole* of 1917 and 1919, the poem was annotated by George Yeats in her copy of the *Collected Poems*: "re-written 1929" ("CCP" 236). Rough at best, the rewritten version consists of only six lines, directed at the old men in the poem's second stanza:

> Shuffle there, ~~&~~ cough in the ink,
> Wear out the carpet with your shoes
> ~~Kn~~ Think what good people think
> Youth could sin, ~~but~~ but old age knows:
> Lord what would you say
> Did your Catullus walk that way. (38v; cf. *VP*337)

This version is unique and was not introduced into Yeats's canon although perhaps recorded in Rapallo C for *Collected Poems* (1933). Juxtaposed to verses on Cracked Mary's passion for Jack the Journeyman on 39r, these old scholars are addressed in a tone of contempt just as Mary addresses the old bishop who had banished Jack. In that sense, the pairing of poems (left and right) is fitting—as they speak to each other.[62]

[37v–38r, 43v] ["Crazy Jane Reproved" and "Mrs. Phillamore" (unpublished)]

Untitled drafts of "Crazy Jane Reproved" (in two stanzas) appear at a single opening (37v–38r), with facsimiles and transcriptions available for viewing in

WFMP 336–38. The epigrammatic lyric "Mrs Phillamore" occurs in two places in the notebook: version 1 at the foot of 38r (*WFMP* 336) and version 2 at the foot of 43v (*WFMP* 400). Only version 2 is transcribed by Clark in a footnote (*WFMP* 401) and in his review of verse rejects ("Castoffs" 13). The date inscribed below "Crazy Jane Reproved" is "March ~~[?]~~ 27" (facing opposite the epigram), which establishes a date for the origin of the poem ("CCP" 241), and this will do for version 1 of "Mrs Phillamore," assuming the two compositions were written on more or less the same day. Version 2 of "Mrs Phillamore," however, would come a few days later, after companion poems "Girl's Song" and "Young Man's Song" were finished.

Like "Cracked Mary & the Bishop," "[Crazy Jane Reproved]" came to Yeats as easy work in the voice of old Mary. The two stanzas on 38r were reasonably fair copies, with small exceptions, before he thought to revise stanza 1 on 37v, initially arrowing the replacement from one leaf to the other, but then striking the whole poem on 38r when he decided to revise stanza 2, also, on 37v—again, the one beneath the other. On comparing the two drafts, side by side, one finds that changes made in lines 4 of each stanza were the crucial business of metrically improving the dramatic turn to rhymed couplets prior to the choral refrain. Rhyming ababcc plus refrain, the only issue at first (aside from accidentals) had been the decision to substitute "Fol de roll, Fol de roll" for "~~Fol de liddle~~ Etc" on 38r.

Beneath this draft activity on 38r, Yeats wrote version 1 of a miniature, slightly acid comedy in ballad measure, as if it were a snatch of actual dialogue:

Mrs Phillamore

"I learned to think in a man's way
And women's toys forget"
   None learned like you that
"~~You learned it well &~~ think to day
              ^
Like the first man you met."

The actual muse of the poem—Lucy ("Lion," née Fitzpatrick) Phillimore, Mrs. Robert Charles—was a formidable personality regarded as an enemy of "great amity" by Yeats.[63] As he insinuated in the letter he dictated to Lady Gregory on March 24, 1929, the fatigue that required his dictating was brought on by the wearying "return journey from Monte Carlo where we had been staying with Mrs, Phillimore" and then by proofreading "my new Cuala book" (*CL IntLex* 5227; see commentary on "Lullaby," above). The first to speak in the poem is Mrs. Phillimore, author of *In the Carpathians*, a travel book of 1912;

the second is Yeats as we imagine him parlaying a truce when allotting himself an equal balance of two lines. Version 2 of the poem (on 43v), though, recasts the jousting in Yeats's favor: she keeps line 1 but forfeits the rest. His three-line rejoinder to her premise claims the match entirely: "'And did so ~~thoroughly~~ <thoroughly> master it / Everything you think today / Is from the first man you met.'" Written for amusement, the two versions engage in sexual politics weighted differently at two places in Rapallo C—the first dominated by Cracked Mary and the second by Young Man ("No withered crone I saw" etc.).

[39v–41r] ["Girl's Song"]

This is the last poem to receive a date inscription before the final draft of "Love's Loneliness" on 50v, with half a dozen undated lyrics interspersed before and after that in Rapallo Notebook C. Requiring two openings in the notebook for three pages of drafting, the composition occupies 39v–40r for the first two pages and 41r for the second, as 40v remains blank beside the almost fair copy of the poem on 41r. The latter is dated "March 29" (now standard in Yeats scholarship: "March 29, 1929"; see "CCP" 241). But George Yeats was less certain in notes she prepared for Joseph Hone: "Girl's Song ('I went out alone') dated March 29 | but was rather later I think" (NLI 30,891).[64] Facsimiles and transcriptions are in *WFMP* 404–09.

George Yeats may have been recalling that some of Yeats's writings from 1929 to the early 1930s found places in parallel sequences under the "Winding Stair" rubric in the *Collected Poems* of 1933. The poem "Before the World Was Made," poem II of the sequence "A Woman Young and Old," gave its title and refrain to line 12 of "Young Man's Song" (see below); and "Girl's Song" concludes (on 41r) echoing the complementary sequences in *The Tower* (1928) and *The Winding Stair* (1933): "Saw I an old man young / Or young man old" (*VP* 515, lines 11–12).[65]

When Yeats began to write "Girl's Song" on 39v, he assumed the voice of a young girl who sings about encountering an old man "yesterday" who "relied" "upon a stick" as "did all his might dec[a]y"—a few catch phrases trying to assemble themselves into verse with rows and columns of rhyme notes at the foot of the page to aid invention (e.g., "~~tongue~~ | —young—song—wrong | long"; "seen | green | been"). The title "Girl song" (*sic*) was written first. Then Yeats shifted right, to the facing recto (leaf 40r), to begin again with a new stanza "I" and to transform textual matter from 39v into stanza "II" with ease. Stanza "I" required a second draft, which was written out beside the first. Beneath the single draft of the second stanza, he went on to write stanza "III" in three stages, the first two apparently struggle to discover the right phrasing for the last two lines. After cancelling those two stages, one after the other, he revised the stanza and achieved a complete version of it, in the right margin, with grammatically balanced closing lines: "Saw I that old man young / Or that young man old" (40r). In copying out the entire poem on 41r, however, those lines were revised for a "musical" effect consistent with the other culminating two-stress lines (4 and 8) in stanzas "I" and "II": "Saw ~~that~~ <an> old man young / Or ~~that~~ young man old" (11–12). Rhythmical adjustment in line 8 ("I sat ~~down &~~ <and> cried") also follows from the four, monosyllabic words of line 4: "And you know who." Yeats shows that the effect of words' own music is everything.

[41v–44r, 45r] ["Young Man's Song"]

Undated in the notebook, this poem was written on the heels of "Girl's Song," soon after March 29, 1929 (see "CCP" 241). Except for the late intervention of the second version of "Mrs Phillamore" (on 43v; see above) and an advanced draft of "Love's Loneliness" (on 44v; see below), "Young Man's Song" occupies a barely interrupted block of writing immediately after "Girl's Song." See *WFMP* 390–403 for facsimiles and transcriptions. As "Young Man's Song" was written consciously as a counterpoint to the latter, the two poems have been locked as a pair since publication in the 1932 Cuala Press edition of *Words for Music Perhaps*, where their order reversed. In the *Collected Poems*, their order reverted, but "A Woman Young and Old" was also introduced to counterpoint the song sequence from *The Tower* called "A Man Young and Old." The logic of the male-female juxtaposition largely derives from the argument Yeats waged in *A Vision* concerning the double-coned truth that he traced to Blake's poem "The Mental Traveller" and thereafter managed to instill into these parallel male and female sequences.[66]

Since, by design, Yeats intended no refrain for this song, its three stanzas required more work than it might have in a ballad because he could not count on the music of repetition. Like "Girl's Song" in its construction of stanzas that are each based on three-stress lines and two alternating end-rhymes, "Young Man's Song" nevertheless extended the length of each stanza by two lines without cutting out a stressed syllable (or word) from the three culminating lines. The poem's rhythms tend to be regular (even iambic) with fewer variations or metrical inversions. Dissonant effects such as the use of eye-rhyme ("show" and "saw") or half-rhyme ("crone" and "lain") were intended as the deliberation process is mirrored in the sets of rhyme notes Yeats made on 41v, 42r, and 42v. Respectively, the writing began at those locations for stanzas 1–3. As we have seen in the genesis of other poems, progress is often measured in stages toward a fair-hand copy although progress might not be made at an even rate.

Starting on 41v, Yeats seemed to know what he wanted and quickly achieved most of it in stanza 1, which would only require a new line 1 and slight refinement of lines 2–3 on 44r, where all three parts of the poem first came together. Turning to stanza 2 on 42r, six lines were similarly obtained but much less to his satisfaction. In all, there are eight draft versions of that stanza up to the final fair copy on 45r. While only four lines of stanza 3 were worked out on 42v (beneath two drafts of stanza 2), it was nearly finished on 43r (above another draft of stanza 2) before slight revision occurred on 44r and the clean copy of 45r. After the three movements of the poem were joined under the title "~~The young mans song~~ ~~Boys~~ <Young Mans> Song" (on 43r), where only stanza 2 was entirely cancelled out, three additional drafts (on 43v) of the fraught stanza were necessary to obtain text for copying into the final version of the poem on 45r. At this penultimate stage in the poem's composition, Yeats posed for himself the task of deciding between three alternative versions of the middle stanza, each rhyming differently from the other two. He chose the one in quotation marks that he had copied in the left margin. To judge from handwriting, this might have occurred at the same time he jotted version 2 of "Mrs Phillamore" in the lower margin (see above). Then he drew vertical strokes through the rejected versions of stanza 2 and turned to leaf 45r, where he made a finished poem out of stanzas 1 and 3 (from 44r) and the chosen stanza 2 (from 43v). In that maneuver, the culminating line of stanza 2 came to echo the poem "Before the World Was Made" (written in February 1928), number II in the sequence "A Woman Young and Old."

[44v] ["Love's Loneliness"; revised from 56v (below)]

At the time Yeats completed "Young Man's Song," the facing page next to it (44v) had been left blank as he began writing the poem "His Confidence" at the next opening (45v–46r). In little more than a fortnight, however, he filled the blank space on 44v with a medial version of "Love's Loneliness" that he had not begun to write until nearing the end of his stay in Rapallo (see "CCP" 241 and *WFMP* 452–53; a facsimile of 44v also appears in Genet 700). Entries below for manuscript pages 50v and 55v–56r are needed to complete the account of this displaced draft in relation to all parts of the composition. Here, the impression of systematic progress from one work to the next seems broken with this first of two displacements since the poem's origin on 56r.

[45v–48r] ["His Confidence" and "Her Anxiety"]

Following "Young Man's Song," Yeats wrote "His Confidence," probably in early April. George Yeats's estimation was also based on the poem's position in the notebook, but, as with several poems in its vicinity, she would only give the date of composition as "1929 [after March 29]" (see "CCP" 241). Its two stanzas evolved, from recto to facing verso to next recto, in just two cycles (i.e., 46r to 45v to 47r, and 47r to 46v to 48r), leaving a temporarily blank page (47v), which the poet promptly put to use by writing "Her Anxiety," a complementary lyric in the Girl's voice. Reproductions and transcriptions are available in *WFMP* 410–21.

"His Confidence" begins on 46r with several cancelled and partly illegible phrasings ("~~Trust n[ot] changeless love~~ || ~~A self torturing cruelty~~ | ~~Had first~~ | All loves [?cruelty] | [?Pierced] [?my] side").[67] More abundant and clear on this page are the four sets of rhyme notes and the gesture of self-violence laid out in the sentence "With my own hand I smote / ~~On my~~ | Upon my hearts hard rock"—with "smote" in place of "struck" (a rhyme for "rock") when the alternative might have been "blow" to rhyme with "know." On 45v (facing left), Yeats worked out both of those options for stanza 2, evidently in two sittings (based on the size and angle of his cursive in the second draft. Not content with the result, he makes three more trial runs at that stanza on 47r and cancels two to produce a quatrain: "I broke my heart in two / ~~B~~ None other struck / Be content to know / How hard this rock." With that much accomplished, he shifted to work on the facing page (leaf 46v) to transform the words "on corners of the eyes / ~~[...]~~ / Daily wrote" into not quite the final version of stanza 1 in two cycles of drafting (as on 45v for stanza 2). Thereafter, on a new leaf (48r), Yeats pulls together all that he has made of the poem so far, revising as he does so, and leaves the poem without title but stanzas in numerals (I and II) for later typing. Miraculously, he does so without rehearsing the closing rhymed couplet that he inserts into each stanza: "What payment were ~~[...]~~ enough / For unending love" (in "I") and "Out of a desolate source / Love leaps upon its course" (in "II").

"Her Anxiety" seems to have been accomplished in a single sitting, perhaps the same day in April on which its companion was finished. Superficially, the stanzas are much the same although their rhyme-schemes differ substantially, distinguishing the voices by personality if not by gender. Their three-stress lines behave differently, as well. For in "Her Anxiety" they are more measured, deliberative, concluding each stanza with a refrain-line ("Prove that I lie") more than equal to the rhetorical force of couplets used in the same places in "His Confidence." In short, untitled and not even close to fair copy on 47v, the one and only version of "Her Anxiety" in Rapallo C is no more revised in its place than is the final version of its mate on 48r although, obviously, written much more quickly.

[48v–50r, 51r] ["Her Dream" and "Symbols"]

By their position in Rapallo C, these poems were clearly written a few days after March 29 but *before* April 17, 1929. Mrs. Yeats safely estimated "Her Dream" to have been written in 1929, at some time "after March 29" ("CCP" 241). Yet she attributed to "Symbols" the incorrect date of "Oct. 1927" ("CCP" 240), thereafter copied by Ellmann.[68] Following work on "Her Dream" for three pages, WBY began writing "Symbols" on 49v before leaving fair-hand versions of both poems on 51r (the one over the other, as shown in *WFMP* 444). As one might expect, pairings of images and transcripts are in separate locations in *WFMP*—on pages 438–45 for "Her Dream" and pages 236–39 for "Symbols." A facsimile of the latter at 49v is also provided in Genet 696, without transcription, whereas Clark collates variants from 51r in the notebook against a loose-leaf version of "Symbols" (NLI 13,590 [7], featured at *WFMP* 238–39 as an intermediate text), without reproducing an image of 51r. Facing the two poems (at left, on 50v) is the final, dated version of "Love's Loneliness" (see next entry, below).

"Her Dream" begins at the opening 48v–49r with false starts (on the right) involving first lines (e.g., "I dreamed upon the break of day / […] That I had shorn my locks away") so reminiscent of early lyrics—and possibly rejected for that reason—but assisted on the left by columns of rhyme notes. Three tiers of revised lines (on the left) about "locks of youth," the shearing away of "ebony locks," and laying of those locks "on loves lettered tomb" are then developed—most decisively on 50r—into the striking image of "Berenices burning hair" for the poem's final line, an achievement twice anticipated on 49r and four times stated on 50r (twice cancelled). The sum of it leads to the last version, on 51r, with the first line left for the poet to choose between the one he wrote in first instance (on 49r but cancelled there) and an alternative—either "I dreamed, as in my bed I lay" or "dreamed for in bed I lay" (cf. *VP* 519).

For "Symbols," composition occurred quickly once the adjectives were worked out for the "old Tower" in line 1 and for the "Blind Hermit" who "rings the hour" in line 2. Once that was decided, the couplet that constitutes stanza 2 ("All destroying sword-blade still / Carried by the Wandering Fool") and the one after that, which gives the poem its zest in double-entendre ("Gold-sown silk on the sword-blade / Beauty & Fool together laid"), might almost have written themselves, as typically Yeatsian as they are. In the margin, however, he directs "no not capitals" in imperative voice, a call for subtlety that he heeds in NLI 13,590 (7) and Rapallo Notebook C, leaf 51r.

[50v] ["Love's Loneliness" copied and revised from 44v (above)]

The final version of this poem, dated "April 17 [1929]" here, is a reworking of stanzas previously assembled on 44v (see "CCP" 241; see also *WFMP* 454–55 and Genet 701). Yeats's initial work on the poem took place on 55v–56r, the last opening in the notebook prior to a longer effort (on 56v–59r) called "[Imagination's Bride]" ("CNGI" 7–12). See the commentary, above, on "Love's Loneliness" (44v) and, below, on the poem's origin at 55v–56r.

[51v–52r] ["{Heavy the Bog}" (unpublished)]

The title of this unfinished lyric was coined by David Clark, whose transcription and notes are in "CNGI" 5–6. As Yeats left it, the poem emulates certain aspects of his dramatic lyric "Towards Break of Day" in *Michael*

Robartes and the Dancer (1921). Perhaps he had thought to repeat such work here in the voice of a bowhunter (or man who dreams of pursuing an archetypal stag that stands on "grey rock" in morning light and leaps "From mountain steep to mountain steep" in the manner of past example and based on "complementary dreams," an idea discussed in *A Vision A* [173–74, *CW13* 140–41], where lines from the older poem were quoted). The rejected line in "Her Dream" (see above) was the opening line of "Towards Break of Day," also, which suggests that "[Heavy the Bog]" might be regarded as an attempt to write complementary verse to counterpoint "Her Dream." Pairing lyrics in composition, after all, follows the nearby precedent of "His Confidence" and "Her Anxiety," for example. Clark suggests that echoing too closely the older poem, written in Enniskerry in the winter of 1918–1919, may be the reason "[Heavy the Bog]" was abandoned after its writing in April 1929.[69] Also, to be generous, two only technically viable fragments on facing pages are not very inspiring. A facsimile of 51v, without transcription of the second stanza, is available in *WFMP* 424 although stanza 1 is omitted there.

[51v–55r] ["His Bargain"]

Beneath the stanzas of the abandoned lyric on 51v–52r are written a few catch-phrases, initiating lines, and rhyme notes for "His Bargain," a poem written in "1929 [after March 29]," according to Mrs. Yeats ("CCP" 241), but clearly in mid-April because of its physical relation to the nearest poems in the notebook. It is the last published poem in it to have been written on contiguous pages as the number of leaves in the notebook grew fewer and time drew nearer the Yeatses' departure for home at the end of the month. Facsimiles and transcriptions are available in *WFMP* 424–37 but also Genet 705–10.

At the opening 52v–53r, most of the writing occurs on 53r, where all but two lines ("A bargain with that hair / And all the windings there" for stanza 2) are destined for stanza 1 (in two drafts), about "Times spindle" (also "Platos famous spindle"). On the left-hand page (52v), two sets of lines bearing the words "swindle" and "dwindle" aim to refine stanza 1, but the rhyme notes on the lower half of the page anticipate the second stanza.

At the opening 53v–54r, Yeats set down (one over the other) two versions of stanza 1, the first concluding "[…] Johny Knave, & Judy lout / Learn to change their loves about" and the second "[…] every knave & lout / Change their loves about." After a space, only three lines relate to stanza 2. So 54r (at right) is used to compose a full stanza 2 in six lines and an alternate version of its first four lines.

Thereafter, at opening 54v–55r, both stanzas are assembled as a poem, revised, and cancelled by means of a vertical stroke on 55r. (Beneath this version of the poem, seven lines record intended revisions for an old poem, "The Two

Trees.") Leaf 54v (facing the cancelled, amended draft of "His Bargain") was then used to preserve a fair-hand copy of the text for later typing. Interestingly, as he copied, Yeats opted for "Dan and Jerry Lout" over "every knave and lout" in stanza 1, line 5.

[55r] ["The Two Trees" (revised lines for *Collected Poems*)]

A reproduction of this holograph fragment is available in Genet 709. Intended for revision, these lines are written at a slant beneath the penultimate draft of "His Bargain." The fragment is correspondent with "The Two Trees," lines 13–18 (*VP* 38, 135). The poem had been written in April 1895, according to George Yeats ("CCP" 231). A single line hovers over it ("There through the bough bewildered ~~air~~ light"), but then, after a small space, the following lines are written:

                        a circle
And there the loves ~~in circles~~ go
The flaming circle flaring circle of our ~~ge~~ day
Here & there & to & fro
In those leaves leafy ways
Remembering all that shaken hair
And how the winged sand[al]s [d]art[70]

[55v–56v] ["Love's Loneliness" (first phase of composition)]

The writing of this poem started on leaf 56r, at the right side of the next opening in the notebook after "His Bargain." But "Love's Loneliness" was suspended in a rough-draft state, interrupted by the call to begin and complete an unpublished poem known eventually as "[Imagination's Bride]" ("CNGI" 7–12). We know with certainty when "Love's Loneliness" had reached its final state in Rapallo C, on leaf 50v (see above), for it is dated "April 17"; close to but before that would be its penultimate state on leaf 44v (see above). Roughly, the length of time between its suspension and its completion in the notebook is equal to the time it took Yeats to write "[Imagination's Bride]" although we cannot know that for certain. Suffice it to say, like "His Bargain," "Love's Loneliness" was conceived in mid-April 1929, several days before its delivery. Facsimiles of the poem's first stage have been presented by Genet (698–702) and by Clark (including transcriptions, in *WFMP* 446–51).

When composition began on 56r, the stuff of stanza 1 struggled to manifest itself in half a dozen lines, all cancelled except for "Grandfathers great grandfathers, ~~all~~" (the first line). After that (and aside from intermittent rhyme notes), only three other lines emerged on that page: "old kindred of our blood, / pray to god that he protects us." On the facing page (55v), Yeats jotted (at top right and lower right) two separate sets of rhyme notes, both considered yet most of the lower set rejected for stanza 1. Sectioned off in the middle of the page are approximately six lines that would evolve later into stanza 2. And then he turned to the next pair of facing pages (both then blank) and launched another assault (in two runs) on 56v—but failed to solve whatever problem he was having with stanza 1. Consequently, he cancelled the effort with drawn lines, as shown in Figure 2.6, and drew a squiggly border around two sides of it as if to set off those lines distinctly (in the upper left corner of that page) from what was to follow. On the other side of that border are now the verses he wrote for the next poem, "[Imagination's Bride]." Perhaps he felt it best to postpone completion of "Love's Loneliness," rather than to abandon it, in order to finish it later on. As half the poem was already forming nicely by 55v, the other half might reasonably come in time.... And so it did, on 44v and 50v, in that order.

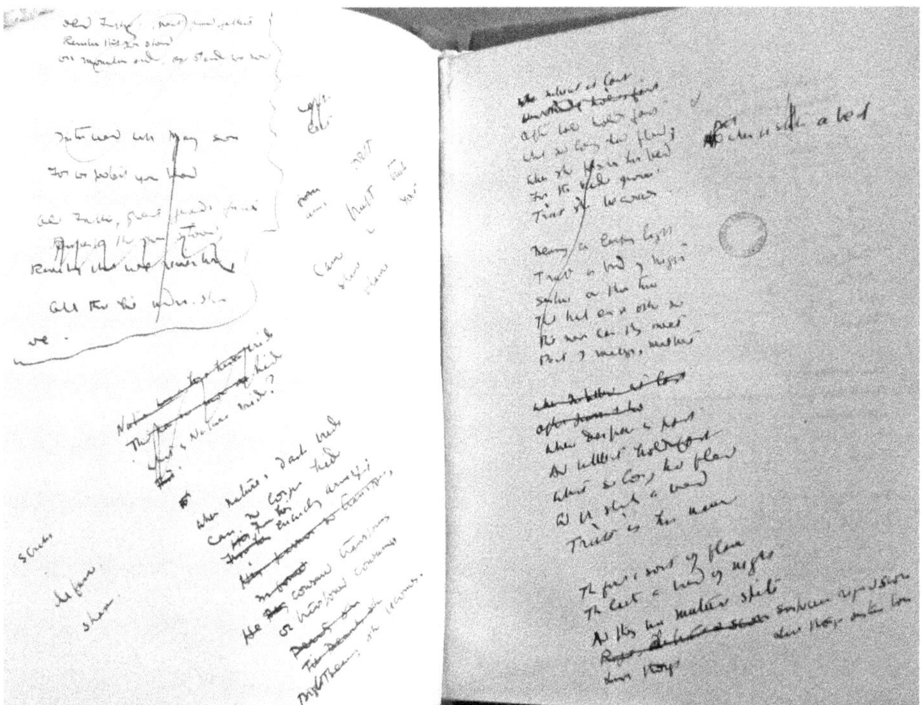

Figure 2.6. Rapallo Notebook C, NLI 13,580, [56v and 57r], in full. Courtesy of NLI; photograph courtesy of Catherine E. Paul. (Circumscribed lines at upper left are part of "Love's Loneliness"; the rest relates to "[Imagination's Bride]." Folio 57r is reproduced for the first time; see below.)

[56v–59r] ["{Imagination's Bride}" (unpublished)]

Genet (701) was first to produce a facsimile of 56v, followed by Clark (*WFMP* 450). Clark's later transcription of the drafts (in "CNGI" 7–12, without comment) produces a final version substantially in agreement with Ellmann's version, first presented in *The Identity of Yeats* to show that a seismic shift had occurred, after four decades, in the way Yeats brought together wisdom and dreams in his poetry. Here, a tranquil "weaving image" of wisdom and dreams is "put aside and a more violent metaphor chosen" (37):

> Now truth (reason's bride) and beauty (imagination's bride), which correspond roughly to wisdom and dreams, are bitter and hostile to each other, in spite of their mutual dependence. The concepts are alive instead of mechanical. Powerful images of sexuality and family hatred suit the mature poet better than flowers and fruits. (38)

We might recall the versions of "Wisdom & Knowledge (or John Hermit & his friends)," Rapallo C, 35v, where the disturbance that Ellmann notes produces commentators like Tom Ratcatcher and Biddy Cockle, or, nearer to hand, compels the speaker in "Love's Loneliness" to bid his "Old fathers great grand fathers / Rise as kindred should" (44v) to "protect your blood" (56v). Too strongly echoing the militant prologue of *Responsibilities* might have been a risk Yeats hesitated to take, just as he might have suppressed a line in "Her Dream" and an entire poem, "[Heavy the Bog]," for artlessly echoing another past achievement. Whatever the reason, the way forward with "Love's Loneliness" was blocked by "[Imagination's Bride]" so that, by the time the latter was finished, Yeats needed to leaf back to available pockets in the notebook (44v and 50v) when taking up the former where he had left it.

Therefore, dating the final unpublished lyric, as well as the first notes in prose after that (starting at 59v), is defined by the material evidence of the notebook and the known dates of Yeats's itinerary. His departure from Rapallo (on April 27, 1929), arrival in London on the twenty-ninth, and busy week visiting friends there before catching up with his wife in Dublin would account for an absence of entries. Moreover, note number "4" in the final prose section of Rapallo C is preceded (on 61r) by a drawn line across the page and the date "May 26"—very likely to signify the resumption of writing in the notebook. "[Imagination's Bride]" had triggered the resumption of prose writing, at that point, due to the philosophical questions it raises that had not been worked out to Yeats's satisfaction in the 1925 edition of *A Vision*.

The poem begins with rhyme notes, the notion of marriage in the assertion that "~~Nature has [...] a hid[d]en~~ bride / ~~That can no more [?]~~ hide" and in the question "What is Natures bride?" (56v). Questions are implied, too, in that poetic assertion: for instance, What is meant by Nature? In what sense is Nature married? And why is that thing (to which Nature is married) hidden from us? Metaphysics aside, with the next lines Yeats set down three sets of rhymed couplets, letting words find meaning in the process while revealing "Beauty" to be the bride, rather conventionally, but breaking with tradition to assign to Nature a masculine gender identity. Not surprisingly, the double-vortex is at the center of invention as Nature takes in "his encircling arms" a "dark bride" that he makes "Bright" paradoxically, for "<He> ~~Being~~ consumed transforms / or transformed consumes" (56v). The gyres are not evident after that, except for a reworking of stanza 1 (cancelled) later on 58r. On 57r, attention is mainly focused on stanza 2 in three stages, much of it cancelled by strikethroughs and a vertical stroke. Keatsian Beauty and Truth contend as sisters "That hate each other so" but are toned down in the stanza (except as "sluts in bed") as the poem deviates from form established in stanza 1 (that of three pairs of rhyming couplets) to that of five-line stanzas interlaced by rhyming the fifth line of stanza 2 with the first line of stanza 3. "Intellect" (later "Reason") begins to take over the place Nature had occupied, eventually becoming "Imagination" by draft three (on 58r).

Draft 2 of the poem (on 57v) is given a title—"The Daimon & <the> Celestial Body"— and is defined by a rewritten first stanza in heightened tones of carnality, active agency, and concrete imagery. The first and last lines of the stanza ("When nature ~~found~~ <holds> his bride" and "Beauty she becomes") survive from draft 1 (with tweaking). Three out of five lines are amended by options provided (at right) beside stanza 2, retaining only the last two lines from draft 1 (57r). All of stanza 3 is retained from draft 1 although the entire poem is cancelled on 57v by a long vertical line drawn through the text.

Following a rejected reworking of stanza 1 based on lines introduced on 56v, Yeats fine-tuned the lyric in a third draft version called "The Passionate & Celestial Body," on leaf 58r. There, he copied out the sixteen lines of the poem (a stanza of six lines and two stanzas of five)[71] much as he had done for draft 2: placing beside stanza 1 four alternative lines (to the right) and beside stanza 2 one such alternative line. Stanza 3 remains unchanged from draft 2. Imagination has taken the place of Nature just as, in the choice of options, "Thought" became "Reason" in the exceptionally fair text that Yeats copied out, finally, on 59r. At left, leaf 58v (a blank page) seems to testify to the poet's general satisfaction with this work, at least for the time being, because this buffer serves no practical purpose other than to suggest finality, after precedents such as the blank pages facing "Those Dancing Days Are Gone" and "Girl's Song" (at 30v and 40v).[72]

6. Conclusion

As we have seen, the prose writings and the poetry composed in Rapallo Notebook C transition into and out of one another as units of work, the former constituting a frame around a core of poetry writing from at least January 23 to April 17, 1929, and possibly longer. Parallels exist between Yeats's notes on the occult "Marriage of Husk & Passionate Body" in relation to "Spirit & Celestial Body" (on 4r through 5r) and his later effort to write a poem about the marriage of *Daimon* (or, alternatively, *Passionate Body*) and *Celestial Body* (on 57v and 58r). Such work also engages with his effort to define these terms in a series of exploratory notes, most of it weeks later (from 59v to the end of the notebook), in notes for "The Soul in Judgment," Book III of *A Vision* (the Macmillan trade edition of 1937). Also, as we have seen, work then underway at the Cuala Press (i.e., *A Packet for Ezra Pound*, the intended introduction for *A Vision*) had produced demands on Yeats's time and energy in Rapallo—including a first-draft essay on Poundian skepticism (6r–8r) for *A Packet*; the text of a postscript for the "End of Cuala book" (11r); both parts of the poem "Meditations upon Death" written to follow the theme on skepticism in the book (9r, 10r); and, in March, the physical challenge of correcting proof copy. The reader need only reflect on Neil Mann's "Rapallo Notebooks A and B," however, to put in perspective the fairly small role Rapallo C plays in the making of the Cuala book.

So the story Rapallo Notebook C tells is partly about the transmutation of *A Vision* 1925 into the Macmillan edition of 1937. But not only that. The story Rapallo C also tells is that the making of poetry is interwoven into the fabric of Yeats's developing philosophy. Back in Dublin, Yeats wrote letters to Olivia Shakespear and Lady Gregory on the same day (July 2, 1929), calculating the progress of his philosophy and his poetry as if they were interchangeable entities. Observing that he had "tidied" the "big table and … desk" of his study so that they were "no longer covered with a disorder of books and loose papers," he reported to Mrs. Shakespear that "I am still putting the philosophy in order but once that is done, and this summer must finish, I believe I shall have a poetical rebirth for as I write about my cones and gyres all kinds of images come before me" (*L* 764; *CL InteLex* 5259).

In his letter to Lady Gregory, he attached a postscript about the progress he was making on the "big book" of philosophy, not knowing that illness would seriously delay progress on this work when he returned to Rapallo in November. He told her, "The moment the big book is finished I shall begin verse again. I have a longish poem in my head about Coole" (*CL InteLex* 5258).

Both letters speak to the moment but in different ways. To Olivia Shakespear, the letter gives an impression of the condition of his study—"disorder of books" etc.—and (he might as well have added) a sense of the phantasmagorical topics addressed in the last ten leaves of Rapallo C. To Lady Gregory, on the other hand, Yeats promised to write, in due course, a magisterial poem: "Coole Park, 1929"—which was a promise he was able to keep by October after turning out more than forty pages of hard work in Rapallo Notebook D (see *WFMP* 609;

"CCP" 240), having filled Rapallo C, as we have seen. In short, after composing twenty-five poems in Rapallo C, Yeats wrote another eight poems in Rapallo D and then one more in Rapallo E, in both cases either for the sequence "Words for Music Perhaps" or for another location in *The Winding Stair* (1933). Consequently, the remainder of a long tale—about certain poems, philosophy, and sundry writings in the Rapallo Notebooks—is entrusted to the next two installments of this series.

Notes

1 Neil Mann's essay first appeared in *International Yeats Studies* 6.1 (2022), 73–183.

2 In alphabetical order, the principal collaborators are Wayne Chapman, Warwick Gould, Margaret Harper, and Neil Mann. Several years ago, we began by discussing a question posed by *IYS* founding editor Lauren Arrington on the feasibility of a project that has since taken shape under the editorship of Rob Doggett. The team works remotely—generally from facilities in Ireland, the US, the UK, and Spain—to prepare a reliable, detailed map of these complexly jumbled notebooks, both from direct observation in the National Library and from a set of digital facsimiles provided by Catherine E. Paul, with, in a few cases, supplements from Jack Quin. Special thanks to Charis Chapman for her expertise setting text and visuals for the series. In addition to these colleagues, there are a number of precursors to acknowledge as fellow collaborators because of their past example. Acknowledgment is therefore made to their work in the text, notes, and appendices below—especially to the unrivaled skill of the late David R. Clark to interpret the handwriting of Yeats in the lyric sequences of *The Winding Stair*.

3 Manuscript notebooks used by Yeats do exist elsewhere, of course. One such, unfortunately owned by an anonymous collector and thus out of circulation, has some bearing on the Rapallo notebooks as a near-contemporary involving some of the same lyric sequences. Accordingly, another precursor to the *IYS* essays was created to assist, in particular, essays on Rapallo Notebooks C and D. Hence, I will sometimes refer readers to my article "Yeats's White Vellum Notebook, 1930–1933," *International Yeats Studies* 2.2 (May 2018), 41–60—an updating of field notes begun by Curtis Bradford, revised by David R. Clark, and then passed down to me by Cornell Yeats general editor Stephen Parrish. For quotations from *A Vision, Revised 1937 Edition* by W. B. Yeats (copyright © 1937 by W. B. Yeats; copyright renewed © 1965 by Bertha Georgie Yeats and Anne Butler Yeats), these are reprinted with the permission of Scribner, a division of Simon & Schuster, Inc. All rights reserved.

4 Clark distinguished between his "interpretative book" (which combined "luxury of interpretation and critical comment") and the great labor to which it was related as humble "by-product." The larger project was no less than "to arrange, transcribe, and edit all the most important manuscripts of Yeats's poems, plays, and prose." By this he meant not simply the Cornell Yeats Series, because he had also envisioned its like at the university press in Amherst before joining the Cornell series and agreeing to edit there three volumes of manuscript materials for poetry. Such editions gave readers all of "Yeats's words," yet it would be up to readers themselves to "take it from there" (*Yeats at Songs and Choruses* xvii). The *luxury*, perhaps the greatest pleasure, is understood to be with the "interpretative" work.

5 I might add that Clark's gifts included dedication to such hard, detailed labor in archival quarries that he voluntarily assisted SUNY librarians in the cataloguing of Yeats's

microfilmed tapes in the Frank Melville Library at Stony Brook, on Long Island, where he spent weeks transcribing poetry for his own use and indexing entries for others.

6 Reminiscent of the title of Robert Chambers's influential study of the transmutation of species, *Vestiges of the Natural History of Creation* (1844), the term is defined by a chapter in Parkinson's *W. B. Yeats: The Later Poetry* (Berkeley and Los Angeles: University of California Press, 1964), 73–113. Though I have sometimes quarreled with Parkinson's tendency to simplify, his masterpiece is in some ways better, in that respect, than Stallworthy's two textual-genetic studies, *Between the Lines: Yeats's Poetry in the Making* (1963) and *Vision and Revision in Yeats's Last Poems* (1969), both published at the Clarendon Press at Oxford. See Wayne K. Chapman, "George Yeats, Thomas Parkinson, and the Legacy of the Archive," in *New Thresholds in Yeats Studies: Yeats Annual* 22, ed. Warwick Gould (Cambridge: Open Book Publishers, forthcoming). I deal with Richard Ellmann's early access to Mrs. Yeats and the manuscripts in *IYS* 2.2 (May 2018), 58n18, as well as in *YA* 15 (2002), 120–58, as reprinted in the final chapter and first appendix of my book *Yeats's Poetry in the Making: "Sing Whatever Is Well Made"* (London: Palgrave Macmillan, 2010), 211–45; hereafter cited as *YPM*.

7 At this writing, Rapallo Notebook D has not been rebound by the Delmas Conservation Bindery and remains loose, like the "'Rapallo' notebook in leather" used for composing *Stories of Michael Robartes and His Friends* (NLI 13,577; "Parkinson's list" II.d). Rapallo D's paper type and cover floral motif also agree with Rapallo C and NLI 13,577.

8 Mann's essay omits the typed cover notice as extraneous. Yet its introduction here is a necessary deferral in the series to account for the notebooks' conservation as they transitioned to the NLI's care. A smaller typed slip (denoting "NOTES ON SYSTEM | INCLUDING COMMENTS | ON <u>THE CAT & THE | MOON</u>" and bearing the handwritten inscription, "See p. 11," in green ink) has been tipped-in just inside the front cover of Rapallo A, too, though the smaller slip belongs clipped to numbered page "11," folio 48r, also amid *Vision* material. See Mann's "Tabular Summary 1: Rapallo Notebook A (NLI 13,578)" in *IYS* 6.1 (2022), 162–71; reprinted as Appendix A, below.

9 Such flags did not exist when Ellmann requested and received from George Yeats an old suitcase loaded with manuscripts (see NLI 30,746, "Miscellaneous cards, notes, etc.," f. 3v), which included the Rapallo notebooks A–E. Selections were subsequently made by Ellmann for microfilming as he prepared to resume teaching at Harvard in academic year 1947/48. Five reels were acquired for the Houghton Library in January 1948. Parkinson, too, had microfilm copies made on two occasions, the first in late 1957 and the second in spring 1958, as he anticipated his return to teaching at Berkeley. Sadly, Parkinson's microfilms have been lost. See Chapman, "George Yeats, Thomas Parkinson, and the Legacy of the Archive," parts 2 and 3.

10 Mann, "Rapallo Notebooks A and B," 73 (rpt. p. 31, below).

11 See David R. Clark, *WFMP* xvii (defined in the "List of Abbreviations"). He notes that Rapallo E includes one poem, "For Anne Gregory," but attributes no date for it. On the authority of Mrs. Yeats, that poem was written in "1930," Sept. 1930 (*YPM* 240). Editors Jared Curtis and Selina Guinness, in *The Resurrection: Manuscript Materials* (Ithaca, NY, and London: Cornell University Press, 2011), argue that Rapallo E has both early and late dates of usage—that it "appears to have been in use from about May or June 1926," or even earlier (xvi), and that Yeats began writing introductions for *Wheels and Butterflies* in "mid-November 1930," with the one on *The Resurrection* to be written in 1931 (xxxix), bridging material in the missing White Vellum Notebook, and producing copy for his typist and copy text for Macmillan in February 1934.

12 WBY to Olivia Shakespear, *L* 748 (*CL InteLex* 5191).

13 WBY to Olivia Shakespear, *L* 758 (*CL InteLex* 5221); WBY to Lady Gregory, *L* 762 (*CL InteLex* 5236).
14 WBY to Olivia Shakespear, *L* 763 (*CL InteLex* 5242).
15 WBY to Lady Gregory, *L* 764 (*CL InteLex* 5252).
16 See *IYS* "List of Abbreviations" at https://tigerprints.clemson.edu/iys/iys_abbreviations.html. The four abbreviations introduced here supplement and are coordinate with abbreviations introduced in the tabular summary at the end of this essay, where (as here) "*YAACTS*" stands for *Yeats: An Annual of Critical and Textual Studies* (ed. Richard J. Finneran; 17 vols.), and where "*IY*" refers to Richard Ellmann, *The Identity of Yeats* (New York: OUP, 1954). Ellmann's dates of composition have been incorporated into my table, "CCP," along with dates provided in texts annotated by Mrs. Yeats. For the abbreviation "*YPM*," see note 6, above.
17 Descriptions are given below according to natural sections of the notebook, whenever possible as indicated by Yeats with headings or directions on a section's intended use. In such cases, headings presented in quotation marks are Yeats's; other supplied details are given in brackets, including folio numbers.
18 See Mann, "Rapallo Notebooks A and B," *IYS* 6.1 162 and 172 (rpt. 120 and 130, below).
19 See "King, John," *Encyclopedia of Occultism and Parapsychology*, via Encyclopedia.com (https://www.encyclopedia.com/science/encyclopedias-almanacs-transcripts-and-maps/king-john). See also Steve L. Adams and George Mills Harper (eds.), "The Manuscript of 'Leo Africanus,'" *YA1* 7 and n10 (rpt. in *YA19* 295 and n10).
20 See Ezra Pound, *Literary Essays of Ezra Pound*, ed. T. S. Eliot (New York: New Directions, 1968), 160.
21 A discussion of Anne Hyde's appearance in 1918 and of the Yeatses' parallel research efforts at the Bodleian Library and the Oxford Union is found in Wayne K. Chapman, "Introduction," *"Something that I read in a book": W. B. Yeats's Annotations at the National Library of Ireland*, 2 vols. (Clemson, SC, and Liverpool: Clemson University Press associated with Liverpool University Press, 2022), xxv (in both vols.); hereafter cited as *YANLI* (with volume number). For an index to the deceased countess' involvement in their research, see *Yeats's* Vision *Papers*, vol. 3: *Sleep and Dream Notebooks,* Vision *Notebooks 1 and 2, Card File*, ed. Robert A. Martinich and Margaret M. Harper (Iowa City: University of Iowa Press, 1992), 239. On the development of the occult system of *A Vision*, Yeats publicly acknowledged for the first time—in *A Packet for Ezra Pound* (Dublin: Cuala Press, 1929), 12—that "On the afternoon of October 24th 1917, four days after my marriage, my wife surprised me by attempting automatic writing" (rpt. in *AVB* 8 and *CW14* 7). The parenthetical "(Four days after my marriage)" recurs in Rapallo C, on 2r, after the starting date for the Script, suggesting that draft materials were at hand for the "INTRODUCTION TO THE GREAT WHEEL," part II, in *A Packet for Ezra Pound*. The elaborate ruse developed for the 1925 edition of *A Vision* to keep this truth from getting out is the story told in *W. B. Yeats's Robartes-Aherne Writings: Featuring the Making of His "Stories of Michael Robartes and His Friends,"* ed. Wayne K. Chapman (London: Bloomsbury Academic, 2018); see 101–64 for the years 1917–1920.
22 See Wayne K. Chapman, *The W. B. and George Yeats Library: A Short-Title Catalog* (Clemson, SC: Clemson University Press, 2006, 2019), 26, items 240 and 241; hereafter cited as *WBGYL*.
23 Just the downstroke of the "9" is completed, but the year 1929 is clearly intended as confirmed by the date of the last entry on 3r.
24 Regarding Yeats's treatment of Lewis in Rapallo Notebook B, see Mann's essay in *IYS* 6.1 111–16 (rpt. 69–74, below). On Yeats's reading familiarity, see Chapman, *YANLI*, vol. 1, where in *Time and Western Man* (item 1136) Yeats was drawn to the last four chapters: "God as Reality," "The Object as King of the Physical World," "Space and Time," and "Conclusion."

The Childermass (item 1129) is the first volume of the unfinished epic "The Human Age," which Lewis presented to Yeats because he had heard from someone that Yeats was reading the other book (1136).

25 See Chapman, *YANLI*, vol. 1, items 1989 and 1989A, pages 360–68.

26 See Pound, *Literary Essays* 16.

27 The quotation intended is probably the quatrain from Swift's "The Progress of Beauty" that Yeats employed in a footnote on art and Lewis's *Time and Western Man*, in "Rapallo," II, *A Packet for Ezra Pound*, page 2 (*AVB* 4; *CW14* 4): "Matter as wise logicians say / Cannot without a form subsist; / And form, say as well as they, / Must fail, if matter brings no grist."

28 Ellmann, *IY* 239. Yeats's writes to Lady Gregory (Nov. 27, [1928]; *CL InteLex* 5194): "I want Lolly to publish next a little book of mine called 'A Packet' almost all written since I came here." See Wade 163 and *CW14* xxxii–xxxvi for dating the booklet's contents by section.

29 The setting copy is at Emory University (SPEC COL PR5906.A553 1929).

30 Catherine E. Paul, "Compiling *A Packet for Ezra Pound*," *Paideuma: Modern and Contemporary Poetry and Poetics* 38 (2011), 45.

31 Paul, "Compiling *A Packet for Ezra Pound*," 46.

32 WBY to Oliver St. John Gogarty, Jan. 6 [1929] (*CL InteLex* 5211); and WBY to Lady Gregory, March 24, 1929 (by dictation: "I have tired myself over the proof-sheets of my new Cuala book"; *CL InteLex* 5227). Near the end of Rapallo Notebook B (on leaves 91r–102r), Mann finds work for parts I-IX of "Introduction to the Great Wheel," pages 11–15 in *A Packet*. Section XV is there.

33 See Mann *IYS* 6.1 118 and 155, n. 171 (rpt. 76 and 113, below).

34 Ellmann reads "of intellectual needs," but his "of" is definitely "&" and the last two obviously misspelled words might be "its technical means" (i.e., prosody). This passage on 7r-8r is also quoted and discussed in Jack Quin's recent study, *W. B. Yeats and the Language of Sculpture* (Oxford: Oxford University Press, 2022), 164.

35 Cf. entries of April 7–26 [1921] in NLI 13,576, ff. 2–4, in Yeats's diary/notebook begun April 7, 1921, at 4 Broad Street, Oxford, wherein he distinguishes between "talking" and "singing" in verse to convey a moment of emotion: "We cannot do this if the poem does not call up the image of sailors, or of horsemen or unhappy lovers, a multitude out of other days" (qtd. in Chapman, *YPM* 10–11).

36 A scene like the one featured in Figure 1.2 (on page 3) in Lauren Arrington's *The Poets of Rapallo: How Mussolini's Italy Shaped British, Irish, and U.S. Writers* (Oxford: Oxford University Press, 2021), or like half a dozen snapshots in the Yeats Collection, MARBL, Emory, filed as "Photographs at Rapallo, 1929."

37 Cf. Ellmann, *IY* 240, for a rectified version of this ending.

38 See *YGYL* 244–45 regarding the BBC Belfast broadcast, made in haste and written in dictation. See also copies of Plutarch's *Lives* and *Morals*, the note's sources in the Yeats library (items 1609–1611a in *WBGYL*).

39 These dates are provided by Ann Saddlemyer, *Becoming George: The Life of Mrs. W. B. Yeats* (Oxford: Oxford University Press, 2002), 417, and by Yeats in letters to Olivia Shakespear (*L* 763 and *CL InteLex* 5242 and 5245).

40 At the National Library of Ireland, the early typescripts are NLI 36,272/6/2a [5–8] and [14–26].

41 See Chapman, *YANLI*, vol. 1, regarding Yeats's acquaintance with Croce's aesthetics: item 355, H. Wildon Carr, *The Philosophy of Benedetto Croce: The Problem of Art and History* (1917; signed by Yeats "Read in 1926"); also, among the English editions of works by Benedetto Croce that Yeats read and annotated, especially item 451, *Aesthetic as Science of Expression and General Linguistic* (1922), and item 455, *Logic as the Science of the Pure*

Concept (1917). Other annotated copies of Croce's books are described in items 454, 456, 457, suggesting close reading by Yeats in the 1920s.

42 Éliphas Lévi, *Transcendental Magic: Its Doctrine and Ritual* (1896; *WBGYL* 1119).

43 As editors Harper and Paul have noted (*CW14* 386), the complicated term "astral light" puzzles because Yeats confutes "astral *spirit*" (probably derived from Paracelsus in the sixteenth century) and "Astral Light" as defined in the nineteenth century by Éliphas Lévi. See note 42, above. On the influence of Dionertes, see *Yeats's Vision Papers*, vol. 2: *The Automatic Script: 25 June 1918–29 March 1920*, ed. Steve L. Adams, Barbara J. Frieling, and Sandra L. Sprayberry (Iowa City, IA: University of Iowa Press, 1992), 510–40 *passim*; hereafter cited as *YVP2*.

44 See Chapman, *YANLI*, vol. 1, regarding Yeats's annotations on dreams, percept, and perception in item 261, Bernard Bosanquet, *The Meeting of Extremes in Contemporary Philosophy* (1924); also in item 1411, John H. Muirhead, ed., *Contemporary British Philosophy* (1924). For the most heavily annotated instances, see item 1815, Bertrand Russell, *An Outline of Philosophy* (1927), 166 *passim* (on Berkeley and Russell) and especially the back flyleaf inscription. Russell is actually cited, finally, on leaf 68v of Rapallo Notebook C, within Yeats's discussion of "Expiation." See note 41 (above) on Croce.

45 Respectively, these are items 158, 678, and 889 in Chapman, *YANLI* 1: 42, 174–75, and 214.

46 The last two bracketed lines and comment are vigorously stricken.

47 Saddlemyer, *Becoming George* 306; see also *YPM* 122 and 318, n51. Both Saddlemyer (404) and Mann ("Rapallo Notebooks A and B," *IYS* 6.1: 76 [rpt. 32, below]) affirm that new "sleeps" occurred in Cannes at the end of 1927 and that Dionertes dominated in them, as Yeats's notes testify in leather manuscript notebook NLI 30,359. Saddlemyer (406) states that these "trances continued, although now rarely, until the second version of *A Vision* was published in 1937," and she quotes the Dublin 1929 entry in Rapallo Notebook C, 66v (illustrated in Figure 2.3), as an unpleasant yet important instance.

48 See *YPM* 138–41 and Chapman, *Yeats's Robartes-Aherne Writings* 43–44.

49 Bertrand Russell, *An Outline of Philosophy* (see note 44, above).

50 Stallworthy, *Between the Lines* 210–12. Without saying so, Stallworthy quotes from Keats's letter to Shelley of August 16, 1820.

51 Clark notes that George Yeats had attributed this date to two slightly later typescripts (*WFMP* 600 and 601), the last ones made before Yeats decided not to publish the poem, possibly at Pound's suggestion (581) or "on the advice of George Russell, among others" (Arrington, *Poets of Rapallo* 99).

52 Arrington's discussion of Yeats's interest in the ballad poetry of Burns in light of younger poets such as Aldington, Bunting, Zukofsky, and MacGreevy is highly recommended (*Poets of Rapallo* 85–104). She notes that of the seven poems published "in the Crazy Jane sequence, five are variations on the ballad" (95) and deal with worldly concerns, reminiscent of Burns, "while the two poems that are not ballads…concern the spiritual plane" (95–96).

53 As Yeats later remarked in a letter to Olivia Shakespear (November 22, 1931; *CL InteLex* 5539), this woman had "an amazing power of audacious speech" and was known to be "the local satirist and a really terrible one." Richard J. Finneran discusses versions of the poem in "The Composition and Final Text of W. B. Yeats's 'Crazy Jane on the King,'" *ICarbS* 4.2 (Spring–Summer 1981), 67–74. A. Norman Jeffares reports, in "Know Your Gogarty," *YA* 4 (2001), 303 and 305n, that Oliver St John Gogarty recited the poem at Tufts University and that it was eventually published in *The Amherst Literary Magazine* 10.2 (Summer 1964), 6–7, where it was taken down from memory (see *WFMP* 581).

54 Quoted in Arrington, *Poets of Rapallo* 30, from Patmore's *My Friends When Young* (1968).

55 Cf. Joseph Hone, *W. B. Yeats, 1865–1939* (New York: Macmillan, 1943), 429. A transcription of the typed list and its use by Hone is found in *YPM* 221–22.

56 The first instance occurs in "On Woman," a Solomon and Sheba poem written in May 21 or 25, 1914 ("CCP" 236), where "stretch and yawn" derive their meaning from the second stanza of Pound's translation of Arnault Daniel's "*Doutz brais e critz*": "I yawn and stretch because of that fair who surpasseth all others" (Clark 52).

57 The refrain also echoes Shakespeare's Sonnet 19: "Devouring Time, blunt thou the lion's paws // ... the fierce tiger's jaws" (in the opening lines) and "Yet do thy worst, old Time: despite thy wrong, / My love shall in my verse ever live young" (in the closing couplet).

58 By the time this letter was written, the nine poems Yeats counted would have included the five he referred to in his letter to Lady Gregory on March 9. The others were "Lullaby," of course, as well as "Cracked Mary & the Bishop," "Crazy Jane Reproved" (untitled but dated), and "Girl's Song"—four lyrics completed between March 27 and 29, 1929. "Wisdom & Knowledge" seems an unlikely fit for the "Words for Music" rubric although chronologically qualified. Bradford's treatment of "Lullaby" makes no mention of the version Yeats sent to Olivia Shakespear and is somewhat loosely attached to his treatment of "The Tower," section III. What Bradford calls "Draft C" and compares with *The New Keepsake* printing of November 1931 (Wade, p. 171) is not in Rapallo Notebook C but is a fair copy on a separate sheet (NLI 13,591 [17]) reproduced and transcribed by Clark (in *WFMP* 488–89). See Curtis B. Bradford, *Yeats at Work* (Carbondale and Edwardsville: Southern Illinois University Press, 1965), 101–13.

59 The poems of this neighborhood in the Yeats canon may be discerned in *WFMP*, Appendix II, [605]–12. Also see Chapman, "Yeats's White Vellum Notebook, 1930–1933," 51–52; and, on Huddon, Duddon, O'Leary, and "Related Matter in the White Vellum Notebook," my *W. B. Yeats's Robartes-Aherne Writings* 272–78.

60 "Heart on sleeve is handsome wear / What evil jack daw bites / But never, never dangle there / The lion & the lights[.]"

61 These are her inscriptions beside the poem in her copy of the *Collected Poems* (*YANLI* 2: 21; "CCP" 241) and typed notes for J. M. Hone in her "Sequence of poems written at Rapallo Feb & March 1929" (NLI 30,891). In the latter, she added, parenthetically: "(after this poem Cracked Mary became Crazy Jane | for obvious reasons)." See note 55, above. Suffice it to say, her note to "See letter to O.S. [etc.]" was in reference to the emergence of a lyric sequence to be called "Twelve poems for music" before the number increased substantially in March and April 1929. See narrative on "Three Things" (20v–23r), above.

62 Stephen Parrish (ed.) transcribes the text from 38v in the apparatus of *The Wild Swans at Coole: Manuscript Materials* (Ithaca, NY, and London: Cornell University Press, 1994), 93. He notes there only that "WBY entered a shortened version, addressed directly to the scholars." No facsimile is provided.

63 Ann Saddlemyer (ed.) notes that "there was always tension and argument between WBY and Mrs Phillimore" (*YGYL* 196n); thus, Yeats wrote to his wife from Galway (on August [3,] [1930]) that "Mrs Phillomore has come & gone & we got on admirably—once established that we are enemies we were in great amity. 'Why do you hate me?' she said. [To which Yeats replied:] 'Because you crush my chickens before they are hatched'" (221). In pencil, George Yeats jotted a note on 38r of Rapallo C to see "Hone p 415" (or 431 in the edition cited above), where Hone quotes Yeats on the pleasures of Monte Carlo in the company of the Phillimores.

64 Cf. Hone 429; *YPM* 222.

65 Yeats noted in *The Winding Stair and Other Poems* that poems in "A Woman Young and Old" were "written before the publication of The Tower, but left out for some reason I cannot recall" (*VP* 831). See Appendix II in *WFMP* 607–12 for lists of poems written in Rapallo Notebooks C–E and MBY 545 (the White Vellum Notebook).

66 On Blake, *A Vision*, and these poetry sequences, see *YPM* 179–85.

67 Clark misreads the first line to be "~~Trust [?in / ?is] chasten~~ love" (*WFMP* 411), the second word is "not" by inference (since neither "in" nor "is" is plausible in context), and the more legible third word is "cha[n]gles[s]" (which affirms Robartes's premise, in *Stories of Michael Robartes*, that only desire remains when love perishes in its attainment (cf. *AVB* 40).

68 Ellmann, *IY* 291 (based on her typescript list of poems, NLI 30,166). How the error happened is apparent in the entry George Yeats made in her copy of *Collected Poems* (*WBGYL* 2344), where, at the title of "Symbols," she wrote: "See letter to O.S. | Oct 2 1927" (Chapman, *YANLI* 2: 19). In her husband's letter to Olivia Shakespear (*L* 728–29), he reports sending off to New York "sixteen or so pages of verse" that eventually appeared in the Fountain Press edition of *The Winding Stair* (1929). "Symbols" was not one of those poems, among many yet to be written for the Cuala Press edition of *Words for Music Perhaps and Other Poems* (1932) and the Macmillan edition of *The Winding Stair* (1933).

69 The datings are mine (see "CCP" 237). Clark notes that the word "bog" is "clearly" what Yeats wrote ("CNGI" note on lines 1 and 9) although it looks like "log." I agree with that but wish he were right when he says, "Yet one wonders whether Yeats meant to write 'bow.'" For more about Yeats and *complementary dreaming* in his poetry and plays in the 1920s, see my chapter "'Metaphors for Poetry': Concerning the Poems of *A Vision* and Certain Plays for Dancers" in *W. B. Yeats's* A Vision*: Explications and Contexts*, ed. Neil Mann, Matthew Gibson, and Claire Nally (Clemson, SC: Clemson University Press, 2012), 217–51, particularly 230–34.

70 See *WFMP* 434 for a good image of 55r. In the second line of my transcription (above), "flaring circle" might be an unintended repetition of "flaming circle"—unless Yeats intended a hypermetric line. His revisions, in any case, are variant with texts after 1929.

71 Clark's streamed transcription partly distorts the layout of these stanzas on leaf 58r (see "CNGI" 10–11) because of limited space between margins on the printed page. The accidental omission of a heading—that is, "[NLI 13,580, 58r]"—is disorienting too.

72 Ellmann claims that "[Imagination's Bride]" is "a poem [Yeats] wrote but did not finish" (*IY* 37). There must have been a reason why Yeats chose not to publish the poem. Mrs. Yeats would have known why, presumably. Had the poem followed the course of other "finished" poems in Rapallo C, one might expect to find it listed in Clark's Appendix III (*WFMP* 613–20), a census of poems typed in Dublin from Rapallo Notebooks C–E and other sources. There is, however, a fair copy of the poem in NLI 13,583, Yeats's dustbin of non-starters. Filed there on a sheet of unlined Swift Brook Bond paper (beside "Knowledge & Wisdom"), this later version substantially differs from the Rapallo version in line 5 only ("There by the bride & grooms" has become "Down by bride & groom"). The later copy bears more punctuation, too, but also a title: "The 2 Passions of the Celestial Bodies." In light of the working titles on 57v and 58r in Rapallo C, this latest version exposes the poem's shaky foundation.

Figure 2.7. A southwesterly aerial view of the harbor at Rapallo and coastline of the Ligurian Sea on the Italian Riviera, c. 1923.

Figure 2.8. Rapallo at twilight, on the Gulf of Tigullio next to the tourist resorts of Santa Margherita Ligure, c. 1929. Compare this image with Figure 2.7, a contemporary colored view from a similar angle.

Rapallo Notebook D: Diary Notes, Poetry, and Other Writings

Wayne K. Chapman and Neil Mann

1. Introduction

Published recently in *International Yeats Studies*, two articles on the contents of Yeats's several Rapallo notebooks[1] inaugurated a series of four analytical digests of which this installment is the third. As such, this essay upholds the model of collaborating scholarship on which the others are based.[2] Out of the five nominal "Rapallo Notebooks," designated by letters A to E, our focus here is on the fourth notebook, "Rapallo Notebook D." Notebooks A–C and E will occasionally be incident to discussion when relevant in some way to Rapallo D. As a rule, diary entries, notes, and philosophical prose related to *A Vision* 1925 and 1937 are common to all five notebooks. Yet poetry written for the lyric sequences of *The Winding Stair and Other Poems* (Macmillan, 1933) is particularly distinctive in defining Yeats's main use of notebooks C and D. As ever, the objective of this series is to guide readers along lines of contiguity that exist in the notebooks while remaining faithful to the principle that manuscripts are valued artifacts involved in an investigative procedure. They are properties curated by the National Library of Ireland, reproduced with the consent of its Trustees, and authorized by United Agents LLP on behalf of Caitríona Yeats and the W. B. Yeats Estate.[3]

Arranged in no definite order, a list maintained by George Yeats to track manuscripts lent to and returned by Richard Ellmann in 1946 presents all five of the Rapallo notebooks as if they had been filed as a group in Yeats's private papers behind a designated "Vision Notebook" (possibly "VNB1" as cited in volume 3 of *Yeats's* Vision *Papers*[4]). Only one of the notebooks, however, is actually referred to by the appellation "Rapallo."[5] During the academic year 1957–58, professor and poet Thomas Parkinson worked with Mrs. Yeats in her home to prepare the manuscripts of Yeats's "later poetry" for the gift she bestowed upon the library in 1964, the year of Parkinson's *W. B. Yeats: The Later Poetry*.[6] Soon after, the NLI adapted its cataloguing system to the organization of the poetry manuscripts ("Parkinson's list," NLI 30,214), including thumbnail listings of fourteen "Bound manuscript books," of which the five Rapallo notebooks are each, for the first time, designated as a "'Rapallo notebook.'"[7] As poetry is given priority in "Parkinson's list," so the first two of the latter are actually notebooks now labelled C and D, implying continuity due to an overly cursory view of content, whereas, in fact, a general transition had occurred between the making of the twenty-five lyric poems in Rapallo Notebook C and the eight poems written in Rapallo Notebook D, interspersed (at intervals) with philosophical diary writings, notes for *A Vision*, and short prose for the Cuala Press. With a single exception at the beginning (see 1r–2r), the extant content of Rapallo D may be seen as continuing from Rapallo C. Mann writes: "Rapallo D was put aside after a few pages, and Rapallo C was [then] the main workbook for the first half of 1929 until July, after which Yeats took D up again in August."[8] The latest dated entry in Rapallo D is "Nov 18 1930" (inscribed beneath a prose "subject for a poem" on 97v).

In 1983, David R. Clark presented a detailed description of the physical construction of Rapallo D, NLI 13,581 (or "Parkinson's list" II.h), in his important work of textual-genetic interpretation, *Yeats at Songs and Choruses*. Appended to support analysis of "Crazy Jane on the Day of Judgment" in chapter 1, the description also served his treatment of "After Long Silence" in chapter 3:

> NLMs. 13,581 is a notebook 30cm. x 22cm. with a patterned paper cover, blue and white on greenish-tan. It contained five signatures of rather heavy unlined white paper with no watermarks. Folios 1–20 comprise Signature 1, but Folios 8 and 9 have been cut out leaving narrow stubs; Folios 21–40 comprise Signature 2, but Folio 33 is cut out; Folios 41–60 comprise Signature 3, but all have been cut out except Folio 41; all of Signature 4, presumably Folios 61–80, has been cut out; Folios 81–98 comprise Signature 5, but Folios 81–83 are cut out. Many of the stubs have ink marks, so that many of the cut out pages contained writing.[9]

At the present time, Rapallo Notebook D has not been rebound for the NLI by the Delmas Conservation Bindery and therefore remains loose, like the "'Rapallo' notebook in leather" used for composing *Stories of Michael Robartes and His Friends* (NLI 13,577; "Parkinson's list" II.d).[10] Rapallo D's cheap paper type and cover floral motif also agree with Rapallo C and NLI 13,577. Hence the following description of the covering, floral design, and general construction of Rapallo C is apposite:

> This is a notebook bound with a greenish tan paper with a design of large and small spots with blue flowers with nine white petals in the large spots [...] [The] signatures are in turn sewn together and then the paper cover glued [...] The inside of each cardboard cover is covered with the same paper as the outside. (*YSC* 244)

On matters of collation—such as position of writings, blank pages, and stubs denoting Yeats's removal of manuscript material from Rapallo D—readers are encouraged to consult regularly the Tabular Summary that is found in Appendix D, below. That subsidiary snapshot of the notebook in abstract is foundational to the main body (Part 4) of this essay.

2. CONTENTS OVERVIEW (MARCH 1928; AUGUST 1929–NOVEMBER 1930)

As we have shown, each of the five manuscript notebooks referred to as the "Rapallo Notebooks" (NLI 13,578–13,582)—acquired in Rapallo, Italy, and in use between 1928 and 1931—had a role to play in the rewriting of *A Vision* (1925). Neil Mann observes that it is indeed "likely that Rapallo Notebooks A, B, and E were all started in 1928" to that end, "with B being the first, while E had all the early material removed,"[11] if E had carried the *Vision* material listed on its cover, and therefore started before Notebooks C and D. Notebook B contains drafts that predate A and declares on its cover that it was "Finished, Oct. 9, 1928." Nevertheless, Rapallo Notebooks C and D, both significant in the making of poetry, are the most serially related to one another in that respect. Rapallo C was "begun. Sept. 23. 1928 in Dublin" (as noted in its initiating diary entry) and "Finished June or July 1929" (as noted on its cover), whereas Yeats began to use Notebook D in Rapallo, briefly, in March 1928, paused for a time, and then took it up again in Dublin in August 1929, its last dated entry being "Nov 18 1930."

We surmise that Yeats did not have Rapallo Notebook D with him during his second sojourn in Rapallo (November 1928–April 1929). Yet, roughly, between August 1929 and November 18, 1930, his whereabouts can be traced from Dublin to Rapallo (on his third trip) and back to Dublin in the notebook. On his arrival in Italy, in late November 1929, he had fallen dangerously ill (as he had in the winter of 1927/28) and wrote little there until he began to recover his strength. While in Rapallo, George Yeats wrote a number of letters to Lennox Robinson that recount the circumstances of her husband's failing health and convalescent state during their stay at Via Americhe 12/8, Rapallo. For instance, on November 30, 1929, she wrote: "There's not much to say about William except that he gets feverish every night (a new trick)," hoping that, after raining [*sic*] stopped long enough for him to get out, he might "buck up a bit," until such time when his main distraction might become "Basel [*sic*] Bunting & Ezra [Pound]'s Momma & Poppa" close by, "parked for the winter in flats (FLATS)."[12] Having arrived cold but still "intact," Yeats gradually grew stronger—so much so that in six months she could humor Robinson (in mock-Poundian dialect) by noting that "William[,] being one of them geniuses that hibernates inside themselves[,] prances all day in a diaphanous silk dressing gown and dresses only when emerging into public life about 7 pm," having risen "at 3 pm in order to bathe" and "swum (swam?) somewhat on his back and somewhat on his front and somewhat under the sea and emerged thankfully and somewhat shaken" (as the danger of losing him, by then, had clearly passed), adding brightly: "I hope it may be repeated tomorrow."[13]

To be sure, the surge of poetic creativity exhibited in Rapallo Notebook C in the spring of 1929—followed intermittently by eight lyrics written in Rapallo D for *The Winding Stair*—had been interrupted by illness and travels, as well as preoccupation with the "big book" of philosophy that resisted completion in the way that he had anticipated in July, when he wrote to Olivia Shakespear (*L* 764, *CL InteLex* 5259). The first three of the poems in Rapallo D were composed in Dublin, in August through October 1929, and four of the five remaining poems were either started or finished in Dublin after Yeats's convalescence in Italy. For example, he is said to have written his "1st prose draft" of "Byzantium" in Rapallo, but, also on the authority of his wife's record-keeping, the "Final MS of poem [was] dated September 1930."[14] On July 3, 1930, they departed for home on a two-week sea voyage. In seven months, the only lyric he had completed in Rapallo was "After Long Silence," which he seems to have begun writing prior to his departure from Dublin when the gravity of his illness began to register with him.

The story of Rapallo D seems best told by addressing its prose and poetry together, with respect to the mixed assortment of a writer's daybook, in principle broadly conceived by Yeats to be a "Diary" of entries and a continuation of the record left in Rapallo C, but differing in that shifts from prose to poetry-writing was more intermittent in D, lacking transitions as the body of work shifted between one mode and then the other. As we have it, with large chunks removed and presumably lost, prose entries in Rapallo D are usually consistent with C on tentative speculations (as in a "Diary of Thought") about fundamental matters intended for a revised edition of *A Vision*. But the prose also includes personal tributes, reading notes, lists of books yet to consult, esoteric calculations from other cultures on the idea of the Great Year, and more. While much of the poetry is occasional, it is also interspersed with prose entries. Alternating the composition of fewer poems than were generated in Rapallo C, Rapallo D has within it a logic that is textually autobiographical and basically chronological, despite notable omissions and generic shifting.

Before describing in detail the contents of Rapallo D, below (in Part 4), the following outline will serve as an overview, differing from the strictly linear limitations of the Appendix. Locations cited by folio (recto and verso) are given here to assist the conceptualization of content in spatial terms. Nonetheless, to outline in abstract the prose and poetry in the notebook—even in a thumbnail sketch—is complicated due to the crisscrossing of drafts at various points. Thus, the substance of Rapallo D is inventoried either by topic or title, listed only once and parenthetically beside the respective work's location (compounded, if necessary, by multiple references).

In three parts, the first entry (on 1r and 2r) appears beneath a heading ("Diary. | [~~...~~] | Rapallo. 1928") and seems a theme on great scenes, a tribute to Lady Ottoline Morrell at Garsington, interspersed (on 1v and at the foot of 2r) with a cluster of possibly related reading notes on the Emperor of China and a list of books "to get" for *A Vision*. The next entries take up the Diary again (in "Dublin. August. 1929"), after more than a year in disuse, with the poem "I am of Ireland" (3r, 4r–6r) and "The Crazed Moon" (3r, finished on 92v–93r). After "I am of Ireland," we find notes on astrological matter, Biblical periods of time, and Hindu eras (6v, 7v, 10r–12v); a draft letter to the editor of *The Irish Statesman* in response to a letter of August 24, 1929 (7r); two missing leaves (8 and 9); a mostly continuous draft of "Coole Park, 1929" (13v–23r, 24v–32v, 34r), interrupted only by "Swift's Epitaph" (21r) and "Astrology and the Nature of Reality" (or "Seven Propositions," 23v–24r, 26r); a missing leaf (33); notes for *A Vision* (34v); drafts of a preface for Oliver St. John Gogarty's *Wild Apples* (35r–36r, 37v–38r, 40r); short reading notes on Fichte and Hegel (36v); a list of engagements for October 28 through November 4, 1929 (37r); drafts of "After Long Silence" with a biographical note (38r, 39v–40r, 41r); a list of engagements for November 4–11, 1929 (38v); drafts of "Crazy Jane on the Day of Judgment" (38v–39v, incomplete until 95v–96r, 97r, 98r); a note for *A Vision* (40v); a list of books and prices for projected reading (41v), as well as a first draft of "Veronica's Napkin" (41v); and then a massive lacuna marked by the stubs of at least forty-two excised leaves (42r–83v). After this rupture, Rapallo Notebook D is intact and progresses with the following entries (including crossovers from above): notes on Spengler for *A Vision* (84r, 85r); "Veronica's Napkin" from 41v (84v–85r, 93v), "Byzantium" (86r–90r, 91r–92r); "Open letter to Lewis," July 1930 (90v); "The Crazed Moon" from 3r (92v–93r); new lines for *The Cat and the Moon* (93v–94r); a memorial tribute to John Quinn (94v–95r); the continuation of "Crazy Jane on the Day of Judgment" from 38v–39v (95v–96r, 97r, 98r); plus, finally, themes for two or more personal poems and a prose subject for an unpublished poem on "the great philosophies, Plato, Spinoza, Hegel," dated "Nov 18 1930" (96v, 97v).

3. Transcription Protocol and Key to Abbreviations

Transcriptions are meant to preserve the idiosyncrasies of Yeats's spelling, punctuation, and revising as much as possible. The whole word is given when that seems intended, even though letters are missing or elided with a stroke, as often with the "-ing" ending. When a precise spelling is unclear, a standard one may be substituted. A word will be left incomplete if Yeats seems to have abandoned it that way. Illegible words are represented thus: [?]. A conjectural reading thus: [?word]. And partly conjectural readings thus: every[?thing]. Yeats's scribal additions are indicated within angle brackets < > whereas ours are given in editorial square brackets [ ]. Yeats's underlinings are retained, as are his strikeouts, which are everywhere indicated with a line through the deleted word, parts of words, parts of lines, whole lines, or sentences, as the case may be. Except in *literatim* transcriptions presented as block quotations, commentary follows the convention of punctuated matter entered in quotation marks (" "). Hence, embedded quotation is indicated by a set of single inverted commas (' '), according to American convention; and end-stop punctuation such as periods will occur within close-quotation marks except in instances where end punctuation is lacking in Yeats's writing. As a rule, use of the slash mark (/), or virgule, follows *The Chicago Manual of Style* (17th ed., section 6.111). However, vertical line marks (|) are used to represent instances of accidental line breaks within texts.

Aside from secondary sources introduced above and in notes thus far, several studies are cited frequently enough in the remaining sections of this essay—either on the dating of poems or for the drafts they present from Rapallo D—that for economy they are identified in the following list of abbreviations:

BTL	Jon Stallworthy, *Between the Lines: Yeats's Poetry in the Making* (Oxford: Clarendon, 1963).
"CCP"	Wayne K. Chapman, "Appendix A: A Chronology of the Composition of the Poems," *YPM* 229–45 (also *YA* 15 [2002]: 138–58).
"CNGI"	David R. Clark, "Yeats: Cast-offs, Non-starters and Gnomic Illegibilities," *YAACTS* 17 (1999; pub. 2003): 1–18.
WFMP	W. B. Yeats, *Words for Music Perhaps and Other Poems: Manuscript Materials*, ed. David R. Clark (Ithaca, NY: Cornell University Press, 1999).
YSC	David R. Clark, *Yeats at Songs and Choruses* (Amherst: University of Massachusetts Press, 1983).

Other acronyms are used as directed in the "List of Abbreviations" posted on this journal's website or as introduced in the endnotes of this essay.

4. Diary Entries, Poetry, and Prose Fragments (in Detail)

[1r–2r] "Diary. | […] | Rapallo. 1928" [with intermittent reading notes and a book list]

The main entry on leaves 1 and 2 barely pre-dates, by a few days, a letter that Yeats wrote to Lady Ottoline Morrell from Albergo Rapallo on March 20, 1928 (*CL InteLex* 5093). Often ailing herself and in 1928 undergoing treatment for bone cancer, she was keenly interested in her friend's condition, which he reported as improved, "almost well again" following a "general breakdown" precipitated by pneumonia and overwork, reflected in the bitterness of *The Tower*. He was by then working "on alternate days & only at what I care for." He acknowledged her kindness and the "great pleasure" that she had given him in a letter from London; and he gave her back a thumbnail of the theme she had inspired:

> I put things in a diary—sometimes a lot of things & then nothing for months. The other day I was writing there that certain moments in Abbey plays had been a principal part of my education—Shaw's "spoilt priest" posed against bog & mountain, Synge's saint at the end of "The Well of the Saints"; two strange people in a play of Lady Gregory's. I had seen them played again & again & sometimes exquisitely until they seemed more vivid than all my friends. Then I asked myself "Has any moment of real life affected me in the same way". Yes I thought at once—Garsington—you, your husband & child in that beautiful room. (*CL InteLex* 5093)[15]

The "Diary" entry to which Yeats refers is paraphrased in the letter. The main thought involves the recollection of scenes triggered by a particular production of Shaw's play *John Bull's Other Island*, which Yeats saw at the Abbey Theatre—a production for which Dolly Robinson (or Dorothy Travers Smith, i.e., Mrs. Lennox Robinson) was credited as Set Designer and Scenic Artist. There were seven performances between September 19 and 24, 1927.[16] The Yeatses arrived in Rapallo in February 1928 and returned to Dublin in early April, so the "Rapallo. 1928." dateline in the diary actually defines a fairly short time span for the entry to have been written before March 20. The theme's first movement came easily:

> Some months ago, at the performance of "John Bulls other Island" | with Dolly Dowdens[17] new scenes[,] I thought Shaws "Spoilt Priest"[18]—seen so | often & with different ~~plays~~ <players> —had probably been an important part of my | education, not ~~perhaps~~ certainly because of anything said—any opinions of his— | ~~them~~ <but> because he seems to rise out <of> ~~the soul soil, out~~ bog & hill | & bring with him, a self possession, a revery that seems asiatic. | Then I

> thought of that other figure—where all is so fine—the Saint | in Well [of] the saints, that has moved me still more as more | vivid in memory though it is years since I have seen it.[19] | Two noble figures separated from all medieval abstractions | & as concrete as ~~Holy~~ <holy-> Well, & roadside cross. | Then I thought of the two mad young people in Lady Gregory's | "Full Moon"[20] as played years ago by Kerrigan & Miss O'Neill | especially as played—that one episode taken out of the play— | in some drawing room. Has any poem or book affected | me so powerfully? Certainly nothing seen on the stage | elsewhere, except it may be De Max in "Phedre"[21] | & that has grown faint with the years, & was always something alian | & noble. Those Abbey persons say something that I long to hear | again—the same thing perhaps that I tried [to] speak in Red Hanrahan | & those early stories[.] (NLI 13,581, 1r)

The next two movements were more difficult, to judge by cancellations. Part "II" was reduced to three sentences, the first two being transitional: "Then I wondered if anything in life seemed comperable. I thought at once of ~~Garssington~~ <Garsington> —that beautiful pannelled Room, Lady Ottoline, her husband & her daughter" (1r–2r). The third sentence struggled with the notion of *fineness* as common to both persons and scene (that is, to the Morrells and the effect of their renowned, red-paneled room) at Garsington Manor, the Morrell country estate near Oxford, of which the Yeatses were fond during the poet's residence near the university during the Anglo-Irish War and from visits long afterward. "Fineness of elaboration & elaborate clarity," he wrote, coalesced into "a clarity of elaborate beauty," resolving the thought so that: "There too persons & scene seemed inseparable[,] a moment eternalized for the memory and grown symbolic[,] a clarity of elaborate beauty that the world sets up against that Asiatic folk-wisdom" (2r).

Part "III" of the theme might stand as its conclusion if it were not for the notes that seem to speak to it in the lower margin and on the facing page. The first sentence came easily enough: "Amy Levi, the jewish novelist that I knew long ago[,] wrote that jews [...] <who> seek Gentile society never know how to pick their company."[22] Bridging this thought with "Aristocratic women" (like Lady Ottoline) who might "pick friends from the class below" proved difficult to the point that six of the eighteen lines of part "III" were cancelled altogether and recast to conclude with a personal compliment: "<Lady Ottoline does> not find [~~...~~] that language of intonation & movement ~~they are~~ <she is> accustomed [to] <among those who interest her> [~~...~~] & so cannot <judge> by character [~~...~~] & has according[ly] been slandered in print & out of it by some she had thought her friends [~~...~~] This graceous, generous & gentle person may [~~...~~] descend to posterity <as> a sort of Lady Carolline Lamb" (2r).[23]

Beneath this tribute to Lady Ottoline, Yeats has drawn a line more than halfway across the page and copied beneath it two lines by St. Gregory of Nazianzen, as translated by Christopher Dawson in his 1929 book, *Progress and Religion*: ["]The end of all art Thou, being One & All & None / Being One ~~th~~ Thou art not all, being All thou art not one" (2r). Beneath this paradox and another drawn line, Yeats sets down more notes drawn from Dawson: "Confucius described 'the ~~ancien~~ Rites' as that where by 'the ancient kings sought to represent the ways of Heaven & to regulate the feelings of men[.]' He who 'violates them may be spoken of as dead' (Lu-Yun, 14,5 and 1,4) '~~They nurture the nature' of man~~ 'In regard to man they nurture his nature'" (2r). However, these notes are incomplete without their complement, on the facing page: "Emperor of China moved from room to room according to the month, changing his dress, his food, his music as he moved to harmonise with the seasons. His palace was 'the house of the Calendar' (C Dawson). In India[,] on the other hand[,] the emphasis of the ritual was on the sacrifice" (1v).[24]

Although clearly copied on a date later than the Rapallo entry of March 1928, it seems certain that there is a connection between "that beautiful pannelled Room" at Garsington Manor—"persons & scene" that seem "a moment eternalized for the memory and grown symbolic" (1r and 2r)—and the Ming T'ang or emperor's "House of the Calendar" in Dawson's account and Yeats's notes (1v and 2r). Lady Ottoline contributed to Yeats's reading via their correspondence and, occasionally, in the lending of books. They continued to follow each other's health problems. For example, on June 5, 1929, from Dublin, he wrote to return to her "Stephens poems" after long delay, hearing that she had "been in a sanitarium & [was] better" and promising to "look up those books you speak of" (*CL InteLex* 5254). Reminiscent of that "Asiatic folk-wisdom" that he set in opposition to the "clarity of elaborate beauty" in part II of his theme but left out of his letter of March 20, 1928, he found the poems of James Stephens, after reading them "a number of times," resembled the Vedas in that Stephens had "found in Ireland something Asiatic & incredibly simple."[25] Moreover, the later but nearby notes that Yeats entered into Rapallo D, on reading Dawson's account of Chinese and Indian rites, suggest that there could be a material connection between them and the entry left unfinished as a tribute to Morrell.

In June 1929, Yeats was rounding out Rapallo Notebook C with prose notes and "Thoughts" for *A Vision*. Perhaps the additional books Lady Ottoline recommended to him were not the ones he listed in Rapallo D (1v), above the Dawson note. If they were to agree with those citations given as "Books to get from R.D.S. [i.e., Royal Dublin Society] or elsewhere," the evidence is circumstantial because her letter has not survived. George Yeats was a life member of the R.D.S., and its archives were close by. Thus, the task might have been given to her to investigate.[26] The seven titles by authors Robert Flint, Georg W. F. Hegel, W. H. R. Rivers, Frederick von Schlegel, and Pierre Duhem have all been reported recently,[27] but the last of these is worth recalling in this connection because, on leaves 52r–58v of Yeats's White Vellum Notebook (WVN), Yeats introduced notes on the Great Year and the precession of the equinoxes taken mainly in autumn 1931, when he demonstrably encountered Duhem's *Le système du monde: histoire des doctrines cosmologiques de Platon à Copernic* (Paris, 1913–14), between working versions of "Crazy Jane and Jack the Journeyman" and part II of the Introduction to *The Words upon the Window-Pane*.[28] Those notes in WVN were entered in October–November 1931, showing how long it might take to follow up a suggestion with actual research. If Yeats's notes on Dawson and the list of "Books to get from R.D.S. or elsewhere" are informed by the March 1928 tribute on 1r and 2r, as well as the associated letter he sent to Lady Ottoline soon after, then the notes and book list were intentionally laid away in the notebook, out of sequence chronologically, and possibly intended for later use. Leaf 2v was left blank as if to punctuate a shift in topic, time, and place, and to mark the return to poetry-writing after the example of Rapallo C.

[3r, 4r–6r] "Dublin. August. 1929" ["I am of Ireland" and unpublished quatrain]

Since July 2, 1929, Yeats had projected that the task of "putting the philosophy in order" might be finished that summer as a prelude to his "poetical rebirth" (*L* 764; *CL InteLex* 5259).[29] Nearly a month later, he announced to Olivia Shakespear that he had "just finished my last bout of hard work at the philosophy" (*CL InteLex* 5266), although he reported to Sturge Moore that he was actually only "writing the last pages of my new 'Vision' with a great sense of a burden thrown off," predicting that "within a month," he expected to "be back at verse again" (July 31, 1929, *CL InteLex* 5267).[30] By mid-September, optimistically, he planned to "finish the book of thirty poems for music[.] I am more than half through. 'For Music' [i.e., 'Words for Music Perhaps'] is only a name, [because] nobody will sing them" (*L* 769; *CL InteLex* 5285)[31] Clark comments: "Actually [Yeats] had done only one new poem for the series" by then, the lyric "I am of Ireland," written in August (*WFMP* xli; see "CCP" 241). Not part of the series, a fragment related to the poem "The Crazed Moon" and an unpublished epigram entitled "a recent incident" intrude without clear relevance upon the first and third pages of Yeats's renewed use of Rapallo D for composition. After the personal diary entry datelined "Rapallo. 1928." (discussed above), a mixed assortment of verses ensued for six pages, beginning beneath a new banner: "Dublin. August. 1929."

("The Crazed Moon" drafts—early and late—are misleading and necessarily discussed below at separate points.)

Of the two dates generally given for “I am of Ireland”—either August 1928 or August 1929 (see “CCP” 241)—the latter is obviously the correct one. The first lines inscribed beneath that date are not so much Yeats’s writing, however, as an approximation in his handwriting of the poem’s source in Irish literature, an old lyric from which a new music might follow from two strong stresses, rephrasings, and redefined lines:

> \ \ [WBY’s stress marks]
> “I am of Ireland
> And the Holy Land of Ireland [close-quote cancelled]
> God [=Good] sir” she cried.
> By St Charity.
> Come dance with me in Ir[e]land (NLI 13,581, 3r)

From seven lines in St. John Seymour’s anthology *Anglo-Irish Literature, 1200–1582* (Cambridge, 1929), Yeats improvised a five-line stanza to serve as a recurrent choral movement for this new poem, which he began to write on leaf 4r, on the right-hand page in the next opening as was his habit. As he was able to refine this refrain there and to progress satisfactorily through a second stanza, leaf 3v was left blank.[32] In other words, as T. R. Henn first observed, Yeats “had heard the ghost of his tune in the old poem; it is snatched up, smoothed, and elaborated, to give harmony with what follows.”[33]

Most of that elaboration occurs on about the first third of leaf 4r, with tweakings on 6r (for two renditions), by which time the choral refrain had reached a state of completion ready to be incorporated in a fair-hand copy of the poem on a loose sheet, numbered “XX” in NLI 13,591 (21). (The following comments will be far clearer alongside the facsimiles and transcriptions in *WFMP* 518–33.) In contrast, stanzas 2 and 4 took a bit longer yet were achieved, by turns, in three integral stages before reaching final status in that loose folio.

In the first stage (for the rest of leaf 4r), much of stanza 2 emerges in rough draft, with interlinear and marginal substitutions occurring to realize an alternating rhyme pattern anticipated, at first, by rhyme notes (“by || eye | said | high”; “by | — | eye”) and carried out in a flexible verse that permits semi-rhymes such as “off” and “rough” in lines 6 and 8 and, more distantly, “alone” and “man” in lines 1 and 3. In the latter instance, the rhymes become decidedly fixed features in the landscape of the poem after three curt revisions of those lines, entered at right angles to the text (at right and left) without resorting to the blank space of facing page 3v.

The next stage of composition involves the rough drafting of stanza 4 on leaf 5r and the thorough revision of its eight lines (on facing page 4v) according to the metrical prescriptions established in stanza 2, but with three particularly strong stresses in each line to accentuate the tempo of those kettle drums and trombones that fiddlers curse in stanza 4 and that make dumb "singers all" to the point where "charity is dry" on 5r. The music is therefore pronounced and loud as Yeats increases tension between the "harpers," brass, and percussionists on 4v, offering alternative versions for lines 5–8 of the stanza. On the one hand, he writes: "Those great trum[p]ets shouted he / Trumpe[t]s & trombones / And cocked a malicious eye / A time runs on, runs on." But, on the other hand, he gives himself the option to choose a slightly transposed version of the male figure's cutting rejoinder: "[']Those trumpets & tromb bones / Those great trumpets' shouted he / 'And time runs runs on' / And cocked a malicious eye" (4v).

(At some point—and long after stanza 4 had been achieved in this second stage—Yeats inscribed an epigram, entitled "A recent incident," in the upper left-hand corner of 4v. This plucky lyric bears no relation to anything else on the page, save for its satirical accent on politics. Written at the same angle as those revised lines of "I am of Ireland," stanza 4—but in a lighter ink and at several centimeters' remove from the other—the poem was clearly jotted down almost two years later. Unpunctuated except for a period at the end, this quatrain in tetrameter directs a Swiftian complaint at men the likes of Jean-Jacques Rousseau and the State—particularly a Catholic-majority one—for condoning the mistreatment of young children: "Rousseau that threw babies in / The foundling basket seemed to sin / But who dare call it that if Rome / Prefer the basket to the home" (4v). Roy Foster quotes the poem, slightly amended as "Upon a recent incident" in the version Yeats copied and sent Lady Gregory on April 24, [1931] (*CL InteLex* 5462),[34] alluding to a case he had just read about "in the paper" involving "a protestant mother" whose "yelling children" were taken from her in "open court" and sent to "catholic institutions." After presenting the text of the poem, Yeats indignantly asserted: "I shall put it [in] my nex[t] book and an appendix with the judges name & all suchlike detail."[35] The book he intended might well have been *Words for Music Perhaps and Other Poems* (Cuala Press, 1932). But the idea had faded by then, so that the unpublished poem remains a matter of scholarship today.)

The third stage of composition for "I am of Ireland" occurs on leaves 6r and 5v, where stanzas 2 and 4 are reconciled for the first time with the refrain (here stanzas 1, 3, and 5). After marking again the heavy accent on "I" in the first line of the poem, Yeats settled matters in the last line of the chorus with a similar promotion of accent by spondaic substitution—revising "& dance with me in Ireland" to "Come dance with me in Ireland." Consequently, stanza 3 was copied from that and stanza 5 dittoed, in its place, with the notation "I am of Ireland Etc." Also on 6r, stanzas 2 and 4 are first assembled from their most advanced state on 4r and 4v, respectively—yet not to Yeats's satisfaction, for he scratched out lines 1–4 of stanza 2 (after indicating beside them the transposition of couplets by arrows and the cue-word "transfer") and did much the same with stanza 4, after trying out (in the lower right-hand margin) the two alternatives that he had weighed as possibilities on 4v. Then, for stanzas 2 and 4, a straight line was drawn from each (traversing the left margin of 6r deeply into 5v) to link up with its corresponding final state. Stanzas 2 and 4 are also partly circumscribed to make certain that whole substitution was understood when viewing this opening in the notebook. After that, all that remained for Yeats to do was to make slight additions such as punctuation when, much later, transferring the poem to a loose sheet (NLI 13,591 [21], recto and verso) for typesetting at the Cuala Press.[36]

[3r] ["The Crazed Moon," anticipating 92v–93r (recovered from "1923," revised August 1930)]

The physical location of an untitled draft fragment of "The Crazed Moon," beneath the dateline "Dublin. August. 1929," is perplexing but not without precedent in Yeats's manuscript notebooks. This unexpected appearance early in Rapallo Notebook D seems inconsistent with a fragment likely written in August or September 1930, with most of the poem composed near the end of the notebook. Clark agrees that the fragment, chronologically the earliest part of the surviving manuscript, "was probably added to this page in 1930" as follows from the note jotted above the poem on leaf 93r: "A lyric written in [?] 1923 & lost | have just found August 1930" (*WFMP* 275n and 278–79). Instances of such displacement to blank pages in a bound notebook have been cited elsewhere in this series.[37] In point of fact, Mrs. Yeats's ascribing the poem's composition to the date "April 1923" (see "CCP" 240) is notable and the only date so far attributed to it by scholars. Yet on what basis? Might she have been mistaken due to conflicting evidence about the poem's origin or possibly misled by her husband's note and memory in relation to the fragment on 3r and the contemporary entries of 1930 on 92v–93r? To be sure, Yeats owned no notebooks purchased in Rapallo before 1927, the year the couple first visited the Italian city. The antecedent would have to have originated someplace else—in some extraneous manuscript.

As the evidence in this case seems mostly to illuminate writing near the end of Rapallo D (at 92v–93r), the making of "The Crazed Moon" is best discussed in that context. Readers will therefore find that discussion, conducted fully in the latter part of this essay, after "Byzantium" and nearer "Crazy Jane on the Day of Judgment." For now, it is sufficient to recognize that only the dateline and "ghost" of the old tune snatched from Seymour's anthology appeared on leaf 3r between August 1929 and August 1930. During that interval, the rest of the page was vacant space.

[7r] [A draft letter to the editor of *The Irish Statesman* in response to a letter of August 24, 1929]

The folio 7r contains a draft of a letter to the *Irish Statesman* in response to a correspondent using the pseudonym "Stall" from August 24, 1929.[38] Entitling the letter "Masks & Music," Yeats defends the masks used in *Fighting the Waves* as "powerful & beautiful," but the letter seems not to have been published, and may never have been written out properly or sent.[39]

> Sir:
> Your correspondent "Stall" thinks that the masks | of Emer & Ethne are guys – no that was not | quite the word but I have heard so many people call ~~Rhodans [=Rodin's] statues guys~~ Epstein women | guys that the words running in my head. Any | how he thinks them ~~frights~~ <gouls>. ~~Whereas I h~~ave | ~~all~~ I ~~am~~ <probably because I> ~~however, who~~ belong to the wretched | post war generation ~~have been going all over~~ | ~~the town [?till]~~ have <[?comitted] my self> all over this town | to the statement that the Emer mask is a most | powerful & beautiful. I think the Etheine mask | lacks not beauty but power, though, ~~I think~~ | if I could but see it here it might not lack | anything. It did not till amidst the stage | lights. But ~~then we~~ do <we> mean to say this | by beauty. (NLI 13,581, 7r)

[6v, 7v, 10r–12v] [Notes on Sepharial zodiac, Hindu eras]

Starting on the verso opposite the draft letter to *The Irish Statesman* (and so probably later), Yeats used the notebook for some five leaves to note his reading of a book by "Sepharial" as well as related articles from *The Encyclopaedia of Religion and Ethics*. Sepharial was the pen name of Theosophist Walter Gorn Old, a writer on astrological and general occult matters, as well as Chinese classics,[40] and Yeats was reading *Hebrew Astrology: A Key to the Study of Prophecy*.[41] It was evidently of interest because of Sepharial's interpretation of long periods of history in astrology and the Bible, and Yeats was clearly looking at traditions to test or corroborate the system of the ages outlined in the automatic script and *A Vision*.

The first page of notes (6v) outlines the Hindu scheme of the Yugas as set out by Sepharial (page 61), compared with that given by H. P. Blavatsky; the planets in relation to the atomic weights of their associated metals and to the days of the week (pages 46–47); symbolic periods from the Bible, including a "prophetic week" of 2,520 years (page 49), as well as the symbolic image of a statue in Nebuchadnezzar's dream as recounted in the Book of Daniel (pages 66–67) and related to the zodiac (pages 78–80). This is continued in the lower part of the following verso (7v), the upper part of which comments more analytically on the contents (see Figure 3.1):

> I notice that Sepharael in his queer mixture of sense & nonsense | devides all periods between creation & ~~Ch~~ Christ into multiples of 36
> I notice especeally 10 periods of 36 [?years] ~~26 AD or~~ [?pased] from | foundation of Alexanders Kingdom <(334)> to begging [=beginning] of Christs ministry (26 A D | ~~cout~~ counting his birth 4 BC). I think of this in connection from something said by one of my spirits though very doubtfully, fealing that they would hate | this ~~form~~ <sort> of ~~calculation~~ jewish calculation. (NLI 13,581, 7v)

It is difficult to be sure what Yeats regarded as sense and what as nonsense in the mixture, but he would no doubt have dismissed Sepharial's identification of the British as a lost tribe of Israel and the British Empire as the stone "not cut by human hands" in Nebuchadnezzar's dream of a statue.[42] Of far more interest to Yeats was the numerological approach to time and his own preoccupation with the transition from the end of the classical *antithetical* dispensation to the start of the *primary* at the beginning of the Christian era. As he indicates here, the first suggestion to appear in the automatic script in January 1918 was tentative, suggesting that the current *primary* dispensation began "2026 years ago but do not rely on this."[43] The reason for giving this date was that the age started "Ten generations before Christ," because "It takes ten generations to prepare for a new religious idea."[44] The period from the "foundation of Alexander's Kingdom"[45] to the start of Christ's ministry would comprise "10 periods of 36 years," which Yeats associates with his ten generations, even though thirty-six years is far longer than the normal reckoning for a generation. Indeed, in Rapallo Notebook A, Yeats had been pondering the same question, with a generation less than half of this, at fifteen years,[46] and most estimates of generations fall between these two figures.

(At this point, two leaves have been cut out—folios 8 and 9—though there is no obvious discontinuity between 7v and 10r and there hardly seems to be enough material in *Hebrew Astrology* to have warranted two more full pages of notes or their removal. Other notebooks show that Yeats sometimes left a page or group of pages blank; it is, therefore, possible that the draft letter appeared on 7r, another draft was on leaves 8 and 9, and leaf 10 was blank, so that, after the two leaves were removed, Yeats could then have come back to insert the notes on Sepharial—as with the notes on Christopher Dawson's book or the "recent incident"—starting on 7v. If that were the case, the notes on folios 11 and 12 on the vast eras of Hindu time from *The Encyclopaedia of Religion and Ethics* might have been there already and prompted the insertion of the Sepharial at this point, or Yeats could have left three leaves blank and added all the material at the same time. However, there is no concrete evidence in any particular direction.)

The notes that follow on 10r consider the symbolism of Aries (♈) in terms of the Bible as set out by Sepharial (pages 91–93), and then the symmetries seen in the planets said to rule over each of the signs of the zodiac, copying a diagram from the book (page 94), and attempting to understand what was known in antiquity.[47] Yeats then concludes the page with a speculation on the concept of the Great Year as understood in antiquity. Though the precession of the equinoxes has come to be the definition of the astrological Great Year and is the measure used in the automatic script and *A Vision*, the concept of a symbolic Great Year long precedes the discovery of the precession. One characteristic of precession, however, is that the equinoxes appear to go through the signs of the zodiac in the opposite order to the apparent passage of the sun during a normal year. Thus, during the year, the sun passes from Aquarius to Pisces to Aries, but, owing to precession, the point of the vernal equinox has passed from Aries to Pisces and will proceed into Aquarius. Yeats therefore speculates:

> It is possible that antiquity without knowing | of Precession had a converse symbolism of the signs | one human one devine. If the annual order is the order | according to the gods the human order would be its | contrary & expressed in the Four Ages. ~~The [?2] living | each others life dying each others death~~ Certainly the | moment they knew of the precession ~~they would~~ <it should have> struck ~~them~~ <somebody> | It would not however be ~~the order in my system for both would | concide at ♈ [Aries]~~ conflict my system suggests between devine & human | for both concide at ♈ [Aries]. In mine they can never coincide. It would be the same if precession were expressed | by movement of Will & the | annual order by C[reative]. M[ind]. (NLI 13,581, 8r)

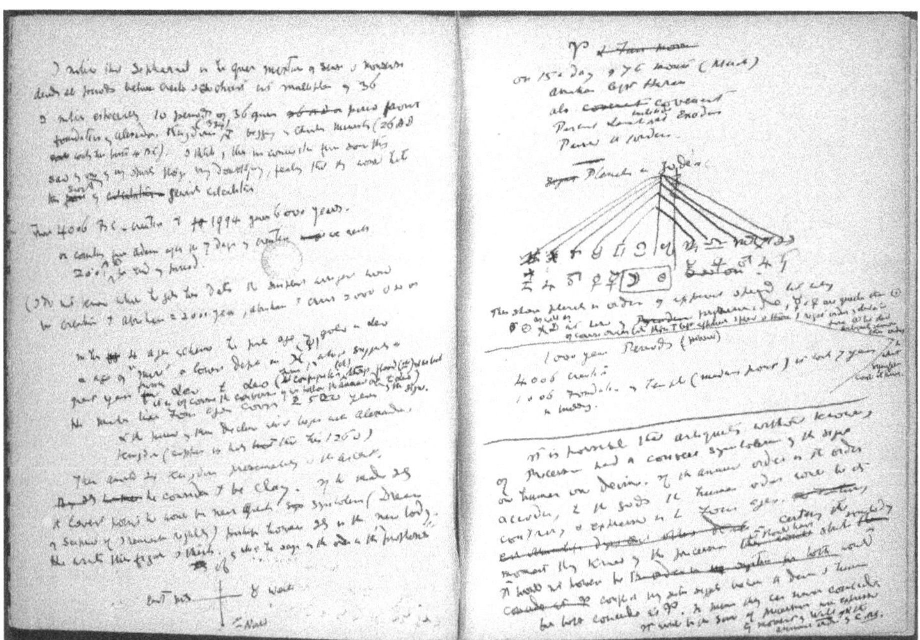

Figure 3.1. Rapallo Notebook D, NLI 13,581, [7v–10r]. Courtesy of the NLI.

(See the lower-right quarter of Figure 3.1—just below the second horizontal line—for this passage.) Yeats conceives of a divine zodiac that goes "forward" from Aries to Taurus, while a human zodiac goes "backward" from Aries to Pisces, and returns to his favorite quotation from Heraclitus—mortals are immortals, immortals mortals, dying each other's life and living each other's death—before rejecting it, possibly because he realizes the two wheels he contemplates do not correspond to the ones in *A Vision*.

This touches on a question that is far from clear in *A Vision B* in the treatment of the *Thirteenth Cone*: that is, whether the "gyre [...] of human life" and "the contrasting cone [...] the 'spiritual objective'" (*AVB* 210, *CW14* 155) run in the same direction or opposite directions. If they go in opposite directions—one counterclockwise and the other clockwise—as in the "converse symbolism of the sign one human one devine" considered in Rapallo D, then they would have to coincide at two points. If, however, they never coincide, this implies that they are always six months apart and run in the same direction. Yeats clearly envisages a form of perpetual opposition, and *A Vision* includes two forms of such opposition, one expressed by *Will* and *Mask* or *Creative Mind* and *Body of Fate*, always diametrically opposed,[48] and the other seen in the way that *Will* and *Creative Mind* move in opposite directions, with *Will* passing counterclockwise through the phases, while *Creative Mind* moves clockwise,[49] with the two coinciding at the New Moon (Phase 1) and the Full Moon (Phase 15).[50] In this notebook, Yeats seems to say that the "conflict my system suggests between devine & human" is the first form of diametrical opposition, moving always in the same direction, so never meeting, while that of precession is the second, as if the equinox's drift were "expressed by movement of <u>Will</u> & the annual order by <u>C. M</u>."

The treatment in *A Vision B*, however, postdates and seems to contradict what Yeats writes here. Unfortunately, the prose explanation is far from perspicuous, and going through the various possibilities that it might be describing is laborious—as is often the case in *A Vision*, a diagram here might have helped readers immensely. In presenting the human and spiritual cones, Yeats writes that "[t]he twelve cycles or months of the second cone are so numbered that its first month is the last of the first cone" (*AVB* 209, *CW14* 254). This implies the movement of wheels in opposite directions, with a year running 1-2-3-etc. matched to one running 12-11-10-etc., each crossing the other at the "New Year" point. The sentence in *A Vision B* continues: "the summer of the one the winter of the other," which implies a correspondence of—approximately—December-January-February to August-July-June and June-July-August to February-January-December, so the "start" of the year is not January.[51] The arrangement implies their crossing at the equinoxes, so that, while winter and summer oppose each other, spring maps onto spring (roughly

March-April-May onto May-April-March) and fall onto fall (September-October-November onto November-October-September), even if they only truly coincide at the respective midpoints.[52]

The paragraph that then follows seems to confirm that Yeats is thinking in terms of wheels numbered in opposite directions: "Although when we are in the first month of this expanding cone we are in the twelfth of the other, when we are in the second in the eleventh of the other, and so on, that month of the other cone which corresponds to ours is always called by my instructors the Thirteenth Cycle or *Thirteenth Cone*, for every month is a cone" (*AVB* 210, *CW14* 155), with the respective months always totaling thirteen: 1+12, 2+11, 3+10, 4+9, 5+8, 6+7, 7+6, 8+5, 9+4, 10+3, 11+2, 12+1. If set around a circle, it is clear that the two parts of the sequence coincide at the transition points between the twelfth and first month and the sixth and seventh. This is what Yeats seems to be denying in Rapallo D, but he evidently found the schematics difficult.

The material that follows in the notebook is in a similar vein to themes suggested by Sepharial's book, going over the great ages of Indian tradition again, but here drawing on *The Encyclopaedia of Religion and Ethics*, which implies that Yeats had access to his books in Dublin.[53] Tracing the symbolic days and nights, he concludes: "Clearly the whole Manvantara system is mere ~~[?]~~ <juggling> to heap age upon age. It would have kept an ~~logical~~ order before the people but not explained it. It had no psychological meaning" (9r). He comments that in the correspondences he has set out in the notes "I think [...] I have left out | some noughts but the process is endless[.] | The whole thing consists ~~in doubling~~ multiply | a 12 or 120 ~~hor~~ hour day & night by 360 to | make a year, & taking 100 of these years for a day | [...] & another 100 for a | night [...] & multiply that by 360 & so on | without end."[54] Despite this apparent cynicism, the following four pages continue to examine the ages and how the lesser periods fit into the greater, using the article by "H. Jacobi in Hastings Encyclopedia of R & E" (9v), which itself characterizes the *manvantara* as "a fanciful system of universal chronology, which passes for orthodox."[55] The calculations spill over onto the page where Yeats started the first prose draft for "Coole Park, 1929."

[13r–23r, 24v–32v, 34r] [A mostly continuous draft of "Coole Park, 1929"]

Between computations on the Great Year (made in the upper-right corner and lower-third portion of leaf 13r), Yeats drew short diagonal lines to set off the prose subject of the poem that he would then write on all but three of the next forty-three pages in the notebook. He had hinted about this project in a letter to Lady Gregory on July 2, 1929: "I have a longish poem in my head about Coole" (*CL InteLex* 5258). Beset by work on *A Vision* and other responsibilities, "Coole Park, 1929" required much of August through at least mid-October to render into verse. Mrs. Yeats cited "MSS. book—1928 [i.e., Rapallo Notebook D] Final version 'Dublin. Sept. 7. 1929'" ("CCP" 240). The prose subject gives the basic concept of the poem and some of its central conceits as a work that was expected to function as a thematic epigraph, or poetic introduction, to the memoir *Coole*, which Lady Gregory had committed to the Cuala Press and which was eventually published there in an abridged edition in 1931.[56] Yeats's outline previews intentions mostly realized in the course of writing the poem in a relatively long period of time:

> Poem on Coole to go with Lady G's | Cuala essays.
> Prose sketch.
> ~~To this house~~ Describe Lady Gregory | ¶ Describe house in first stanza. Here Synge came, | Here Lane, Shaw Taylor, Many names. I too in my timid | youth. Coming & going like the migratory birds. | Then address the swallows flitting in their dream like circles | <~~And she not~~> | Speak of the rarity of the circumstances, that bring together | such concords of men. ~~Each man more than himself~~ | ~~throug[h] whom an unknown life speaks. A circle~~ ever returning | into itself. E[t]c | [followed in right margin by:] Stet [also indicated by underscorings] (NLI 13,581, 13r)

Transcriptions are also provided by Parkinson (*Later Poetry* 80), Stallworthy (*BTL* 180–81), and Clark (*WFMP* 105, with photo-facsimile on 104).[57] Compared favorably with similar prewriting exercises that Yeats undertook after 1913, this one is "generative and suggestive rather than controlling" and not strictly coordinate with the completed poem, which, by the way, "did not devote the first stanza to 'describing' the house; [as] its speaker merely acts as if he were standing in front of the house and speaks primarily of the works and thoughts that it engendered and protected" (Parkinson 80–81). In joining only Douglas Hyde to the company of J. M. Synge and Lady Gregory's nephews Hugh Lane and John Shawe-Taylor, Yeats is said to "minimize any reference to his own youth [...] and to make himself anonymous" (81). Also, significantly, the thought that each man gives voice to an *unknown life* from "depths not his" (regarding the cancelled but restored clauses at the end of the sketch) *does not* finally appear in the poem—a fact justified here by the principle that his prose subject need only produce ideas to test "for probity and pertinence" in the writing of the poem (81). Cited in abstract, these effects are true without accounting for their presence (or absence) in the poem, unless personal circumstance and an obligation to form are also considered parts of the exercise of poetic judgment.

In this case, the writing of the poem progressed alongside production of Lady Gregory's book, which, as Cuala's managing editor, Yeats was at hand to witness and encourage from inception. Writing from Coole to his wife on

August 26, 1928, he noted that their friend was "working on her little essays on the wood, the library & the garden which I am to have for Cuala" (*YGYL* 196, *CL InteLex* 5148). He wrote Gregory three months later, informing her that "I shall have to postpone your Coole essays till some time next year as I want Lolly to publish next a little book of mine called 'A Packet'...I am in a hurry with it as I want to use the 'vision' introduction for the benefit of Cuala & could not after the book itself is published" (November 27, [1928], *CL InteLex* 5194). In compensation for delaying the typesetting of *Coole* with his sister, he added: "I have also an idea of writing—if I may—an introductory poem for your book" (ibid.). In late July 1929, prior to beginning the "longish poem" in his head about Coole, Yeats wrote his wife about distress at the Gregory estate in connection with an article in the *Independent* about the unsettling details of the "Castle Taylor shooting" of 1920—possibly the reason John Shawe-Taylor was included in the poem's cast of characters despite Lady Gregory's failure to cite him by name anywhere in her manuscript.[58] Serious illnesses intervened to delay production of the book until August 23, 1930, when Yeats wrote to her to say that he was letting his sister know the title because Lolly Yeats was anxious to advertise the book with her subscribers and would begin printing as soon as he had finished reading, predicting that it would "become a famous little book" that "people will go back & back to it when they write of the Ireland of our day" (*CL InteLex* 5373). In fact, his delight with this "very touching & moving" book was such that he pledged to have it advertised together with the next project at Cuala, his own *Stories of Michael Robartes and His Friends* (1931).

As Edward Malins notes in his foreword to the complete 1971 edition of *Coole*, the Cuala Press edition of Coole (1931) is shaped according to the Yeatses' interest in publishing: "After Yeats's poem, 'Coole Park,' with which this edition opened, there were three chapters concerned with the Library, the Woods and the Gardens" (7). These were the latest parts of the manuscript that Lady Gregory wrote when Yeats was present and accepted her "little essays on the wood, the library & the garden" for the press and began contemplating the poem he might write based on those focal points. The earlier essays, written in 1927–28, were more than twice the length needed by his sister for a handset booklet and rendered details on the nearly two-hundred-year history of the Gregory family as reflected in rooms of the house, wherein Yeats, Synge, Hyde, Lane, and other contemporaries appear distributed. Omitting these chapters[59] was a practical matter of judgment like that required in writing a preface in verse or prose (e.g., Yeats's preface for Oliver Gogarty's *Wild Apples*, below at 35r–36r, 37v–38r, and 40r).

After the "Prose sketch" on 13r, Yeats began the poem by trying to "describe the house" in a first stanza. As Figure 3.2 indicates with numerous false starts, the task was not easy:

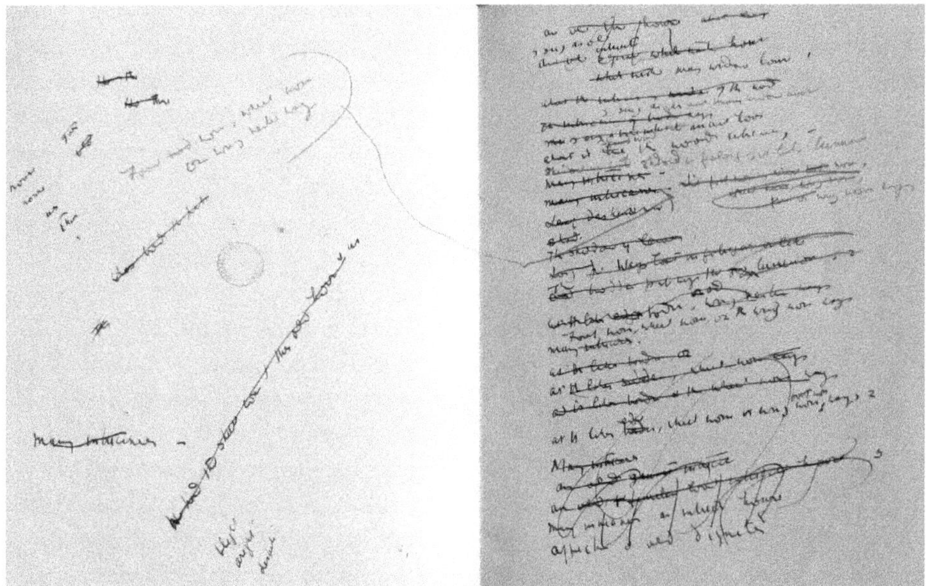

Figure 3.2. Rapallo Notebook D, NLI 13,581, [13v–14r]. Courtesy of the NLI; photograph by Catherine E. Paul.

Little from this effort prevailed by the time he turned the page to the opening at 14v/15r. Hence none of it was included in Stallworthy's study, where the poem's beginning is dismissed as "preliminary scribbles." His transcription begins with the "second verse-draft," at leaf 15r (called "page 4" in *BTL* 181 and so numbered in pencil by Stallworthy on 15r).[60] Parkinson's observation that Yeats "did not devote the first stanza to 'describing' the house" is similarly misleading for not considering the poet's attempt to do that very thing here, in this *first*, verse-draft effort to convert intentions into poetry. Almost everything seems at a dead end, to judge by cancellations, although revisions at a later sitting (in pencil, rendered here in italics) suggest that images of "~~An old~~ square <intricate> ~~white washed house~~ / […] ~~white washed~~ many windowed house […] ~~a bare intricate~~ ancient house" were primary, at first, but soon became engulfed: "About it lie <*~~spread~~ wind*> the woods['] intricacies,— / <*Shadowed in fol[iage] shadowed in foliage, the lake luminous*>" (14r). "Many intricacies" (noted and cancelled on 13v) then becomes the line-initiating catch-phrase for two efforts, of eight and nine lines each on 14r, as a Yeatsian "wheel" takes over, no doubt foreshadowed by that "circle ever returning into itself" at the end of the "Prose sketch." The "square," "old, familiar[,] loved[,] intricate house" has become one with "Many intricacies" involving "Affection & old dignity" by the bottom of the page, part of the "wood[s'] intricacies" of "~~Old trodden pathways that grow luminous~~ / ~~At the lake['s] border, and worn, beaten ways~~" or "Foot worn, wheel worn, or the win<g>~~d~~ worn ways" (affirmed by corrections in pencil, at right, and on 13v, from which "*Foot ~~trod~~ worn, wheel worn or wing [?beat(en)] way*" is indicated for insertion by a long arrow). Leaf 13v is not reproduced by Clark, but see *WFMP* 107 for his complete transcription of 14r.

Rhyme notes on 13v ("house | rouse | us | thus" "bright | aright | despite") join not only the slight correction and drawn arrow cited above, but also remnants of thought bearing on human agency in this intricate landscape: "~~He the~~ | ~~He that~~"; "~~[?those] treading the path~~"; "~~He trod that shall come to this old house & us~~" as a foretaste of the "generations after us" to whom the emerging stanza is dedicated (at first) on 15r. Once there, the "Many intricacies" of 14r have become "miraculous intricacies" of "Amenities of skill, amenities of kind thought." The poet *sings* "Of ancient ~~passions~~ <passion> & intricate thought / A dance like glory that these walls begot" and then (without reference to "generations after us") about "new thoughts knitted to a common thought" (15r). But then (on 14v), "for pleasure" (or "~~my heart[']s sake~~"), he praises again "an intricate house" situated "Among the foliage shadowed, a lake luminous / Old foot worn, wheel worn, <or old> wing worn ways" and largely settles the matter of the first stanza's closing couplet ("Thoughts long knitted into a single thought / A dance like glory that those walls begot") by not choosing to delete the word "long" in an alternative line offered at the bottom of the page: "? or ~~Thought knitted into a single thought~~" (with revision of line 3).[61] Left unfinished at 14v, stanza 1 is not revisited until leaf 19r. Nonetheless, at the foot of 15r, Yeats had already begun to consider the second stanza's integration of content according to the precepts of the *ottava rima* formula (three pairs of interlaced lines of iambic pentameter—or, in other words, linked pairs rhyming alternately—followed by a rhymed couplet):

		~~Lane~~		
		La[ne]		
		~~man~~		
~~Sing~~ Synge	Hyde.	Synge	~~A~~	A
man		man	~~BC~~	1
		imagining	——	
~~Lane~~		~~imagine ing~~	B	B
		Lane	~~BD~~	2
imagining				
Lane		~~thing~~		C
thing		[~~?pride in~~] humility		
continence		[?austerity]		3

(NLI 13,581, 15r. Cf. *WFMP* 108–9 and *BTL* 182.)

From the initial "Prose sketch" and these abstract notes grew a formative text of stanza 2, such as it became over the next four pages (between 15v–17r), before it joined the first assembly of stanzas on leaf 19r.

At the opening 15v/16r, Yeats's introduction of persons seems as tentative and ill-defined as the first stage of stanza 1 had been as shown in Figure 3.2. For that reason, Stallworthy's account is limited to "scribbles" and "fragments of lines" such as "Here Hyde [...] | Those daring men Shaw Taylor and Hugh Lane" (*BTL* 183). Yet see *WFMP* 112–15. Rather, the review began with "audacious" Hugh Lane and Shawe-Taylor "That did great service [?later] in their day" (on 16r) and half a page cancelled before leading with "Here that most medita[tive] John Synge[,] those / Wild hearted men Shaw Taylor & Hugh Lane / Found pride established in humility, / A scene well set & excellent company" ("or," alternatively, "An ordained scene & the best company"). Improvements (on 15v), excluding cancellations, are on the introduction of Hyde and Synge: "Here Hyde, who all that industrious labor first began / That changed his boyish poetry to prose" and "Here that [?profound], vague, meditative man"—anticipating others ("Here many," "Here some perplexed," "Here ~~some~~ <one> long tossed by every wind that blows his mind more running on").

At the next opening (16v/17r), the better part of stanza 2 begins to form in different directions, as Stallworthy explains (*BTL* 184–86) and Clark illustrates in detail (*WFMP* 116–19). In the first instance, projected from the long line entered last on 15v, we have "[...] one long tossed by every wind that blows / ~~Mere~~ <A> weather cock, shuttle cock, ~~comedian~~ comelea[n]" (17r), and after many lines on this same page: "Here I beaten by every wind that blows / The character of my own mind unknown / But hiding under ~~an~~ <youths> embittered pose / That ignorance [...]." Each of the two self-effacing drafts in this manner is heavily redacted by a series of diagonal lines, yet the closing couplet has been decided. Following the recitation of chosen names (also determined but as yet presented in rough form), the couplet delivered the brilliantly withheld predicate of the sentence: "Found pride establis[hed] in humility / A scene well set & excellent company" (17r). Stallworthy reckons that Yeats was wise to abandon a treatment of himself that depended on an unhappy "juxtaposition of cock and chameleon (especially when mis-spelt)" (*BTL* 185), considering that Yeats had confessed in "Hodos Chameliontos" (in *The Trembling of the Veil*, 1922), to having been "lost in that region [that] a cabbalistic manuscript shown me by MacGregor Mathers, had warned me of; astray upon the Path of the Chameleon, upon Hodos Chameliontos" (*Au* 270, *CW3* 215).[62] Thus, Yeats toned down his own share in the esteemed company of "That meditative man John Synge & those / Impetuous men Etc" in two revisions of the stanza on 16v. A humbler cast of himself, as a young man "hiding under an embittered ~~po~~ pose / A boys timidity," is left for tweaking on 19r—but with the understanding that the closing lines of the stanza (from 17r) are implied by "Etc."

On 18r, Yeats turns hastily to stanza 3, mechanically rendering a dozen lines about the flight of swallows as directed in the "Prose sketch" (i.e., "Then address the swallows flitting in their dream like circles")—lines surprisingly faithful to the list of rhyme notes assembled in a column (at upper right) on the facing page ("white | ~~sel~~ skill | night | drille | flight | will | seem | dream"; 17v)—the exercise of a template that requires only to be filled out. The singing declared first in stanza 1 now hesitates with false starts: "~~O swallows~~ / ~~O dusky beam~~ / O blackness with a sudden gleam of white / ~~O swallows~~" (18r). But in turning to those circling migratory birds, Yeats falls too easily into the rhythm of dance, their "deft circles" like "A waltz or old Roger ~~of~~ <or> qu[a]drill[e]" by the fourth line of the stanza. Those three dances—waltz, Roger De Coverley (or Virginia Reel), and quadrille—are from the eighteenth and nineteenth centuries, so the question of form arises from the natural flight patterns of swallows: "Who taught [~~...~~] the mathematics of their flight? / Who taught the sweetness of a common will?" The necessity of closing the stanza with a rhymed couplet produces a third question (addressed to the birds) instead of an answer: "What ~~gre~~ frenzy or what learning makes you seem / A motion with the certainty of a dream." And this is followed by two alternative versions of the couplet, with rhyme notes on 17v for one of them ("attempt" and "dreamt") and verbal emulation of dance-like motion in the other ("turning & returning"). Both options are cancelled on 18r by a single line drawn resolutely through them, whereas Yeats's rhyme notes on the facing leaf (17v) are peculiarly flanked by unrelated inscriptions that convey a sense of distraction. Only 18r is dealt with in *WFMP* 120–21.

(The first distraction is a bit of drollery casually jotted at the center of 17v: "~~An artist painted~~ | A certain friend of mine painted a bather falling from a spring board, [?~~finishing~~] | ~~every al[l]~~ [?possible] muscle & treating flesh with patient refinement—had | the model posed head down ward; ~~when~~ & when ever I saw the picture, & | after a few weeks absence, these words rose to my lips '[?H]as he reached the water yet[?]'" The second tidbit, entered at lower right on the same page, is a glib thought that had just arisen in the course of Yeats's reading for a new play: "I prove in an essay for my Cambridge | lecture that there is only one plausible explanation for the celibacy of Swift— | dre[a]d that his children might inherit | madness.")[63]

Possibly to measure progress on the lyric intended as a preface to Lady Gregory's book of essays, the next stage in composition went straight to the assembly (on 19r) of what had been written so far, with significant revisions of stanzas 1 and 3 carried out on the facing leaf (18v) and a fourth stanza drafted on 19v (over penciled rhyme notes "*sage* | *tude* | *rage* | *good* | ~~*blood*~~ | *newed*"), followed by two substitutions (both cancelled) for the stanza's first five lines. An arrow has been drawn from those lines on 19v, leading to a corresponding fair-hand version at the top of 20r, where they are superimposed in ink on another set of rhyme notes, ones preliminary to a rough sketch of the stanza as it appears in pencil for the better part of this page. The theme, again, is the distinguished house (its "*pillared portico*" noted) and sacred ground recalled from the gospel of Matthew 18.20 ("Where two or three are gathered together in my name, there am I in the midst of them"), but here: "*~~Where two or three are gathered there am I~~ / 'Where two or three are gathered' ~~Jesus said~~ said ~~the~~ <that> sage*" (20r). At this stage in the poem's development, only two stanzas ("I" and "II" on 19r) can be said to resemble their final state. Yet the poem's first title, "Coole House" (inscribed at the top of 19r in this trial assembly of stanzas), is consistent with Yeats's intention to emphasize the great house perhaps more than the great woman in the house, although necessity to honor the latter became imperative, after this, when he wisely abandoned part "IV" from this version to consider Lady Gregory together with nature and the house.[64] (See *WFMP* 122–29; *BTL* 188–92.)

After this, several pages are required for Yeats to find his bearings. The first page (20v) clearly marks this shift in its first line ("The woman of the house was half the tale," wherein "tale" was to rhyme with "seal"), after which five lines emerge from rough jottings to complete an initial sestet for the stanza: "~~A woman here did her own might~~ confer / For half a score once printed by her sea[l] / A woman here had such a character / That half a score ~~once~~ <once printed> by her seal / ~~Nor the inconstant circle of the year~~ <years>" (confirmed at right by a column of rhyme notes). A math exercise jotted below these lines ("36,000 x 12 | = 432,000") shows Yeats's mind, virtually by reflex, drifting back to calculations made on the Great Year much earlier in the notebook. Furthermore, marking almost a dead halt on the progress of the poem here, the facing page (leaf 21r) bears the entire manuscript of "Swift's Epitaph" (see below). Oddly mixing lines from one poem with those of another, two of the lines just quoted were corrected on 21r ("A woman here had such a character / & could so fasten others to her will"), set off by drawn lines between stages of the new poem, written at two or more sittings to judge by the handwriting. (See *WFMP* 130–31 and 240–41.) Soon other interruptions occurred at 23v, 24r, and 26r for "Astrology and the Nature of Reality" (or "Seven Propositions"), scarcely to mention a diary entry on 29v (on Jack Yeats's paintings), before the lyric preface destined for *Coole* regained momentum lost by a wrong turn at 19v–20r.

About the material between 20r and 29r, Stallworthy has little more to say than that the pages he has numbered 16 to 29 "contain scattered and random jottings for stanzas III and IV" (*BTL* 192). He points out that on page "22" (or leaf 24v) Yeats had finally produced a couplet for the new stanza, though, before that (on 25r), following abortive attempts at stanza 4 on 22r, 23r, and 22v (in that order), Yeats had actually written two lines that he thought good enough to share with Lady Gregory, implicitly submitting them to her for an opinion. The lines are: "She ~~sta~~ taught me that straight line that sets a man / Above the crooked journey of the sun" (25r). Having recently returned from Coole, from where he had written his wife about progressing with "some more of the poem for Lady Gregory's book,"[65] he must have felt eager to update his friend too. For, in a week, he wrote cheerfully but apologetically to her as if he thought she were anxious to see the finished work: "I have not written because I had hoped to send you that poem," he said; "—however[,] though it has taken a new leap into life to-day[,] it is not finished—and now I must not delay longer" (*CL InteLex* 5289). The remainder of the letter bestows on her the couplet he produced on leaf 25r of Rapallo D:

> It was very pleasant at Coole but I am too dazed with my day's verse writing to add more now. Here are two lines that may or may not remain in the poem
>
> "She taught me that straight line that sets a man
> Above the crooked journey of the sun." [66]

That was on September 30, 1929. We do not have Lady Gregory's opinion of those lines. She might have been touched and a little baffled with so little text to go on. But we do know that Yeats subsequently drew a vertical line through the partial unit of work with which the couplet is associated on 25r and, similarly, through the textual options offered on 24v, where Stallworthy has spotted the weaker alternative: "That fancies work completed—none could say / Whether her will ~~our~~ or ours had won the day" (*BTL* 192; see *WFMP* 138–41).

Moreover, drawing a line below that ultimately rejected couplet, Yeats advanced the theme of the "unknown traveller" from 25r by focusing on the movement and character of the pilgrim, drawn from recent effort in "Swift's Epitaph" to render into English the Latin word "Viator" as one "World-besotted traveller" (21r; see below). Rough-hewn at best, a cluster of verses mixed with prosy notes on other lines produced the final line for the stanza and poem: "A ~~moments me~~ moments memory to that laurelled head" (24v). In common purpose, the "Viator" in Swift's epitaph and Yeats's "World-besotted" pilgrim blend in the "unknown traveller" (on 25r) to become (on 24v) a "Student or Idler in those days long hence / Com<ing> on some mossgrown, or lea[f] strew[n] stones / [...] Here where the limes shall ever round this shadow stand." Between the lines, the pilgrim is given a predicate: "once [reaching] this house, [?pause] & give" a token of respect (that is, "A moment's memory to that laurelled head"), obviously inspired by association with "the colossal marble bust of Macaenas [*sic*] at the end of the flower bordered gravel walk" at Coole Park (*Coole* 99). Lady Gregory even appears in cameo as "A woman printed with her character / ~~As [?though]~~ / ~~As though that were, a Roman [...] agate se[a]l~~" (24v). The "unknown traveller" or, simply, "Traveller," thereafter becomes an agent of animation for the poet in his descriptive treatment of the garden in several drafts of stanza 4, occurring progressively on leaves 25v, 26r (for one line), 26v (for five lines), 27r, 27v (for two lines), and 28r–29r (astraddle

"Astrology and the Nature of Reality," or "Seven Propositions," as discussed below). At the end of this interrupted phase of writing (see *WFMP* 142–51), Yeats's pilgrim is addressed in three lines extracted from cancellations: "Here student, unknown traveller take your stand / When all the rooms & passages are gone / And saplings rooted in the stony ground" (28v).

At this point, Stallworthy picks up his transcription with a miscue, citing page number "30" (leaf 28v) but quoting text as "ominous prophecy of the future of Coole" (*BTL* 192) as detailed on page "29" (29r). The progress made here on the first and last lines of stanza 4 is remarkable, although, after making three runs at its closing couplet, the conclusion is not quite clinched yet close enough, with revisions on 28v, for the retooling of matter in stanza 3 as a consequence. Thus, Yeats returned to the swallows and made them figurative: "We came like swallows & like swallows went" (30r). Lady Gregory, her character, her house, and her surrounding environment are still the focus, but the circular flight patterns of the birds is downplayed with the arrival of Yeats and literary friends, precursors to the pilgrims afterward addressed as "traveller, scholar, poet" in the final version of stanza 4. What falls out of the poem on 30r and 29v is the recitation of eighteenth- and nineteenth-century dances (waltz, Roger De Coverley, and quadrille) that move in "deft circles" resembling the "mathematics [. . .] of flight" (on 19r). With a diagonal line drawn through Yeats's recasting of stanza 3 on 30r, another line is drawn to set off lyrics reminiscent of those in stanza 1 ("I praise for living ears an ancient house / The woman of that house, her western skies / Stormy cloud-encumbered, luminous")[67] as a reminder of rudiments: house, woman in the house, and brooding sky. In a last revision of the stanza before assembling a draft of the entire poem for the second time (after the first on 19r–20r), Yeats chooses to work on the idea of circling flight, shifting rhymes and the mathematics of dance to the journey of people who, like swallows, "circled" and "wheeled upon a [?counter] <compass> point" toward Lady Gregory's "magic circle" (20v). (For images and transcriptions, see *WFMP* 152–55; see also *BTL* 193–94.)

("Coole Park, 1929" is then interrupted by an interval, a pause of a day or two, perhaps, and by the entry of a diary note set off from the poem by a drawn line on leaf 29v and dated "Oct"—for October 1929. The entry indicates a break in schedule and marks a moment of reflection about the significance of Jack B. Yeats as a painter: "Yesterday I was at my brothers show. He said these pictures are exciting & was full of the word. He was right—it is an art of excitement—I know no other art like it—perhaps it is something that belongs to us here just now. What has happened[?]—until four or five years ago my brother [was] an illustrator, a commentator." As Jack Yeats and his wife, Cottie, had moved to 42 Fitzwilliam Square in fall 1929, visiting was convenient between the siblings because W. B. and George Yeats were neighbors at No. 18. Almost certainly, the "show" of Jack Yeats's paintings referred to in the note is the exhibition held at

Engineers' Hall, Dublin, October 1–14, 1929, for which a two-page pamphlet had been prepared as a visitor's catalogue.[68] WBY is recalling Jack's letter of October 31, 1925, in which he had complained that his drawings for the Cuala Press were "a drag" on his reputation as an artist. By the following spring, he had submitted his last work for the Cuala Prints series. The note on 29v appears to agree with Jack's justification for withdrawing altogether. At the time, he had argued: "You say my painting is now 'great.' Great is a word that may mean so many different things. But I know I am the first living painter in the world."[69] Privately, the diary entry registers a mixture of amazement and fraternal pride after viewing, first-hand, a collection of this *living art*. The entry in Rapallo D, written on the day *after* that occasion, was to be the last obvious interruption before the whole body of "Coole Park, 1929" came together in the next six pages of the notebook, on 30v–32v and 34r—leaf 33 having been removed for some reason.)

This final stage of the poem's composition in the notebook began fully nine pages after the last draft of "Seven Propositions," six of which Yeats forwarded to Frank Pearce Sturm on October 9, 1929 (*CL InteLex* 5291). So, chronologically, the poem advanced to its first full draft around mid-October, more than a month after the September 7 date inscribed beneath the final, fair-hand version that Yeats only slightly edited when copying it out on 32v and 34r. The poem is written out without title, and its four stanzas are at first assigned Roman numerals ("I," "~~II~~ 2," "III," "IV"), though revisions following on 32r (for stanzas 1 and 4) and 31v (for stanza 3), as well as all stanzas in the final draft (on 32v and 34r), are converted to Arabic numbers. On 31r, the most significant changes occur in line 3 ("~~The A windy waters edge~~ <A woman of that house>, ~~the~~ <but> luminous") and in line 6 ("Commend ~~miraculous~~ <unatural> consanguinities"); however, the whole stanza is crossed out there and most of it, save for the closing couplet, afterward rewritten on 32r and tweaked on 32v. The second stanza, on 31r, bears at two points (both in its third line) only two scribal accidents so that its fair-hand rendering easily transferred, verbatim, to the final draft on 32v. Stanza "III," on 31r, proved most in need of revision, for two versions follow on 30v and yet another one on 31v before it was suitably transferred into fair copy on 32v. Notably, "We came like swallows" became "They came like swallows" as Yeats shifts to third-person voice, struggling again with the "geometry" of flight (afterward "the charmed dreaming air" on 30v, then "upon the dreaming air" on 31v and 32v) and weighing options to avoid awkward syntax while achieving a formulaic rhyme from uncommon diction—that is, on "withershin" or "withershins." At first, stanza 3 is scribbled out on 31r, where stanza 4 is crossed out with it. On 32r, the latter is polished with word-choice matters settled in the first six lines, and an alternative for the concluding quatrain is briefly considered but stricken with a diagonal line. As a result, the remainder is copied almost faultlessly to conclude the final draft of the poem on leaf 34r. (See *WFMP* 156–69.) As Stallworthy says: "Lady Gregory, whose epitaph in fact this is, dominates the poem as she formerly dominated Coole"; she is explicitly mentioned in all but stanza 2, and, with substitution of "laurelled" for "sacred" in a "last-minute alteration" at the very end of the poem, she is there only deprived of the "odour of sanctity" (*BTL* 198).

Above this final draft (on 32v), Yeats set the title "Coole Park" (not "Coole House" from 19r). At the end of the poem (on the facing page, 34r), he gave it a puzzling, commemorative dateline—"Dublin. Sept 7. 1929"—when at least a month remained *before* work on the poem actually finished. Closer to the start than anywhere near the day in mid-October on which the final draft was made, "Sept 7" is so specific and corroborated elsewhere[70] that the date implies personal significance. It is displayed prominently, with the poet's name added, when the poem (as "Coole Park") was published as a preface to Lady Gregory's *Coole*. So obviously wrong, the date might have partly served as an act of self-deception since it had taken so unusually long for Yeats to write the poem. Stallworthy remarks, "Few readers of this poem would guess that behind its comparatively simple structure and fluent rhythms lie [approximately] thirty-eight pages of working—more than went into the making of any other poem that I know" (*BTL* 200). This study finds a connection between the difficulty Yeats encountered in writing this poem (as a preface in verse) and his frustration, soon after, delivering a prose preface for Oliver Gogarty's chapbook *Wild Apples* (see below). Yeats complained about fulfilling the latter obligation as editor: "I have no gift of the ready writer & keep composing & recomposing in my head sentences & finding nothing suitable" (to Katharine Tynan Hinkson, Sept. 27, [1929], *CL InteLex* 5288). Similarly, it seems, he had expected to finish much sooner than he did his preface for *Coole*.

[21r] ["Swift's Epitaph"]

The origin of this poem in Rapallo Notebook D was interpreted with some confusion by Mrs. Yeats, with dates of composition variously attributed to "1930," "written at Coole Sept—1929?/1930," "1929 or 1930," and "completed Sept. 1930" ("CCP" 240). In her copy of *The Collected Poems*, she noted (at page 277) at the end of "Swift's Epitaph": "written at Coole | Sept – 1930" (with the year at first superimposed on "1929" and then queried: "1929?").[71] The date of the poem can be established with accuracy, within a day or so, by the position of the manuscript at 21r in relation to the progress of "Coole Park, 1929" at 20v (see above). Clark's transcription and corresponding facsimile of 21r (*WFMP* 240–41) confirm the relationship, including the presence of two amended lines from the longer poem positioned between second and third versions of "Swift's Epitaph." Thus, progress on the former and dating of the latter are pinpointed in the letter Yeats sent from Coole to his wife on September 23, 1929—in which he says: "I have written verse—Swift's epitaph in verse & some more of the poem for Lady Gregory's book & going on with the correction of the account of system" (*CL InteLex* 5287; *YGYL* 209). George Yeats's later confusion over the year is understandable considering the depth of her husband's reading on Swift in 1929 and 1930, and in light of his play *The Words upon the Window-Pane* (1930).

Clark gives a literatim transcription of the Latin epitaph chiseled on Swift's vault in St. Patrick's Cathedral, Dublin, where he is remembered to the traveller ("Viator"): "Ubi saeva Indignatio / Ulterius / Cor lacerare nequit. / Abi Viator / Et imitare, si poteris, / Strenuum pro virili / Libertatis Vindicatorem" (*WFMP* 240n; see also *YP* 599–600). Literally: Where savage indignation is unable to lacerate his heart further. Go forth, traveler, and imitate, if you can, a strong defender of freedom to the best of his ability. Yeats's first recorded translation occurred when commemorating John Synge in 1909: "And is not that epitaph Swift made in Latin for his own tomb more immortal than his pamphlets, perhaps than his great allegory?—'He has gone where fierce indignation can lacerate his heart no more'" (*E&I* 308, *CW4* 223). More recently, in section II of "Blood and the Moon" (written in August 1927), Yeats employed Swift's phrase "*Saeva Indignatio*" to signify "The strength that gives our blood and state magnanimity of its own desire" (*VP* 481: 28–29). And scholars generally credit Yeats for animating "Swift's Epitaph" with departures from the original in its first and fifth lines ("Swift has sailed into his rest" and "World-besotted traveller; he").[72]

Yeats's inventions in those lines seem related to his struggling with the flight of "those travelled swallows" (18v) and the "pilgrims road" (19v) in drafts of stanzas 3 and 4 of "Coole Park, 1929." As he had made a decisive turn from avian flight to the straightforward journey of some future man, some "Unknown traveller" (25r), come to pay tribute in a "moment[']s memory to that laurelled head" (24v), surely Swift's epitaph was raveled into the phantasmagoria to such an extent that Yeats broke off from his labor on the fourth stanza to compose his own version of Swift's memorial before continuing with the longer poem. The evidence is striking. The *Viator* or "Traveller," for several pages after in Rapallo Notebook D, takes center stage before the swallows are dealt a series of adjustments in stanza 3. Yet, here (on 21r), in three stages of work at different sittings (to judge by handwriting), the six lines of verse fell easily into place. The second and fourth lines are invariable while the first and third change with modifications due to the necessity of rhyme: "Jonathan Swift is at the goal" (rhyming with "soul" in line 3) becomes "Jonathan Swift's in port" (semi-rhyming with "heart" in line 3) becomes "Swift ~~has~~ <hath> sailed ~~& found~~ <into> his rest" (rhyming with "breast"). But the fifth line in these drafts affects nothing because it is only the line-initial phrasing and meter (or syllables) that matter—all bearing on the character of the *Viator*. He is in first draft a "World estrangèd man," in second draft a "World besotted ~~ma[n]~~ traveller," and in third draft a "World besotted

~~sailor~~ <traveler>" (21r). The last makes it clear that the *Viator* in the poem is one with the antihero in *Gulliver's Travels*, Swift's "great allegory."[73] The rest is a matter of half a dozen printed variants in the history of Yeats's poem (see *VP* 493).

[23v–24r, 26r] ["Astrology and the Nature of Reality" (or "Seven Propositions")]

Interspersed between the drafts of "Coole Park, 1929," Yeats drafted an important statement of his understanding of astrology and the system of *A Vision*. The first draft of six aphorisms is struck through by a line and occupies the spread 23v/24r. The second draft starts in the lower half of 24r, with the first three propositions, with a further four continued on 26r.[74] A lightly revised version of this latter set is contained in a typescript titled "Seven Propositions,"[75] which was filed with two other sets of apothegmatic schemes, "The Genealogical Tree of Revolution," and "Recent Discoveries in Psychic Phenomena," the latter dated 1938. This dating, with George Yeats's own testimony,[76] led earlier scholars—notably Richard Ellmann,[77] Virginia Moore,[78] and Hazard Adams[79]—to treat the propositions as a late reformulation or revision of Yeats's "ideas a year or so *after* he gave the 1937 *Vision* to his publisher."[80] The correct date and origin is apparent in Yeats's correspondence with Frank Pearce Sturm, where a shorter version of "Six Propositions" accompanies a letter of October 9, 1929 (*CL InteLex* 5291). The dating of the propositions has been corrected in Elizabeth Heine's essay "W. B. Yeats: Poet and Astrologer."[81]

Yeats told Sturm that he had sent his Propositions to George Russell's Hermetic Society and planned to send them "to some of my Kaballists as well as to the Dublin astrologers. I want to find if we are in agreement" (*CL InteLex* 5291).[82] Yeats explained the format and his aim to Sturm: "The Propositions are probably stiff. They are mainly aimed at Æ who in reading my Packet preferred to it certain Indian aphorisms, & seems to think that aphorism [is] the true method."[83] Though Yeats is almost certainly speaking of Russell's privately expressed opinions, in his *Irish Statesman* review of *A Packet for Ezra Pound*, Russell had commented:

> while I would like to know the core of this philosophy I feel I must wait until I come to that intensity of being which, when we attain it, the sage Patangali tells us, will enable us to penetrate to the essential essence of anything, and comprehend it fully merely by directing our attention to it. Then I might know in a second what otherwise must take me many years. I will wait for that myriad instant, and be content with my half knowledge of what the poet means.[84]

Rather than discursive and logical exposition and reception, Russell looks to meditative insight. As a translation of the Sanskrit word *sutra*,[85] aphorism is a deliberately condensed form of teaching meant to be unfolded by teaching and discussion, but also, as Yeats described in *The Aphorisms of Yôga*, for the "pupils to get by heart and put in practice."[86] Yeats himself was drawn to the absurdist formulations and ineffable insights of Zen koans, quoting several of them in *A Vision* and elsewhere, and according to his introduction to *The Aphorisms of Yôga*: "The truth cannot be found by argument, the soul itself is truth."[87]

The Propositions had a second aim, which was to offer to his "fellow students" of Hermetic thought and astrology "the first theoretical justification of Astrology made in modern times, & even that which antiquity must have had has not come down to us" (*CL InteLex* 5291). This was a subject that had been preoccupying him, and it is partly seen in the notes on the planets and zodiac made from Sepharial earlier in this notebook. In Notebook A, he had asserted that "Astrology had its theoretic foundation in some part of great mathematic philosophy that has been lost,"[88] and here he looks to establish some of the fundamental principles underpinning that philosophy. Though the system of *A Vision* is not itself astrological, Yeats incorporates symbolism from astrology into his treatment of several aspects, notably in *A Vision A*. Astrology in general is viewed as overlapping and consistent with the system of *A Vision*, especially in its symbolism—people of the same phase are different because of their astrological chart and the symbolism of the zodiac illuminates Yeats's understanding of the alternating ages of history.[89] Here, Yeats goes further and finds a common ground for both systems, expounding a form of animistic idealism.

The reason that these formulations are so important is that they reformulate the underlying ideas of *A Vision* in such an unexpected way. Most readers, if they were called upon to summarize the system of *A Vision* into fundamental principles, would probably place the antinomies and the gyres at the center of the presentation, and generally readers tend to find their impressions of system dominated by the phases of the moon or the rules governing the Wheel with the *Faculties* and *Principles*. It is unlikely that anyone else could strip away the machinery of *A Vision* so completely as Yeats himself does, showing a depth of engagement with the system that no one else could have, such that even the antinomies are seen as secondary. In their respective treatments of the "Seven Propositions," Moore, Ellmann, and Adams saw these formulations as so evidently different from *A Vision* that they easily accepted a date in the late 1930s and regarded them as clearly a progression beyond *A Vision*. Yet they were actually composed alongside drafts of *A Vision* and before the final drafts.

The Propositions summarize the philosophy underlying the system presented in *A Vision*, but cast in language and terms more reminiscent of McTaggart's and Whitehead's philosophical writings, though clearly in consonance with elements of Spinoza or Berkeley. Despite the major caveat about the mistaken dating, the Propositions are dealt with in some detail by

Moore, Ellmann, and Adams, and often well, though Ellmann in particular has difficulties recognizing that Yeats's conception of Spirits does not exclude human beings, but just includes humans among a wider range of spiritual beings. As the purpose of this essay is more descriptive than analytical, and as Neil Mann has also treated the Propositions elsewhere, both in essay form and online, we shall not repeat that material in detail.[90] It is, however, worth examining here the evolution of the ideas from earlier material in the Rapallo Notebooks and redrafting in Rapallo D.

Rapallo Notebook B, the first of the Rapallo notebooks, contains a draft intended as the opening exposition of the revised version of *A Vision*, explaining the fundamentals of the gyres of space and time, corresponding roughly with "The Principal Symbol" III and IV in the published version (*AVB* 71–72, *CW14* 52–53). In a comment written on a verso for insertion, Yeats added:

> But the mind has two movements one into an imagined space within it self, where all possabilities or passions of the daimon struggle & persist, and one into actual space where all things exclude each other, & has two selves one the universal self, or daimon of daimons, consciousness itself, persisting through time & mirroring space & a separate self set in the midst of space & struggling for room to live & mirroring the Daimon passions. Thought is from the first movement, emotion & sensation from the second. (NLI 13,579, 15v)[91]

This exposition clearly prefigures the formulations of the Propositions, in the distinction of two separate kinds of movement and struggle. The first self is universalizing consciousness, or the *primary* tendency, and the second a separating individuality, or the *antithetical* tendency. The image of reflection is important in all of Yeats's formulations and the phrases here "mirroring space" and "mirroring the Daimon['s] passions" are echoed in the Spirit reflecting the universe and of how a Spirit is reflected into space and time in the Propositions, and also in how *A Vision* states that the "*Principles* are the *Faculties* transferred, as it were, from a concave to a convex mirror, or vice versa" (*AVB* 187, *CW14* 137). The universalizing self and movement are associated with thought, the individuating self and movement with emotion and sensation, ideas developed further in the Propositions, and effectively dividing *A Vision*'s *Spirit* and *Creative Mind* (thought), on the one side, from *Passionate Body* and *Will* (emotion and sensation), on the other.[92] It is evident that the Propositions use more generally accessible language—e.g., recasting Daimons as Spirits but with the same meaning—while equivalents in *A Vision* add technicalities and greater precision.

The first draft of six aphorisms is slightly more astrological than the second, but already clearly expressing an idealist vision of the cosmos in which all is consciousness and mind or spirit. In the closing section of *A Vision A*, Yeats had written that "the ancient philosopher [...] could assume, perhaps even prove, that every condition of mind discovered by analysis, even that which is timeless, spaceless, is present vivid experience to some being, and that we could in some degree communicate with this being while still alive, and after our death share in the experience" and he declares that he "would restore to the philosopher his mythology" (*AVA* 252, *CW13* 207). Here he does not give the full mythology, but the abstracted first principles.

As Elizabeth Heine comments, these aphorisms require "an audience that knows what horoscopes are," in the sense that to the Yeatses a horoscope is not a snippet of writing in a newspaper but a chart recording the positions of the planets, zodiac, and the Earth's diurnal rotation.[93] This first draft also uses terms from the system of *A Vision* ("primary" and "Beatific Vision"), which make it less approachable for a general audience. In fact, all the aphorisms are struck out with a diagonal line, while Aphorisms 1 and 4 are also cancelled with a wavy line (see Figure 3.3):

[23v] Astrology & the Nature of Reality

1. Reality is a timeless & spaceless community of Spirits | Each perceives the others wills them & is willed by them | It is a state of changeless happiness.
2. This reality reflects itself in time as ~~the actua[?]~~ | a series of abstractions. There is unhappiness because | ~~any~~ no abstraction, or moment of time, is a self | subsistent reality. Time must continue ~~the~~ [?*till*] reality has | been completely displayed as a series.
3. My spirit reflects the timeless space less universe | My empirical nature reflects the whole universe, including | itself, as displayed at some one moment. Only | the movements of the stars are sufficiently vast to | permit the mapping of the universe so displayed.
4. At the moment the part which I myself contribute[?] | to this display is reduced almost to nothing. I | am passive, or primary. Hence the state of the universe | as recorded in the horoscope ~~is perpetuates itself~~ | is impressed upon my subjective nature, as the form of | my thought & perception. The channel in which it must flow

[24r]

(5). Human life consists of the turning into timeless & | spaceless existence thought ~~in some form of the fate~~ of the fate, or a vain struggle against. Fate perceived | by Spirit as it self or as timeless and space less reality | is truth. It is the state of the Spirit after the Beatific Vision. | It is followed by birth, & a new fate. ~~E~~ The moment | of birth is not accidental – each new fate is the product | of that which went before it

6. It is impossible to ~~formulat~~ <~~posit~~> <perceive> Fate without ~~positing~~ <expressing> | ~~my~~ freedom. Every possible statement, or perception |

contains both terms – self and that which it perceives – | but the ~~positing~~ perception of fate precedes the expression of freedom. | The horoscope preceeds the life. The body & mind of the | new born child is the reply freedom makes to the horoscope (NLI 13,581, 23v–24r)

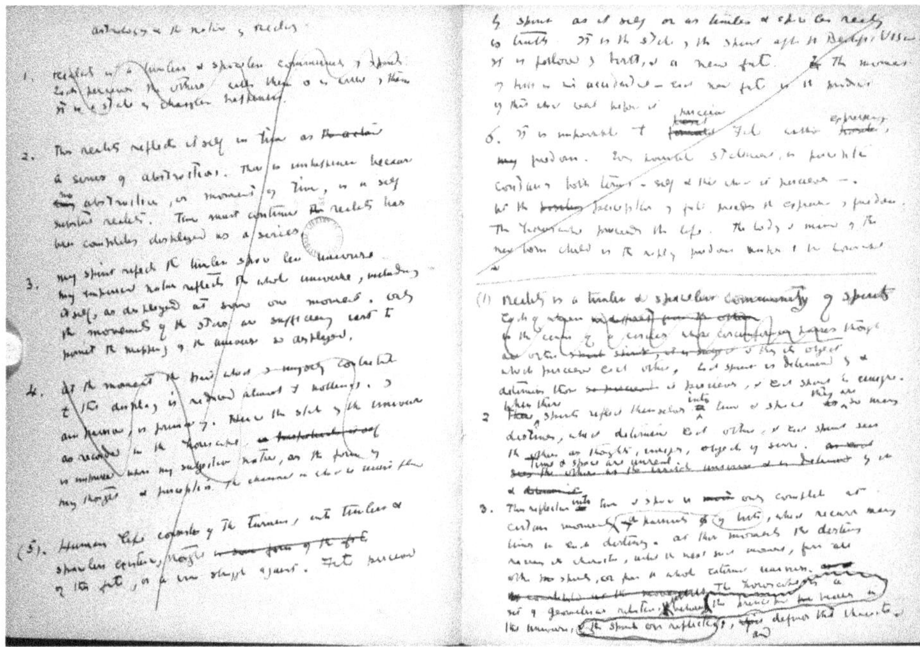

Figure 3.3. Rapallo Notebook D, NLI 13,581, [23v–24r]. Courtesy of the NLI.

Aphorism 1 establishes a community of spirits perceiving and willing one other and their cosmos in eternity and happiness, while Aphorism 2 looks at the reflection of this cosmos into time, which is incomplete and therefore unhappy. For unstated reasons, eternal reality must be expressed piece by piece in time. Aphorism 3 introduces the astrological element, the spirit reflects the universe, and the universe's state is marked by the stars, as therefore is the spirit's, which is expressed in the horoscope or disposition of the planets in the sky in Aphorism 4. Aphorism 5 deals cryptically with the concept of fate expressed in the horoscope, which can either be perceived as itself or as transcendent reality and defined as the truth.[94] Yeats sees a form of reincarnational logic in the time of birth, such that the horoscope corresponds to the fate or the product of foregoing lives and afterlives.[95] Aphorism 6 brings in freedom as the antinomy of fate. Although fate comes first, as does the horoscope, freedom necessarily follows. The actual life lived is the response of freedom to the dictates of fate shown in the birth chart, as a baby will choose and live one set of possibilities from the pattern laid down. This antinomy and the importance of freedom is more clearly expressed in comments attributed to Michael Robartes in the stories that preface *A Vision B* than anywhere in *A Vision* proper.[96] Perhaps as a result, many readers have found the fatalism or determinism of the system overwhelming.

It seems that Yeats returned to "Coole Park, 1929" after the first draft of "Astrology & the Nature of Reality," working on the poem for three pages (24v, 25r, 25v) before returning to the philosophy by drawing a line directly underneath Aphorism 6 (on 24r), making three entries there but then, necessarily, jumping to 26r. There is no title, but Yeats adopted "Six Propositions" in his letter to Frank Pearce Sturm, and then "Seven Propositions" in the typescript that was probably dictated from this second draft.

The second draft continues to seek the precise wording for the concepts, developing some of the ideas considerably and clarifying distinctions, though also obscuring others. In a few places circles and arrows relocate phrases, and the proposition originally numbered 7 is renumbered "4" (with a line inserting it ahead of the former item 4 and with propositions renumbered accordingly). These relocations produce a text that reflects Yeats's later thoughts, but with changes reflected, as far as possible, in the cancellations recorded below.

[24r]

(1). Reality is a timeless & spaceless community of spirits | ~~each of whom is different from the others~~ | ~~is the centre of a circles whose circumference passes through~~ | ~~all others spirit spirit, it is subject & they its object~~ | which percieve each other. Each Spirit is determined by & | determines those ~~so percieved~~ it percieves, & each spirit is unique.

2 ~~These~~ <When these> spirits reflect themselves ~~in~~ <into> time & space as <they are> so many | destinies, which determine each other, & each spirit sees | the others as thoughts, images, objects of sense. ~~As each~~ | ~~sees the others as the visible universe & is determined by it~~ | ~~& determines it~~ <Time & space are unreal.>

3. This reflection ~~in~~ <into> time & space is ~~most~~ only complete at | certain moments <of birth> ~~of~~ <or> passivity ~~or~~, which recurr many | times in each destiny. At the moments the destiny | receives its character, until the next such moment, from all | other ~~pi~~ spirits, or from the whole external universe. ~~As it~~ | ~~is constituted at the moment~~ The horoscope is a | set of geometrical relations between <the spirit on reflection> the principal ~~fo~~ masses in | the universe, ~~which~~ <and> defines that character.

[26r]

→ ~~(7).~~ (4) The emotional character of a timeless & spaceless spirit | reflects itself ~~in~~ as its condition in time | Its intellectual character <reflects>

as its condition in space. | ~~Position~~ The Position of a spirit in space & time | therefore defines character

~~4.~~ 5 Human life is either a struggle ~~of the spirit, or dest~~ <~~the~~ a destiny> | against ~~the ex~~ all other spirits, or destinies or | a transformation of the character, ~~fix fixed upon it~~ <defined in the horoscope> | ~~the moment of birth~~, into time less & spaceless existence | ~~The possible move~~ The whole ~~movement~~ <passage> from birth to | birth should be an epitomy of the whole passage | of the universe ~~from back into its first timeless & | spaceless condition~~ through time & back into its timeless & spaceless condition

(~~5~~6) The ~~nature~~ <acts and> nature of ~~the spirits~~ <a spirit> ~~so reflected in time | & the events of its life~~ during any one life are a section or abstraction | of reality, & are ~~therefore determined~~ unhappy | because incomplete. ~~They are one gu~~ They are ~~one~~ a | gyre or part of a gyre, whereas reality is a sphere

~~(6)~~ (7) Though the spirits are determined by each other | they never completely loose their freedom | Every possible statement or perception contains | both terms — the self & that which is percieved (NLI 13,581, 24r and 26r)[97]

These seven propositions now present a clear sense of process—spirits from the eternal community reflect into time and space, and their characteristics determine the moment and place of birth, registered in the unique configuration of the planets.[98] The use of the word "destiny" introduces a more personal note than the earlier word "fate," since, in Yeats's usage at least, destiny is a more individual, chosen form of necessity than fate, expressing inner qualities rather than being imposed from outside. The introduction of gyre and sphere is slightly idiosyncratic in Yeats's usage, but not overly technical and not out of keeping with aphoristic form. Similarly, the allusion to human life as a microcosmic form of macrocosmic processes hints at greater concepts that lie behind the formulation. The final proposition—omitted in the version sent to Frank Pearce Sturm, so probably also in the version for Æ's Hermetic students—seems a watered-down version of the first draft's vindication of freedom. Possibly the full import is hidden within the wording, as it is in Michael Robartes's declaration "Every action of man declares the soul's ultimate, particular freedom, and the soul's disappearance in God; declares that reality is a congeries of beings and a single being" (*AVB* 52, *CW14* 37).

It is uncertain whether Yeats ever entertained the idea of putting these Propositions, in any form, into *A Vision*, whether as part of the fictions of Michael Robartes or as a separate element in the volume's prefatory "Packet for Ezra Pound." When first putting the system forward in *A Vision A*, Yeats had suggested that his "old fellow students" of Hermetic subjects would be most capable of tackling "what is most technical and explanatory" (*AVA* xii; *CW13* lv). Yet, judging from his comments to Frank Pearce Sturm, he seems to have restricted the relatively direct restatement of his thinking contained in the propositions to such students, rather than offering this summary to a more general audience who might have found it a more approachable introduction to his thought.

[34v] [Notes for *A Vision*]

Taking advantage of a blank verso, Yeats made notes proposed "For 'The Great Wheel,'" the first and main exposition of his system in *A Vision*, though none of these were used. In the upper half of 34v is a passage "From Chapmans translation of Ovids Banquet of Sense."[99] Glossing the phrase "as intellects themselves transite, / To each intelligible quality," Yeats copied out George Chapman's note that "the Philosopher saith *Intellectus in ipsa intellegibilia transit*"—the intellect passes into the intelligible things themselves—and this no doubt relates to his attempts to find ways to illustrate and to find philosophical support for ideas in *A Vision*, specifically here *Creative Mind* and *Spirit*.[100] The other quotation relates to the antinomies and dualities of the system and is one Yeats certainly already knew: "'There is a place where contraries are equally true' | Blake's 'Milton,' Book the Second, line 1." Below that, there is a note that "Coleridge was influenced by Synesius," a late Platonist who was an associate of Hypatia of Alexandria and later a Christian bishop. Indeed, in *Biographia Literaria* Coleridge refers to having translated "eight Hymns of Synesius [...] before my fifteenth year" and the third hymn provides a Greek epigraph for the chapter "On the imagination, or Esemplastic power."[101] Yeats was familiar with Synesius through Ralph Cudworth and the Cambridge Platonists, as he testifies in "Swedenborg, Mediums, and the Desolate Places" (*Ex* 61, *CW5* 67), where he cites Synesius on the spirit's state after death (*Ex* 62–63, *CW5* 68).

[35r–36r, 37v–38r, 40r] [Draft of a preface for Oliver St. John Gogarty's *Wild Apples*]

In 1928, the Cuala Press had published a volume of Oliver St. John Gogarty's poetry titled *Wild Apples* but later agreed to issue a new volume with the same title, including about half of the poems from the earlier collection, along with many more and an introduction by W. B. Yeats.[102]

Yeats's drafting of occasional prose shows a constant struggle with words and meaning, but, unlike work on his poetry or on *A Vision*, it seldom evinces major changes of thought, approach, or theme. The preface for *Wild Apples* that he drafted for the 1930 edition is no exception. This is all the more surprising as he was forced to extend and rethink his original preface, as explained below. Thus, the first sentence of the draft is very much as it appears in the published version and throughout the draft, after a little rephrasing and rethinking, the text corresponds closely to the published version (see *CW6* 172–74).

A few opinions were, however, excised or softened as Yeats tries to do justice to his friend's poetry without giving undeserved praise. Also evident is Yeats's slight exasperation with Gogarty's lack of dedication to the hard work of "stitching and unstitching" (*VP* 204–5) necessary for poetry:

> D Gogarty is a careless writer, often ~~writing <nigh> first drafts~~ <making benumbed first drafts> | of poems rather than poems ~~and I ask have asked~~ myself | ~~of late, why~~ & then the next moment writing with ~~wit~~ animation | ~~care & precission~~. It is much like that in his conversation, except his | conversation is wittier & profound | when public events excite him whereas public events | ~~denumb his poetic faculty, which is best~~ | ~~when it [is] self intoxicated & world begetting~~ ~~make his poetry~~ | ~~dem~~ ~~in the form~~ of some incursion of Augustus Johns perhaps | be numb his poetry. (NLI 13,581, 35r)

It is difficult for the reader to know what Yeats means by "an incursion of Augustus John" (the form that was published, see *CW6* 172)—where it evidently has personal meaning yet relates largely to the poetry that Yeats excluded from his selection of Gogarty's work—and the earlier idea is definitely the clearer formulation, although even then the phrase "self intoxicated & world begetting" smacks more of Yeats than of Gogarty.

Yeats goes on to explain that he recognizes in Gogarty "my opposite"—"a sense of hardship borne and chosen out of pride and joy"—that he had first noted when reading T. E. Lawrence's "description in his 'Revolt in the Desert' of his body guard of young Arabs" (35r, cf. *CW6* 172), which Yeats then quotes accurately, implying that he had the book at hand.[103] He also saw the same quality in the Elizabethans, "though Chapman alone constantly" (36r, cf. *CW6* 172), and Walter Savage Landor. And just as his reading of George Chapman's translations, including "The Banquet of the Senses," may be the reason why he singled this Elizabethan poet out, the portrait sketch of Lawrence by Augustus John at the front of *The Revolt in the Desert* may have prompted Yeats to think of that painter as a representative of the negative influence of the outside world. Some six years later, introducing the *Oxford Book of Modern Verse*, Yeats would identify this quality as expressing "a gay, stoical—no, I will not withhold the word—heroic song" and he placed Gogarty with the "swashbucklers, horsemen, swift indifferent men," and "gave him considerable space" in the anthology, calling him "one of the great lyric poets of our age" (*CW5* 187).[104] It is unclear how far this identification of "my opposite" is a form of antiself—Yeats placed Landor in the same phase of the Great Wheel as himself (see *AVB* 141–45, *CW14* 105–8)—but the description also recalls the sense of a clear-eyed objectivity presented in "The Fisherman" (*VP* 347–48).[105]

At the top of 38r, Yeats wrote the outline for a poem that would become "After Long Silence" (see below). After drawing a line, he continued with the preface, starting section "II" and then moving to the facing verso, as he often did, to carry on. Originally, he appears to have finished about half way down that page (37v), ending with "the gayest of his butterflies" (cf. *CW6* 174). He must have sent Gogarty a copy, probably dictated from this draft for a typist as was his common practice. But Gogarty was not quite satisfied. As Yeats informed his wife in a letter of October 28, 1929: "Gogarty has sent me my preface back that I may defend 'Ringsend' against his enemies" (*CL InteLex* 5298). And he had told his sister at Cuala that "Gogarty is fussing about my preface to his poems. Press on with your printing but reserve ms space for (say) ten more lines to preface" (*CL InteLex* 5297).

Even though it was a short addition, Yeats intended to leave this extra work for when they arrived in Rapallo, but a lung hemorrhage while he was still in London (see below) forced him to delay travel and thus he sent to Cuala for the proofs, telling Gogarty on November 6, "I can now see if I can extend my idea into another paragraph before I leave London. I am not sure, but I'll try. If I do I shall probably be able to commend Ringsend. I cant in any case start for a few days" (*CL InteLex* 5305).[106] There is a change in the handwriting and ink, as Yeats adds his recommendation of the poem "Aphorism" and how he has "found it impossible to forget that Rings End whore's drunken complaint" (37v, cf. *CW6* 174). The brief section III follows below this, but is mainly cancelled and picked up again on 40r—after two pages with several short entries, both poetic and humdrum (see below and see tabular summary). Thankfully, Gogarty was pleased with the revision and found "the extension of the preface as you have written it is excellent. I like it very much," feeling that Yeats's words had "warded off ignorant criticism from Cuala and, incidentally, from myself" (November 13, 1929, *LTWBY* 2: 498).

[36v] [Short reading notes on Fichte and Hegel]

Noted on a verso among the drafts of the first section of the *Wild Apples* preface are two schemes of history taken from George Henry Lewes's *History of Philosophy*.[107] Yeats copies Lewes's summary of Fichte's scheme, in which "[t]he entire life of Humanity has five periods," and Hegel's in which "[t]he great *moments* of History are four."[108] These are evidently related to Yeats's rewriting of *A Vision*, and Hegel's scheme informs the treatment Yeats presents in "The Completed Symbol" IX (*AVB* 202–3, *CW14* 149), although Yeats evidently had other sources for his treatment there. The notes are, however, further evidence of the range of philosophical reading that Yeats was doing in connection with *A Vision*. Lewes's two-volume book is a rapid conspectus of Western philosophy, engagingly written but demanding nonetheless.

[37r, 38v] [A list of engagements]

Yeats lists a series of "Engagements" for two weeks from October 28 through November 11, 1929, when he was staying in London, and much of the activity can also be traced in his letters for this period. The engagements are mainly lunches and dinners arranged with such people as Edmund Dulac, Lord Beaverbrook, Lady Lavery, and tea with Ottoline Morrell. The list appears to include "ghosts" for 2 November, alluding to the annual All Souls' Day meeting of the Ghost Club, though their records indicate he was absent.[109] In a note added later, Yeats records that he had to cancel his commitments on Monday, 4 November, because on Sunday he "got hemmorage of the lungs that afternoon. Ill since. Nov. 1929," and "Could not go" to lunch with Lady Gorell or to an evening performance of *The Silver Tassie* (37r).[110] The appointments for the following week are sketchier (38v), and it seems these dates were made after he had suffered the hemorrhaging, which led him to postpone traveling to Rapallo, though he was apparently well enough to "Dine with Dulac. to meet Sturge Moore" (38v).[111]

[38r, 39v–40r, 41r] [Drafts of "After Long Silence" with a biographical note and anecdote]

Unlike "Coole Park, 1929," dating the poem "After Long Silence" is a relatively easy matter but not without complication because of serious illness, exhaustion, and a short explanation that Yeats left to provide context. On the authority of this notebook, George Yeats reported that the poem was written in November 1929 ("CCP" 241). Like "Lullaby" (written in Rapallo Notebook C), the text of "After Long Silence," once completed, was copied out in a letter sent to Olivia Shakespear from Rapallo. In this case, the letter was dated "Dec 16" and postmarked December 18, 1929 (*L* 771–72; *CL InteLex* 5327). On his journey from Dublin to Rapallo, WBY wrote first a prose draft of the poem while in London (Rapallo D, 38r): "Subject || Your hair is white | My hair is white | Come let us talk of love | What other theme do we know | When we were young | We were in love with one another | ~~& [?s/w]~~ And therefore ignorant." This "Subject" is nestled at the top of the page, preceded by writings of late October (34v–37v), especially his Gogarty preface (continued below the "Subject" on 38r). Photo-facsimiles and transcriptions of three additional pages of work on the poem (mixed, at one point, with preliminary work on "Crazy Jane on the Day of Judgment") are provided in the overall range of *WFMP* 490–97, yet earlier scholarly studies by Stallworthy (*BTL* 209–10) and Parkinson (*Later Poetry* 82–83 and 87–92) also give helpful guidance in the interpretation of the poem's evolution as a text. Parkinson rightly traces the origin of the poem to Yeats's reunion with Olivia Shakespear, late in October, during his layover en route to Rapallo.[112] "After Long Silence" "involves no complicated system of symbolic reference," Parkinson notices, and it "grows immediately from a personal experience that Yeats formulated" in the rhetorical structure of the poem's "summary version" on 38r, which she saw in the course of that visit (83, 87). Parkinson's exegesis of the manuscript as it grew in three pages gives no documentary notice of the physical notebook nor proximity of projects within it that competed for the poet's attention at more or less the same time—for example, his "Subject for a 'Crazy Jane' poem" (dated "Oct 29" on 39r) and "Veronica's Napkin" (on 41v, a page after the "~~Oct~~ <Nov> 1929" final draft of "After Long Silence"). Pinpointing Yeats's activities during his three-week layover in London is partly enabled in Rapallo D by adjacent lists of engagements, for October 28–November 4 (37r) and for November 5–11 (38v) (see above). The third week was evidently scaled back for rest and tests by a doctor. In short, the poem was written between late October and late November 1929, on the verge of one of his most debilitating poetic blackouts, following the episode of lung-hemorrhaging that forced cancellation of appointments in London prior to departure, on November 21, 1929, and a grave condition that committed him to a lengthy convalescence in Italy.[113]

(Nevertheless, at the top of leaf 40r, Yeats jotted an anecdote about T. E. Lawrence for the final section of the *Wild Apples* preface [see above]. Lawrence was a model for gallantry who, in the following year, would be woven into an account of the exploits of Michael Robartes during the First World War.[114] The short anecdote forms section III of the preface: "~~An Arab king sent Lawrence a man for his body guard~~ | ~~saying that he exactly the man~~ ¶ An Arab King sent a man to Lawrence, saying that | as he had just given him a hundred lashes for | over individuality—he had killed an enemy in court | under the eye of the judge—he was exactly the man | Lawrence would [want] for his body guard. Yes we shall | be forgiven our butter flies." [Cf. *CW6* 174])

On November 16, Yeats wrote Lady Gregory from the Knightsbridge Hotel, London, that "I can't at present do a very great deal; I overtired myself yesterday [...] and to-day I have coughed up blood again. That's why I am dictating, for I am in bed again" (*L* 770; *CL InteLex* 5311). As the rescheduled departure for Rapallo was in five days, he hoped to begin new work once there: "I am looking forward very much to the quiet of Rapallo and I long for the sight of a table with my papers arranged upon it and a prospect of so much writing per day. I shall finish the philosophy for I cannot face verse just yet, though I have no lack of themes" (ibid.). On December 16, 1929, he wrote Olivia Shakespear and presented her with the poem in his first letter from Rapallo not dictated. He thought himself "physically well," although "consecutive thought still soon wearies me," and recalled that he was shaky when he got there and "wrote this little poem of which I showed you the prose draft" (*L* 772; *InteLex* 5327). The version follows closely the last draft in Rapallo Notebook D, leaf 41r, anticipated by the intermediate stages worked out on 40r (set off below parallel drawn lines) and on facing page 39v (in ink with interlinear revisions in pencil). See, respectively, *WFMP* 492–93 and 494–95.[115] The full page merits presenting here because of the transitional nature of the poem in the notebook and disturbances foretold (from our point of view) in the biographical note entered, as an explanation, below the drawn line and completed text of "After Long Silence"—yet entered four months after the fact, at "the end of March 1930":

Speach after long silence; —it is right— [first dash cancelled]
All other lovers being estranged [?~~&~~] <or> dead,
Unfriendly lamp-light ~~hid~~ <hid> under its shade
The curtain's drawn ~~upon~~ <upon> unfriendly night—
That we descant & yet again descant
Upon the supreme theme of art & song~~;~~ :
Bodily decrepitude is wisdom [?]; young [conjectural dash or semicolon]
We loved each other & were ignorant
~~Oct~~ <Nov> 1929

~~Often when I~~ | When I wrote this poem, I had already been ill for ~~two or three weeks~~ | ~~but some~~ three weeks or so—I had just arrived in Rapallo | & ~~had to~~ struggled with constant sleepiness—the first stage I suppose | of Malta fever. Now ~~in late M~~ it is the end of March | & for the last five days I have begun to write again | revising ~~the vision~~ "The Vision". I am at Porto-Fino | Vetta ~~ca~~ <and can> look ~~from my~~ <from my> windows out over a vast | tranquil sea, & ~~&~~ a coast dotted with sunlight [=sunlit] house[es] | as far as Genoa. I know seven or eight people at | Rapallo & had stage-fright in my walks of a | few hundred yards[.] Here I can slip in an[d] out without | a word & improve hourly. It is now five months | since my hemorage from the lung in London & I have | written nothing but one poem & doctor says I will <not be well | again> for another ~~three~~ three months, which means I suppose not able to ~~wr~~ write verse[.] (NLI 13,581, 41r; cf. *WFMP* 497–97; *YSC* 86–87)

With accidentals corrected in the lyrics, Yeats then copied and shared them with Olivia Shakespear in mid-December 1929, leaving only the addition of a comma at line 4 and the difference between a semicolon and a colon at line 6 to matter in the comparison. Rather more significantly, in his letter to Lady Gregory of November 16 (quoted above), just a few days before he finished "After Long Silence" in Rapallo, he said there were other "themes" at hand and poems to be made from them, namely a new Crazy Jane poem begun on leaves 38v–39v and "Veronica's Napkin," begun on 41v, at the brink of a great physical gulf near the center of the notebook.

[38v–39v] ["Crazy Jane on the Day of Judgment" (completed at 95v–96r, 97r, 98r)]

This poem began with an entry entitled "Subject for a 'Crazy Jane' Poem" (on 39r), which was dated "Oct 29—[1929]" as confirmed by its position relative to Yeats's prose "Subject" for "After Long Silence" and his lists of engagements in London before journeying on to Rapallo three weeks later. Like "Veronica's Napkin" (see below), the new Crazy Jane poem was soon left in suspension until it came to be finished in October 1930 on leaf 98r. (See "CCP" 241.) The initial prose draft tends to anticipate lines of verse as indicated (though inconsistently) by capital letters and the indicated position of refrain lines. And it very definitely outlines three movements for the poem, thus:

> I
>
> Tell all that history from childhood up | There is nothing that I would not know | No child[?rens] love or hate | or indignity | Love is for wholes whether of body or souls Etc
>
> II
>
> Why do you complain that I am not al[?ways] kind | That some drives me on | To fantastic scenes on & on | or jealousy, all mus[t] I display | Love is for wholes Etc
>
> III
>
> See ~~th~~ in the night, when we meet in | the dark wood, that you touch—all po[r]tions of | my body—every plane & mound—omit | but one I shall think of Jim or John | or some that might take your place | Love is for wholes Etc— || Oct 29— (NLI 13,581, 39r; see *WFMP* 350–51, also *YSC* 9–10 and 34)

As Clark observes, "There is no evidence that Judgement Day had any part in the original idea [...] Though Jane has a listener, the poem is her monologue" (*YSC* 10). This eventually changed, but not until work on the poem resumed the following year.

Meanwhile, at a thirty-degree angle on the facing page (38v), Yeats jotted the words "~~Fo[r]~~ Love is for who[le]" in the middle of his November 4–11 engagements calendar and began to calculate how he might write lines of verse by alternating between three and four accented syllables. Yet when he actually started writing verse at the bottom of the page (and at the same angle), his first four lines are longer than that—indeed longer than the lyrics in the final version. Beside those four lines, he jotted the numbers 4, 5, 4, 4, 5 in a column as if to mark the change, and concluded with two lines of fairly Shakespearean iambic pentameter verse, each beginning with a trochaic inversion: "Love is not love unless it take the whol[e] / Love is not satisfied with less than all" (as Clark thinks, reminiscent of Shakespeare's Sonnet 116: "Love is not love / Which alters when it alteration finds").[116] This locution anticipates another draft (on 39v, above lines for "After Long Silence"), ending with the same two lines but in reverse order. The lines preceding them there are cryptic, partly illegible (even to Clark's astute eye), and employ unusual diction for Crazy Jane (rhyming "aught" and "naught"). And that is as far as the poem went before Yeats suspended its writing for many months. (See *WFMP* 352–55; *YSC* 10–12 and 34–35; especially the narrative below on how the poem came to be completed near the end of the notebook, at 95v–96r, 97r, 98r.)

[40v] [A note for *A Vision*]

On a clean verso, Yeats inserted a "Paragraph to follow page 6 in Soul in Judgement." Labeled "IV," it petered out after a mere seven words: "The later Upanishads describe a fourth state [...]"; yet, even so, it indicates the substance of section IV of that book as published, which starts: "The *Mandukya Upanishad* describes a fourth state [...]" (*AVB* 222, *CW14* 162).[117]

The rest of the page is devoted to a long note that cites, as Yeats summarizes, "Giovanni Gentile—Theory of Mind as Pure Act, English translation, Chap IX" on Kant's perspective on space and time for the note in section III of "The Principal Symbol" (*AVB* 70n, *CW14* 52n).[118] Following the quotation, Yeats comments in his own voice, and the draft is rather fuller than the published version:

> He [*Gentile*] criticises this conception [*of Kant's*], ~~& restates~~ | ~~which seems to me identical~~, ~~and restates it but there is nothing~~ | ~~in his restatement~~ which seems to me that of the | system I am expounding, but there is nothing in [*his*] restatement [~~...~~] | incompatible with that system as it unfolds itself. | The metaphysician ~~must~~ seeks final definition, but a | symbolic system is a drama, which would suggest & evoke | actual experience [~~...~~] & the symbols [~~...~~] can be ex[h]austavel[y] defined as little as can the characters of | a Shakespearean drama. But to us also, though we prefer to | express ourselves in image & display it in two intersecting | ~~ge~~ gyres[,] Time is a [?spaceilising] act. (NLI 13,581, 40v)[119]

This distinction of the system of *A Vision* as a form of drama—albeit philosophical drama—rather than metaphysics is also seen in Notebooks A and B,[120] and in November 1930, in a diary entry for November 16, he maintained that "Because of the antinomy philosophy is drama as is every individual life—all philosophies are true in the measure of their dramatic intensity,"[121] while the sketch of a subject for a poem dated two days later at the end of Rapallo D opens "All the great philosophies, Plato, Spinoza, Hegel are but drama" (see 97v, below).

[41v] [A list of books and prices for projected reading and a draft of "Veronica's Napkin"]

There are two sets of entries on this page: (1) a list of books for reading and (2) first stirrings of lines for "Veronica's Napkin" ("Heavenly circuit! Berenices hair! / Tent pole of eden! The tents drapery" (see *WFMP* 228–29). The first entry is in pencil and consists of the titles of three books and their list prices, indicative of possible purchases for use in Rapallo or later reference. The titles (on art, philosophy, and literature) were chosen perhaps on recommendation as the latest word in those fields. Indeed, none of them had yet been published when the Yeatses made their social calls in London. The first forthcoming title on the list is *A Miniature History of European Art* (London: Milford, Oxford University Press, 1930) by R. H. Wilenski. The second is listed as "A history of philosophy | by George Boas. Harpers," possibly conflating Boas's *Major Traditions of European Philosophy* (1929) with his pending work in the history of ideas, *Our New Ways of Thinking* (1930)—both studies issued in New York and London by Harper and Brothers. The third title is taken down at first as "~~A guide to Ulysses~~" but then corrected to "James Joyces Ulysses. by Stuart Gilbert | [London:] Faber & Faber [1930]." W. B. and George Yeats's library contains a copy of Wilenski's book (signed by WBY) as well as Boas's contemporary *The Adventures of Human Thought: The Major Traditions of European Philosophy* (New York and London: Harper, 1929).[122]

The lyrical entry (in ink) follows beneath a wavy line, as shown in Figure 3.4—perhaps only days after the bibliographic notes were made in London prior to departure. That would make the onset of composition for "Veronica's Napkin," by virtue of this fragment's location on 41v, later than the notes above and nearer the date of the final draft of "After Long Silence" on 41r. The final draft of "Veronica's Napkin" (on 93v) is dated "Oct 1930," establishing that a hiatus of eleven months existed between start and finish, seven months after Yeats had written (on 41r) that a total of eight months in convalescent care was expected and possibly without the capacity to write poetry. Stymied by illness of that severity, it is a wonder that he recovered, like the miracle that the poem celebrates, and developed its theme of apotheosis from the myth of Berenice, which he first explored in drafts of "Her Dream" in Rapallo Notebook C after March 29, 1929 (see "CCP" 241).[123] "Berenice's burning hair" in the precursor poem has become the subject of a series of ejaculations: "Heavenly circuit! Berenices hair! / Tent pole of eden! The tents drapery! / ~~I mock at it for~~ Images of of glory! ~~Greater~~ <Substantial> glories were / Within the circuit of a ~~needs~~ <needles> eye / When ye were first blown ~~of~~ <out upon> the air / [~~…~~] By the great spirits, that great ~~heany~~ <harmony>." These six initial lines are in verse, not a prose draft (or "Subject") as had been used to launch the poems "After Long Silence" and "Crazy Jane on the Day of Judgment." There are rhyme notes at the ends of these lines to confirm the ABABAB pattern of an ottava rima stanza, only the closing couplet of which was work that came less easily on the page. In one pair of lines, "minuit by minuit" (for "minute by minute") is forced to rhyme with "term & Time"—at best a sonorant, alliterative match. In the final effort on 41v, aptly (considering the circumstances), "blood" is rhymed with "road"; so the couplet became "No glory but a napkin dip[p]ed in blood / Thrown by some traveller on a darker road." In form and content, this first draft betrays the residual effect of writing stanzas for so long on "Coole Park, 1929" and of work for nearly half that time developing its "Unknown traveller" based on the Gospel of Matthew and the *Viator* of Swift's epitaph. "Veronica's Napkin" is taken up next at 84v–85r and 93v (see below).

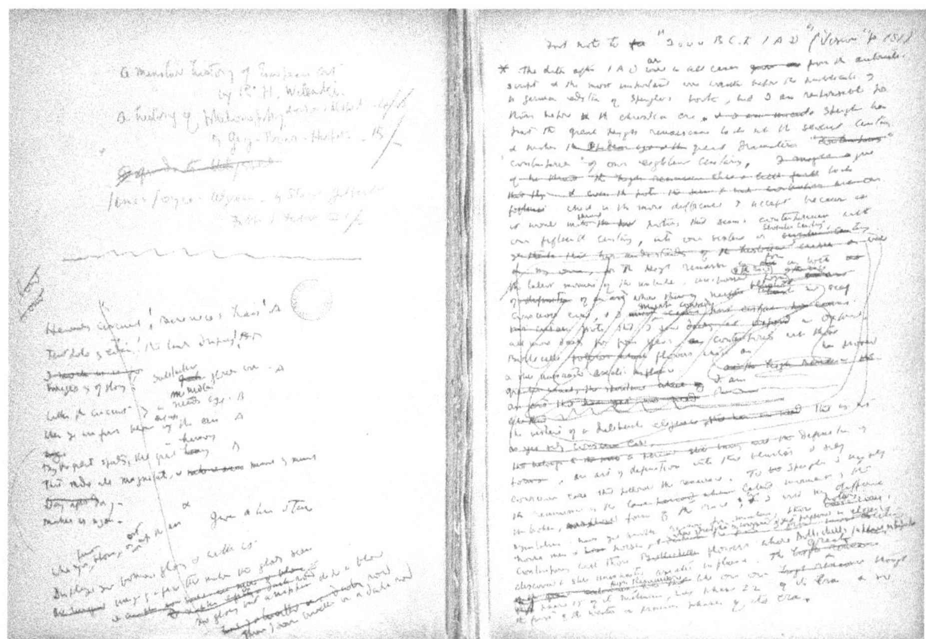

Figure 3.4. Rapallo Notebook D, NLI 13,581, [41v and 84r], with intervening stubs of discarded leaves 42–83. Courtesy of the National Library of Ireland.

[42r–83v] [A massive lacuna marked by the stubs of at least forty-two excised leaves]

It is fruitless to speculate what was on the forty-two-plus leaves that were excised from the notebook[124]—the largest cut from any of the Rapallo notebooks[125]—or why they were removed. The notebook remains particularly rich in content despite the removal, but that makes the gap all the more tantalizing.

[84r, 85r] [Footnotes on Spengler and history for *A Vision*]

After the great gap, the first entry is a single-page "Foot note to '2000 BC to 1 A D' ('Vision' p 181)," referring, of course, to the pagination of *A Vision A* (see Figure 3.4). It notes a discrepancy between the scheme proposed in Oswald Spengler's *The Decline of the West* and that of *A Vision*'s historical gyres with respect to the periods of different historical societies that correspond to each other.

> The dates after 1 A D ~~were~~ <are> in all cases ~~given in~~ from the automatic | script & the most important were written before the publication of | the German edition of Spenglers book, but I am responsible for | those before the Christian Era, & ~~I am uncerta~~ Spengler has | put the Greek High renaiscance back into the seventh century | & makes ~~the Phidian age &~~ the great dramatists ~~"contemporary"~~ | "contemporaries" of our eighteenth century, [~~...~~] | which is more difficult to accept because it | it [*sic*] would ~~make~~ <thrust> ~~the pot~~ pottery that seems contemporaneous with | our fifteenth century into our sixteenth or <seventeenth century> ~~seventeen century~~ | [...] an art of definition into the bluster of self | conscious ease that followed the renaisance. To [?] Spengler & myself | the rennaisance is ~~the last period~~ when latest moment of the | unbroken, ~~as opposed~~ form of the race; ~~&~~ <but> I with my different | symbolism have yet another reason for making those [?~~unconscious~~] <pottery> | horse men & horses ~~& describe the pots I find most exciting~~ <where strength is consumed & yet preserved in elegance>| contemporary with those ~~Bottichelli~~ flowers where Bottichellis [?~~phas~~] <Japanese interpreter> | discovered a still unexhausted Asiatic influence. The ~~high rennaisance of the Greak millennium, like that~~ <Greak High Renaisance> like our own ~~high renaisance~~ though | [?] phase 15 of its milenium, was phase 22 of its era & so | the first of the Western of primary phases of its era. (NLI 13,581, 84r)

Yeats had seen these "pots with strange half supernatural horses" in Oxford's Ashmolean Museum (as is mentioned in the cancelled text), and they had been described in the treatment of *A Vision A*, already slated for repetition in *A Vision B* (see *AVA* 181–82, *CW13* 151; *AVB* 269, *CW14* 195).

On the following recto, there is another, briefer "Foot note to A D 1050 to present day ('Vision' page 196)," this time noting agreement but acknowledging that Spengler's emphasis was perhaps clearer:

> Spengler finds <here>, as I should have found a change of Race | [~~...~~] a begin[nin]g of gothic | predominance. He sees <~~as I do~~ a> ~~the~~ return to all that [~~...~~] | is peasant like & primitive [~~...~~] | all that I call [~~...~~] phase 2 & 3 & 4 | but finds it among the northern flocks & [~~...~~] | villages. He has seen the break with the old more clearly | than I have seen it. (NLI 13,581, 85r)

Yeats evidently decided that it was inappropriate or unnecessary to mention either his discrepancy with Spengler or their mutual corroboration in the new edition of *A Vision*, despite his concern that people would think that he had taken his scheme—or even just the idea of his scheme—from Spengler, as evidenced in a long passage in Rapallo Notebook B, again unused.[126] In the end Yeats may have decided that readers might agree with Gertrude's assessment of the Player Queen in Hamlet's *Mouse-trap*, that "The lady doth protest too much, methinks."[127]

[84v–85r, 93v] ["Veronica's Napkin" from 41v]

When Yeats wrote to Lady Gregory on February 20, 1930, his health had turned for the better after a death-defying winter. Apologizing for writing by dictation (his wife being the typist and silent auditor), he noted that his handwriting was then so illegible that "a cheque that I signed the other day was even for me an incredible signature," and he humored all by joking about lost weight, having "no longer any blood pressure," and having acquired "a beautifully silky beard" (*CL InteLex* 5332) also mentioned in a letter to Olivia Shakespear (on March 4, 1930) as a measure of his descent in illness to the likeness of Buffalo Bill (see *L* 772; *CL InteLex* 5336).[128] Having read by then all the detective fiction "of the world" and having "just started upon the Wild West," Yeats's letter of that date was said to be "the first letter I have written with my own hand since I became ill," and he noted that he was incapable of writing "more than a few words" because "consecutive thought [...] tires me" (*L* 773). By mid-April, however, he declared himself "well again" to George Russell and to be "at work most mornings but dare not yet attempt verse, or anything that would follow me when I laid down the pen" (*L* 774; *CL InteLex* 5342). It is no surprise, then, that poetry-writing resumed in Rapallo Notebook D in proximity to footnotes written in prose on 84r (at right in Figure 3.4) and 85r (see commentary above), and as a continuation of "Veronica's Napkin" based on scratch notes left at 41v (see also Figure 3.4).

On 84v, which is otherwise clean, Yeats tackled the eight lines much as they were, revising as he went along, substituting at first for line 4 "~~When those <great> spirits, that strange harmony~~" and then "When some great spirit, ~~or~~ <~~some~~> <or> wild ~~heere~~ <heirarchy>" (the cancelled line having been line 6 on 41v), whereupon the former line 4 ("Within the circuit of a [~~...~~] needles eye"; transposed to preserve a rhyme) became line 6 ("Stood in the circuit of a needles <needle's> eye"). The new line 5 ("That made all magnitude & [~~...~~] <set> it there") gave a necessary rhyme to line 3, but the new rendering of lines 7–8 is evidence that he may have forgotten that he had intended them to be a rhymed couplet. (Or he might have entertained some thought to discard the ottava rima stanza for so short a poem.) For they do not rhyme in any way:

"Some turn away & find a different pole / And under it a napkin ~~that wiped <dipped in> blood~~ that wiped blood" (84v). Unsatisfied with the pair, they were stroked out apart from the rest of the stanza, and three more attempts were made to restore the rhyme to the couplet, keeping "blood" but rhyming with "stood" instead of "road": "Some ~~found~~ <saught> a different pole & where it stood / A pattern on a ~~ma~~ napkin ~~steeped~~ <steeped> in blood." The latter pairing was forged with much indecision, but a preference among alternatives can be worked out by interpreting the cross-outs, stet-marks, and conjunction "or" on this page. Although the poem had been given a title here ("Veronicas ~~Napkin~~ <Handkechef>"), even more indecisiveness is indicated after Yeats cancelled everything on 84v and moved across that opening in the notebook to 85r. (See *WFMP* 230–33.)

This third draft of the poem is most deviant from the standpoint of form. It was composed in one sitting (to judge by handwriting) as if copied out to make a composite of most viable lines from previous drafts, including some lines that he had rejected. Twelve lines were thus assembled, initially, to fashion a long-form version of the poem, before Yeats recognized that major problems were occurring in lines 5–9. The sitting will have occurred sometime *after* Yeats had already written the Spengler footnote that appears just above it on 85r. The draft is stroked through to indicate rejection of the entire effort, and diagonals and looping scribbles in the vicinity of lines 5–9 point to the problem, as do the strikethroughs and the single diagonal line drawn through an alternative effort to make substitutions for lines 6–8. The result might have been a kind of hyperbolic invention based on ottava rima but extended by a variantly rhyming quatrain at lines 7–10, the whole scheme rhyming a-b-a-b-a-b-c-d-c-d-e-e. If Yeats had been satisfied with this experiment, the poem might have looked something like this:

> Heavenly circuit! Berenice's hair!
> Tentpole of Eden! Eden's drapery!
> Images of glory! Substantial glories were
> Within the circuit of a needle's eye—
> Where ye first blown, like bubbles in the air,
> By those great spirits, that great harmony
> That made all magnitude and minute by minute
> Make it anew and give us term and time[—]
> Displayed your borrowed glory and within it
> Image of a face that made that glory seem
> No drapery where Eden's tentpole stood
> But a torn napkin stained by mire and blood.

Clearly, the poem was in trouble. Rhyme notes were added beside lines 5–8 to help steady the course. But in the effort to salvage "minuit by minuit" and "term & Time" from 41v, Yeats undercut the seriousness of the poem, at this stage, by introducing a disyllabic, comic rhyme ("minute"/"within it"); and in his attempt to make correction at lines 7 and 8, he produced a muddle at the bottom of 85r that, instead of fixing, he chose to leave suspended until a later time—much later as it turned out.

"Veronica's Napkin" was concluded on 93v (see Figure 3.6) with a radical simplification by reversion to its original eight-line structure though shifting some phrases that had developed in the meantime. The notion of pagan "great spirits" and "wild heirarchy" (rather than "great harmony") gave place to "The Father & his angelic heirarchy"; and line 4 (with modification) had shifted to line 6, as rehearsed on 85r, to become "Stood in the circuit of a needle's eye"—all followed by the regenerated closing couplet: "Some ~~saught~~ <found> a different pole & where it stood, / A pattern on a napkin ~~steeped~~ <dipped> in blood." The final pair of lines, however, were broken away from the rest of the poem to form a separate stanza. So the lyric creates only a small sensation by bucking just a little against the norm of its Italian form. The poem's completion is signified by the date "Oct 1930" duly inscribed by Yeats beneath the last line and above new dialogue for his play *The Cat and the Moon* (1924), first performed at the Abbey Theatre on September 21, 1931 (see below). In sum, the poem had required three stages of intermittent writing from November 1929 to October 1930, and it had partially bridged a significant lull in his writing when he began to recover his health in April 1930, declaring himself by then fit but also wary to attempt verse.

[86r–90r, 91r–92r] ["Byzantium"]

Without doubt, a poem of far greater consequence to Yeats's recovery as a poet was "Byzantium," which in the course of its writing bridged the gulf of illness more profoundly than had "Veronica's Napkin" or the yet unfulfilled theme of the new Crazy Jane poem that he had conceived in October 1929 but left as a "Subject" in Rapallo D on 39r. In the 1930 diary, in an entry dated "April, 30, ~~1930~~" (NLI 30,354, 3v and 4r), he introduced two prose summaries, each headed "Subject for a poem," but published posthumously in *Pages from a Diary in 1930* under the single heading "SUBJECT FOR A POEM. APRIL 30TH" as if they coalesced into one. The first was called "Death of a Friend," which was "To describe how mixed with one's grief comes the thought that the witness of some foolish word or act of one's own is gone" (*Ex* 290). The "friend" is Robert Bridges, the late Poet Laureate, who died on April 21, 1930, and was remembered by Yeats in a letter of condolence sent from Rapallo to Bridges's widow on May 7, 1930 (*L* 774–75). Acknowledging slight acquaintance with the deceased, Yeats wrote that her husband "seemed the only poet, whose influence has always heightened and purified the art of others, and all who write with deliberation are his debtors" (*L* 775; cf. *CL InteLex* 5346).

The rough Byzantium "Subject" (simplified here) showed how images were already taking hold of Yeats's imagination, for, more than an idea or sentiment about grief, the poem was to:

> describe Byzantium as it [is/was] in the | system towards the end of the first Christian | maleneum. ~~The worn ascetics on the walls~~ | ~~contrasted with their splendour~~. A walking | mummy— [~~...~~] ||| flames at the street corners | where the soul is purified, | birds of hamme[red] gold singing | in the golden trees | In the harbour [dolphins] offering their | backs to the wailing [?=waiting] dead | that they may carry them to | paradise. (NLI 30,354, 3v–4r; cf. *WFMP* 3)[129]

In other words, the "Subject for a poem" has set the scene for "Byzantium" in a demonstrably elegiac context. Mrs. Yeats noted the history of the poem in several instances, the most extensive being to mark its beginning and completion: "1st prose draft dated April 30, 1930. Final MS of poem dated September 1930" (see "CCP" 240). The trajectory of Yeats's improved health between May and his return to Ireland in mid-July spans a good share of the time he spent working on this poem. Probably not exactly what he meant by "deliberation" in his letter to Mrs. Bridges, his work schedule was in fact deliberate and regular for the remainder of his stay in Rapallo. He told Olivia Shakespear on June 1 (as he planned to sail from Genoa on July 3 and to return home a dozen days later, after a short layover in London) that "I am writing verse again, and pleased with what I am doing [...] working three days and then resting three days" to avoid fatigue (*L* 775, *CL InteLex* 5352).[130] Rehabilitation involved alternating half-weeks of relaxation and work, and his activities included, on the one hand, regaling his children with demonstrations of submersible swimming while tanning to the color of a "meerschaum pipe" (*CL InteLex* 5348),[131] reading popular detective and cowboy fiction for pleasure, and dining out with various expatriate friends, but also, on the other hand, writing creative prose in his diary (NLI 30,354) as well as notes for *A Vision* in Rapallo D, immersive reading in Jonathan Swift for the new play, and thinking out the plot sequence of his Michael Robartes stories for the Cuala Press, which he promised to advertise with Lady Gregory's *Coole*. Poetry-writing, after long hiatus, began again around May 23, the day after he announced to Gregory "My beard came off today," and "Tomorrow I begin the writing of verse and will know much more about myself after a few mornings; I have plenty of subjects" (*CL InteLex* 5348). As noted above, "Veronica's Napkin" appears to be the first poem that Yeats took up again although completing it did not occur until October. "Byzantium," however, was another matter—one beginning successfully with the technicalities of form in stanza 1 (developed at 85v–86r) consistent with content envisioned in its prose subject of April 30. The writing began with rhyme notes on 86r, as shown in Figure 3.5.

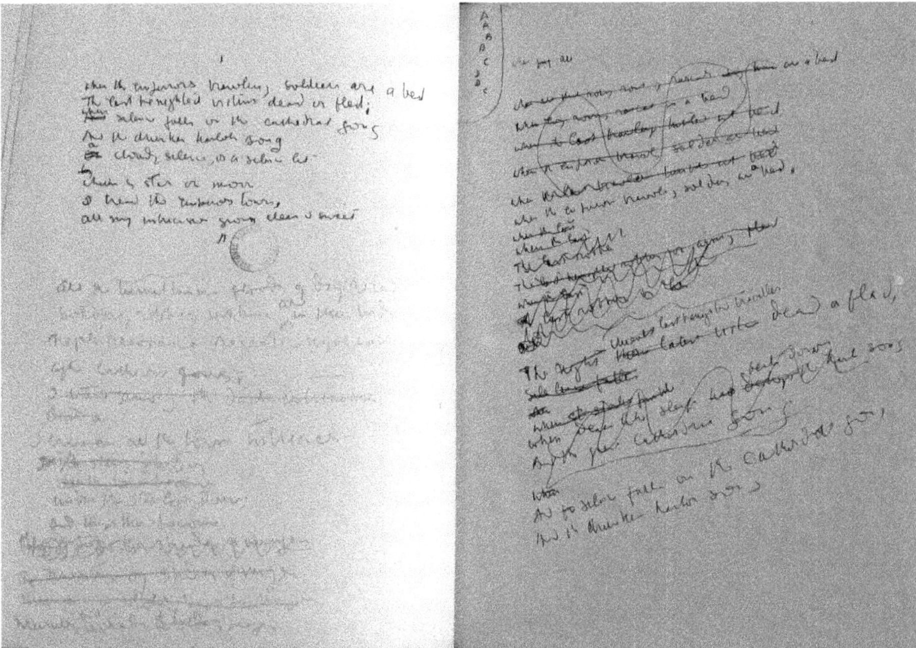

Figure 3.5. Rapallo Notebook D, NLI 13,581, [85v and 86r], cf. *WFMP* 4 and 6. Courtesy of the NLI; photograph courtesy of Catherine E. Paul.

Here, Stallworthy's analysis (in *BTL* 113–36) anticipates Clark's usually better transcriptions in *WFMP* 4–35. Curtis Bradford's 1960 study "Yeats's Byzantium Poems: A Study of Their Development" set out observations on the state of the manuscript that are still useful but involving a methodology that seems of interest mainly as an example of early paleographic innovation in Yeats studies.[132] Bradford, Stallworthy, and Clark start their analysis with the 1930 diary's "Subject for a Poem" mentioned above, although their accounts differ on exact wording.[133] Indisputably, correspondence with Sturge Moore shows that Yeats wished to address a fault in "Sailing to Byzantium" by writing a sequel to it. "Your *Sailing to Byzantium*, magnificent as the first three stanzas are, lets me down in the fourth," Moore wrote on April 16, 1930, "as such a goldsmith's bird is as much nature as a man's body, especially if it only sings like Homer and Shakespeare of what is past or passing or to come to Lords and Ladies" (*TSMC* 162). Shortly after receiving this criticism, Yeats wrote the prose "Subject"; then later, weeks after completing the poem, he confessed to Moore that "[t]he poem originates from a criticism of yours [...] [t]hat showed me that the idea needed exposition" (October 4, 1930, *TSMC* 164; *CL InteLex* 5390).[134]

Encircled rhyme notes "A | A | B | B | C | D | D | C" at 86r (with staggered indentation in a column to indicate longer and shorter lines in the envisioned stanza) defines form as a series of octaves, numbering at least four to constitute the intended sequel to *The Tower* poem. Miscounting the lines indicated by these rhyme notes, Stallworthy nevertheless makes analogy with the stanzas of "In Memory of Major Robert Gregory" and "A Prayer for my Daughter."[135] All the drafting that occurred on 86r (on the right side of Figure 3.5) produced but four lines of the poem, as confirmed by comparing the poem's progress (at right) with the completed stanza labeled "I" on 85v (at left). Stallworthy seems correct in attributing those first four lines (from "When the emperor's brawling soldiers are <a> bed" to "And the drunken harlot's song") to "an obvious echo of Blake's poem about another symbolic city—'London'" (*BTL* 117). As an editor of Blake, Yeats's recollection of "the hapless soldier's sigh" and "the youthful harlot's curse" in Blake's poem would have been reflexive. But the "last benighted traveller" on 86r (or "benighted victim dead or fled" on 85v) would seem to have evolved from Yeats's own device of the "Unknown traveller" in several iterations of "Coole Park, 1929," scarcely to mention his adaptation of the *Viator* (for "World besotted traveller") when writing "Swift's Epitaph." On leaf 85v, therefore, lines 5–8 finish the stanza in the pattern foretold at the outset: "~~On~~ <a> cloudy silence, or a silence lit [a five-stress line with C-rhyme] / Whether by star or moon [a three-stress line with D-rhyme] / I tread the emperor's town [another three-stress line with D-rhyme] / All my intricacies grown clear & sweet [a hypermetric line completing the C-rhyme]." The stanza as a whole produces compression derived from an adaptive complex of influences, a series of antitheses. As Stallworthy notices, this is a remarkable accomplishment for any poet, but especially one with intent to write an ambitious poem after an absence of nearly six months: "soldiers/Victim, cathedral gong/harlot's song, cloudy silence/silence lit, star/moon. An impression of the whole, complicated, physical world is that his port of departure for a spiritual world, [Yeats] has packed into six lines" (*BTL* 118). The stanza's closing lines stand at the threshold of a more tranquil mood as the silence of star and moon are set in contrast with the emperor's dangerous town.

Although the fair-hand version of stanza 1 is followed by the numeral "II" (in the same ink), the remainder of leaf 85v is devoted to a second beginning, rendered at a different sitting and in pencil, as shown in Figure 3.5. The poet in the poem, after the tumult of the day recedes, issues his "night walker[']s song / After cathedral gong"; and the song echoes other phrasings from "Coole Park, 1929," where the "intricacies" of the woods and house at Coole (14r) and the "miraculous intricacies" of skill and thought (at 15r) anticipate new lyrics in a different context: "~~I tread among the dark intricacies~~" and "I traverse all the towns intricacies / […] Under the starlight dome" until "things there become, / ~~Blood begotten shades & images~~ / ~~A mistry of shades & images~~ / ~~Mumies or blood begotten images~~ / Mumies, ~~or~~ <and> shades, ~~or stony~~ <&

hollowed> images" (85v; the uncancelled lines ending in the C-, D-, D-, and C-rhymes of the stanzaic scheme).

On 86v, work on stanza 2 began from a premise that the "walking mummy" of the prose sketch might take its cue from Coleridge, whose *Rime of the Ancient Mariner* Yeats had just been reading to his children for pleasure (see *BG* 429) and whose poetry inspired general entries in his diary of 1930 (see *Ex* 298–301, or parts XII–XIV [June 6–8] and XV [June 19]). In Coleridge's epic ballad, Death and the Nightmare Life-in-Death gamble for the soul of the Ancient Mariner, and Nightmare wins. After jotting the column of the words "cloth | path | light as a breath" (at the top of the page, in ink), Yeats makes several abortive attempts to craft lines for the new stanza, producing three lines that are seminal but not conforming to the rhyme scheme: "Death in life, or that dear Life in Death / And I adore that mystery / Harsh death in life, or that dear life in death" (see *WFMP* 8–9). Following that rehearsal, he begins to work on lines that rhyme according to the established pattern. The first two lines are contrived word-play to form a couplet by rhyming "shade" and "shade" (the stanza's "A"-rhyme), followed by eight cancelled lines (significantly disposing of the word "intricate" in four attempts) before the rest of the stanza takes the form of question and answer: "What if the ~~limbs are~~ <~~bodies~~ limbs are> wound in mummy cloth [B-rhyme] / That know the winding of the path [B-rhyme], / What if the bodies dry the mouths ~~lack breath~~ lack breath [C-rhyme] / That ~~beckons me summons~~ <summons or beckons> me[?] [D-rhyme] / I adore that mystery [D-rhyme] / [...] / And call it death in life, or Life in Death [C-rhyme]." Apart from pencil notes of the kind in the left margin, Yeats inscribed at the bottom of the page: "*That I call death in life*" (in pencil) and "I hail the superhuman, / ~~Or death in life~~ / And call it Etc" (in ink)—duly emphasizing the deliberate adaptation he had executed for stanza 2 at 86v.

For stanza 3, Yeats moved across the opening to leaf 87r and immediately found the A-rhyming couplet that began the stanza's deliberation over the problem Moore had had with the ending of "Sailing to Byzantium" on the emperor's prescient song-birds, here "Miracle, bird or golden handy work / More miracle than bird or handywork." The next lines were more of a problem, however, as they falter over the juxtaposition of nature in "mockery" (with its "mire & blood") against the "petal" and "metal" of "~~golden leaves~~"; without a B-rhyming couplet to articulate the stanza, Yeats comes to a dead end with queries too obviously mimicking Blake[136]—hence rightly cancelled ("~~What great artificars~~ / ~~What mind decreed or hammer shaped the metal~~ / ~~Of golden~~"). Rhetorical artifice here, like that litany of repetition in Blake's "The Tyger," seems aimed at an answer that can only be the inscrutable logic of God. Yeats's heterodox response, though, was to cross out all but the first two lines and to pick up from there with a B-couplet echoing Frazer's *The Golden Bough* and the hint of cancelled words "~~golden leaves~~": "~~Sings all~~ <~~Carrols~~ Mutters> night long out of <a> golden ~~bough~~ <bough> / ~~Or sings~~ What the birds of Hades know" (87r). What remains is to cobble a CDDC-rhyming quatrain from rejected elements that precede the new B-rhyming couplet on the page. By trial and error for several lines, a solution was found and partly copied into the right margin as follows: "Mutters upon a starlight golden bough / What the birds of Hades know / Or by the moon embittered scorns aloud / In glory of changeless metal" (the BBCD-portion of the stanza, or lines 3–6). While these four lines are written vertically, the last lines are squeezed horizontally into the lower right-hand corner of 87r: "Living leaf or petal / And mans intricacy of mire & blood" (the final D- and C-rhymes, respectively, of stanza 3). All of this is laid out in detail in *WFMP* 10–11.

Stanza 4 then came to be executed at the turn of the page, beneath a prose note (at the top of 87v) that served as its "Subject" without any such title:

> And there is a certain square where [?Cold] flames wind & unwind | And in the flamze dance spirits, by that their agony made pure | And though the[y] are all fold[ed] up in flame | It cannot singe a sleeve[.] (NLI 13,581, 87v; see *WFMP* 12–13)

The correlative portion of "Sailing to Byzantium" is its third stanza, regarding "sages standing in God's holy fire / As in the gold mosaic of a wall," augmented by certain passages in both versions of *A Vision* (1925 and 1937) and read in the context of the Condition of Fire ("Anima Mundi," XV–XX, in *Per Amica Silentia Lunae* [1917]).[137] Stallworthy sees and hears additional echoes of the Noh play *Motemezuka*, the plot of which Yeats summarized in his essay of 1914, "Swedenborg, Mediums, and the Desolate Places," for Lady Gregory's *Visions and Beliefs in the West of Ireland*.[138] At the end of the play, the heroine, a spirit, "rushes away enfolded in flames," oblivious to pain because she no longer believes in her punishments" (334). The phrase "folded up in flame" (in the prose subject of 87v) and "enfolded in flames" are nearly identical but also idiomatic English. A Noh source, compounded by diverse others in the poem, does not confirm that the phrase "cannot singe a sleeve" (in both the subject and the verse-draft) derives "of course from the wide Japanese kimono sleeve" and a scene set in the Buddhist purgatory (*BTL* 124).[139] The ease with which stanza 4 emerged, as a counterpoint to stanza III in "Sailing to Byzantium," does show, however, that its content felt familiar to the poet.

As usual, the work began with rhyme notes ("live | [a nib mark] | fla[me?] | sleave"), the image of the square glimpsed in flickering light ("~~Flames upo[n] the marble~~ / ~~A flame on the cathedral [?pavement] flits~~"), and a first line: "At midnight on the marble [?pavement] ~~flits~~ flits" (87v). The A-rhyming second line recaptures the mysterious flame from the cancelled lines and, on the third attempt, produces the line "<A> Flame ~~that~~ <nor> fagot feeds, ~~no mortal~~ <nor taper> lights" (a semi-rhyme, replacing "~~lit~~," for the complement of "flits" in the first line). Line 3 falls in place just after that: "~~No~~ <Nor> breath of wind<s> disturbs & to this that flame" (establishing the B-rhyme). The next line brings minor trouble in deciding between modal auxiliaries "Do," "May," and "Can" for the verb "come" (for the time being chosen as a semi-rhyme to pair with "flame" in line 3), but, in pencil on 88r, the issue is resolved in favor of "*May blood bessoted spirits come*."[140] Also in pencil, the stanza's fifth line is revised there to produce "And ~~all~~ <~~the~~ all> bloods' fury in that flame may leave" (introducing the C-rhyme), with the last three lines left for interlinear revision at the bottom of 87v (wherein the italics below indicate later corrections in pencil):

O [~~*?a*~~]
~~And the the agony of a dan~~ agony of ^ trance! [D-rhyme]
That is a measured ~~dance~~ dance [D-rhyme]
Or *the flame*
~~or~~ agony of ^ ~~fire~~ that cannot singe a sleave! [C-rhyme]
(NLI 13,581, 87; cf. *WFMP* 12–13)

Work on stanza 5—on the "wailing dead" who are carried on the backs of dolphins to Paradise, as forecast in the prose "Subject for a Poem" in Yeats's 1930 diary (NLI 30,354; see *Ex* 290)—brought with it the culmination of the first draft of the poem. Naturally, the great sea of *Anima Mundi* was destined to feature in the conclusion as the repository of images, so that destination might well have been expected for the last line. The stanza itself emerged on consecutive pages 88v–89r, in that order (see *WFMP* 14–17), with the first line (initially cancelled but soon reinstated) establishing control with a quickly found second line: "A straddle on the [?] dolphins mire & blood / [~~...~~] ~~These spirits~~ <The crowds> approach; the marble breaks the ~~b~~<f>lood" (the stanza's A-couplet). The "shades" and "spirits" have come, and so the couplet to follow is rehearsed for six iterations rhyming "emperor" and "floor." The B-couplet is produced after a few trials: "~~The lettered marble of the emperor~~" > "~~The enchanted marble <pavement> of the emperor~~" > "~~The intric[a]t[e] pavement of the emperor~~"; accompanying "~~Shadowy feet upon the floor~~, / Innumerable feet, passion heavy feet [a line without end-rhyme]" > "~~Intricacy of the dancing floor~~" > "~~Flame upon the dancing floor~~ / ~~Simplicity~~"; rendering the couplet "The bronze & marble of the emperor, / Simplicity of the dancing floor" (all for the better part of a page). The lower quarter of 88v focuses on the dolphins and the sea, producing the last line of the stanza in a progressive effort as if by brainstorming: "~~A crowd of spirits~~ / ~~Breaks~~ / ~~The fin tortured~~ / ~~The dolphin~~

~~torn~~ / ~~The dolphin tortured tide breaks~~ / ~~That dolphin tortured flood breaks into spray~~ / ~~That gong tormented current breaks in spray <in foam>~~ / ~~The Dolphin torn, the gong tormented sea.~~" Discovering early the last line of the poem and being out of space on the page, Yeats shifted across the opening in Rapallo D to 89v, where he worked on the intervening lines of the stanza, beginning with "Break the bleak glittering ~~intracesy~~ <intricacy>" (a C-rhyming line to complement one on 88v). After another series of trials to conceive the short D-lines (rhyming "yet" and "beget"), the last three lines of stanza 5 were written to complete the draft: "Where blind images can yet / Blinder images beget / The Dolphin torn & gong tormented sea—" (lines, with many others, yet to be amended in June, August, and possibly September 1930).

The second draft of the poem is a compilation, then, an assembly of the five stanzas from above, copied out and revised in the process (on leaves 89v–90r and 91r), assigned numerals from "I" to "V" in segmental fashion, and dated "June 11" at the end of it. The Yeatses were still in Italy and would remain so for three more weeks. In July, Yeats would draft his "Open letter to [Wyndham] Lewis" (on leaf 91v) at Renvyle, County Galway, Ireland. The interruption is notable for causing the first dogleg in the poem's stream of writing in the notebook, which appears to have continued on a regular basis once it had begun in May. Stallworthy asserts that "an immense advance" occurs in the second draft, for "hardly a line has not been tightened and compressed" and "every objective detail that remains," after "the 'I' figure of the poet has been removed," contributes to one theme (*BTL* 130). In stanza I, following the precedent of "Coole Park, 1929," the word "intricacy" gives place to "complexity" as an aspect of form and does so in stanzas II and V, as well. Until the seemingly displaced matter of 91r, the most altered stanzas are II, III, and IV. However, readers are advised that Stallworthy's difficulty relating the process in his transcriptions is one with his desire for linear narrative. Presenting Rapallo D rectos first, as a draft unit, and only then the constituent verso corrections, gives the impression of a two-stage process and not a complexly integrated one as the handwriting, layout, and clue-lines suggest for at least the first four stanzas. (Clark's treatment in *WFMP* 18–25 is recommended but with a small caveat.)[141]

To take only the most altered stanzas together, we find that on 90r and 89v the amended parts of stanza II affected all but lines 1–2 and line 8; in stanza III, lines 3–4 and 6–8 were clued separately to 89v for corrections; and, in stanza IV, with the last six lines cancelled on 90r, a clued line to revisions on 89v reveals that line 8 hardly changed at all. Also, we see that rewritten portions were built on the underlying forms that Yeats had conceived in first draft—rhyme patterns of longer and shorter lines—with distinct improvements now in diction, syntax, and meter. In stanza II, we obtain "~~A bobbin that is~~ <For Hades bobbin> bound in ~~mul~~ mummy cloth / ~~Can unbind~~ <May unwind> the winding path / A mouth that has no moisture & no breath / Breathing mouths may summon— / I hail the superhuman" (rhyming BBCDD). In stanza III, lines 3–4 become "Planted on a starlit golden bough / Can like the cocks of Hades crow" (the B-couplet), and lines 6–8 are revised to "In ~~all~~ <~~All that~~> ~~simplicity of~~ <glory of changeless> metal / [~~...~~] Common bird or petal / And all complexities of mire or blood" (rhyming DDC). In stanza IV, lines 3–8 are corrected to "Nor breath disturbs [~~...~~] a flame begotten flame / ~~Where~~ <~~There~~ Where> blood begotten spirits come / <And> All complexities of fury leave, / Dying into a dance— / An agony of trance, / <An> [?~~And~~] agony of flame that cannot singe a sleeve" (rhyming BBCDDC). A great effort in such cases has been committed to a more idiomatic marriage of sense and sound.

Stanza V in this draft is written down on leaf 91r and dated "June 11"—at that time leaving 90v to stand alone beside it as a blank page. The dated stanza occupies the top half of the page, beneath which is inscribed a later version dating from Yeats's third draft of the poem, once back in Ireland and after his "Open letter to Lewis" in July (see below). The verses on 91r are therefore literally transitional. As with stanzas I–IV, the text that he copied and revised as he did so from the first draft came to be corrected first by means of a clued interjection (in this case drawn to cancelled lines 3–5 on the "golden smithies" and "~~bleak glittering intricasy~~" of the spiritual dance) but not from the facing verso page. The new lines are introduced, instead, just above the dateline, as follows: "The precious metal of the emperor; / Marble of the dancing floor / Breaks that ~~bleak complexity~~ bright flood, that bleak complexity" (rhyming BBC as before but choosing a slightly different verbal formulation). Below this, probably in August and back in Dublin, Yeats copied the stanza he had just then worked out to satisfaction on 91v, at the end of the final draft of the poem in Rapallo D. The nearly fair copy inscribed at a later sitting only fails to resolve an inconsistency in its fifth line regarding the word "bleak":

> A straddle on the Dolphins mire & blood
> Those crowds approach; smithys break the ~~bl~~ flood,
> The golden smithys of the emperor;
> Marbles of the Dancing floor
> Break ~~bleak~~ bither [=bitter], bleak, aimless complexity,
> Those images that yet
> More images beget,
> That dolphin torn, that gong tormented sea. (NLI 13,581, 91r, in lighter ink; *WFMP* 24–25)

Positioned as it is in the notebook, this version of stanza V misleadingly appears to belong to the second draft of the poem when actually it marks the end of the third (on 92r), which it faces.

Draft 3 is a fair-hand version of the poem, now bearing a title for the first time—"Byzantium"—and "in a blue-gray, almost brown-gray ink, done with a sharp point" (*WFMP* 27n). Overall, few lines are revised beyond spelling and punctuation. The exceptions occur in stanzas I and V (see *WFMP* 26–29) and address small matters of indecision such as shown in lines 4 and 8 of stanza I: respectively, "~~After~~ <~~the~~> <~~And after that~~ After great> Cathedral gong;" and "<The fury and the> ~~All~~ <~~that stupidity th and~~> ~~mere~~ mire ~~& blood~~ of human veins" (92r). In stanza V, as acknowledged above, line 5 struggles to simplify: from "Break bitter, bleak aimless complexity" to "Break the bleak fury ~~of~~ or blind complexity," and then to "Break, ~~bleak, blind~~ <bitter> furies of complexity"—reformulations followed by the recalibration of lines 6 and 7: "Those images that yet / ~~More~~ <~~Fresh~~ More> images beget," revised to "Of images that yet / Fresh images beget" and, finally, "Those images ~~Etc~~ that yet / Fresh images beget" (91v). Draft 3 is not dated, unfortunately, although it has significance as the last treatment of the poem in Rapallo Notebook D in its present state. However, more than sixty years ago, when Curtis Bradford viewed the notebook, there were two loose sheets of holograph inserted at the back of the notebook. These sheets proved to be "a still later MS of 'Byzantium'" bearing variants in stanzas II and V, as well as an intermediate version of stanza IV.[142] Undated, this later manuscript possibly relates to another one, now lost, that Mrs. Yeats reported as "Final MS of poem dated September 1930" ("CCP" 240) or to a portion of the "dummy copy" of poems that Yeats proposed to send Sturge Moore, on "September 26th [1930]," as a sampler of verse to be called *The Winding Stair*, with Moore to create a cover design for Macmillan to match the success of the design that he had drawn for *The Tower* (*TSMC* 163; *CL InteLex* 5387).

That holograph is the last work executed on "Byzantium" to have a connection with the bound pages of Rapallo D without being an actual part of it. By then, Yeats was busy writing again, and, by his own account to his wife, most of that—composed elsewhere—involved "writing notes in diary & correcting Robartes [stories]" (September 13, 1930, *YGYL* 223; *CL InteLex* 5381).[143] By mid-September, he was writing with ease a new poem, "For Anne Gregory" (*YGYL* 224; *CL InteLex* 5382),[144] this time in Rapallo Notebook E (on leaves 31v, 32v–33r, and 34r), because little space remained in Rapallo D. The next entry brings to completion the poem "The Crazed Moon," supposedly recovered in August 1930 from a manuscript source said to have been mislaid since 1923. On September 15, Yeats wrote to his wife from Coole that he was "writing a poem & another of those 'poems for music'"—which might refer to the last two lyrics in the notebook (*YGYL* 225; *CL InteLex* 5383),[145] both completed in October. The last "Subject for a poem" (introduced on 97v) is dated "Nov 18 1930" (a few days before Yeats started writing in the White

Vellum Notebook, on November 23, 1930). By October 4, the significance of "Byzantium" was such that he considered changing the title of his proposed collection, *The Winding Stair*, to *Byzantium*, primarily to avoid confusing the public with a title that another author had taken. Hence, he asked Moore to prepare a second design and submitted to the artist a copy of "Byzantium" "that it may suggest symbolism for the cover" (*TSMC* 164; *CL InteLex* 5390).[146]

[90v] ["Open letter to Lewis," July 1930]

Between drafts of "Veronica's Napkin" and "Byzantium," Yeats drafted an "Open letter to [Wyndham] Lewis" dating it "Renvyle | July." In 1917 Oliver St John Gogarty had purchased Renvyle, a house on the Connemara coast; despite Gogarty's Sinn Fein allegiance, it had been burnt down by Anti-Treaty forces in 1923, but was rebuilt and "reopened as an hotel 1930,"[147] under the management of his wife and son.[148] Yeats was among the first summer's guests, arriving on July 23, to have his portrait painted by Augustus John at Gogarty's suggestion.[149] Yeats must have copied this draft out to send to George for typing on July 27, asking her to "Correct spelling & punctuation I cannot get letters even moderately right after noon & it is now tea time" (*YGYL* 220; *CL InteLex* 5363); however, this letter was delayed and, on August 3, he announced that he would ask Lady Gregory to type it for him when he went to Coole (*YGYL* 221; *CL InteLex* 5367).

Lewis was rallying some of his admirers to defend his satirical novel *The Apes of God*, and solicited contributions from sympathetic names, including H. G. Wells, Augustus John, and Yeats.[150] Yeats sent the open letter to Lewis on August 7, saying that he hoped it was "what you want. I have cursed as well as blessed & think this makes the blessing the more potent. What I have written sounds sincere & is sincere & will be beleived" (*CL InteLex* 5370). It is notable that Yeats's comments are carefully ambiguous and he never actually praises *The Apes of God*, while he takes Lewis to task for his attack on Edith Sitwell. As elsewhere in the notebook, minor leitmotifs are repeated here from writing that is not directly related, including the "benumbing" that was perceived in Gogarty's poetry and the savage indignation of Swift's epitaph (even clearer in cancelled phrases). The selection of Pirandello as a representative of the coming generation also echoes the critique of the historical gyre at Phase 23 in *A Vision A* (*AVA* 211, *CW13* 175). (The following transcription omits cancellations for ease of reading.)

> I read most of your book on a Dutch liner, finished Lord Osmund Party | in the bay of Biscay. I <said> to somebody | the day we passed the Gibraltar I am <reading> an emmense book , which sometimes bores me, some | times exasperates me, some times makes me walk round & round the | deck in

> excitement. Sometimes I think its author a clumsy amateur, sometimes | think if there if there [*sic*] is a great <living> satirist it is he. | Since then I have heard that you attack | individuals, but <that> neither drove me to detraction nor admiration | for I knew nothing of it. I recognised nobody. I spend one week in London every year & | <Your work,> <Like> Pirandello<s>, who alone of living | dramatist[s] <has> unexausted, important material, <both> | portraits [*sic*] the transition from individualism, to universal | plasticity, though your theme is not the flux itself | but <the attempted substitution of> ghastly homunculi | in bottles. Somebody tells me that you have satirized Edith Sitwell. | If that is so, <visionary excitement has benumbed your senses>. When I read her "Gold Coast Customs" a year | [ago] I felt, as <on> first reading "The Apes of God", that something | absent from all literature for a generation was | alive again <passion, & in a form> rare in | in the literature of all times, | A nature enobled by intensity & <by> endurance, <by> wisdom, we had it in one man once; | & he <lies> now in St Patrick under the greatest epitaph in history. (NLI 13,581, 90v)

Lewis quoted the second half of the letter in *Satire and Fiction*, and it is very close to the draft version Yeats had achieved here (cf. *L* 776, *CL InteLex* 5371).

[92v–93r] ["The Crazed Moon," revised c. August 1930 (from 3r, above, and a loose-leaf)]

The origin of this poem is as mysterious as its subject. On the one hand, Yeats's assertion that it is essentially a lost work found must be true. Yet there is no absolute proof, on the other hand, to confirm exactly how and why some composition, allegedly, had occurred seven years prior to its completion in the notebook. As Rapallo D was nearly used up by August or September 1930, it is plausible that a space available on the lower 80 percent of leaf 3r invited the first attempt to renovate an unpublished lyric. However, the first of two columns of new drafting that occur there also appears to be where the poem started, tentatively—with nothing apparently copied from another source—and where consecutive patches of discarded lines produce only a pair of couplets on the left side: "The | A moon is walking there / [~~...~~] The children that [she] bore / [~~...~~] Being wild & strange / Did her wits derange" (with "range" and "change" jotted beside as rhyme notes; see *WFMP* 274–75). From this, Yeats worked out in his head a series of line transpositions that rendered, on the right-hand side of the page, a stanza made of two joined quatrains rhyming ABBACDDC: "A [?moidering] strange / Moon walks there / The children that she bore / Did her wits ~~astrange~~ <derandge>. / And now the [?barren] moon / Can shed such beams about / That[,] hold a finger out[,] / And it seems dri[ed] bone" (end of 3r; slightly edited here for sense).

Clark introduces to the chronology a loose leaf on which a complete draft of the poem (from NLI 13,590, folder [10]) has been made on the basis of the fairly common "Venus and Adonis" stanza for rhyme but with three stresses per line and occasional hypermetric deviation. The logic of progression from 3r to 93r stems from a connection between the "crazy" and "crazed" condition of the moon as she ambles forth in the first stanza (on 3r of Rapallo D and 1r of NLI 13,590). Variations of the sestet (rhyming ABABCC) occur several times prior to 1920 in Yeats's published writings[151] so that "The Crazed Moon" may be seen as an unusual recurrence. In NLI 13,590 (10), 1r, two sittings were required, in which the first two stanzas were written using a pen with a blunt nib and the third stanza came later, "added with a finer pen" beneath a short drawn line and accompanying small adjustments in stanzas 1 and 2 (see *WFMP* 276–77 and 277n). This extraneous, loose sheet is presented by Clark to form a bridge between Rapallo D, leaves 3r and 93r, although the sequence might have been misinterpreted if stanza 1 rehearsals on 3r were really just a dead end, a failed effort by Yeats to *restart* the poem from scratch. If the odd sheet is the key that it seems, the question is: where did it originate? NLI 13,590 is simply a congeries of materials, posthumously sorted by title in twenty-three folders, for poems published in *The Winding Stair*.

At the opening 92v/93r, we find the execution of the full poem in its three stanzas as defined on the loose sheet, first as a fair-hand copy on 93r, with slight amendments interlinearly in stanzas 1 and 2 as copying progressed ("staggering" in line 2 being foreign to the version on 3r but not to the loose sheet). The first line of stanza 2 is the most heavily revised: from "That are dazed or it may be dead" to "Children dazed or dead" (93r). Furthermore, the whole draft on this page appears to have been made with the same "finer pen" that Yeats used when adding stanza 3 to the extraneous sheet, suggesting that the first two stanzas might have constituted the foundation on which he endeavored to construct a finished poem from an extant fragment. Instead of a title, he entered a note at the top of 93r (before or after drawing a long, vertical line through the poem to show that this version was not final. The note ascribes a year (with uncertainty) to the original composition, described as "A lyric written in [?] 1923 & lost"—and on a separate line continues, ambiguously, "have just found August 1930" (implying "I" or "we" to be the grammatical subject of the predicate). From this second draft, an even fairer but also final version of the poem in the notebook was entered on 92v and, this time, assigned a title: "~~The dark fortnight~~" (see *WFMP* 278–81). Not surprisingly, stanza 3 (the most recent part of the work) proved the least stable as he wrote it out, tinkering at first with the last line with four possible outcomes—that is, "Rends ~~all that comes~~ what is in reach. | or | Rends all that comes in reach | or | Rends all that it can reach | or | Rends what is in reach" (92v)—until he struck out all of these options and amended the last three lines instead: "~~Blenched by a~~ <~~Caught in~~ Blenched by that> malicious ~~drea~~ dream / They are spread wide that ~~each~~ each / May rend what comes in ~~reach~~ reach" (92v; cf. "blenched" versus "blenching and trembling" in "A First Confession," a poem written in June 1927 for *The Winding Stair*).

It is possible that Yeats wrote *in error* "1923" in the headnote on 93r—if the unpublished "lyric" recovered in 1930 was written in response to his wife's collapse in April 1924, "the result of accumulated strain" and the effects of various illnesses that necessitated her recuperation in England for weeks as her husband "removed himself to Coole."[152] This might make sense of the rejected title "The dark fortnight" and of her later ascription of "April" to the year 1923, otherwise following the note on 93r in dating "The Crazed Moon" in her copy of *The Collected Poems* ("CCP"240). It is also possible, although unlikely, that "1923" is *correct* and that George Yeats's dating relates to a partly indeterminate episode involving a lost lyric that Professor Grenville Cole[153] brought to Yeats's attention. Sadly, only Yeats's side of the correspondence has survived in two short letters. In the first, he writes: "Yes you may quote that poem, but please say it is from an old unpublished poem of mine—a poem which I have not included in any of my books" (April 20, [1923], *CL InteLex* 4313). In the second letter, dictated to George Yeats but signed, WBY acknowledges delay in responding to a further query from Cole and apologizes for having a poor memory for details: "Forgive me for having overlooked your letter of July 13. I think that was a poem I wrote many years ago, but I dont remember anything about it, & I doubt if it was ever printed—I have certainly no manuscript of it. | I am sorry to give you such an unsatisfactory answer" (August 18, 1923; *CL InteLex* 4360). But this is circumstantial, rather than conclusive, evidence, since Cole's letters have been lost and no connection has been made between this transactional business on Yeats's side and a contemporary pre-textual state of "The Crazed Moon" (presumably NLI 13,590 [10]), other than the coincidence of dates.

[93v–94r] [New lines for *The Cat and the Moon*]

Between the draft of "Veronica's Napkin" dated "Oct 1930" (on 93v) and a tribute to John Quinn (on 94v–95r) with the same date, Yeats includes two short rewrites for *The Cat and the Moon*. The first fragment (on 93v) breaks up a speech by the Blind Beggar, replacing the dialogue of the 1924 Cuala version with that used in *Wheels and Butterflies* (1934).[154] More importantly, on the opposite recto Yeats starts to move toward the play's new ending, where the Lame Beggar's choice of being blessed rather than cured works another miracle. These drafts are not included in the Cornell edition of the manuscript materials. Relying on drafts from 1924 and 1931, Andrew Parkin surmised that when Yeats "realized that his play needed a stronger ending, he eventually composed the bowing sequence" and he suggests that Yeats "probably jotted the new ending on the [1924] typescript and then revised it on hotel notepaper during rehearsals of the play for performances held at Gogarty's Renvyle House Hotel from August 11 to August 18, 1931."[155] Indeed the revised play was then performed at Renvyle before being staged at the Abbey in September 1931.[156] Since the drafts in Rapallo D are clearly from October 1930, they therefore represent an intermediate stage omitted from Parkin's chronology and consideration.[157]

The draft in Rapallo D is in Yeats's most gestural hand—it is unlikely that anyone could discern "First Musician" without knowing that this has to be the reading—so several of the other readings are doubtful, and many lines are cancelled. Yeats also appears to put two parts side by side on the page in places (see Figure 3.6), which is potentially confusing. Clear, however, are two key features that Yeats adds but later dropped: the naming of the compass directions and reference to the "host(s) of heaven."

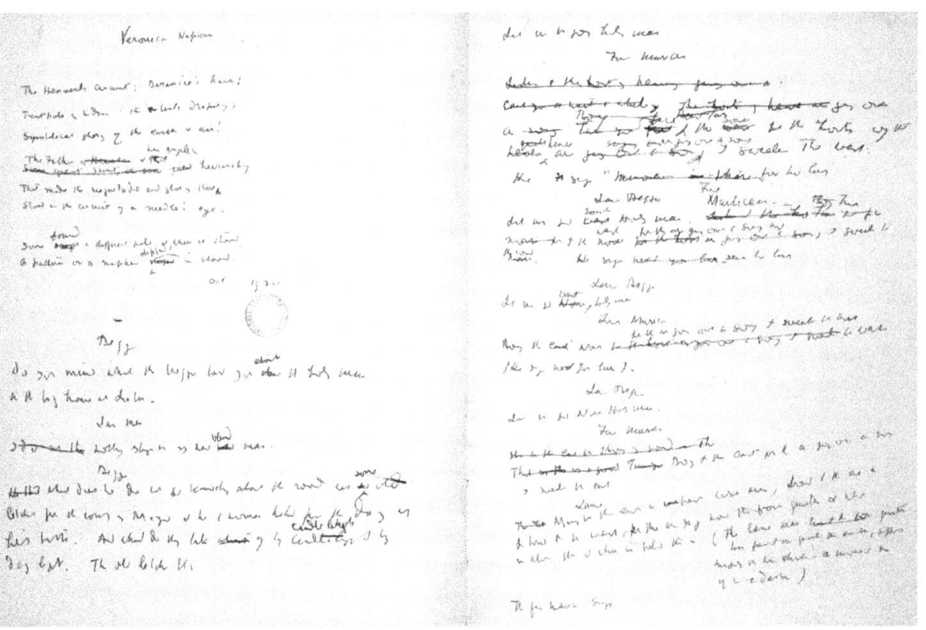

Figure 3.6. Rapallo Notebook D, NLI 13,581, [93v–94r]. Courtesy of the NLI.

The left-hand side of this opening in the notebook, beneath the final draft of "Veronica's Napkin" (on 93v), shows Yeats breaking up the speech of the "Beggar," as described above. The facing page (94r) is presented in *literatim* transcription to help distinguish between parallel entries. Since insertions mix with interlinear material on the page, they are given without the normal convention of pointed brackets:

Let us be going holy man
First Musician
~~Listen to the host of heaven going over a~~
~~Cant you a wait a while~~ ~~The hosts of heaven are~~ going over
[?~~Bowing~~] ~~face Bow~~ Turn south
A ~~song~~ ~~Turn your~~ ~~feet~~ ^ [to] the ~~west~~ for the hosts of the
~~quietly~~ heavn ~~singing a~~ are going over a song
~~heaven~~ ^ are ~~going over a song~~ ^ to sweeten The West
He [?~~h~~] sings "~~Minoulous in phase~~ [?first two lines][158]
Lame Beggar First
south Musician ~~Bow~~ Turn
Let us go ~~west~~ Holy man. ~~Listen to the host~~ ~~Turn~~ ~~yr feet~~
west for they are going over a song no
~~North for~~ to the ~~north~~ ~~for the host~~ are going ~~over a song~~ to sweeten the
the west
~~north~~ He sings ~~next [?four lines~~] — [?seems to ?turn]
Lame Beggar
West
Let us go ~~North~~, holy man
First Musician
[?for they] are going over a song to sweet[en] the west
[?Bowing] the ~~east~~ North ~~for the host is going over a song to sweet~~ the West
(He sings next four lines)
Lame Beggar
Let us go North Holy Man
First Musician
~~Its in the east in xxx of good~~ ~~The~~
~~This is the is a good~~ ~~Turn your~~ Bow to east for the[y] a[re] go[in]g ov[er] a son[g]
to sweet[en] the east
Lame [Beggar]
~~The ea~~ May be the east is ~~we~~ for wise men, I bow to the east &
I bow to the west, for [?they] are [?singing] now the four quarters & what
is above that & what is below that (The lame man ~~bows to the four~~ quarters
[?bows] first to the quarter the [?earth], supports
himself as he shifts – a movement as
if in a dance)
The first musician sings (NLI 13,581, 94r)

Elements here harken back to Yeats's earlier works: the "hosts of heaven" recall work from the 1890s or early 1900s, such as "The Unappeasable Host," or *The Hour Glass* (1903)—"I have made formations of battle with Arithmetic that have put the hosts of Heaven to the rout" (*VPl* 594)—and *The Unicorn from the Stars* (1908)—"There is a fiery moment, perhaps once in a lifetime, and in that moment we see the only thing that matters. It is in that moment the great battles are lost and won, for in that moment we are a part of the host of Heaven" (*VPl* 705). Similarly, the bowing to the four quarters is reminiscent of the rituals of the Golden Dawn.[159]

In the draft on Renvyle writing paper, the compass directions are simplified to "Bless what is before you, what is behind you, what is to left, what is to right of you" and the stage direction's hint of a dance becomes the Holy Man's explicit instruction to dance: "Would it not be a miracle if you could dance [...] Then dance,"[160] and subsequent drafts develop the idea. However, although the "Lame Man bows" in the stage direction, neither character's speech includes "bow" or "bowing." An annotation on the typescript of 1924 version has the First Musician say "Bow to what is in front of you, bow to what is behind you."[161] Parkin places that draft before the Renvyle page, while the Lame Beggar declares "I bow to the east, I bow to the west" in the Rapallo D draft.

Whatever the exact sequence of these amendments, Yeats was already reconsidering the ending of *The Cat and the Moon* a full year before the Renvyle performances in 1931 (and the subsequent Abbey staging in September), so that his revisions were not done in the immediate context of the play's rehearsals—or not only then—but with plenty of forethought.

[94v–95r] [A memorial tribute to John Quinn]

The fragments of the play are followed by a memorial tribute to John Quinn, who had died at the early age of fifty-four on July 28, 1924. It shows, as ever, Yeats wrestling with words to find the right phrasing for his ideas in prose, so the transcription here gives the deleted material, in order to convey the process.

> ~~Like~~ | I ~~try to recall John~~ ~~the~~ <I must recall a> friend of ~~[?*]som~~ many years ~~who I~~ <to> whom I could <so> seldom | speak & ~~whose letters letters himself~~ whose swiftly dictated ~~leters~~ letters ~~so seldom~~ | ~~told me ss of his circumstances~~ ~~told me so little of~~ ~~told me so little~~ for all their <the> forcable | ~~their vivid~~ generalisation <told me little>[162] ~~I thik recall~~ I rember ~~his chief for~~ his generosity, his audacity | ~~courage~~ his ~~irracibility~~ <iracability>. ~~I do not know now~~ ~~At first he was [?]~~ He was at first | one of those vague ~~personalities~~ persons ~~of~~ one thinks so seldom <about> & often with annoyance | who write ~~for an autograph, or to find out one meant in such & such a passage~~ | for an autograph, or a manuscript, or to discover some fact. ~~The~~ <Then> I met him | <at a Galway <u>Feis</u> in honour of the poet Raftery when I was one of the speakers.> | ~~probably at my sisters – my sister Elizabeth has an immense correspondence & in a very short~~ | <Next day he proposed a lecture tour that ~~was to give~~> | ~~time he was an arranging a lecture tour that~~ gave me <~~the~~ my> first substantial ~~su~~ <sum> of money | ~~I ever earned~~. ~~He did~~ All <~~that~~ That>

unpaid work, ~~writing~~ ~~wrote~~ <those> letters to Societies & Universities | all over the United States ~~for a man he had two or three times perhap~~ <he did for a man he met for a few hours on a> ~~day on~~ | ~~a~~ hurried visit to Europe. ~~But~~ But good heaven how irrasible he was. | He made me promise not to go near the University of Chicago – there had been a quarrel | ~~about~~ which he never explained – & ~~no sooner did he get there <that> than~~ <how could I know> a charming deputation | of <young> girls <who> carried me off to their society <belonged to it>. ~~Next day came a denunciatory telegram~~ | ~~yet how could I have known that these were women at the university of Chicago.~~ | They did not look in least <like> the undergraduates & I had never heard of co-education. | ~~At some other time~~ <Once> ~~I had~~ to my great embarrasment ~~to speak lecture~~ <I lectured> to three | middle ladies in a hotel drawing room, I <learned> only weeks afterwards ~~discovered~~ | that they had objected to the date, ~~that~~ but he had refused to listen. ~~to their excuses~~. ~~Once~~ | ~~in~~ <In> later years his audacity & irracability ~~had great public effect~~ | forced British <war> police at propaganda to behave. ~~America had yet~~ | ~~joined the war – public opinion was hesitating~~ ~~German~~ <~~He~~> ~~who has~~ Being at once | pro British & pro Irish, <he had> published a reminiscence ~~of Sir Ro of his friend~~ | of Sir Roger Casement ~~who had been his guest for some weeks~~ <~~who~~ his guest for some weeks>.[163] ~~An E~~ America | had not yet joined the war – public opinion was hesitating & an English | agent, who ~~found that he could not~~ <thought ~~no man~~ nobody should> be pro-British & pro Irish called upon ~~qui~~ him. | ~~Quinn~~. He showed ~~him~~ Quinn a photograph ~~copy~~ of the notorious diary, ~~what~~ | which was not brought into court, or produced anywhere while Sir Roger Casement still | lived, but used afterwards in secret & semi secret. When Quinn had read it the **[continues to 95r]** agent said "~~Now Mr Quinn~~ I dont think you will write any more | articles upon Sir Roger Casement". "You are mistaken" Quinn ~~said~~ | answered "That was only the first of a series. In my second ~~arcticle~~ | I propose to denounce this diary as a ~~forgery~~, [?~~it like~~] forgery – ~~you a~~ <You as its distributor> | ~~for destributing, <the British government for> & I shall after that I shall~~ <and then> describe as an example of | similar propaganda the Piggot ~~forgxxxx~~ <forgeries>."[164] Then came negoceation ~~the~~ | ~~diary dropped out as the agent understood~~ the diary dropped from | English propaganda in the States and Quinn ~~that he would not write that~~ <did not write that> | second article. | —————————— NP [= New Paragraph]

Without anything of Rosevelts creative gift | he <had> something of his temperament, & ~~was~~ though associated in public life | with the Democrats <was> drawn to his side ~~more &~~ <by> sympathy. President | Wilson once ~~told a friend~~ complained to a friend that people thought him | passionless, whereas in reality, he ~~had~~ came to his ~~decein~~ <decisions> only after a hard | struggle with his passions. ~~He~~ Wilson repelled ~~him~~ <Quinn>, ~~Rosevelt~~ | ~~attracted but Rosevelt but Rosevelt had for him the charm,~~ | ~~but shug~~ who shared with Rosevelt the charm ~~surrounding these men~~ <~~surrounding~~ of those> | whose passions ~~&~~ compel <and illuminate> their decisions. Such

> men are | difficult, touchy & I think always important. It is not possible | to forget John Quinn.
>
> WBY | Oct | 1930 (NLI 13,581, 94v–95r)[165]

A typed version of this text, held at the University of Delaware Library, is extremely close to this draft and it was intended to preface a selection of Yeats's letters to John Quinn, as part of a larger project that Lennox Robinson was editing but that was never published. The library's finding aid summarizes as follows:

> The project was undertaken at the behest of Quinn's sister, Mrs. Julia Quinn Anderson, who wished for a selection of Quinn's correspondence to be published, with letters "touching lightly upon his career at the Bar and laying stress upon his friendships with Irish men and women, English and French as well, who were distinguished in the Arts."[166]

Her lawyer engaged Lennox Robinson as editor, and he was then responsible for selecting, asking for permissions, and providing background: "Each group of letters was to be preceded by a short biographical note on the correspondent [...] Although some of these essays were by the original correspondent, most were written by Robinson."[167] We know from Lady Gregory's journals that she received an initial request from Robinson at the end of July,[168] and Yeats wrote to her that he was reading through his letters to Quinn on 4 September 1930 (*CL InteLex* 5377). Yeats evidently preferred to write his own introduction and started this short tribute a month or so later.

Working from Quinn's copies of her letters, Robinson had written to Lady Gregory for a second time, in September, with "85 typed pages" of her letters, asking for her permission to publish from these. Her journals reveal some of the problems that Robinson's request might cause for correspondents, one of which was having the thunder stolen from their own memoirs. She told her biographer, Constant Huntington, that she had chosen "about a thousand words from early letters telling of the work at the Abbey chiefly, and of some talks by Yeats, and sent them to L.R., Yeats approving [...] The later letters to John Quinn are fuller and on more varied subjects. They will come in my memoirs."[169] Other correspondents may have had a similar reluctance to surrender such valued material, which may have contributed to the failure of the project in the end.

[95v–96r, 97r, 98r] ["Crazy Jane on the Day of Judgment" from 38v–39v]

Continuing from 38v–39v, near the gulf of missing leaves that divides Rapallo D between winter 1929 and spring 1930, Yeats finally completed, at the end of the notebook, the new Crazy Jane poem that he had started almost exactly a year before.[170] This shows, with the refurbishment of "The Crazed Moon," that he was beginning to accelerate the production of texts that he intended for Cuala Press and Macmillan. For continuation of this new poem, he would carry forward the idea that nonce stanzas, made in a pattern of shorter and longer lines, could be used to develop Jane's thesis that "Love is not love unless it takes the whole" (last stated on leaf 39v). The final drafts in the notebook were executed in three stages, bordered by the tribute to Quinn (dated "Oct 1930") and shorter prose subjects of October and November. Accordingly, Mrs. Yeats assigned to the poem the date October 1930 ("CCP" 241), as Yeats had suggested at the end of the penultimate draft by inscribing "Oct" (at 97r) before copying out a fair-hand version of the lyric on 98r, incorporating most revisions from the former.

At the opening 95v/96r, the first full draft of the poem occurs, beginning on 95v with stanza 1 and progressing through stanza 3. The alternating refrain lines have been reduced from five beats to four just as the poem has been reconceptualized as a dialogue with the former, silent, male auditor of the prose draft (at 39r) given a voice to respond to Jane's argument. These new refrains are neatly recorded in the upper-right corner of 95v ("And that is what Jane said" and "Thats certainly the case said he") as a distillation of the trials below and as a note of reminder for the expansion of the poem in a fourth stanza on the facing page (beyond the three movements envisioned in the original plan). With refrains contracted, the metrical forms of other lines were seriously reduced from 4, 5, 4, 4, 5 to 2, 2, 3, 2, 4 in a stanza otherwise defined by its ABAAB rhyme scheme. Except for refrain lines, stanzas 1 and 3 caused sufficient difficulty on 95v that most of their lines were cancelled, then fully amended (at right). The whole of stanza 3 was then struck out by a diagonal line. Afterward, on 96r, Yeats pushed on with stanza 4 but, by the middle of the page, fell back to revise stanza 3. Finally, he drew a short horizontal line, as if to set off stanza 3 from the ensuing, fair-hand, alternative lines composed for stanza 4. (See *WFMP* 356–59.)

Naturally, the second, full-draft version of the poem (on 97r) would be an exercise copying and revising constituent parts from 95v and 96r. In each stanza, some changes were made in single lines, such as 1 and 3 in stanza 1, lines 3–4 in stanza 2, line 3 in stanza 3, and line 1 (cancelled then marked stet) in stanza 4. The corrections to stanzas 2 and 4 were substantial enough to require laying them out in the right-hand margin and using clue-lines and arrows to indicate where the substitutions belonged—a technique more common for amendments made on facing verso pages. In this case, however, leaf 96v was already occupied by themes for additional poems (see *WFMP* 360–61 and Figure 3.7, below). As decisive as Crazy Jane is as a persona, Yeats cancelled the first four lines of stanza 4 and made a substitution for them (at right) with an afterthought:

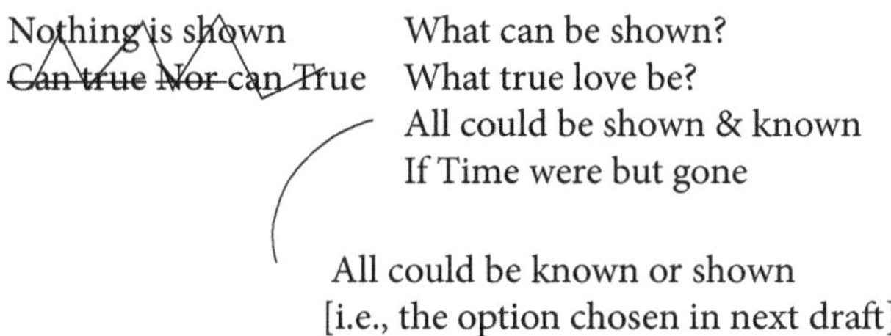

This concluded the draft, with the male persona's refrain left standing, at left, to deliver the final punch: "That<'s> certainly the case, said he." Beneath stanza 4, then, Yeats inscribed the partial date ("Oct"), subsequently drew a vertical line through the whole poem, and advanced to leaf 98r to copy out the poem for the third and final time in Rapallo Notebook D, retooling the man's refrain-line in stanza 2 to agree with the amended one in stanza 4. (See *WFMP* 362–63.) At the top of this third draft, Yeats gave the poem its first title: "Crazy Jane & the End of the World."

[96v, 97v] [Themes for poems and prose subject on "the great philosophies"; "Nov 18 1930"]

Facing 97r and the October-dated, second draft of "Crazy Jane on the Day of Judgment," Yeats introduced themes for new poems. Leaf 96v is accordingly the point where such entries were made on two occasions, both likely prior to his trip to London and busy social calendar while there between November 1 and 17, 1930 (see *YGYL* 228–31). When the draft of the Jane poem had been introduced on 97r, a space would have been left for possible revisions on 96v (as was Yeats's wont). Subsequently, a final copy of the poem was made on 98r, which for a time (until November 18) also left vacant leaf 97v. These blank spaces were filled in with themes for new poems *after* Yeats finished "Crazy Jane on the Day of Judgment," the theme on 97v being his latest. (See Figure 3.7 and Figure 3.8.) From here on, Clark's transcriptions in "CNGI" are recommended as a supplement to the ones below. However, facsimiles are not provided there or in *WFMP*.

On the left side of the wavery, vertical line, we have four self-critical thoughts that are arranged consecutively to suggest the progression of argument in a segmental poem the likes of "Meditations upon Death," composed in 1929 from a tripartite prose subject and eventually splintering into separate poems.[171] Here, the entry entitled "theme for poem" might even be interpreted as "theme[s] for poem[s]" but for the wavery line, which seems to define a discrete work on the left as distinct from the one on the right, called simply "Theme." On the left, we have the following:

theme for poem

—

I so often [?away] in my work | So often forget-full | That I grow ~~inattentive~~, in atentive | that I but see <in> ~~&~~ words & acts | Illustrations of my thought. Then I do & say | Such stupid unkind things.

—

Often my dear a voice in my head | Says that a man needs all his thought | for his life— And then ~~I long most~~ <wish that> I | had been anything but ~~who~~ <what> I am— Perhaps | a millers clerk in Sligo.

—

What is the ~~yous~~ use of of ~~all ones thought~~ <all ones thought> | What is the use of fame, | If ones friends, those who know | Cannot look at ones life & say | He has been good.

—

Not all the fame in the world assu[a]ges <asuages> the pang | that comes upon one, when one has failed to ~~find~~ ~~win~~ win | Some mans, ~~or s[ome]~~ womans, ~~so[me]~~ or childs good will. (NLI 13,581, 96v; cf. "CNGI" 14)

Possibly these thoughts are not the seeds of any one lyric poem, yet they seem to anticipate self-lacerating lyrics such as "The Results of Thought" and "Remorse for Intemperate Speech," both written in the White Vellum Notebook that Yeats began to use on November 23, 1930.[172]

On the right-hand side of 96v (viewed in the upper-left corner of Figure 3.7), we have a confession of a very different stripe and perhaps relevant to the apparently female auditor ("my dear") in the adjacent sketch:

Theme

A phantom to my bed & woke | Had it been been the phantom of | some one who is dead I | should have been at peace— <They depend upon God> | But it was the phantom of | someone who depends upon me | for happiness. All day I | have been in misery— | what hidden pain sent | that phantom to me. (NLI 13,581, 96v; cf. "CNGI" 15)

This theme might seem a foreshadowing of Yeats's "The Apparitions," from his *Last Poems*, with its levitating "*coat upon a coat-hanger*," his "*worst*" premonition of death. But the phantom here proves to be closer to that "hovering thing" in his poem of 1919, "An Image from a Past Life," fashioned on the idea of the Over Shadower that he developed with his wife as they systematized the results of automatic writing in their "Sleep and Dream Notebooks."[173] Interestingly, on October 23, 1930, he wrote to Olivia Shakespear with plans to visit her in London ("about Nov 1"), excusing delay in order to find a typist for *A Vision*. "If I dictate to George it would almost certainly put her nerves all wrong. I

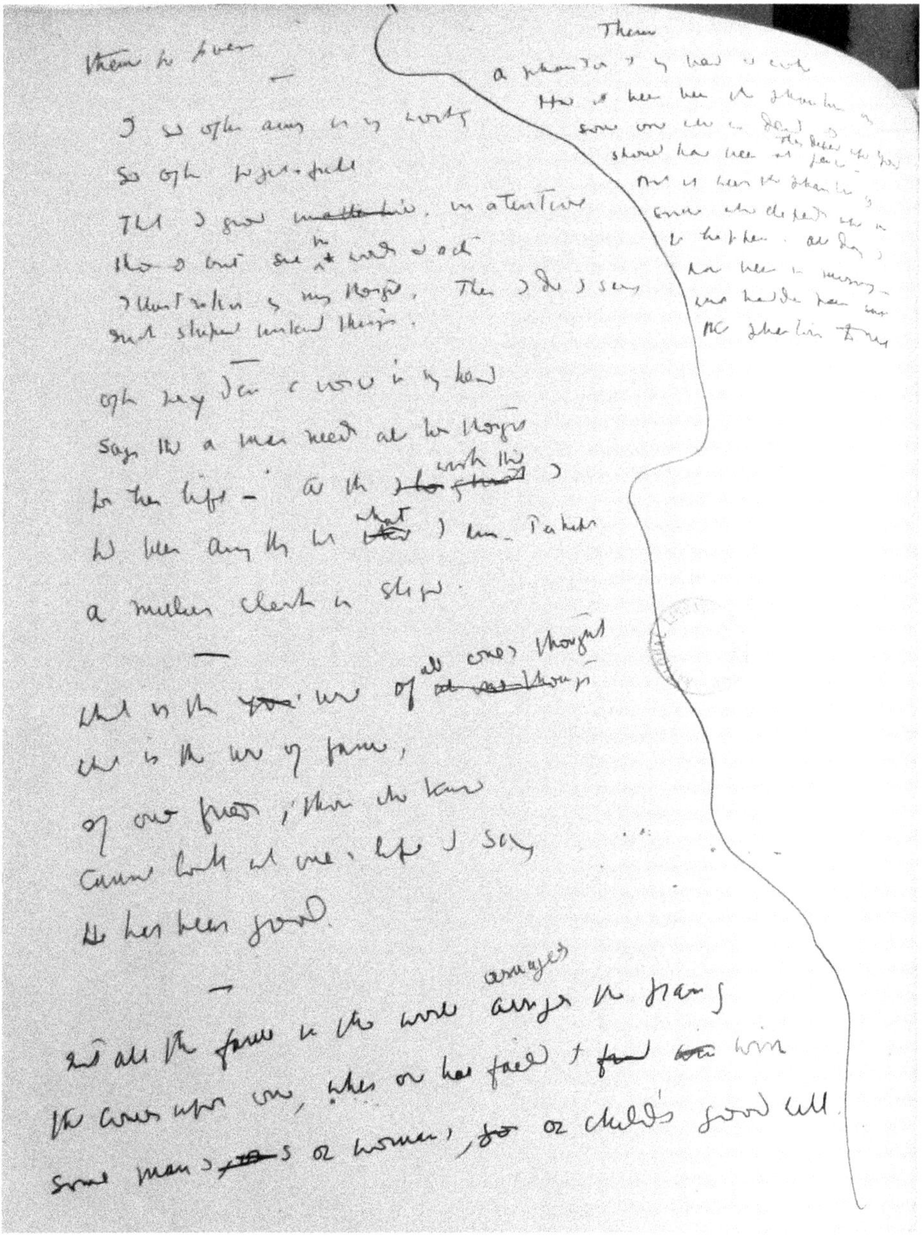

Figure 3.7. Rapallo Notebook D, NLI 13,581, [96v], themes for poetry. Courtesy of the NLI; photograph courtesy of Catherine E. Paul.

don't want any more mediumship" (*L* 777; *CL InteLex* 5394). In postscript, he conveyed an amusing dream, accentuating an account of a doctor's assessment of his "fitness for the London journey" and affirming his own assertion that "I am well and enjoy life" (ibid.).

On this trip, Yeats visited various friends, using the Savile Club as a base and venturing out to stay with John Masefield, new Poet Laureate since May, for several days in Oxford. During that stay, Yeats also visited May Morris at Kelmscott and the Morrells at Garsington, where Lady Ottoline hosted a meeting of several literary friends, including Yeats, Walter de la Mare, and Virginia Woolf. One upshot of the latter event was the poem "Spilt Milk," which Yeats composed inside the back cover of his travel book, Johann Erdmann's *A History of Philosophy* (1880), volume 2: *Modern Philosophy* (third edition, 1924)—and then revised in a letter to his wife on November 8: "We that had such thought; / That such deeds have done, / Must ramble on—thinned out / Like milk on a flat stone" (*CL InteLex* 5404; also *YGYL* 230), taking his metaphor from a suggestion by Lady Ottoline.[174]

On Monday, November 17, 1930, Yeats returned home, "impatient to get to work again," having "seen most of my friends & spent most of my money (*YGYL* 230; *CL InteLex* lacking). The next day, he introduced another topic in prose for an unpublished poem; this time it was on a philosophical subject attuned to recent readings in Erdmann's history. Besides Kant, the book features Leibnitz, Fichte, Schelling, Hegel, and others, not all of whom were of interest to Yeats at that time. Scorings and strokings indicate interest in Leibnitz's notion of monads in relation to God and Kant's relation to Transcendental Aesthetics, Analytics, Metaphysics, and Dialectics.[175] Indeed, the entry in Rapallo D, leaf 97v (shown in Figure 3.8), suggests that Yeats had been reading philosophy through the lens of William Blake (to recall the contrarities of "The Divine Image" and "The Human Abstract").

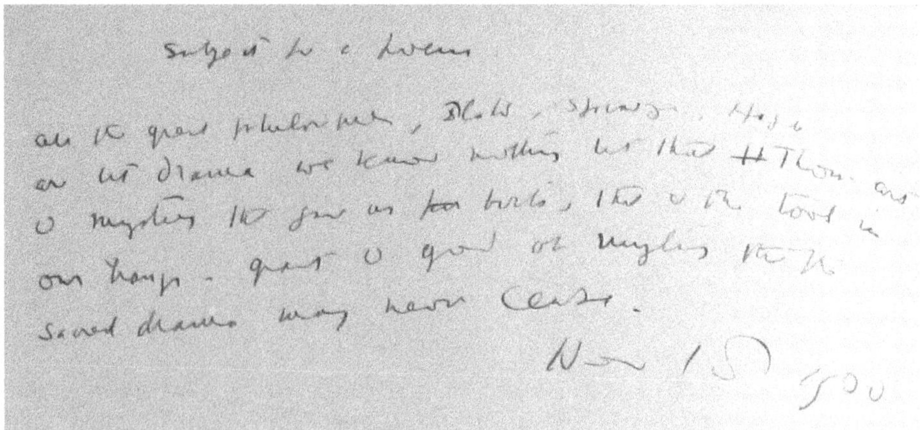

Figure 3.8. Rapallo Notebook D, NLI 13,581, [97v], a prose "Subject for a poem." Courtesy of the NLI.

This theme consists of (1) an impression formed by extensive yet selective readings in philosophy followed by (2) an invocation to the underlying "god or mystery" of it all (or "god of mystery"). In substance, it was both direct and culminating, literally as the chronologically final entry in Rapallo Notebook D:

> Subject for a poem
>
> All the great philosophies, Plato, Spinoza, Hegel | are but drama we know nothing but that ~~th~~ Thou art | O mystery that gave us ~~pir~~ birth, that & the tool[s] in | our hangs [=hands]. Grant O god or mystery that the | sacred drama may never cease.
>
> Nov 18 1930 (NLI 13,581, 97v; cf. "CNGI" 16)

As noted above in the context of a comment made at 40v on Gentile, Yeats wrote in his 1930 diary (on November 16) that "philosophy is drama as is every individual life."[176] Thus the idea emerges here in poetic form. Also, on the same day that he inscribed the last entry in Rapallo Notebook D, he counterpointed it with the final aphoristic entry in his 1930 diary: "NOVEMBER 18TH || Science, separated from philosophy, is the opium of the suburbs" (*Ex* 340). The poem was never written.

[98v] [Note written upside down]

On the final page, Yeats made a stray jotting, entered upside down, to record a "Checque for N. T. S. | £185 . 0 . 0 | signed & returned to Perrin | April 29."[177] J. H. Perrin was the Secretary of the National Theatre Society from at least 1924 until 1934.[178] With an estimated value of nearly £10,000 (or $12,500) in today's money, the amount seems too large for a personal check. Rather, the reference to a signature suggests an official check on behalf of the Abbey Theatre, or possibly some form of endorsement.

5. Conclusion

Those sketchy themes at the end of Rapallo Notebook D might suggest a line of symmetry in view of coincident parallels in the initial "Diary" entry of 1928. At both locations, early and late, we find writing informed by recollected experience and personal affiliation with close friends such as the hospitable Morrells and Masefields in Oxfordshire and intimates such as Olivia Shakespear in London and Lady Gregory at Coole Park. Friendship and editorial responsibility at the Cuala Press are often involved in motivating Yeats's writing in the extant halves of the notebook, straddling a veritable crater at the center of it where many leaves have been cut out. In the first half, the tone of those compositions honoring Lady Gregory and Olivia Shakespear (respectively, "Coole Park, 1929" and "After Long Silence") is mainly elegiac although these friends were still living; and this tone is reflected in the second half of the notebook by a meditation on death and immortality ("Byzantium"), by a reminiscence of the late John Quinn in prose, and by the completion of three lyrics begun in the first half (including "Crazy Jane on the Day of Judgment") and thus conceived prior to Yeats's collapse in the winter of 1929/30. The personal nature of writing can account for difficulties in execution in ordinary circumstances. So it is not surprising that his deep connection with people commemorated in the notebook should compound the toil of writing until persistence and talent eventually prevailed, as they obviously did in "Coole Park, 1929" and "Byzantium," the major achievements of Rapallo D as we have it.

We cannot know of what the entire notebook consisted before much of its content came to be removed—or even when or why leaves 8–9, 33, and 42–83 were cut out and discarded, perhaps at different times. We are left with impressions but nothing tangible beyond correspondence and Yeats's statements that he should not attempt to write poetry during most of his convalescence in Rapallo. Strictly rationing his time, energy, and concentration before returning home in July 1930, he left us but two examples of the prose he had written in the interim: footnotes on "2000 BC to 1 AD" (at 84r) and "AD 150 to [the] present" (at 85r), which are directed as inserts for *A Vision A* at pages "151" and "196," respectively (see above), but not used. Such later notes are consistent with examples found in Rapallo Notebooks A–C, already examined in this series, and characteristic of prose entries appearing in the first half of Rapallo D—for example, notes with calculations on Hindu yugas and esoteric epochs; notes on readings about Fichte and Hegel, and a quotation from Chapman's Ovid for possible use in *A Vision B*—not to mention the drafts of "Astrology and the Nature of Reality" (also known as "Seven Propositions"). Amid these notes (at 84v) is the poet's first attempt, as far as we know, to return to the idled composition "Veronica's Napkin" (from 41v) at the same time, in late April or May 1930, and then the more sustained effort of "Byzantium." Looking back in 1933 in the introduction to *The Winding Stair and Other Poems*, he would remember that having been "ill again, I warmed myself back into life with *Byzantium* and *Veronica's Napkin*, looking for a theme that might befit my years" (*VP* 831). And no doubt, Crazy Jane helped to continue this welcome warming.

When he had written to Lady Gregory on July 2, 1929, Yeats had reported progress on *A Vision*, promising that "[t]he moment the big book is finished I shall begin verse again," adding, tantalizingly: "I have a longish poem in my head about Coole" (*CL InteLex* 5258). That promise should have become the story of Rapallo Notebook D, and it is to a certain extent. As the writing of poetry and philosophy were intertwined for Yeats—both much delayed by illness in this case—the notebook discloses the relationship between the two.

In the end, he projected but never wrote a poem on the premise that "All the great philosophies [...] are but drama" (see above). Yet we still have Rapallo Notebook E to explore in this series—a notebook that contains little poetry, only the lyric "For Anne Gregory"—but highlights Yeats's work on *A Vision* in the context of drama, in a new play for the Abbey Theatre, *The Words upon the Window-Pane* (1930), and a rewritten form of *The Resurrection* (from *The Adelphi*, 1927) for the supplementary "play in prose" at the end of *Stories of Michael Robartes and his Friends: An Extract from a Record by his Pupils: and a play in prose* (1931). The whole of that tale is necessarily entrusted to our final installment.

Notes

1 The first entries in the series are Neil Mann's "Rapallo Notebooks A and B," *International Yeats Studies* 6, no. 1 (2022): 73–183 (and pages 31–118, above); and Wayne K. Chapman's "Rapallo Notebook C: *A Vision*, Poetry, and Sundry Writings," *International Yeats Studies* 7, no. 1 (2023): 211–83 (and 119–80, above).

2 In alphabetical order, the principal collaborators are Wayne Chapman, Warwick Gould, Margaret Harper, and Neil Mann. Years ago, we began discussing the project with *IYS* founding editor Lauren Arrington, but the project took shape under the editorship of Rob Doggett. The team works remotely to prepare a reliable, detailed map of these notebooks from direct observation in the National Library and from a set of digital facsimiles provided by Catherine E. Paul, sometimes supplemented by Jack Quin. Special thanks to Charis Chapman for setting text and visuals in the series. In addition to these colleagues, there are a number of precursors to acknowledge as fellow collaborators because of their example. Acknowledgment is made to their work in the text, notes, and appendix below—especially to the late David R. Clark on interpreting the handwriting of Yeats in the manuscripts of *The Winding Stair*.

3 See Neil Mann, "Yeats's Rapallo Notebooks," in *New Thresholds in Yeats Studies: Yeats Annual* 22, ed. Warwick Gould (Cambridge: Open Book Publishers, forthcoming). Beyond the holdings of the National Library of Ireland, other manuscript notebooks used by Yeats do exist. The most relevant one, owned by an anonymous collector and therefore physically out of circulation, has some bearing on the Rapallo notebooks as a near-contemporary involving some of the same writings. Particularly in relation to poems and notes written in Rapallo Notebooks C and D, we will sometimes direct readers to Wayne K. Chapman, "Yeats's White Vellum Notebook, 1930–1933," *International Yeats Studies* 2.2 (May 2018), 41–60—an updating of field notes begun by Curtis Bradford, passed down to David R. Clark and, thereafter, to Chapman by Cornell Yeats general editor Stephen Parrish.

4 *Yeats's* Vision *Papers*, vol. 3: *Sleep and Dream Notebooks,* Vision *Notebooks 1 and 2, Card File*, ed. Robert Anthony Martinich and Margaret Mills Harper (Iowa City: University of Iowa Press, 1992), 143–82. The location of *Vision* Notebook 1 (VNB1) is unknown at the present time.

5 The exceptional notebook, Rapallo Notebook D, was listed as "Diary Rapallo 1928" on folio 3v of NLI 30,746. The four others noted on George Yeats's list are "Notebook with Resurrection" (Rapallo E), "Notebook D" (Rapallo A), the notebook "Finished Oct. 9, 1928" (Rapallo B), and "Diary Begun Sept. 23, 1928" (Rapallo C). Ellmann's interest is rounded out there with "Kabbalah Unveiled"; "Lily Yeats Ltrs.," letters from Olivia Shakespear, Robert Bridges, and Lady Gregory; "Stories of Michael Robartes" (NLI 13,577); "Unfinished

Play" (NLI 30,427 and NLI 30,488; see *YA17* (2007), 95–179); "Diary April 7, 1921" (NLI 13,576); and, finally, "[Diary] Broad Street, Oxford" (NLI 36,258, *Vision* Notebook 2), in use between July 1923 and November 1927 to preserve *A Vision* material and notes on automatic script.

6 Thomas F. Parkinson, *W. B. Yeats: The Later Poetry* (Berkeley: University of California Press, 1964); hereafter cited as *Later Poetry* to avoid confusing the title with Parkinson's *W. B. Yeats: Self-Critic* (1951), which combined with the later book in 1971. For a detailed account of George Yeats and Thomas Parkinson working together, see Wayne K. Chapman, "George Yeats, Thomas Parkinson, and the Legacy of the Archive," in *Yeats Annual* 22 (forthcoming).

7 On the representation of the five Rapallo notebooks in "Parkinson's list," see Chapman, "Rapallo Notebook C," *IYS* 7.1: 211–14 (and 119–22, above).

8 Mann, "Rapallo Notebooks A and B," *IYS* 6.1: 105 (and 63, above). An error on the estimated date of Yeats's initial entry in Rapallo D is corrected below, in Part 4 [1r–2r].

9 David R. Clark, *Yeats at Songs and Choruses* (Amherst: University of Massachusetts Press, 1983), 243; cited hereafter as *YSC*.

10 See Wayne K. Chapman, *W. B. Yeats's Robartes-Aherne Writings: Featuring the Making of "Stories of Michael Robartes and His Friends"* (London: Bloomsbury Academic, 2018), 165–271; hereafter cited as *YRAW*.

11 Mann, "Rapallo Notebooks A and B," *IYS* 6.1: 73 (and 31, above).

12 George Yeats to Lennox Robinson, November 24 and 30, 1929 (HM 51876–77), Henry E. Huntington Library, San Marino, California.

13 George Yeats to Lennox Robinson, June 7, 1930 (HM 51878), Henry E. Huntington Library, San Marino, CA.

14 See Wayne K. Chapman, *Yeats's Poetry in the Making: "Sing Whatever Is Well Made"* (London: Palgrave Macmillan, 2010), 236; hereafter cited as *YPM*. There, Appendix A collates a dozen sources on the datings of Yeats's poems and is listed as "CCP" in this essay's Key to Abbreviations.

15 Yeats's letter is so close to verbatim that it seems adapted straight out of Rapallo D, 1r and 2r.

16 See Travers Smith, Dorothy (Dolly) on "Cast & Creative" list for the Abbey Theatre production of *John Bull's Other Island* (September 19–24, 1927). Abbey Theatre Archives. Accessed September 10, 2022, at https://www.abbeytheatre.ie/archives/production_detail/3157/.

17 Dolly Robinson was the daughter of spiritualist Hester Travers Smith (née Dowden), daughter of Yeats's mentor and Trinity College, Dublin, don Edward Dowden. Dolly was never, therefore, Dolly Dowden except in WBY's mind.

18 Shaw's "spoilt priest" is later recalled in *On the Boiler* (1939); see *Ex* 411, *CW5* 223.

19 The production of Synge's play *The Well of the Saints* to which Yeats refers here is evidently the one that opened on January 20, 1925. See Abbey Theatre Archives. Accessed September 10, 2022, at https://www.abbeytheatre.ie/archives/production_detail/2969/.

20 Lady Gregory, *The Full Moon. A Comedy in One Act* (Dublin: Abbey Theatre, 1911).

21 Édouard Alexandre de Max (1869–1924), known as De Max on the Parisian stage in the 1890s, was a Romanian actor who frequently played opposite Sarah Bernhardt and was known for his roles in classic plays by Racine and others, including Oscar Wilde.

22 Praised by Oscar Wilde, Amy Judith Levy (1861–1889) was an Anglo-Jewish novelist, essayist, and poet who Yeats remembers from the time when both of them frequented the British Museum's Reading Room and would have encountered one another in London's literary circles of that era.

23 Notorious for her affair with Lord Byron, Lady Caroline Lamb (1785–1828) was also a Gothic novelist and Anglo-Irish aristocrat of the Ponsonby family.

24 See Christopher Dawson, *Progress and Religion: An Historical Enquiry* (London: Sheed and Ward, 1929), 91 for Gregory, 121–22 for Confucius, and 113 for the emperor's palace.

25 Yeats's acquaintance with Stephens's work predates this correspondence, of course. Selections for the *OBMV*, however, were not made from the titles that Yeats possessed and marked for such use in his library. See Wayne K. Chapman, *"Something that I read in a book": W. B. Yeats's Annotations in the National Library of Ireland*, 2 vols. (Clemson, SC: Clemson University Press, 2022), 1: 378; hereafter the volumes are cited as *YANLI* 1 (*Reading Notes*) and *YANLI* 2 (*Yeats Writings*).

26 And plausibly because the only letter from Ottoline Morrell in the National Library of Ireland's W. B. Yeats Collection is found among loose charts, mostly by George Yeats, in the Occult Papers (NLI 36,274/27), "Astrological and Tarot Material."

27 See Chapman, *YANLI* 1 and 2: xxv–xxvi.

28 See Chapman, "Yeats's White Vellum Notebook, 1930–1933," 50.

29 See the concluding section in Chapman, "Rapallo Notebook C," *IYS* 7.1: 263–65 (and 171–73, above).

30 Also see *W. B Yeats and T. Sturge Moore: Their Correspondence 1901–1937*, ed. Ursula Bridge (London: Routledge & Kegan Paul, 1953) 156; hereafter cited as *TSMC*.

31 In this letter to Olivia Shakespear, he hoped to take "a clear type script" of the "new edition" of *A Vision* ("the whole book") to Rapallo "to work at it here and there free at last" as well as begin to write a new version of the Robartes stories."

32 Although Clark believed that the date-line at the top of 3r was intended for "the whole diary, not specifically for the draft of 'I am of Ireland,'" the latter is the only poem in Rapallo Notebook D that Yeats wrote entirely in August 1929, eventually to become part of *Words for Music Perhaps and Other Poems* (1932), the others being of later dates—e.g., "Coole Park, 1929," written from August to mid-October 1929.

33 T. R. Henn, *The Lonely Tower: Studies in the Poetry of W. B. Yeats* (London: Methuen, 1965), 304. The old poem is "The Irish Dancer," which Henn (and Clark after him, in *WFMP* 519n) quotes from Seymour's anthology.

34 See R. F. Foster, *Life2*, 417–18.

35 Ibid. Foster outlines the custody case and press coverage of it in the *Independent* of March 30 and April 21, 1931, in *Life2* 736, note 76.

36 See Clark, Appendix III ("Notes on the Loose Manuscripts"), *WFMP* 615.

37 For example, in Rapallo C, the poems "Nineteenth Century," "Mrs. Phillamore," and especially "Love's Loneliness"; see Chapman, "Rapallo Notebook C," *IYS* 7.1: 238–40, 246, 252–54, 256, 258, and 260–61 (all to be found above on pp. 146–48, 154, 160–62, 164, 166, and 168–69.

38 K. P. S. Jochum, *W. B. Yeats: A Classified Bibliography of Criticism*, 2nd ed. (Urbana: University of Illinois Press, 1990) notes (on page 726) C. P. C[urran]'s review of *Fighting the Waves* in the *Irish Statesman* of August 17, 1929, 475–76. This review elicited a letter from "Stall" on August 24, 1929, *Irish Statesman*, 489–90.

39 It does not appear in the InteLex *Collected Letters* or *Uncollected Prose*, which contains most published letters.

40 Walter Old was an intimate of Helena Blavatsky's and lived with her in London in the late 1880s until her death, making it highly likely that Yeats knew him personally. Blavatsky gave oral expositions of *The Secret Doctrine* between January and June 1889: W. R. Old attended sessions 14, 16, 17, 19, 20, 21, 22, while—tantalizingly—"Mr. Yates" (almost certainly WBY) attended 9 and 15 (see *The Secret Doctrine Dialogues: H. P. Blavatsky's Talks with Students* [Los Angeles: Theosophy Company, 2013], appendices 3 and 4, and Grevel Lindop, "Yeats, Madame Blavatsky, and *The Secret Doctrine*" [*YA22*, forthcoming]). Old left the Theosophical Society acrimoniously and adapted his surname to Gorn or Gorn Old. As well as many magazine articles, he wrote over fifty-eight books, and the Yeatses' library contained four titles, though not the one WBY notes here. See Wayne K. Chapman, *The*

W. B. and George Yeats Library: A Short-title Catalog (Clemson, SC: Clemson University Press, 2019), items 1880–83 (*YL* 1866–69); hereafter cited as *WBGYL*.

41 Sepharial, *Hebrew Astrology: The Key to the Study of Prophecy* (London: Foulsham, [1929]). The chapter titles indicate some of the contents: Chaldean Astrology, Time and Its Measures, The Great Year, The Signs of the Zodiac, How to Set a Horoscope, The Seven Times, Modern Predictions. (The page numbers given here follow the original printing, available online at Hathi Trust, https://babel.hathitrust.org/cgi/pt?id=uc1.b3973615.)

42 See Daniel 2. Sepharial interprets "British as "of Hebrew origin and descent (*Brit*, a covenant) and (*Ish*, a man) from Abraham (*Ibrahim*)" (page 49) and makes "Dan, the pioneer tribe of British enterprise" (page 86).

43 January 27, 1918, in *YVP*1: *The Automatic Script: 5 November 1917–18 June 1918* (Iowa City: University of Iowa Press, 1992), ed. Steve L. Adams, Barbara J. Frieling, and Sandra L. Sprayberry, 296.

44 *Yeats's* Vision *Papers*, vol. 1, 296. Two thousand twenty-six years before 1918 would be 109 BCE, which would not allow for ten generations before Christ, so the unreliability of the date seems to be borne out. See Neil Mann, "Yeats and the Avatars of the New Age," https://www.yeatsvision.com/Yeats_Avatars_of_New_Age.pdf.

45 Alexander succeeded his father to the throne of Macedon in 336 BCE and in 334 crossed the Hellespont to Asia, where he loosed the Gordian Knot and inflicted the first defeats on the Persians. Sepharial actually refers to the defeat of Darius III and the conquest of Babylon, but avoids mentioning dates (333 and 332 BCE, respectively).

46 "My instructors spoke of ten generations from the start of the Great Year to Christ, & if I count 15 years for a generation that being the length according to Heraclitus one gets a date during the life time of Hipparcus [*sic*]," Rapallo Notebook A, NLI 13,578, 23r, page numbered 18. See Mann, "Rapallo Notebooks A and B," *IYS* 6.1: 89 (and 47, above).

47 Each sign of the zodiac is associated with or "ruled" by a particular planet, including moon and sun. The moon and sun are allotted to one sign each (Cancer and Leo), and the others taking two, one on either side of the central sun and moon, "in order of apparent speed" (10r)—Mercury the first two (Gemini and Virgo), Venus the second two (Taurus and Libra), and so on. WBY notes a weakness in the scheme, as Mercury and Venus "are quicker than" the sun, while countering "of course one can take those to left apparent speed & those to right order of distance from ☉ [sun] but did antiquity know this order & what significance could it have" (10r). See Figure 3.1, right-hand page.

48 The phases of *Will* and *Mask* are always fourteen numbers apart (as are those of *Creative Mind* and *Body of Fate*), 1–15, 2–16, 3–17, etc.; the equivalent months or signs of the zodiac would be always six apart.

49 The phases of *Will* and *Creative Mind* always sum to 30 (as do those of *Mask* and *Body of Fate*), 2+28, 3+27, 4+26, etc., with a special case at New Moon (where both are at Phase 1, but it is effectively 1+29); in terms of months or signs the sum would be 14.

50 In *A Vision*, Yeats uses the zodiac in different ways at different points, but in general the solar zodiac runs in the opposite direction to the lunar phases, and *Will*, passing forward through the phases, is passing backward through the zodiac, like the precessing equinoctial point, while *Creative Mind* passes backward through the phases but forward through the signs, in the order of the solar year. However, the point is not presented with any clarity in *A Vision* itself. See Neil Mann, *A Reader's Guide to Yeats's* A Vision (Clemson, SC: Clemson University Press, 2019), Figure 7.11(a), 132 (the paperback version corrects a misprint in diagram 7.11(b), "the passage of *Will* (**counter**clockwise)," 133).

51 Elsewhere Yeats is "told [...] to begin the year like the early Roman year in the lunar month corresponding to March, when days begin to grow longer than nights" (*AVB* 196, *CW14* 144), in other words, after the equinox.

52 A footnote in which Yeats writes of "the lambs of Faery bleating in November" (*AVB* 210n, *CW14* 154n) does not really clarify the matter. If we note that lambing in Ireland normally starts in February or March and Irish Faery is thought to correspond to Ireland itself, earthly November is set over against "lambing-time there" (*AVB* 210n, *CW14* 154n), that is, Faery's February or March. This appears to confirm the 11=2 equivalence.

53 *Encyclopaedia of Religion and Ethics*, ed. James Hastings, 13 vols. (Edinburgh: T. & T. Clark; New York: Charles Scribner's Sons, 1908–1926). See *WBGYL* 864, *YL* 855; Chapman's account of WBY's reading notes indicates quite extensive marking of the pages on "Ages of the World" (see *YANLI* 1: 208–9).

54 Rapallo D, NLI 13,581, 9r. On the mathematics of the heaped ages, see Mann, "Yeats and the Avatars of the New Age."

55 Hermann Jacobi, "Ages of the World (Indian)," in *Encyclopaedia of Religion and Ethics*, vol. 1: 200–202, at 200. This article also provides the details WBY notes on Buddhist and Jain systems, and WBY also refers to E. N. Adler's article on "Ages of the World (Jewish)."

56 Our essay makes occasional use of the full-text version of Lady Gregory's *Coole*, as "completed from the manuscript and edited by Colin Smythe" (Dolmen Editions X; Dublin: Dolmen Press, 1971), hereafter cited as *Coole*.

57 Parkinson's transcription is quoted by A. Norman Jeffares in *A New Commentary on the Poems of W. B. Yeats* (London: Macmillan, 1984), 284, and hence repeated in Jeffares's 6th edition of *Yeats's Poems* (Houndmills, Basingstoke: Palgrave), 598; hereafter cited as *YP*.

58 Yeats to George Yeats, July 26, [1929] (*YGYL* 226, *CL InteLex* 5265); see also further reference to the matter at Coole on Sept. 23, [1929] (*CL InteLex* 5287). The article in the *Independent* appeared on the same day as his first letter. To be clear, the "impetuous" Captain John Shawe-Taylor died in 1911 and is not to be confused with Frank Shawe-Taylor, also related to Lady Gregory and formerly High Sheriff of County Galway. As a land agent necessarily caught up in disputes involving landlords and tenants, the latter member of the Taylor family of Castle Taylor, Ardrahan, was locally gunned downed by IRA soldiers (on March 3, 1920) during the Irish War of Independence. On John Shawe-Taylor, painter and Land Conference organizer, Yeats wrote admiringly in an eponymous essay (*E&I* 343–45, *CW4* 248–49). Lady Gregory treats him as a reformer in her autobiography *Seventy Years*, ed. Colin Smythe (New York: Macmillan, 1974), 402, 429, and 462.

59 In chapters "The Drawing Room" and "The Breakfast Room," as Malins notes, "Lady Gregory not only lists the contents of a room but discusses their personal significance for her," the latter room standing for Gregory family background whereas the former was her particular space as "she wrote [there] her many plays, journals, articles and folk tales, sitting at the great Empire desk, or typed as Yeats dictated" (*Coole* 7).

60 In Stallworthy's book, Rapallo Notebook D is referred to as "Manuscript Book B," and he says that he entered numbers on thirty-eight pages of the notebook that pertain to "Coole Park, 1929." He acknowledges "I have numbered [these pages] 1–38, in their order of composition, although this is not the order in which they occur in the book" (*BTL* 180). These numbers appear in the upper left- or right-hand corners of pages, in pencil, starting with the "Prose sketch" on 13r; and these numbers appear on most of the poem's manuscript facsimiles in *WFMP* 104–68.

61 See *BTL* 183 and *WFMP* 110–11. We aver, with Clark, that Yeats offers and then decides to reject the first of these alternatives.

62 Quoted in *BTL* 185–86, where this line of speculation holds that Yeats might also have "had in mind Keats's remarks about 'The chameleon poet,' who loses all personal identity, so closely does he identify himself with his changing subject-matter" (186).

63 Observations of painters in Rapallo D include an observation (dated "Oct" 1929 on 29v) on the astonishing transformation of Jack B. Yeats's work into "an art of excitement." See below.

On the connection between Swift's celibacy and fear of madness, Yeats's theory is developed in some detail in his Introduction to *The Words upon the Window-Pane* (*VPl* 965–66). But the character John Corbet uses words in the play closely resembling those in Rapallo D, 17v: "In my essay for my Cambridge doctorate I examine all the explanations of Swift's celibacy offered by his biographers and prove that the explanation you selected was the only plausible one" (*VPl* 955: 510–13). The Cambridge essay was thus an imaginary one.

64 Wisdom in this change of direction is considered by Stallworthy, who writes: "Christ's words have, I believe, been taken from their context to provide a link between the idea of the swallows' 'miraculous consanguinity,' and the 'deep amities' existing between Lady Gregory's friends. But if God is at the centre of one circle, and Lady Gregory at the centre of the other, the equation becomes ridiculous. The catalogued paraphernalia of Christianity is as utterly foreign to a poem on Coole, as the introduction of Christ himself: and Yeats very wisely abandons the whole stanza" (*BTL* 191–92).

65 WBY to George Yeats, Sept. 23, 1929 (*CL InteLex* 5287). While at Coole and writing verse, he also cites "Swift's epitaph in verse & [...] going on with the correction of the account of system." See *YGYL* 209, where Saddlemyer dates this letter as from "Monday [16 Sept. 1929]." Yeats returned to Dublin on the 25th.

66 Wade evidently associates "crooked journey" in this discarded couplet with the end of the third stanza as published: "The intellectual sweetness of those lines / That cut through time or cross it withershins" (in *L* 769n).

67 Here we follow Stallworthy (*BTL* 193) while acknowledging the accidentals that tease Clark's transcription in the third line (*WFMP* 155).

68 *Catalogue of Paintings by Jack B. Yeats, Engineers' Hall, Dublin* (Dublin: Browne and Nolan, [n.d.]); Pamphlet volume A62 (2 p.; 8vo) at the National Library of Ireland.

69 Quoted in Hilary Pyle, *Jack B. Yeats: A Biography* (Savage, MD: Barnes and Noble, 1989), 124.

70 Clark's collation lists three other manuscripts at the NLI that also give this date; *WFMP* 169n.

71 Chapman, *YANLI* 2: 20.

72 Donald T. Torchiana, for instance, has remarked: "Of course there is poetic license here—where did the 'World-besotted traveller' come from? Yet in the presence of at least three drafts [in Rapallo Notebook D] and as many more published versions of the poem, we must recognize it for what it is: a distinctly Yeatsian poetic formulation of Swift on liberty"; from *W. B. Yeats and Georgian Ireland* (Evanston, IL: Northwestern University Press, 1966), 141. See also J. V. Luce, "A note on the composition of Swift's epitaph," *Hermathena* 104, Swift Number (Spring 1967): 78-81, https://www.jstor.org/stable/23040176.

73 Yeats's affection for Swift's writings, in particular *Gulliver's Travels*, is indicated by copies of the latter that he kept in his library, volumes edited by Harold Williams (1926) and John Hayward (1934). Yeats also owned Thomas Sheridan's seventeen-volume edition of *The Works of the Rev. Dr. Jonathan Swift, Dean of St. Patrick's, Dublin* (1784). See *WBGYL* 213, *YL* 206.

74 We use "aphorism"—slightly arbitrarily—for the six topics of the first, rougher draft, just to distinguish them more readily from the "propositions" of the second, more finished draft.

75 NLI 30,280. For a fuller account of the drafts and their interpretation, see Neil Mann, "Seven Propositions," https://www.yeatsvision.com/7Propositions.html, consulted December 2022. As that article states, "there are (at least) four versions of the Propositions: the first and second drafts in Rapallo Notebook D, the version sent to Frank Pearce Sturm (also given to Æ's Hermetic Society), [and] a typescript largely identical to the Rapallo Notebook's second draft" (https://www.yeatsvision.com/7Propositions.html).

76 Virginia Moore questioned George Yeats, who was "positive in word and tone" that they were dictated to her "in 1937, at Cannes." See *The Unicorn: W. B. Yeats' Search for Reality* (New York, NY: Macmillan, 1954), 470 n223.

77 Moore, *The Unicorn*, 378–83.

78 Richard Ellmann, *The Identity of Yeats* (London: Oxford University Press, 1954), 235–38.

79 Hazard Adams, *Blake and Yeats: The Contrary Vision* (Ithaca, NY: Cornell University Press, 1955), 287–89.

80 Moore, *The Unicorn*, 378.

81 Elizabeth Heine, "W. B. Yeats: Poet and Astrologer," *Culture and Cosmos* 2.1 (1998), 60–75. Heine emphasizes that these drafts are close to 1930 in date, referring to "Astrology and the Nature of Reality," but she actually cites the later version with the title "Seven Propositions" (this title does not appear in the notebook) at 64–66. See also Heine, "Yeats and Maud Gonne: Marriage and the Astrological Record, 1908–09," *YA13* (1999), 33n15.

82 R. Taylor, ed., *Frank Pearce Sturm: His Life, Letters, and Collected Work* (Urbana: University of Illinois Press, 1969), 100.

83 The "Kaballists" probably refer to members of the Hermes Lodge of the Stella Matutina in Bristol, which WBY visited between October 25 and 27, 1929 (see *CL InteLex* 5295 and 5298). Among WBY's many astrological interests, he was listed as Patron of the Irish Astrological Society (see *CL InteLex* 4334), which was founded by Cyril Fagan, though he turned down the presidency (*CL InteLex* 3857).

84 *The Irish Statesman*, 7 September 1929, 11–12; at https://www.yeatsvision.com/G553.html, accessed December 2022.

85 Indian thought has often been encapsulated in *sutras* (literally "threads" or "rules") to help students remember complex teachings. James Haughton Woods's translation of *The Yoga-System of Patañjali* (1914; Cambridge, MA: Harvard University Press, 1927) (*WBGYL* 1547, *YL* 1536) refers to "The Mnemonic Rules, called Yoga-Sûtras," which are accompanied by canonical comment and explanation.

86 *CW5* 175; *Aphorisms of Yôga by Bhagwān Shree Patanjali done into English from the original Samskrit with a commentary by Shree Purohit Swāmi and an introduction by W. B. Yeats* (London: Faber and Faber, 1938), 11.

87 *CW5* 177; *Aphorisms of Yôga*, 15. WBY also writes about "turning a symbol over in my mind" and drawing "myself up into the symbol," as a way of attempting to penetrate its meaning (*AVB* 301, *CW14* 219).

88 Mann, "Rapallo Notebooks A and B," *IYS* 6.1: 89 (and 47, above), quoting Rapallo A, NLI 13,578, 23r, page numbered 18.

89 Yeats always seems to have viewed the soul-bias of a person's phase as complementing the character shown by the horoscope, so writes of someone being "thwarted by his horoscope" (*AVA* 87, *CW13* 71; *AVB* 153, *CW14* 114), of "some eccentricity (not of phase but horoscope)" (*AVA* 108, *CW13* 88; *AVB* 175, *CW14* 130), and of Æ's intuition being manifested in a particular way "because of the character of his horoscope" (*AVA* 110, *CW13* 89; *AVB* 177, *CW14* 131). The symbolism of planets and zodiac is also used without much glossing or explanation when dealing with the end or opening of a religious dispensation (*AVB* 207–8, *CW14* 152–54).

90 Neil Mann, "'Everywhere that antinomy of the One and the Many': The Foundations of *A Vision*," in *W. B. Yeats's "A Vision": Explications and Contexts*, ed. Neil Mann, Matthew Gibson, and Claire Nally (Clemson, SC: Clemson University Digital Press, 2012), and "The Seven Propositions," https://www.yeatsvision.com/7Propositions.html, consulted February 2023.

91 Omitting cancelled material; the whole passage has a line through it but then "stet" three times down the margin. The end of this long draft on 34r is dated "March 1928." See Mann, "Rapallo Notebooks A and B," *IYS* 6.1: 119 (and 77, above), which quotes the latter part of this. Mann revises his reading of "[?presents]" to "persists."

92 More precisely: *Spirit* and *Creative Mind* (along with *Celestial Body* and *Body of Fate*) are *primary* and associated with thought, while their *antithetical* counterparts, *Passionate Body*

and *Mask*, are associated with emotion and *Husk* and *Will* with sensation, though with much overlap.

93 Heine, "W. B. Yeats: Poet and Astrologer," 64. This birth chart or horoscope is an objective map of the astronomical situation, albeit one that is expressed in archaic form and symbols and given human significance.

94 In terms of *A Vision*, "fate" is particularly expressed in physical life in the *Body of Fate* or in transcendent form in the *Celestial Body*, which is the divine ideas or forms. The *primary* incarnations should accept this fate and the *antithetical* engage in the vain struggle against it.

95 Yeats does not commit himself here to any calculus such as the Theosophists' *karma*, adopted from Hinduism, where past action creates debt or credit, though elsewhere he does use some of these terms. However, he sees the conditions determining the future life as deriving not from virtue or wrong-doing, but mainly from the afterlife or by living life to the full. The term *Beatific Vision* used here refers to the central stage of the afterlife, after the soul has re-experienced all its foregoing life as fully as possible, especially in the *Dreaming Back*: "The more complete the expiation, or the less the need for it, the more fortunate the succeeding life. The more fully a life is lived, the less the need for—or the more complete is—the expiation" (*AVB* 236, *CW14* 172; see also *AVB* 227, *CW14* 165; cf. *AVA* 227, *CW13* 187).

96 *AVB* 52, *CW14* 37. Cf. *Stories of Michael Robartes and His Friends* (Dundrum: Cuala Press, 1931), 21. The stories were finished in September 1930, see *YRAW* xxxi, 220–21, and 291.

97 With the cancellations removed, this is very close to the typescript version given by Moore, Ellmann, Adams, Heine, cited above (for a comparison of the two texts, see Mann, "Seven Propositions," https://www.yeatsvision.com/7Propositions.html, accessed March 2023).

98 Mann, "Seven Propositions" explains how the planets' position with respect to the zodiac effectively represent time, while their position within the framework of the horizon and zenith (the mundane houses) represents space, but notes that the attribution of emotion and intellect, respectively, does not reflect traditional astrology (https://www.yeatsvision.com/7Propositions.html, accessed March 2023).

99 See George Chapman, 3 vols., *The Works of George Chapman*, Vol. 2: *Poems and Minor Translations* (London: Chatto & Windus, 1875), 25 (stanza 24). Yeats had a 1904 printing of this volume (*WBGYL* 379, *YL* *370), and W. K. Chapman (*YANLI* 1: 109) shows that this poem is among the cut pages. Yeats was evidently reading George Chapman at this time, and the introduction drafted on the facing page singles him out from his Elizabethan contemporaries (cf. *CW6* 172).

100 George Chapman quoted the same Latin tag in his "Commentarius" on his translation of the *Iliad* (*Works*, vol. 3 [London: Chatto & Windus, 1885], Bk 14, n3, p. 176; not in the Yeatses' library). It comes from a Latin translation of Themistius's paraphrase of Aristotle's *De Anima* (Bk. 3, Ch. 21); see trans. Hermolaus Barbarus, *Themistii Peripatetici Lucidissimi Paraphrasis in Aristotelis* (Venice: Hieronymus Scotus, 1560), 196.

101 See Samuel Taylor Coleridge, *Biographia Literaria* (London: George Bell, 1876; *WBGYL* 412, *YL* 401), 121n and 139; W. K. Chapman's *YANLI* records no markings for these passages (1: 119–21).

102 The 1928 version contained twenty-seven poems and fifty copies were printed. Eleven of these poems appear in the second version of 1930, along with twenty-two more, and two hundred fifty copies were printed.

103 T. E. Lawrence, *The Revolt in the Desert* (London: Jonathan Cape, 1927) 261 and 265. The title is given as the "Revolt of the Desert" in the Cuala volume (*CW6* 172).

104 Yeats's selection is notorious for its bias, but, in terms of the number of poems, Gogarty, with seventeen, had more poems than any other poet.

105 The poem was published in 1916, at a time when Yeats was thinking of antiself more in the terms presented in *Per Amica Silentia Lunae* or "Ego Dominus Tuus" than those of *A Vision*.

106 The page proofs for *Wild Apples*, NLI MS 30,244, are given erroneously as 1938 in the NLI's Collection List A16.

107 G. H. Lewes, *The History of Philosophy from Thales to Comte*, 2 vols. (London: Longmans, Green & Co., 1867).

108 *The History of Philosophy*, 2: 518–19 and 2: 552.

109 Given the difficulty of WBY's handwriting, the entry almost certainly reads "ghosts" and each member of the club was referred to as a "ghost." The "Rules of the Ghost Club" stipulated "that the November Meeting shall take place on All Souls' Day, on whatever day of the week that may fall" (BL Add MS 52268, see https://blogs.bl.uk/untoldlives/2017/10/the-ghost-of-william-terriss.html, consulted February 2023). My thanks to Tara Stubbs for informing me that WBY was marked as "not present" for 1929's November meeting (Ghost Club Archives vol. XI, BL Add MS 52266, [132/81r–136/83r]); see Stubbs, "W. B. Yeats and the Ghost Club," in Tom Herron, ed., *Irish Writing London*, Vol. 1: *Revival to the Second World War* (London: Bloomsbury, 2013), 21–33.

110 Before her marriage, Lady Gorell's name was Elizabeth (Bessie) Radcliffe. She had been a medium using automatic writing and had worked with Yeats on a number of occasions. See George Mills Harper and John S. Kelly's introduction to and editing of Yeats's unpublished "Preliminary Examination of the Script of E[lizabeth] R[adcliffe]," in ed. G. M. Harper, *Yeats and the Occult* (Toronto: Macmillan, 1975), 130–71. See also WBY's letter to her of October 19, 1929, offering to return some automatic writing when he came to London (*CL InteLex* 5294).

111 GY joined her husband in London on November 4. Ann Saddlemyer gives details of the emergency in *Becoming George: The Life of Mrs. W. B. Yeats* (Oxford: Oxford University Press, 2002), 421; hereafter, this biography is cited as *BG*.

112 Clark's treatment of this point is made in his chapter "After 'Silence', the 'Supreme Theme': Eight Lines of Yeats," in *YSC* 68–69. Critiquing Parkinson's interpretation of the drafts in Rapallo D seems the focus of Clark's illustrated narrative, particularly in part III, pages 77–89; see also Ronald Schuchard, "Yeats and Olivia Revisited: A Pathway to *The Winding Stair and Other Poems*," *South Atlantic Review* 77, no. 1–2 (2014): 122.

113 For details on the delayed departure and the health emergency Mrs. Yeats attended to when she joined her husband in London (on November 4, 1929), see *BG* 421. After recording in his engagements calendar the hemorrhaging episode of afternoon November 3, Yeats struck off the scheduled events of November 4 by drawing a diagonal line through them and annotating simply: "Could not go" (37r).

114 *Stories of Michael Robartes and his Friends* (Cuala Press, 1931), 10; writing completed in September 1930. Rpt. in *AVB* 41, *CW14* 41; see *YRAW* xxxi, 220–21, and 291.

115 See also *YSC* 77–89 for detailed analysis of those intermediate stages of drafting, all or most of which would have occurred in Rapallo, depending on whether transforming the prose "Subject" into verse had been entirely or in some part delayed by Yeats in London. It is also logical that space had been left beneath the final draft in late November to have been filled with the biographical note four months later.

116 Quoted by Clark (*YSC* 11), who adds: "The Day of Judgment figures in [Shakespeare's] sonnet—love 'bears it out even to the edge of doom'—but has not yet entered Yeats's poem" (11–12).

117 The concept of the fourth state of *Turiya* was more fully explored in the introductions to *The Holy Mountain* and to *The Mandukya Upanishad* (*CW5* 139–64, *E&I* 448–85).

118 Giovanni Gentile, trans. H. Wildon Carr, *The Theory of Mind as Pure Act* (London: Macmillan, 1922; *WBGYL* 749, *YL* 742), 126, starting at "Kant said that space is a form of external sense [...]" and ending at "[...] not in space but in time," as quoted in *A Vision*. This passage is marked in the Yeatses' copy, as described in Chapman, *YANLI 1*: 186; however, given WBY's

comment here, it seems probable that in this case the marginal "▽△" are not "the symbols for water and fire," but the gyres of time and space as shown on *AVB* 71, *CW14* 52.

119 Part of the penultimate line has been cancelled but then restored by the proofreader's convention of dashes under the restored text. Two crucial words are hard to decipher, but what looks more or less like "exceustable" is probably "exhaustively" and, going from the printed version, the penultimate word of the passage is probably a form of "spatializing," though the final letters are a simple gesture.

120 See Mann, "Rapallo Notebooks A and B," *IYS* 6.1, esp. 78, 124 (found at 36 and 82, above).

121 NLI 30,354, 1930 diary, final page, entry for "Nov. 16."

122 See Chapman, *WBGYL* items 237 (*YL* 230) and 2290 (*YL* 2274) (on pages 26 and 236).

123 See Chapman, "Rapallo Notebook C," *IYS* 7.1: 257–58 (and 165–66, above). See also the automatic script for November 4 and November 16, 1919, where "the myth of Berenice" symbolizes a critical moment in a woman's life, and "Berenice's hair" was said to signify "desire & sacrifice," summarized in the Card File (C57), *Yeats's* Vision *Papers*, 3: 269. Berenice and Veronica are versions of the same name.

124 As the notebooks appear to have had one hundred leaves initially, the fifty-three leaves of Rapallo D that remain indicate that forty-seven pages were removed in total; given the three missing leaves at 8, 9, and 33, this would point to forty-four other leaves missing, possibly all in this gap. In the documentation in preparation for their Yeats exhibition, which includes images of this notebook, the National Library of Ireland (using page numbering rather than leaves) numbered the last page before the gap 82 and the first page after it 171, indicating a gap of forty-four leaves. However, we follow the numbering used by David R. Clark in *WFMP* to facilitate cross-references with that volume and its reproductions.

125 Rapallo E must have had a significant cut, as its front cover lists contents that are no longer part of the notebook. If one discounts four pages that were loose until the rebinding, and possibly from another source, then Rapallo E has only fifty-nine leaves, but that is still more than Rapallo D's fifty-three leaves.

126 See Mann, "Rapallo Notebooks A and B," 132–33.

127 *Hamlet*, III: 2, line 242, ed. W. J. Craig, *Shakespeare: Complete Works* (London: Oxford University Press, 1943; cf. *WBGYL* 1889, *YL* 1875), 889.

128 For his closest friends, Yeats used humor to dispel worry over his vital signs. His physical state was seriously affected as shown in snapshots taken of him in bed, gaunt-cheeked, and at a cafe with Ezra Pound, in which "I do not recognise myself at all" (WBY to Lady Gregory, March 19, 1930; *CL InteLex* 5337). See also his letter to Sturge Moore (April 7, 1930; *CL InteLex* 5341). Attention paid to this bearded self is particularly self-effacing in light of Edmund Dulac's now-famous portrait of Yeats as bearded Giraldus—a woodcut figure employed as a frontispiece in *AVA* (*CW13* [l]) and, thereafter, moved as an illustrative device to face page 24 in *Stories of Michael Robartes* (where resemblance to Yeats is noted by a character named Duddon) and then relocated to another prominent place in *AVB* 39 (*CW14* 28).

129 We follow Stallworthy and Curtis Bradford in reading "offering their backs" after the word "harbour" (*BTL* 115). Like them, we conjecture that Yeats omitted the word "dolphins" entirely. Clark must have been aware of this reading, but he takes the first word after "harbour" as "[?dolphins]" (with some effort, the shape could be construed as "dlfins"), and his reading of "there beckon" is certainly possible from the contours of the words that we take as "their backs." *WFMP* does not give a photograph of these pages.

130 See also WBY to Lady Gregory, June 27, 1930 (*CL InteLex* 5354).

131 For a charming account of the poet's domestic life in Rapallo, attention to the children, and underwater swimming escapades in May–June 1930, see Saddlemyer, *BG* 427–28.

132 Curtis Bradford, "Yeats's Byzantium Poems: A Study of Their Development," *PMLA* 75, no. 1 (March 1960): 110–25. Apparently only because of its length, Bradford's work was left out of *William Butler Yeats: The Byzantium Poems*, ed. Richard J. Finneran, Merrill Literary Casebook Series (Columbus, OH: Charles E. Merrill Publishing, 1970).

133 In the diary of 1930 (NLI 30,354), the phrase "A walking mummy" is followed by some six lines that are cancelled with almost vertical strokes; as noted by Clark, the lines from "flames" to "paradise" in our transcription are on the opposite recto and "clued in after 'mummy'" (*WFMP* 3n). (Both Bradford and Stallworthy give a misleading description of how these lines supersede the rejected ones: Bradford says that "Yeats cancelled the passage [...] and wrote over it" [111], and Stallworthy follows him in saying that Yeats "wrote over the cancelled lines" [115].) Clark transcribes these cancelled lines as: "A spiritual refinement and perfection amid a rigid world. A sigh of wind—autumn leaves in the streets. The divine life born amidst [?natural/?natures] decay" (*WFMP* 3; these are very similar to *BTL* 115 and Bradford 111, though unaccountably, both Stallworthy and Bradford omit the word "life" that is clearly written between "divine" and "born," and they choose "natural" without qualification).

134 In a postscript, Yeats added: "I wrote this poem last spring: the first thing I wrote after my illness," meaning that it was only the first poem that he had started and finished after his illness, and perhaps nearly up to that date. Yeats asked Moore to design a cover for a collection of poems to be called *Byzantium* as well as for *The Winding Stair*, which was the title they settled on. Moore's design for the latter is introduced by Bridge as an illustration on page 179 of her edition. See Schuchard, "Yeats and Olivia Revisited," 124–32, for a complexly nuanced discussion of the poem and Moore's competing cover designs, both of which are reproduced on pages 128 and 130 (as Figures 3 and 4) and both depicting "birds" and "dolphins" as agents of the soul's transport. These symbols are integrated metaphorically, in Schuchard's essay (at page 125), with the mummy from "All Souls' Night."

135 Stallworthy reports the rhyme scheme incorrectly as "AABBCDDCC" (*BTL* 116) and refers to the manuscript by consecutive pages (from left to right), hence departing from his own procedure, whereby "Coole Park, 1929" is delineated by page numbers that he had inscribed in Rapallo D in the order of composition.

136 See Stallworthy, *BTL* 121–22, where the echo of Blake directs us to "The Tyger," lines 13–14 in Yeats's edition of *The Poems of William Blake* (London: Lawrence and Bullen, 1893; *WBGYL* 216, *YL* 209): "What the hammer? what the chain? / In what furnace was thy brain?"

137 See *AVA* 190–92 (*CW13* 158–61) and *AVB* 279–81 (*CW14* 203–5); also, for Condition of Fire, *Myth* 361–64 (*CW5* 28–30).

138 Lady Gregory, *Visions and Beliefs in the West of Ireland* (1920; rpt. Gerrards Cross, UK: Colin Smythe, 1970); Yeats's summary of the Noh play occurs on page 333–34 (or *CW5* 69–70).

139 Stallworthy's New Critical tendencies seem at odds sometimes with his practice, when he writes a bit too deductively about pretextual evidence. His commentary in this instance seems a little wishful.

140 In this case, Stallworthy's transcription (in *BTL* 124) is more accurate than Clark's, which is given in a note without facsimile in *WFMP* 13.

141 Clark's presentation contains within it a dogleg of its own in layout, owing to practical limits on space. Requiring two pages (21 and 23) instead of one to transcribe 90r, the facsimile is also paired twice (on pages 20 and 22) with half-page transcriptions. Facsimile and transcription of 89v appear *before* both sets with footnotes to acknowledge misplacement "for convenience" and to direct readers to transcriptions two and four pages later. Similarly, at page 25, Clark notes that, for the lower half of 91r, the image on page 24 and transcription

on 25 were "Added later, after completion of NLI 13,581, 91v" (presented on pages 28 and 29). Hence, to follow the convolutions of Yeats's writing process, one is required to compare multiple openings in *WFMP*—a challenging but necessary mental exercise due to the landscape of the notebook itself.

142 See Bradford 122–23; this fair copy of "Byzantium" was photographed in the 1940s for Harvard's microfilm collection; but sometime after Bradford's essay of 1960, the staff of the National Library of Ireland removed these paperclipped sheets from Rapallo Notebook D and gave it the file designation NLI 13,590 (17), 1r, 2r, and 2v. Rust stains from a paperclip are still discernible in the reproductions of the manuscript's recto pages to match Clark's transcriptions (see *WFMP* 30–33). Clark points out in a footnote that "preliminary attempts at ll. 1–3" of stanza IV (mislabeled "V" by Yeats and entirely cancelled) appear on the verso of sheet 2, confirming Bradford's description with a more detailed one. Clark's footnote elsewhere (*WFMP* 29n) is misplaced and belongs on page 31 as it describes physical characteristics of paper, ink, and numbering on sheet 1r: "The draft is in light gray-blue ink on paper 7. The circled '10', top right, is in pencil." "Paper 7" is one of twenty types that Clark coalesces in his Census of Manuscripts as "Paper type A" (xv).

143 Writing was also "about to start on the Swift play."

144 The letter to GY reports on the occasion of the new poem and quotes its last stanza; see also his letter to Miss Byron, September 17, 1930 (*CL InteLex* 5384), in which he quotes the entire poem. An account of its writing in Rapallo E will be made in the final essay planned for this series.

145 The first poem seems not to have been "For Anne Gregory" because Yeats had read that poem to Lady Gregory (as he reported to his wife the day before) "six times in the course of the evening" (see *YGYL* 224; *CL InteLex* 5382, above). The other lyric, intended for "poems for music," might well have been renewed work on "Crazy Jane on the Day of Judgment" (broken off in November 1929 at leaf 39v in Rapallo D).

146 See also *TSMC* 163–66 (*CL InteLex* 5388 and 5393). Both sides of the correspondence are recommended, with the addition of Yeats's letter to his wife (of "Sept 27 [1930]") to explain the situation and ask her opinion on the title change: "Shall I change it & call my book [...] 'Byzantium'[?] In that case I can send Sturge Moore the new Byzantium poem (I have it here) which will give him a mass of symbols. 'Byzantium' would follow up my old 'Sailing to Byzantium' which people liked" (*CL InteLex* 5389). See also note 134, above.

147 See Ulick O'Connor, *Oliver St. John Gogarty: A Poet and His Times* (London: Cape, 1964), 147–49, 199, 256, 268–70.

148 "Celebrating Gogarty's Renvyle House 1983," RTE Archives, consulted Feb. 2023, https://www.rte.ie/archives/2018/0816/985474-oliver-st-john-gogarty-weekend/. John painted two portraits, one now held by Glasgow Art Galleries and the other in private hands.

149 See Gogarty to WBY, June 17, 1930, R. J. Finneran, G. M. Harper, W. M. Murphy, eds., *Letters to W. B. Yeats*, 2 vols. (New York: Columbia University Press, 1977), 2: 510); see also Michael Holroyd, *Augustus John: The New Biography* (New York: Farrar, Straus and Giroux, 1996), 509–10.

150 Wyndham Lewis, *Satire and Fiction: Enemy Pamphlets No. 1* (London: Arthur Press, 1930), 29. This defense was initially provoked by *The New Statesman*'s rejection of Roy Campbell's overly positive review.

151 This particular stanza has close parallels in *The Wild Swans at Coole* (1919). See "Two Songs of a Fool" I (three stanzas written in summer 1918), "Under the Round Tower" (five tetrameter stanzas written in March 1918), and "The Scholars" (two stanzas written in April 1915, revised in 1924, and then rewritten in 1929, to no avail, in Rapallo C; see Chapman, "Rapallo Notebook C," *IYS* 7.1: 251–52 (also 159–60, above).

152 R. F. Foster, *Life2*, 257. The effects of George Yeats's illness were those of pleurisy, recurrent arthritis, and a prior case of scarlet fever resulting in jaundice in 1923 (712n9). Foster allows that Yeats's respite at Coole "could indicate thoughtfulness, or the opposite" (257). His stay was certainly a protracted one, to judge by his letters to her from early April to mid-May (*YGYL* 120–26). Latently, echoes of "The Crazed Moon" occur in "Supernatural Songs" VI ("He and She"; *VP* 559), where "the scared moon" "sidles up," "trips," and "sings" in a version of the new poem that Yeats sent to Olivia Shakespear in a letter on August 25, 1934 (*L* 827–29; *CL InteLex* 6087), where "crazed" appears instead of "scared." In context, "He and She," which Yeats called "a passionate metaphysical sort" of poem about the soul, relates to a thought about his wife and children: "When George spoke of Michael's preoccupation with Life and Anne's with death she may have sub-consciously remembered that her spirits once spoke of the central moment of phase 1 as the Kiss of Life and the central moment of phase 15 (full moon) as the Kiss of Death" (ibid.).

153 Grenville A. J. Cole (1859–1924; geologist, scholar, and sometime poet) was acquainted with Yeats in several respects: as contributors to *The Irish Review*, as honorees invested in the same term at Queens University, Belfast (1922; Cole receiving the DSc and Yeats the DLitt), and perhaps in some government capacity as Director of the Geological Survey of Ireland (from 1905) and President of the Irish Geographical Association (from 1921). Cole was keen to illustrate his books and embraced the cultural and historical significance of Irish places in his works. Yeats and his brother, Jack, owned copies of Cole's *Description of the Raised Map of Ireland* (Dublin, 1909). After Yeats gave Cole the permission he asked to publish whatever piece of Yeats's unpublished work they discussed in 1923, Cole's death, unfortunately, cut short any such intention. Consequently, Cole's last book, *Handbook of the Geology of Ireland* (London: T. Murby, 1924; printed May 30, 1925), was delayed and issued posthumously without any reference to Yeats.

154 *Wheels and Butterflies* (London: Macmillan, 1934), 148 ff.; cf. *VPl* 797.

155 Andrew Parkin, ed., *"At the Hawk's Well" and "The Cat and the Moon": Manuscript Materials* (Ithaca, NY: Cornell University Press, 2010), lii. For Renvyle, see above, "[90v] ["Open letter to Lewis," July 1930]."

156 It premiered at the Abbey Theatre on September 21, 1931, and ran for a week; see https://www.abbeytheatre.ie/archives/production_detail/1458/ (consulted May 2023).

157 The Cornell volume's chronology jumps from 1924 to 1931 (lix) as does the MS documentation, 238ff. It is marginally possible, given Yeats's stay at Renvyle in July 1930, that the draft on "hotel notepaper" could actually date from 1930. However, even though certain elements seem less developed, it probably postdates the Rapallo D draft.

158 Here, and in subsequent entries, Yeats appears to indicate the lines from the poem "The Cat and the Moon" that the Musician should sing. The poem centers on the Gonnes' cat Minnaloushe, whose eyes mimic the moon's phases (*VP* 378–79), and its last twelve lines, starting "Minnaloushe creeps through the grass," accompany the final action of the revised play (see *VP* 804).

159 For instance, "The Lesser Ritual of the Pentagram," described in Israel Regardie, *The Golden Dawn: An Account of Teachings, Rites and Ceremonies*, vol. 1 (Chicago: Aries Press, 1937), 106–7.

160 NLI MS 21,500b, 1r. See Parkin, *"At the Hawk's Well" and "The Cat and the Moon": Manuscript Materials*, 242–43.

161 NLI 21,500a, 14r. See Parkin, *"At the Hawk's Well" and "The Cat and the Moon": Manuscript Materials*, 238–39.

162 For these letters, see Alan Himber, ed., with the assistance of George Mills Harper, *The Letters of John Quinn to William Butler Yeats* (Ann Arbor: UMI Research Press, 1983).

163 Himber notes that the "feature article appeared in *The New York Times Magazine* of 13 August 1916: 'Roger Casement Martyr: Some Notes for a Chapter of History by a Friend Whose Guest He Was When the War Broke Out'" (*The Letters of John Quinn to William Butler Yeats*, 194n15).

164 Some years later, writing to William J. Maloney about a draft chapter of *The Forged Casement Diaries* (Dublin: Talbot Press, 1936), Yeats noted that "Quinn told me that he threatened to open up the question of the Parnell forgeries, and accused the government agent of a similar forgery in the present case. I think that if you were to state this it would give your narrative more force. Quinn would have had a very powerful case" (January 19, 1933, *CL InteLex* 5808).

165 Cf. typescript, University of Delaware Library, Special Collections, "Lennox Robinson papers related to John Quinn," MSS 0212, Box 2, F26.

166 Letter to Cornelius Sullivan, her lawyer, cited in University of Delaware Library, Special Collections, "Lennox Robinson papers related to John Quinn," Finding Aid, "Scope and Content Note," written by the Special Collections staff: https://library.udel.edu/special/findaids/view?docId=ead/mss0212.xml;tab=print (consulted March 2023).

167 University of Delaware Library, "Lennox Robinson papers related to John Quinn," Finding Aid, "Scope and Content Note."

168 Daniel J. Murphy, ed., *Lady Gregory's Journals*, 2 vols. (Gerards Cross: Colin Smythe; New York: Oxford University Press, 1978–87), 2: 546.

169 *Lady Gregory's Journals*, 2: 553–55. There is no evidence that she was concerned that intimations of her affair with Quinn from 1911–12 might emerge. Constant Huntington, director of Putnam's publishing house and designated to oversee her biographical writings, agreed that she would weaken her memoir if important letters were published elsewhere (2: 554–55). Because of uncertainties over her will, however, her autobiography, *Seventy Years*, did not appear until 1974 (see note 58), and Lennox Robinson was the first editor of a selection from *Lady Gregory's Journals 1916–1930*, published by Putnam's in 1946 (with only one mention of John Quinn). See "Lady Gregory's codicil to will: Augusta Gregory (1852–1932), Codicil to Will, ribbon copy, March 1, 1930," New York Public Library, https://www.nypl.org/events/exhibitions/galleries/section-8-blessed-bridget-ocoole/item/2974 (accessed March 2023).

170 Clark allows, but doubts, that some part of the poem might have been drafted in the excised, now lost pages of 42r–83v, because the "number of manuscript pages we have for this poem and the rate of progress in writing the poem accord well with other examples in 'Words for Music Perhaps'" (*YSC* 13). He also allows ambiguity of dating in *YSC*, noting only that "Both Draft 1 and Draft 6 are dated October" (ibid.) but corrects the error in *WFMP* 361n: "The date after [the last line on lead 97r] is in October of 1930. The date of NLI 13,581, 39r, the synopsis with which Yeats began, was 29 October 1929. A year passed before Yeats had finished this poem."

171 See Chapman, "Rapallo Notebook C," *IYS* 7.1: 238–42 (also 146–50, above).

172 Clark notes (in *WFMP* 296n) a "prose germ" or seedling of "The Results of Thought" in the White Vellum Notebook (MBY 545), as well as a shorter one for "Remorse for Intemperate Speech" (quoted in *WFMP* 312n). The poems were written in August 1931 and appear in close proximity to one another. See Chapman, "Yeats's White Vellum Notebook, 1930–1933," 53.

173 See *Yeats's* Vision *Papers*, vol. 3, 348; see also *YRAW* 119–20.

174 For transcription of the draft in Erdmann, including Yeats's annotations in the text, see Chapman, *YANLI* 1: xlvii–xlix and 170–71. For a more detailed discussion of the occasion and the writing, see Wayne K. Chapman, Woolf, Yeats, and the Making of 'Spilt Milk,'" in

Contradictory Woolf, ed. Derek Ryan and Stella Bolaki (Clemson, SC: Clemson University Press, 2012), 265–70.

175 Chapman, *YANLI* 1: 171.

176 NLI 30,354, 1930 diary, final page, entry for "Nov. 16."

177 It could possibly read "Checque to N. T. S." My thanks to Margaret Mills Harper for indicating that the figure is "185" rather than "155." WBY's open 8's can look like 5's (see, for example, the date in Figure 3.8), but the two figures are written differently.

178 The Abbey Theatre archives cite Perrin as "Secretary, National Theatre Society Limited during: 1925? –1930? Business Manager during: 1925–1929" (https://www.abbeytheatre.ie/archives/person_detail/13184/), consulted April 2023. However, the Minute Books, held at NUI Galway, refer to him as Secretary at a meeting on April 15, 1924 (https://digital.library.universityofgalway.ie/p/ms/asset/2111), page 36, consulted April 2023. He appears to have left under a cloud, as the meeting on May 25, 1934, recorded that "The unsatisfactory conduction of the business of the office was considered and it was decided to dispense with the services of the Secretary Mr J. H. Perrin. In view of his long service with the company it was agreed to give him one month's notice and a bonus of six month's salary such notice to be given on June 1st and that if he preferred to leave immediately his request should be granted" (https://digital.library.universityofgalway.ie/p/ms/asset/3603), page 26, consulted April 2023.

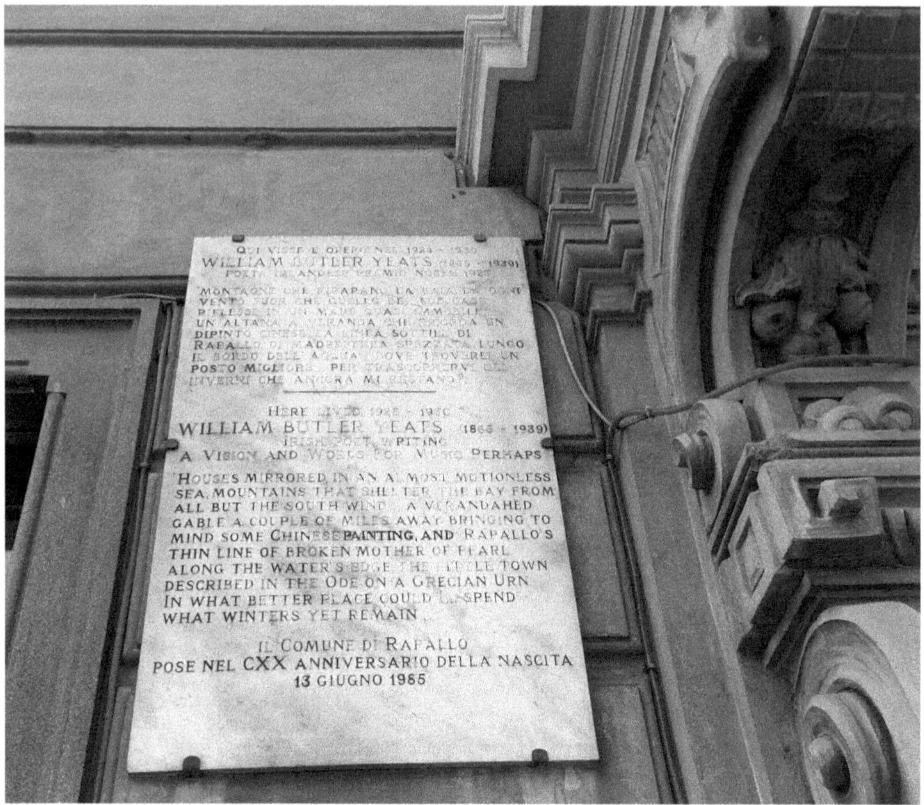

Figure 3.9. A marble plaque in Rapallo commemorates Yeats's residence, at Corso Christoforo Colombo 34 (formerly Via della Americhe 12). Transcription of lower half:

HERE LIVED, 1928–1930
WILLIAM BUTLER YEATS (1865 – 1939)
IRISH POET, WRITING
A VISION AND WORDS FOR MUSIC PERHAPS

'HOUSES MIRRORED IN AN ALMOST MOTIONLESS
SEA, MOUNTAINS THAT SHELTER THE BAY FROM
ALL BUT THE SOUTH WIND...A VERANDAHED
GABLE A COUPLE OF MILES AWAY BRINGING TO
MIND SOME CHINESE PAINTING, AND RAPALLO'S
THIN LINE OF BROKEN MOTHER OF PEARL
ALONG THE WATER'S EDGE, THE LITTLE TOWN
DESCRIBED IN THE ODE ON A GRECIAN URN.
IN WHAT BETTER PLACE COULD I...SPEND
WHAT WINTERS YET REMAIN[?']

IL COMUNE DI RAPALLO
POSE NEL CXX ANNIVERSARIO DELLA NASCITA
13 GUIGNO 1985 [13 June 1985, Yeats's 120th birthday]

The quotation is derived from "Rapallo" I, *A Packet for Ezra Pound* (Cuala, 1929), [1]; cf. *AVB* 3, *CW14* 3. Photograph courtesy of Warwick Gould, taken during a visit in 2019.

Rapallo Notebook E: Supernatural Drama, New and Revisited

Neil Mann and Wayne K. Chapman

Introduction

Coming to Rapallo E as the last volume of the Rapallo Notebooks is both a false ending to a group assembled largely by happenstance and the natural conclusion to a quintet of workbooks with much in common that others do not share. Although the full manuscript draft of *Stories of Michael Robartes and his Friends* was written in a notebook identical to Rapallo Notebooks C and D, it contains only that one work, with all but clean pages removed; and, while the *Stories* are evidently related to the new edition of *A Vision*, they were probably not originally intended for inclusion in *A Vision* itself, nor does the notebook contain drafts of exposition, which constitute one of the linking threads in the five Rapallo Notebooks.[1] Conversely, the White Vellum Notebook has much in common with the Rapallo Notebooks, including their slightly random inclusiveness and the way it overlaps with them in time and certain materials—for instance, a draft of *The Resurrection* that precedes the one in Rapallo E—but its larger format, higher page count, and better quality of paper and binding set it apart as different.[2] The Diary of 1930—"Begun in April, 1930, at Rapallo or rather near it"—was also written alongside much of the material of Rapallo D and E, in particular, and one of its later entries is continued in Rapallo A, but it is distinct in its binding, smaller format, and generally single-minded focus.[3] The *Supernatural Songs* Notebook of 1934 is sometimes referred to as a "Rapallo notebook," but it is separated from the others both in format and in time.[4]

None of these qualifications applies to Rapallo E. Like Notebooks A, B, and C, it continues the struggle to formulate the introductory material for the revised edition of *A Vision*, although, as with C, much of that content has been torn out. It has the same design on the covers as Notebooks A and B, and indeed, like Notebook A, the cover is marked with a letter (see below). With material from 1931, Rapallo E is the last of the notebooks to be finished, except, probably, for the "recent incident" added to Rapallo D in April 1931.[5] It is, however, unique too, as the only notebook containing extended dramatic work, with drafts of two plays in its pages (one initial and one close-to-final version), of which more will be said in later sections of this essay.

Rapallo E has also been distinct for us as researchers because, more than with any of the other notebooks in this series, studying it in detail has thrown up unexpected aspects that entail significant re-evaluations. The major one here concerns the pages that were inserted into the notebook with the cancelled title "The Ressurection" (sic): we started from the assumption adopted by earlier studies that this was a preliminary scenario for the play *The Resurrection*, with the difference in material explained by a complete rethink on Yeats's part in subsequent drafts. But we are now convinced that the outline on the inserted leaves has little or no relation to that play, although the coincidence of titles was no doubt the reason why the pages were lodged here along with a late draft of the play. This entails a major redating of the draft these leaves contain.

Less important, but also involving a reassessment on our part, was that our preliminary study had given an exaggerated sense of the amount of the material that has been removed from the notebook. True, everything listed on the book's cover is in fact missing, but that material was evidently a further redrafting of introductory sections for the revised version of *A Vision*, and actually no more extensive than the quantity of similar material missing from Rapallo C. The excised material had made us conjecture an early starting date compared with similar drafts in Rapallo A and B, which seemed supported by the dating of a fragment of autobiographical prose on the loose pages. Rethinking the status of the missing *Vision* material led us to revise our opinion about when the notebook was started to a slightly later date, and looking at a fragment about walking to the harbor at Cannes led to a reconsideration of how the framing of the sentence could alter the implications of the verb tense being used and, therefore, the likely date of composition.

Other new sidelights that are shed on, or from, the manuscript include a probable source for a particular "spirit photograph" of Yeats that has been reproduced several times, as well as a re-evaluation of the sources of and inspiration for *The Words upon the Window-Pane*.

In addition to insights into the manuscript itself, there has been the realization that there were more extant microfilms of Yeats manuscripts than were generally known. With help, we chased down these elusive films, including photographs of not just Rapallo E but also the White Vellum Notebook, specifically copies made for David R. Clark and used in the production of the Cornell manuscripts series. These comparatively clean images of Rapallo E were used in *"The Resurrection": Manuscript Materials*, edited by Selina Guinness and Jared Curtis,[6] the latter of whom was particularly generous in assisting us in our search, as were Katherine Reagan and Grace Bichler at Cornell University Libraries, the current repository of Clark's films.

In this closing chapter of our project, we would also like to reiterate our gratitude to Catherine E. Paul for sharing with us her recent photographs of the manuscripts and allowing their use to illustrate the articles in this series, as well as thanks to Jack Quin for checking the physical descriptions of the notebooks for us when Covid restrictions made our traveling to the National Library in Dublin impossible. Finally, we are also grateful to Lauren Arrington for initiating the project and including us in it, and to Meg Harper and Warwick Gould for their support and input at various points.

CONTENTS: OVERVIEW

As noted already, what distinguishes Rapallo E (NLI 13,582) from the other notebooks is its dramatic content, as it includes the first drafts of one of Yeats's most successful plays, *The Words upon the Window-Pane*, and the last handwritten draft of *The Resurrection*. A preliminary scenario on the topic of Christ's death has also been inserted. In addition to *The Resurrection*'s opening and closing lyrics, the notebook contains the poem "For Anne Gregory" but otherwise lacks the poetic richness of Notebooks C and D. In common with all the other Rapallo Notebooks, it also contains substantial drafts for the revised edition of *A Vision*, as well as Yeats's notes on his reading and miscellaneous records—including a page on consultations with London clairvoyants.

Curtis Bradford treated both plays extensively in *Yeats at Work* (1965),[7] transcribing large portions of the notebook, though in a text that was smoothed with regard to spelling and gaps, and without reference to cancellations. Since then, both plays have, of course, featured in the Cornell Manuscripts Materials series: *The Words upon the Window Pane* in 2002, edited by Mary FitzGerald,[8] and *The Resurrection* in 2011, edited by Jared Curtis and Selina Guinness. The songs from *The Resurrection* are also printed in the Cornell series volume dedicated to *The Tower* (2007), edited by Richard J. Finneran with Jared Curtis and Ann Saddlemyer.[9] The other poem in the book, "For Anne Gregory," appears with many lyrics from Rapallo Notebooks C and D in *Words for Music Perhaps*, edited by David R. Clark. The book's opening notes on Leo Frobenius's *The Voice of Africa* constitute an appendix in *Yeats, Philosophy, and the Occult*, transcribed and commented on by Matthew Gibson. As with the other Rapallo Notebooks, the material that has not been transcribed or commented on to any significant extent elsewhere comprises drafts for *A Vision B* and extraneous notes.

A number of factors make Rapallo E interesting in terms of its physical structure and make-up. The main ones are a swath of pages removed from the beginning of the notebook and a group of four leaves—almost certainly from another book—that have been inserted. The nature and style of the removals mean that the notebook's original form is easy to reconstruct, though not necessarily apparent to a person examining the rebound notebook today, so that caution is important in order to avoid a false impression.

Dating

External evidence makes it relatively straightforward to date the major drafts contained in Rapallo Notebook E, even though the only date in the notebook proper lacks a year. (There are also two dates on the four loose leaves, but we shall return to that matter shortly.)

Although Curtis Bradford dates the drafts he examines to 1930 and 1930–31, he does not give the notebook itself any date. In the Cornell series, David Clark states that Notebook E contains "entries from about 9 May [1928] to about January 1929," a span endorsed in the introductions by Mary FitzGerald and Richard Finneran, Jared Curtis, and Ann Saddlemyer.[10] We agree that the notebook could well have been started in 1928, but would amend the anchor date given to "9 May [1929]" and assume that, when Clark and the other editors give January 1929 as the last date, they are referring solely to the entries that are actually dated, since, as indicated by Bradford's dating and external evidence, major drafts are clearly from 1930 and 1931.

To complicate matters, four loose pages (two folded bifolia) carry a dramatic scenario that has been inserted into the notebook. This scenario is entitled "Ressurection" (as cited above), but that title is cancelled and amended to "Dance Play," above the prose sketch of a play in which Christ enters an afterlife process where he meets other sacrificed saviors. Different interpretations of these pages give rise to a major difference in dating: Does the scenario represent a very early idea for *The Resurrection*, later superseded by the version Lady Gregory heard in 1925, where the disciples experience the phantom's beating heart? Or is it a fresh variation on the theme of Christ's death, like *Calvary* or the mooted play on Jesus and Judas, and therefore independent of the drafts for *The Resurrection* itself? In either case, these pages are not an integral part of the notebook, so their dating does not bear directly on the notebook in its original form. Conservation work has altered this state insofar as the loose pages are now bound into the notebook, although we shall continue to treat the four leaves as extraneous and, of course, shall examine evidence relating to these pages in the appropriate section below.

Indeed, fuller details will be given in our examination of all the relevant sections, but the following are the key points about content as it relates to dating the notebook as a whole:

- The first pages of the book are taken up with notes on Leo Frobenius, whom Yeats mentions once in his extant correspondence, in a letter to Sturge Moore from Rapallo in April 1929 (*CL InteLex* 5328). Though indicative, the reference is not conclusive.
- Folio [2v] gives an account of "Clairvoyance on May 9," indicating (as will be outlined later) that Yeats was in London. This makes it likely that

we are dealing with May 1929, when Yeats was in London until May 16, as he was in Dublin in early May of every year from 1923 to 1928.[11]

- The notebook is then missing some sixteen leaves that contained material for a new introduction to *A Vision* (as indicated by cancelled titles on the book's cover). The draft then continues over another fourteen extant leaves, carrying on from similar attempts in Rapallo B and Rapallo A to find a way into the initial presentation of the system. Similarities between the covers of Rapallo A and E make it possible that this draft could be roughly contemporary with those two books, which were started in the spring of 1928 (as was Rapallo D) and continued in use until late in 1928. In this case, Yeats might have left blank Rapallo E's first two leaves, which were filled later with the notes on Frobenius and clairvoyance—a conjecture that has no evidence, but remains a possibility.
- There are then some thirteen leaves used for initial drafts of *The Words upon the Window-Pane*; these are interrupted by three pages of drafting "For Anne Gregory." We know from correspondence that Yeats was working on the draft of *The Words upon the Window-Pane* between August and October 1930; he wrote "For Anne Gregory" in September 1930.
- Following on immediately from the draft of *The Words upon the Window-Pane*, there is a draft of *The Resurrection*, which occupies seventeen leaves and is Yeats's final handwritten version before dictating the play to a typist. He probably finished this draft at the very beginning of 1931.
- Following *The Resurrection*, there are four leaves on the afterlife for *A Vision*, which are what remains of a draft of fifteen leaves, probably from early 1931.
- There are ten leaves that are completely blank at the end of the book, a point of similarity with Rapallo A.
- The loose leaves are extraneous to Rapallo E itself, but could date from some years earlier or be roughly contemporary with the drafts in the notebook.

In sum, therefore, a conservative estimate would have the notebook starting in April or May of 1929, being used until early 1931 and providing material for dictation to a typist in March 1931 (*Res* xxxviii), although it could have been started in 1928. Four leaves from elsewhere were inserted into the notebook at some stage.

Structure and State

As noted above in the context of dating, the beginning of the notebook is missing a large sequence of pages. With a total number of seventy-two leaves (plus the additional four), it is still more complete than either Rapallo Notebooks C or D, with seventy and fifty-three leaves respectively, though in Rapallo E only sixty-two of them are written on. In this case, we can be relatively sure about what the missing pages at the beginning contained, since they would correspond to the headings that appear scratched out on the notebook's cover and would have contained material leading into the exposition of *A Vision* that follows.

Other features of the notebook's structure can be made out from the 1940s microfilm held at Harvard's Houghton Library,[12] particularly the original stitching. It is also possible to see where pages lack their counterpart across the fold, and we can discern the location of the other pages that have been removed from this book among the notebook's final drafts (on the afterlife for *A Vision*), at a location just prior to the blank pages.[13]

The four additional leaves that contain the scenario on Christ are recorded by Curtis Bradford as having been "written on loose sheets of paper" and "filed" in an envelope; when he "examined it, it had been placed with the final manuscript of the play (MS. 4) written in 1930–31 in the Rapallo Notebook labelled 'E'" (*YAW* 239). This is also the arrangement in the Harvard microfilm (probably in the late 1940s), where it can be seen that they are two folded bifolia that precede "the final manuscript of the play." However, when the notebook was microfilmed for David Clark (ca. 1958), the pages were placed ***after*** the final MS draft,[14] which has been their position since the notebook was rebound in 2005 by the Delmas Conservation Bindery.[15] These pages were bound between the fourth and the fifth gatherings, following the late draft of *The Resurrection*, but after the start of material on the afterlife for *A Vision*. Following some radical culling by Yeats, only five leaves remain of this draft, but the first three sides of writing ([58v], [59r], and [59v]) are now separated from the rest ([67r], [69r], and [74r]) by the four extraneous leaves ([60-bis] through [63-bis]) (see the detailed description below, as well as the leaf-by-leaf collation described in the Appendix).

Thus, while restoration has slightly obscured gaps in general and the loose leaves' looseness, the stubs of the Japanese paper used to anchor single pages testify to missing pages; moreover, worn edges and discoloration bear witness to the wear and tear suffered by leaves not sewn into the block. The placement of the loose pages makes sense structurally, but it also falsifies the sequence of the notebook and causes minor problems with labeling or referring to the pages. Placing the pages outside the main block at the beginning or at the end of the book might have been more logical, but it is only after prolonged study that we have been able to gain a clearer picture of the pages' relation to the notebook.

Pagination

Like all of the Rapallo notebooks, Notebook E has a total of five gatherings, originally each with ten folded double leaves (i.e., twenty leaves),[16] sewn with thread that is visible on microfilm in the first four gatherings (the central seam of the fifth gathering fell between blank pages, so the relevant spread was not photographed). Only four leaves remain from the first gathering, and if we were to be consistent about counting *known* missing pages, we should probably number the extant leaves 1, 2, 19, and 20.[17] However, elsewhere we have relied on stubs and have not hypothecated missing pages when both counterparts of a folded leaf have been lost. Such renumbering would also interfere significantly with cross-referencing our work with that of the Cornell editions—effectively marring the functionality of this analysis and its associated table in the Appendix.

Similarly, it might seem appropriate to number the four loose leaves in a separate series, but again, doing so would make any cross-referencing to *"The Resurrection": Manuscript Materials* more confusing. In order to show the shape of the notebook itself and to keep the numbering used by the Cornell edition, which is the sequence of the rebound notebook, we have repeated the numbering for the added pages: 60bis–63bis.[18] Since leaves 60 to 64 of the notebook are missing, it could be argued that it would be less cumbersome to use the "bis" for the missing leaves, but that would create a false impression as to which are the extraneous leaves. We shall, therefore, limit any attempt at reconstruction to the following table.

Table 4.1: Rapallo Notebook E, current configuration and missing leaves.

Gathering	Number of extant leaves	Bifolia	Leaves removed
First	4	= 2	16
Second	20	= 10	0
Third	20	= 10	0
Fourth	15	= 5 and 5 halves	5
*loose**	*4*	*= 2*	*n/a*
Fifth	13	= 3 and 7 halves	7
total without loose	**72**	**= 30 and 12 halves**	**28**
total	**76**	**= 32 and 12 halves**	**28**

* The loose bifolia have been rebound between the fourth and fifth gatherings of the notebook.

It seems almost impossible that the loose pages came from the notebook itself, as the leaves are joined folds and the only folded bifolia removed from Rapallo E would have had to come from the first gathering, where the pages were numbered by Yeats—as indicated by the extant page numbers—and dedicated to *Vision* material. Therefore, these leaves appear to come from another notebook with the same size of paper and format.

It is possible that they come from a notebook that was discarded, as it appears that Rapallo Notebooks A and E are two survivors from a larger group. Notebooks A and E are the only notebooks with a designating letter on their cover—though to muddy matters slightly, what is now called Notebook A (from the letter on its title page) also has a large letter "D" on its cover.[19] This "D," in turn, is similar in execution to the "E" on the cover of Notebook E, made of multiple lines from a fine nib (see Figure 4.1). It seems probable, therefore, that there were other notebooks similarly labeled A, B, and C. Those would have been different from the notebooks that we now assign those letters: as noted, what is now Rapallo A was labeled "D," while Rapallo B, which predates Rapallo A slightly, has the same cover diamond-chain design and format but no letter on its cover; Notebooks C and D have paper of the same size and format but have differently patterned covers, and, again, neither has a letter on the cover or anywhere in the book.[20]

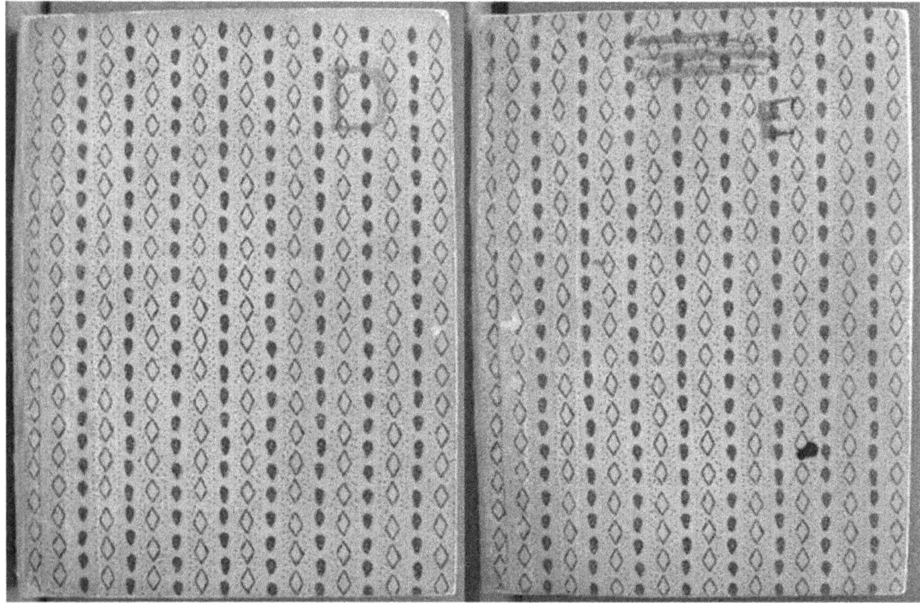

Figure 4.1. The front covers of NLI 13,578 (Rapallo A) and NLI 13,582 (Rapallo E). Courtesy of the National Library of Ireland (NLI). Photographs courtesy of Catherine E. Paul.

Another possibility, which may be more tenuous, arises from the dating on the pages, which would fit into the center of the first gathering of Rapallo C, which happens to lack four leaves. The material also shows other points of contact, but the details of this possibility are left for a fuller examination later.

TRANSCRIPTION PROTOCOL AND KEY TO ABBREVIATIONS

Our editorial transcriptions are meant to preserve as much as possible the idiosyncrasies of Yeats's spelling, punctuation, and revising. The whole word is given when that seems intended, even though letters may be missing or elided with a stroke, as often with the "-ing" ending. When a precise spelling is unclear, a standard one may be substituted. A word will be left incomplete if Yeats seems to have abandoned it that way. Illegible words are represented thus: [?]. A conjectural reading thus: [?word]. And partly conjectural readings thus: every[?thing]. Yeats's scribal additions are indicated within angle brackets < >, and in the case of insertions above the line the accompanying caret mark is omitted. Our own interventions are given in editorial square brackets [ ], including our numbering of the book's pages by folio or leaf (Yeats's own page numbers are placed in quotation marks); text supplied in transcriptions to aid understanding is italicized within the brackets. Curly braces { } and slightly offset margins are used within long, blocked transcriptions to interpolate matter from a facing page of the notebook. Yeats's underlinings are retained, as are his strikeouts, which are everywhere indicated with a line through the deleted word, parts of words, parts of lines, whole lines, or sentences, as the case may be; where they are illegible, fragments and false starts may be substituted with ~~xx~~ in cancelled text. Where possible, earlier stages of cancellation are indicated with double strike-throughs. Vertical line marks (|) represent accidental line breaks within texts.

Except in transcriptions presented as block quotations, citations follow the American convention of entering commas and periods inside quotation marks (" "), with embedded quotation indicated by single inverted commas (' '). As a rule, in quotation within our commentary, the slash mark or virgule (/) is used to indicate a poetic or dramatic line break that is deliberate on Yeats's part, following *The Chicago Manual of Style*, our general guide on matters of style.[21]

Aside from secondary sources introduced above and in notes thus far, several studies, already signaled in the notes, are cited frequently enough in the remaining sections of this essay to merit repetition here for convenience:

Res — W. B. Yeats, "*The Resurrection*": *Manuscript Materials*, ed. Jared Curtis and Selina Guinness (Ithaca and London: Cornell University Press, 2011).

WFMP — W. B. Yeats, "*Words for Music Perhaps and Other Poems*": *Manuscript Materials*, ed. David R. Clark (Ithaca and London: Cornell University Press, 1999).

WUWP — W. B. Yeats, "*Words Upon the Window Pane*": *Manuscript Materials*, ed. Mary FitzGerald (Ithaca and London: Cornell University Press, 2002).

YAW Curtis Bradford, *Yeats at Work* (Carbondale and Edwardsville, IL: Southern Illinois University Press, 1965).

Other abbreviations are used as directed in the "List of Abbreviations" posted on this journal's website or as introduced in the endnotes of this essay.

IN GREATER DETAIL

[Cover]

As observed above, the notebook shares its cover design with Rapallo Notebooks A and B, while the letter "E" drawn with multiple strokes of a pen is similar to the "D" on the cover of Rapallo A.

The cover also bears a list of contents, which has been scratched out: "Principle Symbols," "hourglass and diamond," "T[?he] [?Diagram of the] Great Wheel." Clearly indicating introductory exposition for *A Vision*, little or none of this material is extant; however, the continuation of the draft is ([3r–17r]), testifying that these titles give a good indication of what was on the missing pages, evidently a redrafting of topics dealt with in Notebooks A and B. In this sense, the notebook is similar to Rapallo C, where the gist of the pages removed from what is now the end can be surmised from the cancelled "Contents" page ([78r], which would originally have been [1v] when the book was the other way round and the back was the notebook's beginning). In both cases, too, these lists show that the removed pages were drafts for the revised version of *A Vision*. In contrast, what was written on the pages removed from Rapallo D is harder to surmise; yet, if there is any pattern, we can console ourselves that those pages were more likely to have contained drafts for *A Vision* than lost poetry.

[1r–2r] [notes on Leo Frobenius, *The Voice of Africa*]

In comparison with the other notebooks, which often have titles or dates on the first page, the opening of Rapallo E is rather abrupt, with three pages of notes on Leo Frobenius's *The Voice of Africa* (1913), but nothing has been removed before these leaves, which must always have been the first ones in the book.[22] As these pages have been examined in depth by Matthew Gibson in *Yeats, Philosophy, and the Occult*, the treatment here will be relatively brief.[23]

Yeats mentions Frobenius in a letter to Thomas Sturge Moore from Rapallo in April 1929, indicating that his knowledge of the German anthropologist came through Ezra Pound, whose enthusiasm for his work seems to have been relatively recent, making it unlikely that Yeats's own investigation would have gone back further. Certainly, Yeats would have relied on Pound or George Yeats for knowledge of Frobenius's *Paideuma* (1921), which was then untranslated from German.

> Ezra Pound has just been in. He says "Spengler is a Wells who has founded himself on German scholourship instead of English journalism." He is sunk in Frobenius Spenglers German source & finds him a most interesting person. Frobenius originated the idea that cultures (including arts & sciences) arise out of races, express those races as if they were fruit & leaves in a pre-ordained order & perish with them; & the two main symbols that of the Cavern & that of the Boundless. He proved from his logic — some German told Ezra — that a certain civilization must have once existed at a certain spot in Africa & then went and dug it up. He proves his case all through by African research. I cannot read German & so must get him second hand. He has confirmed a conception I have had for years, a conception that has freed me from British liberalism & all its dreams. (*CL InteLex* 5328).

Though Yeats's account involves an element of hearsay, he had already latched on to the idea of the Cavern and its counterpart that he would use in *A Vision* (*AVB* 258–60, *CW14* 189–90). Enthused by Spengler's *Decline of the West*, Yeats was also wary of acknowledging parallels in print for fear of appearing derivative, even though he was clear that these were cases of simultaneous revelation.[24]

> When in 1926 the English translation of Spengler's book came out, some weeks after *A Vision*, I found that not only were dates that I had been given the same as his but whole metaphors and symbols that had seemed my work alone[....] I knew of no common source, no link between him and me, unless through
>
> The elemental things that go
> About my table to and fro. (*PEP* 24–25; *AVB* 18–19, *CW14* 15)

Though he might speculate about spirit inspiration, going back to "Spenglers German source" obviated accusations of direct influence and potential accusations of plagiarism.

The Voice of Africa had been translated into English, meaning that it was accessible to Yeats. As Gibson observes, Yeats copied here mainly quotations and diagrams "taken from chapters 10, 12, and 15" on Yoruba culture (*YPO* 309). The notes focus on the development of civilization, "The great ages of universal history," for instance, and parallels between the Yoruba and ancient Phoenician, Etruscan, and Gaulish cultures, and in particular the concept of "The Templum (earth navel – crossing roads 4 cardinal points. 16 devisions of the circle of the heavens Etc)" ([1r]), noting "Templum at the root of ideas of the universe in Babylonia Troy & Etruria" ([2r]). Additional notes cover the relation between the four cardinal directions and the Ifa oracle, deities (Orishas), and the calendar ([1v–2r]), possibly reflecting the interests of a younger Yeats as a ritual magician in the Golden Dawn and creator of Celtic Mysteries, where the four cardinal directions are an essential element in organizing rites and correspondences. Yeats also notes gods' attributes, including ram-headed storm and sun gods in North and West Africa.[25] In the lower right-hand corner of the third page, Yeats squeezes in an observation of his own, with relation to the gods' tools: "Two of old Irish Talismans here stone & sword" ([2r]), again perhaps looking back to his use of the Lia-Fáil and the Sword of Nuada in creating the rituals of the Celtic Mysteries.[26]

[2v] "Clairvoyance on May 9"

The verso of the second leaf is taken up with notes on "Clairvoyance on May 9 Mrs Caulton Trance." "Caulton" is the most honest reading we can make of what Yeats wrote, yet, given the illegibility of Yeats's handwriting and his tendency to misremember names, it seems probable that he is referring to "Mrs H. Cantlon Trance Medium, Clairvoyance and Pyschometry" (as she advertised in magazines such as the spiritualist journal *Light* and *The Occult*

228 LIGHT May 12, 1928

LONDON SPIRITUALIST ALLIANCE, LTD.

16 Queensberry Place,
South Kensington,
London——S.W. 7.

ANNUAL SUBSCRIPTION, ONE GUINEA, payable on the 1st of January.

ADVANTAGES OF MEMBERSHIP. Use of Circulating and Reference Libraries (3 books at a time). [illegible] admission to ordinary lectures. Reduced fees for psychic experiments, various circles and study classes. [illegible] of comfortable premises, opportunity of meeting those interested in Spiritualism and allied subjects.

LIBRARY SUBSCRIPTION for the personal exchange of one book at a time, 3 months 7/6; 6 months 12/6; 12 months 21/- The usual advantages of membership are not included.

INQUIRERS are invited to write or call for the Syllabus and a Pamphlet giving a short explanation of the [illegible] and purpose of modern Spiritualism, and a brief history of the L.S.A. which had its rise in the early days, being founded by the pioneers of the movement. The Secretary, Miss Mercy Phillimore, attends every day except Saturday, and is at all times prepared to meet inquirers.

A BIBLIOGRAPHY of Spiritualism and Psychic Research has been issued under the auspices of the L.S.A. Price 1½d. post free. It is classified, and is a useful guide in a wise selection of books for the student.

NOTICES.

LECTURE

THURSDAY, MAY 17th, 1928

AT 8 P.M.,
VICE-ADMIRAL J. C. ARMSTRONG, on
"Survival of Personality."
Chair: Lieut.-Col. C. DAVIDSON.

EXPERIMENTAL WORK.

PRIVATE SITTINGS (Professional)
TRANCE ... Mrs. J. W. Garrett, Mrs. Mason, Mrs. Cantlon
NORMAL ... Mr. T. E. Austin, Mrs. Minnie Nordica
AUTOMATIC WRITING ... Mrs. Cantlon
HEALING ... Mrs. E. A. Cannock
PRIVATE SITTINGS (Non-Professional, for Members only).
NORMAL ... Mrs. E. R. Richards
TRANCE ... Mrs. Morrel
CRYSTAL GAZING ... Mrs. Moon
CIRCLE SITTING. (Clairvoyance, Psychometry, etc.).
Tuesdays, at 8 p.m. ... Mr. T. E. Austin
(Members 2s. 6d.; Non-Members 3s. 6d.; limited to 8 sitters)

MEETINGS FOR DEMONSTRATION OF CLAIRVOYANCE, Etc.
Every Tuesday at 3.15 p.m. Members free; Non-Members 2s.
Tuesday, May 15th ... Mr. T. E. Austin

TRAINING OF THE PSYCHIC FACULTIES.
CLASS FOR GENERAL DEVELOPMENT.
Tuesdays, at 8 p.m. ... Mr. C. Glover Botham
CLASS FOR AUTOMATIC WRITING.
Wednesdays, at 2.30 ... Mrs. Cantlon
(For fees and particulars, apply Secretary.)

TRANCE ADDRESSES.
Wednesdays, at 5 p.m. (Through the Mediumship of Mr. W. E. Foster.)
April 25th to July 11th inclusive.
Answers to written questions of a general and impersonal character concerning the Life of Spirits and Their Surroundings.
Admission, including tea served from 3.30-4.45 p.m.: Members 1s.; Non-Members 2s.

AT HOME, Wednesdays, 3.30-6 p.m.
For the purpose of introductions among Spiritualists and friends.
HOSTESSES: Ladies of the House Committee.

IMPORTANT NOTICE.—Non-Members cannot be admitted to any meeting except on the presentation of a ticket purchased before the day of the meeting, or as the guest of a member.

No Private Sitting or place in a circle can be definitely booked until the fee is paid.

CARD GUESSING EXPERIMENT: A further appeal. Many thanks are due to all those who most kindly took part in the card guessing experiment for which an appeal was made in LIGHT. As the experiment continues to yield interesting and suggestive results, this further appeal is made to readers of LIGHT who have not yet taken the experiment to ask if they would help both by doing the experiment themselves and by persuading friends to try also.

A scoring sheet for recording guesses and a stamped addressed envelope will be sent on application to Miss [illegible], c/o the Secretary, The London Spiritualist Alliance, 16, Queensberry Place, S.W.7.

A considerable number of data has already been collected, but [illegible] are essential before any definite conclusions can safely be drawn.

Figure 4.2. Advertisement for the London Spiritualist Alliance in *Light*, with Mrs. Cantlon listed for "Trance" private sittings, as well as Automatic Writing and a Class for Automatic Writing. *Light: A Journal of Psychical, Occult, and Mystical Research* 48.2470 (May 12, 1928): 228.

Review). She conducted "private sittings" at the London Spiritualist Alliance in South Kensington (see Figure 4.2), as well as at her own premises near Sloane Square. The fact that Yeats mentions going to a different medium at the "same place" the following week would indicate that he was attending the LSA, though in the later instance he does not even mention a name. Yeats dismissed the session as:

> Mostly vague – many names – Christian names – given of which I | knew nothing. Control seemed fishing most of the time. | Did however give a fair description of my father & his Christian name & | saw an easel. <My father gave name "Gifford" "as a test."> Said that my father had known a cripple called | Laurence — a retainer. cripled hip. I know nothing of this. ([2v])

This assessment of a form of "cold reading" finds an echo in H. Dennis Bradley's book of 1931 examining psychics: the chapter on Claire Cantlon is entitled "The Gentle Art of Fishing."[27] Such chicanery would be enough for any skeptically minded witness to dismiss the séance as a form of fraud; however, since Yeats worked from an assumption that the medium was acting in good faith but that mediumship itself might involve forms of telepathy and dramatization, his account offers possible reasons to explain her unconvincing performance. Thus, when he was told that he "would go into a Bazar – somewhere in Egypt – through a curtain door to where there was an old cross legged holy man with a crystal," Yeats found that "A good deal of what was said there was an attempt to symbolize my philosophical research – perhaps this old holy man symbolized some guide or other." Yet he went on to note that, "This symbolization did not however come until I asked some question, which showed the nature of my studies."[28] Further down the page, he writes that, "A week later [he] saw a young clairvoyant at same place," and again the session was "Practically a failure" with "one definite statement" about "A long journey," which he judged "All most improbable," but, again, he sought to explain the misdirection as "Probably an echo of an aborted project of going to Japan" ([2v]).

Between these two disappointing meetings with mediocre mediums, he also noted another psychic visit "On Monday," which probably refers to the one preceding the May 9 visit to the clairvoyant: "On Monday I got a spirit photograph with Mrs Deane but the print has not yet come. I asked mentally for Mabel Beardsley." After an interval of a week or so, he recorded: "Psychic print – has a charming girls head – not Mabel Beardsley but the most charming I have seen in print of the kind. An unknown head" ([2v]).[29] This is very probably the spirit photograph of Yeats that has been reproduced in several places,[30] sometimes attributed to Eva Carrière and Juliette Bisson and dated 1914, when Yeats visited them.[31] However, based on Yeats's appearance, William

H. O'Donnell is right to observe that the photograph was "made probably in the late 1920s" (*CW5* 355 n35d). When placed next to photographs known to have been produced by Ada Deane and those by Juliette Bisson (see Figure 4.3), the photograph of Yeats has far more in common with the former.[32]

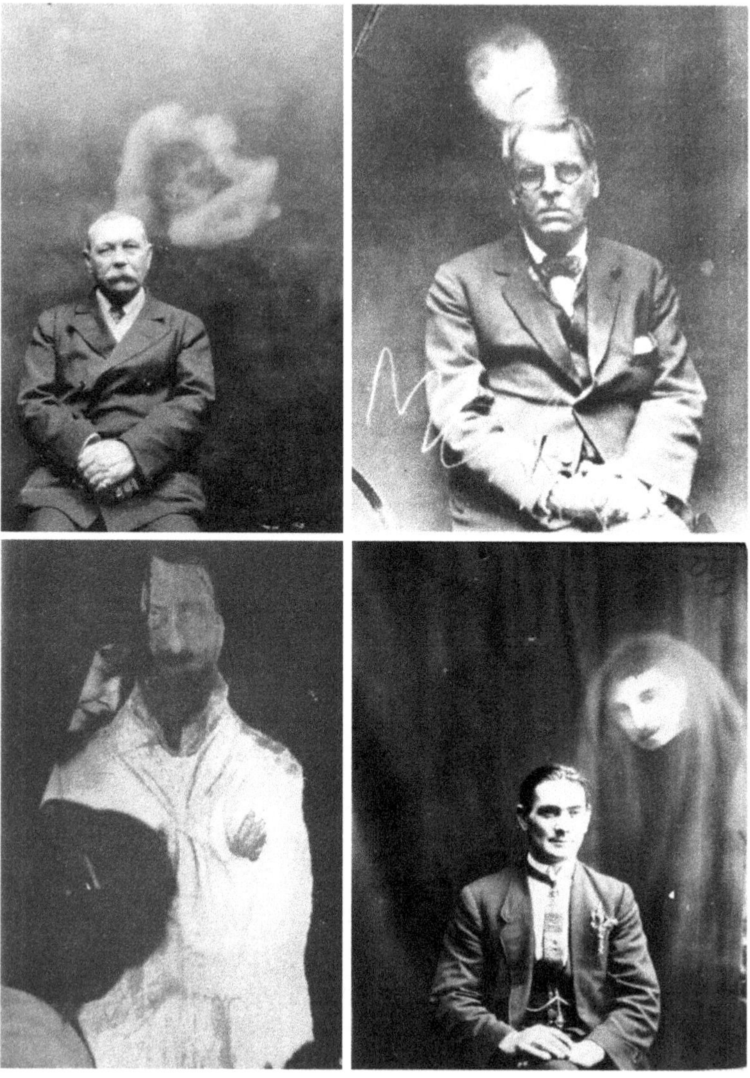

Figure 4.3. Spirit or psychic photographs, clockwise from top left: Sir Arthur Conan Doyle, photographed by Ada Deane, 1922; WBY, photographer and date unknown; William Thomas, photographed by William Hope; Eva C. (a medium), photographed by Juliette Bisson, c. 1913.[33]

Though the name "Cantlon" may be based on unclear handwriting and an element of conjecture, that of "Mrs Deane" is far more clearly attested. Ada Emma Deane won some fame for photographs showing the spirits of the war dead crowding around the London Armistice Day ceremonies in the early 1920s,[34] and she was also well known for spirit photographs.[35] As Ada Deane was based in London,[36] this fact again points to the year being 1929, when Yeats was present in London until May 16 (see *ChronY*),[37] as he was elsewhere in early May 1927, 1928, and 1930.[38]

Some corroboration comes in a letter to George Yeats, sent from the Savile Club in London on May 9, 1929, when Yeats notes that he had "been to a couple of mediums. At the last medium somebody, who seems to be my father, came & said 'You have a son who is slow to learn but he is slow & sure. When older he will be brilliant'" (*CL InteLex* 5251). This ties in with the notebook account, which also refers to his father's apparent presence, although giving other details and without the message.

Since "May 9" is the only date given in the notebook proper, it is of some importance. However, as Yeats sometimes inserted material on pages that he had left blank,[39] it is also possible that the notebook was started earlier with blank pages at the beginning, or at least leaving a blank verso here, which Yeats then used later on. Still, the notebook was clearly in use no later than May 1929.

Without any deliberate intention, it is as if Yeats was doing background research for *The Words upon the Window-Pane*, the first drafts of which appear later in this notebook. He had no need for research, of course, being an inveterate habitué of sittings; indeed, if he was ever advised to "write what you know," a play based on a séance would have been an obvious choice. In psychic matters, he thought himself to be a sympathetic but objective investigator; however, reading his accounts of séances, automatic writing, and bleeding oleographs,[40] or even just his comments on a "spirit photograph" as above, it is clear that he was looking for confirmation of his convictions rather than approaching the practice with any scientific skepticism. The same is true for the extended experiment in automatic script and sleeps with his wife. Yet he was also trying to understand the phenomena and ascertain what was actually happening, not perhaps scientifically but from within, as it were, willing to take the spiritists' own terms and explanations as a starting point, while treating them analytically.

In writings such as "Swedenborg, Mediums, and the Desolate Places," *A Packet for Ezra Pound*, and the Introduction to *The Words upon the Window-Pane*, Yeats enters into the imperfection of human attempts to communicate with the spirits of the dead. Following lore and tradition, he expects and tolerates deceit in both human beings and spirits—"Because mediumship is dramatisation: even honest mediums cheat at times either deliberately or because some part of the body has freed itself from the control of the waking will, and almost always truth and lies are mixed together" (*VPl* 968, *CW2* 719–20). Also, he wrote: "I remember that Swedenborg has described all those between the celestial state and death as plastic, fantastic and deceitful, the dramatis personae of our dreams; that Cornelius Agrippa attributes to Orpheus these words: 'The Gates of Pluto must not be unlocked, within is a people of dreams'" (*PEP* 30; *AVB* 23, *CW14* 18). One spirit had warned Yeats: "'Remember we will deceive you if we can'" (*PEP* 18; *AVB* 13, *CW14* 11).[41] Ultimately, he accepts Hermes as the god of mysteries and psychopomp of the dead, but also as a trickster and the god of thieves. Yet what is a fatal handicap for him as a credible investigator of psychic phenomena works to his advantage as a creative artist.

Doubt about mediums (even his own wife) and about spirits (even his own Instructors and their revelation) underlies *A Vision* itself, and a rejected opening stated: "This book would be different if it had not come from those who claim to have died many times and in all they say assume their own existence." Yeats had a habit of revising away from commitment to spiritual statements,[42] but even this abandoned statement just refers to "those" it has come from, to their "claims" and their "assumption"—they may not be the spirits of the dead and could be the people of dreams or temporary dramatizations.[43] The introduction to *The Words upon the Window-Pane*, which first appeared in *The Dublin Magazine* (1931–32) and then in revised form in *Wheels and Butterflies* (1934), is a sensitive and nuanced approach to what Yeats thought might be involved in mediumship, far from the simple credulity that he is sometimes ascribed, but also far from skepticism.[44]

[3r–17r] [drafts for *A Vision*, introductory material]

The first pair of leaves [1r–2v] is followed by fifteen leaves devoted to the revised version of *A Vision* [3r–17r], opening on a page which Yeats numbered "17" and continuing up to "29" and an unnumbered page 30. This should indicate that sixteen previous leaves of material have been removed, almost certainly numbered, in accordance with Yeats's practice in Rapallo A and B, on the rectos from 1 to 16. Indeed, the notebook's first gathering is missing eight conjugate leaves from the center (i.e., eight leaves on either side of the seam).[45] The missing pages evidently contained introductory material for *A Vision*, as Yeats continued in his struggle to clarify and simplify his presentation of the system's fundamentals, as indicated by the headings on the notebook's cover, which have been scratched out: "Principle Symbols," "hourglass and diamond," "T[?he] [?Diagram of the] Great Wheel."[46] The first extant page includes a diagram of the hourglass and diamond in the wheel, and could plausibly answer to the second or third heading, but this part of the draft has probably already moved beyond the initial exposition those titles indicate. Certainly, the following sections are not connected with the titles on the cover, so it appears that Yeats has removed all or most of the material summarized in the cancelled headings.

There is a corrected typescript that appears to be based on the text from this notebook, entitled "Book III THE COMPLETED SYMBOL," and the notebook's page "17" corresponds to page "3" of the typescript.[47] The first two pages of the typescript could therefore account for four or more pages of the notebook's foregoing material (depending upon cancellations), but this possibility makes it likely that the bulk of the missing pages belonged to an earlier "book"—Book II—corresponding to the titles or headings from the cover. Indeed, Yeats refers backwards to an earlier exposition when explaining the figure of the hourglass and diamond within a wheel: "This is the complicated geometric figure I <mention> in Book II chapter [*blank left*] " ([3r]; see Figure 4.4).[48] The material that follows—much of it cancelled, rewritten, and reordered—outlines how the *Faculties* move within this diagram. *Will* and *Mask* on the hourglass move toward the center and back to the periphery, or circumference, alternating in dominance with *Creative Mind* and *Body of Fate*, in a formulation very close to that applied to the *Principles* in the published version (*AVB* 198–99, *CW14* 146).

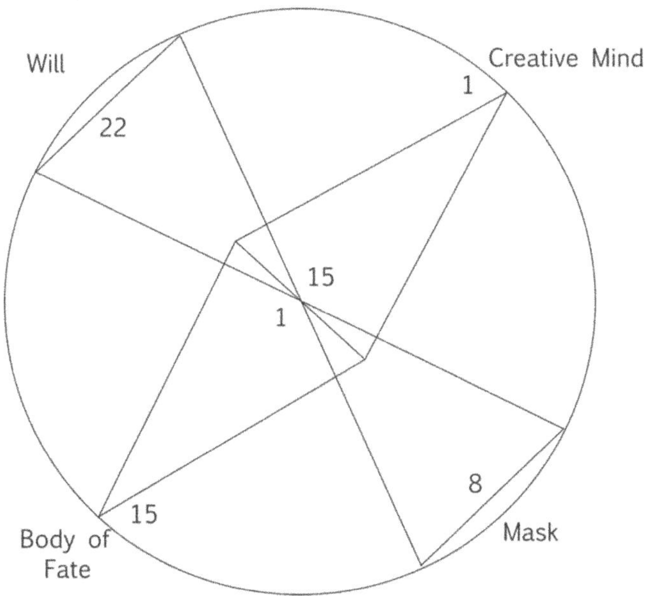

Figure 4.4. Redrawn from NLI 13,582 (Rapallo Notebook E), [3r]. Cf. *AVB* 199 and 200, *CW14* 146 and 147.

As part of the description, Yeats states that "Will & Mask meet at the centre of the figure at Phase 15, they are when so united the Daimon itself" ([3r]), and, though this detail does not appear in the published edition, it does indicate a key to Yeats's conception of Unity of Being—also mentioned in cancelled text—which is that it channels the *Daimon*. As put forward in *A Vision B*, Unity of Being is possible from Phase 13 to Phase 17, thus centering on Phase 15, the full moon. One phase is most privileged, however: Yeats's own Phase 17, where "Unity of Being, and consequent expression of *Daimonic* thought, is now more easy than at any other phase" (*AVA* 75, *CW13* 63; *AVB* 140, *CW14* 105). In the treatment presented in this draft, the central point of the hourglass, in *antithetical* mode (i.e., while *Will* is predominantly *antithetical*), pivots on Phase 15 and is *daimonic*; in *primary* mode, its focus is Phase 1, where "darkness" and "abstraction prevails" ([3v]).

> The figure is unlike the other cones I have described | ~~because~~ in that the expansion of the lunar cones like that of the solar | [*is*] spatial. All is related to the center ~~of the sphere~~, & | it represents a pulsation or expanding & contracting of the sphere | itself. Its greatest expansion is at phase 8 & phase 22 | where intellect, or sun attempts to grasp the totality of fact[,] | its greatest contraction phase 1 & phase 15 where it is withdrawn | into the One, or into the personality. The dark of the Moon | where desire ceases & Will [?obeys] is the dark night | of St John of the Cross. ([5r])

This passage recalls the following comment in *A Vision*: "The diamond is a convenient substitute for a sphere, the hour-glass for two meeting spheres. Taken in relation to the wheel, the diamond and the hour-glass are two pulsations, one expanding, one contracting. I can see them like jelly-fish in clear water" (*AVB* 199–200, *CW14* 147). Here in the draft, Yeats's explanation of the *Faculties*—or *Principles*—moving inwards and outwards on the hourglass and diamond helps to elucidate the image and how it came to him.

The next section was originally entitled "The daimon," but that heading has been replaced simply by a Roman numeral "II." This part addresses various themes, some of which survived into the final version, though most are significantly modified, and there is no section devoted to the *Daimon* in *A Vision B*. In this sense, the draft here looks back to *A Vision A*'s treatment of "The Daimon, the Sexes, Unity of Being, Natural and Supernatural Unity," which expounds the equivalence of human *Faculties* with their *daimonic* counterparts, such as *Will* with *Mask* and *Mask* with *Will* (*AVA* 26–27, *CW13* 24–25). Yet this draft also looks forward to the treatment of the *Thirteenth Cone* or cycle as a single, spiritual counterpart to the human cycles—a concept which only appears in *A Vision B*, though the term itself is repeatedly revised out of the drafts here. Other aspects, such as an analysis of how judging art relates to the *Faculties* and to consciousness, reappear in several drafts of this period but were not used in the published version (the following transcription omits cancelled material).

> Only the logical faculty <— Creative Mind —>[49] | my instructors tell me is concious. As I stand in front | of a picture I say "That is well painted" —"That

> <shoulder is out | of drawing" "<That is> a beautiful face" "That lace colour [=*collar*] must [*have*] taken a long time"> | & but for these judgements I would <note †>dream as if in my bed at night. <When these judgements> | <The antithetical being only exists in action &> these faint contacts of the known & the knower, or of the is & | ought <may> at the <crisis of an action> awaken the entire being, so the consciousness is | flooded with the daimon.
>
> {† Once when my instructors had set me a theme for meditation they told me to pay | especial attention to the secondary images, because through these spirits communicate. Eastern | philosophers, they said, confined attention to the primary image that they might | get "all out of the individual will"} ([6r] and [5v])[50]

The treatment continues with questions of the nature of consciousness, the relation of the *Daimon* to spiritual perfection, the relation of the *Daimon* to the Four *Principles*, death, and the Ghostly Self (including cancellations):

> After death | the daimon is called the ghostly self, because of an association | I have yet to explain between the 13th Cone & ~~the Holy~~ the third person | of the Trinity, as that Trinity is thought by let us say Plotinus | & ~~is then in~~ there, in a state analogous to dreamless state, | being ~~free~~ purified even of the half ~~waking~~ <waking> that we call | dream ~~is united to the whole of being & therefore free~~ | is <re->united to the whole of being. Or rather it knows itself | for what is & has always been. ([9r])

In *A Vision B*, the connection of the Ghostly Self with the Holy Ghost is relegated to the introductory material of *A Packet for Ezra Pound*, and the concept itself is named but not explained. Yeats may have abandoned identifying it as the afterlife form of the *Daimon* because doing so oversimplified his understanding (or uncertainty) about this term; however, using the phrase without any clear presentation can only leave readers confused. Indeed, despite echoes in the published edition, relatively little of this material was used, so that the figure of the *Daimon* is consequently hazier and glimpsed rather than seen.[51] Similarly, the description of the dreamless state of the afterlife—the *Beatitude* of *A Vision B*—has a positivity that is missing from the published version.

Yet immediately following this explanation, Yeats gives vent to a mixture of frustration and resignation in a pair of sentences that are cancelled by a vertical line:

> I have toiled over ~~this account of the daimon~~ <these thoughts> | & am well aware of it ~~inaqed inaquacy~~ <inadequacy>, but the best | part of ~~what~~ attention, & that of my instructors was spent | on the 28 phases, & or the geometrical symbols. | ~~& the xx few sentences xx~~ ~~& the little~~ What they said of

> the | daimon, & it was little, long ~~saw~~ seemed unintelligible. | I once said "Will I ever understand" & the Spirit replied | "Not while you live". ([9r])

Such words are testimony to Yeats's unwillingness to misrepresent ideas that he did not feel fully his own, and it is perhaps natural that he should have decided to scant his treatment of something he could never hope to understand fully. All the same, it might have been helpful to his readers to have retained more of this candor in the published edition.

The following eight pages are dedicated to exposition of "The Four Principles." Like the *Daimon*, the *Principles* have sometimes been put to one side by commentators on *A Vision*, if not actually dismissed as an unnecessary complication or duplication of the *Faculties*.[52] This can be attributed in large part to the organization of *A Vision B*, where they are introduced at a point where the presentation of yet more barbarous terms and arcane technicalities may fatigue many readers' patience. Yeats, like most of his "old fellow students" in the Theosophical Society or the Golden Dawn (*AVA* xii, *CW13* lv), was used to taking on quantities of abstruse terminology and definition, so he may not have realized how uninviting they can be to a reader. The *Principles* are actually more straightforward than the *Faculties* and more conventional in many ways, largely in line with general esoteric schemes of spiritual bodies. However, it is probable that fewer readers of *A Vision* are familiar with esoteric thought than Yeats expected or intended, nor does Yeats make the parallels clear even for those who are familiar with such thought.[53]

The opening statement in the draft here does not agree with the final formulation of *A Vision B*, but does certainly offer a clearer sense of the human constitution (here the cancelled text has been omitted):

> <Man> is expressed in the Four Faculties | the daimon in the Four Principles. The Principles | show what is visable to sense, or a necessity of | mind, or has value in it self, all that needs no evidence | <all that is sufficient to it self>. When Pater in a famous | passage considered those who were devoted to works of philanthropy | as less fortunate than those devoted the arts he | abased the faculties <or> human activity for its | pre-occupation with ways & means, with | the artificial & the arbitrary. The Four Principles are Husk | and Passionate Body, Spirit & Celestial Body, & the first | two[,] in that they constitute <the> particular, have an afinity with Will & Mask, the second two | have it <being universal> with Creative Mind & Body of Fate | though in other characters they are different. ([10r])

This presentation is not necessarily clearer than the published version (*AVB* 187–89; *CW14* 137–39), but it contains elements that might have made it easier for readers to understand the importance and role of the *Principles*. With a little further elaboration, the reference to Pater is potentially illuminating, alluding to the Conclusion of *The Renaissance*, which considers the transience of human life:

> we have an interval, and then our place knows us no more. Some spend this interval in listlessness, some in high passions, the wisest in art and song. [...] High passions give one this quickened sense of life, ecstasy and sorrow of love, political or religious enthusiasm, or the "enthusiasm of humanity." [...] Of this wisdom, the poetic passion, the desire of beauty, the love of art for art's sake has most; for art comes to you professing frankly to give nothing but the highest quality to your moments as they pass, and simply for those moments' sake.[54]

Yeats interprets "the enthusiasm of humanity" as philanthropy in his draft, and, though it may yield a "quickened sense of life," he sees it as less favored than devotion to "art or song," which "give nothing but the highest quality" to the passing moments. For Pater, "the poetic passion" is part of the "high passions," but Yeats here—possibly recalling rather partially—takes Pater to be putting the more practical enthusiasms, which he associates with "ways and means, with the artificial & the arbitrary" and therefore his *Faculties*, below the *Principles*' ideal reality, as reflected in the arts.[55]

Yeats goes on to explore the *Principles*, specifically *Husk* and *Passionate Body* in terms of light as a product of mind, a theme that recurs in the drafts of the late 1920s,[56] but ended up as little more than a footnote in *A Vision B* (*AVB* 190–91, *CW14* 140). (A single cancellation is included in the following transcription in order to give a verb its subject.)

> The popular mysticism of | the nineteenth century borrowed from I | think some eighteenth century writer – perhaps Henri Martin – | the term astral light, & without understanding its origin | gave it a world wide currency. The light is astral | because antiquity thought of our souls as stars | omitting [=*emitting*] light, but this light displays not merely those forms to that come in dream & | vision, but eall [*sic*] that is visable. It is the Passionate | Body expressed or made visable by the Husk | & is the double being, that made such writers as Eliphas | Levi describe in that Pseudo scientific language that hides | its dependence on the perceiving mind, as negative & Posative | and compare it to the two serpents upon Mercuries Wand. | Older writers have I think compared it to | images in a mirror. | Those images, are as it were the reflections Spirit & Celestial Body, | Passionate Body is matter, the matter of Aristotle & of the middle ages | <which confers actual existence which is alone the unchanging states or forms of the Spirit> Yet without these forms, Husk could | express nothing, for it would know neither space | nor cause & effect, nor identity & difference, & last night | my instructors, [?fearing] that ~~I give to~~ granted a too independent energy to | perception, compared them to [?facet reflected] | by the sun. Yet <Passionate Body is but as it were Celestial Body in motley>[.] ([11r–12r])

This exploration includes a slightly confused version of what A. E. Waite had told Yeats about the origins of the term "astral light" in 1914,[57] with Yeats putting *Henri* Martin—a contemporary Symbolist painter[58]—in place of Louis-Claude de Saint Martin.[59] In *A Vision B*, the "eighteenth century writer" was revised to "some seventeenth-century Platonist" (*AVB* 191, *CW14* 140), as Yeats decided to refer the idea vaguely back to Henry More and the Cambridge Platonists, a connection he had made when writing notes for Lady Gregory's *Visions and Beliefs in the West of Ireland*.[60]

One significant point is that Yeats writes here of communication from his instructors "last night," emphasizing how the Yeatses continued to engage in "Sleeps" during the late 1920s. These appear to be particularly in response to what Yeats was writing in his revisions, to confirm, reject, or refine, as he is doing here.[61] Some of these Sleeps are reported but they are not logged as systematically as those of the early 1920s, when the Yeatses kept dedicated notebooks, so that summaries are scattered rather haphazardly. Other sessions seem to have fed into the ongoing process of Yeats's writing without necessarily being recorded separately, unless, as here, we learn of them tangentially.

The comment that "Passionate Body is but as it were Celestial Body in motley" is surprising, at least from the perspective of Yeats's later presentation of the *Principles*, where the connection between the two seems to lie in the *Spirit* cleaving to one in life and to the other after death. It makes sense, however, in a form of transmuted reconfiguration, and the phrase substitutes a cancelled simpler expression, that "Celestial Body & Passionate Body are one ~~more~~ may be called the same being <body under different conditions>" ([12r]). These ideas are actually contained in the symbolic formulations of "The Completed Symbol" as published, but in extremely condensed form, as expressions of the relationship of the *Principles* and the *Daimonic* world that is the total spiritual reality (*AVB* 189, *CW14* 138–39).[62] Each of the *Principles* can be viewed as enabling or reflecting a particular aspect of the *Daimonic* world. At a fundamental level, the *Daimons* that make up reality can be perceived as many or one: as the many, the "*Passionate Body* is the sum of those *Daimons*" that the individual *Daimon* seeks "to make apparent to itself,"[63] while as the one, the *Celestial Body* is "all other *Daimons* as the Divine Ideas in their unity" (*AVB* 189, *CW14* 138–39).[64] Alternatively, the One can put on the motley of multiplicity. If the *Daimons* are perceived "as *Passionate Body*," they manifest in terms of "time and space, cause and effect," the illusory but physical universe; if they are known or understood by *Spirit* in a unified vision, they are "intellectual necessity" or *Celestial Body*. Yet perceiving must precede knowing, for without perception there would be no way out of the self-enclosed circle—that is, "the *Passionate Body* exists that it may 'save the *Celestial Body* from solitude'" (*AVB* 189, *CW14* 139).

Yeats appears to view this interdependence in mythic terms, using several interlinked myths, including one in which *Passionate Body* grows young as *Celestial Body* ages (*AVB* 189, *CW14* 139), enacting aspects of Blake's "The Mental Traveller" (examined further below). Another mythic image is that of *Celestial Body* and *Passionate Body* as sisters and rivals for a lover, as explored in the drafts of the poem in Rapallo C, "Imagination's Bride."[65] There the *Passionate Body* (or *Daimon*) and the *Celestial Body* are treated as vying for the attentions of *Spirit*: *Spirit* chooses *Passionate Body* in incarnate life—becoming Imagination, while she is Beauty—but after death moves toward *Celestial Body*—becoming Reason, while she is Truth. Here, in a passage that is largely cancelled ([12r]), Yeats puts forward a similar but different dynamic, with *Celestial Body* being lured from her husband *Spirit* to *Husk* as a lover, and it may be that Yeats here is still sorting out his understanding of the *Principles*, giving the formulations greater fluidity. He then returns to the image of the union of *Spirit* with *Celestial Body*, which is "our body in Paradise, that <Paradise> we possess in some degree between one phisical life and another <& wholly when the twelve cycles end> Or we may prefer <to> call the Celestial Boddy the Bride <and>, Talk of its marriage to the Spirit, <as my instructors do> with it, a garment <leant> to the Spirit, which falls away to reveal universal man, Christ" ([12r]), referring to the central stage of the afterlife, *Beatitude* or *Marriage* (*AVB* 232, *CW14* 169).[66]

Yeats moves on then to a contemplation of the *Beatitude* itself and how it is that the *Spirit* passes from this state of union to the less perfect states that precede birth.

> At the consummation of her marriage <she [=*Celestial Body*] is> undevided Time, | [~~...~~] Time where there is neither past present nor future, a single unbroken state | [~~...~~]. <To tell otherwise> consciousness, in that | ~~supr~~ supreme moment ~~of its abstraction~~ <is conscious> of nothing but an idea of | self — "Celestial Body is that one portion of eternity that can be separated" | was my instructors phrase. ~~& then the light rises before it, for the light is the Celestial Body turning from its this monoty~~ | ~~& so as it were foams & rises & the light which has been~~ | ~~compared from time imemoreal to the sea, foams & resounds.~~ | ~~Nothing but as ever~~ <Then there comes an unbroken> brightness, which cannot even be called brightness | because there is [*no*] darkness there to give a measure, [?rythms] [~~...~~] <so lost in> | their own unity that all sound is | gone, [~~...~~] delineations [~~...~~] so filled & | hightened that they have vanished. Then this light which has | been compared [~~...~~] <as often to the sea as to a mirror>, |[~~...~~] begins to foam & resound, | ~~or if we – Paul Valery metaphor~~ – ~~or prefer we may think of it as~~ | ~~a still brightness, breaking up mirroring Spirit [...]~~ —, | <to break up into> in endless images. But gradually the Spirit finds its allies[,] is | drawn from the whole to certain images that come to it | with

> ~~its own~~ from its own past, & though at first it can | mould them as it will, they assert more & more their customary | form, until at last Spirit, ~~dominated also by the past~~<its recurring states also from the past> | is separated from the whole, ~~foretels its freedom~~ & is born into | that image we call its body [~~…~~] among those images we | call its fate. ([13r])

These images illustrate and vivify the sense of the *Spirit* being drawn from the timeless completeness of unity with its "true love," *Celestial Body*, to the multiplicity of fragmented images and to the familiar patterns of its previous lives, and thus towards a new birth in the physical world, succumbing to the lure of *Passionate Body*.

The brightness recalls "pure light" reached "in contemplation and in wakefulness," the "fourth state" of consciousness,[67] "wherein the soul, as much ancient symbolism testifies, is united to the blessed dead" (*AVB* 223, *CW14* 162). Yeats then imagines this pure light multiplying like the sea breaking into waves and foam or the mirror shattering.[68] As the deleted reference to "Paul Valery['s] metaphor" indicates, this is in many respects the reverse of what appears in the opening sections of the "The Soul in Judgment" as published in *A Vision B*, where Yeats is thinking about death rather than birth.

> Paul Valéry in the *Cimitière Marin* describes a seaside cemetery. […] The midday light is the changeless absolute and its reflection in the sea the "ouvrages purs d'une éternelle cause." The sea breaks into the ephemeral foam of life. […] The *Spirit* is not those changing images—sometimes in ancient thought as in the *Cimitière Marin* symbolised by the sea—but the light, and at last draws backward into itself, into its own changeless purity, all it has felt or known. (*AVB* 219–20, *CW14* 159–60)

The next consideration shows Yeats wrestling with the angel and trying to pin the *Principles* down further, including material that constitutes a preliminary version of Section III of "The Completed Symbol" (*AVB* 191–93, *CW14* 140–41). Our transcription (below) starts with a few words on [13r], and then carries on over two more rectos, with insertions from opposite versos; we have included Yeats's numbers (at right) to indicate the beginning of new pages, with curly brackets indicating, as usual, matter inserted from facing versos.

> It is still Spirit that which
>
> 28
>
> contemplates the imovable whole [~~…~~] though now | but symbolized as an image~~, & from its suffering come~~ | ~~the Four Faculties, & the active world~~. ~~There~~ All images so contemplated | & demobilized are symbols of spiritual states, or we can | say that state & image grow conscious & visable

to | gether, but [~~...~~] their growing & desolving, ~~there~~ | are expressed in the ~~four~~ Four Faculties, which are forms of | suffering. [~~...~~] They are not realities, but relations | between realities, ~~which~~ which substitute projects for images | [~~...~~] words <&ideas> for states. [~~...~~] ~~There is yet another <a> symbolism that that carries tasks my mind, so~~ | ~~little capable of abstraction, even more beyond its capacity.~~ |

{In the Passionate Body, the Celestial Body, or ~~Spirit~~ consciousness seen | ~~as from without~~ by itself as from without & so as fate ~~those~~ lets fall | ~~from itself~~ an inverted reflection Passionate Body, freedom multitudinous | possability, whereas ~~Spirit~~ consciousness itself, Spirit, the [?final] freedom | lets fall to Husk which is but our expression of destiny[.] | There is yet another symbolism, which tasks my mind so | little capable of abstraction beyond its capacity}

~~Spirit is the future~~ <Spirit> because its states ~~are the ea~~ — joy, peace, | love, ~~what you will~~ — are the aims we pursue in all our actions | is <called the> future & so ~~in a certain sense~~ <almost> the daimon itself. | [~~....~~] <whereas> the Husk, because | [~~...~~] it takes | images from the indivisible, unforeseeable present <~~or Passionate Body~~>, & makes them | dead seperate & knowable is called the Past.

{~~hence its name~~ <& has from this its name> as if it were something shed off | by the growing seed.}

~~But~~ The present, | a moment different from all other moments is the Passionate Body | as contrasted with the Celestial Body which is the eternal | moment. These atributions are reversed among the Faculties | for ~~there the~~ Mask or Image ~~is~~ <which reflects ~~Husk~~ <the> Passionate Body ~~are~~ is called> the future, because in this | ~~word or~~ world of ways & means, we represent the future by an image | whereas the Critical Moment - where Spirit reflects itself - <is called the past> | <because> silogism & concept, can only judge, what is dead & separate. | The Will - the ego the normal man <->is ~~clearly~~ <called> the present

29

& instead of the other present - the spirits idea of itself, that which | can be seperated from eternity, ~~is~~ stands the Body of Fate, ~~the Spac~~ | Space as it is known to each individual man, his totality | of fact. But as ~~the Four Faculties <later>~~<~~as~~ a whole>, ~~are caused by~~ | ~~the domination of~~ <we can call> Husk & Passionate Body, <which is> | [~~...~~] "corporeality ~~it~~ <or> that of which corporeality is | made" Space, & Spirit & Celestial Body <Time>, & | & [*sic*] so discover antithesis between Husk & Passionate Body | & their ~~reflections~~ temporal *reflections Will & Mask, & between Spirit & | Celestial Body & their spatial reflections Creative Mind & | Body of Fate.

{* ~~It is this~~ Because of this inverted reflection that Spenglers historical ~~skeme~~ sceme seems | the exact opposite. His mind, trained by german philosophy to discover ~~every where~~ | first ~~reality~~ realities everywhere, [~~...~~] <~~whereas~~ as I> explain history | [~~...~~] as, because all ways & | means, antithetical to those realities, I find, as will be seen presently, Time not Space | in the Greek mind and in the modern Space not time.} ([13r, 14r, 13v, 15r, 14v])

If such considerations do not tax the mind of readers by their abstraction, then the convoluted thought and cross-correspondences involved will almost certainly try their patience, yet there are insights that are revealing that were lost in revision. The published version of these observations retains mainly the correspondences with past, present, and future,[69] but the main question is why Yeats found these categories worth preserving into the printed edition, while other material that explains the *Principles* a little more was shed. The answer seems to lie in that passion he had for categorization and correspondence fundamental to symbolic thought, particularly to the occultism of Theosophy and the cabalistic Rosicrucianism of the Golden Dawn. In the Theosophical Society's Esoteric Section, Yeats had studied "tables of oriental symbolism" where "the seven principles which made the human soul and body corresponded to the seven colours and the planets and the notes of the musical scale" (*Mem* 23) and, despite complaining of "the abstraction of what were called 'esoteric teachings'"(*Au* 181–82, *CW3* 158), he seems to have found the tables and organization both congenial and useful.[70] The preparatory notebooks and card indexes, as well as the book of *A Vision* bear testimony to a way of understanding that uses schematic correspondence to shed light on relationships, even if this procedure sometimes creates "an arbitrary, harsh, difficult symbolism" (*PEP* 31; *AVB* 21, *CW14* 18).

The final page and a half of this draft for *A Vision* are entitled "The Cones of the Principles," and Yeats outlines there the movements that he explains in Sections VI and VII of *A Vision B* (*AVB* 198–201, *CW14* 146–48). Indeed, the diagram that he uses to illustrate the explanation (see Figure 4.5) is a slightly fuller version of the one that appears on *AVB* 201, *CW14* 148.

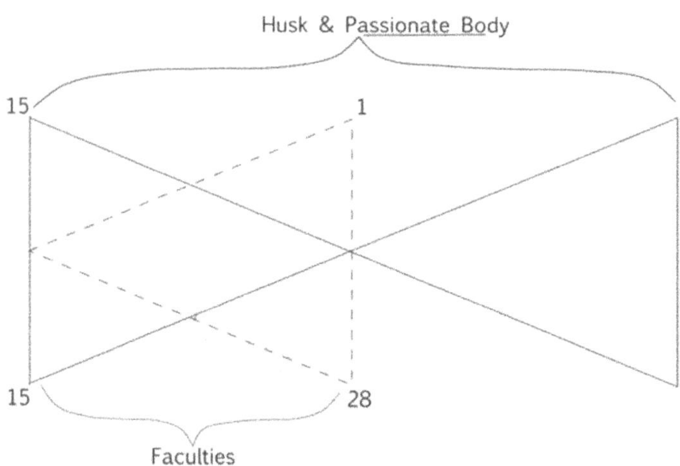

Figure 4.5. Redrawn from NLI 13,582 (Rapallo Notebook E), [15r].

As in *A Vision*, along with the geometry, Yeats traces the archetypal cycles of the year, month and day, life and death, and he introduces the myth of the

Blake's "The Mental Traveller," in which one figure ages as its counterpart grows younger and then vice versa:

> At death Husk & Passionate body | [~~...~~] at phase 15, are united as Will & Mask are | at phase 15 of the Great Wheel, for at death Passionate Body has been | ~~completely~~ expressed <& studied to the utmost> [~~...~~] | & then the counter movement begins, ~~&~~ <till> Celestial Body is completely known <in its turn>. | This is symbolized by the statement that [~~...~~] when we die the Passionate | Body has reached old age, & the Celestial Body extreme youth | & that when wer [=*we are*] born the Celestial Body has grown ~~old in turn~~ & the | Passionate Body young. [...] While Celestial Body | <is young> we are bling [=*?blind*] to the necesary truths, but rich in those that come from Husk & Passionate Body acting upon the Faculties, | much knowledge & little wisdom. When it is old we have | wisdom & little knowledge. ~~At <From phase 1 to> phase 15 Spirit & Celestial Body are <sub>unconscious~~ | ~~[...] from phase 15 to phase 1 Husk & Passionate Body. The Spirits enter our world through our~~ | ~~images, we enter theirs in abstract contemplation~~
>
> {We are subconscious to the dead & they to the living, they enter | into our world through images we into theirs through abstract contemplation}([16r], [15v])

This certainly helps to understand how Yeats expected his readers to interpret his gnomic assertions about Blake's images and how, "when I understood the double cones, I had understood ['The Mental Traveller'] also" (*AVA* 134, *CW13* 108). There is also a hint of Yeats's tendency to conflate spirits of the dead and *Spirits*, and indeed the question of how much he thought they should be distinguished. Since the *Principle* of *Spirit* is the animating center of the whole being and what remains constant from one incarnation to the next (along with the more impersonal *Celestial Body*), it is in most senses the distinguishing aspect of the spirits of the dead. In another sense, spirit is reserved for the afterlife states in which the dead have shed the old *Husk* and *Passionate Body*: "The *Spirits* before the *Marriage* are spoken of as the dead. After that they are spirits, using that word as it is used in common speech" (*AVB* 235, *CW14* 171).[71]

Though direct contact with the dead through a medium was fraught with deceptions, Yeats was convinced that there were more natural forms of interchange that took place on a daily basis in the images of dream and inspiration, with no real boundaries between the living and the dead. The dead are present in the unconscious minds of the living, and "Those who inhabit the 'unconscious mind' are the complement or opposite of that mind's consciousness and are there [...] because of spiritual affinity or bonds created during past lives" (*AVB* 237, *CW14* 172). The dead rely on the living to achieve the aims of the afterlife, and the living are inspired to action or creation by the dead. Earlier in this same draft, Yeats recounts how his Instructors had told him "to pay especial attention to the secondary images" in meditation "because through these spirits communicate" ([5v]),[72] and, elsewhere, he agrees with "Sir Thomas Browne 'that many mysteries ascribed to our own invention have been the courteous revelations of spirits'" (*Ex* 60, *CW5* 66).[73] Yeats's terminology follows that of Christian tradition and his Golden Dawn training, with "meditation" involving visualization—and potentially welcoming secondary images that arose, as in dreaming—while "contemplation" was higher and more abstract. One of the opening sections of *A Vision B*'s "The Soul in Judgment" discusses the "pure light" of contemplation (mentioned above); Yeats mentions briefly there that, in the past, the living had discovered "the still unpurified dead through their own and others' dreams"—referring to those in the first three stages of the afterlife—"and those in freedom through contemplation"—indicating also those in the later stages and, perhaps, those freed from incarnation altogether (*AVB* 223, *CW14* 162). It is a rise from the level of image and forms to that of the ideal and pure light. As in "Paul Valery['s] metaphor," the "light is the changeless absolute" fractured by the waves and sea foam (*AVB* 219–20, *CW14* 159–60), and incarnation is descent to the world of foam and image, while the afterlife is a gradual purification and return to light. Indirectly, therefore, Yeats's examination of the *Principles* here prepares for Rapallo E's other block of work on *A Vision*—after a gap of months—a draft on the soul's states during the afterlife: see the section headed "[58v–74r] [drafts for *A Vision* on the afterlife]," below.

In sum, the thirty-odd pages of draft material that Yeats created in this notebook (of which we now have half) were yet another iteration of his relentless hammering at the exposition of *A Vision* in an attempt to improve its clarity and coherence without sacrificing accuracy to his sources. The many repetitions of the material, with major and minor variations, bear witness to his dissatisfaction with the organization and formulations that he managed and to an almost obsessive impulse to improve understanding and expression of the themes. In that respect, these pages are very different from most of Yeats's prose, in which, despite heavy revision, he usually discovered the organization quickly and even the expression required only a few drafts at most.

[17v–31r, 32r, 33r] "Jonathan Swift" [scenario and part of the first-draft version of *The Words upon the Window-Pane*]

At folios [17v/18r], Yeats shifted to playwriting, away from notes and writings for *A Vision B*. By 1957/1958, this shift had caught the attention of George Yeats and Thomas Parkinson so that two typed slips were attached to [17v] to highlight the contents of the notebook. The smaller slip, labeled "WORDS UPON THE | WINDOW PANE," was clipped at upper right, and the larger slip, serving as a short, general Contents for Rapallo E, was attached at left (by two paper clips), having been prepared in the same format as an extant slip in Rapallo A.[74]

Although now loose, the Rapallo E slips were still attached to [17v] when photos were obtained for Mary FitzGerald's Cornell Yeats volume, *The Words upon the Window Pane* (see *WUWP* 4 and compare with Figure 4.6, below).[75]

We know from Yeats's correspondence that the holograph versions of the play—from the early sketch through two later drafts—were written between August and October of 1930, with the lyric "For Anne Gregory" interspersed (at [31v], [32v–34r]) in September 1930. By late September, Yeats had written well into the second draft, now in the Houghton Library, Harvard University (f MS Eng 338.9). Our account of the early draft scenario and the first full draft of the play is thus only a partial account of the whole play because much rewriting and at least one major redaction of key material from Rapallo E occurred in the Harvard manuscript. To compensate, a general summary of such changes is given in our analysis of folios [34v–41v] of the first draft (see below).

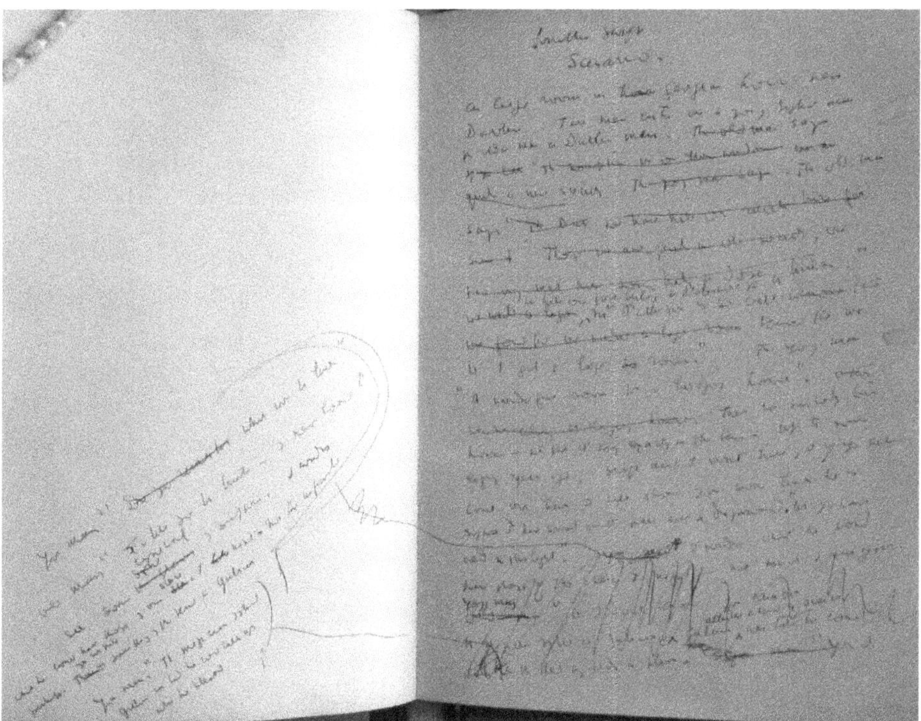

Figure 4.6. NLI 13,582 (Rapallo Notebook E), [17v–18r]. Courtesy of NLI; photograph courtesy of Catherine Paul E. Paul. (See *WUWP* 4–7.)

Yeats's lifelong encounter with the works of Jonathan Swift has been established by many scholars, and some even cite books on or by Swift in Yeats's personal collection.[76] Before Yeats began "Jonathan Swift | Scenario" on these pages, he had already written at Coole Park his verse-translation "Swift's Epitaph" in mid-September 1929. He had also jotted in Rapallo Notebook D a note (dated "Oct" 1929) in language resembling words used by the character John Corbet on Swift's fear of passing madness on as justification for his remaining celibate.[77] Yeats's immersive reading of Swift for the play was evidently stimulated by Shane Leslie's *The Skull of Swift: An Extempore Exhumation*, which Yeats read while at Coole in late August 1928, quite soon after its publication.[78] Such background reading continued, at intervals, into spring 1930, when he said convalescence in Rapallo involved "read[ing] daily from Swift's *Letters* and his *Journal to Stella*."[79] Especially suggestive were the translations of Swift's Latin epitaph that are made to recur as echoes at crucial points in Leslie's narrative. It was, experimentally, one of the organizing devices of *The Skull of Swift*, a novelistic "new biography" in the manner of Lytton Strachey's *Elizabeth and Essex: A Tragic History* (1928). In Leslie's treatment, Swift's central conflict as a character is in battling opposites and in controlling tension between affairs of the "heart" (carnal and platonic) and of the "skull" (political and intellectual) to forge an outsized reputation for himself. He foolishly restrains the one but exercises the other, too successfully, until the skull is inevitably emptied of "memory [...] within its own phantasmagoria," and words begin to fade "into emptiness beyond words" (Leslie 328). Not mad but isolated in almost total deafness, he rages passionately until the end. In death, the old Dean leaves behind his epitaph and all his published writings to become a ghost, joined by "crouching" Vanessa and wife-like Stella, to pass "together into the void" (Leslie 337).[80]

Yeats's nearest literary project involving romantic triangles, or triads, woven into its plot structure (albeit for comic effect) was a work of prose fiction, "Stories of Michael Robartes and His Friends," a work planned in mid-September 1929 but incomplete until Yeats reported to his wife from Coole (on September 13, 1930) that "I have been writing notes in diary & correcting Robartes. Robartes is finished [....] I will send it on Monday" (*CL InteLex* 5381). Preceding this visit to Coole, Yeats had written to Lady Gregory with promising news: "When I have finished my present task[,] 'Stories of Michael Robartes & his friends' [...] I shall begin my spiritistic play about Swift" (August 23, [1930], *CL InteLex* 5373).[81] Between mid-August and mid-September 1930, then, the play *Words upon the Window-Pane* began to take shape quickly with preliminary sketching at Rapallo E, [18r]. Already by September 4, 1930, Yeats was able to report to Lady Gregory: "I have finished the first sketch, a very full scenario, of a one act play on Swift. I hope to finish it at Coole" (*CL InteLex* 5377). Thereafter, work on the play continued, although interrupted briefly by several drafts of the lyric poem "For Anne Gregory." The day before that, on September 13, 1930, he reported to his wife that he was just "about to start on the Swift play" proper (*CL InteLex* 5381)—that is, he had reached the vicinity of folios [30r–31r] in the notebook.

The "Scenario" begins by identifying three key elements of the play: a haunted house "near Dublin," verse scratched by Swift on a pane of glass in that house, and the raising of spirits from the dead as told in Part III of *Gulliver's Travels*. The house was not one of those distant houses that Yeats knew to be haunted such as Renvyle House in Connemara or Castle Leslie in County Monaghan.[82] A Swift connection required a setting in or near Dublin, and the Deanery of Saint Patrick's Cathedral would have been an absurdity, because of the séance, and offensive to Abbey Theatre audiences.[83] Hence the setting became "A large room in ~~house~~ Georgian house near Dublin" ([18r]; see *WUWP* 6–7). It was, as "Young Man" (an Englishman) says, "'A wonderful room for a lodging house.'" "Old Man" (a Dubliner) explains that the discreet society to which he belongs had first met in a building on Molesworth Street but then moved to this new location to gain a "larger room" due to Mrs. Patterson's growing popularity as a medium. Although the old location was in the center of Dublin and an easy walk to the Cathedral and Deanery, the current site is a mile away and once had been "somebody['s] town house—not that it was exactly in the town—up to some eighty years ago. Swift used to visit here." Without explicitly saying so, Old Man relates details associated locally with the Dean as a frequent guest at a Queen Anne manor, "Fairfield," in Glasnevin, a property belonging to the Gogarty family in 1909, when Yeats took up lodgings there and discovered writing on a pane of glass.[84] In the "Scenario," the Englishman is invited next to view the inscription, "some lines he [Swift] is supposed to have scored on the pane with a diymond," but the light is too dim. In five lines (cancelled at the bottom of the page), the conversation turns to what opinion Swift might have had of the "sceance to night" in light of "the Magicians Island in Guliver. – Guliver <attended a kind of sceance,> was told he could raise from the dead any body he pleased." On [17v] (at a slant and with clue-lines drawn to show where revisions were to be inserted on the facing page), it is Old Man who recalls first that *Gulliver's Travels* may provide an answer to this question: "~~There is~~ <Is not there> some thing of the kind in Gulliver[?]" To this Young Man replies: "'The Magicians Island[.] Gulliver was told he could call up who he pleased'" (*WUWP* 4–5).

Yeats has in mind two chapters, VII and VIII, in *Gulliver's Travels*, Part III, "A Voyage to Laputa, Balnibari, Glubbdubdrib, Luggnagg, and Japan," where Gulliver is introduced to the Governor of Glubbdubdrib, a small "Island of *Sorcerers* or *Magicians*."[85] All of the Governor's attendants are spirits who vanish "with a turn of his finger," and at Gulliver's request this host summons "scenes of pomp and magnificence" by raising great men of antiquity to participate, at first in a form of pageant, with Alexander the Great at the head of his army, followed by Hannibal, Caesar, and Pompey leading their armies.[86] By the same means, Caesar and Brutus are summoned in particular, and the latter explains to Gulliver "that his ancestor Junius, Socrates, Epaminondas, Cato the younger, Sir Thomas More and himself [Brutus] were perpetually together: a *sextumvirate* to which all the ages of the world cannot add a seventh" (159). In Yeats's "Scenario," the younger and the older man are mistaken on number as they recall that Swift "chose seven men, then [...] he declared the world could not add an eighth" (folio [19r]; *WUWP* 10–11). The number remains in error, and the membership of Swift's select group becomes imprecise with correction on [18v]: "Half a dozen old Romans & then ~~Brutus, Cato, Etc &~~ Sir Thomas Moore" (*WUWP* 8–9). Old Man asserts that Swift was pagan, but Young Man counters: "No no no— he was a deeply religious man, but he despised ordinary men. Those seven men, ~~were Brutus, Cato, Blessed Sir Thomas More & the rest~~ <Cato, Brutus & the rest> were martyred because they saw more than their fellows" ([19r]).[87]

In the longer, more philosophical Chapter VIII, Gulliver gives us "Ancient and modern history corrected," with the appearance of Homer and Aristotle and the latter's assessment of an imaginary presentation by Pierre Gassendi (1592–1655) on Epicurus and another on "the *vortices* of Descartes" as told by the ghost of René Descartes (1596–1650).[88] Significantly, at a pivotal turn in *The Skull of Swift*, Shane Leslie uses this episode to establish one of the fundamentals of the last phase of Swift's tortured life—an inner-life for portrayal in fictionalized biography:

> The seances in Glubbdubdrib enabled Gulliver to introduce Homer to his commentators and Aristotle to Descartes. [...] Aristotle predicted that the Doctrine of Attraction, otherwise Newton's Gravitation, would be exploded and that "new systems of Nature were but new fashions, which would vary in every age, and even those, who pretend to demonstrate them from mathematical principles, would flourish but a short period of time." By the necromancy of his pen the Dean could lean back in his chair and question the history and learning of the past.[89]

As indicated by cancellations in Yeats's sketch, a dialogue between characters becomes more of a monologue as Young Man begins to lecture on Gulliver's (*qua* Swift's) depiction of "Nature made perfect by intellect" in the land of Houyhnhnms (here "hynanmes")—"not what we call intellect now, but as Plato understood it," as "Some[thing] perhaps that all possessed in the Golden Age, or in Edan perhaps"; for "He" (Swift?) "thought <Something> the Roman Senate had it in its great day. ~~He was the opposite~~ of ~~Russeu~~ Rouseu in Everything [....] Rousseu,[90] ~~who~~ was the opposite in everything, [...] preffered some sort of untutored savage, or primitive man to the Roman Senate" ([19r]). To this, Old Man replies, perhaps impatiently: "What a lot you read—I read Swift when I was young but ~~since~~ have not time to read anything now." (To Old Man's thinking, the opposite of an "untutored savage" is understood to be Aristotle, Plato's pupil.) Thus in self-defense, the young Englishman (himself a student) brings this discussion to a close with four lines at the top of [20r]:

> Young Man ~~But~~ "But it does not need any great reading to see | how different they were. ~~Swift~~ Rous[*seau*] did not call up seven | to show the world could not add the eight[*h*], but the uneducated mob. | ~~Old~~ All that is satirized in Gulliver & The Tale of a Tub.[91]

Thus the idea for a play about Jonathan Swift manifested through a modern-day séance is clearly formulated from the beginning (from [18r]), with the action set up by an observation that the location of the meeting belonged to friends of Swift's in the eighteenth century and by lines ostensibly cut by him with a diamond on a window-pane. The "Scenario," like a prose Subject of any number of Yeats's poems, anticipates the plot-line of the play (at [20r], with an insertion from [19v]) in rough outline, continuing, in part "II" (on [20r]) to explore the main action, which involves a medium who appears to voice the spirits of Swift and Vanessa. Part "II" extends the action to a version of the play's close (at [27r–28r]) with visitors leaving a supposedly "failed" séance and with the medium left alone (at [29r]) but still projecting speech in the voice of Dean Swift.

With the dialogue between Young Man and Old Man ending on the topic of Swift's satires (as related above), Yeats skipped a couple of spaces to begin a much longer, second part of the "Scenario" by entering the numeral "II." (centered) and continuing to relate the arrival of other persons who have come for the séance. At some time, however, Yeats might have thought either to make a new start on part I by simplifying it into main points (on facing page [19v]) or to remind himself of the progress he had made thus far by jotting details as a prelude to writing the action. At the top of [19v], he reintroduced an abbreviated title ("Swift.") and, beneath that, the heading "Scenario." Thereafter, he made the following entry but cancelled it in four strokes, as shown:

> Conversation between old Dublin man, & young Cambridge man. ~~Swifts signature~~ | on ~~window.~~ ~~Fine room for a lodging house~~ Are sceance always here. Yes | Always. Fine room. History of house. Swifts name on window pane. | What is it does not no [=*know*]. Cannot see in this light. Would he have thought | much of sceance or me to attend one. O I dont know the Magicians Island. | ~~What a Pagan he was was. Seven men one Christian~~. That was different | more modern. He was pure intellect, how he would have hated | all your patter about loved ones, & dear departed & all the rest. | His love of intellect & what a pagan he was. (See *WUWP* 12–13.)[92]

Although part "II." of the "Scenario" continues directly from [20r], [19v] produces fifteen lines of prose to be inserted before that, as indicated by clue-lines drawn to the facing page. As "People have been coming in" ([19v]), Old Man begins to introduce the "young Cambridge man" as "a young friend of mine <M^{r} S> —from Oxford—thinks we are some kind of jugglers but we all have to make a beg[inn]ing." The first person "M^{r} S" meets within the insert is "M^{rs} L," a new character not having been anticipated on [20r]. She gives testimony to the effectiveness of "M^{rs} P" (or Mrs. Patterson, the medium, named both on [18r] and [20r]) in communicating with Mrs. L's husband, who "was killed in a flying accident two years ago." She comes to ask her husband's "advice about every thing" and to visit their deceased child ("Our son [...] is with him—he died when he was a little boy but he has grown up there—he looks my husband tells me as if he was thirty years ~~age~~ old—he will never grow [continuing to 20v] any older than that"). The inserted matter on folio [20v] is of equal length to that on [19v] and shows that Yeats continued to expand dialogue into the scenario, possibly because otherwise his initial sketch of the action (on [21r]) was proceeding too quickly toward the séance. The dialogue between Young Man ("Mr S") and Mrs. L is thus extended, though with some of Old Man's comments cancelled or reassigned. Young Man asks, "Do you all ~~come here~~ to sceances to meet somebody who is dead"? To this Mrs. L complicates matters by recalling the function of the medium's control, Silver Cloud:

> That <old> man sitting ~~by~~ by the door had ~~lost all religious~~ <no religi[*ous*]> | belief, ~~but~~ he thou[*ght*] the grave ended everything~~—he has got something~~ | he had a horror of death, ~~but now he is a religious~~ man | ~~He wants to die – says it will be a great relief~~ – Now he wants to | die. He told me the other night that there are horse races there[,] | says Silver Cloud told him that – ~~but I dont belev she did~~ – ([20v])

On this observation, a certain amount of comic repartee is effected between Old Man and Mrs. L, to the detriment of both Silver Cloud and the deaf man seated by the door. Whether the man "is deaf enough to have mistaken what Silver Cloud was saying," Mrs. L allows that "There are deceiving spirits"—but also that "all who can should join" in because "It does not matter if you cannot sing very well [...] a hymn is always a great help" (cf. *WUWP* 16–17, where the clue-lines on [20v] are shown to direct the complicated interjection of speakers and lines of dialogue at this point). All of this follows inserted matter on [19v] to complete the second page of an insert to go into the "Scenario" at the beginning of part II. Its wry last words caution that "a lyer does not cease to be a liar because he is dead" and that "<a good> control like Silver Cloud 'should be able to ~~help~~ & select.' May I introduce Miss Y our secretary."

On [20r], just as Old Man observes that "people are late to night," a "Young [?ish] woman" interrupts to say that the others have all arrived "before their time. It is early for every thing." She "Is introduced to young man." "It is his first sceance. He asks questions" and shows his skepticism, as natural at first, but "[s]ometimes they give good descriptions <[they] describe sitters> Etc." The open-endedness of the elliptical "Etc.," as a substitution for something so well-known that it might be left to fill in later, indicates Yeats's familiarity with the subject-matter rather than the opposite. (See, for example, his note on "Clairvoyance" at [2v], above, or a note on the medium's voice, in Rapallo C, [1r].)[93] The young woman cuts straight to the problem at hand: "Lately [a] horrid spirit has upset things[....] M[rs] Patterson ~~thinks it is [...] somebody connected with the house~~ <says connected with house perhaps> ~~but nobody can think of any body~~" ([20r]). There are the cases of "Abraham Wallace & the [?~~Jambler~~] <gambler>," an example that Yeats himself uses in *A Vision* (*AVB* 225, *CW14* 163). "But it is not always the moment of death[....] There are spirits who go over & over guilty events of their past lives" ([20r]). Old Man adds: "they have suffered so much, that they are drawn back as it were must repeat some past action, just as we back up things that made us suffer."[94] In a cancelled line, he cites a book about Marie Antoinette by an "~~Oxford~~ Lady" inspired by a vision,[95] replaced by the young scholar's citing the mourning "Achilles in a black cloud" in Homer's *Iliad*,[96] to adduce a classical example. Young woman is convinced that "this spirit is bad," for he has "spoilt two sceances" and "would do nothing but pour out a lot of abuse, [?abusing] some woman," to such an extent that "~~Some~~ <Two> of their members [had] resigned." (*WUWP* 14–15.)

Folio [21r] continues the "Scenario" from [20r]. We learn then that at least half a dozen persons have arrived and are seated, and the "young woman" (Miss Y, the group's secretary) points out and greets Mrs. Patterson, an "old ~~woman~~ <medium>" who begins the ceremony with greetings, short remarks including instructions, and a hymn by "Miss X" (another member, evidently assigned this task in past séances):

> [N]ow my dear friends we will begin. There [are] some strangers among us[.] | I want to explain that I do call up spirits – I make the right | conditions that is all & they come. I do not know who is going to | come – they ~~mu~~ decide that – ~~but~~ the guides ~~all ways try to~~ do | ~~something~~ do their best, <but they cannot always succeed just at once> [~~...~~] If you want to speak to some | dear one who has passed on they will find for you but you [*must*] have | patience. If they do not find [*you*] to night, they may the next time [~~...~~] <Now we will begin>[.] You need not hold hands – | but nobody should move their leggs[;] that interferes with the | magnetism. <Now Miss X, a hymn please, the same

> verse we had | last time will do. (hymn)> (Cf. *WUWP* 18–19; the speech is simplified here for sense and as indicated on [21r].)

Miss X narrates the signs of Mrs. Patterson's progress into a trance—that she "always snores like that when she is going off[.] She will be in ~~the~~ trance in a moment." Then the medium speaks in a "Child Spirit" voice: "'Glad to see you friends. [...] Good evening everybody,'" which Miss X explains for the others is the voice of "Silver Cloud," Mrs. Patterson's child. "Child S" (for "Child Spirit," or Silver Cloud) concludes this page by announcing the presence of two more spirits: "There is somebody here for Lady ~~over there~~ by the door"—a spirit "recognised"—but also a "Third spirit not recognized." This one disturbs her, and she says, "drive that old man away - Who does he [*want?*] he is an old [continuing on 22r] but I say that he is a horrid old man - [?] Nobody want him here."

Thus Swift makes his entrance after Miss X notes that the "horrid old man" is "the spirit I told you of" and that "She [Mrs. Patterson or Silver Cloud] could not get rid of him last time" ([22r]). Silver Cloud has tried to go on with "Another description"—a "description recognised & message received"—but her effort is deflected by "somebody not recognised." Then we have "Suddenly Swifts voice speaking through medium. 'You have written to her - [?want to] [*know*] if she & I are married - what write [*sic*] have you to ask questions'"—in response to which Miss X interjects, "'That is the spirit that spoils everything[']," as Swift goes on to identify the spirit he addresses in detail and by name:

> I found you an ignorant little girl, without intellectual | or moral ambition, & ~~have~~ that I might teach you | I have left great mens houses, how many times | did I not stay away [from] my Lord Treasurer ~~neg~~ neglect | affairs of the greatest moment, that we might read Plutarch | together. I taught you to think in every situation of | life, not what Hester Van Homrigh should shou [*sic*] do | in that situation, but what Cato would & Brutus would | & now you peep & peer like any common slut | ~~Yes~~ a common slut I say a common slut, | ~~a common tavern slut caught peer[*ing*] through a~~ key | ~~whole, a~~ <common tavern slut> her ear against the key whole. ([22r], cf. *WUWP* 20–21)[97]

Young Man informs the group of the abused spirit's identity: "Did you catch the name of Hester Van Homrigh? That was the woman he called Vanessa"—a dramatic cue for the entrance of Vanessa: "Medium in Vanessas voice 'Why did you make me love you[?']" ([22r], last line).

Folio [23r] begins with Vanessa pleading with a question: "Why did you let me spend hour after hour in your company[?]" But the voices of the living (Young Man and Mrs. Patterson) and the dead (Silver Cloud and Swift) are interwoven for half a page, drawing attention away from the question, until

Yeats refocuses the dialogue. He accomplishes this by deleting fourteen lines in a combination of strikethroughs and wavy, vertical strokes and revising these exchanges below and on the facing page (folio [22v]). Young Man protests that the "old woman," Mrs Patterson, "wants us to believe that Vanessa is there too speaking through her Mouth" ([23r]); and Old Man offers that "~~Maybe these Spirits are dreaming~~ [...] Perhaps Vanessa is not here, ~~perhaps its Swifts dream~~ <perhaps its all Swift>" ([22v]; see *WUWP* 22–23). After that, the medium, in the voice of Swift, responds to Vanessa: "My god—do you think it is easy to me. I am a man in whom is strong, & [~~...~~] I swore that I would never marry" ([23r]). And, for the remainder of the page and a bit beyond, Vanessa articulates her complaint as the woman in Swift's autobiographic poem "Cadenus and Vanessa":

> "If you are not married Cadenus | why should we not live like other men & women. ~~When I | followed you to Ireland, I left~~ It is ~~five years now since~~ You | came to my mother's house, & began to teach me. I loved you | from the first moment. I thought it would just [*be*] enough to be near | you & speak to you. I followed to Ireland, five years ago & I | can bear no longer. It is not enough | to see enough, not enough to see & speak to you, nor enough to see | & speak, & touch your hands when we meet | [continuing to 24r] or part. Cadenus – Cadenus I am a woman, nor were the | women Cato <Cato> & Brutus loved <Brutus loved> any different. ([23r–24r]; see *WUWP* 24–27)[98]

At this, Old Woman (Mrs. Patterson) "stands up" and answers back (in "Swifts Voice") to blame ill health ("I have that within me no child must never [=ever] inherit") and to cite an instance of dizziness in London that Vanessa would recall ("I had to hold on to the book case I almost fell") and Dr. Arbuthnot's explanation "of those attacks, & other things worse things," which Pope ("because I told him") put in a line of verse ([24r]). Vanessa recites the line adroitly ("Great wits are ~~und~~ unto madness near allied")[99] and assures Swift that the Vanhomrigh "blood has been healthy for generations," which prompts the medium to rise to her feet again as Swift responds: "What if it be healthy [...] ~~What if it drown all that is Jonathan Swift~~ [...] so I add to all the common crowd, cattle that fill the fields[?]" In response to his fear,[100] Vanessa is consoling but also alluring: "Look at me Swift it is your [?courage/?arrogance] that keeps you from me, give your hand [...] Give me your both your hands – I am [*?woman*] put this hand upon my breast – O it is white, white as are the Gamblers dice, the little ivory dice ~~they threw throw~~."

Vanessa continues in this vein at the next opening in the notebook ([24v/25r]), where she proves to be as much of a disruptive agent in the proceedings as the spirit of Swift has been. At [25r], she continues: "It is the uncertainty, that ~~keeps me the gambling makes them throw the dice draws them to the table~~ brings them [*i.e., men*] to the table. A man child perhaps – perhaps not perhaps no Cadenus" ([25r]). In cancelled lines, the medium briefly stands again and, in Swift's voice, threatens to leave, which seems an unintentionally comic threat and therefore cut. Instead, Yeats chose to postpone Mrs. Patterson's latest rise to issue two more statements in Vanessa's voice: "What ~~have~~ does intellect matter with its load[*ed*] dice[?] I am the common ivory dice – white – white – white ivory" (the skin of her bosom) ([25r]). Then a line is drawn to a circumscribed passage on the facing page to extend Vanessa's speech for most of folio [24v]. This is her last speech in the "Scenario":

> Old woman rises & then sinks back again – Vanessa voice | ~~No No Cadenus – I You do not Do not think it is | the strength of my arm that pulls you back Cadenus | it is my love~~ It is not my hands that pull you back | Cadenus. You love & I love – You are [?growing] old | [?and] you want to grow old without children. Old | people are very solitary – their friends that remain are old too | & solitary – They ~~love~~ turn towards the young, but only their | children, or their childrens child – will endure an old man. | But you are not yet old Cadenus if you love | —white dice, white ivory dice. (The old woman | sits up talking (Swifts Voice[).][101]

Back on [25r], Swift is defiant in cancelled lines about bequeathing his intellect to mankind and directing Vanessa to "find some young coxcomb – healthy blood – that is safe" (see *WUWP* 30–31); however, this is amended to become "O god hear my prayer grant to Jonathan Swift this afflicted man that he may leave to posterity nothing but the intellect that came to him from heaven." Mixing stage directions and voices, Yeats has the "Old woman" move toward and beat upon the closed door, which had been open previously, and wails as Swift ("My god I am shut in with my enemy <with Venessa who hates my soul>") but "crouches" like Vanessa ("She crouches at door"), just as the ghost of Vanessa does at the end of *The Skull of Swift*, when the Dean dies.[102] Yet, instead of Swift's or Vanessa's voice, the next one that Mrs. Patterson assumes is that of her control, Silver Cloud.[103] She complains about the intrusion of "Bad old man. Big chief once ~~but~~ – bad old man [?not] know he is dead"—which inspires a short, derisive summation on [24v] (cancelled) about Swift's "Talk to another [~~...~~] squaw that he the big chief has many squaws." Then, back on [25r] and a few lines on [26r] ([25v] being a blank page) Silver Cloud tries to prevent the return of Swift (who uses up power) by imploring the group to sing to keep him away. "(Some one leads old woman back to her chair)" and Silver Cloud bids them all to "do another verse of hymn – Every body. Sing" ([25r]) to "bring good influence" ([26r]). And the scene ends with a direction and a mere prompt: "(Verse sung – Old Woman begins to speak during singing – singing falters & stops). Swifts Voice" (see *WUWP* 32–33).

For the remainder of folio [26r], the "Scenario" is notably sketchy. Three short entries are made there between drawn lines. The first entry suggests that Yeats knows what he wants but lacks having the material at hand to be more specific when outlining, mostly in third-person and in choppy sentences, what he wants said as Swift considers Stella, who makes no appearance in the play other than in a few lines of her verse. Yeats can only calculate next moves:

> The[n] follows scene in which Swift speaks to Stella | quoting her poem. He ~~do~~ has most wronged her. He asks | her assurance. But no he has her poem. She has had | no children – but she has her intellect – many friends – | If she had married – where would she be now. Would her face | give so much light. He begs [*her*] to out live him – to close | his eyes – ~~then it will be as though~~ His life has been always | solitary but for her – Many friends & yet solitary – begs her | & [=*at?*] the end. Repeats her poem – Yes that is right to come | to her soon. ([26r]; cf. *WUWP* 32–33)

In a few weeks, the poem "Stella to Dr. Swift on his birth-day November 30, 1721" was received by Yeats in two forms—the first in his wife's hand, as copied from text in the National Library of Ireland, and the other a typed copy[104]—from which selected lines were copied into the final draft, i.e., into the Harvard MS, at [16r] and [17r] (see *WUWP* 126–31). Without Stella's poem at hand in early September 1930, Yeats drew a short, horizontal line below the paragraph above and jotted a note of apology for Silver Cloud to say at the planned scene's conclusion and to mark the end of the séance: "Power all gone. Silver Cloud can do nothing more to night. Good by friends – Silver Cloud very sorry – bad old man—["] ([26r]). This is followed by two lines at the bottom of the page (after another even shorter horizontal line, almost a dash) to initiate the exit sequence: "The[n] ~~people in sceance come to say good by~~ – Miss X – says well Mrs P you tried your best – puts down money" (cf. *WUWP* 33, lines 17–18).

After this, the exit sequence was written with comparative ease, to judge by penmanship and the relative infrequency of cancellations on [27r], [28r], and [29r]. Folio pages [26v], [27v], and [28v] are blank and therefore devoid of supplements or revisions on facing pages, from this point to the end of the "Scenario" on [29r]. In a way, this sequence is the reverse of the one worked out for the arrivals and introductions of part II ([19v–21r]), where more invention was required to imagine and launch the action of the play. At this turn, the main characters had already been established, and Mr. S, an avowed skeptic from the beginning, gives money for a good show although the others attending consider the séance a failure. Ironically, as both Yeats and his wife looked askance at professional mediums, the ensuing sequence developed from a suggestion made by Mrs. Yeats. In an entry of September 13, 1930, in his *Pages from a Diary Written in Nineteen Hundred and Thirty* (*Ex* 322), Yeats recalled meeting in July with a clairvoyant who spoke suggestively about an imminent work: “Is this my Swift play? My wife who urged me to do it added the detail about the medium refusing money and then looking to see what each gave.”[105] The scene was sketched with such rapidity that speeches and directions meld into a kind of automatic script:

> Old woman [Mrs. P] says cannot accept it after a sceance like that | [Mr. S:] “No no – You must – Whether sceance is good or bad it | exausts you just the same. People who had put down money | & taken it up again ‘Now put it down –’[”] They [the others] go one by one | Young man [Mr. S] says “I thought it a wonderful sceance[,] Mrs | P. You know I ~~am doing my~~ get my Doctorate | by an essay on Swift – that is what brought me to | Dublin.[”] Old Woman [Mrs. P:] “I should not take your | money – I should not really.” ~~He puts it down~~ – She | ~~(looks)~~ I will not take anything. He says look | I have given you twice as much as your regular fee | now I will make it three times as much. ([27r], with editing in brackets for sense; cf. *WUWP* 34–35)

Yeats’s sympathy elsewhere for the hybrid role of the medium and the inevitable imperfection of communication undermines any attempt at scientific skepticism about the validity of phenomena involved when he is an investigator, but it creates a poignant paradox in *The Words upon the Window-Pane*, where the only person to realize who the voices are dismisses the medium’s channeling as mere performance, while the majority of the believers do not understand what the voices signify and view the séance as a failure. After the others have gone, Young Man tries to press Mrs. P to explain how she knows “so much about Swift” when “Hardly any body knows anything about that poem of Stellas,” so like Donne “in places,” until questioning leaves Mrs. P bewildered.

As Young Man becomes more aggressive on [28r] (“Do you remember the story about the negress,” etc.), the writing becomes fraught with assertions, denials, and cancellations for nearly half a page. “‘Who are you talking about Sir.’ Why about Swift of course – [~~…~~] Old Woman ‘I dont know [~~…~~] anybody called Swift[”] [~~…~~] ‘O yes you do’ ‘Nobody of that name here – but in Glasgow, I am a Glasgow woman, a great many people come to the sceances. [~~…~~] Or is it somebody who has passed on’” ([28r]). To which Young Man insists emphatically: “Swift Jonathan Swift – the spirit that was here to night – You gave a wonderful impersonation”—with Mrs. Patterson partly conceding some knowledge of the subject, but only as a medium: “What that man, that dirty old man, dont talk of him, its not lucky to talk of him. Dont think of him – A bad spirit like that – to talk of them or think of them brings them.” Given her obvious agitation, Young Man breaks off this interview as courteously as he can with the words: “Ah well – I see you are very tired. We will have our talk some other day – Good night You are certainly a genius (EXIT)” ([28r]; cf. *WUWP* 36–37).

After the exit sequence comes the dramatic curtain scene on [29r], a short solo featuring the medium, who unawares still bears the presence of Swift's spirit:

> She lowers the ~~lamp or blows out the can[*dles*]~~ gass – | or blows out the candles. [~~…~~] | & puts on kettle [~~…~~]. Swifts Voice[:] | Harley gone, [?Bolingbroke] gone, the Duke of Ormond <Godolphin> gone[106] – | Counting on fingers "five great ministers, ten great ministers ~~I | have not fingers enough to count up the~~ that I have known | I have not fingers enough to count up the great ministers | that I have known & that are gone". Old Woman wakes | with a start takes down tea pot & cup & go to fire | to arrange kettle better. Swifts ~~voic~~ v[o]ice "Perish the | day on which I was born Etc ([29r]; cf. *WUWP* 38–39)

The "Etc" signifies the possibility of following Shane Leslie's example by quoting more than the third verse of Job chapter 3 from the King James translation of the Bible ("Let the day perish wherein I was born") to dramatize Swift's "uttering imprecations upon himself."[107] In later drafts, Yeats drops in references to Job via other characters to prepare for his adaptation of Job 3:3 in the play's powerful curtain-line. The most effective of these, an elliptical allusion by the medium herself, is not introduced until Harvard MS, [18r]: "His clothes were dirty, his face dirty, his face covered with boils. It was horrible. Some disease ~~what~~ had made one of his eyes swell up. It stood out from his face like a hens-egg" (*WUWP* 134–35; cf. *VPl* 955: 531–33). Although Wilde has been cited as a possible source, Leslie seems a nearer one in portraying Swift's condition before he died: "One final spasm of pain smote him. Like Job his body was covered with boils. One of his eyes swelled to an egg and five pairs of hands could scarce keep him from tearing it out. The eye sank back into the tortured skull" (327).[108] The names of Swift's Tory allies are dropped from the play but not the five or ten "great ministers" of his hands.

At this time, Yeats was also busy preparing copytext for *Stories of Michael Robartes and His Friends*, as noted above, and arranging poems and cover designs for *The Winding Stair* from matter generated in Rapallo Notebooks C and D. He looked forward to a respite at Coole, where he intended to concentrate on finishing this new play. And so, on September 4, 1930, he wrote to Lady Gregory about a prolonged visit, to start on Wednesday, September 10. He added: "I have finished the first sketch, a very full scenario, of a one act play on Swift. I hope to finish it at Coole" (*CL InteLex* 5377). As shown in Figure 4.7 (below), beyond the long "Scenario" of [17v–29r], the next phase of the play's writing began with a restatement of the setting (on [30r]) and characters defined in dialogue (at right) and by the list of "Characters" and projected action (at left, on [29v]). This first scene involves Young Man (here named James Corbet) and Old Man (named John Lefanu but amended to John Mackenna) from the early sketch. Some of the others are anticipated, most importantly Mrs. Henderson (formerly Mrs. Patterson), the medium, although some never appear in the action drafted in the Rapallo E manuscript—Mrs. James and even Mrs. Henderson, for example. The following facsimile of folios [29v] and [30r] (viewed together as Figure 4.7) presents a layout that must have helped Yeats convert the material of his rough outline into stage-reality.

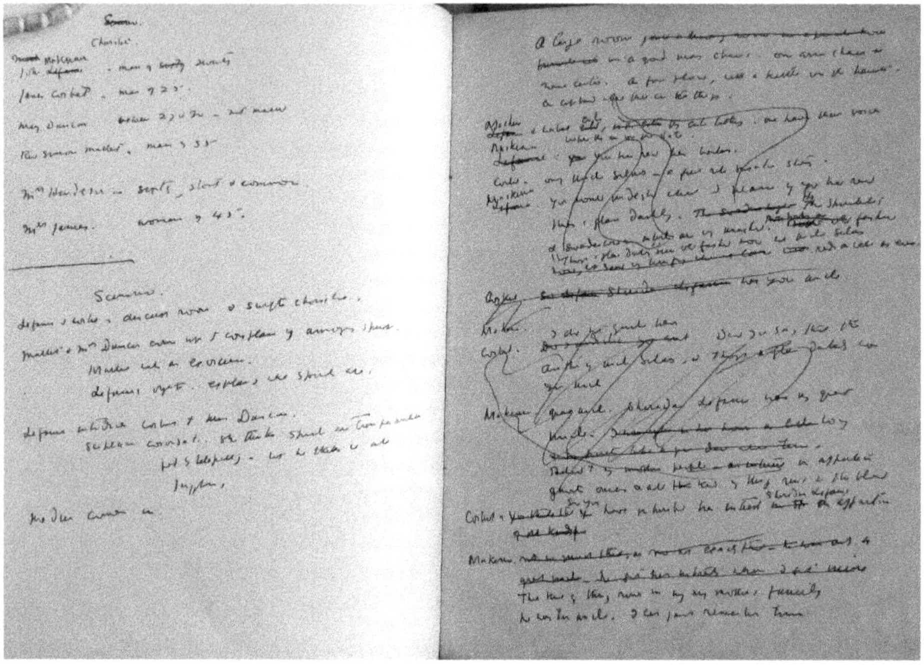

Figure 4.7. NLI 13,582 (Rapallo Notebook E), [29v–30r]. Courtesy of NLI; photograph courtesy of Catherine Paul E. Paul. (See *WUWP* 40–43.)

To begin on the left side of the opening, Yeats wrote "Scenario." at the top, but cancelled and replaced it with the word "Characters." Beneath this is a *dramatis personae* of six persons: "John ~~Lefanu~~ <~~Mack~~ McKenna> – man of ~~sixty~~ seventy"; "James Corbet – man of 25"; "Mary Duncan [–] between 27 & 30 – not married"; "Rev Simon Mallet – man of 35"; "Mrs Hende[r]son – sixty, stout & common"; and "Mrs James. woman of 45." Beneath this is a short drawn-line to separate the list of persons from an abbreviated "Scenario" (so-called but consisting of notes for only four stages of the play's action up to, but not including, the séance). These are (1) "Lefanu & Corbet – discuss room & Swifts character"; (2) "Mallet & Miss Duncan come up to complain of annoying spirit – | Mallet wants an exorcism. | Lefanu [i.e., Mackenna] objects. – explains what spirits are"; (3) "Lefanu [=Mackenna] introduces Corbet to Miss Duncan. | Swiftian conversation. She thinks spirits are Trance personalities fed by telepathy – but he thinks it all juggling"; and (4) "Medium comes in" ([29v]; cf. *WUWP* 40–41).

On the right side (on [30r]), the setting is defined, almost abstractly, to be "A large room, ~~once a drawing room in a private house furnished with~~ – a good many chairs – one arm chair ~~is~~ near center. A fire place, with a kettle on the hearth. A cupboard where there are tea things." By the end of the first exchange of lines between old Lefanu and young Corbet (heard talking before they are seen on stage), Yeats has decided to change the name of the former to Mackenna and to make him the great-nephew, instead, of the Irish mystery writer and Swedenborgian, Sheridan Le Fanu (1814–73). They speak critically of Le Fanu's novels *Uncle Silas* (1864) and *In a Glass Darkly* (1872, cited in error here as "Through a glass darkly"). Cancelling this first exchange, Yeats revises to suggest the Mackenna family's affinity to Le Fanu and his occult interests: "~~I was often in his house as little boy & my parents talked a great deal about him~~. Belonged to my mothers people – an interest in apparitions ghosts omens & all ~~that~~ kind of things runs in the blood." Yeats cancels this exchange, too, but concludes the page with Corbet inferring that the old man's interest in apparitions is an inherited one. To this, Mackenna demurs: "~~Not so much that, as No not exactly that – he was only a great uncle – he got his interests where I got mine~~ That kind of thing runs in my my mothers family he was her uncle. I can just remember him" ([30r]; cf. *WUWP* 42–43).[109]

At the next opening ([30v/31r]), Yeats starts over at the top of [31r] by reducing the setting to three words: "A large room" (also in large script). A clean stage direction follows: "Corbet & Mackennas voices heard at first outside the door in what follows." As before but in simplified speeches, they are discussing the novels *In a Glass Darkly* and *Uncle Silas*, with Corbet commenting that Mackenna's great-uncle, Sheridan Le Fanu, shows his sympathies in the latter novel by making "the one good influence" a Swedenborgian. In this vein, Mackenna acknowledges "~~I can just remember him when I was a child~~" and then shifts his attention to comment that "~~We must put the chairs right~~" for the séance. After striking these statements on [31r], a sixteen-line insertion was prepared on [30v], then clued by drawn lines and an arrow to make clear the substitution. Mackenna gives, then, an account of his own involvement with spiritualist activities: "If you had heard the talk I have heard from my mother & from my old aunts you would understand how in after life such things became an obsession" ([30v]). He has a business, which occupies little thought. "My great interest in life has been what people call apparitions – all that relates between man & the supernatur[al] which philosophy & the Church ignore." He concedes that his "study has been mainly theoretical for there are no good mediums in Ireland." So he values the opportunity to "get one from across the water," especially Mrs. Henderson "come from Glasgow at her own ~~expense~~ risk"—a circumstance justifying commensurate payment: "We are all to give her what we can. She lives very economically & does not expect a great deal" ([30v]; *WUWP* 44–45). He asks Corbet (back on [31r]) to assist with the chairs, and the young man remarks, as he had at his first entrance in the early "Scenario": "A wonderful room for a lo[d]ging house" ([31r]; cf. [18r]). And on that note, Mackenna gives background on the house in words also resembling those of Old Man in Yeats's first sketch. Here, he says: "It was a private house until about forty years ago – it was not so near the town in those days, there are quite large stables at the back. It was an important place in the eighteenth century." On their task to set up chairs around the medium's armchair, Mackenna says that they have done enough before Mrs. Henderson comes and "~~until we know how many people are coming~~" ([31r]; *WUWP* 46–47). Hence the chair count is deferred.

But as there are not to be empty chairs at a séance, in the next scene Mackenna and Miss Duncan take up this business when she and Mr. Mallet make their entrance on folio [32r], where Mackenna also begins to speak of Swift's connection with the house: "~~Swift was often in this room, & Stella~~ <Friends of John Swift lived here> In ~~the first part of~~ the eighteenth century the house belonged ~~Swift was often here~~, & Stella & her companion Tingley often sat at cards in this very room."[110] Though Yeats cancels these speeches, deferring the entrance of Duncan and Mallet indefinitely, Mackenna and Corbet are allowed to expand upon the setting's Swiftian association and to introduce the theme of words etched on a window-pane. McKenna says that the house was owned by "friends of Swift" in the "early" eighteenth century and mentioned "in the Journal to Stella several times." Several lines are cut after that, however, including the following:

> There is something on this window pane, ~~which~~ [?~~was~~] cut with a diamond by Swift | after Stellas death. ~~There~~ Somebody else may have cut them there in memory | of them both for they are not the kind of ~~joclar thing swift Swift~~ | bitter jocular thing Swift cut in window panes. ([32r]; cf. *WUWP* 48–49)[111]

Corbet expresses excitement because of the coincidence of his dissertation topic: "I am hoping to get my doctorate at Oxford by an essay on Swift & Stella[.] That is what brought me to Dublin." To this news, Mackenna notes the presence of "some lines of Swifts cut on the window with a diamond" (revised to "some lines from a poem of Stellas cut on that window with a diamond"). Mackenna's expression of doubt that the lines were carved by Swift, like the cancelled lines of Mackenna's preceding speech, are stricken, leaving him to "wonder what Swift would think of our work to night." "Not much I think," Corbet replies (also on [32r]), giving us the scene's last line except for a stray clause at the top of folio [33r] ("how many do you expect Miss Duncan"), a question posed by old Mackenna in his first cancelled speech on [32r].

Although not for long, work on Yeats's Swift play came to a stop here, perhaps for only a day or so. The pause was just long enough to draft and polish an amusing lyric poem, "For Anne Gregory," destined to join others of its kind in *Words for Music Perhaps* (Cuala Press, 1932).

[31v, 32v–34r] [drafts of "For Anne Gregory]

Thus, interspersed in the Rapallo E draft of *The Words upon the Window-Pane* are drafts of "For Anne Gregory," the only poem in the notebook apart from songs that Yeats wrote for *The Resurrection.* Three days after arriving at Coole, Yeats wrote his wife, saying "I am about to start on the Swift play" (*YGYL* 224; *CL InteLex* 5381), when in truth he had advanced its writing to folio [33r] in the notebook. The next day (September 14, 1930), he wrote to her again to request that, when joining him, she bring with her a copy of "Swift's verse," adding that he had written "a poem, half mockery & half wholly complimentary about Anne Gregory's 'yellow hair'" (*YGYL* 224; *CL InteLex* 5382). He said that the new poem consisted of three "verses" (or stanzas), the following being the last:

> I heard an old religious man
> Yesternight declare
> That he had found a text to prove
> That only god, my dear,
> Could love you for your self alone
> And not your yellow hair. (*YGYL* 224; *CL InteLex* 5382)

Then he boasted: "Lady Gregory made me read it to her six times in the course of one evening, & would have insisted upon a seventh had not bed time come." And on Monday, September 15 (the next day), he explained in yet another letter to his wife: "I am writing a poem, another of those 'poems for music.' […] I have done little at the play[.] A first draft is always a hateful job & one puts it off" (*YGYL* 224–25; *CL InteLex* 5383).

The poem's composition began with its last stanza, which seems natural to the process of creating a refrain with a dazzling compliment for its designated first audience, Lady Gregory's nineteen-year-old granddaughter. Facing, on [31v], a full page of dialogue from the play up to that point, the most difficult for Yeats were the first two lines. After three trials, the quaint expression "yester night," sacrificed after two trials, is restored in the fourth just as the speaker, a "rambling monk," becomes an "old religious man" in the course of the same four stages. From the first, the poem was to have the rhythm of a ballad (alternating tetrameter and trimeter lines); and lines 3–6 fell into place just as Yeats quoted the stanza back to his wife on September 14 (except for two commas added in the latter). Spondaic substitution in the first line of the refrain (on "love you") retards and intensifies the three iambic stresses of the last line: "And not your yellow hair" ([31v]; *WFMP* 198–99).

At the next opening ([32v/33r]), stanzas 1 and 2 were worked out, respectively. At first (on [32v]), Yeats jotted a set of rhyme notes ("—dear | alone | hair") to remind himself of the last word in each of the three final lines of the stanza he had just written on [31v]. Beside these rhyme notes, he produced four lines of verse (lines 3–6), only the first two of which are new because 5 and 6 were from the refrain. Of the other two ("While such a ~~pile~~ <heap> of honey lock / A rampart at your ear"), line 4 is the more stable when comparing it here with its next iteration near the bottom of the page. Between these two points, Yeats fashions a rough first stanza by adding two lines to signify a young male perspective ("Many a lad," "any young man," "the youngster") "T[h]rown into despair" ([32v]; see *WFMP* 200–201).

On folio [33r], well below the vagrant line from the play, the second stanza is written at a slant and without evidence of much labor. After a rejected attempt at the first line in the voice of the girl ("~~But I will get a [?hair] [?die]~~"), Yeats is able to deliver a version of the whole stanza (with trouble only in line 3, where "Such ~~brown of~~ <brown>" is deleted), intact but without any punctuation despite the line's parenthetical relation to her sentence. So the residual verse is much as Yeats would have it later:

> But I can get a hair die
> And set such colour there
> Brown or black or carrot
> That young men in despair
> Shall love [*me*] for my self alone
> And not my yellow hair (cf. *WFMP* 202–203)

At the next opening in the notebook, Yeats put it all together by copying all three parts of the poem on folio [34r], substituting "coloured" for "pale" in stanza 1, "dye" for "die" in stanza 2, and little else that he did not cancel before he finished there. On the facing folio ([33v]), he jotted possible substitutions that are clued to stanza 1, lines 1 and 5 (respectively, "My dear there[s] not a man alive" and "Could love Etc"), though these were never implemented. He experimented with modal auxiliaries *may*, *shall*, *can*, and *could* to the verb *love* in the refrains of two stanzas (2 and 3). And in line 3 of stanza 1, he played with a manner of a rhetorical delivery whereby stress marks were placed over the words "By those" in order to give emphasis to the "honey-coloured / Ramparts" of Anne's hair. In fact, an *accent grave* was actually placed over "those" in the fair-hand copy of the poem that Yeats inscribed, initialed, and dated "Sept 1930" (NLI 13,590

(13), [1r]), as well as in a holograph copy made for Lady Gregory that he left in her personal archive, on a blank page of his *Selected Poems* (1929).[112] By shifting voices in the poem from male to female and back again, Yeats managed to write another successful song (a ballad) in dialogue, like those of Crazy Jane and other personae in lyrics he was then collecting for *Words for Music Perhaps*. When read aloud by the poet for the first time, "For Anne Gregory" had a different title and was an instant sensation among those who witnessed it at the Gregory estate.[113] Much later, Anne de Winton (née Gregory) recalled the jitters that accompanied her particular audience with the poet:

> Mr Yeats sent a message for me to go up to his sitting-room, and then said that he had written a poem called "Yellow Hair" and that he had dedicated it to me, and proceeded to read it, in his "humming" voice. We used to hear his voice "humming" away for hours while he wrote his verse. He used to hum the rhythm of a verse before he wrote the words, [...] but on this occasion I was petrified. I had no idea that he was going to write a poem to me, and I had no idea at all what one should say when he had read it aloud.
>
> It was agony! For once, I think I did the right thing. Nearly in tears for fear of doing something silly, "Read it again," I pleaded, "oh do read it to me again."
>
> Obviously this was all right, for Yeats beamed, put on his pince nez attached to the broad black silk ribbon, and read it through again.
>
> [She quotes the poem from *VP* 492.]
>
> This time I was able to stutter: "Wonderful. Thank you so much. Wonderful. I must go and wash my hair," and crashed out.[114]

[34v–41v] "Swift" [the entrance sequence (3rd version), *The Words upon the Window-Pane*]

When Yeats took up the play again (on [35r]), it was to relaunch the entrance sequence for the third time since its initial rehearsal in the long "Scenario" of [17v–29r]. The central idea seems clearer with development by combining, or blending, the speeches of characters from the first and second drafts of [29v–32r]. The writing now seems to have come more easily to him—unlike that of his more usual mythical plays—because he was able to draw on his own wide experience visiting séances for the set-up, atmosphere, and action of the play. Although this third draft of the scenes preceding the séance is fraught with revisions and with insertions on verso pages, by the time the writing reached the one and only full-length draft of the play in holograph (the Harvard MS), the blended work of Rapallo E, [34v–41r] had become the basis for most of Yeats's fair-hand copying into the latter manuscript. ([41v] is exceptional as shall be explained in due course.) In this third version of the opening sequence, names for most of his characters had moved closer to their final forms just as the setting became more firmly established with details associated with Swift's life.

At [35r], the working title "Swift" is still used (appearing at the top), followed by a stage direction: "Peter Trench & William Corbet enter." Originally referred to simply as Old Man and Young Man, they were introduced as "John ~~Lefanu~~ <Mackenna>" and "James Corbet" on [29v] and are given new names here. (They are yet to become "~~William~~ <Dr> Trench" and "John Corbet," respectively, in Harvard MS [at 1r], where the working title is amended to "The words upon the window pane"; cf. *WUWP* 78–81.) Trench and Corbet have become leading parts, and they discuss (as on [30v]) the absence of "good mediums in Ireland" at a reasonable cost, as well as Mrs. Henderson's origin in Glasgow. Trench has not any connection with the Swedenborgian Sheridan Le Fanu here but offers that he is "chairman of the 'Dublin Spiritualists Association'" and that "this is the first of the sceances I have been able to attend"—which is new, along with information conveyed to Corbet about Henderson's trance mediumship and her method used to differentiate between speakers by "some mannerisms, some trick of phrase, or even of movement" ([35r]; *WUWP* 52–53). Indeed, this is new material that Yeats expands on the facing folio, where Trench explains:

> This is the first of <of her> sceanses that I have been able to attend | but I saw a great deal of the movement as a young man—I knew Hume [=Home; i.e., D. D. Home] | the Fox sisters, Eglinton all great mediums.[115] That is why they have made | me chairman of the Dublin Spiritualists Society. ([34v])

Before returning to [35r] and, by now, familiar dialogue from [18r] and subsequent exchanges on the good state of the room "for a lodging house" that actually had been "a private house until ~~forty~~ <fifty> years ago," Trench supposes that the young man believes "it all juggling" (to which Corbet agrees) but adds:

> I thought the same but one soon gets over that[.] | If you get nothing to night you must come again. Several is | [?better] evidence. Sometimes a sceance is spoilt – Mrs | Hendersons sceances have been a good deal spoilt – a | disturbing influence of some kind. She is a trance | medium, & ~~whe~~ <if> all goes well
> {You may get some good evidence to night} ([35r], [34v]; *WUWP* 50–51)

The first two-thirds of folio [36r] bring into this draft a reworking of matter from [32r] on the house in its relation to Swift's Dublin friends, on his playing cards with Stella there (as mentioned in *Journal to Stella*), and on lines of her poetry etched into the window-pane. Here, Trench observes that "Somebody cut <with a diamond> two lines from a poem of hers on the window paine" (see *WUWP* 56–57). But in transferring speech from one place to another, Yeats forgets, for a few lines, that Trench is now speaking, not Miss Mackenna, who will not be introduced until the interjections are prepared on the facing page (on [35v]).[116] Trench directs Corbet's attention to the etched lines ("you can hardly see them in this light"), and Corbet asserts, without seeing them clearly, that they are "two lines" from a birthday poem written for Swift in the manner of Donne and Crashaw, she being "a much greater poet than Swift" ([36r]). Space is left to fill in later Stella's verse. Corbet announces, as before, that he is writing "an essay on Swift & Stella [...] for his doctorate at the university." He asks Trench for his opinion on what Swift might think of their séance, which Yeats takes as a cue to introduce the topic of Swift's "kind of sceance," described in *Gulliver's Travels*, Part III, Chapters VII and VIII, about "The Magicians Island"—matter not seen in the drafts of Rapallo Notebook E since part [I] of the early "Scenario" (at [17v–20r]). Most of that reprised material now follows on folios [36v–38r].

Yet before that, Miss Mackenna (formerly Duncan) and Johnson (formerly Rev. Simon Mallet, later Abraham Johnson) make their appearance in a short scene interjected, from [35v] to [36r], into position immediately after Trench calls Corbet's attention to Stella's lines in the glass. As indicated by clue lines drawn around each of two separate entries on [35v], their order should be transposed. The Johnson and Mackenna entrance would be defined in purpose by the note in the short scenario on [29v] (for Mallet and Duncan), indicating that they were to complain about an "annoying spirit" that warranted an "exorcism." Here (on [35v]), that deferred scene was developed, with speeches to be arranged in the following order:

[(]Johnson & Miss Mackenna enter)
Johnson
Where is Mrs Hendeson
Mackenna
She is ~~lying down~~ up stairs – she always rests before a sceance
Johnson
I ~~mu~~ must see her before the sceance. We must get of[*f*] that evil | influence which has disturbed the last two sceances. I know that has to be done
Mackenna
~~You must not speak about it~~. If you speak to her, you will upset her nerves & | then there will be no sceance at all
Johnson Where is Mrs Mallet, she is I am told an experienced spiritualist, I will | consult – (A bell rings or knock sounds ~~& then a~~

> Miss Mackenna. There she is now & she has probably [?noticed/?heard] our thoughts [~~...~~] <You can bring him into the smoking room.> | her voice is heard[)] "~~We~~ So glad to see you Mrs Mallet – there is some [?tea]["] etc)
>
> They stare at window – Trench points out the exact spot | Corbet [?stoops] down & sees [~~...~~][117] ([35v]; cf. *WUWP* 54–55)

From [36v] to [38r], then, the play's dialogue consists of a largely academic display of learning by Dr. Trench and William Corbet on the subject of Swift's worthies by analogy to Gulliver's meeting with the spirits of great men on Glubbdubdrib, or "The Island of *Sorcerers* or *Magicians*." In Leslie (258), this episode denotes the "necromancy" of Swift's pen, a theme that, on the first pages of Yeats's "Scenario," had been projected as key to the interpretation of a character who does not *appear* though his words are given voice by a clairvoyant medium. As much of this has been discussed already, from Yeats's scratch notes on folios [17v–20r], our focus now will be on how a hypothesis was reached in dialogue by Trench and Corbet, given the twists, turns, and amplifications of Yeats's composing process. That hypothesis is essentially the idea that is to animate Corbet's doctoral thesis, which will argue that Swift's writings mark "the highest point of intellectual achievement" reached by a European author of his time ([37v]).

On [37r], then, Yeats at first confuses Swift and Gulliver in Corbet's account of the *sextumvirate* of worthy men that (since [18v/19r]) has been mistaken in Yeats's count: "~~Swift~~ <Gulliver> was told that he call back from the dead anybody he liked, & asked for Brutus, Cato Sir Thomas Moore seven men, & except for Sir Thomas Moore all Greek or Roman ~~Se~~ worthies – men to whom as Swift says the world could not add an eighth" ([37r]; see *WUWP* 60–61). Corbet says that to "call up such men"—and prove one's ability to do so—would empower a movement to "conquer the world" but, for ten more lines, fails to articulate doubt. Hence those ten lines are stricken in preference to an insert on science and religion (on [36v]) but clued in to follow a weak protest by Trench: "~~S So Swift made~~ <So> Gulliver ~~sumen~~ <called up seven> men, to ~~whom~~ the world ~~could add an eighth~~. The seven men out of all history most admired by Swift, & there was only one Christian among the Seven. What a Pagan Swift was" ([37r]).

On the facing verso ([36v]), Trench counters Corbet and defends the spiritualists' movement "not as a science but as a religious movement" that "enables [...] ~~quite~~ ordinary people to speak accross the great barrier, to other ordinary people whom they had known & loved." At first, "<a great many> people ~~deluded themselves~~ thought they could ~~speak~~ to ~~just such~~ call up just such spirits as Gulliver called up on the Magicians Island." However, in that phase, members of the movement faced "every kind" of delusion. And on that note, Corbet comments: "Swift hated the ordinary man. 'I hate lawyers, I hate doctors' he was accustomed to say though I love judge so & so Dr So & So" (cf. *WUWP* 58–59), joining his amended speech, at the bottom of [37r], to assert that Swift's seven (sic) worthies were

> martyred because they ~~saw more than their fellows~~ <were not ordinary men>. He calls | the hynamys [=Houyhnhnms] ~~the perfection of nature~~ his ideal people, the perfection of | nature, merely by their nature ~~made perfect by intellect~~, bred, trained | and disciplined, nature made perfect by intellect. He thought the Roman | Senate ~~that nature~~ had it in its great day. In my essay | [text continues to 38r:] ~~I contrast Swift & Rousseu~~ (cf. [19r])

Corbet finishes his sentence on the next folio, noting that his thesis "contrast[s] Swift & Rousseau," and goes on to say (just as Young Man does on [19r]), that Rousseau had preferred "some sort untutored savage, or primitive man" ([38r]). Trench replies as his prototype (Old Man) had done earlier, provoking young Corbet to express (perhaps too vehemently) that his hatred for Rousseau, which "is so strong that Swift ~~attracts me~~ <attracts> - attracts me, draws me upwards to some thing cold, arrogant & pure" ([38r]; *WUWP* 64–65). This exchange is cancelled by a wavy line and clued to its replacement, the first of three insertions on the facing verso:

> ~~I hope to~~ p | ~~My essay will be much more than an essay on~~ the | I hope to prove in my essay that in Swifts day Europe had reached its | highest point of intellectual achievement. ~~Swift dreaded the~~ ruin that ~~was to~~ | ~~follow, Democracy, Rousseau & all the rest~~. I can prove from Swifts every | work that he for saw the ruin to come, Democracy, Rousseau, the French | Revolution. That is why he ~~hated~~ <hated> ordinary men, that is why he [?~~wo~~] wrote | Gulliver, that is why he wore out his brain, thats where he got Saevo | in~~i~~nato [=*indignatio*], that is why he sleeps now under the greatest epitaph in history[.] | You remember how it runs: ["]He has gone where f fierce indignation | can lacerate his heart no more" ([37v]; *WUWP* 62–63)[118]

Given the prominence of Gulliver's séance and Swift's worthies as a counterpoint to ordinary people in Yeats's "Scenario," this scene, and the complete draft only weeks ahead, it is ironic that much of it had been cut—but to good effect—by September 27, 1930, when he wrote to his wife to say: "After you left I shortened by a whole page the Swift exposition & read what I have written to Lady Gregory. She was enthusiastic, & has several times returned to the subject. She says there is not a word too much, that it is 'powerful' & full of a sense of something coming" (*YGYL* 226; *CL InteLex* 5389). Related blocks of text were cancelled in the Harvard MS, [4r–4v].

Back on [38r], Dr. Trench and John Corbet are then joined by Rev. Johnson ("a minister of the gospel by profession"), Miss Mackenna, and Mrs. Mallet. Clued in from [37v] is Johnson's complaint, directed to Trench and Mallet ("experienced spiritualist," [35v]), that "Something will have to be done Mr Trench to drive away the influence that has been disturbing the sceances. I have come here at considerable expence week after week" ([37v]). Johnson goes on (back on [38r]) to cite his work with the "poorer classes" by producing a "great effect" by singing and preaching after the example of "the great revivalist preacher <Mr> Sankey" with whom he hopes to speak "through some medium" ([38r]),[119] having been directed in Belfast by a "fortune teller, who has a great gift with the cards, [...] to speak to Mr Sankey" in Dublin, but without success. At the foot of the page, Mrs. Mallet begins to reflect on Mrs. Henderson's past interruption—a reflection lengthened (as follows) by a third insertion clued from the notebook's opposing leaf:

> Mrs Mallet. What Mr Johnson says is quite true[;] the last | two sceances have been completely spoilt by a spirit, which | says a lot of unintelligible, & does not pay the slightest attention to
> { what we say. Just after the sceance has ~~started it~~ begun | the spirit begins talking ~~as as~~ though there are I think two spirits. There is a | long unintel-l[ig]ible quarrel – & poor Mrs Henderson is tost & thrown | here & there in the most horifying way.
> Trench. Did this spirit, or these spirits say the same thing every night
> Mrs Mallet. Yes just as they were characters in a play but a very ~~horple~~ | horible play } ([38r] and [37v]; cf. *WUWP* 62–65)

On [39r], Mr. Johnson follows this exchange with a formal request for an exorcism, having "brought a book for the purpose," asking Trench "as President of the Dublin Spiritualists Association to permit me to go through a ceremony of exorcism," but this speech is cancelled with the substitution of a clued speech by a newly invented character on [38v], a Mr. Rogers (eventually renamed Cornelius Patterson in the Harvard MS). A gambler, Rogers is a foil to the religiosity of Johnson and the solemnity of Mrs. Mallet. Rogers's tone is colloquial:

> Mr Rogers: I never did like the ~~sort~~ heaven they talk about [*in*] the Churges [=*Churches*] | but then Mrs Mallet ~~Old Rogers began to like about the su~~ told about | the summer land – told [?Mrs] that her husband Mr Mallet that was | asked to leave, & beautiful houses & even to drink just as when he lived | I said ~~that is the world for old Rogers~~ why not the [?horses] why not the dogs |

> That is the world for old Rogers I said, but I dont like new spirit – | ~~We dont understand him & he talks like a kind of parson he~~ <he gets angry & goes> gets up in her head | talks like a kind of parson ([38v]; cf. *WUWP* 66–67)

Although in a rough state here, the first draft of Corny Patterson's speech will be substantially revised in Harvard MS ([7r]) toward the text in *VPl* 943–44, lines 174–80.

On returning to [39r] after the insertion above, we notice that the handwriting is legible for the remainder of the page, with few strikethroughs and only two additional, clued additions from the facing page, both in speeches by Trench and tending to enhance his authority as a spiritualist leader. In the first instance, after asserting that "We Spiritualists do not admit there are any evil spirits"—that "Spirits are just ordinary people" ([39r])—he adds that "We do not permit the spirits that come to us to be driven away with curses, or violence of any kind" ([38v]). He continues, then (back on [39r]), to describe the condition of spirits after death. Essentially, he says: "When a spirit comes back through the medium for the first time it reenacts the pains of death"—a claim that Mrs. Mallet supports by testifying that, "When my husband came first [in a séance], he seemed to gasp & struggle as he was drowning – as the medium had to do the same it was most painful to watch" ([39r]). Trench goes on to articulate the doctrine of dreaming back,[120] when "a spirit re-enacts some painful or passionate moment of its life"—such as murderers or robbers repeating their crimes, a lover seeming "to make love once more," or a soldier "to hear the word of command" ([39r]). For spirits that mutter "unintelligible things," Trench says (in the final insertion of [38v]): "We write rescaet [=*requiescat*] in pace [i.e., may he/she rest in peace] on the tombs but they cannot rest[.] If I were a Catholic I would say that such spirits were [here the text returns to 39r:] such spirits do not often come to sceances unless those sceances take place, in the house where the event reenacted took place." Dr. Trench concludes by prescribing humane treatment in difficult cases: "This spirit, who speaks unintelligible words, who does not answer when spoken to If it was such a spirit, we can help it by patience & friendly thoughts. It wears out its remorse, or passion by reenacting it" ([39r]; *WUWP* 68–69).

Again, to judge from legibility and the relative lack of significant interventions to amend text on folio [40r] ([39v] being blank save for the name "Trench"), we may infer that most of the writing from [38v] through the first eighteen lines of [40r] (roughly equivalent to the content of *VPl* 943–45, lines 157–226) came easily to Yeats. The back-and-forth between Johnson and Trench on [40r] is uncomplicated, except for the complication of a delayed entrance by the medium, Mrs. Henderson. Trench explains that praying for protection from an evil spirit is unnecessary because "every good medium is protected by her controls," Silver Cloud (later Lulu) being "very able & experienced," and she is Henderson's "personal" control. The persons gathered for the séance take their places, and Dr. Trench introduces Mrs. Henderson to "Mr Corbet, a young man from Cambrid[g]e" and a skeptic, as well as "Miss Mackenna our secretary" ([40r]), though Corbet and Mackenna had been introduced to each other already, on folio [35v] (cf. Harvard MS, [1r]). With Mackenna welcoming the young man's skepticism because she does "not know what to think," the draft is both more broadly discrepant with the next draft (the Harvard MS) and more fraught with cancellations (see *WUWP* 70–73) to the end of the scene (on [41r]), just prior to the séance.

The idea of heaven, from old, ordinary Rogers's "summer land" to the young, educated Corbet's preference for the "heaven of Bo[t]acheili" (Sandro Botticelli), or "an utterly impossible & preposterous heaven" of the Spiritualist, is discussed by Miss Mackenna and John Corbet for an entire page ([41r], including two lines inserted at the end of it from [40v]), most of it stricken or scribbled out in blocks as an indication of difficulty. In part, Yeats is milking comic material he introduced with Rogers (first on [38v]), the view that "Everything they do here they [~~...~~] expect to do there" (in the afterlife); for example, if "old Rogers lost every penny he had on horses," he "expects to find a Bold dog & horses in the grave where he can win back his money" by betting at the races. Miss Mackenna finds the idea of "a new heaven" rather terrifying, noting that "<Old> Rogers & Mrs Mallet [~~...~~] dont want be ~~transform[ed] into~~ Boccelli [=Botticelli] angels" ([41r]). She acknowledges the vacillation of her own beliefs about the existence of a popular heaven: "Sometimes I think that & then I dont mind, but at other times I think just as Mr Trench does & then I am terrified[.] You remember the words of Job 'A spirit passes before my face The hair of my head stood up[']" ([41r]; *WUWP* 72–73).[121] They end their colloquy agreeably, and, given the opportunity in the Harvard MS, will choose to sit next to each other before the séance begins. From [40v], Mackenna's last speech in Rapallo E expresses her comfort in his company: "It makes me feel safer. I came here rather terrified—as if something might happen tonight."

With that, Yeats's drafting of the longest continuous segment of the play (his third since [29v]) comes to an end in the notebook. The fourth iteration (that of the Harvard MS) is the only one to include the séance sequence, largely an expansion of what he had roughed out rapidly in the "Scenario" on leaves [21r–26r]. At some point before reaching the anticlimax, or the departure sequence after the séance in the Harvard draft, Yeats prepared for Corbet's exit in the departure sequence by rehearsing in Rapallo Notebook E, on folio [41v], this character's most significant speech, which is addressed to Mrs. Henderson. This rough draft has been circumscribed and evidently written in two stages (separated by a short drawn line), but it amounts to a sort of free-floating text followed by new writing for *The Resurrection* (see Figure 4.8, below).[122] One of the editors' additions to FitzGerald's introduction is not exactly true,[123] as Rapallo E and the Harvard MS do not *both* present drafts of "the entire play" unless one counts the prewriting of the "Scenario" as a draft, whereas Yeats thought the actual writing of the play began at Rapallo E [29v], with two fresh starts after that. The third start breaks off just before the main event in the action (at [41r]), but he has left at the end a fragment of Corbet's exit speech (at [41v]) to incorporate into the Harvard MS (at [18r]; *WUWP* 134–35, lines 8–21). This last phase of composition was possibly reached on or near October 4, 1930, when Yeats wrote to his wife with news that he had just "finished the play as completely as it can be finished without your criticism," and he asked: "Could you bring down your type-writer, & let me dictate a clean copy" (*YGYL* 227; *CL InteLex* 5391). On the penultimate page of the Harvard holograph, he then carefully copied into Corbet's dialogue with Mrs. Henderson a fair-hand version of the residual fragment from Rapallo E, transcribed here and viewed in the upper left-hand quarter of Figure 4.8, below.

> "You have excited me beyond words. ~~Spirits may have~~ ~~Were there spirits~~ <Were there actually spirits> | ~~Perhaps what I saw to night was~~ <~~perhaps~~ There> ~~I have seen~~ <or did you> ~~a spirit, but~~ <as> I prefer to think, | ~~that it was you~~ create <it all when> ~~either~~ a wake or asleep. I would like to compliment your scholar ship | ~~on your selection, of what I consider~~ of your explanation of Swifts [?] celebacy, ~~that~~ | an explanation ~~which I have [?advocated] myself~~ which I ~~shall~~ proved in my essay for my doctorate at | ~~Cambridge~~ to [be] the only plausible explanation. But there is something that I want to ask. | ~~In Swifts day European intellect reached its climax, free from superstition at last | – no where of Swift If ever Swift thought himself If regarded himself the intellect, & | forsaw its collapse he might~~
>
> ---
>
> Swift was the chief representative of the intellect of his epoch – | ~~the <arrogant> intellect~~ which | had ~~for the first time during the Christian Era over[come] superstition; he forsaw~~ the collapse | of ~~the intellect~~, the intellect arrogant [in] its triumph over superstition, he for saw | its collapse. ~~Was that why~~ Did he refuse to beget children out of dread of | ~~the~~ <that> future. ~~Was that his madness or w~~ Was Swift mad or was it the | intellect it self that was mad. ([41v]; cf. *WUWP* 74–75)

The issues of madness and celibacy, in the view of Yeats *vis-à-vis* Shane Leslie, were aired in later months, when Yeats began writing his introduction that was published in the *Dublin Magazine* in the fall of 1931, and then later in Macmillan's *Wheels and Butterflies* and the 1934 Cuala Press edition of the play (*WUWP* 233–34; *VPl* 966–67).[124] It must also be said that the play itself went into production at the Abbey Theatre at a phenomenal pace, with Yeats reporting to Lady Gregory, on October 29, 1930, that the work was already in rehearsal (*L* 778; *CL InteLex* 5398), and to Olivia Shakespear, on December 2, 1930, that the play had opened and was "a much greater success than I ever hoped and beautifully acted" (*L* 779; *CL InteLex* 5414).

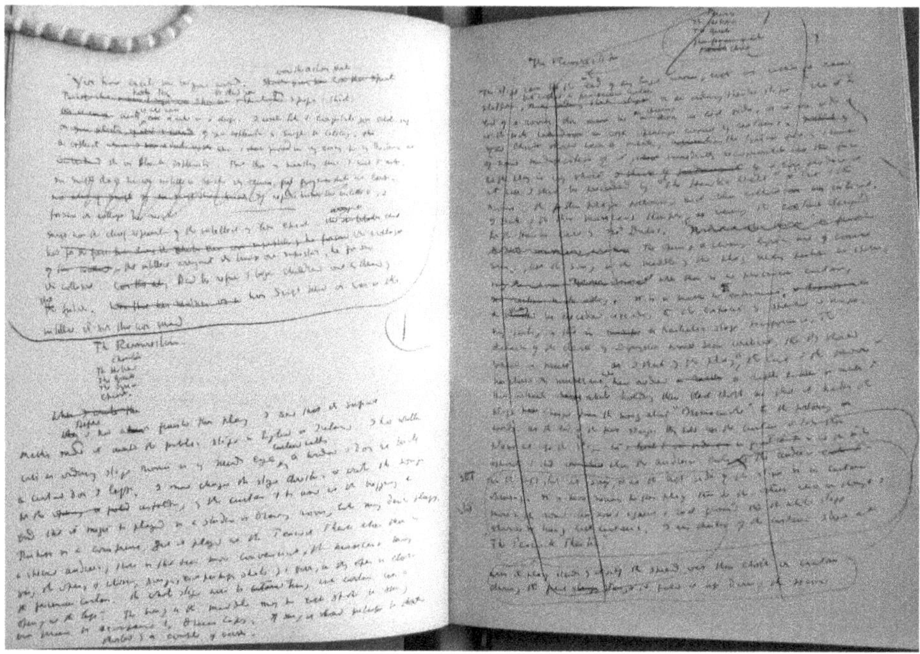

Figure 4.8. NLI 13,582 (Rapallo Notebook E), [41v–42r]. Courtesy of the NLI; photograph courtesy of Catherine Paul E. Paul.

[41v–58r] "The Ressurrection" [draft of *The Resurrection*]

The end of this early draft of *The Words upon the Window-Pane* almost collides with the opening of the last handwritten draft of *The Resurrection*, with elements of both crammed onto the same page. And though they are very different in development, matter, and style, both plays dramatize the occurrence of something supernatural in the framework of ordinary human life, using skeptical characters to emphasize the nature of the extra-ordinary that they witness.

Unlike the apparently rapid and relatively smooth genesis of *The Words upon the Window-Pane* and its transition to stage, in *The Resurrection* Yeats was returning to a play that he had started some five years earlier in 1925 and had already published in 1927, though it would not be produced in a theater until 1934. The collision of the two plays is not entirely accidental, however, for Jared Curtis and Selina Guinness indicate that, "Spurred on by the Abbey's success with *The Words Upon the Window Pane* in mid-November 1930, Yeats returned to *The Resurrection* in the early weeks of December" (*Res* xxx), first in the White Vellum Notebook and then with this redrafted version in Rapallo E.

The rewriting was also perhaps spurred by a sense that he was finishing his revisions for *A Vision* (as he thought[125]), a context recalling the play's genesis, announced to Lady Gregory on April 23, 1925:

> Yesterday I finished my book; handed it over to George to make the diagrams & pack off to the publisher. I then cleared all loose papers & rejected pages from my table, & this morning started life afresh. I have even begun to write letters for the first time for months[....] I am planning a one act play on Christs appearance to his diciples after the crucifixion — I think it will turn out a play of beleif & yet modern in temper. I however do not think of it for the Abbey. We shall probably play it here in the drawing room. (*CL InteLex* 4714)

Indeed, he told her, a few days before arriving at Coole in May, that he had "started [his] new play — that about the Resurrection, a sort of overflow from the book" of *A Vision* ([May 11, 1925], *CL InteLex* 4725). Within a week of his arrival, Lady Gregory was noting that "He has finished the first draft of his little play *The heart of the Phantom beats*,"[126] and recorded that he read her "his Resurrection play" on 22 May, "very good I think, direct and leading up with a strain of expectation to the beating heart."[127] The following day he presented a lyric that he "meant to be a poem of Christianity and it has come out like this," and she quotes the stanza "Another Troy must rise and set," which was complemented two days later by the stanza "In pity for man's darkening thought."[128] We shall return to details of this genesis when considering the inserted material, but for now turn attention to Yeats's renewed interest in the play.

As he started reworking the play, he wrote to Lady Gregory from Dublin in December 1930, indicating that another factor in his renewed focus was the play's inclusion in his collection of *Wheels and Butterflies*—the butterflies of dramatic art being broken on the wheels of theoretical prefaces and introductions[129]—even though this book did not, in the end, appear until 1934 (Wade 175; 1935 in the USA, Wade 176):

> I have almost finished "my wheels & butterflies" — Macmillan may want it at once. I will know in a few days. I am now rewriting one of the plays in it — a thing called "The Resurection" I wrote a few years ago & rather bad. I am making an impressive play of it or think so. (December 22, [1930], *CL InteLex* 5427)

A few days later he wrote with equal satisfaction to Olivia Shakespear:

> At the moment I am putting the last touches to a play called "The Resurrection" — young men talking[,] the Apostles in the next room overwhelmed by the crucifixion Christ newly arisen passes silently through. I wrote a chaotic dialogue on this theme some years ago. But now I have dramatic tension through out. (December 27, [1930], cf. *CL InteLex* 5428, cf. *L* 780–81)[130]

In revising the play, Yeats sought to focus the characters' differing perspectives on the crucifixion, tighten the drama created by Christ's appearance, and add to the shock of the phantom's beating heart.[131] The *Adelphi* script of 1927 was certainly wordier and included more detail that was incidental or extraneous, featuring ideas that Yeats kept returning to—the role of Judas, Leda's unhatched egg, and humans' difference from gods—that were not germane to the play's narrative thrust. In the *Adelphi* script, as in the final version, the main characters take the contrasting positions that Christ was purely god with a phantom body (the Egyptian), purely human (the Hebrew), and both god and human (the Syrian), but occasionally, as Bradford comments, Yeats's phrasing "sounds like something from *A Vision* put into dialogue. It is far too talky."[132]

The first redrafting in the White Vellum Notebook (WVN) started with a skeleton outline of the play's action, in which the "Egyptian" changes halfway through into the "Greek," as he had been in the first drafts of 1925. In the WVN, the script moves closer to the version Yeats would publish in 1931, with fuller dramatization of the themes, but with many revisions and cancellations, and with some material out of sequence, for insertion elsewhere. Even for the author (or those with hindsight), it was difficult to put these pages into sequence, and the material clearly needed to be reorganized and presented in more comprehensible form for dictation. As Curtis and Guinness state, "the revised version of *The Resurrection* found [in the WVN] approximates the underlying text of the second draft in Rapallo Notebook E,"[133] which began "as a fair—or at least legible—copy, though he soon fell to revision heavily, particularly in the second half of the play" (*Res* xxxv).

Yeats began dictating *The Resurrection* to Alan Duncan from this handwritten draft in Rapallo E on March 4, 1931 (see *Res* 451). This represents a *terminus ad quem* with respect to dating the draft itself; with respect to the *terminus a quo*, we can really only state that the Rapallo E draft follows that of the WVN—a notebook that was apparently "Begun November 23 1930" and where the *The Resurrection* runs from page 185 to 230, roughly halfway through the volume.[134] Though Yeats did not necessarily use the WVN in sequence, it still seems highly unlikely that the WVN draft could have been started before December 1930.[135] The play is last referred to in correspondence on December 27, 1930, when Yeats wrote to Olivia Shakespear that he was "putting the last touches to a play called 'The Resurrection'" (*CL InteLex* 5428; *L* 780–81), and on January 5, 1931, when he told Augusta Gregory about adding to the closing song.[136] If these comments refer to the Rapallo E draft, Yeats would need to have worked at high speed to be finishing this second version so soon; if they refer to the WVN draft, then the Rapallo E draft probably dates from the early months 1931, but in the end the difference is slight.

On the recto opposite the final drafted lines of *The Words upon the Window-Pane* (see Figure 4.8), Yeats outlined the staging he envisaged for the play, how Christ should appear, and a performance program that projects a production (along with *At the Hawk's Well* and *The Cat and the Moon*) and imagines a transition from "the song about 'Minalushe' to the following words" (which appear on the next recto): "I saw a staring virgin stand / Where holy Dionysius died" ([42r–43r]). However, he cancelled the opening comments and squeezed a new version onto the facing verso underneath the close of *The Words upon the Window-Pane*; the opening half is very close to the "Prologue and Stage Directions" as they appear in the Cuala printing of *Stories of Michael Robartes and His Friends: An Extract from a Record Made by His Pupils: and a Play in Prose* (1931; Wade 167).[137] Clue lines then indicate that this is to be followed by cancelled text on the recto marked "stet," with an introductory sentence inserted from the bottom of the page.

The draft is generally easy to follow in *"The Resurrection": Manuscript Materials*, with admirably clear facsimiles of the original, and we have only a few quibbles with the transcriptions. One feature that is harder to appreciate, however, due to the default layout of the Cornell volumes, is Yeats's usual method of writing on rectos and using the opposite versos for insertions or replacements. These are generally clued in with balloons and lines to the relevant insertion point, but necessarily precede the page they are supplementing. The first four rectos of the text, as transferred from the WVN into Rapallo E, entailed only minor changes on the page ([43r–46r]), though Yeats started to need the versos opposite for replacement text on the pages numbered 6, 7, and 8 ([47r–49r]). The following two rectos again involved a little cancellation and rewriting ([50r–51r]), but the next opening gives one of the more extreme examples of using the full spread to work out the themes (see Figure 4.9 below).

This is a key moment in the play, as the Greek reveals that he has "sent the Syrian to the tomb to find out" what has happened to Christ's body ([49r], *Res* 406–407) and then describes the followers of Dionysus filling the streets with noise and threat of violence, with "monstrous ceremonies" in which they "sing of the death of the god & pray for his resurrection" ([50r], *Res* 408–409). The Greek rejects this ecstatic worship of Dionysus as un-Greek in its "self surrender and self abasement" ([51r], *Res* 412–13), characterizing the true Greek approach by using one of Yeats's favorite vignettes from *The Iliad*:[138]

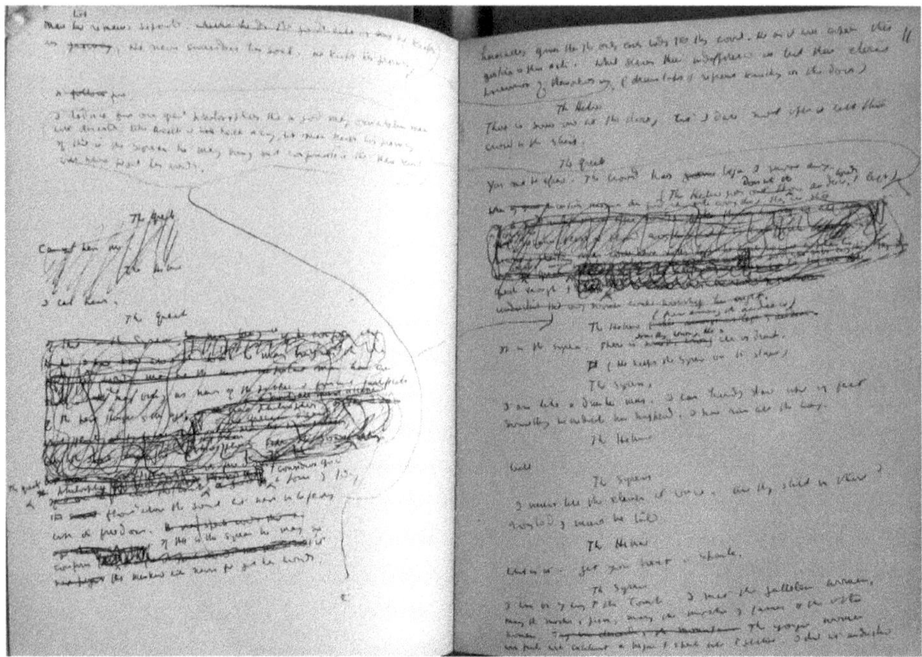

Figure 4.9. NLI 13,582 (Rapallo Notebook E), [51v–52r]. Courtesy of NLI; photograph courtesy of Catherine Paul E. Paul. See *Res* 414–17.

~~The godess~~ <When the> goddess came to Achilles in the battle ~~took~~ she | took him by his yellow hair; she did not interfere with his soul. | Lucretius thinks that the gods [*appear*] in visions of the day & night | but are indifferent to human fate. That is the exageration of a Roman | rhetorician. ~~They are always present to our souls~~ They can be | discovered by contemplation, in their faces a high keen joy like the | cry of a bat & ~~it is we who give them body~~ the man who lives

11

heroically gives them the only earthy body that they covet. He as it were copies their | gestures & their acts. What seems their indifference is but their eternal | possession of themselves

{Man ~~too~~ <too> remains separate; ~~whether he do the gods will or not~~ he keeps | his ~~privacy~~; He never surrenders his soul. He keeps his privacy}

(drum taps to represent knocking on the door) |

The Hebrew

There is some one at the door, but I dare not open it with this | crowd in the street.

The Greek

You not be afraid. The crowd has ~~gone~~ begun to move away.

(the Hebrew goes ~~out through~~ <down into the> audience to <towards> left) ([51r, 52r, 51v], *Res* 412–17)

In the time needed for the Hebrew to go and bring the Syrian into the room, Yeats decided to have the Greek continue talking to the Hebrew offstage—effectively to himself—on the boundary between the divine and the human. This speech effectively replaces the one in the *Adelphi* version that had introduced the theme of the beating heart to the play—"it is the heart, that swirl of blood, that separates mankind from Divinity" (*Res* 260–61, *VPl* 920), a foreshadowing of the play's closing line: "The Heart of a Phantom is beating!" (*Res* 266–67, *VPl* 930)—which Yeats may have judged premature. In the WVN, this was replaced with the idea of human privacy and hints at the play's new ending with Yeats's favorite Heraclitean paradox—"God and Man die each others life live each others death" (WVN 225, *Res* 356–57)—stating that "If a god interfered with mens soul, if he thrust himself upon all their acts, it is we men who would become phantoms" (WVN 209, *Res* 328–29, omitting cancellations).

This was the starting point of the Rapallo draft (the first line given below was inserted later), but Yeats then wove themes of incarnation and Dionysian self-sacrifice into the speech:

> <When ~~my Greek~~ ancestors imagine their god, who asks everything they are still> | ~~If a god interfered with mens souls, if he thrust himself in all their acts | <or if he> or became flesh & blood every thing would be transfigured man would | become a phantom man would have nothing left he would become a phantom | When Ase <Asiatic> Greeks <imagined> <invented a religion of self sacrifice that imagined a god who asks everything, they still>~~ | ~~imagined a god that interferes with their souls, they were still~~ | Greek enough to ~~think <say> <believe> that he could only be worship [?for women]~~ | ~~understand that only women could worship him aright.~~ ([52r], *Res* 416–17)

If we clear away most of the cancellation in the text above, Yeats finished with a line explaining the Dionysian rites, but with an underlying Nietzschean dismissal of Dionysian slave morality: "When my ancestors imagine their god who asks everything, they are still Greek enough to understand that only women could worship him aright."[139] As is clear from the multiple layers of cancellation, however, Yeats was already wrestling with this formulation, and he started a new tack of thought on the facing page (see Figure 4.9), introducing a greater sense of expectation of the Syrian's news, before he decided to move that element to follow a comment on Greek ideas of divinity:

> { ~~The Greek~~
> ~~Can you hear me.~~
> ~~—The Hebrew~~
> ~~I can hear.~~

> The Greek
>
> ~~If that is the Syrean, he may bring u~~ | ~~if he confirms what~~ | ~~he he I had said about the tomb he may bring us the~~ | ~~most his words may be the most important man has ever~~ | ~~spoken. He <he> may bring us news of public & final justification~~ | ~~of the best thought of the age. as the great philosophers, <a proof all must accept> of the dream~~ | ~~<of the Grecian dream>~~ | ~~which floats always before the souls of men but never [?intrudes],~~ | ~~before the soul, & yet but & <be that dream> which floats before the soul always~~ | ~~but does not interfere with its freedom~~
>
> ~~If I am right about the tomb~~ | <The Greek> ~~Its~~ philosoph~~ery~~ ~~<has declared that believes that>~~ ~~a god~~ <considers god a form of joy | that ~~seems to~~ float<s> above the soul but never interfears | with its freedom. ~~He may speak words that no~~ | ~~age should never forget.~~ If that is the Syrean he may so | confirm ~~that <what I> thought & speak words mankind will it~~ | ~~never forget~~ that mankind will never for get his words.} ([51v], *Res* 414–15)

Even this reworking is heavily cancelled in different stages, so that Yeats reformulated the two elements again, a little more succinctly, further up the page:

> {I deduce from our great philosophers that a god may overwhelm man | with disaster, take wealth & ~~hel~~ health away, but man keeps his privacy. | If this is the Syrean he may bring such confirmation that man kind | will never forget his words.} ([51v], *Res* 414–15)

This short summary of a Greek philosophical conception of the proper limits of divine action is more direct in its thought—dealing with life's disasters, wealth, and health, not forms of joy floating above the soul—but then immediately moves the focus of the action to the Syrian and his news.

> The Hebrew ~~(still amongst at left of audience)~~ <(from among the audience)>
>
> It is the Syrian. There is ~~something wrong~~ <something wrong. He is> ill or drunk.
>
> ~~Th~~ (He helps the Syrean on the stage)
>
> The Syrian
>
> I am like a drunken man. I can hardly stand upon my feet | Something incredible has happened. I have run all the way.
>
> The Hebrew
>
> Well.
>
> The Syrean
>
> I must tell the eleven at once. Are they still in there? | Everybody must be told.
>
> The Hebrew
>
> What is it. get your breath & speak.
>
> The Syrian
>
> I was on my way to the Tomb. I met the gallelean women, | Mary the mother of Jesus, Mary the mother of James & the other | women. ~~They were descending~~

> ~~the mountain.~~ The younger women | were pale with excitement & began to speak all together. ([52r], *Res* 416–17)

As the Syrian goes on to describe the miracle of the resurrection, the text is more certain, with a few corrections on the rectos themselves. The evidence of the rolled-back stone introduces the third term between the Hebrew's view of Jesus as a self-deceiving saint and the Greek's idea of a docetic phantom: a man not a phantom has risen from the tomb in defiance of everything we know. He also brings in the theme of eternal return and echoes the song that opens the play: "What matter if it contradicts all human knowledge – another Argo seeks another fleece another Troy is sacked. (laughing as he speaks)" ([54r], *Res* 420–21; cf. WVN p. 219, *Res* 344–45). The Syrian's laughter continues, to the irritation of the Hebrew, but the Syrian himself thinks it comes from outside, and it is unclear whether this is a form of hysteria or the laughter of "tragic joy."

In "The Gyres" (1938), tragic joy is the response as "ancient lineaments are blotted out. / Irrational streams of blood are staining the earth" and Troy burns: "We that look on but laugh in tragic joy" (*VP* 564). As Curtis and Guinness underline in their introduction to *The Resurrection: Manuscript Materials*, the concept of the irrational, while always present in the play, grew in importance as Yeats revised. The *Adelphi* version had closed with the Egyptian's words:

> Never before did the Heart of a Phantom beat. How terrible! Reason itself is dead. (In a loud voice.) Rome, Greece, Egypt—it has come, the miracle, that which must destroy you, irrational force, the Heart of a Phantom is beating! (*VPl* 930, *Res* 266–67).

The term "irrational force" comes straight from *A Vision*'s meditation on the impetus that inaugurates a new religious age, used three times in connection with the arrival of Christianity and twice in relation to the new dispensation:[140] because Christ is "more than man He controlled what Neo-Pythagorean and Stoic could not—irrational force" (*AVA* 186, *CW13* 155), and later, prefiguring the play, Yeats notes that Christianity triumphs over Neo-Platonism "because the Judean miracle has a stronger hold upon the masses than Alexandrian thaumaturgy" (*AVA* 189, *CW13* 157–58).

In the White Vellum Notebook, the play's close was adapted to remove the reference to irrational force:

> Greece, Egypt, rome some thing has come to destroy you <Man has begun to die for> the heart of a phantom is beating [~~....~~] — Your words are clear to me at last O Heraclitus God & Man die each others life live each other death (WVN p. 225; *Res* 356–57)

But in the WVN version, the idea had entered the play earlier, when the Syrian challenges the Greek's world of "knowledge" and logic.

> What if ~~things if always when everything seems known, when every thing seem explained~~ <there is always> ~~What if some~~ some thing that lies out side knowledge, out side ~~reason~~ & <order>
> {what if always at the moment when order seems finally established, every thing finally explained, that something appears}
> ~~what if wen when it seems that everything~~ <~~is~~> <~~seems~~> ~~appears just when~~ <~~it seems that~~ > ~~so order seems forever established that some thing appears~~ (he ~~begins <to> laugh)~~ (He begins to laugh) (WVN pp. 219 and 218; *Res* 346–47)

As Yeats rewrote this section in Rapallo E, an insertion from the facing verso brings back the word "irrational" to the Syrian's speech:

> But what if there is some thing it cannot explain, some thing more important | than anything else.
>
> The Greek
>
> You mean the barbarian would come back.
>
> The Syrean
>
> What if there is always some thing that lies out side knowledge, | outside order. What if at the moment when order seems finally ~~established, every thing finally~~ | ~~explained~~ <knowledge & order seem complete>, that some thing appears.
>
> (He begins to laugh)
>
> { The Hebrew
>
> Stop laughing
>
> The Syrean
>
> What if the ~~irrational return~~ irrational return, what if the circle | begin again.
>
> The Hebrew
>
> Stop }
>
> He laughed when Christs body was nailed to the | cross & now you laugh. ([55r] and [54v], *Res* 422–25)

This insertion was the line that Yeats picked out to open the final section of his introduction to the play for *Wheels and Butterflies*, drafted in the WVN, quoting directly:

> "What if there is always some thing outside knowledge, outside order [....] What if the irrational return? What if the circle begin again?" Years ago I read in Sir William Crookes' "Studies in Psychical Research," after excluding every possible fraud he touched a materialised form & felt the heart beating. I felt as I read, though my intellect rejected what I read the terror of the supernatural described in Job. (WVN p. 93, *Res* 526–27)

As Homer's Athene physically pulls hair and Lucretius was said by the Greek to hold that the gods appear "in visions of the day & night" ([51r]), Yeats here recalls the story of contact with a spirit told by Eliphaz, the first of Job's infamous "comforters": "In thoughts from the visions of the night, when deep sleep falleth on men, fear came upon me, and trembling, which made all my bones to shake. Then a spirit passed before my face; the hair of my flesh stood up" (Job 4:13–15).

These verses are also quoted (slightly inaccurately) by Miss Mackenna in *The Words upon the Window-Pane*,[141] and it is no accident that Yeats's source for the beating heart of a phantom was a form of séance. The terror of the resurrection may be on a different scale, but Yeats seeks to convey that experience of the supernatural is not comfortable, but an experience akin to the awe and vertigo inspired by the sublime: it is "life at its most intense moment [...] in which one discovers something supernatural, a stirring as it were of the roots of the hair" (*Au* 320, *CW3* 247). Both *The Resurrection* and *The Words upon the Window-Pane* seek to explore the unease we may feel when the world reveals things that go beyond the rational order of our reality and what we think we know.

[58v–74r] [drafts for *A Vision* on the afterlife]

Drafts for A Vision *concerning the afterlife, start immediately following the end of the final handwritten draft of* The Resurrection, *but will be dealt with after the inserted leaves.*

[60bis-r–63bis-r] "Dance Play" [scenario titled "Ressurrection," cancelled]

At some stage, four leaves were removed from a notebook of the same format as the Rapallo notebooks. These leaves were still joined in the middle and are actually two bifolia. They were then inserted into Rapallo E at a relatively early date, as the earliest microfilms show them placed within the book, and it is very probable that the insertion was done by the Yeatses themselves. The reason for putting them into Rapallo E was evidently the fact that the scenario they contain was titled "Ressurection" and it was seen as associated with the play, perhaps even an early version of the play itself.

This draft focuses on Christ's experience following death in a psychic landscape among the world's other sacrificed saviors, making it very different from the play as written and also from the scenario Yeats outlined to Lady Gregory in his letter of April 23, 1925 (*CL InteLex* 4714, see above). However, given its title, it appears to make sense that it must be a preliminary scenario of *The Resurrection*, and it is presented as such by Curtis Bradford in *Yeats at Work* and Jared Curtis and Selina Guinness in *The Resurrection: Manuscript Materials*. In this case, it would have to date from early in 1925, as Curtis and

Guinness evince (*Res* xviii); their dating process is essentially the same as Curtis Bradford's, but earlier than the date of 1926 that he ventured (*YAW* xxx), because of a letter to Lady Gregory of which he was unaware and a journal entry that was misdated by Lennox Robinson in the 1947 selection from her journals (see n143).

However, the date at the head of the first folio gives combinations of day and month that are problematic unless it comes from January 1929 and, apart from the (cancelled) title, there is no essential reason to link this scenario with the play of *The Resurrection* in either its 1925 drafts or the new version that Yeats drafted in Rapallo E. Although the title presents a stumbling block, it is certainly worth exploring the possibility that the draft is a completely separate engagement with the crucial figure of Christ. Indeed, there is every reason to associate it with a scenario that Yeats described to Lady Gregory in a letter from Rapallo of January 1929:

> Now that the philosophy is finished I am writing prose drafts for poems. I have a senario of a dramatic poem — very short — of Christ coming out of the tomb, & am trying to make a draft for a series of personal lyrics. But the start after a long interval — is always difficult. (January 21, [1929], *CL InteLex* 5213)

This scenario would potentially resemble *Calvary* or other treatments of the relationship between Judas and Christ intimated in the automatic script. The draft we have on the loose sheets is called a "Dance Play," but it is quite possible Yeats did not make a major distinction from a "dramatic poem" in his mind when writing his letter.

A date in January 1929 would place this dramatic poem before Yeats's renewed interest in *The Resurrection* as sparked by his work on *The Words upon the Window-Pane* and the introductions he was drafting for *Wheels and Butterflies*. But, as had happened in 1925, the fact that he thought that "the philosophy [was] finished" seems to have given an impetus to write creatively about Christ as the avatar who ushered in a *primary* religious dispensation, as explained in *A Vision*'s "Dove or Swan." And the date of this letter to Augusta Gregory coincides with one of the dates at the head of the scenario—dates that present problems to Curtis Bradford, as well as to Jared Curtis and Selina Guinness, when they attempt to tie this scenario to a point in time early enough for it be a preliminary sketch for the play of *The Resurrection*. Abandoning that assumption removes almost all of the problems.

It appears that the date was originally written as "Sunday" followed, slightly separately, by "Jan 20"; in 1929, January 20 was a Sunday (see Figure 4.10). Then both Sunday and 20 were cancelled, with "21 & 22" added, indicating, perhaps,

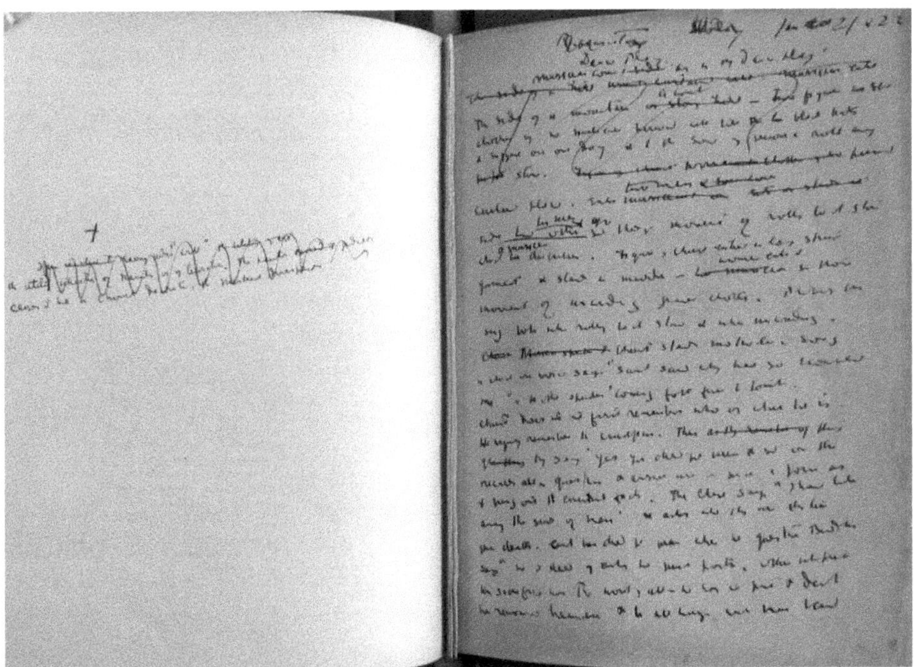

Figure 4.10. NLI 13,582 (Rapallo Notebook E), [59v–60bis-r]. The four loose leaves [60bis–63bis] have been inserted between the notebook's fourth and fifth gatherings. Courtesy of NLI; photograph courtesy of Catherine Paul E. Paul.

how "the start after a long interval — is always difficult" (see *CL InteLex* 5213 above). The combination of "Jan 22" is repeated three leaves later on the last recto of the loose material, where Yeats appears to have added a year in different ink—"(?1929)"—in a retroactive attempt to date this piece of writing.

Curtis Bradford, seeking to reconcile a date that was consistent with these leaves pre-dating the early drafts of *The Resurrection* he knew about, proposed that the date was probably from 1926 and was therefore almost certainly "Sunday Jun 20" (which was the only feasible combination from that year).[142] This claim is untenable because the letters to and comments by Lady Gregory indicate that the play was already being drafted in early 1925,[143] so Jared Curtis and Selina Guinness propose jettisoning the dates altogether: "it may be wiser to trust Yeats's deletions of 'Sunday' and '20' as simple errors made while traveling between Sicily, Naples, and Capri, and assume that the scenario was written January 21 and 22, 1925" (*Res* xxi).[144]

Following the dramatic scenario, there is other material on the last leaf—both recto and verso—which definitely appears to belong to the late 1920s. The passage headed "Jan 22 (?1929)" explores how artists are molded by early experience, referring to John Masefield, J. M. Synge, and Ezra Pound. It relates most closely to ideas expressed in drafts in Rapallo C about Ezra Pound and skepticism, passages that may have been considered for *A Packet for Ezra Pound*, along with the poem "Meditations upon Death," which appeared in the Cuala edition of that work (Rapallo C, [8v–10v]).[145]

While this paragraph is potentially connected to preparation for "Rapallo in Spring" and *A Packet for Ezra Pound*, this is definitely the case for the note on the verso of this leaf, as it is a version of one that also appears in Rapallo B, Rapallo C, and in the published version of *A Packet for Ezra Pound* (*PEP* 27; *AVB* 20, *CW14* 16): "At Aliceras [*sic*] I could walk two mins [=*miles*], at Canne I can walk but one—soon I shall but walk the garden path, & the mile to to [*sic*] the harbor where the yacts are shall seem incredible romance" (Rapallo E, [63bis-v]). Although the phrasing of the sentence appears to place it in early 1928, it seems to be a line extracted and quoted from earlier writing, and the examination below will show that it could certainly be from January 1929, along with the rest of the inserted pages.

Having belabored these externalities somewhat, we should turn at least briefly to the actual content. Even if the pages have nothing to do with *The Resurrection* beyond showing Yeats's interest in the person and significance of Christ, they probably did prepare the ground for returning to the *Adelphi* play the following year. Curtis's and Guinness's Cornell volume gives good reproductions and transcriptions of the inserted pages, so the quotations in the following discussion will focus on the "final" state, ignoring cancellations and revisions.

The details of the scenario make it clear that Yeats already envisaged a dance play rather than the "dramatic poem" he mentioned to Lady Gregory, with cancelled directions for "Two figures in black clothes of no particular period with tall black hats & suggest our own day & to the sound of music roll away [~~...~~] stone" and then specifying a "Curtained place" ([60bis-r], *Res* 4–5). These figures then unwind the grave clothes of Christ, with a "Song in which one voice says 'Saul said why have you troubled me' & the other speaks 'Coming forth from the tomb. Christ does not at first remember who or where he is. He vaguely remembers the crucifixion"—a closing quotation mark is missing, so it is unclear whether these last two sentences were conceived as commentary to be spoken aloud or whether the speech stops earlier, perhaps after "tomb." There is a little confusion in the reference to the words of Samuel's spirit when invoked by the medium or witch of Endor on Saul's behalf (1 Sam 28:15)—though simply omitting the word "said" (Saul, why…) or giving Samuel rather than Saul (Samuel said…) would correct the allusion—and the same instance was in Yeats's mind later in the year when he was writing the *Stories of Michael Robartes and His Friends*.[146] Among Robartes's bombastic sayings, as recalled by his followers, is a meditation on the Many and the One, and the lure to reincarnate: "We come at birth into a multitude and after death would perish into the One did not a witch of Endor call us back, nor would she repent did we shriek with Samuel: 'Why hast thou disquieted me?' instead of slumbering upon that breast" (*SMRF* 21; *AVB* 52, *CW14* 37).

Christ remembers that he has "taken away the sins of men" and, in contrast, Buddha says he "died of eating too much pork," yet the others there state that Buddha's "sacrifice was the worst of all – he was not put to death he renounced heaven to be all ways with man kind" ([60bis-r], *Res* 4–5).[147] Buddha is the only one who remains with Christ as he agonizes over "the endless sin & misery of men – for who the gods die in vain," later bringing him to the Three Marys, before whom "Christ hesitates & then says I am the way & the life" ([60bis-r–61bis-r], *Res* 4–7).

At this point, Yeats appears to have taken stock and thought: "On the other hand it could be made a dance play for the ordinary stage, in which a god would be represented not merely suggested," before restarting with the figures rolling away the stone ([61bis-r], *Res* 6–7). Again, the grave clothes are unwound and he remembers he has "taken away the sins of men," asking the others he sees, Dionysus, Buddha, and "perhaps a third," about themselves ([62bis-r], *Res* 10–11).

There is a hint of Yeats's favorite Heraclitean paradox as he considers gods who die for humans or humans who become gods (the following text omits cancellations):

> "It is a tragedy for men to die & to the | gods to be born" Then Christ sees many persons coming. | he asks who are these & is told Gods | who have died for men. He is about to kneel but Buddha stops him. He answers I am still a man. Buddha | says only the god who suffers lives
>
> {or only the act is | divine – in that we put on divinity | now one now another as the turning heavens | decree}
>
> They pass singing before him & bow as | they pass. Their song is "why have you troubled me | said Saul" enlarged to a stanza or chorus – and the verses | about the risen Christ" ([62bis-r and 61bis-v], *Res* 8–11)

Again the Three Marys are brought to him and he tells them "I am the life & the way," a version of the statement from John's gospel "I am the way, the truth, and the life," though without the continuation that "no one comes to the Father except by me" (John 14:6). Thus Yeats pauses at the same emphatic point as before, which may have been the piece's conclusion or just where the initial impulse petered out.

The two drafts are brought together in a single page of typescript that stops at the point where Christ says, "I am still a man"; below this is typed: "(the rest has been torn off.)," evidently referring to an intermediate draft on loose paper.[148] The typescript bears a title and date: "Resurrection. Dance Play (Jan

21 & 22)" with "1929" added in ink, very probably in Yeats's hand. The Cornell editors' note continues: "If '1929' is correct, WBY returned to the idea of a dance play on the themes of *The Resurrection* after he had composed and then published the *Adelphi* version in 1927," but they evidently think the dating mistaken (*Res* 15n).

While the scenario as outlined is closer to a dance play than to the dramatic poem mentioned to Lady Gregory, it clearly lacks dramatic tension and direction as it stands, functioning more as a tableau in which Dionysus, as in *The Resurrection*, represents the other slain gods and the Buddha, other compassionate teachers. Yeats recognized in Christ a unique conjunction of teaching and sacrifice. Christ's first spoken words focus on dying for the sins of humanity. Yet the unique is at the same time part of the cyclical as Buddha emphasizes how forms of divinity change "as the turning heavens decree." Though he may believe in Christ, Yeats is hardly a Christian. His position here is closest to that of the Syrian in *The Resurrection*, where Christ is both god and man, and he understands that there has been a major dislocation of the laws of cause and effect, the logic of nature, through the irrational or suprarational force that Christ represents.

[63bis-r] [paragraph on Masefield, Synge, and Pound]

Below the final statement of "I am the life & the way," Yeats drew a line and added an unconnected paragraph, which is dated "Jan 22" with "(?1929)" added afterwards. This was almost certainly from the same days in January as the preceding scenario, dated "Jan 21 & 22," and the day before the prose outline of "Meditations on Death" in Rapallo C, dated "Jan 23."[149] We agree with Curtis and Guinness that it "may be part of the preparatory work for *A Packet for Ezra Pound*" (*Res* 13n), but are not quite so certain that Yeats "finished it [i.e., *PEP*] in August 1928." The latest date attached to prose in the "Packet" is "November 23rd. 1928," but on January 6, 1929, Yeats told Oliver St. John Gogarty that *A Packet for Ezra Pound* was "just finished" (*CL InteLex* 5211), and the poems published under the title "Meditations upon Death" (on pages 9 to 11 of the Cuala printing) are dated February 4th and 9th 1929, so there was evidently still some leeway.[150]

Jan 22 *(?1929)*

> Masefield was, as he ~~believs~~ believes tirannized over by an ~~hard~~ <~~harsh~~> <old> aunt & I have always | been convinced that this aunt is the evil in all his plays, himself the suffering | hero or heroine. Long ago I ~~usd t~~ <used to> compare him ~~wit~~ <with> Synge, who | had no hatred for the ~~bad~~ <worst> persons in his plays. But the act which | ~~fixed~~ <moulded> Masefield ~~natur~~ occured while he was an ~~instnctv~~ <instinctive> & imaginative | being alone, while he was a boy, & so his intellect & practical capacity | are not effected.

> Ezra's ~~moulng~~ <moulding> act occured in early manhood – | an act of persecution in America, & neglect in England – & therefore effects his | intellect & practical capacity while it leaves his imagination & | ~~emotional nature~~ <instinct> free – hence "Cathay" & the "Propertius" poems. | How far does the sense of being a victim enter ~~into all~~ <into ~~all~~> dramatic creation? | Can anything else enable the creator to identify himself with | with [*sic*] those in the fable who suffer? What enabled Shakespeare to | identify himself with phantastic [~~?Mercutio~~] & raving – ~~Lear~~ suffering? | Synges life was a strugle with ill health & a premonition of death | his characters do not act tragically but ~~phantasticl~~ <phantastically> upon one another. | Tragedy comes from beyond them. Had his "Deirdre" been finished | I think ~~tht~~ <that> would have been ~~plain~~ <plane> there also. He thought of making Concubar | drunk.

Such meditations were probably somewhere between diary and draft, and quite possibly not intended for any particular form of publication. They could easily fit into the musings of his autobiographical writing or into an essay as a digression, falling somewhere between the schematizing of *A Vision*'s gyrating *Faculties* and a freer form of psychological speculation on the personal and artistic consequences of formative trauma, which still betrays Yeats's tendency to schematic oppositions. As he noted in 1922, when sending Maud Gonne the autobiographical *The Trembling of the Veil*, "You will find that I use my philosophy throughout but in a summery way & without the mathematical foundation which gives it precission."[151]

As already observed, the sentence on the final verso is a version of one that appears in *A Packet for Ezra Pound*. Its content would, therefore, seem to place the moment of writing a year earlier than the rest of the insert—that is, in Cannes in early 1928:[152]

> At Aliceras I could walk two mins [=*miles*], at Canne I can walk but | one—soon I shall but walk the garden path, & the mile | to to [*sic*] the harbor where the yacts are shall seem | incredible romance. ([63bis-v]).

Given Yeats's handwriting (see Figure 4.11), it would be unwise to place too much reliance on the tense of "I can walk," yet it does seem unlikely to be "could" and the line appears to relate to the harbor in Cannes because of the one mile to the harbor that is mentioned (see the published version and Rapallo B below). Indeed, within a week of their arrival in Rapallo on February 17, 1928, Yeats seems to have felt (slightly) reinvigorated: "Though still capable of very little at a time, I am at last recovering strength visibly. [...] I can walk about the harbour here for an hour without fatigue" ([February 24, 1928], *CL InteLex* 5081).

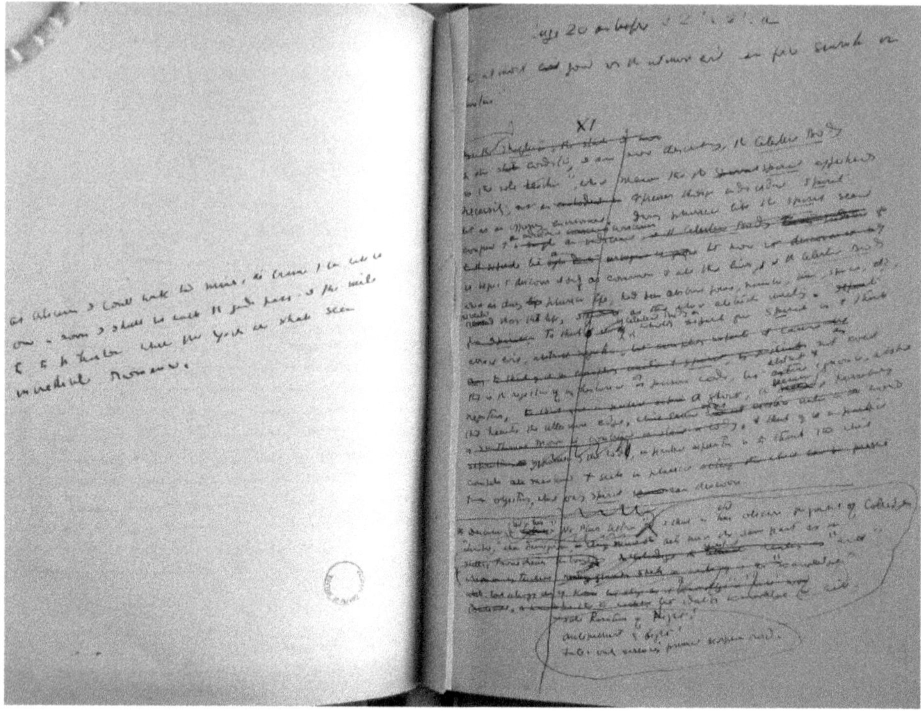

Figure 4.11. NLI 13,582 (Rapallo Notebook E), [63bis-v]–[66r]. (Courtesy of the NLI; photograph courtesy of Catherine E. Paul.) [63bis-v], on the left, shows the fragment starting "At Aliceras I could walk…"

A version of this line appears in Rapallo B—probably written in the fall of 1928[153]—where it is placed at a particular moment when communications from the Instructors intruded again, slipping briefly into a form of historic present:

> I might have read for two or three more years but for something | that happened last February at Cannes[.]
>
> VII
>
> September twe[*l*]ve mons [=*months*] was very ill with [?bronco] pneumonia & | [~~…~~] my wife took me first Spain & then to | Southern France. I ~~was almost~~ <seemed> well for a time & then was ill again | the ~~xx~~ neumonia had been followed by general nervous break down. | I got up for but a short time in each day and began to study | a gradually narrowing circle. Two months ago in Aliceras I | walked two miles, a month ago when I first came here I got as | far as the harbour and that must be a mile, but now I find the | two hundred yards to the sea more than enough some days. Then my | circle [*widened*] again very slowly, & it had grown but little wider | when one after noon at a quarter to five I heard my wife | lock her bed room door […] | in a trance, & in a moment the spirit was speaking. (NLI 13,579, Rapallo B, [99r–100r])[154]

Clearly, therefore, "Two months ago" refers to two months before an incident of February 1928 recounted in the leather notebook which he had brought (containing poems such as "A Dialogue of Self and Soul") under the heading "3 Sleaps. Cannes.":

> Some trouble at first. George while asleap locked | doors of both rooms & then "apple" began to talk | – [?mainly] it seemed to make link again. It was in the | afternoon, & nurse came to the door with | Michael at 5.30. George half woke & | fell on floor – I had thought she was awake. | I unlocked door & George now awake said | we had been at work. George did not recover | from the shock for days. (NLI 30,359, [13r])

When the moment was elaborated slightly further in section XI of *A Packet for Ezra Pound*—where the nurse brings "our daughter" rather than Michael—Yeats shifts the tenses into the past for greater clarity, but still uses "ago" and "now": "Two months ago I had walked to the harbour at Algeciras, two miles; a month ago to the harbour at Cannes, a mile; and now thought two hundred yards enough" (*PEP* 27; *AVB* 20, *CW14* 16).

Yeats evidently liked this line enough to repeat it in various forms, so it seems likely that he was uncertain about where or how he would use it, but use it he would. A less particularized version appears cancelled in "Lyric Sequence," the prose subject that Yeats drafted for "Meditations on Death" in Rapallo C. Opening, as in the published form, with Algeciras and its herons, at this stage the preliminary outline considers evidence of age—"~~An old man is like a child – he turns to god as a child to his nurse~~"—as well as the wisdom of personal experience "I have a little wisod. Plato's king — something of Sankarya, & something has been spoken to me alone" ([9r]). His declining health and narrowing horizons were briefly considered as a theme: "~~At Cannes. Ka | Algeciras I I could walk a couple of miles & now a mile~~" ([9r]).[155]

There is even the tantalizing possibility that the note on the loose pages in Rapallo E once faced the cancelled lines in Rapallo C, in other words that these loose pages were the central four leaves of the first gathering of Rapallo Notebook C. The single line has the appearance of the kind of stray note Yeats would put on a verso opposite a cancelled line to correct or substitute—in this case the prose subject of "Meditations on Death."[156] If that were the case, Rapallo C would open as a "Diary of Thought | begun. Sept 23. 1928 | in Dublin," including material that would become part of the "Introduction to the Great Wheel" in *A Packet for Ezra Pound* on [2r]. Folio [3r] contains *Vision* material dated "Jan 1929" and, after more *Vision*-related writing, folio [6r] starts to explore how "Ezra Pound bases his scepticism upon the statement, that we know nothing but sequences."[157] This continues over three rectos with a few notes on the versos. Following the blank verso [8v], we suggest that there would be the scenario for the "Dance Play" or "dramatic poem" on leaves conjectured as [9], [10], and [11], these last two forming the central folded sheet of the gathering. Leaf [12r] would contain the end of the scenario and the paragraph on Masefield, Synge, and Pound, dated "Jan. 22 (1929?)." The verso of this leaf would have the stray lines about Algeciras and Cannes, and opposite them would appear a similar line, cancelled in the preliminary prose for "Meditations upon Death," date "Jan 23" (see Figure 4.12).

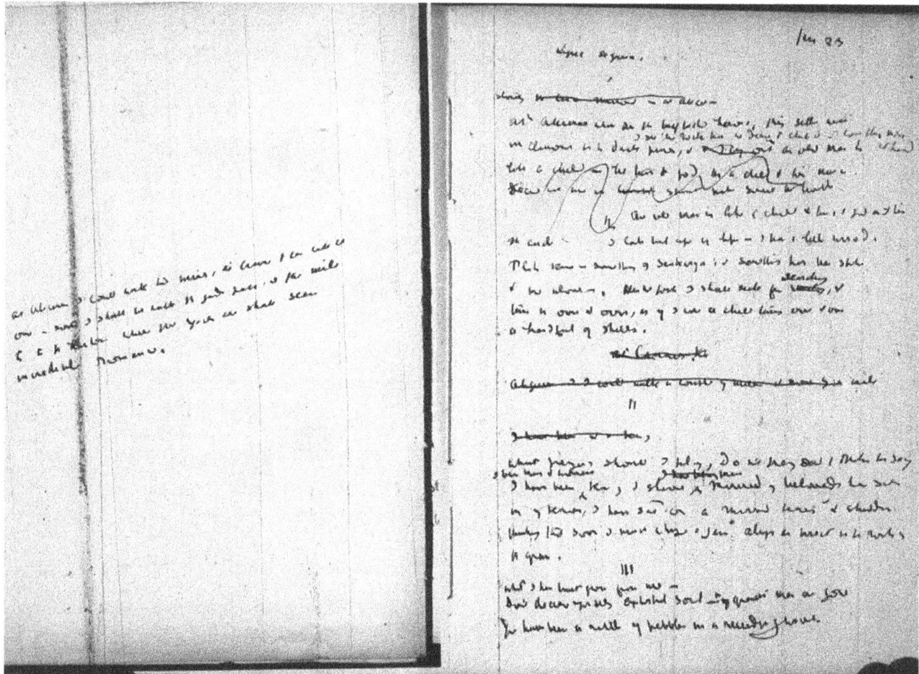

Figure 4.12. NLI 13, 582 (Rapallo Notebook E) folio [63bis-v] (left) placed opposite NLI 13,580 (Rapallo Notebook C) folio [9r] (right). These microfilm images show the binding thread at the center of the gathering in Rapallo C and the loose leaves in Rapallo E. They are not aligned here, in order to make the separate elements clearer.

That is one possibility, and it is appealing, but these four pages are uniform with the Rapallo notebooks generally, all the extant notebooks are missing pages (though relatively few are missing folded bifolia), and there are also probably notebooks that are missing, so there are a number of places the leaves could have come from. It is, however, unlikely that the leaves "were at some time removed from the notebook" (Rapallo E itself) and then reinserted later as Curtis and Guinness suggest (*Res* xvi), since there is really nowhere that they could come from in Notebook E, as the sixteen leaves removed from the first gathering were almost certainly numbered and contained introductory material for *A Vision*. The notebook's other missing pages would not be folded pairs.

The renewal of contact with the communicators is also an important consideration in the reasons for the amount of energy Yeats devoted to the redrafting of *A Vision* in the Rapallo notebooks generally. As he indicates, his philosophical reading had been ample during 1926 and 1927, and there is no reason to think that he could not "have gone on reading for some two or three years more but for something that happened at Cannes" (*PEP* 27; *AVB* 20, *CW14* 16). In his own estimation, the sessions that followed were important in clarifying his thinking, but they are also suggestive evidence that George Yeats was not deliberately controlling her husband through these communications, as she would have had little reason to disturb the sleeping dog so long after Yeats had accepted that the "Exposition in sleep came to an end in 1920" (*PEP* 23; *AVB* 17, *CW14* 14).

[58v–74r] [drafts for *A Vision* on the afterlife]

This second block of material on *A Vision* starts immediately after the end of the draft of the play *The Resurrection*, on a verso, [58v], replacing the writing on [59r]; there is a three-line comment (cancelled) on the following verso, [59v], after which comes a gap of seven pages [60–66] (with the interpolated four leaves now in their place).[158] There is then another single side of writing, [67r], a gap of one leaf [68], another single page of writing, [69r], followed by four missing leaves [70–73], and a final page with writing, [74r]. There are therefore five full sides of drafting in total, one verso and four rectos, a large part of which is cancelled, along with a cancelled snippet. (The following treatment will ignore the interpolated pages and treat leaves [58] to [74] as if the insertion were not there—as they appear, for instance, in the photographs of the Harvard microfilm.)

It seems likely that the drafting was continuous, as sections are numbered and the progression fits with the gaps, so that the pages were probably removed after the draft was completed.[159] Given its position after the final manuscript draft of *The Resurrection*—which, as outlined above, comes after the draft in the White Vellum Notebook, itself "begun Nov 23 1930"—this work for *A Vision* probably dates from early in 1931, possibly before he told Ezra Pound that he was going "to Dublin tomorrow to dictate from the now finished MSS of 'A Vision.' I have cast off the burden of years" (February 5, [1931], *CL InteLex* 5441).[160] We now know that it would be some years before *A Vision B* was actually published, and that Yeats would continue the process of redrafting, but, at this stage in 1931, he evidently felt that the bulk of the revision had been done, though the drafts needed typing, with the inevitable refinement that came with the process of dictation.[161]

If this was the case, the writing of this material seems surprisingly uncertain, with large stretches of what little text remains being cancelled and with even larger gaps of removed pages. Yeats had long felt that what he had written on the afterlife was inadequate, but also that he did not have enough material or understanding to write with more confidence. So, not only has the "book" on the afterlife in *A Vision A* been almost entirely rewritten in *A Vision B*, but the concepts and their organization have been completely overhauled. He had written in Rapallo B that "The Gates of Pluto" in *A Vision A* filled him "with shame," such that he resolved to "postpone the theme till my instructors come to me again or my own thought take fire," and to content himself in that notebook "with a few rambling comments."[162] The text contained in the few isolated pages extant here indicates a state that is significantly more developed than those "rambling comments" and, in at least one aspect, it is even clearer than the published version of *A Vision B*, as it gives a brief, lucid enumeration of the six stages of the afterlife before starting on the description.[163] And for the general reader, labeling the stages with months of the year (as here), rather than zodiac signs (as in *A Vision B*), also probably makes clearer the relationship of the afterlife to summer and incarnate life to winter, although the mystification of astrological symbolism may be part of the point in *A Vision B*.

Having started his drafts on the first recto after the play, Yeats appears to have given this section a Roman "V," which was then cancelled, along with much of the associated text, but repeated at the top of the text replacing it on the opposite verso. This indicates that Yeats had already drafted and was satisfied with four preceding sections.[164] The "Contents" in Rapallo C ([78r]) indicate that the removed material included the "Soul in Judgement (continued from loose leaf book) 12 pages," so the four sections might have been in this loose-leaf book or carried on similar loose pages.[165]

Still, as already mentioned, this first page is isolated, with seven leaves after it torn out (a few of the stubs bear word fragments); the next leaf, [67r], references "page 20 or before & 21 & 21.a," probably referring to loose-leaf drafts. A single line of text precedes a new section numbered "XI" dealing with the third afterlife state, "The Shiftings," with many cancellations and a decisive final vertical line through the whole text. After another gap of one leaf, a section numbered "XII" on [69r] is focused on the fourth state, "The Beatitude." Four more leaves are removed before the final page, headed "XIV," which describes an unnamed state—identifiable as the fifth stage, "The Purification"—and almost all is cancelled. Though the treatment may total five sides of draft, it is so discontinuous and fragmented that it is unclear why Yeats left these pages rather than removing them all. Yet, because the treatment of the afterlife is so generally scanty, the material contained here that Yeats considered but later rejected provides valuable insights into his thinking.

The draft on [59r] broaches the subject of the different stages of the afterlife, with a large insertion from the opposite page, and substantial footnote (that occupies more than half the page). It starts:

> ~~My instructors~~ I shall [~~...~~] explore by a series of analogies* [~~...~~] | drawn from the double cones, the state of the soul | between death [~~...~~] & birth; | [~~...~~] if anything is stated | by my teachers, ~~it~~ I shall point out that it is so stated because I do not | yet understand. [~~...~~] In what I have written hitherto ~~I have~~ <I have> looked | [~~...~~] for confirmation <mainly> to my readers | general knowledge of life, if life seemed to fit with the patterns I had made | that was sufficient, but [~~...~~] we must now explore a | theme, that owes it existance perhaps to the experience of visionaries. ([59r])

This opening is then followed by text inserted from the opposite verso that, despite appearing to continue the theme is headed with the number "V," as if opening a section. Despite differences of terminology and reference, the six-stage scheme it outlines is recognizable as almost exactly the same as that presented in *A Vision B*, radically different from *A Vision A* and a significant development from the formulations in the earlier Rapallo Notebooks.

> { V
> The state between death & birth can be measured out, upon the wheel of | the Faculties. Upon that wheel they run from phase 15 to phase 28 | and constitute a dark fortnight or a fortnight when the moon decreases | in light [~~...~~] but as we pass at Death from the control | of the Faculties & [~~...~~] we | measure this out upon the wheel of the Principles. In the wheel of the Principles | the Spirit is the male or active principle, & Celestial Body is related to it as | Mask is to Will [~~....~~] & solar symbolism | predominates over lunar. The period from death to birth is measured according to the months | & constitutes the summer from [~~...~~] | the begin[*nin*]g of March to the end of August, what the antithetical phases | are in the wheel of the Faculties these months are in that of the Principles. | [~~...~~] Death [~~...~~] thus ocurs, when phase 8 ocurs on the wheel of the | Faculties, & at Death Spirit regains freedom, [~~...~~] & begins to oppose the | Celestial Body [~~...~~] to the | Passionate Body, [~~...~~] which is at[*?=as it*] were the Body of Fate. March or death | has two moments "The Vision of the Blood Kindred" & "The Vision of the Celestial Body["] <and begins the separation from Nature [~~...~~]>. | The second state, or April, is called the Return and the ~~Re~~ Dreaming Back, & completes the | separation from Nature, The third state of May is the separation from good & evil & is called | The Shiftings. June, the fourth or central state is ~~pure intellect, & so~~ called now "The | Beatitude" now "The Beatific Vision." July or the Fifth state plunges the soul once more into | good & evil & is called "The Purification["]; August or the sixth state plunges it into nature | and is ~~called~~ may be called "The Preparation."} ([58v])

As noted above, this succinct summary of the stages might have helped many readers, and it persists into quite advanced drafts, making its omission in the published edition of *A Vision B* all the more perplexing.[166]

A footnote to the "series of analogies" in the first line of [59r] looks to the extended epistolary debate that Yeats had with Thomas Sturge Moore, focusing particularly on Yeats's understanding of Kant:

> * ~~In~~ I write for a few students. One of them, [...] | when I gave him my poem "Byzantium" [...] said that its analogies | told us nothing about reality.[167] <Though in The> later Kant thought that we ~~could~~ <probably> know the [...] <numinous> | through analogies, though we can not prove them true; but that [...] <seems> self deception <to my friend> | ~~a disciple of George Moore, the Cambridge metaphysician, he thought~~ The Kant of | the Critic of Pure Reason like Admiral [?Cochrans] ship, when it got between two | enemies, [...] <had> raked ~~in a single instant~~ ~~all~~ past & future philosophers.[168] | The substance of Spinoza, the Absolute of Hegel <Time & Space> were alike [...] <subjective fabrications ~~and that alone~~>. I now put | to him this problem. [...] Who fabricates? [....] | Experiences ~~unknown to~~ | ~~Kant, or~~ rejected without examination by the educated classes of Kants day are now | classified as studies. ~~If the ego~~ ~~I know from personal experience~~ I am convinced | my own & <by> the experience of others that ~~the ego~~ <the mind> [...] <can know without the intervention of sense what others think>[,] | [...] that the eye can ~~sometimes~~ ~~sea~~ see | past distant & future events[,] | [....] | <that> the impersonal ego of Kants day, forever bound to its own dark | lanthorn does not exist.[169] If [*we*] are to think at all I must | substitute we for I & that we are the fabricators or that our [*end of page*] ([59r])

Yeats appears to be thinking of research on telepathic forms of perception at a distance, reinforced by his own experiences, as putting the world model of the Enlightenment in doubt, and the missing conclusion of the note probably gave a version of how "we," the "community of spirits," collectively co-create reality through perception, as epitomized in Rapallo D's "Seven Propositions."[170] The end of the note on missing folio [60r] may also have contained some consideration of aesthetics, as the page opposite [59v] gives a sentence for insertion, all cancelled with a wavy line: "I am ~~inclined to~~ classify under 'Will' ~~the utility of art~~ the utility whether of painting or of literature. The painter ~~ceased to~~ gradually ceases to be a Church decorator, the minstrel disappears."

The pages that followed presumably dealt with the soul's existence in the first two stages between death and birth, corresponding to March and April in the scheme on [58v], as, after a gap of seven leaves (and disregarding the inserted leaves), the next section, XI, presents the "third state of May [which] is the separation from good & evil & is called The Shiftings," though Yeats's "evil" here is not so much moral as conceptual.

page 20 ~~or before~~ & 21 & 21.a

the utmost ~~evil~~ good nor the utmost evil can force sensation or emotion"

XI

~~In the Shiftings, the state I now~~ |
In the ~~state~~ condition I am now describing, the Celestial Body | "is the sole teacher", which means that the ~~Spirrit~~ Spirit apprehends | Necessity, not as ~~embodied in~~ expressed through individual Spirit | but as an opposing environment. During phisical life the Spirit seemed | confined to ~~a single an individual~~ <an individual ~~consceness~~ consciousness>, | [~~...~~] but now [~~...~~] it | begins to discover itself as common to all that lives, & in the Celestial Body | which ~~as~~ during ~~life~~ phisical life, had been abstract forms, number, time, space, etc., | ~~revead~~ <revealed> through that life, ~~stands it~~ as that which abstracts unity. | [~~...~~] To think <of> ~~it a~~ <~~if~~ Celestial Body as> wholly separate from Spirit is to think | abstract evil, [~~...~~] | not <an> evil | that is rejection of an historical or personal code, but ~~astrac~~ <abstract>* ignorance, abstract | negation, [~~...~~] A ghost, a ~~seemng~~ <seeming> possibility that haunts the uttermost edge ~~which cannot come into existence <exist> unless in the words~~ | ~~of Sir Thomas Brown it contrive or steal a body~~, to think of it is | [~~...~~] in partial separation is to think that which | compels all mankind to seek in phisical [~~...~~] | objectivity, which only Spirit ~~knows~~ can discover. ([67r])

The asterisk attached to "abstract ignorance, abstract negation" points to a note at the foot of the page, involving a complicated web of balloons and arrows to rearrange the writing and then revise the rearrangement—the following transcription attempts to give something close to the intended final form:

*Described in Coleridge's "Ne Plus Ultra" [~~...~~]

Sole Posative of Night!
Antipathist of Light!
Fates only essence! primal scorpion rod.

[&] I think in ~~his~~ <that> obscure fragment of Coleridges "Limbo", where Demogorgon [~~...~~] acts much the same part as in Shelleys "Prometheus Unbound". ~~In Coleridge the ultimate <spiritual> reality is "Will" whereas my teachers [...] generally speak or write of it as "knowledge" [...] but always as if "knowledge" & "will" were identical, a knowledge that is willed~~, but identify knowledge & will. ([67r])[171]

As *Spirit* seeks to transcend good and evil, evil is seen as concrete absence, unyielding Necessity, personified by the implacable Demogorgon of Coleridge or Shelley. The implication is that *Celestial Body*, while divine in origin and ideal in essence, is on its own sterile and therefore "evil" in the particular sense apprehended by the philosophical mind of Coleridge and referred to in "Limbo" as "*positive Negation*."[172]

The state of the *Shiftings*, described here, follows the *Return*, which is associated with the gaining understanding of motives and consequences, causes and effects, exhausting pain, pleasure, and emotion, completing "the emotional and moral life," so that it "can be dismissed" (*AVB* 231, *CW14* 168). In the *Shiftings*, the *Spirit* seeks to move beyond the confines of culture and context and, more specifically, beyond good and evil, although the meaning remains hard to understand or accept because the insistence on exchanging good for evil and vice versa is difficult to view except in moral terms. Even Yeats comments, in one draft, that "The conception is so strange [...] harsh and paradoxical."[173] Otherwise, however, this state involves a clear shift away from personal experience to generalized, using "an opposing environment" of Necessity as a way of discovering what is "common to all lives."

The reversal is clearly important, because, without it, the next life will repeat the same circumstances and motives, and it must also be apprehended and understood, or the reversal itself will be repeated.

> XII 29
>
> Should the Spirit fail to reverse envorment [=*environment*] & motive, it must incarnate | with the old motive the old invirnment, should it make reversal | without understanding it & that which it displaced | as part of the same reality, it would incarnate with the new motive | the new invirnment. ([69r], cancellations omitted)

Like Blake's *Marriage of Heaven and Hell*, the complementing of good and evil results in a form of balanced unity and a more universal experience, leading to the potential union of the *Celestial Body* and *Spirit* in the brief (though timeless) central stage, called the *Beatitude, Beatific Vision*, or *Marriage*: "When it sees all as one, <it allows before or after> the Beatitude or Beatific Vision, a unity of Being created by the Spirits of the 13th Cone or Sphere, where all antinomies are solved" ([69r]).

The rest of the page is filled with a note that appears to be keyed to text from the preceding (missing) page, examining an apparent "confusion in the script tween the absorbtion of Celestial Body at the close of the return, & the Devine Marriage of equal union of the 13th cone." Yeats introduces the quotation from the script that he repeated in both printed versions—"'The Celestial Body is the Devine Cloak lent to all; at the consummation the cloak fall for the Christ is revealed'"—which he connects with Bardaisan's "Hymn of the Pearl," indicating that "It was a mistake in symbolism however to speak of such a cloak as discarded, a cloak lent not found." He then recounts a personal experience:

> I awoke one night, when I was a young man to find my body rigid | and to hear my own voice, or some strange voice speaking through my lips | as seemed, speak these words "we make an image of him who sleeps | and it is not him who sleeps & we call it Emmanuel." | The <u>Celestial Body</u> only returns into that condition when it has deserved a name ~~when it is the body of intellect, or the bride of spirit or the bride of~~ intellect, Wisdom, the Heavenly Maiden of the Rennaissance poets. ([69r]).[174]

This experience was of particular importance to Yeats and was repeated in his autobiographical writing, as well as in *A Vision B*, where it illustrates how "A living man sees the *Celestial Body* through the *Mask*" (*AVB* 233 n, *CW14* 169 n), although the variant wording here indicates Yeats was quoting from memory.[175] As in the writing of *The Resurrection* or the dance play draft, we see that, although Yeats was not a Christian in terms of religion, the figure of Christ, or Emmanuel, represents perfected or transformed humanity.

After a gap of another four pages, the draft picks up at section "XIV," which examines the afterlife's fifth stage, the *Purification*, with the progressive disappearance of individual qualities or "denudation," but also continuing concerns of the previous passage, with the *Spirit* compelled to repeat what has remained unresolved from one life to another. Apart from an opening phrase, the first third of the page is cancelled completely, and, while the lower text is largely clear, the first half is cancelled with a single wavy line:

> An intellectual ~~purification~~ <denudation> ~~similar to~~ <has accompanied> this shedding off of ~~[....]~~
> the present moment, of the fated image, the <u>Spirit</u> has become more | & more ~~anybodys~~ <everybodys> spirit, ~~[...]~~ | & as it has done so has | ~~been~~ has as it were unstitched the web it wove when living (~~[...]~~ | phases ~~2, 3, 4~~, <1, 2, 13 [=3]> of the spiritual ~~cone~~ cone ~~are~~ <confront> phases 26, 27, 28 of the phisical cone). | ~~Human life~~ <It may> begins with <outer & inner> freedom ~~[...]~~ & receives [?undistinguishable] mere formless sensation everywhere | & after the ~~mythical~~ life of children, which corresponds to the mythic epoch ~~[...]~~ <of every civilization>, | the ~~[...]~~ conflicts of youth, which correspond to the heroic age ~~of every civilization~~ | he becomes the man set in cause effect, necessity or nature everywhere. After | that in man & civilization alike comes ~~the~~ phisical decline & the growth of | reflection the beg[inn]ing of the return into the whole. At the end of the <u>Beatitude</u> the <u>Spirit</u> | has lived back <through> the project of its late life ~~[...]~~ | but what was the source is now the end, what was the seed is now the exfoliation | & because all that was done amiss during prevents the [?climbing] back, the <u>Spirit</u> | has been through out dependent upon the help of the living, & will be compelled where | has not been found [...] to weave that | same web again. Because the spiritual end is always the opposite of that | phisical source (think of Blakes contrast between

> those ~~brought forth in so~~ | begotten in sorrow & brought forth in joy & those begotten in joy & brought forth in | sorrow) it reaches complete freedom ~~from nature or necessity~~ at the moment when | is ~~most fated~~ is most bound to necessity. ([74r])

The parallel of human life and the progress of civilizations recalls Vico's three ages[176] and, of course, Oswald Spengler, who held that "Every Culture passes through the age-phases of the individual man. Each has its childhood, youth, manhood and old age."[177]

Though it is cancelled and the details are unclear,[178] the concept of the soul's spiritual cone or wheel running opposite to the physical again embodies a form of paradox and reversal, shifting from age and infancy to sorrow and joy, so that "what was the source is now the end," age runs to infancy, and what is begun in sorrow attains joy. Also crucial here is the reliance of the dead upon the living to complete the necessary purifications of the afterlife, so that if it "has not been found" they will be compelled "to weave that same web again." This recalls part of Olivia Shakespear's reaction to *A Vision A*, "I think it is rather terrible—all so unending & no rest or peace till one attains an unattainable goal" (February 14, 1926; *LTWBY 2* 467–68), or George Russell's observation that the "great wheel turns ceaselessly, and that I and all others drop into inevitable groove after groove."[179] Indeed, some readers of *A Vision* have found, like Russell, that it leaves little room for "the idea of Free Will," and it may be in response to such criticisms that Yeats repeats assertions of the soul's freedom through the drafts, though that freedom is expressed as a spiritual paradox: Yeats speaks of the *Beatitude*, where *Spirit* unites with its individual form of fate, the *Celestial Body*, as attaining "complete freedom at the moment when [*it*] is most bound to necessity," echoing the Book of Common Prayer's Collect for Peace, which states that the service of God is perfect freedom.[180]

[74v–85v] [blank pages]

This is not the end of the processes involved in the afterlife, but Rapallo E's drafts stop here, although there are another ten blank pages available, a point of similarity with Rapallo A, which closes with sixteen blank pages. As in that case, it shows that this notebook was evidently put to one side as Yeats used other materials to carry on with his drafting, including loose-leaf binders and other notebooks, including the White Vellum Notebook.

Conclusion

As stated at the outset of this essay, Rapallo Notebook E forms a fitting close to the quintet of the Rapallo Notebooks and our examinations of them—fitting for its important literary material as well as in the way it fades out inconclusively with a mutilated, unfinished draft and blank pages. The Rapallo Notebooks are workbooks, made special by their survival and contents.

Like the other four notebooks, in Rapallo E the *Vision* drafts are both repetitive and illuminating for the light that they shed on the system of *A Vision* and some knotty problems that the published material leaves unresolved. The massive work that has been done on the automatic script and the early drafts for *A Vision A* has helped readers to understand the genesis of the work and thought. The working papers from 1926 onwards are more scattered and less coherent, but no less important in understanding how Yeats's thinking developed, informing many aspects of his creative work and competing with it for his time and attention.

The reading notes from Frobenius—like those from other writers in the other notebooks from Mackenna's Plotinus to "Sepharial" to George Henry Lewes—show Yeats testing his thought against others and using his own ideas to explore points of contact or possibly to create what Harold Bloom would regard as a "strong misreading" that could be useful.[181] The diary accounts of séances in London show Yeats's fascination with psychic phenomena, an interest which is then transmuted creatively into the play of a Dublin séance interrupted by an obsessive thought-form or ghost, Swift in *The Words upon the Window-Pane*, and, at the turning point of the ages, the beating heart of a phantom. The notebook also harbors the pages containing an abandoned tableau of Christ among the dead saviors, which underlines the importance of Christ in the history of the world and its soul, a thread which runs through the automatic script, *Calvary*, *The Resurrection* in its two versions, and this scenario.

As with all the notebooks, what engages the reader most is perhaps the heterogeneity of the thought and writing. Even when attention turns from something that engages our interest to a topic that is less immediately attractive, the notebook makes us aware of the writer in time, juggling the concerns of politics, reading, friendships, dinners, personal interests, with creative or philosophical projects. On the one hand, there is "the bundle of accident and incoherence that sits down to breakfast" or deals with day-to-day business and, on the other, the artist "reborn as an idea, something intended, complete" (*E&I* 509, *CW5* 204), yet these are the same person and these aspects collide and overlap as the notebook brings those separate moments and states of mind together.

In Yeats's view, when the artist fully participates in a work of art and its production, both artist and art embody idea, intention, and completeness. Rapallo Notebook B elaborates what such completeness means: it is a folding in, where all the elements produce a symbolic common multiple, each one related by harmonic integers to the others, or where multiple cycles finish together in a great conjunction. Explaining the Great Year's totality, Yeats compares it to how "in the work of art each separate line, color, or thought is related to [*the*] whole, is as it were multiplied into it,"[182] a formulation revised in Rapallo A to "a work of art where every thing is a part of everything, flows as it were into the whole."[183] Indeed Yeats's conception of human Unity of Being[184] is a fundamentally aesthetic judgment, treating a person like a work of art that exhibits proportion and coherence.

Though the artist presents the achieved work, in the cases where that achievement is sufficiently compelling, critics are interested in how that point is reached and in the variations of the way that the creative process may play out in different cases, with masterful poetry sometimes achieved almost immediately and at other times only after long wrestling. Appreciating the processes involved in the drafts within the notebooks relies on some familiarity with the published works that they pre-figure and also on the readers' interest in those works. Yet in the context of the notebooks, they have an interest and aesthetic appeal of their own.

In the general introduction to this collection of essays, we looked to "The Circus Animals' Desertion" to refer to the notebooks as the "mound of refuse or the sweepings of a street" that Yeats locates as the beginning of the "masterful images" that "because complete / Grew in pure mind" (*VP* 630). That comparison seems even more true at the end of this project, as we see the poet's search for a theme and for inspiration in the jumble of "the foul rag-and-bone shop of the heart" (*VP* 630). This rag-and-bone shop combines the rags and tatters in the "mortal dress" that make "Soul clap its hands and sing, and louder sing" in "Sailing to Byzantium" (*VP* 407) with the bones that sing their memories of human love retained beyond death in "Three Things" (*VP* 521).[185]

In that overview we cited Louis Hay's idea of a draft as one of the possible manifestations of the text, which thus represents a multiplication of modes of expression.[186] If drafts multiply possibility, notebooks expand such diversity further by their juxtaposition of disparate stimulations, notes, workplans, revisions, and drafts within their covers, where even the removed pages show part of the process of writing and erasure in a way that loose pages never can. Each set of drafts is also in play with the drafts and notes alongside within the workbook and the five Rapallo Notebooks, along with the contemporary manuscript books, together offer further interplay across volumes.

Notes

1 Thomas Parkinson's list of manuscript notebooks referred to NLI MS 13,577 as a "'Rapallo' notebook in leather," indicating a board-covered notebook in a leather sleeve (NLI 30,214, item II.c); see Wayne K. Chapman "George Yeats, Thomas Parkinson, and the Legacy of the Archive" in *YA22* (forthcoming). For facsimiles of NLI 13,577, see Wayne K. Chapman, ed., *W. B. Yeats's Robartes-Aherne Writings: Featuring the Writings of His "Stories of Michael Robartes and His Friends"* (London: Bloomsbury Academic, 2018), 188–271; hereafter cited as *YRAW*. For a summary of the extant notebooks and their characteristics, see Mann, "Appendix: Yeats's Notebooks" in *YA22* (forthcoming).

2 Item II.l in Parkinson's list (NLI 30,214) and formerly MBY 545 in Michael Butler Yeats's cataloguing, it is now in unknown private hands. There are microfilm copies available at Harvard's Houghton Library, the Melville Library at the State University of New York at Stony Brook, the National Library of Ireland, and Cornell University Library, the last of these not totally complete. See Chapman, "Yeats's White Vellum Notebook, 1930–1933," *IYS* 2.2 (2017).

3 The Diary, NLI MS 30,354, contains, for instance, the first prose draft of "Byzantium" before work continued in Rapallo D (see "Rapallo Notebook D," *IYS* 8.1: 173–83; also 231–41 above), and Notebook A also contains a late addition that continues a diary entry from October 1930 (see "Rapallo Notebooks A and B," *IYS* 6.1: 104; also 62 above).

4 Parkinson describes it as a "Brown leather-bound notebook, begun in Rapallo in June, 1934" (item II.n in his list NLI 30,214). Formerly MBY 351, it is now in Boston College's Burns Library, where it is catalogued as "*Supernatural Songs*, notebook, 1934-1934" (https://findingaids.bc.edu/repositories/2/archival_objects/20846). It is also described by Richard Allen Cave as a "notebook (usually referred to as the 'Rapallo notebook') in an octavo album format with leather boards imitating a medieval design with a series of three mock 'hinges,' embossed with stylized flowers, to front and back covers. The leaves are of cream laid paper, measuring 24.1 by 15.8 cm," see *"The King of the Great Clock Tower" and "A Full Moon in March": Manuscript Materials* (Ithaca, NY: Cornell University Press, 2007), xvi. The first recto of the notebook is headed "Rapallo. June. 1934" (ibid., 88–89).

5 See "Rapallo Notebook D," *IYS* 8.1: 132, 134, and 137 (also 190, 192, and 195 above).

6 *"The Resurrection": Manuscript Materials*, ed. Jared Curtis and Selina Guinness (Ithaca, NY, and London: Cornell University Press, 2011); hereafter cited as *Res*.

7 Curtis Bradford, *Yeats at Work* (Carbondale and Edwardsville, IL: Southern Illinois University Press, 1965), 217–267; hereafter cited as *YAW*.

8 *"The Words upon the Window Pane": Manuscript Materials*, ed. Mary FitzGerald (Ithaca, NY, and London: Cornell University Press, 2002); hereafter cited as *WUWP*. The punctuation of the title—specifically the hyphenation of "Window-pane" and capitalization of the second element—varies in different versions. Mary FitzGerald follows the first publication by the Cuala Press, which gives *The Words upon the Window Pane* (1934). Macmillan's *Wheels and Butterflies* (1934) gives *The Words upon the Window-pane*, the form subsequent editions from Macmillan have tended to favor. In the Scribner *Collected Works* (*CW2*), David R. and Rosalind E. Clark use *The Words upon the Window-Pane*, which we have adopted as the standard form outside direct quotation.

9 *"The Tower" (1928): Manuscript Materials*, ed. Richard J. Finneran with Jared Curtis and Ann Saddlemyer (Ithaca, NY, and London: Cornell University Press, 2007).

10 David R. Clark *"Words for Music Perhaps": Manuscript Materials* (Ithaca, NY, and London: Cornell University Press, 1999), xvii; hereafter cited as *WFMP*. The wording in *WUWP* is almost identical: "*NLI 13,582 Rapallo Notebook E* containing entries from about May 9, 1928, to about January 1929" (xii), as is that of Richard Finneran, Jared Curtis, and Ann

Saddlemyer in *"The Tower" (1928): Manuscript Materials.* Mary FitzGerald sadly died in 2000, before the volume she was editing was finished, and her husband, Richard Finneran, passed in 2005, before finishing the volume he was editing; in both cases, therefore, the census probably represents a default repetition of the descriptions used elsewhere in the series rather than these scholars' considered comments.

11 See John S. Kelly, *A W. B. Yeats Chronology* (London: Palgrave, 2003), 241–65; hereafter cited as *ChronY*.

12 The microfilm of WBY's notebooks held at Harvard University's Houghton Library was made in the late 1940s (probably for Richard Ellmann). See Wayne K. Chapman, "Yeats's White Vellum Notebook, 1930–1933," *IYS* 2.2 (2018): 58 n18.

13 It can sometimes be difficult to discern precise details, and the final blank pages are not photographed.

14 Most of Rapallo Notebook E, starting at [17v] onward (the beginning of the draft of *The Words upon the Window-Pane*), was filmed at the request of David R. Clark, ca. 1958; see Microfilms, Box 9, M0027, Cornell Yeats editorial records, Cornell University Library, Ithaca, NY.

15 The conservation note for Notebook E is dated December 2005, as are those for B and C; that for A is dated February 2006. The restoration of D has been less extensive.

16 Oddly, the last gathering of Rapallo B appears to have twenty-two leaves, making it something of a sport.

17 Although the microfilms appear to show some breakage between the book's cover and the first leaf, the second gathering starts with a page numbered "19," following directly from the preceding pages, implying that the extant folios are the two outer ones.

18 As intact folded double leaves, these are different from the leaves in Rapallo Notebook A ([39–44], [74]), which became loose because their counterpart on the other side of the sewing had been removed.

19 WBY also refers to Rapallo A as "book D" in his diary of 1930 (NLI 30,354) to indicate where he continued the text of his entry for October 20 (see "Rapallo Notebooks A and B," *IYS* 6.1:104; also 62 above).

20 Thomas Parkinson (in NLI 30,214) did not use letters, referring to Rapallo C as "'Rapallo' notebook with notation 'Diary' on cover. Diary of Thought begun Sept. 23," and Rapallo D as "'Rapallo' notebook. Diary begun in Rapallo, 1928. Contains many versions of poems in The Winding Stair, including 'Byzantium.'" Rapallo C and D's covers share the pattern found on Yeats's "'Rapallo' notebook in leather, containing Stories of Michael Robartes and his Friends," now NLI 13,577 (the leather refers to an external slip-cover for the notebook).

21 Though the 18th edition of *The Chicago Manual of Style* appeared in 2024, for consistency we continue to follow 17th edition, which was current for the preceding essays in the series, as there are changes in policy. The paragraph on the use of the slash for poetry is unchanged except for numbering: 6.111 (17th ed.), 6.118 (18th ed.).

22 Since restoration, however, they are preceded by two added blank leaves (so that Gibson counts the first page as [3r] rather than [1r] used here; see note 25). Our numbering discounts the added leaves, as do the Cornell volumes.

23 See Matthew Gibson in Appendix II of ed. Matthew Gibson and Neil Mann, *Yeats, Philosophy, and the Occult* (Clemson, SC: Clemson University Press, 2016); hereafter cited as *YPO*.

24 See also Rapallo B (NLI 13,579) [71r], cit. "Rapallo Notebooks A and B," *IYS* 6.1: 133 and 158 n214 (and 91 and 116 n214 above).

25 Gibson counts the leaves added for rebinding, so his leaf numbers start with [3r]. We disagree with him on one point of transcription, where association with the zodiac and a "bull god" has led him to read "Taurus" in place of "Tunis," close to the site of ancient

Carthage: "Ram also as chief deity at Tunis in Pre-Carthaginian religions (Replaced by bull god from east)" ([2r]).

26 See Lucy Kalogera, "Yeats's Celtic Mysteries," (PhD dissertation, Florida State University, 1977), 41 and 142, and ed. John Kelly, Warwick Gould, and Deirdre Toomey, *W. B. Yeats: Collected Letters*, vol. 2 (Oxford: Clarendon Press, 1997): "the talismans of the Tuatha de Danaan….the Lia-Fail or stone of destiny, the sword of Lugh [sic *for* "Nuada" *or* "Light"], the spear of Lugh, and the cauldron of Dagda" (665) were central to the "four Outer Order rituals" written by WBY (667–68).

27 H. Dennis Bradley,…*And After* (London: T. Werner Laurie, 1931), 54–62.

28 A member of the London Spiritualist Alliance, Claire Frances Cantlon had faced trial in 1928 under the vagrancy act for "professing to tell fortunes." At her trial, women police officers who had visited her undercover gave accounts of less than impressive séances; Cantlon pleaded guilty to a technicality (see *Light*, 21 July–4 Aug. 1928, 340–41; 352–53; 362–64, 366, 372, and a recent account in *Psypioneer Journal* 11:1 [Jan. 2015], 11–33 [http://iapsop.com/psypioneer/psypioneer_v11_n1_jan_2015.pdf]). Cantlon was also honorary secretary of the Faery Investigation Society.

29 Mabel Beardsley had died in 1916 after a long illness, during which WBY visited her, writing to Lady Gregory on January 8, 1913, "Strange that just after writing those lines of the Rhymers who 'unrepenting faced their ends' I should be at the bedside of the dying sister of [Aubrey] Beardsley, who was practically one of us" (*CL InteLex* 2056, *L* 573). She was the subject of the poem "Upon a Dying Lady" (1917, *VP* 362–67).

30 See Kathleen Raine, "Hades Wrapped in Cloud," *Yeats the Initiate* (Mountrath: Dolmen; London: George Allen & Unwin, 1986), 23; *YO* plate 1 (facing 122); and *Life1* Plate 31.

31 Roy Foster suggests it came from Juliette Bisson (*Life1* Plate 31) and Yeats visited her in 1914 (*Life1* 517–18); cf. George Mills Harper and John S. Kelly, "Preliminary Examination of the Script of E[lizabeth] R[adcliffe], in *YO*, 137. Eva Carrière was a medium who specialized in materializing ectoplasm, and Bisson photographed her (see Juliette Alexandre-Bisson, *Les phénomènes dits de matérialisation* [Alcan: Paris, 1914], esp. ch. 1, and https://www.metmuseum.org/art/collection/search/284437); for a skeptical summary, see Harry Price, *Fifty Years of Psychical Research* (London: Longmans, Green, 1939), 87.

32 Another candidate is William Hope, investigated by the Society for Psychical Research in 1922. The style of his photographs is certainly closer to Deane's, but there is no evidence of WBY visiting him.

33 Sir Arthur Conan Doyle by Ada Deane, 1922, https://en.m.wikipedia.org/wiki/File:Photo_of_Sir_Arthur_Conan_Doyle_with_Spirit,_by_Ada_Deane.jpg (consulted May 2024); *YO*, facing 122; William Thomas by William Hope, https://flashbak.com/spirit-photography-in-1920s-england-when-william-hope-conned-arthur-conan-doyle-36092/ (consulted May 2024); Eva C. by Juliette Alexandre-Bisson, *Les phénomènes dits de matérialisation* 188–89, https://archive.org/details/lesphnomensd00biss/page/188/ (consulted May 2024).

34 Ada Emma Deane (1862–1957) produced photographs showing misty spirit light and even faces at the Armistice ceremonies in 1921, 1922, and 1923. In 1924, the *Daily Sketch* outbid its rivals to publish Deane's Remembrance Day photograph, which appeared on November 13. Two days later, the same newspaper's front page ran the story "How the Daily Sketch Exposed 'Spirit Photography,'" proving the photograph was fraudulent, with supposed soldiers being the faces of sportsmen from the press. Her supporters, including Arthur Keith and Arthur Conan Doyle, dismissed the exposé, as recounted by her collaborator, Estelle Stead, in *Faces of the Living Dead: Remembrance Day messages and photographs, etc.* (Manchester: Two Worlds Publishing, 1925). For a more recent assessment, see Andreas Fischer, "'The most disreputable camera in the world': Spirit Photography in the United Kingdom in the Early Twentieth Century" in *The Perfect Medium: Photography and the*

Occult, ed. Clément Chéroux (New Haven: Yale University Press, 2004), in association with an exhibition at the Metropolitan Museum of Art in New York. See also Martyn Jolly, *Faces of the Living Dead: The Belief in Spirit Photography* (London: British Library Publishing, 2006) and "Photographing the Dead," https://martynjolly.com/2013/10/03/photographing-the-dead/ consulted March 2024.

35 The Metropolitan Museum in New York holds an album of Deane's spirit photographs (which, owing to restrictions, can only be glimpsed at https://www.metmuseum.org/art/collection/search/286461), though a number of her photographs are available through a simple search online. See also Allerton S. Cushman, "An Evidential Case of Spirit Photography" in *Light*, May 13, 1922; F. W. Warrick, *Experiments in Psychics: Practical Studies in Direct Writing, Supernormal Photography and Other Phenomena* (New York: E. P. Dutton, 1939); and Meredith K. Reddy, "Artful Mediums: Women, Séance Photography, and Materialization Phenomena, 1880–1930," PhD thesis, University of Toronto, 2015, which includes several of Deane's photographs.

36 The "W. T. Stead" Borderland Library in Smith Square, Westminster, advertised Deane's "Psychic Photography" in the spiritualist weekly *Light*.

37 If the identification of Claire Cantlon is correct, she was also in London. In the year 1929, May 9 was a Thursday, so that would imply a visit to Mrs. Deane on Monday May 6, and the second visit to South Kensington in the week of May 13–17. WBY told his wife on May 9 (*CL InteLex* 5251) that he would "come home Monday or Tuesday" (i.e., May 13 or 14), but he appears to have arrived on Thursday, May 16 (*ChronY* 265).

38 May 9, 1928, sees Yeats at the Abbey in Dublin writing to Seán O'Casey about the success of *The Plough and the Stars* (*CL InteLex* 5110), while on May 9, 1927, he wrote to his sister from Coole (*CL InteLex* 4994), and on May 7, 1930, he was in Rapallo (*CL InteLex* 5346 and 5347).

39 For a clear example, see Rapallo D, where "A recent incident" in April 1931 is inserted among material from August 1929 (NLI 13,581, [4v]; see "Rapallo Notebook D," *IYS* 8.1: 132, 134, and 137 [also 190, 192, and 195 above]). Similarly, a clearly dated "note made Sept 18, 1915 at Coole" appears on a verso amid accounts of dreams and séances from 1913 in the PIAL Notebook (NLI 36,276/2, [28v]).

40 See, for instance, Arnold Goldman, "Yeats, Spiritualism, and Psychical Research" in *YO*, as well as that volume's edited versions of WBY's reports by G. M. Harper and J. S. Kelly, "'Preliminary Examination of the Script of E[lizabeth] R[adcliffe]'" and G. M. Harper, "'A Subject of Investigation': Miracle at Mirebeau." See also Neil Mann, "Yeats, Dreams, and the Dead," in *YPO*.

41 Margaret Mills Harper quotes "A stray note filed with the automatic script of Elizabeth Radcliffe": "'I ask what is the cause of the deception—'a spirit' who seems to have given every proof of goodness will deceive.…I am looking for some theory that will reconcile belief in spirits, in whom I believe, with evidence of deception'" (*Wisdom of Two: The Spiritual and Literary Collaboration of George and W. B. Yeats* [Oxford: Oxford University Press, 2006], 33n).

42 See, for example, the successive drafts of the section on belief in *A Packet for Ezra Pound*, in Catherine E. Paul, "W. B. Yeats and the Problem of Belief," *YA21* (2018), 297–311.

43 For the question of mediums and spirits in relation to *A Vision*, see Neil Mann, *A Reader's Guide to Yeats's "A Vision"* (Clemson, SC: Clemson University Press), 32–34; hereafter cited as *ARGYV*. WBY's understanding of Madame Blavatsky's Hidden Masters evinces a similar complexity; see Appendix A of the *Memoirs* (*Mem* 281).

44 See *VPl* 957–77, *CW2* 706–723. Versions of the introduction first appeared as "A Commentary" in the *Dublin Magazine* 6:4 (October–December 1931) and 7:1 (January–March 1932, with text not included later, except in the *Variorum Plays*), and in the Cuala

edition of the play in 1934. The introduction was drafted in the White Vellum Notebook on the pages numbered [1–29], [32–36], [95–97], [117–29], this last dated November 1, 1931 (see Chapman, "Yeats's White Vellum Notebook," *IYS* 2.2, items 1, 5, 19, and 22). The Yeatses' correspondence of November 1931 includes debate on the nature of mediumship arising from their disagreement about what was involved (*YGYL* 270–72).

45 WBY's practice in numbering pages does not always include every recto and very occasionally he also numbers a verso if it is significant. However, as it appears that eight bifolia are missing from the first gathering, this only allows for sixteen leaves. The central stitching is visible in the microfilm photographs.

46 The "Principle Symbols" recalls *AVB*'s Book I, "Part I: The Principal Symbol," while "The Diagram of the Great Wheel" recalls "Part II: Examination of the Wheel"; "Part III: The Twenty-Eight Incarnations" remained largely unchanged between *AVA* and *AVB*.

47 NLI 36,272/24. They begin to diverge after about seven or eight pages, however.

48 Since this section was titled "Book III THE COMPLETED SYMBOL," the reference is to the preceding book.

49 In the typescript, this is changed to "Only the logical faculty – 'creative mind' conjoined to 'will' – my instructors tell me is conscious" (NLI 36,272/24, page numbered 9).

50 Page "20" ([6r]) has two notes indicated, one with an asterisk and the second with a dagger; both the actual notes on [5v] are marked with asterisks, so I have emended the mark for the second note on [5v] to a dagger for clarity. WBY's note references are normally placed *before* the word or phrase that is being noted. The note here alludes to Sleeps from 1920: "The Solar group spoke last night (Tuesday 28th [1920]) through Dionertes. We were to meditate for 5 minutes between 2 & 3 pm on the subject of 'The Heir' & to do this lying on our backs. We were to attend to the secondary images that arose from the first idea. The Indian insistance on the first idea means that they wish to get all out of themselves, but it is through the secondary ideas that spiritual beings communicate" ("Sleep of Sept 26 27 & 28," written "September 29. 1920," *YVP3* 49).

51 See, for instance, Graham Hough's opinion that "The Daimon is an elusive concept," *The Mystery Religion of W. B. Yeats* (Brighton: Harvester, 1984), 110.

52 For instance, Helen Vendler describes them as "irritatingly similar to the Four Faculties," *Yeats's "Vision" and the Later Plays* (Harvard: Harvard University Press, 1963), 26, while Graham Hough finds that "try as I will I cannot fit them into the system or see them as anything but shadows or echoes of the Faculties," *The Mystery Religion of W. B. Yeats*, 110.

53 In correspondence to Iseult Gonne, for instance, he glosses his term "Passionate Body" with the Theosophical "astral body" (February 9, [1918], *CL InteLex* 3408).

54 This is the version of the first edition, *Studies in the History of the Renaissance* (London: Macmillan, 1873), 212–13, which reworked elements from Pater's review of "Poems by William Morris" in *The Westminster Review* (1868). Omitted in the second edition, the conclusion was later restored a slightly adapted version of the original.

55 This aesthetic aspect of his pneumatology is seen less clearly in a paragraph on "interactions of *Faculties* and *Principles*" in *A Vision* (*AVB* 195, *CW14* 143–44).

56 See NLI 13,578 (Rapallo A) [46r–48r], treated in "Rapallo Notebooks A and B," 96–97 (and 54–55 above); NLI 13,579 (Rapallo B) [17r]; and NLI 13,580 (Rapallo C) [63r–67v] for WBY's notes on problems in his understanding of the system of *A Vision*, particularly points 7 and 8 and continuation, [63r]ff: "I must make light include supernatural light in which are the forms of spirits at 15 forms of [?uneasy] perfection" [63r], and "Light so understood is Astral Light & now for the first time I see the derivation of astral light from that light which Grossestete calls corporeality it self or that of which corporeality is made, & from the light which Bonaventure identified with all the senses" [64r] ("Rapallo Notebook C," *IYS* 7.1: 230–35 [and 138–43 above]).

57 WBY had asked A. E. Waite about the origins of the "astral light" in 1913 or 1914—Waite's reply arrived on January 31, 1914, giving Éliphas Lévi as the primary source and mentioning (but dismissing) a work by Louis-Claude de Saint Martin; see *Letters to W. B. Yeats*, vol. 1, ed. Richard J. Finneran, George Mills Harper, and William M. Murphy (London: Macmillan, 1977), 279–80; See notes 59 and 60, below. On the astral light, see note 56, above.

58 Henri Martin was a contemporary of WBY's (1860–1943) and was associated with Joséphin Peladan's Salon de la Rose+Croix. It seems to be a simple confusion of names.

59 Martinism, a form of masonic mysticism, has a complex history, being refounded several times. The original Martinism was expounded by Martinez de Pasqually (1727?–1774), but a reformed version was taught by Louis-Claude de Saint Martin (1743–1803). WBY was certainly familiar with Martinists from his stay in Paris in December 1896, when he records his first experiences of taking "Indian hemp with certain followers of Saint-Martin" at "the meeting place of the Martinists" (*E&I* 281, *CW4* 204–205; cf. *Au* 347, *CW3* 264).

60 WBY's inquiry to A. E. Waite (see note 57) seems to have been in connection with his work for Lady Gregory's *Visions and Beliefs in the West of Ireland*. There, his Note 12 examines the concept of "pictures in the astral light" and considers Henry More's concept of "*Spiritus Mundi*," stating that "The name 'Astral Light' was given to this air or spirit by…Éliphas Lévi" (*CW5* 271). See *CW14* 385–87 n12.

61 From what WBY writes in section XI of "Introduction to The Great Wheel" (*PEP* 27–29; cf. *AVB* 20–22, *CW14* 16–17), these renewed sessions appear to have started in Cannes in February 1928 and are recorded as "3 Sleaps Cannes" in NLI 30,359, along with two later on, headed "Sleap . March Rapallo."

62 There is an element of the aphoristic or *sutra* style of presentation, with ultra-condensed formulations designed for extensive unfolding by a teacher—not that Yeats offers much by way of expansion. See "Rapallo Notebook D," *IYS* 8.1: 153–60 (and 211–18 above).

63 This is in turn elucidated slightly by the "Seven Propositions" (see Rapallo D, [24r] and [26r]). The *Daimons* or Spirits represent all of reality, including the physical universe: "1. Reality is a timeless & spaceless community of spirits which percieve each other. Each Spirit is determined by & determines those it percieves, & each spirit is unique. 2 When these spirits reflect themselves into time & space they are so many destinies, which determine each other, & each spirit sees the others as thoughts, images, objects of sense. ~~As each sees the others as the visible universe & is determined by it & determines it~~ Time & space are unreal." ("Rapallo Notebook D," *IYS* 8.1: 158; and 216 above).

64 See Mann, "'Everywhere that antinomy of the One and the Many': The Foundations of *A Vision*" in *W. B. Yeats's "A Vision": Explications and Contexts*, ed. Neil Mann, Matthew Gibson, and Claire Nally (Clemson, SC: Clemson University Press, 2012), 1–21.

65 There are some four drafts in Rapallo Notebook C, NLI 13,580, [56v–59r], the first untitled, the second titled "The Daimon & the Celestial Body," the third "The Passionate & Celestial Body," and the fourth untitled; the last two have "Imaginations bride" as their first line. See Jacqueline Genet, *William Butler Yeats: Les fondements et l'évolution de la création poetique* (Villeneuve-d'Ascq, France: Université de Lille III, 1976), 701; David R. Clark, "Yeats: Cast-offs, Non-starters and Gnomic Illegibilities," *YAACTS* 17, 7–12; "Rapallo Notebook C," *IYS* 7.1: 261–63 (and 169–71 above).

66 The non-physical incarnation at Phase 15 is said to be in a body of "the greatest possible beauty, being indeed that body which the soul will permanently inhabit, when all its phases have been repeated according to the number allotted: that which we call the clarified or Celestial Body" (*AVA* 71, *AVB* 136; "Celestial Body" is italicized in *CW13* 59 and *CW14* 102) and the description of the *Beatitude* states that "My instructors have described the *Marriage* as follows: 'The *Celestial Body* is the Divine Cloak lent to all, it falls away at the

consummation and Christ is revealed'" (*AVB* 232, *CW14* 169), and a very similar passage is attributed to Owen Aherne in *AVA* (*AVA* 236, *CW13* 194).

67 The "Introduction to *The Holy Mountain*" (*E&I* 448–73, *CW5* 139–55) uses the term *Turiyā*, while the "Introduction to the *Mandukya Upanishad*" (*E&I* 474–85, *CW5* 156–64) refers to the "fourth state" or conscious *Samādhi*.

68 Both the sea and the mirror were important early on for Yeats, featuring in *The Shadowy Waters* and the story "*Rosa Alchemica*," where the protagonist writes of holding himself "apart, individual, indissoluble, a mirror of polished steel" (*The Secret Rose, Stories by W. B. Yeats: A Variorum Edition*, ed. Warwick Gould, Phillip L. Marcus, and Michael J. Sidnell, 2nd ed. [London: Macmillan, 1992], 127–28) but has a vision in which "the mirror is broken" into two, four, and "numberless pieces" (ibid. 135); hereafter cited as *VSR*.

69 In the published version "*Spirit* is the future, *Passionate Body* the present, *Husk* the past" as here and WBY notes that "My teachers do not characterise the *Celestial Body*, but it is doubtless timeless"; "In the *Faculties*, *Mask*…is apparently the timeless, *Will* the future, *Body of Fate*, or Fact, the present, *Creative Mind* the past" (*AVB* 191–92, *CW14* 140–41), so that only *Creative Mind* keeps the same attribution.

70 For example, he used indigo, "the symbol of one of the seven principles into which they divided human nature," to provoke appropriate dreams (*Au* 181–82, *CW3* 158) or visions (*Mem* 23) in fellow members, in order to identify the appropriate visionary symbols to control his own meditations.

71 WBY does make the distinction in a draft of this passage: "My instructors speak of those in the states before the <u>Beatitude</u> as the dead and confine the word spirit (as distinct from <u>Spirit</u>) to those in the <u>Beatitude</u> or later states" (NLI 36,272/6/2a, cit. *CW14* 286).

72 See p. 291 and note 50 above.

73 Thomas Browne, *Religio Medici* (part I, section XXXI). The Yeatses' library contained three copies, including *Religio Medici, and Urn-Burial*, Temple Classics, ed. Israel Gollancz (London: Dent, 1896; *WBGYL* 297, *YL* 289), 46. See "Rapallo Notebooks A and B," *IYS* 6.1: 158 n214 (and 116 n214 above). In a very early draft of the *Vision* material, Yeats suggested coincidence of ideas might be owing to "the courteous communication of spirits" (*YVP4* 45).

74 See "Rapallo Notebook C," *IYS* 7.1: 213 (and 121 above).

75 Corresponding clip marks can be seen at the top and left edges of folio [17v], as recorded in Figure 4.6. The larger slip (now also loose) presents highlights in Rapallo E as follows: "From || 'RAPALLO' NOTEBOOK CONTAINING MS OF | <u>RESURRECTION</u>, WORK ON <u>A VISION</u>. | (Parkinson's List II, K) || THIS ALSO CONTAINS DRAFTS OF <u>WORDS UPON</u> | <u>THE WINDOW PANE</u>"; a few spaces below this is a notice of copyright on behalf of Mrs. W. B. Yeats "or her executors." Almost certainly, every Rapallo notebook was provided with such slips by George Yeats and Thomas Parkinson, as recently confirmed by selections from eight of Yeats's manuscript notebooks (including Rapallo A, D, and E) that were filmed at the request of David R. Clark, c.1958; see Microfilms, Box 9, M0027, Cornell Yeats editorial records, Cornell University Library, Ithaca, NY.

76 See, for example, Douglas N. Archibald, "*The Words upon the Window-pane* and Yeats's Encounter with Jonathan Swift," *Yeats and the Theatre*, ed. Robert O'Driscoll and Lorna Reynolds (Toronto: Macmillan Company of Canada, 1975), 176–214, and a host of scholars listed in FitzGerald's "Introduction" (*WUWP* xvii, n7), rpt. from her essay "'Out of a medium's mouth': The Writing of *The Words upon the Window-pane*," *Colby Library Quarterly* 17.2 (June 1981): 61–73 (cf. n6). While Archibald's interpretations of Swift seem generally more useful than his treatment of Yeats's evolving view of Swift, the catalogues of early Yeats scholarship (1948–1975) provided by Archibald are recommended, particularly his footnote 5, on books by and about Swift in Yeats's library. On the latter, see also note 73 in "Rapallo Notebook D," *IYS* 8.1: 204 (and 262 above).

77 See "Rapallo Notebook D," *IYS* 8.1: 146, 203 n63 (and 204, 261 n63 above).

78 Shane Leslie is the pen-name of Sir John Randolph Leslie, prolific critic, biographer, and poet, as well as Yeats's friend, fellow Anglo-Irish nationalist, paranormalist, and member of the Irish Academy of Letters. *The Skull of Swift: An Extempore Exhumation* was co-published in 1928 by Chatto and Windus (London) and Bobbs-Merrill (Indianapolis, IN). References in the text are given hereafter as "Leslie" in parenthesis. On August 26, 1928, Yeats reported to his wife that he was then "reading Shawn [*sic*] Leslie on Swift," which Ann Saddlemyer identifies as *The Skull of Swift*, noting that in its detailed treatment of Swift's relationship with Vanessa and Stella the book "may well have influenced WBY's *The Words upon the Window-Pane*, begun in August 1930" (in *YGYL* 197 and n5). Significance lies in the extent to which Leslie's book—rather than (as FitzGerald has argued in *WUWP* xvii *et passim*) a mere dramatic scene entitled "Swift and Stella" by C. E. Lawrence—might account for the apparent ease with which Yeats wrote his Swift play. The problem with Lawrence as antecedent is that there is no solid evidence that Yeats or Lady Gregory actually read the play in *Cornhill Magazine* (June 1926): 672–81, and the inference that at least Lady Gregory did is unsupported by an uncut, complimentary copy that FitzGerald cites from the play's reprinting in Boston (1927), currently an item in the Berg Collection, NYPL (see *WUWP* xvii, 11n). The Leslie text has far more to offer in evidence of Yeats's actual encounters with it. The introduction to FitzGerald's volume repurposes an essay that she had published twenty-one years before in *Colby Library Quarterly*, acknowledged by Cornell general editors Parrish and Saddlemyer out of respect for her memory (*WUWP* ix) because she had died before she was able to write a new introduction. The emphasis placed on the possibility that Yeats was inspired by or used another writer's play about Swift and Stella, once appropriate to the essay, is perhaps misplaced in the Cornell introduction, where it has borne the authority of the Yeats series since 2002.

79 On Yeats's convalescent reading of Swift's *Letters* and his *Journal to Stella*, see letter 134, Yeats to Sturge Moore, in *W. B Yeats and T. Sturge Moore: Their Correspondence 1901–1937*, ed. Ursula Bridge (London: Routledge & Kegan Paul, 1953) 160; hereafter cited as *TSMC*. See also *CL InteLex* 5341, where the letter is dated April 7, 1930.

80 Cf. Mrs. Henderson (in Swift's voice) observing Vanessa in Yeats's play, near the beginning of the séance: "You sit crouching there" (*VPl* 948: 321).

81 See *YRAW* 167.

82 See W. B. Yeats, *"The Dreaming of the Bones" and "Calvary:" Manuscript Materials*, ed. Wayne K. Chapman (Ithaca, NY, and London: Cornell University Press, 2003), xxxviii–xxxix and 117, for Yeats's pen-and-ink drawing and account of a disturbance of spirits that interrupted his recitation of *Calvary* at Renvyle in 1927. The house was owned by Oliver St. John Gogarty. The Leslie family estate in Monaghan is also haunted, as Yeats would have heard. In late August 1926, he spent a week with "fellow travelers" Shane Leslie and his American wife as guests at Muckross House, County Kerry, where the two poets got on well together, as Yeats attested to his wife (addressed as "Dobbs") in a letter of August 27, 1926: "I have got to like Leslie very much—he is quite simple & friendly & is regarded by his wife very much as Gogorty [sic] is by his wife" (*YGYL* 172). Besides their common friendship with Gogarty and keen interest in Swift, they probably discussed their experiences as investigators of unexplained phenomenon. Leslie's fictional and factual accounts were published as ghost stories, his latest collection at that time being *Masquerades: Studies in the Morbid* (1924). He might well have spoken to Yeats about *The Skull of Swift* when it was yet a work in progress. Later, a more documentary book, *Shane Leslie's Ghost Book* appeared in 1955 (London: Hollis and Carter).

83 C. E. Lawrence's "Swift and Stella" is set in "The Library of the Deanery of St. Patrick's Cathedral in the early spring of 1723" (*Cornhill Magazine*, June 1926, 672), the year Vanessa

(Esther Vanhomrigh) died. The dialogue between Swift and Stella (Esther Johnson) is decorously stilted, possibly in keeping with the setting. Theater critic Norman Marshall gave the play a notice of two sentences: "Mr. Lawrence's dialogue between Swift and Stella had better remain on the printed page. It is good reading but 'poor theatre'" (*Drama* 6.8 [May 1928], 122). Shane Leslie, who very likely read this scene in *Cornhill Magazine*, later offered to the Abbey Theatre his own dramatic treatment of the Vanessa-Swift-Stella conflict. Leslie's play in three acts is called "The Dean of Saint Patricks" (*sic*) and is set, by turns, within and just outside the Deanery around 1720, permitting Leslie to enliven the conflict by introducing both Vanessa and Stella to the audience as rivals competing for Swift's hand in marriage. The play contains some decent Irish dialect between Mrs. Sherman (housekeeper) and Rafferty (the Sexton) and functions, for the most part, as a comedy with farcical moments concerning the publication of one of Swift's satires. On January 21 or 22, 1931, after the success of Yeats's play, Lady Gregory noted that she at first hesitated to reject Leslie's play, "trying to find polite words in which to say it was not worth doing." But asked by Lennox Robinson for her opinion, she was relieved when Yeats interjected: "It is no use at all—rubbish" (*Lady Gregory's Journals*, vol. 2, ed. Daniel J. Murphy [New York: Oxford University Press, 1978], 588 and n91). "The Dean of Saint Patricks" was never published and survives in typescript (29 pages, annotated) as MS 50,867/9 in the National Library of Ireland's Typescript Collection. No doubt, Leslie was also aware of Arthur R. Power's one-act play *The Drapier Letters*, performed at the Abbey Theatre on August 22, 1927, after its initial rejection there. Yeats alluded to the play in his Preface to Arland Ussher's translation of *The Midnight Court* (1926), the plot of which is based on Swift's "Cadenus and Vanessa." In a note, Yeats observed: "I think it was Sir Walter Scott who first suggested 'a constitutional infirmity' to account for Swift's emotional entanglement, but this suggestion is not supported by Irish tradition. Some years ago a one-act play was submitted to the Abbey Theatre reading committee which showed Swift saved from English soldiers at the time of the *Drapier Letters* [1724–25] by a young harlot he was accustomed to visit" (*CW6* 291–92). On the strength of this veiled notice, Power successfully resubmitted his play (292 n2d). In 1934, Scott's, Leslie's, and Yeats's theories were first discussed in the Introduction to the Cuala Press edition of *The Words upon the Window Pane* (*WUWP* 233–34; cf. *VPl* 963–64).

84 See R. F. Foster, *Life1* 412, 606 n47, and *Life2* 410. Foster gives the house as "'Fairfield,' Botanic Road, near Dr Delaney's 'Delville,' where Swift had been a frequent visitor. *Thom's Directory* describes it as 'vacant' in 1909, but the Gogarty family owned it and let out rooms in it" (*Life1* 606 n47). Yeats's room was let to him for fifteen shillings a week (*Life1* 412). To that, Ulick O'Connor adds that "Dean Swift was said to have stayed there and cut an epigram in praise of a servant-girl on the window of the closet: this legend forms the basis for Yeats's play" (*Oliver St John Gogarty: A Poet and His Times* [Dublin: O'Brien Press, 2000], 13). A. Norman Jeffares and A. S. Knowland give the epigram as follows: "Mary Kilpatrick—very young / Ugly face and pleasant tongue" (*A Commentary on the Collected Plays of W. B. Yeats* [Macmillan Press, 1975], 595; hereafter as *CCPl*). The old house was demolished in 1928 to make way for the Mobhi Road. Gogarty, who grew up in the house, may have spun the story (see Glasnevin Heritage | Facebook, "Fairfield, Glasnevin.—W. B. Yeats, James Joyce, and 'Buck Mulligan' [i.e., Gogarty]," https://m.facebook.com/GlasnevinHeritage/photos/a.182651638552178/303603663123641/?type=3 [accessed Jan. 5, 2024]). For details on Yeats's occupancy, see WBY to Lady Gregory (Oct. 12, [1909]), *CL5* 611 n1; and WBY to Martin Harvey ([Oct. 25, 1909]), *CL5* 615 n1.

85 We refer to the Riverside Edition of *Gulliver's Travels and Other Writings*, edited by Louis A. Landa (Boston: Houghton Mifflin, 1960), hereafter *Gulliver*. The relevant chapters occur on

pages 156–63. For the editions of *Gulliver's Travels* in Yeats's library, see "Rapallo Notebook D," *IYS* 8.1: 204, 66 n73 (and 261 above).

86 *Gulliver* 157–58.

87 Yeats later corrected this error in number by listing the spirits Gulliver "calls up from the dead" but slightly misquotes Swift on their distinction as "'a sexumvirate to which all the ages of the world cannot add a seventh'" (*WUWP* 231; cf. *VPl* 963, where the correct spelling of "*sextumvirate*" is given, following correction in *Wheels and Butterflies*).

88 *Gulliver* 159–60.

89 Leslie 257–58. Incidentally, Yeats owned and presumably read his copy of Leslie Stephen's biography, *Swift*, from Macmillan's English Men of Letters series (1927; see *WBGYL* 2009 [*YL* 1996]), a Victorian classic from 1882 by the first editor of the *Dictionary of National Biography* (1882–1891) and father of Virginia Woolf. Stephen's strictly fact-oriented study of Swift epitomizes the art of biography as later counterpointed in the practice of "new biographers" such as Shane Leslie. Stephen makes no reference whatsoever to Gulliver's imaginary experiences in the land of Sorcerers or Magicians.

90 As a philosopher and political theorist, Jean-Jacques Rousseau (1712–1778) was reviled by Yeats in the unpublished epigram "A recent incident," which was copied into Rapallo Notebook D, at folio [4v], for possible use in the Cuala Press edition of *The Words Upon the Window Pane: A Play in One Act, with Notes upon the Play and Its Subject* (1932). See "Rapallo Notebook D," *IYS* 8.1: 134 (and 192 above); see also *Life2* 417–18. In his Introduction to the play, Yeats queried: "Did not Rousseau within two years of the death of Swift publish his *Discourse Upon Arts and Sciences* and discover the instinctive harmony not in heroic effort, not in Cato and Brutus, not among impossible animals [...] but among savages?" (*WUWP* 234; cf. *VPl* 967).

91 *A Tale of a Tub* (1710), rpt. in *Gulliver* 241–353. Particularly of interest in connection with Part III, Chapters VII and VIII in *Gulliver's Travels* are pages 329–33 (and notes on 526–27) in Section IX ("A Digression concerning the Original, the Use, and Improvement of Madness in a Commonwealth") in *A Tale of a Tub*.

92 A third possibility is that this paragraph is a displaced specimen of prewriting that actually precedes the entry on [18r], chronologically.

93 See "Rapallo Notebook C," *IYS* 7.1: 218 (and 126 above). About the Rapallo C item on mediumship ("Mediums have a few fixed types of controls"), see also Donald T. Torchiana, *W. B. Yeats and Georgian Ireland* (Evanston, IL: Northwestern University Press, 1966), 139 n65.

94 In *Four Plays for Dancers* (1921), Yeats dramatized the eternal penance paid in reenactment by the ghosts of Dervorgilla and Dermot, who, with Young Man, are the sole persons of the one-act play *The Dreaming of the Bones*. In his Note on the play, Yeats says: "The conception of the play is derived from the world-wide belief that the dead dream back, for a certain time, through the more personal thoughts and deeds of life" (129). See *YRAW* 128–30. Similarly, in the Introduction for *The Words upon the Window-Pane*, first published in the Cuala Press edition of 1934, Yeats observed: "I have not heard of spirits in a European séance room re-enacting their past lives; our séances take their characteristics from the desire of those present to speak to or perhaps obtain the counsel of their dead; yet under the conditions described in my play such re-enacting might occur, indeed most hauntings are of that nature" (*WUWP* 236; cf. *VPl* 969).

95 *An Adventure* (London: Macmillan, 1911) by Charlotte Moberly and Eleanor Jourdain tells of their encounter with the queen and courtiers at Versailles in 1901 (it is cited in *A Vision B* [*AVB* 227n, *CW14* 165n] and a later edition was in the Yeatses' library: 4th ed. rev.; London: Faber and Faber, 1931; *WBGYL* 1340; *YL* 1327). While in Oxford, WBY visited Jourdain, principal of St Hugh's. See *Life2* 23, 114.

96 Homer describes the "black cloud of grief" that enshrouds Achilles when he learns of Patroclus's death in the *Iliad*, book 18:24. The same expression is used of Hector at 17:591.

97 The Lord Treasurer is Robert Harley, Earl of Oxford (1661–1724). An interesting translation of Plutarch (AD 46–AD 120), by Thomas North, exists in the eight volumes of *The Lives of the Noble Grecians and Romanes* (Stratford-upon-Avon: Basil Blackwell for the Shakespeare Head Press, 1928), from which Yeats cut and read sections on "Alcibiades," "Cato Utican," "Cicero," "Scipio African," and "Epaminondas"; see item 1609 in Chapman, *"Something that I read in a book": Yeats's Annotations in the National Library of Ireland* (Clemson, SC: Clemson University Press, 2022), 1:319. Cato, Brutus, and Epaminondas we have already met in *Gulliver's Travels* Part III, Chapter VII (see above and notes 84–87). For Hester Van Homrigh, see Esther Vanhomrigh (a.k.a. "Vanessa") as discussed in note 83, above. Also see Leslie's account of this woman's complicated relationship with Swift in "Vanessa and the Dean," chapter X of *The Skull of Swift* (178–208, esp. 196–200), where the possible carnal nature of the relationship is explored, including whether the woman wished most to be Swift's servant, mistress, or wife. Yeats responds to Leslie's interpretation in *VPl* 966 (cf. *WUWP* 233).

98 FitzGerald writes that Yeats's play might be indebted to C. E. Lawrence's "Swift and Stella" for the use of four words: "I am a woman." In Yeats, it appears on [24r] as "Cadenus - Cadenus I am a woman" etc., and eventually as "Jonathan, Jonathan, I am a woman" (*VPl* 949; see *WUWP* xx). In "Swift and Stella," the line is "I am a woman, Jonathan, and I have loved you since you were a tutor and I was that child" (Lawrence 679). Of course, a significant difference is that the speakers are not the same. Vanessa's assertion in Yeats's play follows from Swift's claim to be "a man of strong passions [...] sworn never to marry" (*VPl* 949); a woman of age at their first meeting, Vanessa is not like Lawrence's Stella, who claims to be already Swift's wife ("even as that child") due to her "womanly love" and because "always in my thoughts and my heart I have been your wife" (Lawrence 679).

99 However, either Yeats, the spirits, or the medium confuses Alexander Pope's "An Epistle from Mr. Pope, to Dr. Arbuthnot" with John Dryden's *Absalom and Achitophel*: "Great wits are sure to madness near allied, / And thin partitions do their bounds divide" (1: 163–64)." In Pope's verse-epistle, Arbuthnot asks: "Who breaks a Butterfly upon a Wheel?" (308), anticipating the title of Yeats's 1934 collection of plays, *Wheels and Butterflies*. The misattribution of Pope for Dryden was not corrected by Yeats until typesetting the play occurred for the 1934 Cuala Press edition (see *WUWP* 215).

100 Swift's fear of madness is a form of psychosomatic obsession, according to Leslie, with the natural decline of advancing age contributing: "Lucid and logical though he remained in his own mind, his insanity took the form of belief that he was becoming insane. Dizziness and deafness stunned his brain or set it buzzing" (276). For Yeats's view of the question, we have John Corbet (or Young Man in the "Scenario") to opine on later pages. In the play's Introduction, Yeats deals with the old and new theories of Samuel Johnson, Walter Scott, Shane Leslie, and an unnamed friend (see parts IX and X in *WUWP* 233–34, coalesced in part I in *VPl* 965–67; cf. *CCPl* 237–40).

101 See *WUWP* 28–29. Vanessa's appeal is erotic but also imagistically reminiscent of the siren in "The Rime of the Ancyent Marinere (1798)" ("Her skin is as white as leprosy, / And she is far liker Death than he"; III.188–89), in which Coleridge's siren dices with Death on the Spectre-ship to gain the life of the accursed mariner ("The naked Hulk alongside came, / And the Twain were playing dice"; III.191–92). Yeats read the ballad to his children while in Rapallo, in spring 1930, after recovering from illness. See "Rapallo Notebook D," *IYS* 8.1: 177 (and 235 above); as well as Samuel Taylor Coleridge, *The Complete Poems*, ed. William Keach (London: Penguin, 1997), 153—cf. lines 192–93, 195–96, and marginal note from the

1834 version, found on page 173. Coleridge's poem is located in three collections found in the Yeats library: *WBGYL* 414–16 (*YL* *403–405).

102 "But if the Muses did not come to escort him homeward, the spirit of Vanessa was crouching that night outside the Cathedral porch to kiss his lonely feet" (Leslie 337).

103 In the Harvard manuscript, "Mrs Henderson sinks to the ~~grou~~ floor & then speaks as Lulu" (*WUWP* 122–23).

104 WBY to GY (Coole Park [Oct. ?4, 1930]): "I have finished the play as completely as it can be finished without your criticism. [...] Swift or as I call it 'Words Upon the Window Pane' being finished I am enjoying a pleasant day of idleness. It was very good of you to send me that poem I am afraid you had to copy it twice—once in the National Library & then upon the type-writer" (*YGYL* 227; *CL InteLex* 5391). The full text of Esther Johnson's poem is available (with another and a citation for a third poem to her credit) in *CCPl* 223–25.

105 See *BG* 432–33 on Yeats's acknowledged debt to his wife for this scene, as well as on their later disagreement about interpreting the play's séance "in light of Plotinus Ennead V.7"; see also *Life2* 410.

106 The four "great ministers" recalled from the "galaxy" of associates paraded in Leslie's final chapter "Golgotha the Place of the Skull (1734–1745)" (320–22) are, respectively, Robert Harley, Earl of Oxford (see note 97, above); Henry St. John, 1st Viscount Bolingbroke (1678–1751); James Butler, 2nd Duke of Ormonde (1685–1745); and Sidney Godolphin, 1st Earl of Godolphin (1645–1712). In Leslie's narrative (322), Swift next recalls the making of his own epitaph and related lines 345–48 from his satirical "Verses on the Death of Dr. Swift, D.S.P.D." See *CCPl* 230.

107 In Leslie (312–13), a good many verses are selected and consolidated. These are verses 3, 5, 6, 7, 11, 13, 17, 18, 24, and 25. After the array of these lines in block-quotes, references to Job become a regular part of the apparatus in the biography's last chapter, wherein "the words of Job the Patriarch were upon him" (Swift) as if "[h]is birthday prayer had been ironically heard" (324–25). In a letter to Mrs. Whiteway of Nov. 27, 1738, Swift refers to the habit of reading Job 3 on his birthday: "I hope at least things will be better on Thursday [his birthday], else I shall be full of the spleen, because it is a day you seem to regard, although I detest it, and I read the third chapter of Job that morning. I am deafer than when you saw me last, and indeed am quite cast down." Yeats refers to reading the *Letters* (see note 79, above). Swift's letter to Whiteway in the Yeats library is in vol. 13 of the 1784 edition of *The Works of the Rev. Dr. Jonathan Swift, Dean of St. Patrick's, Dublin*, arranged, revised, and corrected by Thomas Sheridan; *WBGYL* 2055 (*YL* 2043). C. E. Lawrence ends the script of "Swift and Stella" with the Dean reciting Job 3:3–6 with the "anger of passion" in his voice (681). Leslie is likely to have read the *Cornhill Magazine* version of Lawrence's play in 1926, even if Yeats did not.

108 Jeffares and Knowland say that "comment on the swollen eye" by Mrs. Henderson (formerly Mrs. Patterson, or Old Woman, in the "Scenario") "may have been suggested by Wilde" (*CCPl* 243).

109 The name change from Lefanu to Mackenna, emphasizing the distaff side of the older man's genealogy, makes his interest in spiritualism align with the matrilineality of Yeats's own (that is, from his mother's Pollexfen branch of the family). Mackenna's explanation introduces the idea of heredity, in case Yeats had been planning to write a scene about Swift's supposed madness as symptomatic of an inherited disease carried to him by "blood" and uncertain lineage. See *WUWP* 233–34 and *VPl* 965–66.

110 On the house, see note 84, above; by Stella's "companion Tingley," Yeats refers to Rebecca Dingley, frequently mentioned in Swift's *Journals to Stella*. Leslie (285) calls Dingley Swift's "third in the Platonic partnership" (285).

111 Again, see note 84, above, on the servant girl who inspired an epigram, possibly etched by Swift on the glass pane of a closet at Fairfield, Glasnevin.

112 A facsimile and transcription of the fair copy (NLI 13,590, [1r]) appear in *WFMP* 206–207. Lines from the holograph version in *Selected Poems* are collated in Clark's *apparatus criticus*. See Box 1, folder 31, "Yellow Hair; For Anne Gregory" ("For Anne Gregory"), with revisions and deletions, 1930 September. Three stanzas of six lines each, on p. vi, Lady Gregory's copy of Yeats's *Selected Poems, Lyrical and Narrative* (1929; PR5902.M3 1929). AMsS, 1 p. (poem)," in Manuscript Collection No. 600, MARBL, Emory University.

113 On Yeats's behalf, George Yeats sent a typed copy of the poem (by then retitled "For Anne Gregory," punctuated, and divided into parts I, II, and III) to a Miss Byron from Dublin (Sept. 17, [1930]; *CL InteLex* 5384). Mrs. Yeats's cover note said: "My husband is away – I will give him your letter as soon as he returns on Sept. 19th. And in the meantime I enclose a typed copy of the poem you liked. It has not yet been published. This is only to tell you that your letter arrived safely." From context and dating, Miss Byron must have heard Yeats read the poem at Coole almost as soon as he had finished writing it.

114 Anne Gregory, *Me and Nu: Childhood at Coole*, illustrated by Joyce Dennys, with prefatory note by Maurice Collis (Gerrards Cross, Bucks: Colin Smythe, 1978), 29–30.

115 These were all nineteenth-century perpetrators of spiritualist hoaxes: Daniel Dunglas Home, a well-known Scottish medium accused of fraudulent practices, though never proven; the Fox sisters, Margaret and Catherine, who "rapped" during séances by cracking their toes; and British medium William Eglinton, who was exposed as a fraud.

116 The mistake is understandable because Dr. Trench was called John Mackenna on [32r], and Miss Duncan, there, transmutes to Miss Mackenna when her character is introduced on [35v].

117 The last stage direction ("They stare at window" etc.) is all that remains of the upper entry on [35v], made before it was transposed and after Yeats cancelled almost nine lines, including a short speech by Johnson to Miss Mackenna in which he voices his concern to her that, like the "last sceance," the present one might be "spoilt" and that, as "new secretary of the 'Society['] ~~I think you should speak to Mrs Hendeson~~ I have some thing to present" (perhaps the request for exorcism). What Corbet "sees" is Stella's words cut on the window-pane, as per the clued arrow drawn on [36r] to show where the combined entries of [35v] were to be inserted.

118 For a general gloss on this passage, see *CCPl* 231–34, where a full transcription of the Latin on Swift's tomb is transcribed over Yeats's shorter translation (from 1929). On Yeats composing "Swift's Epitaph," see "Rapallo Notebook D," *IYS* 8.1: 151–53, 204 n65 (also 209–11, 262 n65, above). In one of Leslie's earliest evocations of the relevant Latin in *The Skull of Swift* (38), an esteemed Irish physician and historian is quoted in such a way as to relate to the discussion Corbet and Trench are having at this point in the play: "Swift had no wiser or gentler friend in modern times than Sir Norman Moore, but Sir Norman could only say that Swift 'had arrived at a conclusion, unaffected, horrible but to him irresistible, to hate mankind not out of mere inhumanity but as a result of long observation, a conclusion that made him wretched till he reached the place *"ubi sæva indignatio ulterius cor lacerare nequit"*'" (Leslie 38).

119 Ira David Sankey (1840–1908), American Evangelist; see *CCPl* 234.

120 This is also seen in the *Dreaming Back* as a stage within the *Return* during the afterlife expounded in *A Vision B* (*AVB* 226 ff., *CW14* 164 ff.).

121 Having planned in the long "Scenario" (at [29v]) the play's curtain line adapted from Job 3:3, Yeats is here anticipating that line by making a similar adaptation from Job 4:15: "a spirit passed before my face; the hair of my flesh stood up." See Harvard MS, [9r] (*WUWP* 110–11).

122 See Chapman, *YRAW* 167–69, 171–73, and 274–79 on the interrelationship between Yeats's "Stories of Michael Robartes"—which had been sent finished to George Yeats on September 15, 1930—and the play *The Resurrection,* rewritten and published with "Stories" in 1931.

123 See Stephen Parrish and Ann Saddlemyer, "Acknowledgments," in *WUWP* ix, as well as xxiii–xxiv (paras. 3–6) and xxvii–xxviii (substituted for the last paragraph of Mary FitzGerald's 1981 essay). See notes 75 and 77, above. Still, FitzGerald's impression seems valid that, for much of the Rapallo E manuscript, "close examination" of Yeats's "handwriting shows no hesitation in the writing of the central action involving Swift and Vanessa. It [i.e., the "Scenario" of 17v–29r] is clearly a first draft, but it is a draft obviously informed by a fairly complete idea of the play" (*WUWP* xvii). Some later efforts (between [29v] and [41v]) seem to be even more confident.

124 On madness, Leslie had answered the question in *The Skull of Swift* (328): "The Dean was not really mad, not utterly distraught, not a lunatic. [...] His memory moved within his own phantasmagoria, though the words, which he would say, failed his lips and those, which he could say, failed his thought." Leslie was willing to accept the premise that Swift might have been unchaste in his relationship with Vanessa, based on a theory that Yeats disputes in the introduction to the Cuala edition ("Shane Leslie thinks" etc.; *WUWP* 233 and *VPl* 966). In his gloss to the questions "Was Swift mad? or was it the intellect itself that was mad?" Yeats alludes to Leslie as "a scholar in whose imagination Swift has a pre-eminence scarcely possible outside Ireland" and presents a recent conversation between them in which the latter had said: "I sometimes feel that there is a black cloud about to overwhelm me, and then comes a great jet of life; Swift had that black cloud and no jet. He was terrified." To this remark, Yeats replied: "Terrified perhaps of everything but death," and his friend agreed that Swift "was not afraid of death but of life." The anecdote leads to Yeats's observation about the play: "I have put a cognate thought into the mind of John Corbet. He imagines, though but for a moment, that the intellect of Swift's age, persuaded that the mechanicians mocked by Gulliver would prevail, that its moment of freedom could not last, so dreaded the historic process that it became in the half mad mind of Swift a dread of parentage" (*WUWP* 234; *VPl* 966–67). See also note 97, above.

125 See his letter to Olivia Shakespear, February [9, 1931] (*CL InteLex* 5444, *L* 781)—but also his letter to Augusta Gregory, January 21, [1929] (*CL InteLex* 5213).

126 *Lady Gregory's Journals*, "19 May" [1925], 2:11

127 *Lady Gregory's Journals*, "23 May" [1925], 2:12. Cf. WBY's letter to GY: "I read my play to Lady Gregory yesterday — she approves very fully. Thinks it right as it is without lyrics" (May 23, [1925], *CL InteLex* 4734).

128 *Lady Gregory's Journals* 24 and 26 May [1925], 2:12. Cf. WBY's letter to GY: "I have a fine lyrical opening to the play. I hope to do the rest of the lyrical part before we meet. The worst is that the lyrics have without any intention of mine become much less Christian than the play" ([May 25, 1925], *CL InteLex* 4735).

129 The source is in Alexander Pope's "Epistle to Dr. Arbuthnot," as noted above in note 99. See *IYS* 5.1, which is devoted to *Wheels and Butterflies* (London: Macmillan, 1934), especially Margaret Mills Harper's opening essay, "Introduction to the Introductions: *Wheels and Butterflies* as Comedy," and Alexandra Poulain's "'[...] but a play': Laughter and the Reinvention of Theater in *The Resurrection*."

130 Transcription adapted from *CL InteLex*, based on the letter at the NLI; see https://digital.nli.ie/Record/vtls000833354 (consulted March 2024). Our reading is closer to that of Wade's *Letters*.

131 See *Res* xxiii–xxxix and *YAW* 237–67.

132 *YAW* 250. The *Variorum Edition of the Plays* prints the two versions on facing pages, 900–31.

133 As Curtis and Guinness take the loose pages as a first draft of *The Resurrection* and part of Rapallo E, they refer to the late draft contained in the notebook proper as "the second draft."
134 Penciled page numbering of the volume (probably by Curtis Bradford) runs from 1 to 387; see Chapman, "Yeats's White Vellum Notebook, 1930–1933," 53. See "Dating the White Vellum Notebook and Rapallo Notebook E Drafts," *Res* xxx–xxxi.
135 Position and date are not always clearly linked in the WVN: for example, on page 129, a draft of the Introduction to *The Words upon the Window-Pane* is dated "November 1, 1931" and, on page 137, a draft of "Crazy Jane Talks with the Bishop" is dated "Nov 1931," but then, on page 179, a "Memo for Vision" is dated "~~Nov~~ Dec 1930" (see Chapman, "The White Vellum Notebook," 50–52). Some of the dating was added later, and not always accurately.
136 See *CL InteLex* 5429; *Lady Gregory's Journals* 2: 582.
137 *Stories of Michael Robartes and His Friends* was completed at the Cuala Press, according to the colophon, on October 31, 1931, and it was published the following March (see Wade, *A Bibliography*, item 167, p. 168). *YRAW* gives the Cuala material pertaining to the stories (279–310), including details about the proofs, NLI 30,019.
138 *The Iliad*, bk. 1, l. 197, though the moment is Achilles' confrontation with Agamemnon, not in battle as WBY writes here. In *A Vision A*, Yeats sees the shift from the *primary* era of Christianity to the *antithetical* age will see "the ecstasy of the Saint…recede" but "men may be long content with those more trivial supernatural benedictions as when Athena took Achilles by his yellow hair" (*AVA* 215, *CW13* 177). See also: "Eleven pass, and then / Athena takes Achilles by the hair, / Hector is in the dust, Nietzsche is born, / Because the hero's crescent is the twelfth" ("The Phases of the Moon," *VP* 374).
139 WVN introduces the line "They imitate women that they may attain in worship a womans self abandonment" (WVN p. 206, *Res* 320–21; Rapallo E [50r], *Res* 408–409; cf. *VPl* 915, ll. 172–74). This echoes the epigraph of "*Rosa Alchemica*" taken from Euripides' *Bacchae* (*VSR* 125, *Myth* 264), but with a sexist gloss.
140 This count applies to *A Vision A*: the first three were retained into the revised version of *A Vision B*, but the latter two were removed along with the consideration of the near future.
141 See discussion of folio [41r], above, just prior to Figure 4.8 (*WUWP* 72–73; cf. *VPl* 945).
142 Bradford's interpretation of "Jan" as "Jun" is ingenious but made less likely by the far clearer "Jan" on the last of loose leaves ([63bis-r]). Looking at the possible combinations in the years under consideration, Sundays include: 1925 (Jan 18, 25; Jun 21, 28), 1926 (Jan 17, 24; Jun 20, 27), 1927 (Jan 16, 23; Jun 19, 26), 1928 (Jan 15, 22; Jun 17, 24), 1929 (Jan 20, 27; Jun 16, 23).
143 In dating the genesis of *The Resurrection*, Bradford was also misled by a journal entry from "24 May" by "Lady Gregory, notoriously reliable about dates," and dated to 1926, as trumping the testimony that pointed to 1925 from "Yeats and [Joseph] Hone, both notoriously unreliable about dates" (*YAW* 239; cit. *Res* xxi). However, the journal entry in question was misdated in Lennox Robinson's edited selection from *Lady Gregory's Journals* (New York: Macmillan, 1947), 263, and is actually from 1925, see ed. Daniel J. Murphy, *Lady Gregory's Journals* 2: 12.
144 This option would also need to assume a lost notebook with the same size and type of paper bought on this earlier Italian trip to match the Rapallo "Italian MSS books" ([August 17, 1928], *CL InteLex* 5145; cf. *YGYL* 194); see "Rapallo Notebooks A and B," *IYS* 6.1: 73, 142 n2 (and 31, 100 n2, above).
145 See "Rapallo Notebook C," 7.1: 238–41 (and 146–49 above).
146 See also *YRAW* 254–55; 304. Letters to Lady Gregory and his wife indicate that WBY was writing of the stories in the summer of 1930, referring to "my present task 'Stories of Michael Robartes & his friends'" (August 23, [1930], *CL InteLex* 5373) and later to

"correcting Robartes. Robartes is finished—they get me a registered envelope in Gort today. I will send it on Monday" (September 13, [1930], *CL InteLex* 5381).

147 The Buddha died of a form of dysentery following a meal of *sukara-maddava*—"pig's delicacies"—a term variously taken as pork tenders, truffles, or yams. Theosophists repeated the story of "too much pork" in order to pour scorn on Europeans' literal reading of sacred texts: e.g., in H. P. Blavatsky's (anonymous) criticism of "the remarks of Sir M[onier] Williams concerning the death of Buddha 'said to have been caused by eating too much pork...'" in her article "Christian Lecturers on Buddhism," *Lucifer* 2.8 (April 15, 1888): 145. Elsewhere, Blavatsky states that it is an "allegorical statement that makes Gautama, the Buddha, die very unpoetically from the effects of too much pork," which referred to his having revealed certain secrets, such that "he preferred, instead of availing himself of Nirvâna, to leave his earthly form, remaining still in the sphere of the living, in order to help humanity to progress" (*The Secret Doctrine* vol. 3 [London: Theosophical Publishing, 1897], 3:89n). WBY here takes both the pork and the renunciation of nirvana, without the allegory. See also A. P. Sinnett, *The Growth of the Soul* (1896; 2nd enlarged, London/ Benares: Theosophical Publishing, 1905), 73.

148 NLI MS 30,769, reproduced on *Res* 14.

149 NLI MS 13,580 [9r]. See "Rapallo Notebook C," *IYS* 7.1: 223 (and 131 above).

150 The colophon dates the printing to June 1929 and it was published in August 1929 (Wade 163).

151 Letter to Maud Gonne MacBride, October 21, [1922], *CL InteLex* 4194.

152 The Yeatses were in Algeciras in November 1927, arriving in Cannes at the end of that month and moving on to Rapallo in February 1928; see *ChronY* 257–58.

153 Rapallo B's cover states that it was "Finished, Oct 9, 1928" and this page comes some four pages from the end of the notebook.

154 The word "widened" is supplied on the authority of NLI MS 30,758, a typescript based on this version. WBY indicated in ink that first sentence quoted here is moved to the start of following section (here VII), which continues (with ink corrections in italics): "I was ill after <~~*broncial*~~> pneumonia and general nervous breakdown had partly recovered but fallen ill again and ~~now~~ spent most of the days in bed considering a slowly narrowing circle. ~~At Algeciras t~~<*T*>wo months ago I had walked <*to the [?~~Harbour two~~] the harbour at Algeciras*> two miles, a month ago to the harbour at Cannes, ~~almost~~ a mile, and now two hundred yards ~~well~~ <were> enough. Then it ~~began to widen again but was still almost at its narrowest~~ <*just began to widen*> when I lay in bed ~~after a brief saunter in the garden and~~ at a quarter to five in the afternoon <*after a brief saunter*> I heard my wife locking her room door" (page numbered 15).

155 See *WFMP* 214–15 and "Rapallo Notebook C," *IYS* 7.1: 239 (and 147 above).

156 GY wrote to Lennox Robinson in November 1927 that her husband was thinking about death and "making his last will & testament at all hours of day & night. [...] However in the same breath he talks of writing a poem on the herons at Algeciras 'in a few years time' [...] What a pillaloo!" cited in *Life2* 354.

157 "Rapallo Notebook C," *IYS* 7.1: 222ff (and 130ff).

158 In the rebinding, the interpolated leaves are inserted after five of the removed leaves [60–64] (fourth gathering), and before the last two [65–66] (fifth gathering).

159 See the tabular summary in the Appendix for the numbering and gaps. Only pages [69r] and [74r] are numbered, but they are "29" and "24" respectively—one is almost certainly a slip and the two pages should be either 19 and 24, or 29 and 34. In either case, however, the numbering could not have started with the first page of this draft ([59r], which would be either 9 or 19). As the draft starts with section "V" ([59r/58v]), continuing the numbering of an earlier version, the pages might follow suit; or the numbering could start on [67r]

which is headed "page 20 ~~or before~~ & 21 & 21.a," probably indicating a point for insertion or where the draft picks up from previous material.

160 He repeats much the same news to Olivia Shakespear—"I have really finished 'A VISION' – I turn over the pages & find nothing to add"—on February [9, 1931] (*CL InteLex* 5444, *L* 781) and to Lady Gregory—"I am dictating the final version of 'A Vision'"—on February 19, 1931 (*CL InteLex* 5447).

161 See Connie Kelly Hood, "A Search for Authority: Prolegomena to a Definitive Critical Edition of W. B. Yeats's *A Vision* (1937)," PhD dissertation, University of Tennessee, 1983, esp. 41–54 and "The Remaking of *A Vision*," *YAACTS* 1 (1983): 33–67, esp. 48–52. See also Harper's and Paul's introduction in *CW14*, esp. xxix–xxxii.

162 NLI 13,579 (Rapallo B), [88r]. See "Rapallo Notebooks A and B," 136 (and 94 above). A typescript dated "December 21st. 1928" echoes these sentiments, but also hints at personal concerns: "I have written fragmentary paragraphs wishing to postpone almost all that concerns the dead till greater knowledge comes, or greater strength for a meditation that is followed by sleepless nights, and because the resolution to discuss in their detail events tha[t] I had sooner consider my secret is still lacking" (NLI MS 36,272/5/1, page numbered 16).

163 From *A Vision B* itself, it is difficult to tell whether the *Meditation* is part of the first or second stage, and the relationship between the *Return*, the *Dreaming Back*, and the *Phantasmagoria* as parts of the second stage is not particularly clear. It is so unclear that readers often take the *Meditation* as the overall name for the second stage of the afterlife including *Return*, *Dreaming Back*, and *Phantasmagoria*, and these include perceptive critics such as Helen Vendler in *Yeats's "Vision" and the Later Plays*, e.g., 75–78 and 249–50, and Harold Bloom in *Yeats* (Oxford: Oxford University Press, 1970), 268–70, as well as in the later introduction to *William Butler Yeats (Modern Critical Views)* (New York: Chelsea House, 1986), 18–19.

164 The wording resembles sections numbered "5" or "V" in typescripts which show the structure of the introduction to *A Vision B*'s "The Soul in Judgment" already in place, with references to Valéry's "*Le cimitière marin*" and the Indian concept of "Turiyā," (e.g., NLI 36,272/22 and 36,272/23; see Peter Kenny, National Library of Ireland Collection List No. 60, "Occult Papers of W. B. Yeats," 43). It is coincidental that Rapallo B has four sections of "Soul in Judgement"—cut short by the start of the draft of the "Introduction" destined for *A Packet for Ezra Pound*—as these were probably written in the fall of 1928 and Yeats certainly worked on this subject matter during 1929 and 1930, prior to this 1931 draft. The treatment in Rapallo B covers fifteen leaves ([76r–90r]), and its section IV also outlines the stages of the afterlife and in different form from section V here. See NLI 13,579, [76r–90r], and "Rapallo Notebooks A and B," *IYS* 6.1: 133–37 (and 91–95 above).

165 For example, one extant loose-leaf draft is NLI 30,319(3), nineteen pages long, and titled "Book IV | The Soul in Judgement," with the last section numbered "IX."

166 See drafts such as "Notes Upon Life After Death": "5 | The states between death and birth as I explained in the preceding Book measured on a Wheel of the Faculties run from Phase 15 to Phase 28; but as we pass at death from the Faculties to the Principles we shall think of it as marked upon their Wheel. When so measured it contains six states corresponding to the six months from March to August" (NLI 36,272/22, page 6). The late typescript treatment that Harper and Paul give in *CW14* Appendix II, still uses the months of the year and shows continuing fluidity in the names of the six states (NLI 36,272/6/2a, *CW14* 281–83).

167 Yeats here appears to paraphrase Thomas Sturge Moore's criticism of the analogies or symbols in "Sailing to Byzantium": "I prefer with Wittgenstein, whom I dont understand, to think that nothing at all can be said about ultimates, or reality in an ultimate sense. Anyway I can say nothing that approaches giving me satisfaction, nor am I satisfied by what others say. Your Sailing to Byzantium, magnificent as the first three stanzas are, lets me down in the fourth, as such a goldsmith's bird is as much nature as a man's body, especially if it only sings

like Homer and Shakespeare of what is past or passing or to come to Lords and Ladies" (*TSMC* 162). This critique led WBY to write "Byzantium" (October 4, [1930], *TSMC* 164; *CL InteLex* 5390)

168 WBY is referring to Immanuel Kant's *Critique of Pure Reason* (*Critik der reinen Vernunft* [Riga: Hartknoch, 1781]), and his reading of Kant was important, not least for his adoption of the term "antinomy," which became a key term in *A Vision B*. He mentions Kant in a number of letters to Sturge Moore (see February 2, [1928]; February 12, [1928]; February 23, [1928]; [June 1928]; March 24, 1929; April 9, [1929]; *TSMC* 121, 122, 124, 131, 149, *CL InteLex* 5072, 5076, 5080, 5127, 5229, 5234, respectively). The reference to Admiral Cochrane, in an uncertain reading, seems to attribute a deed of naval bravado to a historical figure renowned for daring—in this case Thomas Cochrane (1775–1860)—rather than necessarily the correct one. The feat of firing simultaneous broadsides between two enemy vessels is recorded in the case of Admiral Piet Hein (1577–1629) of the Dutch Republic.

169 The metaphor of the "dark lanthorn" comes from Samuel Butler's *Hudibras*: " 'Tis a *dark-Lanthorn* of the Spirit, / Which none see by but those who bear it…" (I.i.505–506). See, for example, ed. A. R. Waller, *Hudibras* (Cambridge: Cambridge University Press, 1905), 16.

170 See "Rapallo Notebook D," *IYS* 8.1: 159 (and 217 above). NLI MS 30,280 contains notes from December 1938 where Yeats writes about recent advances in psychic research.

171 See *The Poetical Works of Samuel Taylor Coleridge*, ed. James Dykes Campbell (London: Macmillan, 1893 [cf. *WBGYL* 415, *YL* 404, an edition from 1925]): "Ne Plus Ultra," 199–200 and "Limbo," 189–90.

172 A later typescript gives this passage as: "Completely dominant over Spirit it [*Celestial Body*] is absolute necessity, absolute evil, a seeming possibility haunting the utmost edge, Coleridge's 'Ne Plus Ultra,'" quoting the same opening lines of the poem and contrasting it with "Celestial Body in Spirit, the abstract good" (NLI 36,272/22, pp. 24–24a).

173 NLI 36,272/22, typescript "Notes Upon Life After Death," p. 23.

174 See the commentary on the poems centered on "Imagination's Bride" in "Rapallo Notebook C," *IYS* 7.1: 261–63 (and 169–71 above), transcribed in full by David R. Clark in "Cast-offs, Non-starters, and Gnomic Illegibilities," 7–12.

175 The experience of September 7, 1898, was recorded in the "Vision" notebooks ("Visions, begun July 11, 1898"), see *ChronY* 52. It appears in autobiography (*Mem* 126; *Au* 379, *CW3* 284); it is also quoted in *Per Amica Silentia Lunae* (*Myth* 366, *CW5* 32) and in "The Manuscript of 'Leo Africanus,'" ed. Steve L. Adams and George Mills Harper, *YA1*, repr. *YA19* (2015), 323; and it is fictionalized in *The Speckled Bird*, ed. W. H. O'Donnell (Basingstoke: Palgrave, 2003), 25.

176 WBY relied on Benedetto Croce's *The Philosophy of Giambattista Vico*, trans. R. G. Collingwood (London: Howard Latimer, 1913), which GY gave him in August 1924 (see *WBGYL* 456, *YL* 445).

177 Oswald Spengler, tr. C. F. Atkinson, 2 vols., *The Decline of the West* (London: George Allen & Unwin, 1926; *WBGYL* 1989, *YL* 1975), 1:107.

178 Since Phase 1 is usually taken separately, WBY's first option of 2, 3, 4 follows the normal pattern, with the opposing phases presumably running in reverse 28, 27, 26. Yet he seems to have doubted that the opposition of physical and spiritual cones followed this scheme, bringing Phase 1 into the first series.

179 George Russell had felt that "to follow in the wake of Mr. Yeats' mind is to surrender oneself to the idea of Fate and to part from the idea of Free Will" (review, *The Irish Statesman*, February 1926, https://www.yeatsvision.com/G482.html, consulted April 2024).

180 This line is present in prayers attributed to the Christian saints Augustine and Gelasius, but the idea is also present in the concept of Islam itself (submission to the will of God) and the *mitzvoth* of Judaism.

181 See, for example, Harold Bloom, *Yeats* (Oxford: Oxford University Press, 1970) and *The Anxiety of Influence: A Theory of Poetry* (New Haven: Yale University Press, 1973).

182 NLI 13,579 (Rapallo B), [69r], page numbered 16, see "Rapallo Notebooks A and B," *IYS* 6.1: 132 (and 90 above). Hazard Adams cites a similar passage from "a rejected typescript for *A Vision*," in *Blake and Yeats: The Contrary Vision* (1955; New York NY: Russell & Russell, 1968), 175–76. Cf. "My instructors compare [the Great Year] & those perfect numbers [of Plato] alike to a work of art because in a work of art each separate line, colour or thought is related to the whole is as it were multiplied into it, & to their Daimonic sphere, while lesser periods & the numbers that leave a fraction over are gyres, a part of the suffering of the Four Faculties" (loose-leaf draft, NLI 30,322, page numbered 4).

183 NLI 13,578 (Rapallo A), [22r], section X, page numbered 17, see "Rapallo Notebooks A and B," *IYS* 6.1: 87–88 (and 45–46 above). The coming together of all the cycles in the Great Year is an image of eternity, expressed poetically in "There" (*VP* 557).

184 WBY derives the term from Dante's *Convito*, claiming that Dante compares it to "'a perfectly proportioned human body'" (*AVB* 82, *CW14* 61; see *CW14* 353 n37). It is defined in the automatic script as "Complete Harmony between physical body intellect & spiritual desire – *all may be imperfect* but if harmony is perfect it is unity" (*YVP2* 41), and in *The Trembling of the Veil*, WBY compares it to "a musical instrument so strung that if we touch a string all the strings murmur faintly" (*Au* 190, *CW3* 164; cf. GY's note *YVP3* 27). See *ARGYV* §6.4, 103–108.

185 See the drafts in "Rapallo Notebook C," *IYS* 7.1: 244–45 (and 152–53 above).

186 *"Mais la genèse nous révèle en même temps que cette œuvre première et différente était l'un des possibles du texte, sans se trouver pour autant inclus ou subsumé dans l'œuvre seconde,"* Louis Hay, "'*Le texte n'existe pas.' Réflexions sur la critique génétique*," 158; cf. Matthew Jocelyn's translation, "Does 'Text' Exist?" at 75). See "General Overview," above, 19–20.

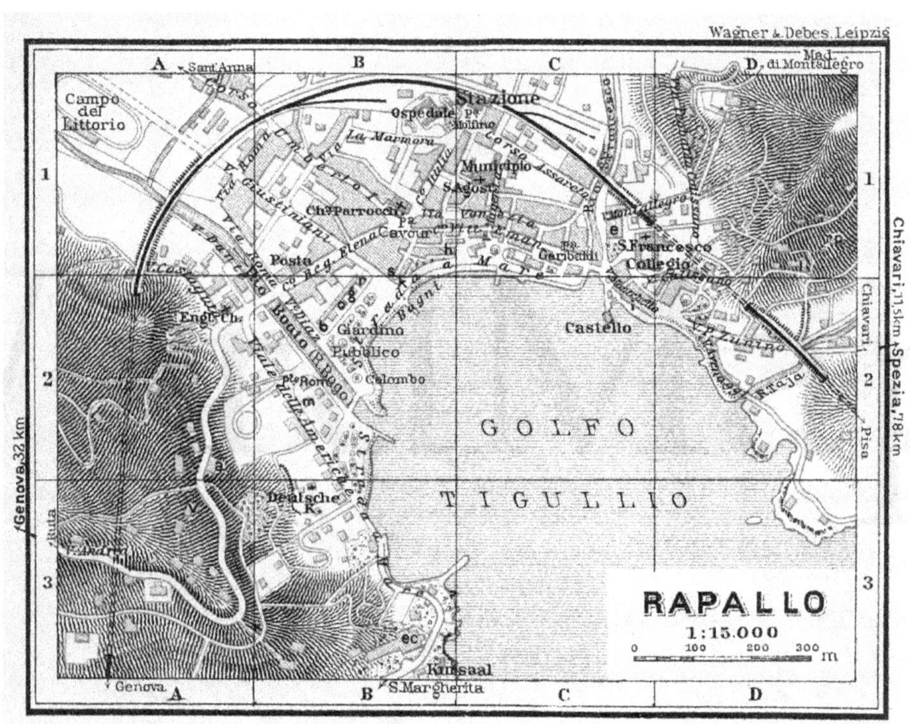

Figure 4.13. Map of Rapallo, 1930, by Wagner & Debes, Leipzig.

Appendix A

Tabular Summary: Rapallo Notebook A (NLI 13,578)

Neil Mann

The following table gives a listing of the notebook's leaves by:

1. **Leaf number**.
2. A **brief description**, indicating the corresponding work.
3. A summary of the **title** or the **section** number.
4. The **page number** as given by Yeats.
5. The first uncancelled line(s) of **text** (cancelled text is included where there is no uncancelled text).
6. **Notes** give points of physical description, including pages which are cancelled *in toto*, and indicate if the page includes a date.
7. The final column records where **published** transcriptions or final versions appear. Besides the standard *IYS* abbreviations used in the table (see https://tigerprints.clemson.edu/iys/iys_abbreviations.html), the following abbreviations are also used:

   PD1930 = *Pages from a Diary Written in Ninteen Hundred and Thirty* (Dublin: Cuala, 1944);
   UP2 = *Uncollected Prose by W. B. Yeats*, ed. John P. Frayne and Colton Johnson, vol. 2 (New York: Columbia University Press, 1976);
   WPQ = Curtis Bradford, *W. B. Yeats: The Writing of "The Player Queen"* (DeKalb: Northern Illinois University Press, 1977).

Please note:

- **Blank pages** are included, giving both recto and verso.
- Evidently **missing pages** are also included (with a single leaf number). Following restoration, most of these are now indicated by stubs of Japanese paper used to fix the counterparts on the other side of the stitching.
- Pages added at the beginning and end of the book during the rebinding process are indicated but not counted.

RAPALLO NOTEBOOK A (NLI 13,578)

Folio	Description	Title/ Content	WBY p. no.	First line of page (uncancelled)	Note	Pub.
Cover	Patterned	*Marked* "D"				
Inside	Patterned					
0	Flyleaf/ endpaper			papers added in restoration		
0	Rebinding					
1r	[Title]	*Marked* "A"	—	*A*		
1v	Contents	Contents (notes on Plotinus)		*Contents* *Great Year (final version) 20 pages*		
2r	Notes	[MacKenna *Plotinus IV-Fifth Ennead*]	—	*Plot IV p 10 top of intellect symbolized by [circle] sensation by line*		
2v	[Blank]					
3r	[Blank]					
3v	[Blank]					
4r	*A Vision* material	Great Year | I	1	*The Great Year | I |* *To the time when Marius sat at home planning a sedition that began the . . .*		cf. *AVB* 243–45, *CW14* 177–79 (cf. also notes to *The Resurrection*)
4v	[Blank]					
5r	*A Vision* material	[§I cont.]	2	*interpreting oracles had thought of anouncing in the Senate House that . . .*		
5v	Text to insert opposite			*at some star, that marks the transition from the constellation . . .*		
6r	*A Vision* material	[§I cont.]	3	*& Virgil goden [sic] age needed a longer gestation.*		
6v	[Blank]					
7r	*A Vision* material	[~~H~~] II	4	*II | It is upon Annus Platonicus that my instructors have founded their . . .*		
7v	[Blank]					cf. *AVB* 243–45, *CW14* 177–79 (cf. also notes to *The Resurrection*)
8r	*A Vision* material	[§II cont.] III	5	*In* [gap] *instance a writer of the time of Marcus Aurelius translated by . . .*		
8v	[Blank]					

Rapallo Notebook A (NLI 13,578)

Folio	Description	Title/ Content	WBY p. no.	First line of page (uncancelled)	Note	Pub.
9r	*A Vision* material	IV	6	*IV | The circle of twenty six thousand years is for one half the Great Wheel . . .*	Lower part (2 tables) all cancelled	
9v	[Blank]					
10r	*A Vision* material	[§IV cont.]	—	~~*Phase 15*~~ ~~*Phases 16.17.18*~~ ~~*Phases*~~	All cancelled (tables)	
10v	Calculations, cancelled			*Stet* [for cancelled para. opposite]		
11r	*A Vision* material	[§IV cont.]	7	*The months run as follows* *The first month coincides with phase 15 mid spring*		
11v	Cont. from previous recto & cancelled start to §V & text to insert opposite			*between phase 18 & phase 19 it will reach the climax of the next movement . . .*		
12r	*A Vision* material	V	8	*V | We have four symbols of change, the double cone, the wheel formed . . .*		
12v	[Blank]					
13r	*A Vision* material	[§V cont.]	9	*It is the contrary of the lunar & subjective Hourglass figure; expands . . .*		
13v	[Blank]					
14r	*A Vision* material	[§V cont.] VI	10	*The widest part is the Celestial Body or rather the whole cone is Celestial Body*		
14v	Text to insert opposite			*In the diamond there is only one gyre, because primary thought, needs . . .*		
15r	*A Vision* material	[§VI cont.]	11	*At Phase 15 they coincide — Spirit & Husk at one end Celestial Body & . . .*		
15v	Substitute text, start §VII & text to insert opposite & stet for text opposite			~~*VII | But a civilization belong to its Husk (or Will) to its phase*~~ . . .	All cancelled	
16r	*A Vision* material	~~VII~~	—	~~*VII | If we take the halves of each symbol nearest Husk & Spirit*~~ . . .	All cancelled	

RAPALLO NOTEBOOK A (NLI 13,578)

Folio	Description	Title/ Content	WBY p. no.	First line of page (uncancelled)	Note	Pub.
16v	Substitute text & text to insert opposite			*But each ~~civilization~~, or period of 2200 years, belongs to its phase to its Husk . . .*		
17r	*A Vision* material	[~~VII cont.~~] VII	12	*~~VIII~~ VII | So far I have considered the wheel of the Great Year as if its . . .*		
17v	Text to insert opposite			*drama renewed, the Heraclitean antythesis rediscovered, Hegel & Karl . . .*		
18r	*A Vision* material	[§VII cont.]	13	*can be drawn through all four faculties [diagram] I have shaded the cone, which . . .*		
18v	Diagram			*[intersecting triangles]*		
19r	*A Vision* material	[§VII cont.]	14	*When religious thought refuses to be Mask & Body of Fate when it insists . . .*		cf. *AVB* 256, *CW14* 187
19v	Text to insert opposite			*But even were it possible I would not follow beyond the range of concrete. . .*		
20r	*A Vision* material	[§VII cont.] VIII	15	*cones for period, where the Faculties of some larger cone fall, as I am told . . .*		
20v	[Blank]					
21r	*A Vision* material	IX	16	*~~VII~~ IX | The diagrams frequently make each of these months a half . . .*		
21v	[Blank]					
22r	*A Vision* material	X	17	*X | I reconstruct the wheel of the twenty eight incarnations till it . . .*		cf. *AVB* 202, 248, *CW14* 149, 181
22v	Text to insert opposite			*a point that remains fixed like the ascend of the indiual horoscope*		cf. *AVB* 253n, *CW14* 184n
23r	*A Vision* material	[§X cont.] XI	18	*is now passing from phase 22 to phase 23, but a nation or individual or . . .*		
23v	[Blank]					

Rapallo Notebook A (NLI 13,578)

Folio	Description	Title/ Content	WBY p. no.	First line of page (uncancelled)	Note	Pub.
24r	*A Vision* material	XII	19	*XII | They tell me that the primary revelation comes soon after the . . .*		
24v	Text to insert opposite			*great nameless mountains, cattaracts falls through cloud into cloud an . . .*		
25r	*A Vision* material	[§XII cont.]	20	*When Christianity lost its first character when ecclesiastics became . . .*	Dated "Nov 1928"	
25v	[Blank]					
26r	? *A Vision* material	[?cont.]	—	~~*Plotinus in Samkara, but a Plotinus in Sankara its Plotinus*~~ . . .	All cancelled	
26v	[Blank]					
27r	[Blank]					
27v	[Blank]					
28r	[Blank]					
28v	[Blank]					
29r	[Blank]					
29v	[Blank]					
30r	[Blank]					
30v	Text to insert opposite			*Had Prof Trench made I would understand for he is as Ruskin said . . .*		cf. *CW10* 211–13; *UP2* 477–80
31r	Article	The Censorship & St Thomas Acquinas I, II	1	*The Censorship & St Thomas Acquinas. | I | "The Censorship of Publications Bill" declares in its preliminary section that "the word . . .*		
31v	Text to insert opposite			*Nobody can stray into that little Byzantine chappel at Palermo . . .*		
32r	Article	[§II cont.] III	—	*For centuries Byzantium, & Platonic Theology had dominated the thought . . .*		
32v	Text to insert opposite			*a corresponding change in tecnique [?evolved] here to [?imagine] her not . . .*		cf. *CW10* 211–13; *UP2* 477–80
33r	Article	[§III cont.] III [=IV]	2	*As if liberated from a conviction that only ideas were real, from the time of . . .*		

RAPALLO NOTEBOOK A (NLI 13,578)

Folio	Description	Title/ Content	WBY p. no.	First line of page (uncancelled)	Note	Pub.
33v	[Blank]					
34r	[Blank]					
34v	[Blank]					
35r	[Blank]					
35v	[Blank]					
36r	[Blank]					
36v	[Blank]					
37r	[Blank]					
37v	Text to insert opposite			~~*In obedience to their will*~~ ~~*I remain a dramatist*~~ ~~*and if I define a thing*~~	All cancelled	
38	*Missing leaf*					
39r	*A Vision* material	[First Things] [§II cont.] III	2	*angry & said that each is perfect. I did not dare to ask why if each be perfect . . .*	ff. 39–44 were loose (see Harvard microfilm)	
39v	[Blank]					
40r	*A Vision* material	[§III cont.] IV	3	*and its desire is expressed by a vortex or gyre. Though the gyre always touches . . .*		
40v	Text to insert opposite			*that the Ought is unimpeded or unified emotion—Beauty—the Known thought . . .*		
41r	*A Vision* material	[§IV cont.]	4	*Time or subject [diagram cone] Space or object* *The mind only gathers it self up into it self by something that resists nor can . . .*		
41v	[Blank]					
42r	*A Vision* material	[§IV cont.] IV [bis]	5	*as they come war retires to the extreme boundary. . . . in proportion as it runs out a soft immortal stream of boundless . . .*		
42v	[Blank]					
43r	*A Vision* material	[§IV bis cont.] V	6	*by fire when the expanding gyre of Love escapes in its turn, & its Vernal . . .*		
43v	[Blank]					

Rapallo Notebook A (NLI 13,578)

Folio	Description	Title/ Content	WBY p. no.	First line of page (uncancelled)	Note	Pub.
44r	*A Vision* material	[§V cont.]	7	*[diagram intersecting triangles]* *We have therefore four gyres AB . CD . . .*		
44v	Text to insert opposite			~~*If I did my instructors*~~ ~~*If he did*~~	All cancelled	
45r	*A Vision* material	[§V cont.]	8	*When Spirit has reached the narrow end of its cone, & Husk the broad end . . .*		
45v	Text to insert opposite			*It could not indeed be one did it not play that part, for it is action that . . .*		
46r	*A Vision* material	VI	9	*VI | The* <u>*Husk*</u> *emanates light that seen when we rub our eyes, that seen . . .*		cf. *AVB* 190–91, *CW14* 139–40
46v	Text to insert opposite			*I repeat familiar speculations to relate what many believe with a forgotten . . .*		
47r	*A Vision* material	[§VI cont.] VII VIII	10	*Because no tint & shade, no quality, can exist without a surface, though it . . .*		
47v	[Blank]					
48r	*A Vision* material	[§VIII cont.]	11	*and behind the picture only, behind fruit or tiger but behind all their . . .*		cf. *The Cat and the Moon*
48v	Text to insert opposite			*At midwinter Christ is born Christs Annunciation is in spring & . . .*	All cancelled	cf. *CW13* 133; *CW14* 156
49r	*A Vision* material	IX	12	*IX | When the Four Principles are one in the daimon there is no greater or . . .*		
49v	*A Vision* material	[Cont.] X		~~*X | At midwinter Christ is born, at midsummer St John,*~~	All cancelled	cf. *CW13* 133; *CW14* 156
50	[Page stub]					
51	[Page stub]					
52	[Page stub]					
53	[Page stub]					
54	[Page stub]					
55	[Page stub]					

Rapallo Notebook A (NLI 13,578)

Folio	Description	Title/ Content	WBY p. no.	First line of page (uncancelled)	Note	Pub.
56	[Page stub]					
57	[Page stub]					
58r	Play	*Player Queen*	1	*Player Queen | corrections for sake of dancers | Page 403*	Page nos. are those of US *Plays in Prose and Verse* (1924)	*WPQ* "Draft 32" 447–51 Transcribed (without cancelled text) *WPQ* 447–48
58v	Text to insert opposite			*1 P | It is of me that they are*		*WPQ* 448
59r	Play	[Cont.] Page 407	2	~~*but no no step I will . . .*~~ *Yet what do I care who it is*		*WPQ* 448
59v	[Blank]					
60r	Play	[Cont.]	3	~~*in the old Play the Burning of Troy*~~	All cancelled	
60v	[Blank]					
61r	Play	[Cont.] page 409 & 410	4	*page 409 | "delete cloak of Noah*		*WPQ* 449
61v	Play	[Cont.]		*cast him beyond the border*		*WPQ* 449
62r	Play	[Cont.]	5	*Player Queen |* ~~*Yes let all be banished*~~		
62v	Text to insert opposite			*P.Q. | Let them well rewarded*		*WPQ* 449–50
63r	Play	[Cont.]	6	~~*Look It fits me as if. . . .*~~ *I am told she was such a woman*		*WPQ* 450
63v	Substitute text & text to insert opposite			*Milles & Maestrovic the famous Servian sculptor & medalist*		
64r	Article	Editorial [Essay on coinage]	1	*Editorial | What advice should we give the government . . .*		cf. *CW6* 166–71
64v	Substitute text & text to insert opposite			*for Charles Ricketts had recommended Carline, we selected on the . . .*		

RAPALLO NOTEBOOK A (NLI 13,578)

Folio	Description	Title/ Content	WBY p. no.	First line of page (uncancelled)	Note	Pub.
65r	Article	[§I cont.] II	2	*but after some hesitation for Charles Ricketts, & the secretary of the school . . .*		cf. *CW6* 166–71
65v	Insert			*quote Blake*		
66r	Article	[§II cont.]	3	*as the deputy master of the mint has commended, a precaution which . . .*		
66v	Text to substitute opposite			*The other night I woke with a sense of well being of recovered health & vigour.*		cf. *CW10* 214–18; *UP2* 480–85
67r	Article	"The Irish Censorship" I	1	*The Irish Censorship | I*	All cancelled	
67v	Text to insert opposite			*some of these ecclesiastics are of an incredible ignorance*		
68r	Article	[§I cont.] II	2	*upon them . . . by ecclesiastics who shy at the modern world as horses in my . . .*		
68v	Text to insert opposite			*& under this section "The Spectator" "The Nation" "The New Statesman" . . .*		
69r	Article	[§II cont.] ~~III~~ IV	3	*subject for judgment book or periodical. These five persons must then say . . .*		
69v	Text to insert opposite			*Though it was almost inevitable that the one remaining Catholic [?county] . . .*		
70r	Article	[§IV cont.]	4	*are right who say that in a hundred years the population will overtake . . .*		
70v	Substitute text & text to insert opposite			*permits him to exclude such works as the Origin of Species, Mr Marxs . . .*		
71r	Article	III	6	*III | This bill, if it becomes law will give one man, the Minister of Justice . . .*		
71v	Substitute text & text to insert opposite			*Neither the government, nor the comission on which the bill based, nor . . .*		

RAPALLO NOTEBOOK A (NLI 13,578)

Folio	Description	Title/ Content	WBY p. no.	First line of page (uncancelled)	Note	Pub.
72r	Article	[§III cont.]	7	*But in legislation intentions are nothing & the letter of the law is everything.*		cf. *CW10* 214–18; *UP2* 480–85
72v	Substitute text & text to insert opposite			*an educated press, & a [?better] understanding among creative writers* . . .		
73r	Article	V	8	*V | The fanatics, who hold trains are no doubt influenced in some sense* . . .		
73v	[Blank]					
74r	Notes	VI [1 line cancelled] [notes on kalpas]	—	~~*VI | Yet I am not such that*~~ *I would have them | Indian ages of world*	Loose leaf; at end of vol. in Harvard microfilm	
74v	[Notes on kalpas etc.]			*A manvantara of which 14 = Kalpa*		
75r	Article	[§V cont.] VI	9	*There is no remedy but better education, & taste for reading, & enough mature* . . .		cf. *CW10* 217–18; *UP2* 484–85
75v	[Blank]					
76r	Article	[§VI cont.]	10	*The power to create great character, or possess cannot long survive the certainty* . . .	Signed "W B Yeats"	
76v	[Blank]					
77r	[Draft letter]	[Letter in reply to Miss H (on Wagner)]	—	*Dear Sr | Miss Horniman is quite right to say that Wagner got part of the* . . .		cf. *CLInteLex* 5176; *UP2* 485–86
77v	[Blank]					
78r	Note for article	[Note from essay on coinage]	—	*Mestrovic was in Checko-Slovakia & one letter went astray. He made one* . . .		cf. *CW6* 297n10
78v	[Blank]					
79r	Diary	Diary (Oct 20 continued)	—	*Diary (Oct 20 continued) | . . . Dogmatic protestantism. Much of the emotional energy in our civil war* . . .	Diary of 1930	*PD1930* 56–57; *Ex* 338-39

RAPALLO NOTEBOOK A (NLI 13,578)

Folio	Description	Title/ Content	WBY p. no.	First line of page (uncancelled)	Note	Pub.
79v	[Blank]					
80r	[Blank]					
80v	[Blank]					
81r	[Blank]					
81v	[Blank]					
82r	[Blank]					
82v	[Blank]					
83r	[Blank]					
83v	[Blank]					
84r	[Blank]					
84v	[Blank]					
85r	[Blank]					
85v	[Blank]					
86r	[Blank]					
86v	[Blank]					
87r	[Blank]					
87v	[Blank]					
88r	[Blank]					
88v	[Blank]					
89r	[Blank]					
89v	[Blank]					
90r	[Blank]					
90v	[Blank]					
91r	[Blank]					
91v	[Blank]					
92r	[Blank]					
92v	[Blank]					
93r	[Blank]					
93v	[Blank]					
94r	[Blank]					
94v	[Blank]					
95r	[Blank]					
95v	[Blank]					
0	Binding					
0	Flyleaf/ endpaper					
Inside	Patterned	[Conservation summary]				
Cover	Patterned					

Appendix B

Tabular Summary: Rapallo Notebook B (NLI 13,579)

Neil Mann

The following table gives a listing of the notebook's leaves by:

1. **Leaf number.**
2. A **brief description**, indicating the corresponding work.
3. A summary of the **title** or the **section** number.
4. The **page number** as given by Yeats.
5. The first uncancelled line(s) of **text** (cancelled text is included where there is no uncancelled text).
6. **Notes** give points of physical description, including pages which are cancelled *in toto*, and indicate if the page includes a date.
7. The final column records where **published** transcriptions or final versions appear. Besides the standard *IYS* abbreviations used in the table (see https://tigerprints.clemson.edu/iys/iys_abbreviations.html), the following abbreviation is also used:

   PEP = *A Packet for Ezra Pound* (Dublin: Cuala, 1929).

Please note:

- **Blank pages** are included, giving both recto and verso.
- Evidently **missing pages** are also included (with a single leaf number). Following restoration, most of these are now indicated by stubs of Japanese paper used to fix the counterparts on the other side of the stitching.
- Pages added at the beginning and end of the book during the rebinding process are indicated but not counted.

RAPALLO NOTEBOOK B (NLI 13,579)

Folio	Description	Title/ section	WBY p. no.	First line of page (uncancelled)	Note	Pub.
Cover	Patterned			Finished, Oct 9, | 1928		
Inside	Patterned					
0	Flyleaf/ endpaper			Papers added in restoration		
0	Rebinding					
1r			—	*B | Prose | ?Siris*		
1v	Contents		—	*Contents* *~~Notes on Rapallo~~* *Rapallo in Spring 9 pages* *First 4 to be used*		
2r	Rapallo in Spring/*PEP*	I	1	*~~Siris~~ Rapallo in Spring*		cf. *PEP* 1–5, *AVB* 3–6, *CW14* 3–6
2v	Revisions for insertion on opposite page	II		*Foot note – Mr Wyndham Lewis*		
3r	Rapallo in Spring/*PEP*		2	*I shall not lack conversation, for ~~Ezra Pound~~ a man with whom I should quarell more than with anybody . . .*		
3v	Text to insert opposite			*To explain, a structure that is musical or perhaps one should say . . .*		
4r	Rapallo in Spring/*PEP*	[§II cont.] III	3	*ABCDJ then JKLM & then each set of letters reflected, & then ABCD . . .*		
4v	Text to insert opposite			*He ~~no knows their~~ all their histories. That fat grey cat is the an hotel . . .*		
5r	Rapallo in Spring/*PEP*	[§III cont.] IV	4	*seeking expression without ornament or emphasis not inherent in the . . .*		
5v	Text to insert opposite			*I was accustomed to compare such poetry with that painting . . .*		
6r	Rapallo in Spring/*PEP*	[§IV cont.] ~~V~~	5	*~~confounding all together in his powerful invented symbols & metaphor~~*	All cancelled	
6v	[Blank]					
7r	Rapallo in Spring/*PEP*	[§IV cont.]	6	*A friend tells me that Cezanne deduced his art from certain passages in Balzac Chef D'oevre Inconnu*		
7v	[Blank]					

Rapallo Notebook B (NLI 13,579)

Folio	Description	Title/ section	WBY p. no.	First line of page (uncancelled)	Note	Pub.
8r	Rapallo in Spring/*PEP*	V	7	*In the sixteen[th] & seven[teen]th centuries imagination recovered its autonomy*		
8v	[Blank]					
9r	Rapallo in Spring/*PEP*	[§V cont.]	8	*As we talked ~~dreams~~ of my youth return to me, & I remembered . . .*		
9v	[Blank]					
10r	Rapallo in Spring/*PEP*		9	*all promising rest from the self creating all creating soul . . .*		
10v	Text to insert opposite	I		*I* | *This book would be different if it had not come from those, who claim to have died many times . . .*		
11r	*A Vision* material	I	1	*First things* *II* *I begin with the daimon & of the daimon I know little, but content . . .*		
11v	Text to insert opposite			*At first the daimon knows all other daimons within itself as separate . . .*	All or most cancelled	
12	Page removed					
13	Stub			*a* | *one* | *exis* | *to. . . .*		
14	Page removed					
15r	*A Vision* material	III	2	*III* *A line is movemt without extension . . .*		
15v	Text to insert opposite			*But the mind has two movements one into an imagined space within it self*	Cancelled but "stet"	
16r	*A Vision* material	[§III cont.]	3	*perpetually gives way a mere limit, but creates itself through continual conflict or finds its object through . . .*		
16v	*A Vision* material	~~III~~ IV	4	*IV* *At roots of all most all that I have to say is pchologial truth which I cannot prove by abstract exposition . . .*		

Rapallo Notebook B (NLI 13,579)

Folio	Description	Title/ section	WBY p. no.	First line of page (uncancelled)	Note	Pub.
17r	*A Vision* material	[?I~~V~~]	6	~~*to first devide it into Four Principles, which elaborate & are the creation of natural things.*~~ | ~~*V*~~ | ~~*The devide into War & Love is too simple . . .*~~	All cancelled	
17v	Text to insert on previous page		5	*insert at top of previous page In the shaded cone, which are called Spirit & Celestial Body . . .*		
18r	*A Vision* material		7	~~*with substance, cause & effect,*~~	All cancelled	
18v	Text to insert opposite		~~8~~ 9	*When Spirit & Celestial Body are united in contemplation . . .*		
19r	*A Vision* material	VII	10	*When we are in Spirit & Celestial Body whether in meditation or the in the purification state . . .*		
19v	Notes for opposite			**1 The Double vortex is the year . . .*		
20r	*A Vision* material	VIII	11	*define Fate as all things determined from without & describe it as Daimon*		
20v	Text to insert opposite (i.e., 22r)			*Nature, where the subjective experience of the diamon— mirror of all daimons— are reflected as all animate & incarnate bodies*	Arrows connect 20v to 22r, so postdate removal of leaf 21	
21	Page removed					
22r	*A Vision* material	V	6	*V* *In the gyre or cone of Husk & Passionate Body is light phisical light*		
22v	Text to insert opposite		6.a	*the source of the light, which reveals that being as in a mirror . . .*		
23r	*A Vision* material	VI	7	*VI* *It is comestary* [sic] *to deny or affirm a substratum behind sensation . . .*	Much cancelled	
23v	Text to insert?			~~*Therefore Husk too it had separate shape . . .*~~	Cancelled	

Rapallo Notebook B (NLI 13,579)

Folio	Description	Title/ section	WBY p. no.	First line of page (uncancelled)	Note	Pub.
24r	*A Vision* material	[§VI cont.]	~~6~~ 8	*Passionate Body and Celestial Body exceeds human emotion & human intellect alike. . . .* *(for 9, 10 Etc see some pages back)*		
24v	Text to insert opposite			*No moment of the light is the same as any other, & the Spirit seeks to . . .*		
25r	*A Vision* material	~~VIII IX~~	12	~~*The Principles show what ever? is its own evidence, [?all this] is born . . .*~~	All cancelled	
25v	Text to insert			*Husk from birth to death, living events in the order of time, finds . . .*		
26r	*A Vision* material	IX	9	*The Principles show what is visable to sense necessary of thought, all . . .*	Much cancelled	
26v	?Text to insert	at head of Chap III		*at head of Chap III* *Between this symbol & the next given by my instructors, the double vortex. . . .*		
27r	*A Vision* material		—	~~*when we substitute discursive mind argument & silogism, classification. . .*~~	All cancelled	
27v	Sentences to insert opposite			*Principles alone cannot distinguish between fact & hallucination . . .*		
28r	*A Vision* material		10	*Husk gives way to Will, in all that is done to prolong our existence . . .*		
28v	Text to insert opposite	[X]		*[?Morality] is the submission of our Will & Creative Mind to the body of . . .*		
29r	*A Vision* material		—	*Spirit & Celestial are alive, intellect masculine, Husk & Passionate . . .*	Upper part all cancelled	
29v	Diagram to insert			[3 diagrams of double cones (all but central one cancelled)]		
30r	*A Vision* material	X	11	*The Four Principles include in the the* [sic] *Double Vortex the figure . . .*		
30v	Sentence to insert			*after each complete year or month of the faculties, there is the change . . .*		

Rapallo Notebook B (NLI 13,579)

Folio	Description	Title/ section	WBY p. no.	First line of page (uncancelled)	Note	Pub.
31r	*A Vision* material	[§X cont.] XI	12	*are human life alone when united to Husk & Passionate Body, are & . . .*		
31v	Text to insert			*We can represent man & woman so opposed as part of the same vortex . . .*		
32r	*A Vision* material	[§XI cont.]	13	*Each however is antithetical to itself, & sees the other as its object & . . .*		
32v	Text to insert			*The God, "boundless love" the universal self is always . . .*		
33r	*A Vision* material	[§XI cont.] XII	14	*Coventry Patmore called St John "natural love" & . . .*		
33v	Text to insert			*At first we are subject to Destiny, or Passionate Body, to Fate or . . .*		
34r	*A Vision* material	[§XII cont.] XIII	15	*an ideal history, determined by the nature of the mind alone, and I . . .*	Dated "March 1928"	
34v	Text to add			*I am a dramatist & symbolist, & often content with such definition. . . .*		
35r	*A Vision* material			~~*Religio Poetae*~~ | ~~*Book II*~~ | ~~*1. The Great Wheel*~~ | ~~*The double vortex of Heraclitus was too simple, we . . .*~~	All cancelled	
35v	[Blank]					
36r	*A Vision* material		1	~~*Siris*~~ | ~~*a Foundation*~~ | *Book II | I. The Great Wheel | When my instructors began, I was taught to . . .*		
36v	[Blank]					
37r	*A Vision* material		2	~~*A Foundation*~~ | ~~*I*~~ | ~~*This book would be different*~~ | *& PB, Will & Mask moves from left to right & Spirit . . .*		
37v	[Blank]					
38r	*A Vision* material			~~*When for many weeks, after*~~ | ~~*when my instructors first taught me, they*~~	All cancelled	
38v	Text to substitute			*(I) Introduction. I have used hitherto the double cone & four gyres . . .*		

RAPALLO NOTEBOOK B (NLI 13,579)

Folio	Description	Title/ section	WBY p. no.	First line of page (uncancelled)	Note	Pub.
39r	*A Vision* material		3	*I. Introduction | The Great Wheel is a circle of 28 lunar phases or of 27 phases and a moonless night . . .*		
39v	Text to substitute			*the cone of objective life & it lives in the same degree for Creative Mind*		
40r	*A Vision* material		4	*When I wrote my second Book as it was for the first edition of this book . . .*		
40v	[Blank]					
41r	*A Vision* material		5	*I wrote this book in my first excitement when it seemed that I . . .*		
41v	[Blank]					
42r	*A Vision* material		6	*So far as this second book is concerned the Great Wheel is the 28 types of incarnation, that are one . . .*	Cancelled text contains date: May 1928	
42v	[Blank]					
43r	*A Vision* material		7	*& the moment of this possible attainment "could in found . . .*	May 1928	
43v	Notes, referring to *AVA*			[diagram of cones] *Page 12 | line 6 | put "picturesque" before "method". full stop after . . .*		
44r	Notes, referring to *AVA*		7	*Page 14 | line 3 | after subjective read I understand by the word . . .*		
44v	[Blank]					
45	Page removed?					
46	Page removed?					
47	Page removed?					
48r	*Vision* material	II	~~8~~	~~*II. In the Great Wheel there are alternate of Primary & Antithetical*~~	All cancelled	
48v	[Almost blank]			[triangle]		
49r	*A Vision* material			~~*the religious life contracts into a point, & begins to expand once more*~~	All cancelled	
49v	[Blank]					
50r	*A Vision* material			~~*such a symbol would show at the birth of Christ the greatest . . .*~~	All cancelled	
50v	[Blank]					

Rapallo Notebook B (NLI 13,579)

Folio	Description	Title/ section	WBY p. no.	First line of page (uncancelled)	Note	Pub.
51r	*A Vision* material			~~*(II.)"By common custom" Cicero wrote in the Dream of Scipio "men . . .*~~	All cancelled	
51v	Text to insert opposite			*and foretold the future of civilization believing their mind made & not . . .*		
52r	*A Vision* material		1	*II. I do not know all that was in my instructors mind when they decided . . .*		
52v	Text to insert opposite			*an abstract ideal is e* **I do not know when the map was . . .*		
53r	*A Vision* material		2	*Their Great Year starts where the Fishes of the star map touch the . . .*		
53v	[Blank]					
54r	*A Vision* material	~~III~~ III	3	*An ideal separated from its opposite is lyrical & its phantastic imobility . . .*		
54v	Text to insert opposite			*Phase 1, mid autumn, Solar West* *[Libra] begins at central point*		
55r	*A Vision* material		4	*The following is the table of the months, & of the solar signs—I leave . . .*		
55v	Text to insert opposite			*The Faculties have overpowered ~~the Principles as all are out of phase~~*	All cancelled	
56r	*A Vision* material		5	*Phases 23.24.25* *[Leo] " " "* *Phases 26.27.28* *[Virgo] " " "*	Cancelled after first two lines	
56v	Text to insert opposite			*It is as it were the astrological horoscope of a spiritual . . .*		
57r	*A Vision* material		6	*The Great Year began with <u>Husk</u> in the middle of phase Fifteen and . . .*		
57v	Text to insert opposite			*~~Our civilizations must move through the moment of greatest intectual~~ . . .*	All cancelled	
58r	*A Vision* material		7	*the world was therefore at phase 15, or rather between phases 14 & 16 . . .*		

RAPALLO NOTEBOOK B (NLI 13,579)

Folio	Description	Title/ section	WBY p. no.	First line of page (uncancelled)	Note	Pub.
58v	Text to insert opposite			*The early Christians had some similar thought when they alloted . . .*	All cancelled	
59r	*A Vision* material		8	~~*Early Christian They face one another again as early Christian*~~ . . .	All cancelled	
59v	[Blank]					
60r	*A Vision* material		—	*I am puzzled by a symbolism which Patmore must have though that of . . .*	All cancelled	
60v	Text to insert opposite			*We are now all but through one twelvth part and as the signs and . . .*	All cancelled	
61r	*A Vision* material		8	*Hitherto we have had three symbols of change that of the double cone . . .*		
61v	Text to insert opposite			[diagrams] *The antithetical life passes [?away] into its object, & is [?loss from] it . . .*		
62r	*A Vision* material		9	*The other is in a diamond shaped figure which passess through the . . .*		
62v	Text to insert opposite			*We can can consider half cone as containing [?our one] gyre that of . . .*		
63r	*A Vision* material		10	*Sometimes the documents from which this book is made represent the . . .*		
63v	Text to insert opposite			*<u>Will</u> & <u>CM</u> now make their cone constitute secular or political . . .*		
64r	*A Vision* material		11	*the cones drawn between Husk and Body of Fate & contain both the . . .*		
64v	[Blank]					
65r	*A Vision* material		12	*of this shaded cone. As antithetical life, Particular & Universal Self . . .*		
65v	Text to insert opposite			*It was a long time before I understood the line with the four . . .*		
66r	*A Vision* material		13	*tenth century or greatest expansion, while the gyre of civilization had . . .*		

RAPALLO NOTEBOOK B (NLI 13,579)

Folio	Description	Title/ section	WBY p. no.	First line of page (uncancelled)	Note	Pub.
66v	Notes (for a talk/lecture?)			*? Materlinck do not touch me ?what about Lang, Etc.*		
67r	*A Vision* material		14	*the date upon the line fell into the places of its Four Faculties*		
67v	[Almost blank]			~~*[when] [would return]*~~		
68r	*A Vision* material	III	15	*I reconstruct the wheel of incarnations but it . . .*		
68v	Text to insert opposite			*In pure "sequence["] there is no "allusion" all is from the whole & . . .*		
69r	*A Vision* material		16	*of number to a work of art, because in the work of art each separate . . .*		
69v	[Blank]					
70r	*A Vision* material		17	*I do not know when the wheel which has Christian history for the first . . .*		
70v	[Blank]					
71r	*A Vision* material		18	*I have left what follows, except for the change of Fountain into . . .*		
71v	Line to insert			*360 days of a hundred years apiece*		
72r	*A Vision* material		19	*insert at A What Great Year was coming to an end. An Etruscan cycle of some . . .*		
72v	[Blank]					
73r	*A Vision* material		20	*writers usually attributed to the first & second centuries, & [?one knows] . . .*		
73v	[Blank]					
74r	*A Vision* material		21	*not [?be] spoken from exact knowledge, or any other knowledge . . .*		
74v	[Blank]					
75r	[Blank]					
75v	[Blank]					
76r	*A Vision* material	I	1	*Soul in Judgement | ~~Life after Death~~ | I | Coventry Patmore thought Da Vinci had a philosophical intention . . .*		
76v	[Blank]					

Rapallo Notebook B (NLI 13,579)

Folio	Description	Title/ section	WBY p. no.	First line of page (uncancelled)	Note	Pub.
77r	*A Vision* material		2	*when in the middle moment between Life and Death it is called back . . .*		
77v	[Blank]					
78r	*A Vision* material		3	~~*before I must once more consider the symbolism of life before passing to . . .*~~	All cancelled	
78v	Text to substitute			*Phase 15 & phase 1 are now called Critical Moments & phases or gyres . . .*		
79r	*A Vision* material			~~*the man. In the first moment & before the woman in the second is . . .*~~	All cancelled	
79v	[Blank]					
80r	*A Vision* material			~~*If I place it upon the great wheel itslef a gyre in a greater cone, & . . .*~~	All cancelled	
80v	[Blank]					
81r	*A Vision* material			~~*At this moment the soul, which might be dragged from historic phase*~~	All cancelled	
81v	[Blank]					
82r	*A Vision* material	II	3	*The Wheel of the Incarnations, has the same geometric structure as . . .*		
82v	[Blank]					
83r	*A Vision* material		4	*and we consider the movements of the Faculties round the circle as . . .*		
83v	[Blank]					
84r	*A Vision* material		5	*fortnight to the dark; . . . The 13th sphere is the present dwelling place . . .*		
84v	Cancelled note			~~*Each equinox or equinoctial sign has [?at the] first has the side of . . .*~~	All cancelled	
85r	*A Vision* material		6	*When the gyre of Spirit moving from right to left is at [Libra] of shaded . . .*		
85v	[Blank]					
86r	*A Vision* material	III	7	~~*[?arrow] that Anne cone is at phase 16 of Creative Mind & Michael . . .*~~	All cancelled	
86v	[Blank]					

Rapallo Notebook B (NLI 13,579)

Folio	Description	Title/ section	WBY p. no.	First line of page (uncancelled)	Note	Pub.
87r	*A Vision* material		7	*That the Principles contain in their complete movement life as the . . .*		
87v	[Blank]					
88r	*A Vision* material	IV	8	*St John of Cross had the same thought when he said . . .*		
88v	[Blank]					
89r	*A Vision* material		9	*haunting the place where they had lived that fill the poetry & prose . . .*		
89v	Text to insert			*Even while we live, the more our state aproximates to phase 15 . . .*		
90r	*A Vision* material		10	*at "the opening of the Tinctures" it seeks a reverse past experience . . .*		
90v	[Blank]					
91r	*PEP/A Vision* material		1	*Introduction | I | The other day Lady Gregory said to me "you are a much better educated man than . . .*		cf. *PEP* 11–25, *AVB* 8–19, *CW14* 7–14
91v	Text to insert			*as a little later almost all communication took place in that . . .*		
92r	*PEP/A Vision* material		2	*My wife bored & fatigued by the almost daily task I think & talking . . .*		
92v	[Blank]					
93r	*PEP/A Vision* material		3	*upon the interaction of two cones, & . . . Just when I was interested in . . .*		
93v	Text to insert			*was never adequately explained, for the explanation in Book IV leaves . . .*		
94r	*PEP/A Vision* material		4	*two or three of the principal Platonic dialogues I know no philosophy . . .*		
94v	Text to insert			*was he was constrained by a drama which was part of the conditions . . .*		
95r	*PEP/A Vision* material	IV	5	*Whether my question has to be asked before his own mind cleared or if he . . .*		
95v	Text to insert			*I noticed that their sweet smells came more often when we were passing . . .*		

RAPALLO NOTEBOOK B (NLI 13,579)

Folio	Description	Title/ section	WBY p. no.	First line of page (uncancelled)	Note	Pub.
96r	*PEP/A Vision* material		6	*was sometimes shown approval for something said or thought as when . . .*		cf. *PEP* 11–25, *AVB* 8–19, *CW14* 7–14
96v	Text to insert	V		*V | When I prepared for publication the first confused incomplete . . .*		
97r	*PEP/A Vision* material	[V] VI	7	*though I had mastered nothing but the 28 phases, & the general ideas . . .*		
97v	[Blank]					
98r	*PEP/A Vision* material		8	*soldier, who had a little later to turn his own house in fort told me that . . .*		
98v	[Blank]					
99r	*PEP/A Vision* material	VII	9	*I might have read for two or three more years but for something that . . .*		
99v	[Blank]					
100r	*PEP/A Vision* material		10	*& then having locked the door of bedroom lay down upon the edge of . . .*		
100v	Text to insert			*It was obvious that though he tolerated my philosophical studies . . .*		
101r	*PEP/A Vision* material		11	*as my embarrassment was increased by his irritability —from Plato & . . .*		
101v	Text to insert opposite			*without acquiring meaning, —sometimes she spoke with her own . . .*		
102r	*PEP/A Vision* material	VIII	12	~~*Beginning for account of origin of system | I | A friend sad the other . . .*~~ *After a fortnight of communication made possible they explained . . .*		
102v	*PEP/A Vision* material	IX		*given in this book, or rather touched & skimmed for I find I understand . . .*		
0	*Binding page*					
0	*Binding page*					
Inside	Patterned					
Cover	Patterned					

Appendix C

Tabular Summary: Rapallo Notebook C (NLI 13,580)

Neil Mann and Wayne K. Chapman

The following table provides a listing of the 70 extant leaves (by recto and verso) and eight stubs in this notebook in relation to its covers and conservation papers. This listing is generally consistent with the corresponding summaries of "Rapallo Notebooks A and B" (Appendix), *International Yeats Studies* 6.1 (2022), 161–83. As Yeats did not number the pages in Rapallo C, the column for page numbers in the tables for Rapallo A, B, and E (column 4 there) does not appear in this table; therefore, the six columns here (from left to right) list the leaves of Rapallo Notebook C by:

1. **Leaf number**.
2. A **brief description**, indicating the corresponding work.
3. A summary of the **title** or the **section** number.
4. The first uncancelled line(s) of **text** (cancelled text is included where there is no uncancelled text).
5. **Notes** that give points of physical description, including pages which are cancelled *in toto*, and indicate if the page includes a date.
6. The final column records where **published** transcriptions or final versions appear. Besides the standard *IYS* abbreviations used in columns 2, 5, and 6 (see https://tigerprints.clemson.edu/iys/iys_abbreviations.html), the following abbreviations are used:

   Hone = Joseph Hone, *W. B. Yeats, 1865–1939* (London: Macmillan, 1943);
   IY = Richard Ellmann, *The Identity of Yeats* (Oxford: Oxford University Press, 1954);
   PEP = *A Packet for Ezra Pound* (Dublin: Cuala, 1929);
   WFMP = W. B. Yeats, "*Words for Music Perhaps*": *Manuscript Materials*, ed. David R. Clark (Ithaca and London: Cornell University Press, 1999);
   WSC = "*The Wild Swans at Coole*": *Manuscript Materials*, ed. Stephen Parrish (Ithaca and London: Cornell University Press, 1996); and
   YAACTS17 = *Yeats: An Annual of Critical and Textual Studies* XVII, ed. Richard J. Finneran (Ann Arbor, MI: University of Michigan Press, 2003).

Please note:

- **Blank pages** are included.
- Evidently **missing pages** are also included (with a single leaf number). Following restoration, most of these are now indicated by stubs of Japanese paper used to fix the counterparts on the other side of the stitching.
- **Pages added** at the beginning and end of the book during the rebinding process are indicated but not counted.

We are extremely grateful to Jack Quin for his help in checking the physical copy of this notebook at the National Library of Ireland at a time when travel was impossible, and for helping to ensure the accuracy of this table.

Rapallo C (NLI 13,580)

Folio	**Description**	**Title/ section**	**First line of page (uncancelled)**	**Note**	**Pub.**
Cover	Patterned board		*DIARY*		
Inside	Patterned board				
0	Conservation leaf				
0	Conservation leaf				
1r	Notes related to *A Vision*?	(1), (2)	~~*Contents*~~ *Diary of Thought | begun. Sept 23. 1928 | in Dublin*		
1v	Notes related to *A Vision*		*Anne came Feb 3 1918.*	[Anne Hyde]	
2r	Notes related to *A Vision*	(3)	*3. The passage about light I quote on....*		
	PEP		*Script began Oct 24 1917. (Four days after my marriage)*		cf. *PEP* 12, *AVB* 8, *CW14* 7
2v	[Blank]				
3r	Notes related to revising text of *A Vision A*		*Book II. Correction Delete all up to end of first paragraph on page 17.*	Date: Jan 1929	*AVA* 16–17, 26–30, 213; *CW13* 16–17, 24–27, 176
3v	Text to add to text of *A Vision A*		*Page 180 Foote note "The Great Wheel & *history*		*AVA* 180, *CW13* 150
4r	*A Vision*		*As <u>Husk</u> & <u>Passionate Body</u> approach one another*		
4v	Text to revise cancelled text opposite		*is abstract empty unity. It cannot act would change the <u>Celestial Body</u>*		

RAPALLO C (NLI 13,580)

Folio	Description	Title/ section	First line of page (uncancelled)	Note	Pub.
5r	*A Vision*		*Husk is perception, medieval "matter". makes all concrete particular multitudinous*	Almost all cancelled	
5v	Text to insert opposite		*Any philosophy, which holds the universe but a sequence in the mind*		
6r	Notes on EP and skepticism		*Jan 1929* *Ezra Pound bases his scepticism upon the statement that we know nothing but sequence.*	Date: Jan 1929	*IY* 239, cf. *PEP* 7–9, "Rapallo" VI?
6v	[Almost blank]		~~*when Copernicus [?re]*~~		
7r	Notes on EP and skepticism		*and being more moral than intellectual*		*IY* 239–40
7v	Text to insert opposite		*nor do I think that I differ from others except in so far as my preoccupation with poetry makes me different.*		*IY* 240
8r	Notes on EP and skepticism		*We even more than Elliot require tradition & though it may include…*		*IY* 240
8v	[Blank]				
9r	"Meditations upon Death" [At Algeciras/ Mohini Chatterjee]		*Jan 23* *Lyric sequence* *At Aleciras where on the bay wild herons*	Date: Jan 23	*WFMP* 208–209
9v	"The Nineteenth Century and After"		*Though the great men return no more*		*WFMP* 262–63
10r	"Meditations upon Death" [At Algeciras/ Mohini Chatterjee]		*Meditations upon death* *I* *The heron-billed pale Cattle Birds*	Date: Feb 4. 1929	*WFMP* 210–11
10v	[Blank]				
11r	*PEP*		*End of Cuala book* *PS.* *Oedipus was certainly as well known to the common people as Raftery*		*PEP* 36n, *AVB* 28n, *CW14* 21n
11v	Note for *A Vision*		*First note to Book I of Great Wheel page 21 (Type script in orange envelope).*		

RAPALLO C (NLI 13,580)

Folio	Description	Title/ section	First line of page (uncancelled)	Note	Pub.
12r	"Meditations upon Death" [Mohini Chatterjee]		*I* *I asked if* [I] *should pray* *But the Brahman said*		*WFMP* 216–17
12v	Text related to opposite		*Where well out we stand* *After a miriad graves*		*WFMP* 218–19
13r	"Meditations upon Death" [Mohini Chatterjee]		*Eyes remembered bright* *Feet in old days light shall* *Once more be bright or light*		*WFMP* 220–21
13v	"Mad as the Mist and Snow"		*Bolt & bar the shutter* *For the foul winds blow*	Most cancelled	*WFMP* 498–99
14r	"Meditations upon Death" [Mohini Chatterjee]		~~*Old soliders to face to face*~~ ~~*In grim strategic though*~~		*WFMP* 222–23
	"Mad as the Mist and Snow"		*The classics on the book shelf there* *Glimmer row & & row*	Most cancelled	*WFMP* 500–501
14v	[Just title]		*Meditations upon Death* *I*	*WFMP* 225n	
15r	"Meditations upon Death" [Mohini Chatterjee]		*Meditations upon death* *II* *I asked if I should pray*	Date: Feb 9 1929	*WFMP* 224–25
15v	Text to insert opposite		*Horace there by Homer stands* *Plato stands below*	*WFMP* 503n	
16r	"Mad as the Mist and Snow"		*I* *Bolt & bar the shutter* *For the foul winds blow*	Date: Feb 12 1929	*WFMP* 503–504
16v	Notes for opposite		*Nualas boat of ivory*	*WFMP* 583n	
17r	"Crazy Jane on the King"		*King Nualas ivory magic boat* *On Udan Adan lay a float*		*WFMP* 582–83
17v	Revision of text opposite?		*O King Nuala & his boat* *On Udan Adan lake a float*		*WFMP* 586–87
18r	"Crazy Jane on the King"		*O King Nuala green glass boat* *On Udan Adan lake a float*		*WFMP* 584–85
18v	Revision of text opposite?		*The sevene sages wait the ship* *O the finger on the lip*		*WFMP* 590–91
19r	"Crazy Jane on the King"		~~*Did Nualas ship of glass*~~ ~~*Over Udan Adan pass?*~~	All cancelled	*WFMP* 588–89
19v	[Blank]				
20r	"Crazy Jane on the King"		~~*The childs The bad girl's*~~ ~~*refusal to cheer for the King*~~ ~~*King Nuala*~~	All cancelled	*WFMP* 592–93

RAPALLO C (NLI 13,580)

Folio	Description	Title/ section	First line of page (uncancelled)	Note	Pub.
20v	Text revising opposite		*A man found if I held him there* *When my arms were yet alive*		*WFMP* 460–61
21r	"Three Things"		*For this thing I held lif [sic] dear* *Sang a bone cast up on the shore*		*WFMP* 458–59
21v	Rhyme notes		*bless | ness | less | yes | ches | dress*	*WFMP* 463n	
22r	"Three Things"		*Three dear things that I think on yet* *Cried a bone cast up on the shore*		*WFMP* 462–63
22v	Text revising opposite		*I* *O cruel death give three things back* *Sang a bone upon the shore*		*WFMP* 462–63
23r	"Three Things"		*I* *O cruel death give three things back* *Cried a bone cast on the shore*	All cancelled	*WFMP* 464–65
23v	"Crazy Jane on the King"		*Then I thought some great event* *Had called him up & hither sent*		*WFMP* 596–97
24r	"Crazy Jane on the King"		*Yester night I saw in a vision* *Those Long bodied Tuatha de Dannan*		*WFMP* 594–95
24v	"Crazy Jane on the King"		*I* *Cracked Mary's Vision* *Yesternight I saw in a vision*	Date: Feb 24	*WFMP* 598–99
25r	"The Nineteenth Century and After"		*Though that great song return no more* *There's keen delight in what we have*	Date: March 2	*WFMP* 264–65
25v	Text revising opposite		*When I saw them dancing there* *& Some sort of Indea dance it seemed*		*WFMP* 378–79
26r	"Crazy Jane Grown Old Looks at the Dancers"		*I dreamed I saw them dancing there* *Love is like the lower of the lily*		*WFMP* 376–77
26v	Text revising opposite?		*I saw in a crowd of dancers* *In bitter sweetness of their youth*		*WFMP* 380–81
27r	"Crazy Jane Grown Old Looks at the Dancers"		*When she—although it seemed she played* *I knew if all for murder truth*		*WFMP* 382–83
27v	Revised version of opposite		*Cracked Mary & the dancers* *I* *I found that ivory image there* *Dancing with her his chosen youth*	Date: March 6	*WFMP* 386–87

Rapallo C (NLI 13,580)

Folio	Description	Title/ section	First line of page (uncancelled)	Note	Pub.
28r	"Crazy Jane Grown Old Looks at the Dancers"		~~*Cracked Mary & the dancers*~~ ~~*I*~~ ~~*I found a couple dancing*~~ ~~*In bitter sweetness of their youth*~~	All cancelled	*WFMP* 384–85
28v	?Revision for opposite		*Your husband now I sing to her*		*WFMP* 508–509
29r	"Those Dancing Days Are Gone"		*What songs I made that woman there* *That is a wretched crone*		*WFMP* 506–507
29v	Revising opposite?		*What can I sing but what I know* *Though this be my last song*		*WFMP* 512–13
30r	"Those Dancing Days Are Gone"		*I'll sing into that woman ear* *There all her dancing gone*		*WFMP* 510–11
30v	[Almost blank]		*5 | 6 | 7 | 5*		
31r	"Those Dancing Days Are Gone"		*I* *Come let me sing into your ear* *Those dancing days are gone*	Date: March 8	*WFMP* 514–15
31v	Continuing opposite		*Thus sang | sleap | alarm | deep | bed | arms* *Thus a mother sang to sleap*		*WFMP* 472–73
32r	"Lullaby"		*As Paris slept* *That first night*		*WFMP* 470–71
32v	"Lullaby"		~~*Sleap beloved sleap*~~ ~~*Sleap where you have fed*~~	All cancelled	*WFMP* 474–75
33r	"Lullaby"		*Beloved may your sleap be sound* *That have found it where you*		*WFMP* 476–77
33v	Revision for opposite		*Found the potions work being done* *When birds could sing, when dear could weep*	Most cancelled	*WFMP* 480–81
34r	"Lullaby"		~~*Sleap beloved such a sleap*~~ ~~*As Tristan that famed forester fell*~~	All cancelled	*WFMP* 478–79
34v	Revision for opposite		~~*Such sleap as Leada tried to guard*~~ ~~*When Eurotas bank*~~	Most cancelled	*WFMP* 482–83
35r	"Lullaby"		*Sleap beloved such a sleap* *As did that wild Tristan know*		*WFMP* 484–85
35v	[Unpublished poem: "Wisdom & Knowledge"]		*Wisdom & Knowledge (or John Hermit & his friends)* *John Hermit stays at home for he*	Date: March 29 [?27] twice	*IY* 166, *YAACTS17* 2–3
36r	"Lullaby"		*Lullaby* *I* *Beloved may your sleap be sound*	Date: March 1929	*WFMP* 486–87

RAPALLO C (NLI 13,580)

Folio	Description	Title/ section	First line of page (uncancelled)	Note	Pub.
36v	Continues & substitutes opposite		*IV* *Bring me to that wall for he*		*WFMP* 330–31
37r	"Crazy Jane and the Bishop"		*Crack Mary & the Bishop* *II* *Nor was he the bishop when his ban*		*WFMP* 328–29
37v	Substitutes opposite		*I* *I care not what the sailors say*	Date: March 27	*WFMP* 338–39
38r	"Crazy Jane Reproved"		~~*I care not what the sailors say*~~		*WFMP* 336–37
	[Unpub: "Mrs Phillamore"]		*Mrs Phillamore* *"I learned to think in a man's way*		Hone 415, *YAACTS17* 13
38v	"The Scholars"		*Shuffle there, cough in the ink* *Wear out the carpet with your shoes*	*WSC* 93n	
39r	"Crazy Jane and the Bishop"		*Cracked Mary & the Bishop* *I* *Bring me to the chapel wall* *That at midnight I may call*		*WFMP* 332–33
39v	"Girl's Song"		*Girl song* *A met an old man yeterday [sic]*		*WFMP* 404–405
40r	"Girl's Song"		*I* *I went out alone* *To sing a song or two*		*WFMP* 406–407
40v	[Blank]				
41r	"Girl's Song"		*Girls Song* *I* *I went out alone* *To sing a song or two*	Date: March 29	*WFMP* 408–409
41v	"Young Man's Song"		*My love must be at last* *Even like the old crone*		*WFMP* 390–91
42r	"Young Man's Song"		*Stupid fool* *The world was not yet*		*WFMP* 392–93
42v	"Young Man's Song"		*When the world was not yet* *That stalking thing I saw*		*WFMP* 394–95
43r	"Young Man's Song"		*Abashed by that report* *For the heart cannot lie*		*WFMP* 396–97
43v	Revising opposite		*"Uplift those eyes & throw* *Those glances unafraid*		*WFMP* 400–401
	[Unpub: Mrs Phillamore]		*Mrs Phillamore* *"I learned to think in a mans way"*		Hone 415, *YAACTS17* 13
44r	"Young Man's Song"		*Young mans Boys song* *She will change I cried*		*WFMP* 398–99
44v	"Love's Loneliness"		*Old fathers great grand fathers* *Rise as kindred should*		*WFMP* 452–53

RAPALLO C (NLI 13,580)

Folio	Description	Title/ section	First line of page (uncancelled)	Note	Pub.
45r	"Young Man's Song"		*Young Mans Song* *She will change I cried*		*WFMP* 402–403
45v	"His Confidence"		*on corners of the eye* *wrote I much*		*WFMP* 412–13
46r	"His Confidence"		*shame | side | came | tide* *All loves cruelty* *Paid my side*		*WFMP* 410–11
46v	"His Confidence"		*with* *on corners of the eyes* *Daily wrote*		*WFMP* 416–17
47r	"His Confidence"		*I broke my heart in two* *None other struck*		*WFMP* 414–15
47v	"Her Anxiety"		*Earth in beauty dressed* *Awaits returning spring*		*WFMP* 420–21
48r	"His Confidence"		*I* *Unending love to buy*		*WFMP* 418–19
48v	Notes for opposite		*room come | tear | Tomb |* *day | say ray | high | there |* *sky | hair* *I cut the locks of youth away*		*WFMP* 440–41
49r	"Her Dream"		*I dreamed, on my bed I lay* *Midnight and its wisdom come*		*WFMP* 438–39
49v	"Symbols"		*Symbols* *A storm battered world old Tower* *The blind hermit rings the hour*		*WFMP* 236–37
50r	"Her Dream"		*I dreamed as in my bed I lay* *Nights fathomless wisdom come*		*WFMP* 442–43
50v	"Love's Loneliness"		*Old Fathers, great grand Fathers* *Rise as kindred should*	Date: April 17	*WFMP* 454–55
51r	"Symbols"		*Symbols | I* *A storm beaten old watch-tower*	Ref. *WFMP* 237	*WFMP* 444
	"Her Dream"		*Berenice* *I dreamed as in my bed I lay*		*WFMP* 444–45
51v	[Unpublished]		*I thought to have crept up him there*		*YAACTS17* 6
	"His Bargain"		*Before the almighty will | had unbound*		*WFMP* 424–25
52r	[Unpublished]		*Heavy the bog & the wind is high* *The wind is high & the arrows few*		*YAACTS17* 5
52v	Notes for opposite		*Before heavy hours unwound* *From times [?great] spindle shaft*		*WFMP* 428–29
53r	"His Bargain"		*Before I saw times spindle* *Turn once round*		*WFMP* 426–27

RAPALLO C (NLI 13,580)

Folio	Description	Title/ section	First line of page (uncancelled)	Note	Pub.
53v	"His Bargain"		*Plato describles [sic] a spindle* *Some body twirls round*		*WFMP* 430–31
54r	"His Bargain"		*I made & will not break it,* *And time had not begun*		*WFMP* 432–33
54v	Revised version of opposite		*Who talks of Plato's spindle;* *What set it it [sic] whirling round?*		*WFMP* 436–37
55r	"His Bargain"		~~*Who talks of Plato's spindle;*~~ ~~*What set it whirling round*~~		*WFMP* 434–35
	"The Two Trees"		*There through the bough bewildered light* *And there the loves a circle go,* *That flaming circle flaring circle of our day*		
55v	Revision for opposite		*crouched alone upon | the bare hill side*		*WFMP* 448–49
56r	"Love's Loneliness"		*Grandfathers great grand fathers*		*WFMP* 446–47
56v	"Love's Loneliness"		~~*Old Fathers, great grand fathers*~~	Circum-scribed by wavy lines	*WFMP* 450–51
	[Unpublished]		*When Natures dark bride* *Can no longer hide*		*YAACTS17* 7, *WFMP* 450
57r	[Unpublished]		*Intellect at last* *After [?bold] holds fast*		*YAACTS17* 8
57v	[Unpub: The Daimon & the Celestial Body]		*The Daimon & the Celestial Body* *When Nature holds his bride*	All cancelled	*YAACTS17* 9
58r	[Unpub: The Passionate & Celestial Body]		*The Passionate & Celestial Body* *Imaginations bride*		*YAACTS17* 10–11
58v	[Blank]				
59r	[Unpublished]		*Imaginations bride* *Having thrown aside*		*YAACTS17* 12
59v	*A Vision* notes	(1)	*Note (1) |* *When automatic script began, a spirit said the "Funnell" contains "no images".*		
60r	*A Vision* notes (cont.)	(1) cont.	*reality of this state, though [?dreamed]....*		
		(2)	*(2) | Husk is light (though also hearing etc.)....*		
		(3)	*(3) | After death the Spirits act in common....*		

RAPALLO C (NLI 13,580)

Folio	Description	Title/ section	First line of page (uncancelled)	Note	Pub.
60v	*A Vision* notes (cont.)	(3) cont.	*Identical with the ends of human endevour they are ceaselessly present to the human mind…*		
61r	*A Vision* notes (cont.)	(3) cont.	*A spirit spoke of the form of art as "correspondential" to the state of the dead.*		
		(4)	*May 26 (4) | The spirit last night after giving sign confirmed statement that spirits….*	Date: May 26	
61v	*A Vision* notes (cont.)	(4) cont.	*Can I consider "dreams" as our emotion acting [*to*] connect with what remains "sensuous"….*		
		(5)	*(5) | Who are the Teaching Spirits of the Return?*		
62r	*A Vision* notes (cont.)	(5) cont.	*Am I to assume that the Teaching Spirits are beings who have passed beyond our sphere….*		
		(6)	*(6) | In comment on (2). The Images (PB) grow contingent more & more after death….*		
62v	*A Vision* notes (cont.)	(6) cont.	*& from Husk which gave them separate existence.*		
63r	*A Vision* notes (cont.)	[~~(7)~~], (7)	*7 | I am tempted to transfer light from Husk to P.B. by the fact Spirits speak of dreaming back forms etc as in light.*		
63v	*A Vision* notes (cont.)	(7) cont.	*seems [?unlimited] & limited perception.*		
64r	*A Vision* notes (cont.)	(7) cont.	*primary two freedoms, that of the individual that of the one….*		
		(8)	*8. | Light so understood is Astral Light….*		
64v	*A Vision* notes (cont.)	(8) cont.	*"Astral light" the stream of images can be assumed as becoming pure undifferentiated….*		
65r	*A Vision* notes (cont.)	(8) cont.	*We say that PB persists in the "Dreaming Back" but what persists is PB imobalized by Spirit….*		

RAPALLO C (NLI 13,580)

Folio	Description	Title/ section	First line of page (uncancelled)	Note	Pub.
65v	*A Vision* notes (cont.)	(8) cont.	~~*The Daimon is Spirit fully expressed in Matter (PB)*~~	All cancelled	
66r	*A Vision* notes (cont.)	(8) cont.	*I must distinguish between the forms expressed, drawn forth out of the light....*		
66v	*A Vision* notes (cont.)	(8) cont.	*or perhaps | Husk = Expression. B.B.* [sic] *Potential form | In which case the daimon*		
	Sleep	[sleep]	*an unpleasant but important interview with Dionertes. He was petulant & distressed–*		
67r	Sleep (cont.)	[sleep cont.]	*was to ephemeral for such a word. Then he objected to a careless phrase of mine about....*		
67v	Sleep (cont.)	[sleep cont.]	*must think out for myself.*		
	A Vision notes (cont.)	Notes	*June | Expiation A Spirit joined to its C. B lives through its life....*	Date: June	
68r	*A Vision* notes (cont.)	[cont.]	*are symbols, is metaphoric because it is seperated from the Record & has memory alone.*		
68v	*A Vision* notes (cont.)	[cont.]	*The system denies I think the existence of anything which we know unconsciously.*		
69r	*A Vision* notes (cont.)	[cont.]	*Is not sympathy itself a reversal of being but voluntary whereas that in expiation is involuntary.*		
69v	*A Vision* notes (cont.)	[cont.]	*phases of the daimon*~~*—its life constituting a year—28 phases devided into 12*~~*. We are in....*		
70	Missing pages—8 strips				
71					
72					
73					
74					
75					
76					
77					

RAPALLO C (NLI 13,580)

Folio	Description	Title/ section	First line of page (uncancelled)	Note	Pub.
78r	Contents		*Contents* | ~~*Introduction to Great Wheel. page 13 (detached from rest)*~~ | *Soul in Judgement (continued from loose leaf book) 12 pages*	Upside down	
78v	Title page		*Diary Diary [larger written over smaller]*	Upside down	
0	Conservation leaf				
0	Conservation leaf				
Inside	Patterned board				
Cover	Patterned board		*Finished June or July 1929*	Date: June/July 1929	

Appendix D

Tabular Summary: Rapallo Notebook D (NLI 13,581)

Neil Mann and Wayne K. Chapman

The following table provides a listing of the 53 leaves (recto and verso) and forty-five stubs in this notebook in relation to its covers and conservation papers. This listing is generally consistent with the corresponding summaries of "Rapallo Notebooks A and B" (Appendix), *International Yeats Studies* 6.1 (2022), 161–183. As Yeats did not number the pages in Rapallo D, the column for page numbers in the tables for Rapallo A, B, and E (column 4) does not appear; therefore, the six columns here (from left to right) list the leaves of Rapallo Notebook D by:

1. **Leaf number**.
2. A **brief description**, indicating the corresponding work.
3. A summary of the **title** or the **section** number.
4. The first uncancelled line(s) of **text** (cancelled text is included where there is no uncancelled text).
5. **Notes** give points of physical description, including pages which are cancelled *in toto*, and indicate if the page includes a date.
6. The final column records where **published** transcriptions or final versions appear. Besides the standard *IYS* abbreviations used in columns 5 and 6 (see https://tigerprints.clemson.edu/iys/iys_abbreviations.html), the following abbreviations are used:

   "SP" = Neil Mann, "Seven Propositions" (rev. Apr. 2009), The System of Yeats's *A Vision*, https://www.yeatsvision.com/7Propositions.html.
   WFMP = W. B. Yeats, *Words for Music Perhaps: Manuscript Materials*, ed. David R. Clark (Ithaca and London: Cornell University Press, 1999); and
   YAACTS = *Yeats: An Annual of Critical and Textual Studies* XVII, ed. Richard J. Finneran (Ann Arbor, MI: University of Michigan Press, 2003).

Please note:

- **Blank pages** are included, giving both recto and verso.
- Evidently **missing pages** are also included (with a single leaf number). Following restoration, most of these are now indicated by stubs of Japanese paper used to fix the counterparts on the other side of the stitching.

- **Pages added** at the beginning and end of the book during the rebinding process are indicated but not counted.

We are extremely grateful to Jack Quin for his help in checking the physical copy of this notebook at the National Library of Ireland at a time when travel was impossible, and for helping to ensure the accuracy of this table.

Rapallo D (NLI 13,581)

Folio	**Description**	**Title/ section**	**First line of page (uncancelled)**	**Note**	**Pub.**
Cover	Patterned				
Inside	Patterned				
1r	Diary entry refers to theater matters, Lady Ottoline Morrel	I, II	*Diary.* *Rapallo. 1928* *I* *Some months ago, at the performance of "John Bulls other Island" with Dolly Dowdens new scenes*	Date: Rapallo, 1928; cf. WBY to O. Morrell, 20 March [1928], *CL InteLex* 5093	
1v	Notes for reading philosophy		*Books to get from R. D. S. or else where*		
2r	1r cont.; notes St Gregory/ Confucius	II cont., III	*Room, Lady Ottoline, her husband & her daughter. There too persons & scene...*		
2v	[Blank]				
3r	Draft of "I am of Ireland", "The Crazed Moon"		*Dublin. August. 1929* *"I am of Ireland* *And the Holy Land of Ireland...*	Date: August 1929	*WFMP* 518–19, 274–75
3v	[Blank]				
4r	"I am of Ireland"		*she sat by the road* *I am of Ireland*		*WFMP* 520–21
4v	Quatrain (unpublished)		*A recent incident* *Rousseau that threw babies in*	cf. WBY to AG, 24 April [1931], *CL InteLex* 5462	*WFMP* 524–25
	"I am of Ireland"		*The harpers are all thumbs* *The fiddlers all a curst*		*WFMP* 524–25
5r	"I am of Ireland"		*All the lutes are cracked* *All the drumbs burst cried he*		*WFMP* 522–23
5v	"I am of Ireland"		*One man & one man alone* *in that outlandish gear*		*WFMP* 528–29
6r	"I am of Ireland"		*I am of Ireland* *O the Holy Land of Ireland*		*WFMP* 526–27

Rapallo D (NLI 13,581)

Folio	Description	Title/ section	First line of page (uncancelled)	Note	Pub.
6v	Notes on Sepharial, zodiac, Hindu eras		*Sepharial in Hebrew Astrology gives this table*	*Hebrew Astrology* (1929)	
7r	Draft of letter in response to letter in *Irish Statesman*, 24 August 1929		*Masks & Musics* *Sir:* *Your correspondent "Stall" thinks that the Masks of Emer & Eithne are guys*	Letter cancelled	
	Notes on Sepharial		*Sepharial goes on* *Seven times 300 or 70x36 years*		
7v	Notes on Sepharial, zodiac, eras		*I notice that Sepharial in his queer mixture of sense & nonsense*		
8	[Leaf missing]				
9	[Leaf missing]				
10r	Astrological notes, zodiac, Sepharial		*[Aries] on 15th day & 7th month (March)*		
10v	Notes on Indian epochs, periods of time		*a day & night of Brahma = 2 Maya Yugas*		
11r	Notes on Indian epochs, periods of time		*A day & night of Brahma = 2 Maya Yugas 120 year* *360 such days & nights = 43200* *A year of Brahma*		
11v	Notes on Indian epochs, periods of time		*H. Jacobi in Hastings Encyclopedia of R & E gives to a Maya Uga 12,000 years*		
12r	Notes on Indian epochs, periods of time		*we are now in the 457th Yuga (Maya Uga) of the 28th of the…*		
12v	Notes on Indian epochs, periods of time		*We are in Kalpa or the Boar which began when we were half way through life of Brahma*		
13r	"Coole Park, 1929"		*497 | [-]<u>457</u> | 40* *Poem on Coole to go with Lady Gs Cuala essays.* *Prose sketch.*		*WFMP* 104–05
	Calculations (of Maha yugas)		*43,200,000*		
13v	Text to insert opposite		*Foot worn, wheel worn or wing [?beat{en}] way*		*WFMP* 105n

Rapallo D (NLI 13,581)

Folio	Description	Title/ section	First line of page (uncancelled)	Note	Pub.
14r	"Coole Park, 1929"		*About it wind the woods intricacies* *Shadowed in foliage, a lake luminous*		*WFMP* 106–07
14v	Text to insert opposite		*Among the foliage shadowed, a lake luminous* *Old foot ways wheel worn, or old wing worn ways*		*WFMP* 110–11
15r	"Coole Park, 1929"		~~*But for the generations after us*~~ ~~*I sing miraculous intricacies*~~	All cancelled	*WFMP* 108–09
15v	Text to insert opposite		*Here Hyde who all that industrious labor first began*		*WFMP* 114–15
16r	"Coole Park, 1929"		*Here that most medita[tive] Man John Synge Those* *Wild hearted men Shaw Taylor & Hugh Lane*		*WFMP* 112–13
16v	Text to insert opposite		*Here Hyde before he had beaten into prose* *That noble blade the muses busked on*		*WFMP* 118–19
17r	"Coole Park, 1929"		*Most daring men Shaw Taylor & Hugh Lane Etc.* *Found pride establis in humility*	Almost all cancelled	*WFMP* 116–17
17v	Rhyme scheme, prose fragments		*a curtain fell of more of painted* *& lacked fully for a spring board*	*WFMP* 121n	
18r	"Coole Park, 1929"		*O blackness with a sudden gleam of white* *O wild reversing swallow than can fill*		*WFMP* 120–21
18v	Text to insert opposite		*Among the nest, under the luminous* *Storm tormented cloudy Connaght skies*		*WFMP* 124–25
19r	"Coole Park, 1929"		*Coole House* *I* *I praise for living ears that ancient house*		*WFMP* 122–23
19v	Text to insert opposite	IV	*Protecting with that cloudy heritage* *Those great characters of the living word*	Most cancelled	*WFMP* 126–27
20r	"Coole Park, 1929"		*"Where two or three are gathered"—He bestowed* *That blinding tempest of the middle age*	*WFMP* 127n	*WFMP* 128–29

Rapallo D (NLI 13,581)

Folio	Description	Title/ section	First line of page (uncancelled)	Note	Pub.
20v	Further ideas		*The woman of the house was half the tale…*		*WFMP* 130–31
21r	"Swift's Epitaph"		*Jonathan Swift's in port / Savage indignation there…*		*WFMP* 240–41
	"Coole Park, 1929"		*A woman here had such a character…*	WFMP 131n	
21v	Reworked lines		*Gave something of her character to all*	WFMP 133n	
22r	"Coole Park, 1929"		*And here the mistress of that house put into all* *And here that woman now grown old & frail*		*WFMP* 132–33
22v	"Coole Park, 1929"		*Had such a [?character] such patience that she gave* *Some thing of her [?character] to all*		*WFMP* 136–37
23r	"Coole Park, 1929"		*A womans house had such a character | seal* *was set on all the devout fancies there*		*WFMP* 134–35
23v	"Astrology and the Nature of Reality", drafts of Seven Propositions		*Astrology & the Nature of Reality* ~~*1. Reality is a timeless & spaceless community of spirits.*~~ ~~*Each perceives the others wills them & is willed by them.*~~	All cancelled (except title)	"SP"
24r	Seven Propositions		*(1) Reality is a timeless & spaceless community of spirits which perceive each other.*		"SP"
24v	"Coole Park, 1929"		*this shadow stand* *A moments memory to that laurelled head*	Almost all cancelled	*WFMP* 140–41
25r	"Coole Park, 1929"		*She taught me that straight line that sets a man* *above the crooked journey of the sun*	All cancelled	*WFMP* 138–39
25v	"Coole Park, 1929"		*Come here & dedicate — here when the sun* *Whitens the stone long upon the ground*	Almost all cancelled	*WFMP* 142–43
26r	Line of "Coole Park, 1929"		*and every oak & Illacks a balloon.*	WFMP 143n	
	Seven Propositions		*5. Human life is either a struggle of a destiny against all other destinies…*		"SP"

Rapallo D (NLI 13,581)

Folio	Description	Title/ section	First line of page (uncancelled)	Note	Pub.
26v	"Coole Park, 1929"		*Here traveller when some shapeless mound*		*WFMP* 145n
27r	"Coole Park, 1929"		*Here Traveller, when this spot of ground* *Here Traveller, here on this spot of ground*		*WFMP* 144–45
27v	"Coole Park, 1929"		*Here traveller dedicate—here when a mound*		*WFMP* 147n
28r	"Coole Park, 1929"		~~*When bits of briar*~~ ~~*When briar & nettle & bits of brozen broken stone*~~	All cancelled	*WFMP* 146–47
28v	"Coole Park, 1929"		~~*Withdraw in fancy from this planted ground*~~ ~~*From all that resurrection of the sun*~~	All cancelled	*WFMP* 150–51
29r	"Coole Park, 1929"		~~*Here student, unknown traveller take your stand*~~ ~~*When strong ash shaplings root among the stone*~~	All cancelled	*WFMP* 148–49
29v	"Coole Park, 1929"		~~*We came like swallows & like swallows went*~~		*WFMP* 154–55
	Diary entry		*Oct | Yesterday I was at my brothers show.*	Date: Oct.	
30r	"Coole Park, 1929"		*I praise for living ears an ancient house* *The woman of that house, her western skies*	Almost all cancelled	*WFMP* 152–53
30v	"Coole Park, 1929"		*They came like swallows & like swallows went* *Yet half a dozen in formation there*	All cancelled	*WFMP* 158–59
31r	"Coole Park, 1929"		*Here Hyde before he had beaten into prose* *That noble blade the Muses buckled on*	Most cancelled	*WFMP* 156–57
31v	"Coole Park, 1929"		*They like swallows & like swallows went*		*WFMP* 162–63
32r	"Coole Park, 1929"		*A sycamore and* *I meditate upon the swallow flight*		*WFMP* 160–61
32v	Fair copy "Coole Park, 1929", stanzas 1–3		*Coole Park* *I* *I meditate upon a swallows flight*		*WFMP* 164–67
33	[Cut out]				
34r	Fair copy "Coole Park, 1929"		*4* *Here traveller, scholar, poet take your stand* *When all those rooms & passages are gone*	Date: Dublin. Sept 7. 1929	*WFMP* 168–69

Rapallo D (NLI 13,581)

Folio	Description	Title/ section	First line of page (uncancelled)	Note	Pub.
34v	Notes for *A Vision*		*For "The Great Wheel"* *From Chapmans translation of Ovids Banquet of Sense....* *"There is a place where contraries..."...* *Coleridge was influenced by Synesius*		
35r	Preface to *Wild Apples*	[I]	*Some years ago, I made a selection from Dr Gogartys poetry for the Cuala press...*		cf. *CW6* 172
35v	Arithmetic		*430* *36 x 12*		
	Quotation to insert opposite		*"She does not know her hair* *Is golden with a hint* *Of Trojan ashes in it"*		
36r	Preface to *Wild Apples*	[I cont.]	*I have been brought up in that soft twilight—"magic casements—" "siren there"*		cf. *CW6* 172–73
36v	Notes on Fichte and Hegel from G. H. Lewes's *History of Philosophy*		*Fichtes historical scheme summarized by G. H. Lewis in his "History of Philosophy"*		
37r	Engagements for Oct. 28–Nov. 4 1929		*Engagements* *Monday Oct 28 Lunch — Gynn*	Dates: Oct. 28–Nov. 4 [1929]	
37v	Preface to *Wild Apples*	[II cont.], III	*And Synge state the greatest man of the school sang of himself*		cf. *CW6* 172–73
38r	Theme for "After Long Silence"		*Subjet [sic] | Your hair is white | My hair is white*		*WFMP* 490–91
	Preface to *Wild Apples*	II	*II | The other day I was asked why....*		cf. *CW6* 173
38v	Engagements for Nov. 5–Nov. 11 1929		*Tuesd Nov 5*	Dates: Nov. 5–11	
	"Crazy Jane on the Day of Judgement"		*Love is for who*		*WFMP* 352–53
39r	"Crazy Jane on the Day of Judgment"		*Subject for a "Crazy Jane' poem* *I* *Tell all that history from childhood up*	Date: Oct 29	*WFMP* 350–51

RAPALLO D (NLI 13,581)

Folio	Description	Title/ section	First line of page (uncancelled)	Note	Pub.
39v	"Crazy Jane on the Day of Judgement"		*Escape your touch & that*		*WFMP* 354–55
	"After Long Silence"		*Un friendly lamplight hidden by its shade*		*WFMP* 494–95
40r	Preface to *Wild Apples*, section III		*An Arab King sent a man to Lawrence…*		cf. *CW6* 174
	"After Long Silence"		*Those other lovers being dead & gone*		*WFMP* 492–93
40v	Note for *A Vision*		*Note to be inserted where Antithetical & Primary are associated with Time & Space in "Principal Symbols" | *Giovani Gentile…*		cf. *AVB* 70
41r	"After Long Silence"		*Speach after long silence; it is right All other lovers being estranged or dead…*	Date: Nov 1929	*WFMP* 496–97
	Note on circumstances of poem		*When I wrote this poem, I had already been ill for three weeks or so & I had just arrived in Rapallo & struggled with constant sleepiness—the first stages of suffering from Malta fever.*		*WFMP* 496–97
41v	List of books and prices		*A minature history of European Art by R. H. Wilenski*		
	"Veronica's Napkin"		*Heavenly circuit, Berenices hair A*		*WFMP* 228–29
	[42 leaves excised (Clark); NLI counted 44 leaves]		*[numbering to follow Clark WFMP]*		
84r	Note on Spengler for *A Vision*		*Foot note to "2000 B C to 1A D" ("Vision" p 151) *The dates after 1 A D are in all cases from the automatic script & the most important*		
84v	"Veronica's Napkin"		*Veronica Handkerchief Heavenly circuit! Berenices hair!*	All cancelled	*WFMP* 230–31
85r	Note on Spengler for *A Vision*		*Foot note to A D 1050 to present day ("Vision" page 196. *Spengler finds here, as I should have found…*		
	"Veronica's Napkin"		*Heavenly circuit! Berenice's hair!*		*WFMP* 232–33

Rapallo D (NLI 13,581)

Folio	Description	Title/ section	First line of page (uncancelled)	Note	Pub.
85v	"Byzantium"		*When the emperors brawling soldiers are a bed* *The last benighted victim dead or fled*		*WFMP* 6–7
86r	"Byzantium"		*When the emperor brawling soldiers are a bed* *last benighted traveller*	Most cancelled	*WFMP* 4–5
86v	"Byzantium"		*His breath body beckons me* *And I adore that mystery*		*WFMP* 8–9
87r	"Byzantium"		*Miracle, bird on golden handy work* *More miracle than bird or handy work*		*WFMP* 10–11
87v	"Byzantium"		*And there is a certain square where tall flames wind & unwind* *And in them plunge dance spirits, by that their agony made pure*		*WFMP* 12–13
88r	For insertion opposite		*May blood bessoted spirits come* *And all bloods fury in that flame may leave*		*WFMP* 13n
88v	"Byzantium"		*A straddle on the dolphin mire & blood* *The crowds approach; the marble breaks the flood*		*WFMP* 14–15
89r	"Byzantium"		*Break the bleak glittering intricacy* *Where blind images can yet*		*WFMP* 16–17
89v	For insertion opposite		*For Hades bobbin bound in mummy cloth* *May unwind the winding path*		*WFMP* 18–19
90r	"Byzantium"		*I* *The unpurged images of day receed* *The emperors drunken soldiers are a bed*		*WFMP* 20–23
90v	Open letter to Wyndham Lewis		*Renvyle* *July* *Open letter to Lewis*	Date: July	see Lewis, *Satire & Fiction*, 29; part in Wade, *Letters*, 776
91r	"Byzantium"		*V* *A straddle on the dolphins mire & blood* *Those crowds approach; metal breaks the flood*		*WFMP* 24–25

RAPALLO D (NLI 13,581)

Folio	Description	Title/ section	First line of page (uncancelled)	Note	Pub.
91v	"Byzantium"		*V* *A straddle on the dolphins mire & blood* *Those crowds approach; smithys break the flood*		*WFMP* 28–29
92r	"Byzantium"		*Byzantium* *I* *The unpurged images of day recede;*		*WFMP* 26–27
92v	"The Crazed Moon"		*Crazed through much child-bearing* *The moon is staggering in the sky*		*WFMP* 280–81
93r	"The Crazed Moon"		*A lyric written in 1923 & lost have just found it August 1930*		*WFMP* 278–79
93v	"Veronica's Napkin"		*Veronica Napkin*	Date: Oct 1930	*WFMP* 234–35
	The Cat and the Moon		*Beggar* *Do you mind what the beggar told you about the holy man*		cf. *VPl* 797
94r	*The Cat and the Moon*		*Let us be going holy man*		
94v	Memorial of John Quinn		*I must recall a friend of many years to whom I could seldom speak,*		
95r	John Quinn, continued		*agent said "I dont think you will write any more article upon Sir Roger Casement".*	Date: Oct 1930	
95v	"Crazy Jane on the Day of Judgement"		*And that is what Jane said.* *Thats certainly the case said he*		*WFMP* 356–57
96r	"Crazy Jane on the Day of Judgement"		*Mouths thirst on* *But mouths thirst on*		*WFMP* 358–59
96v	Themes for poems (unpublished)		*theme for poem* *I so often [?away] in my work* *So often forget-full* *[Separated vertically by a line]* *Theme* *a phantom to my bed I woke*		*YAACTS17* 14–15
97r	"Crazy Jane on the Day of Judgement"		*I can scoff & lower* *or scold for an hour*	Most cancelled. Date: Oct	*WFMP* 360–61
97v	Subject for a poem (unpublished)		*subject for a poem* *All the great philosophie, Plato, Spinoza, Hegel are but drama we know nothing but that*	Date: Nov 18 1930	*YAACTS17* 16

Rapallo D (NLI 13,581)

Folio	Description	Title/ section	First line of page (uncancelled)	Note	Pub.
98r	"Crazy Jane on the Day of Judgement"		*Crazy Jane & the End of the World 'Love is all Unsatisfied*		*WFMP* 362–63
98v	Upside down, note about cheque for NTS		*Checque [*sic*] for N. T. S.* £185.0.0	Date: April 29	
Inside cover					
Cover					

Appendix E

Tabular Summary: Rapallo Notebook E (NLI 13,582)

Neil Mann and Wayne K. Chapman

The following table provides a listing of all leaves (recto and verso), including blank pages and stubs in Rapallo Notebook E (National Library of Ireland MS 13,582). This notebook was rebound at the Delmas Conservation Bindery in 2005.

The following abbreviations are used in this table:

PEP = *A Packet for Ezra Pound* (Dublin: Cuala, 1929);
Res = W. B. Yeats, *"The Resurrection": Manuscript Materials*, ed. Jared Curtis and Selina Guinness (Ithaca and London: Cornell University Press, 2011);
WFMP = W. B. Yeats, *"Words for Music Perhaps": Manuscript Materials*, ed. David R. Clark (Ithaca and London: Cornell University Press, 1999);
WUWP = W. B. Yeats, *"The Words upon the Window Pane": Manuscript Materials*, ed. Mary FitzGerald (Ithaca and London: Cornell University Press, 2002); and
YPO = *Yeats, Philosophy, and the Occult*, eds. Matthew Gibson and Neil Mann (Clemson, SC: Clemson University Press, 2017).

Please note:

- **Blank leaves** are included, giving both recto and verso.
- **Missing leaves** that can be reckoned reliably from stubs are generally included in the page count with a single leaf number. Although sixteen leaves can be identified as missing from the first gathering, there are no stubs and they are **not included here** to maintain consistency with the numbering used in the three associated volumes of the Cornell Manuscript Materials.
- **Four leaves inserted** into this notebook by the Yeatses have been numbered as "60bis" to "63bis," to reflect the fact that they are not integral to the notebook and could have been bound elsewhere, but the numbering reflects that used in Cornell's *"The Resurrection": Manuscript Materials* and their actual position in the rebound notebook.
- **Leaves added** at the beginning and end of the book during the rebinding process are indicated (0) but not counted.
- **Text quoted** is generally the first uncancelled material on the page, except where there is no uncancelled material or where cancelled words are necessary to understand the phrasing.

RAPALLO E (NLI 13,582)

Folio	Description	Title/section	WBY p. no.	First line of page (uncancelled)	Note	Pub.
Cover	Patterned board	*Marked* "E"		~~*Principle symbols*~~ ~~*hourglass & diamond*~~ ~~*T[?he Diagram of the]*~~ ~~*Great Wheel*~~ *E*		
Inside	Patterned board					
0	Conservation leaf					
0	Conservation leaf					
1r	Passages from and notes on Leo Frobenius, *The Voice of Africa*			*"The great ages of universal history are not measured by the duration of their years, but by their style..."*		*YPO* 310 (as 3r)
1v	*The Voice of Africa*			*Frobenius quotes from Pliny "When we (Romans) prey we bring our right hand to our mouth & turn our..."*		*YPO* 311 (as 3v)
2r	*The Voice of Africa*			*Templum at the root of ideas, the universe in Babylone, Troy, Etruria.*		*YPO* 312 (as 4r)
2v	Account of séances and spirit photography	Clairvoyance on May 9		*Clairvoyance on May 9 Mrs Caulton Trance Mostly vague – many names...*	Caulton [=Cantlon?] Dated "May 9"	
3r	*A Vision*: introductory material	[?§I]	17	*[diagram: hourglass & diamond in circle] <The gyres are> sometimes considered to complete the double <movement> in <24 hours>...*		
3v	Text to substitute opposite page			*at the same moment Creative Mind and Body of Fate <moving> in cones, which have their bases touching...*		
4r	*A Vision*: introductory	[§I cont.]	18	*at the same moment Creative Mind reaches the centre of its figure & Body of Fate...*	All cancelled	

RAPALLO E (NLI 13,582)

Folio	Description	Title/section	WBY p. no.	First line of page (uncancelled)	Note	Pub.
4v	Text to insert opposite			*Much that I say here is in Herakleitos though the form is different "Homer was wrong..."*		
5r	*A Vision*: introductory	[§I cont.] ~~The Daimon~~ II	19	*The figure is unlike the other cones I have described in that the expansion of the lunar cone...*		
5v	Note to insert opposite			**My instructors cannot mean that these can be anything not present...*	Written sideways	
6r	*A Vision*: introductory	[§II cont.]	20	*as of the spiritual cone into twelve cycles exists but in relation to man...*		
6v	Text to insert opposite			*But sexual love is the only action that can <give> antithetical man knowledge of his individual daimon...*		
7r	*A Vision*: introductory	[§II cont.] III	21	*But the lover <claim> such perfection <for> the object of his love & fails again to find it there...*		
7v	Text to insert opposite			*When it <animates> the waking man, it <compells him to find> in woman <and there awake>...*		
8r	*A Vision*: introductory	[§III cont.]	22	*Where there is <sexual> domination without expression, <one or other is> out of phase, & the daimon...*	All but last lines cancelled	
8v	Text to insert opposite			*man as a sexual being is always antithetical & the woman always primary, but each as subject...*		
9r	*A Vision*: introductory	[§III cont.]	23	*those conflicts of races nature & schools of thought where the daimons of races nature & schools...*		
9v	[Blank]					

RAPALLO E (NLI 13,582)

Folio	Description	Title/section	WBY p. no.	First line of page (uncancelled)	Note	Pub.
10r	*A Vision*: introductory	The Four Principles	24	*The Four Principles <Man> is expressed in the Four Faculties the daimon in the* *<u>Four Principles</u>.*		
10v	[Blank]					
11r	*A Vision*: introductory	[§I cont.]	25	*or that of which corporeality is made. But the light must be thought of as coming from the mind...*		
11v	[Blank]					
12r	*A Vision*: introductory	[§I cont.]	26	*<which confers actual existence which is always change, upon the unchanging states or forms...>*		
12v	Text to insert opposite			*~~itself as different as the~~*	All 4 lines cancelled	
13r	*A Vision*: introductory	[§I cont.]	27	*At the consummation of her marriage, <she is> undevided Time, Time when there is neither past...*		
13v	Text to insert opposite			*In the <u>Passionate Body</u>, the <u>Celestial Body</u>, or conscience seen by itself as from without & so as <u>fate</u> lets fall...*		
14r	*A Vision*: introductory	[§I cont.]	28	*contemplates the imovable whole, though now but symbolised as an image.*		
14v	Note to insert opposite			**Because of this inverted reflection that Spenglers historical sceme seems the exact opposite.*	Written sideways	
15r	*A Vision*: introductory	The Cones of the Principles	29	*& instead of the other present – the spirits idea of itself, that which can be separated from eternity...*		
15v	Short text to insert opposite			*We are subconscious to the dead & they to the living, they enter into our world through image...*		

Rapallo E (NLI 13,582)

<table>
<tr><th>Folio</th><th>Description</th><th>Title/section</th><th>WBY p. no.</th><th>First line of page (uncancelled)</th><th>Note</th><th>Pub.</th></tr>
<tr><td>16r</td><td>A Vision: introductory</td><td>[cont.]</td><td>—</td><td>as the movement takes the time, which passes phase 1 & phase 15 of the cones of the Principles…</td><td></td><td></td></tr>
<tr><td>16v</td><td>[Blank]</td><td></td><td></td><td></td><td></td><td></td></tr>
<tr><td>17r</td><td>A Vision: introductory</td><td></td><td>—</td><td>The relations between Faculties & Principles Insert here page 20 & 21 | from yellow envelope</td><td>Almost blank</td><td></td></tr>
<tr><td>17v</td><td>Text to insert opposite</td><td></td><td></td><td>Young man “What were the lines” Old man: “To live for the truth….”</td><td></td><td>WUWP 4–5</td></tr>
<tr><td>18r</td><td>The Words upon the Window-pane first draft; see WUWP xvii.</td><td>Jonathan Swift Scenario</td><td>—</td><td>Jonathan Swift | Scenario. | A large room in Georgian house near Dublin. Two men enter one a young English man the older man a Dublin man.</td><td></td><td>WUWP 6–7</td></tr>
<tr><td>18v</td><td>Text to insert opposite</td><td></td><td></td><td>half a dozen old Romans & then Sir Thomas Moore.</td><td></td><td>WUWP 8–9</td></tr>
<tr><td>19r</td><td>The Words upon the Window-pane</td><td></td><td>—</td><td>chose seven men, then he declared the world could not add an eighth. <Old Man “but only one of> seven was a Christian”</td><td></td><td>WUWP 10–11</td></tr>
<tr><td>19v</td><td>Revision & text to insert opposite</td><td><s>Swift |</s> <s>Scenario</s></td><td></td><td>People have been coming in. Old man introduces Mrs L. Here is a young friend of mine <Mr G> – from Oxford – thinks we are some kind of jugglers but we all have to make…</td><td>Swift | Scenario in upper half cancelled</td><td>WUWP 12–13</td></tr>
<tr><td>20r</td><td>The Words upon the Window-pane</td><td>II</td><td>—</td><td>Young man But it does not need any great reading to see how different they were. Rouso did not call up…</td><td></td><td>WUWP 14–15</td></tr>
<tr><td>20v</td><td>Continues from 19v</td><td></td><td></td><td>any older than that. Young Man. Do you all <s>come here</s> to scence to meet somebody who is dead</td><td></td><td>WUWP 16–17</td></tr>
</table>

Rapallo E (NLI 13,582)

Folio	Description	Title/section	WBY p. no.	First line of page (uncancelled)	Note	Pub.
21r	*The Words upon the Window-pane*		—	*While they have been speaking various persons half a dozen perhaps more have come & taken seats.*		*WUWP* 18–19
21v	[Blank]					
22r	*The Words upon the Window-pane*		—	*but I say that he is a horrid old man – nobody will hear her. Thank you – thank you. (Mrs X that the spirit…*		*WUWP* 20–21
22v	For insertion opposite?			*Old Man* [cancelled text, except:] *Perhaps Vanessa is not here, <perhaps it all Swift> dream perhaps her dream.*		*WUWP* 22–23
23r	*The Words upon the Window-pane*		—	*Why do you let me spend hour after hour in your company.… YM | That old woman wants us to believe that Vanessa is there too…*		*WUWP* 24–25
23v	[Blank]					
24r	*The Words upon the Window-pane*		—	*or part. Cadenus – Cadenus I am a woman, nor were the women Cato Brutus loved any different.*		*WUWP* 26–27
24v	Text to insert opposite			*Old woman rises & then sinks back again – Vanessa voice It is not my hands that pull you back Cadenus.*		*WUWP* 28–29
25r	*The Words upon the Window-pane*		—	*It is the uncertainty, that brings them to the table. A man child perhaps – perhaps not perhaps not Cadenus.*		*WUWP* 30–31
25v	[Blank]					
26r	*The Words upon the Window-pane*			*bring good influence (Verse sung – Old woman begins to speak during singing – singing falters & stops).*		*WUWP* 32–33
26v	[Blank]					

Rapallo E (NLI 13,582)

Folio	Description	Title/section	WBY p. no.	First line of page (uncancelled)	Note	Pub.
27r	*The Words upon the Window-pane*			*old woman says cannot accep it after a scence like that "No no – you must – whether scene is good or bad…*		*WUWP* 34–35
27v	[Blank]					
28r	*The Words upon the Window-pane*			*old Dublin tradition. Do you remember that story about the negress. "What are you talking about sir."*		*WUWP* 36–37
28v	[Blank]					
29r	*The Words upon the Window-pane*			*she lowers the gass – or blows out the candles. ~~She finds a tea pot &~~ cup & puts on kettle. Swifts voice: Harley gone…*		*WUWP* 38–39
29v	*The Words upon the Window-pane* dramatis personae	~~Scenario~~ Characters; Scenario		*Characters John <McKnna> – man of seventy James Corbet – man of 25*		*WUWP* 40–41
30r	*The Words upon the Window-pane*		—	*A large room and a good many chairs. One arm chair near curtain. A fire place, with a kettle on the hearth.*		*WUWP* 42–43
30v	Text to insert opposite			*If you had heard the talk I have heard from my mother & from my old aunt you would understand how…*		*WUWP* 44–45
31r	*The Words upon the Window-pane*			*A large room | Corbet & Mackens voices heard at first outside the door in what follows.*		*WUWP* 46–47
31v	Draft of "For Anne Gregory"			*I heard a rambling monk of d But yester night declare That though the church think other*		*WFMP* 198–199
32r	*The Words upon the Window-pane*			*Yes I think that should be enough. I do not expect many people. In the early eighteenth century this house…*		*WUWP* 48–49

Rapallo E (NLI 13,582)

Folio	Description	Title/section	WBY p. no.	First line of page (uncancelled)	Note	Pub.
32v	Draft of "For Anne Gregory"			*While such a <heap> of honey lock A rampart at your ear & love you for self alone*		*WFMP* 200–201
33r	*The Words upon the Window-pane*			*how many do you expect Miss Duncan.*		*WFMP* 202, 203n; *WUWP* 49n
	Draft of "For Anne Gregory"			*But I can get a hair die And set such colour there Brown or black or carrot*		*WFMP* 202–203
33v	Lines to insert opposite			*My dear there not a man alive* *Could love Etc*	Fragments	*WFMP* 205n
34r	Draft of "For Anne Gregory"			*Never shall a young man Thrown into despair By those great honey coloured*		*WFMP* 204–205
34v	Text to insert opposite			*There is the first <of her> seance that I have been able to attend*		*WUWP* 50–51
35r	*The Words upon the Window-pane*			*Swift* *Peter Trench & William Corbet enter.* *Peter Trench: We have no good mediums in Ireland...*		*WUWP* 52–53
35v	Text to insert opposite			*They stare at window – Trench points out the exact spot Corbet stoops down to see.*		*WUWP* 54–55
36r	*The Words upon the Window-pane*			*here in the eighteenth century. It once belonged to friends of Swift – it is mentioned in the journal to Stella...*		*WUWP* 56–57
36v	Text to insert opposite			*Trench: The power of the <spiritualists> considered not as a scence but as a religious movement...*		*WUWP* 58–59
37r	*The Words upon the Window-pane*			*Trench: something like our scene to night* *Corbet: <Gulliver>was told that he call back from the dead anybody...*		*WUWP* 60–61

RAPALLO E (NLI 13,582)

Folio	Description	Title/section	WBY p. no.	First line of page (uncancelled)	Note	Pub.
37v	Text to insert opposite			*I hope to prove in my essay that in Swifts day Europe had reached its highest point of intellectual achievement.*		*WUWP* 62–63
38r	*The Words upon the Window-pane*			*(Johns return & comes up to Trench follow by Mrs Makenn & two or three other persons.)*		*WUWP* 64–65
38v	Text to insert opposite			*We do not permit the spirits that come to us to be driven away with curses, or violence of any kind*		*WUWP* 66–67
39r	*The Words upon the Window-pane*			*Mr Trench. We spiritualists do not admit there are any evil spirits. The spirits are just ordinary people…*		*WUWP* 68–69
39v	[Almost blank]			*Trench*	One word	
40r				*Johnson: spirit I am concerned that the spirit which has spoilt the last two scence is an evil spirit.*		*WUWP* 70–71
40v	Text to insert opposite			*Corbet: You said you are glad I am a sceptic. Mrs Macken: It makes me feel safer.*		
41r	*The Words upon the Window-pane*			*the summer land is just the kind of garden <some people desire>. Everything they do here they expect…*		*WUWP* 72–73
41v	*The Words upon the Window-pane* for previous?		1	*You have excite me beyond words. <Were they actual spirits> <or did you> <as> I prefer to think create…*		*WUWP* 74–75
	The Resurrection			*The Ressurrection Characters The Hebrew The Greek….*		*Res* 380–81

Rapallo E (NLI 13,582)

Folio	Description	Title/section	WBY p. no.	First line of page (uncancelled)	Note	Pub.
42r	*The Resurrection* final ms. draft, basis for Cuala printing; see *Res* xxxv			~~*The Ressurrection*~~ ~~*Persons*~~ ~~*The Hebrew*~~ ~~*The Greek*~~ ~~*The figure of Chr Jesus Christ*~~	All cancelled	*Res* 382–85
42v	[Blank]					
43r	*The Resurrection*			*The <unfolding> & <folding> of the curtain* *I saw a staring virgin stand* *Where holy Dionysus died*		*Res* 386–87
43v	[Blank]					
44r	*The Resurrection*		3	*& now are wandering through the streets like a pack of wolves. The <mob was> terrified by their frenzy...*		*Res* 388–89
44v	[Blank]					
45r	*The Resurrection*		4	*The Greek | Is it true that when the soldier asked him if he were a follower of Jesus he denied it.*		*Res* 390–91
45v	[Blank]					
46r	*The Resurrection*		5	*He spoke, but he had said nothing <if I had merely looked at him> it would have been all the same.*		*Res* 392–93
46v	Text to insert opposite			*The Hebrew* *The country people everywhere have such tales but who is to prove them true?*		*Res* 394–95
47r	*The Resurrection*		6	*as though it were all gathered together in the spot of a burning glass.*		*Res* 396–97
47v	Text to insert opposite			*she may lost some dear loved child & brood over Then she may have heard of this god that seemed a man...*		*Res* 398–99
48r	*The Resurrection*		7	*The Greek* *When I saw them raise him to the cross I think they were driving the nails through <the> hands...*		*Res* 400–403

Rapallo E (NLI 13,582)

Folio	Description	Title/section	WBY p. no.	First line of page (uncancelled)	Note	Pub.
48v	Text to insert opposite			*one has to sacrifice everything, that the divine suffering might , as it were descend into our mind & soul…*		*Res* 404–405
49r	*The Resurrection*		8	*The Greek* *I think there is nothing in the tomb*		*Res* 406–407
49v	[Blank]					
50r	*The Resurrection*		9	*The Greek (who is standing facing the audience & looking out over their heads) It is the worshippers of Dionysus.*		*Res* 408–409
50v	[Blank]					
51r	*The Resurrection*		10	*The Song* *Astrea's holy child* *<A rattle in> in a wood*		*Res* 410–13
51v	Text to insert opposite			*Man <too> remains separate: he keeps his He never surrenders his soul. He keeps his privacy.*		*Res* 414–15
52r	*The Resurrection*		11	*heroically gives them the only earthly body that they covet. He as it were copies their gestures & their acts.*		*Res* 416–17
52v	[Blank]					
53r	*The Resurrection*		12	*what they were saying; but Mary the mother of James said they had been to the tomb at daybreak…*		*Res* 418–19
53v	[Blank]					
54r	*The Resurrection*		13	*The Greek* *I said that we must all be convinced, but there is another reason why you must not tell them anything.*		*Res* 420–21
54v	Text to insert opposite			*The Hebrew* *Stop laughing* *The Syrean* *What if the irrational return…*		*Res* 422–23

RAPALLO E (NLI 13,582)

Folio	Description	Title/section	WBY p. no.	First line of page (uncancelled)	Note	Pub.
55r	*The Resurrection*		14	*The Syrean* *But what if there is something it cannot explain, something more important than anything else.*		*Res* 424–25
55v	[Blank]					
56r	*The Resurrection*		15	*I have seen in Alexandria. They are almost under the window now.*		*Res* 426–27
56v	[Blank]					
57r	*The Resurrection*		16	*(The figure of Christ, wearing a recognisable but stylised mask enters through the curtain…*		*Res* 428–29
57v	[Blank]					
58r	*The Resurrection*		17	*The Song of the unfolding & folding of the curtain* *In pity for mans darkening thought*		*Res* 430–31
58v	Text to insert opposite	V		*V* *The states between death & birth can be measured out, upon the wheel of the Faculties.*		
59r	*A Vision*: on afterlife	V		*I shall explore by a series of analogies drawn from the double cones, the state of the soul between death & birth.*		
59v	Additional text			*~~I am inclined to classify under "will" the utility of art the utility whether of painting or literature.~~*	All cancelled	
60	Thin strips of paper, with some ink markings visible					
61						
62						
63						
64						
60bis-r	Dance scenario (Resurrection)			*~~Ressurection Sunday~~ Jan ~~20~~ 21 & 22* *Dance Play* *Musician comes as in my dance plays*	Dated Jan 21 & 22	*Res* 4–5 [as 60r]; see *Res* xxi
60bis-v	[Blank]					

Rapallo E (NLI 13,582)

Folio	Description	Title/section	WBY p. no.	First line of page (uncancelled)	Note	Pub.
61bis-r	Dance scenario (Resurrection)			*Christ out in agony again the endless sin & misery of men — for whom the gods die in vain.*		*Res* 6–7 [as 61r]
61bis-v	Dance scenario (Resurrection)			*or only the act is the devine — in that we put on divinity now one now another as the turning heavens decree*		*Res* 8–9 [as 61v]
62bis-r	Dance scenario (Resurrection)			*dance slowly unwinding the grave clothes. Christ when <unwound> does <not> know where he is.*		*Res* 10–11 [as 62r]
62bis-v	[Blank]					
63bis-r	Dance scenario (Resurrection)			*Christ burst out about the eternal sin of man & his vain suffering. Buddha who alone of the men remains…*		*Res* 12–13 [as 63r]
	Notes on Masefield, Synge, and Pound			*Jan 22 (?1929) Masefield was as he <believes> tirranized over by an <old> aunt & I have always…*	Dated "Jan 22 (?1929)"; year added in different ink	cf. *PEP* 7–9, "Rapallo" VI?
63bis-v	Notes for *PEP*?			*At Aliceras I could walk two mins, at Canne I can walk but one - soon I shall but walk the garden path…*	cf. NLI 13,579 [99r]; 13,580 [9r], dated Jan. 23 [1929] (*WFMP* 208–209)	cf. *PEP* 27, *AVB* 20, *CW14* 16
65	Leaf removed					
66	Leaf removed					
67r	*A Vision* material on afterlife	[cont. §X] XI		*page 20 ~~or before~~ & 21 & 21a the utmost good nor the utmost evil can force sensation or emotion.*		
67v	[Blank]					
68	Leaf removed					
69r	*A Vision*: on afterlife	XII	29	*XII Should the Spirit fail to reverse inviroment & motive, it must incarnate with the old motive…*		
69v	[Blank]					

Rapallo E (NLI 13,582)

Folio	Description	Title/section	WBY p. no.	First line of page (uncancelled)	Note	Pub.
70	Leaf removed					
71	Leaf removed					
72	Leaf removed					
73	Leaf removed					
74r	*A Vision*: on afterlife	XIV	24	*the present moment, of the fated image, the Spirit has become more & more <every bodies> spirit…*	Much cancelled; page numbering, 24 [= 34]	
74v	[Blank]					
75r	[Blank]					
75v	[Blank]					
76r	[Blank]					
76v	[Blank]					
77r	[Blank]					
77v	[Blank]					
78r	[Blank]					
78v	[Blank]					
79r	[Blank]					
79v	[Blank]					
80r	[Blank]					
80v	[Blank]					
81r	[Blank]					
81v	[Blank]					
82r	[Blank]					
82v	[Blank]					
83r	[Blank]					
83v	[Blank]					
84r	[Blank]					
84v	[Blank]					
0	Conservation leaf					
0	Conservation leaf					
Inside	Patterned board					
Cover	Patterned board					

Notes on Contributors

Wayne K. Chapman is Professor Emeritus of English at Clemson University, founding director of Clemson University Press (2000–2016), and editor of *The South Carolina Review* (1996–2016). He has written or edited numerous books on Yeats, including: *Yeats and English Renaissance Literature* (Macmillan Press, 1991); *"The Countess Cathleen": Manuscript Materials*, with Michael Sidnell (Cornell University Press, 1999); *Yeats's Collaborations, Yeats Annual* 15, with Warwick Gould (Palgrave Macmillan, 2003); *"The Dreaming of the Bones" and "Calvary": Manuscript Materials* (Cornell University Press, 2003); *The W. B. and George Yeats Library: A Short-title Catalog* (Clemson University Press, 2006, rev. 2019); *Yeats's Poetry in the Making: "Sing Whatever Is Well Made"* (Palgrave Macmillan, 2010); *Rewriting "The Hour-Glass": A Play Written in Prose and Verse Versions* (Clemson University Press, 2016); *W. B. Yeats's Robartes-Aherne Writings: Featuring the Making of His "Stories of Michael Robartes and His Friends"* (Bloomsbury Academic, 2018), and *"Something that I read in a book": W. B. Yeats's Annotations at the National Library of Ireland*, 2 volumes (Clemson University Press, 2022).

Neil Mann has written extensively on Yeats's esoteric interests and *A Vision*, with articles in the *Yeats Annual* and *International Yeats Studies*. He created the website yeatsvision.com in 2002 and edited the following collections of essays: with Matthew Gibson and Claire Nally, *Yeats's "A Vision": Explications and Contexts* (Clemson University Press, 2012); and with Matthew Gibson, *Yeats, Philosophy, and the Occult* (Clemson University Press, 2016). His book *A Reader's Guide to Yeats's "A Vision"* (Clemson University Press) came out in 2019. He works as a professional editor and translator.

www.ingramcontent.com/pod-product-compliance
Lightning Source LLC
Chambersburg PA
CBHW061253230426
43665CB00027B/2924